ID0938719

The Russian Revolution
of February 1917

The Russian Revolution of February 1917

Marc Ferro

Translated by J. L. Richards

Notes and bibliography translated by Nicole Stone

London

Routledge & Kegan Paul

First published in Great Britain 1972
by Routledge & Kegan Paul Ltd
Broadway House, 68–74 Carter Lane
London EC4V 5EL
Printed by Unwin Brothers Limited
The Gresham Press, Old Woking, Surrey, England
A member of the Staples Printing Group

ISBN 0 7100 7307 0

CONTENTS

★ ★ ★ ★ ★ ★

PREFACE

The year 1917 was crucial in the history of modern times. The Russian October Revolution set forth the guidelines for any evaluation of the future evolution of our society. Many books have been written to explain this event. After fifty years, interest in this study has not abated. Nevertheless, there still remains a vast untapped body of documents, and the interpretation of facts as well as of the attitudes of participants in the Revolution is still a subject of controversy. The outline of historical reconstruction, which dims the picture of precisely those periods most closely studied, is still open to question.

This is the reason for the present study, devoted to the study of the first few months of the Provisional Government from February to June, when the failure of the bourgeois Republic, which depended upon the support of moderate revolutionaries, created the conditions that made the Bolshevik victory possible. This study is a colorful, lively, and detailed narrative, giving new points of view by systematically utilizing for the first time a mass of documents which express the opinion of the country during the months of uncertainty and anarchy. The reader will find at the end of the volume, in the Documents Section, a number of unedited and not previously translated texts, the inclusion of which is intended to illuminate the history of the period.

By their character, their temperaments, and their nature, men occasionally have a decisive influence on events during troubled times. One of the merits of Marc Ferro's narrative is to bring to life the personalities of the Revolution, to place them psychologically, and to explain their motivations. On the eve of the liquidation of Tsarism, the most advanced elements of the Duma and the newly elected Soviet were divided between the exuberance of victory and the fear of tomorrow: "Facing the task before them, the leaders of the day knew that they had to choose between the Tsar and the Revolution. At the end was either power or the gallows and their hearts were troubled." This elation over an unexpected success is understandable among revolutionary leaders who had hardly imagined that "the road from Siberian jails to the seat of power was so short." Their hesitation to choose the really revolutionary means also is understandable, inasmuch as most of them interpreted the Russian situation in the light of lessons of the past: in France, in the days of June 1848, hadn't the dictatorship of the "Montagne" brought on Bonapartism? And didn't the failure, in Russia, of the 1905 Revolution encourage them to maintain a "conciliatory" and reforming attitude?

Further, Marc Ferro's study of the 1917 Revolution shows clearly that the hypothesis of "two powers" after the Revolution of February and the fall of Tsarism doesn't conform to reality. In fact, if it was not the Duma, it was at least the spirit of the Duma, which, faced with the timidity of a Soviet almost astounded by its success, brought on a policy of hesitation, a refusal of responsibilities, and a strategy that consisted mainly of passively waiting. The result was to put off to beyond the projected Constitutional Assembly the most urgent problem—that of land reform in particular. The pseudo-revolutionary Soviet's failure to act and the abandonment of its Socialist ideals reinforced among the bourgeoisie, who were attempting to seize power, the certainty that the Revolution would go no further and that the new republic would not repudiate capitalism.

But while worries assailed the leaders, who were divided by their social and political adherences, the whole country reacted spontaneously, in the enthusiasm of liberty, by sending telegrams, motions, and reports containing approval, criticism, and suggestions. The most original part of Marc Ferro's study concerns this spontaneous movement, triggered by the events of February, which reveals a high level of political and civic consciousness.

Certainly the picture of a passive Russia driven by new shepherds has long been abandoned. But only the examination of innumerable facts verifying the general participation in the events could account for the liveliness of popular conviction and the fervor of popular sentiments as well as the moderation of the claims in the context of the incontestable class struggle. The peasants, violently hostile to the nobility, showed their attachment to property. The soldiers condemned the war while admitting, patriotically, its necessity. The workers demanded the eight-hour day, and later the control of factories, although they did not demand confiscation. What is most typical is the multiplication and the sudden proliferation of the "soviets" over the whole territory, taking charge of true local self-government in all sectors of the administration and the economy. Marc Ferro insists on the spontaneous nature of this reaction, while admitting the determining initiative of the militant revolutionaries.

In this fusing of forces, tolerating rather than opposing each other, Bolshevism was not too apparent. Lenin's activity developed from April on, but he appeared then as an extremist figure and as a demagogue playing into the hands of the reactionaries by his excesses. Lieber, the Menshevik, says of him: "If Lenin had not existed, the bourgeoisie would have invented him." And when, at the Soviet Congress in June, Lenin suggested arresting a certain number of millionaires and giving power to the soviets, he was ridiculed by Kerensky.

Still it can be asserted that he alone had a lucid view of the situation. In a few months the atmosphere changed. The honeymoon period of the Revolution was finished as well as the waiting period. Kerensky—"the Balalaika of the régime," as Lenin called him—could no longer turn back the crowds with his persuasive voice. The popular claims became more pressing and more uncompromising. While the Socialist ideal disgraced itself at the government level, and while a nationwide reaction grew, paralyzing all reforming activity, public opinion outran government power. To satisfy this impatient opinion the political genius of Lenin—the word isn't too strong—provided a program of immediate action.

Thus, as far as the author is concerned, it is not the conflict of the two powers which characterizes the period. As long as the Soviet and the Duma were opposed by the big parties and numerous groups whose various overlapping or contradictory programs Marc Ferro clearly distinguishes, popular opinion, the opinion of the street—realistic, worried about efficiency, and increasingly exasperated by the government's incapacity—was equally hostile to both sides. June marked the decline of the revolutionary parties which had until then seemed to run the Revolution. The confrontation then took place between the two powers, with their various and conflicting programs, and an anonymous revolutionary mass represented by Lenin and the Boleshevik party, with their practical solutions destined to solve the crisis of the country. The tests of public opinion show definitely that Lenin's program, adapted to the moment, showed the way for a very large majority of this Revolutionary mass.

Roger Portal

FOREWORD

If it were necessary to describe this study I would say that in it I have tried to analyze the relationship which existed between the aspirations which tore up Russian society in 1917, the programs of the political parties which claimed to represent it, and the acts of its leaders.

Such a study of political and social relationships would inevitably be so similar to a description of revolutionary events that it seemed artificial to isolate the analytic from the narrative elements. The analysis of social and political structures and the chronological development of events thus form a whole.

Further, it was necessary to bring the material into focus because in the last ten years the publication of innumerable volumes of documents from archives, notably in the USSR, and the appearance of the latest Soviet or Western historical works have updated information and perspectives heretofore tinged by the posthumous testimony of the principals of the Revolution. Direct access to the archives of Moscow, Leningrad, Amsterdam, and Paris, as well as the systematic stripping of the Russian section of the B.D.I.C., so rich in unedited newspapers and brochures, permitted us to compile and compare information gathered from documents whose contents are frequently found to vary according to the prejudices of the moment.

Although our initial aim was to focus the knowledge acquired in the fifty years since the success of the October Revolution, and to present faithfully the documents on men and facts, we have been brought by this very documentation to expand our task. The existence of a mass of unedited information on the aspirations of the people of Russia has allowed us to reconsider the conduct of the groups, social classes, and individuals, and to stack the wishes of the populace against the programs or the acts of organizations and politicians. We have used this information as a source of a unique perspective on the history of the Revolution. In effect, the wishes of the French nation certainly were expressed in 1789, but they were expressed within the context of the Old Order, before the Revolution broke out and succeeded. In Russia, on the contrary, the populace made its wishes known as soon as—but not before—it learned of the fall of Nicholas II. Upon examination, these popular expressions can be seen to be independent of the objectives of the political parties, which were known long ago. Twelve days after the fall of the Tsar, *Isvestya* already had received ten thousand messages of this nature; Kerensky received some, as did the soviets in Moscow and other places. Motions came out of factories or regiments as well as from the locksmiths of Tiflis and the bank directors of the Caucasus, from domestic servants and technical students. At this date, when neither the political parties nor the trade unions had yet had their meetings, when the organizations obliterated by the police were not even able to circulate their slogans, there can be no doubt as to the spontaneity of the messages. To show this, let us cite the message to *Pravda* inviting its readers to "firmly defend the country," or the calls from isolated factories asking the Soviet for instructions and directives. Furthermore, the films kept in the motion picture archives attest that in 1917 virtually every Russian citizen and citizeness had a plan all ready for the country's regeneration.

It is these projects, these petitions, read at the meetings which we will use in this work. These texts permit us to obtain a fair idea of the authentic aspirations of the Russian people in 1917. In comparing them to the programs of the parties, to the motions of the soviets, where the necessities of political action and the different trends of opinion clashed and were reconciled, we can directly evaluate the failure of some and the clarity of others. We can also interpret, in retrospect, the causes of the Revolution and the conditions and circumstances which were to lead to the defeat of the victors of February.

The time to show my appreciation to those who have helped me has been delayed too long; that they will accept my expression of thanks will suffice. I will first name the librarians of the B.D.I.C., who for the last five years have helped in thousands of ways; their colleagues of the Bibliothèque Nationale and the Libraries Saltikov-Schedrin and the Fondamentalnaya, who guided my first steps, as well as the archivists of Moscow, Leningrad, Amsterdam, and the Ministry of War. I also must thank my seniors, colleagues, and friends—both historians and nonhistorians—who at the various stages of the drafting of this work have read my text, discussed it with me, and helped me to improve it; these include A. Bennigsen, A. Besançon, H. Carrère d'Encausse, F. Chatelet, J. Cohen, G. Dagron, G. Haupt. Cl. Heller, H. Miakotine, P. Nora, A. Romano, P. Souyri, Y. Trabut, L. Valensi, and our deceased friends F. de Liencourt and P. Stibbe.

I do not know if custom permits me to mention my indebtedness to my teachers as well, but I must acknowledge my gratitude to those who showed friendliness or confidence in me during the long years of solitary exile: P. Angrand, M. Crouzet, J. Egret, J. Gadrat, A. Labaste, R. Latouche, and those who are now deceased—M. Merleau-Ponty, R. Balanchard and E. Esmonin.

Also my present teachers: Dean Renouvin, who has agreed to direct my principal thesis and whose work was for me a model of exactitude, loyalty, and liberalism; the director of this work, R. Portal, Professor at the Sorbonne, who suggested I write it, corrected the economics, showed me its shortcomings, and was willing to write the Preface; J. B. Duroselle, Professor at the Sorbonne, whose kindly approval brought me the necessary support; Henri Michel, Director of Research at CNRS, who gave me the opportunity to know and utilize the enormous amount of motion pictures at his disposal; the Director of the Collection, Paul Lemerle, Professor at the Sorbonne, who knew how to request all the necessary revisions with firmness and friendliness. I must add that words fail to express what I owe to Mr. and Mrs. F. Braudel who made me feel like a son and encouraged the writing of this history of events in Russia.

ABBREVIATIONS

S. D. Social Democrat
K. D. Cadet, or Constitutional-Democrat
B. Bolshevik
Z. Zimmerwaldian
S. R. Socialist-Revolutionary
M. Menshevik
U. Unitarian

INTRODUCTION

Three Russias have been born successively: the Russia of the rivers and cities, which was born first; that of the forest appeared later; finally, the Russia of the steppes and of the Empire. The Revolution reached them one by one.

First came the Russian Revolution of the cities, the rivers, and the sea coasts—thanks to the action of the old urban populations who were sensitive to foreign winds; thanks to the sailors and soldiers. These overthrew Tsarism, established "bourgeois" liberties, and became intoxicated with their success. That was in February.

Then, upsetting the old Russian society and changing it profoundly, the Revolution reached the zone of the forest and clearings. It got its second wind in the cities, reviving among the elements just freshly arrived from the countryside the Pugachev tradition. That was in October.

Later the Revolution flamed through the steppes and the surrounding mountains where, under the pretext of resisting the awakening of national minorities, "the whip of the Cossacks and Asiatic despotism joined forces." Foreign intervention reinforced the camp of the enemies of Bolshevism. That was the time of the Civil War.

This Russian Revolution was a European revolution as well; the heiress of 1789, of 1848, and of the tradition of the Commune, she had for her principal craftsmen the members of the Communist International. Their ideal was the founding of Socialism— first in liberal Europe, then in backward Russia.

Daughter of the First World War, the Russian Revolution wanted to end the conflict which had stained the whole earth with blood. In that she didn't succeed, but at least she assured her survival in Russia itself and did not permit herself to be stifled. Nineteen-seventeen was no longer "1917," the beginning of a new era, but simply Year One of the Russian Revolution.

EPIGRAPH

The Russian is poorer than the Bedouin, poorer than the Hebrew. There is nothing to be reconciled with, nothing to console him. Therein lies the secret of his revolutionary vocation.

Detached from the life of the common people by European civilization and cut off from Europe by despotism, he is too weak to overthrow it and the only thing left is flight.

But where can he go? Not everyone is able to play cards night and day, or to drink until the fumes of alcohol smother his sorrow or put his mind to sleep. . . . Then there are those who escape by reading—in the study of the West.

We are slaves because we have not the means of liberating ourselves. Anyway, we'll accept nothing from the enemy.

Russia will never be Protestant.

Russia will never be the Golden Mean.

Russia will never revolt with the sole objective of getting rid of Tsar Nicholas and obtaining as a reward for victory Tsarist representatives, Tsarist courts, or Tsarist laws.

Herzen
(Letter to Michelet, February 7, 1854)

PART ONE

★

THE FALL OF TSARISM

★

CHAPTER ONE

FROM WAR TO REVOLUTION

1. THE ILLUSIONS OF 1914

The prestige of Russia had never seemed greater than in 1913, the year of the tricentennial of the Romanov accession to the throne. Tocqueville's prediction had indeed come true: America and Russia were the emerging powers of the future. Russia led the way in many fields. In Paris, Stravinsky's *Sacre du Printemps* and Diaghilev's Ballets Russes had made history. The Russian economy, into which French investors eagerly tossed their money, was making giant strides forward. After the disaster of 1905, the Russian army had been reorganized. The régime appeared to be stable since the Tsar himself had made necessary concessions and instituted a Duma. Not everyone agreed that the situation had really improved, but the memory of 1905 was rapidly fading. The few Russian expatriates who were still voicing their hatred of the régime went unheeded by the rest of Europe. With the declaration of war in August 1914, the Socialist International, their last hope, crumbled, bringing all its promises down with it. Instead of "making war on war," its members rushed against the enemy along with everyone else.

Russia differed in one important aspect from both her allies and her opponents. In the West, a number of revolutions had changed society, built nations, and given hope. For these nations the concepts of "fatherland" and "liberty" were closely bound to one another. This was not the case in Russia, where "the homeland was a stepmother as well as a mother." The immense Russian territory, circled by mountains, deserts, and oceans, ice-bound for six months, served as a prison for its inhabitants. On this soil where nothing changed, autocracy had succeeded for three centuries in keeping the people from being conscious of their misfortune and their boundless misery. The only result of the peasant flare-ups of the eighteenth century was to brand the flesh of the Russian people with red-hot iron; already they prophesied that in Russia the revolution would be of a secular and social nature. The defeat of the Decembrists in 1825 showed at least that the minds of Russia's young people were open to the idea of progress. This was the birth of the intelligentsia, which was to teach the people through the whole nineteenth century that they could be masters of their own destiny. This was a role which redounded to its honor, even if, according to Bakunin, by accepting exile and by liberating the peasants and the city workers, the intelligentsia hoped to seize power for itself. Thereafter, neither the reforms of 1861, nor the defeat of 1905, nor the efforts of the State to give new life to the country could exorcise the specter of revolution. Revolution had become a *raison d'être* as instinctive as the defense of the native soil, a passion all the more violent because of the equally desperate means that Tsarism used to repress it.

In going off to war, the Russian soldier of 1914 was doing his duty. The defeat made him consider it his responsibility to punish the men in charge. Performing both duties, on the domestic and on the foreign front, meant defeating the enemies of his freedom. Some agreed with Lenin that in declaring war the Tsar had made the best possible contribution to the Revolution. But this was hard to believe at the outbreak of hostilities, when the economy had taken on new life and the army had been reorganized in the face of a collapsing opposition.

FIRST ILLUSION:
The Knell of the Revolutionary Movement

Fifteen million soldiers faithfully answered the Tsar's call. One million deserters had been predicted, but there were barely a few thousand. Russian soldiers had neither the somewhat vain reckless-ness of the French, the easy-going manner of the English, nor the self-assurance of the Germans. As one in their desire to defend their native soil, their singleness of purpose engendered the belief that for Russia the era of unrest was definitely over. Russian opinion was that the country was fighting for a just cause, honor-ing the promise it had made to the Serbian "little brother." The alliance with the Western democracies led the Russians to hope that after the war their government would pattern itself on the Western model. Even Georgi Plekhanov, the "father of Russian Social-Democracy," thought that the fight against German imper-ialism should come first, and so he invited the revolutionaries to suspend the fight against Tsarism in order not to hinder the war effort against the Germany of Wilhelm II.

Still all opposition had not disappeared. From the first, certain émigrés—Lenin, Trotsky, and Martov—had condemned the "imper-ialist war" and denounced both sides as responsible for it. In any event, while his companions were content to urge an immediate peace, Lenin, beginning in September 1914, demanded "the trans-formation of the imperialist war into a civil war." For Russia the absolute evil was Tsarism, and victory could only consolidate it.

4

Thus the revolutionaries should fight for the defeat of the government. Such a tactic, according to Lenin, was valid not only for Russia's revolutionaries. This defeatism (*porazhentsvo*) received short shrift. In Paris, some émigré Bolsheviks who were more responsive to the calls of Plekhanov or Grigori Alexinsky than to those of Trotsky or the *Nashe Slovo* (Our Word)* group, enlisted in the French Army. In Russia there was the same patriotic contagion. True, the Social-Democrats voted against military credits and the "Trudoviks" (Workers) walked out of a meeting of the Duma, but that did not prevent them from announcing that they would contribute to the national defense. Only the Bolsheviks remained absolutely opposed.

These outbursts had little effect. When the government of I. L. Goremykin had the five Bolshevik deputies deported to Siberia, there was hardly a murmur. Only a few factories went on strike at the behest of the party. Had the war sounded the knell of the revolutionary movement? Actually, weakened by the defeat of 1905, the movement seemed to owe its failure as much to the cleverness of the authorities as to its own divisiveness.

In the first place, the revolutionaries were divided into Westerners and Slavophiles. The former thought that the history of the West forecast the future of Russia and that certain mistakes which led to the defeat of the revolutions of 1848 could be avoided. The latter insisted on the unique character of the Russian past. They thought that Russia would have to find the road to revolution within herself. Thus, in the second half of the nineteenth century, the Marxists thought that inevitably Russia would have to go through a long phase of capitalistic development. The Populists, on the other hand, thought it was possible to pass directly to Socialism; the Narodnaya Volya (Narodnik) movement shared the same objectives, although its tactics were the opposite. These differences augured serious complications in any plan of action. The Marxists placed the future of the revolution squarely on the shoulders of the emerging industrial working class. The Populists, on the other hand, were counting on the peasantry, which already had been initiated into socialism through such collective institutions as the *Mir*. There were clashes and quarrels: the Marxists quit the Narodnaya Volya movement as soon as it became apparent that specifically Russian methods, such as terrorism and the "movement toward the people," had failed completely. From 1883 on, each was to go his own way. This fundamental choice had resulted, on the eve of 1905, in the formation of two separate socialist organizations, the Social-Democratic party, created by

5

Plekhanov in 1898, and the Socialist-Revolutionary party, founded a little later.

From the time they were formed, these two parties became the subject of controversy on the forms which revolutionary action should take, its main objectives, and the organization of the party.

The Socialist-Revolutionaries quarreled about revolutionary tactics. Was terrorist action to be directed solely at the "enemies of the people," or were the crops and the railroads to be included? The effectiveness of certain acts of sabotage was recognized by most members of the party, but it was clear that terrorism was on the wane. To confuse matters, the majority also rejected all participation in legal political activities.

In leaving the populist movement, the Social-Democrats had broken with terrorist methods. But was it necessary to educate the working class and prepare them for revolutionary action (*propaganda*), or should one only exploit the workers' dissatisfaction to the fullest (*agitacia*)? The "politicians," such as Plekhanov had not yet won out over the "activists" when another quarrel caused a further split. The Russian revisionists—notably M. Tugan-Baronovsky, Nicholas Berdyaev, and Peter Struve, who were disciples of the German socialist Edward Bernstein—thought that in order to speed the formation of a powerful working class it was necessary first to contribute to the development of capitalism in Russia and to uphold the demands of the bourgeoisie. Hence it was useless to call for illegal action or terrorism. These "legal" Marxists went against the revolutionary sensibilities of the militants. Castigated by Plekhanov and Paul Axelrod, they left the party. The "economists" followed suit. According to A. S. Martynov and E. D. Kuskova, no action could be expected from the working class except in the economic sphere. Political fighting should be left to the bourgeoisie. In their polemics with the economists, Plekhanov and Axelrod had the support of a newcomer, Vladimir Ulyanov—the future Lenin.

These uncertainties caused the revolutionaries' course of action to waver dangerously. More than ever they needed singleness of purpose. To prove this, Lenin then wrote *What Is to Be Done?*, a little pamphlet which was to determine the future of the working-class movement. He examined the problems confronting the organization of a revolutionary party. Should one swell one's ranks, as the Germans did, in order to win over a majority in the country and then seize power, or should one form a party of professional revolutionaries having only a limited number of trained militants, which would be maneuverable like an army in the field and which would instigate insurrection as soon as conditions were ripe for success? No accord could be reached between the partisans of democratic organization and the champions of a centralized party. The latter, who were in the majority in 1903, formed a separate political unit known as Bolsheviks (majority). Martov and Axelrod became the leaders of the minority, or Mensheviks. Plekhanov thought, as did Martov, that the Leninist conception of a revolutionary party would lead to a one-man dictatorship over the party. But the old leader, believing that Lenin's ideas could not take hold and hoping to pave the way for the reunification of the party under his direction, did not condemn them outright. At that time no one thought that Lenin's ideas bore the seed of the division of the Marxist parties into Socialists and Communists. It was thought only that they manifested the scorn of the Bolshevik leaders for revolutionary spontaneity among workers, even organized workers.

During the revolution of 1905 the differences between Bolsheviks and Mensheviks encompassed not only party organization but objectives and tactics as well. In his *Two Tactics* Lenin stated that at this stage of development Russia was undergoing a bourgeois revolution, much like the French Revolution of 1789. Nevertheless, it was dangerous to entrust Russia's fate to the bourgeoisie, who had neither the will nor the strength to smash the feudal system and bring about a true social transformation. Only the proletariat, in conjunction with the peasantry, could force the bourgeoisie to carry out this revolution. Lenin urged that as soon as Tsarism was overthrown a provisional government should be set up which would be the expression of "revolutionary democratic dictatorship of the proletariat and peasantry." It was to be a democratic dictatorship, since the forward-looking elements of the bourgeoisie would be ready to collaborate with it. According to him, this régime would be a necessary stage on the way to the establishment of a socialist republic, an objective attainable only on the day when backward Russia would be backed by a more advanced Europe and when the proletariat had assumed power.

Opposed to a premature socialist revolution, "which would not be the work of the workers themselves, but of those leading them," Plekhanov and the Mensheviks drew an opposite conclusion from the 1905 experience. The events of 1905 confirmed Plekhanov and the Mensheviks in their belief that the peasantry could not be relied upon and that the bourgeoisie would go over to the reactionaries as soon as trouble broke out in cities or in the countryside. Since revolution was unfeasible under these conditions, the first step was to help the bourgeoisie overthrow Tsarism, which meant that the bourgeoisie should not be frightened. Ultimately a way would have to be paved for a socialist revolution and means would have to be found to prevent the middle class from decreeing anti-worker policies. To this end the Mensheviks recommended the establishment of soviets, which were to be the agents for the overthrow of Tsarism during the bourgeois phase of the revolution, and then bastions of proletarian strength in the bourgeois country during the period of preparation for the transition to socialism.

The Bolsheviks had taken no particular stand on the setting up of the soviets, since in their conception the role of working-class leadership was left to the party. On the other hand, they had definite ideas on the functions of the soviets; they thought that these institutions must not limit themselves to organizing the proletariat and protecting it against the bourgeoisie but must also become the embryos of the revolutionary-democratic dictatorship of the proletariat.

Trotsky, who had been the chairman of the Petersburg Soviet in 1905, agreed along with "Parvus" (A. L. Helphand) that, having led the revolution during its bourgeois phase, the Russian proletariat would certainly not wait for the triumph of the social revolution in Europe to establish socialism. However, left to itself, this second revolution would be doomed. Therefore, as soon as Tsarism had been overthrown, it was essential to start a socialist revolution in Europe. According to this theory, known as the theory of permanent revolution, the fate of the Russian Revolution depended somewhat upon the action of a Continental workers' movement. This theory had few followers.

Having learned its lesson from the events of 1905, the Tsarist government had instituted a pseudo-constitutional state. It thus quieted that section of the opposition which trusted Nicholas II, hoping he would respect the terms of the manifesto of October 1906. The Constitutional-Democrats or Cadets (K.D.), who were more radical than the Octobrists, howled their distaste for a régime which left little freedom of opinion and little power to the Duma. Nevertheless, they conscientiously took their seats, and, as in the local administration organizations (*Zemstvos*) which they partly controlled, they cooperated more and more with the régime. Actually, they cooperated because the events of 1905 had made them realize to what lengths a revolution could lead. The leaders of these "bourgeois" parties, the Octobrist Alexander Guchkov and the Cadets Pavel Milyukov and Fyodor Kokoshkin, nevertheless kept fighting for a Russia endowed with a truly Western-style parliamentary régime. However, neither the Tsar nor the bureaucracy allowed them to develop their propaganda. Since the State controlled part of the economy, the Octobrists and the Cadets considered themselves victims of the régime. They consequently turned to the revolutionary parties.

These liberals adopted two opposing attitudes. At times they cooperated with the State, which was the source of progress since Peter the Great and which, thanks to Count Witte and Premier Stolypin, remained more advanced than the social order. At other times they rejected any cooperation with it, judging it incapable of injecting new life into the country. Before 1905, the liberal opposition had been faced with a much more radical choice: mostly members of the intelligentsia, those who were impressed by the reforms of the Tsar's government, became part of the bureaucracy, while those who thought the reforms insufficient became revolutionaries. These two segments of the intelligentsia hated one another intensely, although they were striving for the same ideal, the reform of the country. But in the heat of battle, they lost sight of their objective; indeed, in promulgating his reforms, Stolypin's intention had been precisely to smash the revolutionary movement in this way. At the opposite extreme, the enemies of the régime aimed more at scuttling the régime than at improving the lot of the people. No communication was possible between those who were using the State to transform Russia and those who were exploiting the discontent of the country to conquer the State. They were all intractable; on the one hand the bureaucrats saw the revolutionary spirit percolate all the way up to the Grand Duke; on the other, the revolutionaries suspected treachery from even the most dedicated among them.

During these years the bureaucracy had scored some points. The better to rally the bourgeoisie, it stimulated industrial development, attracted foreign capital, and developed public education. By dint of agrarian reform, Stolypin neutralized a part of the peasantry. He had broken the rural commune (*obshchina*), promoted the development of a class of small property-owners, and encouraged the peasants to enclose their lots. He also helped the pioneers who wanted to go to Siberia. In this way, he had released a part of the energy which drove the peasants and changed their attitude toward the State. Undoubtedly rural emigration had swelled the flow of the discontented into the cities, but these unskilled workers did not have the same problems as the workers who were already organized. Consequently management was able to take advantage of their disunity. Under these conditions, it appeared that the working class, battered since 1906, politically isolated, and socially divided, would hardly be a menace to the régime. Even its leaders were beginning to wonder about the value of their doctrines and about the future of the revolution. With the working-class movement weakened, the peasants about to give in, the bourgeoisie tamed, and the intellectuals and artists disillusioned, the chances for the opposition lessened each year. The only compensation was that the opposition could now lean on the mounting discontent of the racial minorities.

These minorities resented the policy of "Russification," which they considered a deliberate act of aggression on the part of the Tsarist régime. This policy had merely reinforced the intense nationalism of the Ukrainians, the Tartars, the Buriates, the Mari, etc., and provoked them to join forces with the Poles, Finns, Balts, Georgians, Jews, etc., in their long-standing struggle for their rights. Although for centuries these minorities had been downtrodden and repeatedly beaten, they had never united and were thus easy prey for the bureaucrats, who set the Ukrainians against the Jews, the Bashkirs against the Tartars, and the Georgians against the Armenians. Moreover, each minority had its own gamut of parties, often divided along the lines of the Russian revolutionary movement. Among the Poles, for example, the subdivisions were infinite. No one, to this day, has been able to count them.

Divided, paralyzed by the isolation which a clever administration had been able to impose upon them, the racial minorities remained inactive while the police destroyed political groups and trade unions. Nevertheless, it was apparent to many observers that the régime was too intensely hated and the wretchedness too general for there to be any chance of its indefinitely postponing the ultimate explosion which would destroy the bars of the "prison of the people"; it remained only to discover the formula that would put the different groups into motion.

Meanwhile the defeated leaders of 1905 found themselves once again on the road to exile. They bore an undying hatred for Tsarism. Having lost everything—family, home, country—they considered themselves citizens of another country. They recognized only their own laws, their own code of honor, their own ceremonies, meetings, and hierarchy. Like the first Christian sects, their kingdom was not of this world, and if their promised land remained Russia, as long as the Tsar reigned they were not permitted to enter it. As in ancient Christian times, each chief had his own church and each church its renegades and pariahs, each stigmatized with the sign of his own ideology.

During the period of reaction which followed the aborted uprising of 1905, the group leaders, who were already divided on the role which the peasantry and the proletariat were to play in the coming revolution, quarreled about the future of their movement, about the possibility of using legal political action, about the role to be played by the cooperative movement and by the racial minorities in the struggle against the autocratic régime.

The morale of the revolutionaries was low, for subversive methods had failed. By what means could the struggle be taken up again? To be sure, there was now a parliament, the Duma, but in making use of that body would they not be playing into the hands of the opposition? On the other hand, was it not equally dangerous to leave the use of the Duma to the bourgeois parties and organizations of the extreme right, like the Union of Russian People or the Union of the Archangel Michael? The majority of Social-Democratic leaders leaned toward participation in the electoral battles. Certain Mensheviks even thought of liquidating the old party and fighting the State with new methods, copied from the West. With Leonid Martov, they thought the hour of Russian revisionism had finally arrived, but they wanted to redouble the *agitacia* so as not to be swallowed up by the old "legal" Marxists.

The Bolsheviks denounced these "liquidators." The most dedicated ones formed the "Capri Group," which centered around the figure of Maxim Gorky; with Anatoli Lunacharsky, Grigori Alexinsky, Alexander Bogdanov, and Nikolai Bukharin. They condemned all participation in legal politics. Isolated between the "Capri Group" and the Mensheviks, Lenin believed that all means which would lead to revolution should be used, legal or illegal. He alone, uninfluenced by his more conventional companions, did not conceal his admiration for the terroristic exploits of the young Koba-Stalin, so long as these exploits were for the benefit of his team. This somewhat crude cynicism, which could be tolerated from Plekhanov, was shocking when it came from Lenin. Hence his isolation deepened and he came to insist that he had nothing in common with the other Social-Democrats. On the contrary, he reaffirmed his hostility to any reunification of the party and presented the Bolsheviks as the only champions of "action at any price." This drew him the sympathy of the young and impatient.

Despite the efforts of Viktor Chernov, the Socialist-Revolutionaries (S.R.) were divided by similar quarrels. Their ranks included

11

former proponents of direct action who would not let them forego terrorism and urged the immediate application of all the points of the S.R. program as soon as power was seized. Known as the "Maximalists," this faction did not leave the party, but stopped obeying it. Conversely, those who had ignored the objections and taken part in the elections to the Duma left the party and formed the Trudovik group, directed by Alexander Kerensky. Another break developed after 1906 when the party, fearing that the reforms of Stolypin were going to rally the peasantry to private ownership, drew up its agrarian program. A. V. Peshekhonov thought that the socialization of the land should no longer be urged, but that a democracy of small landowners should be instituted. His advice went unheeded, and he broke away to form the Socialist-Populist party.

Though not very numerous, the Anarchists themselves were split into rival groups who interpreted the teachings of Bakunin, Kropotkin, or Malatesta differently. Although outside of Russia, they were all connected with the Revolutionary Syndicalist movement, the only opinion they shared in common was their condemnation of political parties which, under pretext of defending the workers, acted and decided in their name. They noted that these self-styled "friends of the People" actually adhered to strongly organized parties from which they could exert party-machine control. Thus Peter Kropotkin urged the workers to agitate within the cooperative movement or in the trade-unions, which he thought would be a more effective path to emancipation than direct political action.

Hectored by the bureaucracy, syndicalism (trade unionism) had not developed freely in Russia. On the other hand, the cooperative movement, especially in rural areas, had been progressing at full steam since 1905. The political parties viewed cooperatives with suspicion because they tended to slow down the momentum of popular demands, although Tugan-Baronovsky, an old Marxist converted to reformism and the theory of cooperatism, congratulated himself for precisely this development. Consequently the extremists preferred to cooperate with the political organizations of the national minorities, no matter how suspect their actions appeared.

Unlike the trade-unions and the cooperatives, the nationalist organizations had never been considered by the Russians as a branch of the revolutionary movement. They were shown the sympathy reserved for oppressed people, for the revolutionaries frowned upon the policy of Russification as practiced by the Tsarist government. At best, the revolutionaries conceded that the

12

nationalists could play the role of a reserve army in the struggle against autocracy. They were so far from admitting that the minority groups could have their own problems that they looked upon them with suspicion the moment they formed any opinion which differed from revolutionary orthodoxy. The Social-Democrats even accused the nationalist movement of harboring petit-bourgeois sentiments and of being anti-Socialist, thereby increasing the gap between the people instead of closing it. Even the avowedly Socialist Jewish *Bund* was suspect. It was feared that it would play too important a role at the core of Social-Democracy. The Socialist-Revolutionaries were thought to be more favorably inclined to nationalist movements, but like the Social-Democrats, they thought that the national independence movement, if it succeeded, could only result in strengthening the feudal system. However, with the development of a federalist strain of thought in the S.R., in which Cadet liberalism was pretty well reconciled to the aspirations of the nationalist organizations, the differences between Russian and non-Russian revolutionaries did not always emerge very clearly.

The Revolution of 1905 had revealed the power of the nationalist organizations, and the Russian parties, which had then been made powerless, did not want to lose their support. Without further ado, they recognized the right of these people to self-determination. In spite of Plekhanov's objections, the Mensheviks wrote into their program the national and cultural autonomy claimed by the *Bund*, while the S.R. talked of their preference for a federal solution. Lenin, along with the Bolsheviks, went even further. They had a double objective: to put into action the disintegrating force of the nationalist groups and to tighten proletarian solidarity. Therefore the right to independence of minority groups had to be recognized, although this did not necessarily mean that this right would be exercised once the revolution had triumphed. Just as the right to divorce does not inevitably lead to divorce proceedings, so the right to secede would not necessarily lead to secession if the Russian Revolution, like the French Revolution, could prove attractive to the people of the neighboring countries. Asked by Lenin to clarify this doctrine, Stalin first defined a nation as a community with a territorial base; consequently the Jews did not constitute a real nation and therefore their claims for autonomy were groundless. Later Lenin specified that the right of secession should be accorded to other minority groups even if the demand for autonomy had been instigated by the bourgeoisie, for he felt that the insurrection resulting from this demand would end in weakening the oppressor State. Thus the Russian revolutionaries should help in the nationalist movement and the minority group revolutionaries should pave the way for return to the Socialist mother country as soon as the revolution had triumphed in Russia. The followers of Rosa Luxemburg—that is, the left wing of the nationalist Social-Democrats—did not share these views and kept their traditional veiled hostility to the nationalist movement. The voices of Lenin and Stalin were drowned out and the Bolsheviks were looked upon as the most uncompromising enemies of the nationalist independence movement.

Paralyzed by their differences, the revolutionaries were unable to bring about the downfall of Tsarism, and it was finally the state itself which contributed most effectively to fulfilling the revolutionaries' dreams. Agricultural reforms had neglected an important segment: the peasants who had not emigrated to Siberia surged into the cities where the new metallurgical and chemical industries were creating a demand for manual labor. In St. Petersburg and Moscow these workers became a sort of subproletariat which injected new blood into the workers' movement, turning it away from the revisionist ideas then in favor among numerous militants. The Mensheviks maintained their position of dominance in the Caucasus (except in the seaport city of Baku) and in numerous middle-sized towns, but they lost ground gradually in the large cities, where the Bolsheviks took over the leadership of the large federations (e.g., metallurgical workers, typographical workers, etc.). This surge of Bolshevism among the young and the peasants who had recently settled in the suburbs was understandable; Lenin's party was not postponing the revolution indefinitely and was emerging as a disciplined and active organization. The uninitiated confused Bolshevism and Maximalism, a sign that the most radical of the organized parties was taking over the Russian revolutionary tradition.

During the last prewar months the strike movement took on renewed vigor, vibrant with revolutionary overtones. One wonders if the war did not interrupt a course that would otherwise have been steady; although this question must remain an historians' quarrel because with the coming of war, patriotic fervor completely deflected revolutionary development in this quarter. In sharp contrast to the increase in number of strikers from 46,643 in 1910 to 1,449,234 for the first six months of 1914, the number of strikers fell to 34,752 on a day when the mobilization still had reached only a small part of the population. Along with this, the leaders of the revolutionary parties were again divided; there were "patriots," "internationalists," "defeatists," each group casting anathemas on the others. The fragmentation was such that the revolutionary movement risked total paralysis.

In brief, the question was whether Russian society could manage to absorb the revolutionary ferment along with the World War. Having rehabilitated the working class, was it going to rid itself of those parasites, the leaders without troops who were shivering in Siberia or in the bitterness of exile? It seemed quite likely, for the renovation of the economy seemed to have opened infinite possibilities to the Russian people.

MORE ILLUSIONS:
The Surge of the Economy and the Rebuilding of the Army

When war broke out, economic development in Russia was increasing remarkably. From 1885 to 1913, the rate of industrial growth exceeded 5 percent a year, an exceptional rate for so long a period of time. It was inconceivable that after two years of hostilities the whole system should collapse, without the allies even being able to help.

In 1914 certain sectors of the economy were well developed, especially industry, but the system into which they fitted was still archaic. For example, outstanding progress was made in heavy metallurgy from 1900 to 1914. Was Russia going to be the new America which Wilhelm II wanted to destroy before it was too late? The production of steel alone had been quintupled, and its growth accelerated during the war. Its process of industrial concentration was particularly rapid, reaching the machine-tool sector, munitions, and related areas. Certain firms, such as Med, Snoryado-Soyus, Pridvagon, and Krovlya, controlled as many as twenty enormous factories which accounted for a large part of the production. The same spectacular improvement took place in the drilling for petroleum, where the technical progress of the Russians astounded foreign experts. This phenomenal growth reached the point at which there were proportionately more workers employed in what were then considered giant industries in Russia than there were in their counterparts in the United States. Likewise at the other end, the smallest industries employed only half as many workers as their American analogues. Virtual conglomerates came into being, exerting pressure on the administration to leave them a free hand. In 1916, in order to prepare for real state capitalism, the "Textile King" Rabushinsky drew up a plan of industrial economy that was to be under the control of its directors. This was the logical outcome for a country in which the State had always played the chief economic role.

In agriculture as well certain factors were significant: Russia, which was then the greatest producer and exporter of cereals in the world, ranked high also in the production and export of flax, hemp, and cattle. After 1906 the reforms of Stolypin had triggered a process of agricultural change which the administration watched closely through a veritable army of expert statisticians. The Ministry of Agriculture multiplied experimental stations, model farms, and agricultural schools, which increased from 21 in 1907 to 1,657 in 1913. The war highlighted the image of a rural Russia undergoing change; with several million peasants mobilized and more than two million horses requisitioned, the level of agricultural production held steady for two years, despite a hard winter. Thanks to the influx of Austro-Hungarian prisoners, the landowners were able to obtain cheap manual labor, profits increased, and a market for harvest was assured, even if the exports did suffer because of the war. All this was important and constituted a clear advantage.

Unfortunately, there was also another side to the agricultural picture. In relation to the amount of space available or to the needs of the population, the level of production was mediocre: the wheat harvest was less than eight metric hundredweight per hectare (approximately 2.5 acres), as compared to fifteen in the West where natural conditions were often less favorable. Agricultural production in other areas was equally disappointing. In fact, farming was still only sightly mechanized and production had been improved for only a small part of the rural population. The dominant image of Russian rural life was still one of misery. In addition, life expectancy for a population which was five-sixths rural was only thirty-six years, as against Western Europe's fifty-five. The infant mortality rate was 273 per thousand. Poorly equipped and cut off from the rest of the country, the peasants lived in a world untouched by progress. Other statistics bear this out: cotton production zoomed, but the per capita consumption was one-tenth that of the English, one-third that of the French or Germans. It was the same with other raw materials.

The rise of industrial production was equally illusory. In an epoch when "coal was king," Russia produced one-sixteenth the amount produced by the United States, one-ninth that of Great Britain, and one-sixth that of Germany. She ranked sixth in the production of iron, yet manufactured only 6 percent of the world production of steel. The scarcity of means of transport paralyzed all attempts to modernize the economy; Germany had eleven kilometers of railroads per hundred square kilometers, France had eight or nine, while Russia had only four hundred meters, excluding Siberia. The State was partly responsible for this situation, for it controlled two-thirds of the rail network and had made an effort to modernize it only in Poland, the better to ensure the defense of the territory in case of war with Germany.

The war brought out some unpleasant surprises. Having recovered from its defeat in 1905, the army seemed to be in excellent condition. In accordance with the pacts made with France, the general staff moved against Germany according to schedule. Taken by surprise, the Germans were badly hit at Gumbinnen and were forced to modify the "Schlieffen Plan" and recall some troops from the Western front. This helped Generals Joffre and Gallieni win the battle of the Marne. Thanks to these reinforcements and to some clever strategy, however, the Germans were able to push back the Russians and take 60,000 prisoners at the battle of Tannenberg. For Germany the peril was past. Although the armies of Grand Duke Nicholas lost another 20,000 men, they nevertheless fell back in an orderly fashion, and in the end it was the Central Powers who were put on the spot, as witnessed by the myth of Field Marshal von Hindenburg, "Savior of the Fatherland." Thus the Tsar's Court believed the army was in top form, and some success on the Austrian front and a bitter resistance in East Prussia at the start of 1915 strengthened this illusion.

2. THE DISINTEGRATION

A MILITARY DISASTER

It was at first thought that the war would not last, but by the beginning of 1915 there was nothing to augur an early end to hostilities. For Russia the entry of Japan and of Turkey into the war canceled each other out, at least in the short run. But it foretold a long war, which Russia wouldn't be able to sustain. Lacking a sizable corps of reserve officers, the army could no longer find replacements for the troops which had been decimated during the summer of 1914. Moreover, the inferiority of Russian artillery turned out to be catastrophic. Matériel had been accumulated for a twelve-week campaign and the factories could fill only a third of the needs. The closing of the Dardanelles wiped out any possibility of filling orders placed abroad and was generally a disaster for Russia.

Thus paralyzed, the general staff had to improvise while waiting for the wartime economy to get into gear. It tried to avoid major battles, but the joint offensive of Hindenburg, Hötzendorf, and Enver-Pacha rapidly put the Russian army in a desperate situation.

> For more than twelve days, the Germans swept our lines and we were unable to fire back because we had nothing. . . . Completely exhausted, our regiments fought with bayonets. . . . Blood flowed everywhere. . . . Our ranks were thinned. Two regiments were almost completely destroyed by artillery. When, after three days of silence, our battery received *fifty shells*, all the regiments and companies were immediately informed and the men were overcome with joy and relief.

The high command managed to avoid being wiped out altogether, but half of the army was disabled—151,000 killed, 683,000 wounded, 895,000 taken prisoner. Such an unprecedented disaster lowered the morale of the troops and their commanders. The responsibility for it was laid on those in the rear—that is to say, on the government.

The retreat had grave consequences. Lithuania, Poland, and Galicia came under control of the Central Powers, who made the most of the situation by professing solicitude for the rights of the national minorities. They allowed representatives of these groups to be present at the Lausanne Conference where they greatly outnumbered the delegates of the Austro-Hungarian minorities. But the stratagem boomeranged, for the delegates turned against their sponsors. Its most active members, those from Poland, Lithuania, and Ukrainia, started the publication of a *Bulletin of Russian Minorities* in which Tsarism and its allies were sharply criticized. Germany followed up its advantage by organizing a *Finnish Legion*, which went off to fight against the Russians. It did the same with the Ukrainians and the Tartars and recognized Polish independence on November 3, 1916. The purpose of this was to organize an army to fight on the Russian Front. Although the Poles saw through the tactic, nevertheless they were aware that Germany was opening up new horizons for them, as well as for the Finns, the Balts, and the Ukrainians. The main thrust of the Central Powers was aimed at weakening the Russian state, which had already been badly shaken up by the events of 1915.

Meanwhile Grand Duke Nicholas and his chief of staff, General Zhanuskevitch, tried to keep up appearances. They likened the 1915 retreat to that of 1812, as if, once again, they were acting out a preconceived plan. They systematically used scorched earth tactics, the upshot of which was that the experts of the general staff added their own destruction to that of the enemy; women and children swelled the columns of retreating troops. Thousands of refugees drifted toward the rear where they were not expected and no arrangements had been made for them. A. V. Krivoshein, the Minister of Agriculture, predicted that "This great migration, organized by headquarters, will drive Russia to the brink, to revolution, to perdition." In effect, the moment of truth rang for the old Régime. Would the economy be able to supply the army's wants? Would it bow to popular demand and make concessions to opinion which would encourage the Russian people to make new sacrifices?

THE ECONOMIC SYSTEM CEASES TO FUNCTION

The requirements of sixteen million soldiers called for a reconversion of the economy, one that was to be unmatched anywhere outside of Russia. More than 80 percent of the factories were taken over to supply war needs. However, there was no rise in production because the new labor force, recruited from farms, was unused to factory work; in fact, output fell about 30 percent. Agricultural production, predictably, also fell off. Six hundred thousand prisoners and countless refugees did not adequately compensate for the loss of skilled farm workers, and land under cultivation was reduced by a fifth.

The loss of the western provinces meant the loss to Russia of Polish industrial production. The retreat aggravated the already precarious situation of rolling stock. In 1916, out of a hundred locomotives, eighteen had already been destroyed or were in the hands of the enemy, and five were out of commission. In Russia itself, rail traffic decreased 32 percent in 1915, 22 percent more in 1916; in the Donbas, an important region economically, it was less than 59 percent of that of 1914.

In addition, the Russian economy suffered from another handicap—the stranglehold of foreign capital. Before the war, more attention had been paid to economic penetration than to financial take-over because low-priced goods, especially from Germany, were competing with those made in Russia. It was now plain that the capital squeeze, which had been less obvious, was tight. Foreign firms controlled nearly half the investments; 90 percent in mining, 42 percent in iron works, 28 percent in textiles, 50 percent in chemicals, and comparable figures in other industries. The fact that the Allies were holding 68 percent of these funds was bound to have its effect on the foreign policy of the managerial class. These conditions of capital ownership also indicated the urgent need for a conversion in the economy. Russia had to repay these debts with raw materials, which were therefore given priority. But because of the German blockade and the closure of the Dardanelles, the Russian debt increased. Furthermore, the cost of the material delivered by the allies spiraled upward. To make up the deficit, Russia had to provide fresh troops for the fronts in Champagne and in Salonica. They landed in Marseilles, to the shock of the Russians on the home front. Russian capitalists were more successful in resisting a French syndicate which had proposed the establishment of some kind of control over Russian railroads. Imports became rarer, as allied industry was barely able to supply its own needs on the Western front. Deliveries decreased even before the submarine war was launched; in 1916 they had fallen to 36 percent of the 1914 level.

The necessity for a realignment of the economy in line with the needs of the army seemed all the more imperative since the allies' interests were also involved. Given over completely to defense needs, industry was no longer able to take care of civilian requirements. With industry so concentrated and rigid, there was no safety valve. In a few months the rear had no manufactured products. Thus the back of the Russian economy was broken, with the most far-reaching consequences. Unable to buy industrial products, the peasants slowed their deliveries to the cities. What good were rubles? There was nothing to spend them on. In the larger cities agricultural prices rose as fast as industrial prices. By 1917 they were three to five times as high as they had been in 1914:

Product	Before War	April 1917
Rye Flour (one bag)	6r. 50k.	40r.
Wheat Flour (one *pud*, i.e. 36 lbs)	2r. 50k.	16r.
Potatoes (one bag)	1r.	7r.
Meat (one lb)	10-12k.	60-70k.
Fat	12-15k.	90k.
Kerosene	4-5k.	11-12k.
Pair of shoes	5-8r.	40r.
Yard Goods (one *arsin*)	10-12k.	50-70k.
Two cubic meters of firewood	6r.	40r.

Salaries did not keep up with prices, because the influx of workers from the countryside kept wages down. In January 1917 in the factories of Novy Lessner, in Petrograd, less than 10 percent of the workers received a minimum living wage—i.e., two hundred rubles a month. Half got less than a hundred rubles, which was the average wage of the best paid workers in the provinces, the typographers. The following is a typical budget of a "privileged" family of Kharkov.

1. Average salary per month: 1913: 43 to 55 rubles
   1916-1917: 90 to 111 rubles
2. Average consumption of a family of four:

	Pre-War Price	Price on April 15, 1917
4 lbs bread	16 k	60 k
1½ lbs meat	28 k	1r 50 k
½ lb fat	13 k	50 k
Other food	10 k	50 k
1 herring	5 k	30 k
Tea and sugar	7 k	15 k
2 *puds* kerosene	10 k	20 k
2 glasses milk	6 k	26 k
Entertainment	10 k	20 k
Daily Expense	1 ruble 5 k	4 rubles 2 k
Monthly Expense:		
Rent	15r	30r
Laundry	1r 50 k	6r
Miscellaneous expense	50 k	2r
Dues and sickness insurance	1r	2r
	18 rubles	40 rubles
Total for Month	63 rubles	166 rubles 30 k

On an average, workers received wages which leveled around 44 to 50 rubles in 1916, or about half that of the typographers of Kharkov; this was a quarter of the minimum living wage. Figured in gold rubles, this wage remained identical with that of 1914, the rise in price being compensated by the rise in wages. Management thought that it had made enough concessions. The workers did not, and the number of strikers skyrocketed:

August-December 1914	34,752
1915	553,094
1916	1,086,354

The salaries of white-collar workers and civil servants lagged even further behind the rise in prices. The buying power of the middle class and the petite bourgeoisie sank to rock bottom, as is shown in the following table:

		WORKERS' WAGES		WHITE-COLLAR WAGES	
Year	Price Index	Actual	Real	Actual	Real
1913	100	21-22	21-22	85.5	85.5
1914	101	22.9	22.7	85.5	84.6
1915	130	27-32	21-24	103	79.2
1916	203	44-50	22-25	142	69.8
1917	673	142-143	21.2	255	38.0

Four times higher than those of laborers in 1914, the salaries of civil servants and white-collar workers had decreased relatively by half. The laborers were not paid any better than they had been in the past. As for the white-collar workers, they were much worse off and were just as angry with the régime as were the laborers. When working-class demonstrators organized a march in 1917, white-collar workers and tradesmen joined the parade, something they had not done in 1905.

There were price increases, shortages, queues. The economic system was paralyzed at every level: production, distribution, and consumption. The reconversion effort had made a mess of revenues and reawakened demands for social justice. How were the State and the ruling classes going to react?

THE STATE DISINTEGRATES:
The People Take Over

Upon the declaration of war, Nicholas II had given the high command tremendous military power. With the 1915 setback these powers extended right into the heart of Russia, to the capital (St. Petersburg, renamed Petrograd). Trouble mounted as the army chided the administration for its lack of foresight, and the administration in turn accused the army of creating chaos. No one knew who was in charge. There was a vacuum in the government which the ruling classes lost no time in filling.

Shorn of a part of his powers, Prime Minister Goremykin, an old man, tried to hold the resentment of his colleagues in check. Nicholas II did not care for recriminations and was very angry. Jealous of the Grand Duke Nicholas's position as supreme commander, he held him responsible for his country's misfortunes and decided to take over the supreme command himself. God had spoken to him and his job was to lead the troops to victory. The court, as well as the people, were appalled; everyone knew his indolence and his incompetence in military matters. Moreover, it was easy to foresee that once the Tsar left Tsarskoe-Selo, the cabinet would lose all authority, because the Tsarina would hire and fire ministers as she pleased. Members of the government begged Goremykin to forestall this catastrophe, to ask Nicholas II to change his mind. Goremykin protested; the ministers offered their resignations, but the Tsar refused to accept them and they remained in office. A few weeks later, Nicholas II dismissed them. Deprived of even the right to resign, the ministers had lost all authority. The Tsar's presence in the capital had created the illusion that it was the seat of government; with him gone to the wars, even that illusion evaporated.

The Tsar's departure contributed to the government's disintegration. Having taken command of the armies, he led a new life in the field which seemed to agree with him. He gave the impression of being on vacation. This did not keep him from exposing himself to enemy fire. His duty as sovereign demanded it, and he never shirked. But once away from the government, from the city, and from business, he showed no desire to be kept informed; this was the prime minister's job. He was not importuned because of his well-known aversion to administrative work. Cut off from reality in his special train somewhere near Mogilev, Nicholas II relied upon Alexandra, his wife, who liked politics and often showed more firmness than her husband.

Unfortunately, the Tsarina was very unpopular. Being of German origin, haughty and devout, she inspired little confidence among the Russians, who wrongfully suspected her of Germanophilia. But what they especially held against her was her involvement with the clique ruled by the monk Rasputin. This peasant had insinuated himself into the court by his mysticism and by his claim that he knew about "the real feelings of Russia." Listening to him was more appealing than having to hear complaints emanating from the cities. More or less a healer, he earned the gratitude of Alexandra and of her husband for saving the life of their son Alexis. At Tsarskoe-Selo, pandering to the taste of the court for the occult, he showed the pious, especially the women, the way to salvation. Husbands could profit from his connections with their wives because he saw to it that they got ahead in their careers. Within a few years, the government was filled with his "creatures." Council President Boris Stürmer, and Minister of the Interior Alexander Protopopov were among the ouija-board addicts.

Just as in the famous "Diamond Necklace Affair" on the eve of the French Revolution, public rumor exaggerated, when it did not actually invent, court excesses. In 1916 the court clique was accused of arranging a separate peace or knowingly opening the way for enemy invasion. Rasputin was held responsible for all the country's misfortunes at that time. Some compared Nicholas II with Louis XVI and Alexandra with Marie-Antoinette. Nicholas, with his unassuming manner, his deep love for his wife, his devoutness, and his solicitude for his children, gave the impression of being a "good king."

Actually the Tsar was an autocratic, lazy ruler who was bored by cabinet meetings and wearied by any edifying conversation. Like Alexandra, he was uncomfortable in the company of any but mediocrities. The more talented his ministers, the sooner he became irritated with them. Far from being the easygoing sovereign depicted by his admirers, Nicholas II was always defending his prerogatives. His father and the absolutist ideologue Konstantin Pobedonostsev had taught him that he was the autocratic Tsar, that God had willed it so, and that any concessions to the times were sacrilegious. Ashamed of having been forced to set up a Duma in 1905, Nicholas felt not the slightest remorse about having ordered the people to be fired on; in fact, he bore them a grudge for having rebelled against his "majesty" and debated whether or not to forgive them. Timid and uncommunicative, the Tsar governed Russia in ritual fashion. Alexandra exclaimed: "What! Share the power with the Duma? That's ridiculous! Nicolas is an autocratic Tsar. How could he share his divine right with anyone?" After the revolution of 1905 had been quelled, the ruler in Nicholas fell into a deep sleep. Until the last minute he devoted himself to his wife, to his children's health, and to his personal appearance. He took a daily walk, and in his diary he made observations about the rain or the good weather.

The country reacted violently against this neglect. It wanted to safeguard its heritage and save the land, but this had to be done slowly and carefully, without upsetting the bureaucrats, who clung to their prerogatives. Thus sprang up private associations, concerned with the public interest, which tried to obtain from the Tsar or from highly placed officials the guarantees which would allow them to act without interference. The "Red Cross Committee" set the example. It started out modestly, but little by little took over the administration of public health and became a branch of the Ministry of Public Health. The *zemstvos* also intervened, giving the newly formed associations their support. After 1914 the delegates of thirty-five of these met in Moscow and became a "Pan-Russian Union of *Zemstvos*" to help sick and wounded soldiers. Directed by Prince Lvov, the activities of the Union soon went beyond this first phase and became quite popular. A "Union of cities" was also founded, through which the town mayors were able to coordinate the reception of refugees, the deployment of prisoners of war, and other related functions. Then a "Committee of War Industries" was formed in Moscow by Alexander Guchkov. Its objective was the streamlining of war production. These representatives of commerce and industry became a sort of parallel ministry, having branches in all the big cities. The "Union of *Zemstvos* and Cities" was then organized for the purpose of provisioning the army and supplying it with munitions. This union also formed the *"Zemgor"* which served to assist the "Committee of War Industries."

Thanks to all this activity, the army was better supplied in 1916 than in 1915. General Brusilov was even able to carry out a victorious offensive in Galicia. However, his progress was interrupted again because of a shortage of supplies. Once more the enemy had the advantage of a crushing artillery superiority of three-to-one at certain places on the front. The allies had reduced their deliveries in spite of the desperate appeals of the Russian high command. Thus France, in 1916, supplied only 56 out of 592 promised airplanes and 612 motorized units out of 4,194 ordered. This matériel was only 5 percent of the needs of the army and the country was able to supply only half the orders. Financial aid from the allies also decreased. When Minister of Finance Bark came to Paris in 1916 to apply for a loan, he was received coolly— Russia did not seem to be fighting with the same energy as France at Verdun.

The rear did not know about the temporary improvement at the front. Consumers became better organized and the already well developed cooperative movement spread. The difficulties of everyday life, the price increases, the endless queues spurred the formation of giant cooperatives of twenty to thirty thousand members. They grew like mushrooms, and the largest ones merged. The workers' cooperatives, which were weaker, were threatened with absorption and, in 1917, Kropotkin urged them to fuse with the trade-unions to form "Communities of Cooperation." At this time, Russia had 35,000 cooperative societies, totaling nearly ten million members.

The government viewed all these proofs of the vitality of the Russian people with suspicion. The administration watched helplessly as it was slowly being divested of its powers. Every working group became organized: big business, industry, the professions, etc.—"all this without authorization," noted a police report. Without realizing it, the Russians were beginning to govern themselves: the army on one side, the producers and consumers on the other.

The revolution had not yet been thought out, but it existed in fact.

3. THE IDEA OF REVOLUTION IS ACCEPTED

THE GROWTH OF THE LEGAL OPPOSITION

In 1914 there was nothing to indicate that the Duma would play a decisive role in the downfall of the régime. "Badly elected," this fourth Duma had no prestige. It lost the little authority it might have commanded when it failed to protest the abuse of Article 87 which allowed the government to withdraw its right to oversee public affairs. However, the government was unable to keep its President, Mikhail Rodzianko, from requesting an audience with the Tsar. Conscious of his importance and rather tending to exaggerate it, Rodzianko did not hesitate to use his prerogative. This irritated Nicholas II, who was constantly being recalled to his duties as sovereign. The Duma also tried to act on the cabinet. Its members, who had joined haphazardly the various committees and associations created since 1914, had asked the prime minister for the necessary authorizations. Was this the beginning of cooperation? Goremykin reluctantly accepted this intrusion of the Duma into the affairs of State. He gave the "Committee for the Aid of the Victims of War" to understand that the situation was not serious and that the pessimism of the committee was harmful to the morale of the nation. General Vladimir Sukhomlinov and N. Maklakov considered their zeal out of place. "Either the government is hiding the truth and is deceiving us, or it is blind, which is a sign of ineptitude," commented Milyukov.

This marked the end of the political truce of 1914. Encouraged by the Octobrists, a majority of those elected formed a "Progressive Bloc" to which some members of the "Council of the Empire" and even some ministers rallied. The objectives of the "Bloc" remained modest since they did not dare demand a responsible minister but merely a "government by trust." Their aim was to get rid of the ministers whom Goremykin himself had singled out as expendable. Always vigilant when it came to defending the prerogatives of the autocracy, the prime minister not only disapproved of the attitude of the "Bloc" but even decided that it was illegally constituted. Subsequently the "Bloc" campaigned against the government, forcing the ministers who supported it to resign. Goremykin had won this round and the Duma was then adjourned.

In a move that seemed deliberately provoking to the assembly,

Alexandra and Nicholas chose as replacement for Goremykin, whom they now considered useless, a protégé of Rasputin's, Governor Stürmer, a veteran of the Okhrana (the secret police), who prided himself on being a reactionary.

Not missing a chance, liberal opinion criticized the ineptitude of the administration and demanded a more responsible government. Although the sessions of the Duma were getting shorter and shorter, they seemed like a breath of fresh air in this reactionary atmosphere. Benefitting from an unprecedented opportunity to be heard, the assembly shone to such a point that the Social-Democrats themselves declared, along with the prominent Menshevik Nikolai Chkheidze, that "nothing hereafter could be done without it."

The court maneuvered. Well aware, as V. Maklakov showed in a famous parable, that the legal opposition was too timorous to change horses in midstream, it persuaded Nicholas II to overcome his prejudice against the Duma and to be present at its next opening session. Flattered by his presence, the deputies would not dare show their feelings about Sturmer. In fact they did not, for essentially they were faithful to the régime and only hoped to make it more liberal.

Still, there were some who wondered whether, in order to save Tsarism and Russia, it would not be necessary to get rid of Nicholas II, who was falling more and more under the influence of the court clique of Alexandra and Rasputin. The latter had even managed to have the paranoid Protopopov appointed to serve in the Ministry of the Interior. A league was formed against "inept" ministers and even the Union of the Russian People set up a hue and cry against Rasputin. Then it was Milyukov's turn to denounce the government officials: "taken separately, each of their acts was senseless, but taken together, they amounted to treason." Despite the censorship, the press printed these philippics. S. I. Shydlovsky, in the name of the "Progressist Bloc," accused the government of starving the capital on purpose to incite the riots which would be an excuse for concluding a separate peace. Kerensky demanded the dismissal of "all ministers [who were] traitors to the country," and Chkheidze stated that "the hour has come to side with the people against the government or with the government against the people." At the beginning of 1917 Nicholas II yielded to public opinion and dismissed Sturmer. He chose as his successor Prince Golytsin, who "declined the honor," requesting that a prime minister be selected who would have the confidence of the country. Nonetheless, he was forced to accept the appointment.

The court now blamed everything on Rasputin. In keeping with tradition, it hatched a plot and thus the favorite was felled by assassins. The execution of Rasputin was hailed as a first step toward the rehabilitation of the country, although in the Duma it was feared that the Romanovs would seek a cruel revenge—as indeed they did. At this point the opposition decided to strike at the top by replacing Nicholas II and erecting a constitutional monarchy with Prince Lvov or Milyukov as prime minister. The plot brought together several personalities who did not always see eye to eye. There were industrialists like Alexander Konovalov and M. I. Tereshchenko (the latter had close ties with the British Embassy), parliamentarians like Guchkov, Kerensky, and N.V. Nekrassov, and soldiers like Generals Brusilov and Alexeiev. All felt that the rupture of the ruling classes with the Tsar and his court clique was unavoidable; by joining together they had chosen sides.

There was talk of a "Palace Revolution." They were all against a popular uprising for fear of seeing the mass movement veer to the extreme Left, creating difficulties in the prosecution of the war.

Other plots were hatched, but there was some hestitation about bringing Grand Dukes into them and about ways and means. No hurry was felt because it was thought that the illegal opposition would not revive and that the nation would not rise spontaneously.

REVIVAL OF THE UNDERGROUND OPPOSITION

The strikes started up again in extraordinary numbers. The lack of money, the decline in purchasing power, and the wave of political repression all gave rise to a growing discontent. The people were war weary, but the workers hesitated to show their yearning for peace, for it ran against their patriotic feelings and would make the Duma suspicious. The strikes had political motives as well as economic ones, and represented a sort of return to prewar revolutionary tradition. The timing of these demonstrations showed that there was a central organization behind them, consisting of secret groups in Russia that were controlled from abroad. Conversely, the quarrels of the Socialists abroad had their repercussions in Russia, "disrupting the movement while great things were afoot."

Plekhanov and Lenin were at opposite poles. Faithful to the social-patriot position adopted in 1914, the former saw his authority weakened in *émigré* circles. A police report noted that in Paris the number of voluntary enlistments was decreasing because of the influence of the Internationalists. Plekhanov's group at that time included Alexinsky and Leon Deutsch, who along with the Socialist-Revolutionary N. D. Avxentiev edited *Privyz*. Its only success was the rallying of Vera Zasulich to their side, although she too considered Plekhanov's position too chauvinistic. At the other pole, alone by choice, Lenin refused to have anything to do with those responsible for the failure of the Second International. As a concession to Russian patriotism, he no longer stressed defeat, but merely "transformation of the imperialist war into civil war." There he was in disagreement with the majority of Internationalists who, behind Martov, Axelrod, Chernov, and Natanson (Bobrov), wanted first of all to reorganize the International so as to force all governments to conclude a peace without annexations. Their only point of agreement was their condemnation of the Social-Patriots, whom they described as Social-Chauvinists.

At Zimmerwald, in September 1915, an international convention of revolutionaries holding similar views was held. There were few participants because the majority of Socialists and Syndicalists had adhered to the "Sacred Union" (in German, *Burgfriede*). In spite of Camille Huysmans, who along with the International Bureau was of the opinion that under these conditions a convention was premature, certain delegates showed up at Zimmerwald, mainly Russians, Italians, and some neutrals. The manifesto produced by this convention and addressed to the whole world nevertheless had quite an impact. Condemning the policies of the "Sacred Union," it issued a call for a peace campaign, pointing out the imperialistic character of the war. All the Russian Socialists except the Plekhanov-Avxentiev group subscribed to this call. A "leftist group" organized by Lenin, Karl Radek, and Nikolai Bukharin considered this manifesto insufficient. They had reservations as well on the second manifesto issued by the Zimmerwaldians at Kienthal in 1916, despite its somewhat firmer tone. Henceforth, this "Zimmerwaldian Left" refused to cooperate with those who, while condemning the "scuttlers" of the International, had not broken with them. Martov and his friends considered this position too strong, for it isolated the workers from their leaders, and they felt it was essential that all those fighting Tsarism close ranks. The militants who edited *Nashe Slovo*, the organ of Trotsky's "Unitarians," like the Bolshevik group of *Novy Mir* in New York, were of the same opinion. Lenin's "sectarianism" worried even Dmitri Manuilsky, Bukharin, and V. Maisky, who leaned toward Martov and his friends.

Judging that events were beginning to justify his position, Lenin stood firm. On August 23, 1915, he wrote to Alexander Shlyapnikov, in Russia:

> The military setbacks help in the disintegration of Tsarism and facilitate the union of the revolutionary Russian workers with other countries. . . .
> 1. Our victory will strengthen the Leftist movement in Germany a hundredfold.
> 2. As soon as Tsarism is defeated, we will propose peace on a democratic basis to all belligerents, and in case of refusal, we will start a revolutionary war.

In 1916, finishing the draft of *Imperialism, the Highest Stage of Capitalism*, Lenin opined that a revolution would break out, not in a country where capitalism was strongest, but in a state economically undeveloped. The war would thus reverse Marxist dogma and made the explosion more likely to occur in Russia than elsewhere. Lenin thought also that the uprising of the racial minorities would contribute to it, and that such an uprising therefore should be encouraged. On this point Radek, Bukharin, and Grigori Pyatakov disagreed with Lenin, who remained practically alone, even at the core of the "Zimmerwaldian Left." The only ones to share these views were Grigori Zinoviev and Alexandra Kollantay, as expressed in *Komu Nuzhna Voyna? (Who Needs the War?)*

These exiles, who had been preparing since 1914, were the prime movers of all the pacifist and activist movements of Europe. They were without peer when it came to publishing illegal pamphlets, changing residence or identity. The team of "professional revolutionaries" of which Lenin had dreamed was already in existence. However, they were not all on his side and their opposite numbers in Russia were equally divided into irreconcilable groups. But in Russia the pressure from the masses was stronger than their internal divisions.

This had not always been the case. In 1915 a bourgeois proposal from the "Committee of War Industries" had revived all the controversies of the first years of war. The committee had proposed that workers' representatives form a "worker group" to participate in the committee's activities. This unprecedented suggestion posed a serious problem to the working class because an acceptance would enable the ruling class to take the place of the State, which had proven itself unable to save the country. It would also enable the ruling class to lead the struggle against the régime. For these reasons the Bolsheviks came out against acceptance. Cooperation with bourgeois imperialism was unthinkable because victory would reinforce its power as well as that of Tsarism; defeat, on the other hand, would lead to revolution more certainly than victory. Those who wanted victory must be fought.

The Social-Patriots took a contrary stand: because the principal enemy of the international workers' movement was German imperialism, a truce must be arranged with the bourgeoisie as it had been with Tsarism. And so they recommended acceptance. The majority of the revolutionaries rejected either of these extreme proposals, for defeatism was unpopular and the workers instinctively tended to defend their country, but they still did not want to cooperate with the "class enemy." The upshot was that six or seven organizations thought it advisable to accept the bourgeois proposals but to remain alert. This was the position of Vera Zasulich and the *Samozashchita (Self-Defense)* group. Militants like K. A. Gvozdev, Volsky (N. Valentinov), Cherevanin, and V. Potressov were willing to make a temporary agreement with the bourgeoisie in order to prepare the attack on Tsarism and to safeguard the status of the workers in the future régime. Martov, Axelrod, Maisky, and others who were against any such cooperation wanted to give a "class content" to their participation by helping war victims and so forth.

In September 1915, after several months of discussion, a vote was taken. A strong majority in Petrograd was against acceptance. The result was a surprise. At a time when all the extremist organizations were in complete disarray, the vote did not so much express the growing influence of Bolshevik slogans as the fact that the Bolsheviks had adapted to the wishes of the masses. Still, at the elections in November, the principle of the formation of workers groups' was affirmed, but its supporters were somewhat discredited for the Zimmerwaldians had refused to take part. To regain the confidence of the people, those elected, among whom were Gvozdev and V. Bogdanov, waged an active campaign against Tsarism. They regained enough ground to cause the police, informed of their intentions by the Menshevik Abrossimov, to decide to take steps to neutralize them. The group was arrested in January 1917.

The quarrels between the factions split the workers movement wide open, although it was unanimous in its hatred of the régime. Any strike ordered by the Bolsheviks was doomed to failure because the "Defensists" condemned it under the pretext that it favored the victory of German imperialism and ruined the chances of democracy and socialism, while the Zimmerwaldians claimed that it was anarchistic and warned against it. Moreover, as the Bolshevik strength came from the big factories, manned by new-comers who had no workingman's tradition, their rivals insinuated at every opportunity that they were merely the tools of agitators. If, on the other hand, a demonstration came from "Defensist" circles, was it in response to a call from the Duma? In this case neither the Bolsheviks nor the other "Internationalists" would have anything to do with it; they had nothing but suspicion for the bourgeois and imperialist Duma who would abandon them at the first chance. If an action originated with Martov's friends, or Chernov's or Trotsky's, the Bolsheviks and the workers' group refused to participate—the first, so as not to cooperate with the militants who would not formally denounce social patriotism; the second, so as not to "play into the hands of the extremists." Under these conditions, the party members could swear eternal hatred to autocracy, but this accomplished nothing. No one thought that a series of contradictory slogans could lead to revolution.

"THE HOUSE TOTTERS"

A police report dated at the beginning of 1917 describes the feelings of the working class, the difficulties of living, and the weariness caused by the war:

According to the spokesman for the war industry workers' group, the proletariat in the capital is on the verge of despair. It is believed that the slightest disturbance, on the smallest pretext, will lead to uncontrollable riots with thousands of victims. In fact, the conditions for such an explosion already exist. The economic condition of the masses, in spite of large raises in wages, is near the point of distress. . . . Even if wages are doubled, the cost of living has trebled. The impossibility of obtaining goods, the loss of time spent queueing up in front of stores, the increasing mortality rate because of poor housing conditions, the cold and dampness resulting from lack of coal . . . —all these conditions have created such a situation that the mass of industrial workers is ready to break out in the most savage of hunger riots.

The political discontent went even further:

The legal restrictions which weigh on the workers have become unbearable and intolerable. Forbidding changes of employment from one factory to another or from one job to another has reduced the workers to a chattel state, good only for "cannon fodder." Restrictions on all meetings, even for the purpose of organizing cooperatives or canteens, and the closing of unions are the reasons why the workers, led by the more educated and perhaps the more revolutionary among them, adopt an openly hostile attitude to the government and protest against the continuation of the war.

They wanted a confrontation. After the arrest of the "worker group," Protopopov and General Belayev, Ministers of Interior and War, decided, with General Khabalov, Regional Military Commander of Petrograd, to send for reinforcements. They outlined the jobs of the police, the Cossacks, and the army. Because of the lack of barracks, however, they were unable to increase the garrison as much as they wished. This worried them a little because the reserves, recruited locally, were not very reliable.

The discontent spread from the rear to the troops, from front lines to reserves. Already irritated with the officers who were held responsible for the slaughter of 1915, the soldiers blamed the "barines" (gentlemen) for all their misfortunes. Their letters were full of invectives against those in charge and they spoke of a "settling of accounts" when the war was over, or even sooner.

After the workers and the soldiers, the idea of a needed change had entered the heads of even those most hostile to revolutionary ideas. Prince Mansyrev hoped to enlarge the activities of literary groups like the "St. Petersburg Club" or the "Society of the Year 1914" in order to prepare the way for a political revolution. "Revolutionary ideas insinuated themselves even among people who had nothing in common with the Socialists. It was the fashion. One began to notice indifference to the troops' success. The calls to freedom got more response than the patriotic appeals." Like the advanced wing of the Duma, the conservatives wanted to prepare the changeover themselves in order to prevent the effects of a revolution originating in the streets. They fought all movements which they did not originate themselves but they were powerless. During this time, inflamatory speeches shook the structure.

"The house totters," noted the poetess Zinaida Hippius, the

wife of the writer Dmitri Merezhkovsky. "Should not the liberals help with their own hands to destroy what is doomed to destruction, so that the building won't collapse entirely and bury us all in the rubble?" But who, in February 1917, could believe in the intuition of a poet?

CHAPTER TWO

★

THE FALL OF THE ANCIEN RÉGIME

1. THE PETROGRAD INSURRECTION: THE "FIVE DAYS"

In Petrograd, around mid-February, only a ten-days' supply of flour remained. The Regional Commander, General Khabalov, decided, along with the municipal authorities, to set up a rationing system. The crowd learned of it and the following morning, February 16, the lines stretched out in front of the bakers' shops, then in front of all food stores. Emptied in a few hours, some stores closed their steel shutters. Crowds gathered and store windows were broken into. In the days following, these incidents recurred. They happened mostly after long hours of waiting, in twenty below weather, when the crowd heard the dreaded *"n'et-u"* ("there isn't any more").

The Duma had just had its opening session on February 14. Andrei Shingarev (Progressist) and M. I. Skobelev (Menshevik) challenged the "unfit ministers." They urged them to leave, adding that in France "the people of yore had known how to sweep the throne." The deputies blamed the government for the fact that the management of the Putilov factories had dismissed thousands of workers following a strike; during periods of scarcity it left whole families in want, without aiding them. These speeches, however, were made to empty seats. For some time, the President of the Council and his ministers had gotten into the habit of showing their contempt for the deputies by not even coming to the meetings.

Foreseeing the storm, the leftist deputies tried to establish contact with the clandestine organizations. It was the lawyer N. D. Sokolov's idea to meet at Gorky's. Kerensky and Chkheidze came as representatives of the Duma Left and Shlyapnikov and K. K. Zhurenev of the clandestine organizations. Also present were publishers and cooperative and party delegates, including V. Zenzinov (S.R.) and A. V. Peshekhonov (Socialist Populist). "Nothing but gossip," Zhurenev observed; nevertheless, contact was established between the two opposition movements. The Bolsheviks, united and long-standing enemies of the workers' group, refused to be associated with Duma demonstrations. Once more the movement had run aground. A few days later at Gorky's house Kerensky and Shlyapnikov had words.

Meanwhile, the parties and the trade-unions were trying to

35

organize a demonstration for February 23, called "Workers' Day." For the occasion an organizing committee had been put together under the aegis of the Unitarians. Were they going to organize a strike or a parade? After the failure of the preceding week's demonstration, the Bolsheviks were somewhat reluctant. They thought the attempt premature. On the morning of the 23rd, seeing the strikers, men and women, lining up in formation, they decided to take part.

On the first day, the women's demonstration was swelled by the workers dismissed from Putilov, who were soon followed by thousands of other workers. Fearing trouble in the center of town, the authorities had ordered the closing of offices and stores. The city employees were asked not to report for work; thus they were present at the demonstration and, like many curious bystanders, followed the parade. "The strikers were serious and dignified," remarked Marylin Markovitch. Thus the Petersburg petite-bourgeoisie joined the workers of Vyborg to demonstrate against Tsarism. On that day the Russian working class came out of the ghetto.

The mood was somewhat gay. "It looked like a holiday," noted an eyewitness. The streetcars were stopped. The Cossacks patrolled and were greeted in a friendly fashion. The passiveness of the police surprised everyone. In fact, underestimating the importance of the demands—they weren't merely demanding bread or work, but peace and the end of Tsarism—the authorities thought the demonstration reflected only worry about lack of food. During the night of the 23rd and 24th they had placards posted reassuring the populace on the availability of breadstuff.

On the second day the wives of the workers once more played an essential role. For everybody, it was a question of parading on the Nevsky Prospect and attracting as many people as possible. The workers set off at eight o'clock from points of departure at Vyborg, Petrogradsky, and Vassily Island, the main worker quarters of Petrograd. This time the police were stationed so as to prevent the demonstrators from crossing the Neva bridges. Going past the bridges, the demonstrators crossed the river on the ice and reformed on the other side. With their red flag in the lead, they chanted *La Marseillaise*. In Russia this revolutionary hymn had kept its original meaning; it was sung with faith and determination. An immense crowd gathered at Znamenskaya Square, shouting "Long Live the Republic." The Cossacks appeared and were acclaimed. Kazhurov, a Bolshevik worker, saw one of them nod as one would to an accomplice, and he wondered what it meant. But the mounted police arrived; they yelled "Keep moving," and with swords drawn they charged, wounding and killing many. The demonstrators ran in every direction, escaping as best they could. Snarling, the police didn't pursue; they didn't know what to do, for they had been given no instructions.

Polite society did not know that the night of the 24th to the 25th would be the last *soirée* of Petersburg. At the meeting for the aid of the prisoners of war, as at the "Anglo-Russian Society," no one spoke of the day's events. Meanwhile at the Council of Ministers, Protopopov assured his colleagues that these popular demonstrations meant nothing, that in twenty-four hours they would be brought to heel. Prince Golytsin evaded a meeting with Guchkov who had sought him out. The Octobrist leader had learned that the police were to emplace machine guns on the roofs of buildings to disperse the demonstration predicted for the morrow. He left a message at the home of the President of the Council saying that if those machine guns weren't withdrawn he would not guarantee the fate of the dynasty. The message remained unanswered.

On the third day the Bolsheviks were the main organizers of the strikes and parades. The strikers returned with exceptional force. Had they heard the call of the parties? Whatever it was, at dawn the posters stuck up by General Khabalov had been torn down. Around ten o'clock everyone was afoot. This time the role of the organizations was obvious.

The War Minister, General Belayev, had recommended that the demonstrators be prevented from crossing the Neva. They must not shoot at them, "because of the impression it would make on the Allies; instead, they should break the ice in front of them." However, Khabalov gave no specific instructions. As on the day before, the working-class crowd rolled toward town. Everyone was watching the reactions of the Cossacks, of the army, and of the mounted police (Pharaohs). Kept in reserve, the army intervened very little. More aggressive than on Friday, the Pharaohs wounded and killed some; harassed by various projectiles, they charged viciously, chasing the stragglers. Commissioner Krylov was killed. One could see the difference between the mounted police and the Cossacks, who always went through gaps opened by the crowd. "Hurray," yelled the crowd. The Cossacks pranced near them, as though to protect them. Twice already they had refused to back the police. At about three o'clock that afternoon they were the heroes of a memorable exploit. On Znamenskaya Square a speaker was lecturing the demonstrators, when the Pharaohs arrived to disperse them. No one moved. One of the Pharaohs aimed his weapon at the orator. The crowd began screaming. Then in a cloud of snow and dust, a Cossack charged forward and cut the Pharaoh down. Others surged in and put the police to rout. The crowd remained thunderstruck, not knowing what to think.

That evening at the Council of Ministers the discussion was stormy. Protopopov was furious because Golytsin had met Rodzianko in his absence and because the food supply for the capital had been turned over to the Municipal Council. "I'll have him arrested, your Rodzianko, and will dissolve the Duma," he sputtered. On this point the ministers agreed, but they first wanted to get rid of Protopopov, who could no longer control his temper and who was known to be unpopular. The high point of this meeting was the arrival of General Khabalov, who had just received a telegram from the Tsar:

I ORDER THAT YOU STOP THESE DISORDERS IN THE CAPITAL AS OF TOMORROW. THIS SHOULD NOT BE TOLERATED IN THIS GRAVE HOUR IN THE WAR AGAINST GERMANY AND AUSTRIA. NICHOLAS

Later, Khabalov explained:

This telegram, how could I say it, to be frank and sincere, was for me like a sledge-hammer blow. "To stop as of tomorrow." How? What was I going to do? How "stop"? When they asked for bread, we gave bread, and that was the end of it. But when the flags are inscribed "down with autocracy" it's no longer a question of bread. But what then? The Tsar had ordered—we had to shoot.

During the night the Okhrana, the Tsarist secret police, proceeded with numerous arrests. This time there was no longer any doubt; the next few days would be decisive. In the minds of Khabalov and Vassilev, the Chief of Police, it was a dead-end situation. Conversely, the workers' leaders thought the insurrection was going to be "liquidated." Both sides agreed only on one point—from here on everything depended on the attitude of the army.

The leaders of the underground organization, expecting something, were astounded by the events. "We got no orders from the [Bolshevik] Party Center," wrote Kazhurov. "The Petrograd Committee was imprisoned and the representative of the Central Committee, Shlyapnikov, was in no position to give orders for the next day. . . ." As for the other parties, they had been disabled and were disorganized. Once more the old quarrels started up. Under these circumstances no one thought that a revolution would break out, much less succeed, as a result of some more or less anonymous demonstrations which weren't really controlled by any organization. At the most, people suggested the idea of organizing a Soviet. The Menshevik Cherevanin was the apostle of this idea. The Bolsheviks, anxious to keep contact with the avant-garde of the working class, then urged making "soviets" the slogan to be passed on to the masses, but the Mensheviks thought unity would be better achieved on the platform of the Constituent Assembly. Once more, they couldn't decide anything in common.

The fourth day was Sunday. The city got up later than usual, but when it did it found the soldiers at their combat posts. Khabalov had already sent a telegram to the Stavka (General Headquarters): "Today, February 26, calm reigns in the city since morning." But before noon the working-class quarters got under way and in the center of the city the population went into the streets. "The soldiers were across the avenues," reports an eyewitness, "watching the sidewalks. The orders were issued by bugles from the rear." The crowd approached them, speaking amicably, and they answered. The officers increased the number of orders to stop these conversations, but they started up again with other participants. The Command was irritated, nervous, and feeling a weakening of authority.

A soldier of the Volynski Regiment describes what happened:

The soldiers hoped that they had only been brought for show, to frighten. But when the railway station clock sounded noon, the doubts evaporated. The order to fire was given. A salvo was fired. The workers dispersed. The first salvos were harmless; the soldiers, by a tacit agreement, had fired into the air. . . .

"But how are you shooting? Let everyone fire in turn, so that I can see him shoot. Aim for the heart," shouted an officer. He ran through the ranks, seizing first one rifle then another, shooting himself. . . . Suddenly a machine gun aimed at the crowd by the officers started crackling and the workers' blood reddened the snow on the esplanade. The demonstrators fled in disorder into the courtyards of the buildings, crushing one another.

There were forty killed and forty wounded on Znamenskaya Square and more than a hundred and fifty during the day. The soldiers were indignant. But the demonstrators, harassed and feverish, defeated and apparently vanquished, went home. Then the government decided to order a state of seige and adjourn the Duma. It rejected Maklakov's plan, which proposed proceeding simultaneously with the resignation of the ministry, a three-day suspension of the Duma, and the establishment of a "government of confidence," with a popular general like Alexeiev at its head. He thought the situation was well in hand, that there would be no fifth day.

More exasperated than discouraged, fearing some provocation, the Party men felt the gravity of the situation. What were they going to do tomorrow? Some "Unitarian" and "Bolshevik" tracts called on the soldiers to fraternize with the crowd. Would this be enough? They discussed it the whole night of the 26th to the 27th, in Bolshevik headquarters at Vyborg and at Kerensky's house, where a sort of general staff of the revolution met. This general staff lacked only troops. In the working-class quarters it was rather the leaders who were missing.

The Bolsheviks had little confidence in this movement, which they had not entirely incited, but only followed, because it was alien to the method of armed insurrection which alone, according to them, could succeed.

No doubt they had stirred things up on Saturday, but on the evening of the 26th only one thing was clear to Kazhurov: "The Revolution is petering out. The demonstrators are disarmed, no one can do anything to the government now that it has taken decisive action."

Everyone didn't share this pessimism, and there were many who wanted to continue the uprising. A tract was drawn up calling for the continuation of the struggle; "otherwise it would be condemning the soldiers to be shot." The objective was the overthrow of Tsarism and the formation of a Soviet which would make up a government. But did they believe this? When Chugurin proposed forming "armed commandos," Shlyapnikov opposed it. He feared that some thoughtless act would exasperate the soldiers with the workers; already they hadn't hesitated to fire on the crowd. It was even rumored that one regiment had mutinied. But what good would these "pistols" be tomorrow when the troops from the front would enter the capital? To sum it up, it would be better to "continue the work of propaganda" to win over the soldiers and paralyze Tsarism. Convinced that a revolution could not succeed, badly informed of the latest writing of Lenin which showed the opposite, and underestimating the movement, especially because it was anonymous and because they had no control over it, the Bolshevik leaders, apt at organizing masses, confessed their inability to take the political initiative unless they had instructions. As they were reluctant to collaborate with the "Defensists," they did nothing further. Lenin had forbidden Shlyapnikov to collaborate, at any price, with Chkheidze or Skobelev or their friends. "I was convinced when I saw them," wrote Nikolai Sukhanov, "that the most influential workers' organization in Petersburg, which urged the most extreme solutions on the questions of power in those days, hadn't formulated any set policies and that we could not expect from them any energetic slogans with respect to a prepared plan."

At the same time, at Kerensky's, all shades of militant revolutionaries met—from Populists to Defeatists. For several months these men had met at each other's places to accomplish an impossible unity. By an irony of fate, the only movement which had grown at all was not the accomplishment of any act of any one of them, nor the fruit of any joint resolutions. Heatedly, they commented on the day's events—the repression, the Pavlovsky mutiny, the adjournment of the Duma by Prince Golytsin. How would the deputies react tomorrow to the Tsar's ukase? For the last few days the Duma had been demanding responsibility for the food supply of the town. But hadn't Rodzianko also addressed alarmed petitions to the Tsar? The riot frightened the Duma, but then, "driven by the Nation," as Milyukov said it would, "take extreme measures." The Duma seemed, then—except for the minority of the extreme Left—more anxious about reestablishing order than about its own prerogatives. Yet except for the extremists, everyone was counting on the Duma. Only the day before, didn't Chkheidze say that they should rely on the Duma under all circumstances? The dialogue then becomes stormy. The representatives of the clandestine organization—Zhurenev and Sokolovsky (Unitarians); V. Alexandrovich (S.R., Defeatist)—reproached Kerensky and his friends for their enthusiasm, Kerensky especially for his hysteria. Zhurenev and Alexandrovich, who presented themselves along with the Bolsheviks as the only representatives of Socialism, were skeptical about everything. According to them the "troop movement amounts to nothing."

"Reaction is increasing; the uneasiness in the factories is secondary. It is clear that the workers and the soldiers don't have the same objectives. One shouldn't daydream about the revolution, but prepare for better days by means of a systematic propaganda in the factories." These words were like throwing cold water on the discussion, Zenzinov remarked. Briefly, while some wanted to go forward, "to participate in the events" (Kerensky, Zenzinov, Erlich), Zhurenev wanted to wait and see. They disbanded; nothing had been decided.

"During the first few hours of the 27th," the fifth day, writes Trotsky, "the workers thought the solution of the problem of insurrection much further than it was in reality. More precisely, they thought everything still had to be done, whereas their task was already nine-tenths accomplished. The revolutionary thrust of the workers in the vicinity of the barracks coincided with the movement of the soldiers who walked on the street."

In town, echoes were heard of the incident which occurred the day before between officers and men of the 4th Company of the Pavlovsky Regiment. Aroused over the order to shoot demonstrators, the soldiers wanted to return to barracks and demanded a cease-fire. The chaplain was called to quiet them. They agreed to leave their weapons, but twenty-one of them didn't heed the call. It was a sign of things to come. The night of the 26th to the 27th, the fever had infected all the barracks. Afterward the Pavlovksy, Preobrazhensky, and Volynsky Regiments all commented, livid with anger, on the shootings of the day. Never again would they shoot at the people. One of the participants reported:

On the morning of the 27th, around six o'clock, our detachment assembled. Kirpichnikov spoke; he told us how to act and what needed to be done. At that moment, the sound of spurs was heard in the hall. Second Lieutenant Kolokolov, a former student newly arrived at the Regiment, entered. The men answered his salute as usual. Behind him, Commandant Lashkevich entered. Everyone froze, listening. In response to the form of salute "Good morning, brothers," a "hurra" burst out, as had been arranged. Sensing something awry, he repeated the formula, and once more a vigorous, fearful "hurra" resounded. Lashkevich sharply demanded of Sergeant Markov what this signified. Markov, reaching for his bayonet, replied firmly: "Hurra, it's a signal to disobey your oders." The rifle butts crashed on the asphalt floor of the barracks, the bolts clicked. "Get out while you can," yelled the soldiers. Lashkevich tried to yell: "Attention!" but no one obeyed. He asked to reestablish order in order to read them a telegram from *His Majesty, Nicholas II*. But his words were useless. Having lost all hope of bringing the men to heel, Lashkevich and Kolokolov left, running. Quickly, Markov and Orlov opened the transom over the window, aimed their rifles, and when the officers came into sight, two shots rang out. Lashkevich was stretched out full by the entrance.

The alarm was sounded. With the officers fleeing, the way was clear and the detachment came out of the barracks. In the street it met other soldiers, some Litovkys, some Preobranzhenskys.

During this time, the workers descended on the town. Advancing carefully, they perceived in the distance a group of soldiers. A rumor spread—"they're without officers." Immediately workers and soldiers began to fraternize. Elsewhere, shots were heard. Was it a misunderstanding? A soldier called to a worker, "Don't be afraid, come on, come with us." Together they crossed the Neva bridges.

Around twelve o'clock this impassioned procession began to plow through the city. Soldiers, under their officers' eyes, distributed their weapons to the crowd, who shouted their approval. In the distance, at around one o'clock, black smoke could be seen rising from the Civil Tribunal, which was in flames. At two o'clock all the bridges had been crossed and the enormous Volynsky contingent arrived on the Liteiny Prospect. There it met up with the Semenovsky Regiment, who had remained loyal. Barricades were put up, but there was vacillation among the Semenovskys. Mutineers in cars passed nearby and invited them to join the insurgents. Shooting went on here and there, and some were killed. But after a short fight, the insurgents carried the day. They entered the arsenal and soon the crowd was armed with forty thousand rifles. In a few hours, the old order tumbled and Petrograd was almost wholly in the hands of the insurgents. An eyewitness, the Count de Chambrun, wrote to his fiancée in France:

> While the Palace of Justice was burning, the Pavlovsky Regiment marched from its quarters, with its band playing. I watched these battalions pass in close order, led by non-coms. Instinctively, I followed them. To my surprise, they marched toward the Winter Palace, went in, saluted by the sentries, and invaded and occupied it. I waited a few moments and saw the imperial flag come down slowly, drawn by invisible hands. Soon after, alone on this snow-clad square, my heart heavy, I saw a red rag floating over the palace.

2. THE INITIATIVE

Meanwhile, the Duma deputies learned that by the Tsar's ukase its session was suspended. In order to let the government know what they thought of it, they decided, as did the Constituent Assembly of 1789, to pay no attention to this order and began their session. However, so as not to disobey their Tsar's order, they decided not to meet in the meeting hall, but in the semi-circular hall beside it. Until the last moment, Rodzianko, the Duma President, had made moving appeals to the Tsar. On the 26th, he closed the first one "praying to God, that the responsibility for these events would not fall back on the Monarch." Once more he asked Nicholas II to form a government of confidence. This telegram was unanswered. He sent another one on the 27th:

THE SITUATION WORSENS. MEASURES MUST BE TAKEN IMMED-IATELY. THE LAST HOUR HAS COME WHEN THE FATE OF THE COUNTRY AND THE DYNASTY IS TO BE DECIDED. TOMORROW WILL BE TOO LATE.

In this message there is not a hint of a start of revolt. No one reproached him, but they had taken counsel. Grouped around Rodzianko's desk, the deputies agreed, in view of the situation, to limit speeches to five minutes for each speaker. Extremely tense, they took turns speaking, interrupted only by the chatter of rifle fire. Nekrassov made the first proposal. "We no longer have a government. We must form one which has popular confidence." He proposed to entrust General Manikovsky, along with members of the Duma, with the task of forming it. The Cossack chief Karaulov proposed the election of a commission which would be entrusted with forming it. The Progressivist Rievsky thought it would be awkward to entrust this government in the hands of a general of the Old Régime, as Nekrassov proposed. N. T. Savich put up the name of General Polivanov, older, less energetic, but popular. Dzhiubinsky proposed that the Assembly of Deans take over, and this suggestion was acclaimed. At this moment Kerensky arrived. He asked that the Assembly delegate him, along with Chkheidze, to address the soldiers. Chkheidze was agreeable, but not the suspicious Assembly. They were waiting for the opinion of Milyukov. He came out against all of the proposals, judging that the hour to form another government had not yet arrived; but he had no other suggestions to offer. Ready to follow the suggestions of the Cadet leader, the deputies were disappointed; instead of taking things in hand, Milyukov had beat around the bush. What was to be done now?

At that moment 20,000 demonstrators entered the Tauride Palace gardens. The delegates lost their heads. Some of them, fearing for their lives, went into the streets to mix with the crowd. Others, like Milyukov, thought it more dignified to stay, to hold their heads high. They hoped that the Duma would impress the demonstrators. Hadn't the Tsar, by ukase, ordered its dissolution? V. V. Sulgin well described his anxiety: Was this army coming to protect or attack them? Worried, distressed, taking comfort from one another, even those who had fought for years against the autocracy felt suddenly that there was something terrifying, dangerous, which was threatening them all. That something was "the Mob."

Still, it was only a matter of small groups. And the palace guard hesitated. The insurgents were armed. An incident was about to occur, when, coatless, hatless, defeated, a few deputies, among them Karaulov, a Cossack officer, came out. He went up to the demonstrators and spoke to them a few moments, stopping their advance. Skobelev, Chkheidze, and Kerensky greeted the insurgents from a distance. "As I was, without my hat, I leaped ahead toward the soldiers whom I had been wishing for so long," says Kerensky. "Startled sentries stood on the steps. I welcomed the troops and the people in the name of the Duma and myself. Only their union could save the situation."

But plainly, the crowd was paying more attention to the rifle shots which announced the arrival of more determined contingents. Some of the more outspoken groups of soldiers and civilians asked Kerensky: "Give us some orders, tell us what to do." The large battalions were advancing now. Cries rang out while they acclaimed Chkheidze, Skobelev, and Kerensky. "They belong to us! They belong to us!" And further on they again asked for "instructions, directives." Suddenly Kerensky roared loudly, "Arrest the ministers, seize the post offices, the telegraphs, the telephones! Occupy the railway stations, the government offices!" It was then that Rodzianko appeared. He announced that the Assembly was going to have a meeting and assured the demonstrators "that the main task was to replace the old régime with a new government." "Good God!" someone said, "they are finally deciding!"

Among the civil and military insurgents who collected in the Tauride Gardens were "The Workers' Group of the War Committee," who had just been freed from the Krestys Prison. Had they simply followed the stream of the movement, or, as Trotsky and the Bolsheviks suggested, did they head toward the Duma "in order to play a historic role there while our comrades led the victory in the streets, among the workers and soldiers?" There are no witnesses to answer this question. Only Cherkasky reports that "some trucks brought political prisoners," but he does not specify if the "Workers' Group" was among them. In any case, when they arrived at the Tauride Palace, Gvozdev and his comrades rejoined their Menshevik friends, Deputies Skobelev and Chkheidze. In view of the turn of events, they planned to form a Soviet. It was impossible to act in this mob and they asked Kerensky to intercede with the President of the Duma so that they could meet somewhere else. Room 13, belonging to the Budget Commission, was vacant and Rodzianko gave them permission to use it. "He said we could stay," reported a worker. "Thus it was by our cooperation," bitterly comments Prince Mansyrev, "that a little group of suspects was able to proclaim itself the Soviet."

"There were in this room seven or eight men in rags," Prince Mansyrev went on.

> They spoke of the formation of a Soviet presided over by [Georgi] Khrustalev-Nosar. He yelled, they answered. Suddenly he saw Milyukov in the crowd, pale, but clean-shaven and dignified. Khrustalev rushed at him, yelling. "What do they want from me? To put me at the head of the movement? What movement? What's wanted from me?"

Who, then, was in that Room 13 at the Tauride Palace? First, the "bosses," all Mensheviks—Gvozdev and his sidekicks (B. O. Bogdanov, Breido), and the two Social-Democrat deputies (Chkheidze, Skobelev). Then, arriving alone, Khrustalev-Nosar. Kapelinsky, from the cooperative movement (Internationalist) was there also. Among the "radical left" of Petrograd were the lawyer Sokolov, who was rather close to the Internationalists; V. P. Grinevich, who was also a Menshevik sympathizer; Erlich, from the *Bund*, V. G. Grohman, Frankorussky (who were connected with the Mensheviks), Sokolovsky, and Pankov.

The idea of forming a Soviet may have been running into difficulties. Three hours later, when the Bolshevik leader Shlyapnikov arrived, they were still arguing. He said there was no hurry and that they could afford to wait for the "workers' representatives." They agreed to delay the meeting by two hours—that is, until nine o'clock that evening. In fact, however, the pre-Soviet had already issued a proclamation at 3 P.M., under the name of "Workers' Soviet," inviting the workers' delegates to the Tauride Palace for a meeting at seven that evening. With the permission of Chkheidze and Kerensky, the Newsmen's Committee of Petrograd spread the news.

The pre-Soviet of three o'clock also decided to form a Food Supply Commission, which included Grohman and Frankorussky.

This commission sent a call to the population to feed the rebellious soldiers and began to make an inventory of the stocks on hand in the city. The Soviet decided to create a military commission to take charge of the defense of the revolution. Under the direction of a Socialist-Revolutionary officer, S. D. Mstislavsky, and aided by a naval officer, Lieutenant Filippovsky, it tried to form a plan for the defense of the Duma and Petrograd. Sokolov reorganized some delegates from the insurgent regiments, furnishing them with brassards and mission orders on Duma letterhead. After taking an inventory of weapons on hand, they spread out a map of Petrograd to get a good view of the situation. Most of the regiments had revolted; only the cavalry was in doubt, because the Cossacks weren't as sure as they had been in the preceding days. It would only take one loyalist regiment to sweep away this "crazy multitude," because there weren't even a hundred men available to protect it. They wondered what tactics to use. They were determined but powerless to act in this yelling mob, which should have been the militia of the revolution. Those to whom missions were entrusted disappeared, or didn't know how to accomplish them, while unknowns brought back the first prisoners, well guarded.

For their part, the Bolsheviks issued a manifesto. Traditionally this manifesto is dated the 26th—erroneously, as shown by Burdzhavlov, since the preamble could only have been written after the army's uprising. The manifesto must be dated the morning of the 27th at the earliest, but at the latest the evening of the 27th, since it was to be distributed on the 28th, as Supplement No. 1 to *Izvestya*. We know from Sukhanov and Shlyapnikov that it was between four and five o'clock when Shlyapnikov—who had typewritten the manifesto, composed by Khakorev, Kazhurov, V. V. Schmidt, and Vyacheslav Molotov—went to the Duma after learning by telephone of the formation of a Soviet, and did not leave the Tauride Palace until very late that night. This manifesto thus was composed, *before* the Bolsheviks learned of the formation of the Soviet of 3 P.M. In the manifesto the Bolsheviks invited their representative to form the "Provisional Revolutionary Government"; it was no longer a question of a "Soviet."

To explain their absence at the three-o'clock Soviet, the Bolsheviks showed that, on the 27th, "The Menshevik patriots went to the Duma, where the roles and positions were assigned. The Bolsheviks went into the districts where the workers and soldiers were, to work out the revolution with them." To justify his lateness, Shlyapnikov underlined the fact that there were no workers at the Duma on that day. Elsewhere, he points out that the picket lines of soldiers remaining loyal would not permit the crowd from the working-class quarters to get to the center of the city. And when he arrived at the pre-Soviet of 3 P.M., he asked at once that they wait for the workers' delegates. No one protested, which implied that no workers' group had as yet arrived.

The accuracy of this account cannot be verified until the truth is established from another context.

Before the revolution was accomplished, anxious to be in the fore of the workers' movement, the Bolsheviks were not hostile to the idea of the Soviet. But on the day when the insurrection triumphed and the Mensheviks formed the Soviet, the Bolsheviks deemed that this stage should be bypassed. They spelled out their own program of action, which was strictly Leninist in its inspiration. They wanted to proceed immediately to the election of a Provisional Revolutionary Government, in which they would eventually participate. But the revolution had broken out under such conditions that, from then on, along the road to power lay not only the Duma, but the Soviet as well.

3. THE NIGHT OF DECISION

While the Soviet of 3 P.M. was being formed, the Duma, worried, continued to deliberate. It willingly recognized that it represented the opposition to autocracy. It also made plain to the Tsar that it was the only force which would be able to serve as arbiter between the nation and him. Hoping that Nicholas would entrust it with the power, the Duma figured that if Nicholas' resistance brought it to extreme measures, it would have the support of the whole country. But at the critical moment the Duma faltered.

After debates in which the loyalists seemed to carry the day, a revolutionary action was decided on, but only to oppose the Revolution more effectively. Thus was established the Committee for the Reestablishment of Order and Communications with Institutions and Personalities, whose name itself constituted its program. Made up of leaders of the political parties of the Duma (except for the extreme right), this committee delegated its president, Rodzianko, to meet Prime Minister Golytsin. In Golytsin's presence Rodzianko was to meet Prince Michael. All three hoped that the Tsar would end his silence with the proclamation of the formation of a "Ministry of Confidence." Startled by his own powerlessness, Golytsin had agreed; at about six o'clock he had submitted his resignation to the Tsar, but Nicholas refused it.

Ignorant of the Petrograd events, the Tsar was relying on the optimistic report War Minister Belayev had sent him on the 26th. He thanked his brother Michael, who had offered his services, and answered that he himself would come to Petrograd the next day. Of course, he didn't know that there was no longer a government. Dispersed somewhere in the capital, the government had disappeared, the ministers had fled, and the police were hiding. At midnight Belayev had only about 1,500 to 2,000 soldiers. Nevertheless, he expected to organize the resistance around the Admiralty, while waiting for help which never arrived.

Rodzianko had returned to the Tauride Palace. Distressed, he came back to tell the committee of the failure of his last appeal to the Emperor. During his absence, the Duma was filled by the day's victors—demonstrators, workers, and soldiers who were occupying the Tauride Palace. They didn't know that already they had assured the revolution's success.

In the crowd which climbed the Tauride Palace stairs were the delegates of the Petrograd Workers' Soviet. They were bringing fresh news from the workers' quarters, but they were also asking about the situation in the city, the Marie Palace (the government seat), and the Stavka (general headquarters). All sorts of rumors were circulating: General Alexeiev had just been named President of the Council; the Tsar was going to accompany him to Petrograd to settle the situation in person; Grand Duke Nicholas was once more commander-in-chief; the loyalist troops were marching on Petrograd, where the 17th Infantry Regiment had already arrived, and had taken over the Peter-Paul Fortress. It was also said that the capital had been abandoned on purpose, and so on. Everyone wondered what the Tsar would attempt. What would be the reaction at the front? In Petrograd they didn't know whether this was an ephemeral riot or a revolution, whether tomorrow the people would support those who took the risk of leading the movement. "We are finished," whispered Grinevich, one of the Soviet orators, into the ear of Sukhanov. "Now it's the gallows," thought Peshekhonov, with a dryness in his throat, mounting the stairs.

It was under these circumstances that the Soviet session opened at nine o'clock, sometimes interrupted by the shouts of the mutinous soldiers who had come to yell their revolt, sometimes chilled by the news which was circulating. Powerless, Sokolov tried in vain to keep order in the debates. At least it was possible to thin down the crowd in the hall which led to the round auditorium where, without a by-your-leave to the Duma, the Soviet had set themselves up. A "committee" controlled the entrances, giving each delegate, according to the credentials he was carrying, an advisory or a voting voice. Shlyapnikov cast a doubt on the representativeness of those elected on the grounds that the workers were not in the factories at the time of the "elections"; he insisted that the representatives were only provisional.

In the hall there were about fifty delegates and perhaps two hundred to two hundred and fifty observers when Sokolov decided to start the session. The differences which afflicted the democratic camp appeared immediately. By continuous reference to "his" action in 1905, Khrustalev-Nosar irritated the audience and was excluded from the Political Bureau by a vote of thirty-six to ten. Then they proceeded to the real elections. Each group voted only for the candidate of its own party or even for an independent, but never for a candidate of an opposing faction. The independents thus obtained more votes than the members of the parties, so that J. M. Steklov, Kapelinsky, and Sukhanov were elected at the head of the list. At the end of the list were Shlyapnikov and Alexandrovich, with twenty-five and twenty-three votes respectively. The latter, who arrived with a group of workers, was chosen over Zenzinov, a fellow Socialist-Revolutionary, but a "Defensist." Included in the Political Bureau were the seven members of the Presidium; thus Chkheidze was nominated president of the Soviet; Kerensky and Skobelev, vice-presidents; Gvozdev, Sokolov, Pankov, and Grinevich, secretaries. Over-all, the Mensheviks seem to have gotten the best of it. Shlyapnikov then proposed strengthening the committee by adding to it members of the workers' parties. Bolsheviks, Mensheviks, and Social-Revolutionaries would be entitled to three supplementary representatives. Molotov (B.) and Zhurenev (U.) took their seats that evening; the others came later. It was in the middle of these elections—to which, according to Shlyapnikov, not enough interest has been paid—that the representatives of the mutinous regiments appeared, including Volhynians, Engineers, Finns, and others. They were to follow each other on the speaker's stand all night long, increasing the diatribes, calls, and proclamations that continuously interrupted the debate. Nevertheless, the Soviet Bureau was able to confirm the mission of the committees formed in the afternoon and to decide on the creation of a workers' militia under the command of commissars and on the publication of a revolutionary daily, *Izvestya*. The first issue immediately sent out an appeal for the struggle against Tsarism and proposed the gathering of a Constituent Assembly.

At the same time, the "right" of the Tauride Palace went into action. The Duma Committee felt that in order not to lose prestige it would have to put itself at the head of a revolutionary movement with which it was unfamiliar. Knowing of the existence of the Soviet, it wanted to prevent its acting, because the Duma still carried great authority. Loyalists like Sulgin urged the Committee to seize power in the name of the Tsar; with the formation of the Soviet, the "left" was beginning to balk. Kerensky declared that he could go along with his colleagues only insofar as it did not conflict with his position as President of the Soviet. After a long hesitation, Rodzianko went over to the side of those urging a coup. And it was thus that, with a triumphant look and a suppressed smile, Milyukov was able to announce to the Soviet that the Duma had assumed power. The Soviet Literary Committee was the first to learn the news and applauded it—although in Stekhlov's case merely out of politeness, as Peshekhonov tells us. It was already midnight. Immediately Rodzianko announced to the Military Committee of the Soviet the nomination of Colonel Engelhardt as Commandant of Petrograd. Sokolov protested: "There is already a Military Committee led by Mstislavsky." Voices were raised. Did the two powers born of the same revolution oppose each other already? Not yet. Mstislavsky yielded, accepting the authority of Engelhardt because he felt it was necessary to unite against Tsarism. Another triumph for the Duma.

At the Soviet Chkheidze chaired the debate. It was late. The workers' delegates, thinking these repeated effusions somewhat useless, left the premises. To achieve privacy the Bureau curtained off a corner.

It was during this meeting that Molotov, in the name of the Bolshevik Party, brought up the question of the representation of the soldiers in the Soviet. He proposed that the soldiers elect representatives who would constitute the "Military Section of the Soviet." The Mensheviks opposed this, fearing anarchy in the army, but the majority overruled them. At four o'clock in the morning the Executive Committee, exhausted, recessed until noon.

4. THE TWO-POWER STRUCTURE

During the next two days the insurgents mopped up the city. Around the Admiralty, General Zankevich commanded about a thousand men. Having learned by telegraph of the nomination of General Nikolai Ivanov as Dictator of the Capital, he thought of retiring to the Peter-Paul Fortress where he could await reinforcements. The bridge was blocked. Putting on his best uniform, he appeared before his soldiers. Gauging their attitude, he felt that he could not rely on them to break down the roadblock, and decided to go to the Tsar's Palace, to die alone. On his side, threatened with bombardment by the guns of the fortress in the hands of the Revolution, the Navy Minister decided not to prolong resistance. At 2:30 P.M. he sent his last telegram to the Stavka:

AROUND NOON, FOUR COMPANIES, ONE *SOTNJA* [one hundred Cossacks] , TWO BATTERIES, ONE MACHINE-GUN COMPANY, THE LAST FAITHFUL TROOPS, EVACUATED THE ADMIRALTY. I DID NOT DEEM IT WISE TO TRANSPORT THEM ELSEWHERE, BECAUSE THEY WERE NOT ABSOLUTELY RELIABLE. WILL BE QUARTERED IN BARRACKS. THE KEYS ARE AT THE NAVY MINISTRY.

At dawn on the 1st of March the entire city was in the hands of the insurgents. There were several small actions on the Sampsonev-sky and at the Narva Gate, but these apparently were due to a misunderstanding, for even the most "loyal" troops had gone over to the Revolution. A few lone policemen, disguised as soldiers and hiding on the roofs of buildings, would have continued to machine-gun the crowds, but they were pursued and massacred. Some violence was committed against officers and carriage owners, and apartments were looted. Baron Stackelberg was murdered. The Tsar's ministers were arrested and brought to the Duma.

Under pretext of putting them under close watch, Kerensky sent them to a back room of the Tauride Palace. He didn't want bloodshed, and liked to repeat that he did not want to be the Marat of the Revolution. He saved Protopopov, then Sukhomli-nov. "They came and told me he was at the Duma," Kerensky reported. "The soldiers were in a terribly overexcited state. They looked as though they would tear him to pieces."

Kerensky wanted to do as he had done a few moments earlier with Protopopov: "Seeing that its victim was going to escape, the crowd rushed upon us," he related. "I hastened to shield Sukhomli-nov with my body. There was only myself between him and the assailants. I yelled that I would not allow them to kill him and thus dishonor the Revolution. I said that they would reach him over my dead body. The crowd backed off and we were able to shove Sukhomlinov out the door which opened behind us and which was closed while the guards crossed bayonets."

The clashes had ended and the whole city rejoiced. On the Nevsky Prospect, crowded with people, not a single carriage was to be seen. Parades formed singing the *Marseillaise*. People embraced, weeping with joy. It was the first of March, Springtime.

Neither the Duma nor the Soviet shared this euphoria. Facing the task before them, the leaders of the day knew that they had to choose between the Tsar and the Revolution. At the end was either power or the gallows and their hearts were troubled.

THE DUMA'S MANEUVERS

Having assumed power, the Duma Committee tried to implement it. It nominated "commissars" to reestablish order. Holding back the Revolution was more important than consolidating it. It hoped thus to slide into power, with the agreement of the Old Order and thus without creating any problem of continuity. Rodzianko even thought that he would be put at the head of the new government, thus realizing his dream of a "Government of Confidence." Guchkov confided to Sir George Buchanan, the British Ambassador, "that he didn't consider the situation desperate, if only the Emperor would follow the advice given him, and reorganize the government." If not, the Duma would be obliged to save the monarchy in spite of Nicholas II. Guchkov wanted to avoid his violent overthrow, preferring that he abdicate "spontaneously," which would prevent a violent shake-up and permit the continuation of the war. "Certainly, we aren't masters of the situation," confided Vice-President Shydlovsky to an American newspaperman; "the people and the soldiers are in control. We must act cautiously."

The first priority was to keep events from taking an irreversible course. Thus Rodzianko corrected an appeal sent out by A. A. Bublikov, the Communications Commissar, over the railway telegraph system: "The Monarchy having fallen, the Duma has assumed power," read the text. "No," explained Rodzianko, "we must say, 'The Monarchy showing itself powerless, the Duma assumed power.'" To keep up the ambiguity, he sent a message to General Nikolai Russky, Northern Front Commander: "The Committee has taken governmental authority in view of the elimination of the old Council of Ministers." Rodzianko thus continued the old dream of the "Progressive Bloc," as if in the meantime there hadn't been a revolution.

The Tsar, who had agreed to install the Duma as a responsible government, decided to go in person to the Stavka. Shydlovsky was to accompany him. But, seeing them arrive at the station, the railway employees alerted the Soviet, and the Soviet, fearing a trap, would not allow them to proceed. The incident had serious repercussions. Did Kerensky misunderstand Rodzianko's motives? He was upset, repeating that the Soviet was going to hold up the Tsar's abdication, which was now certain. Shaken, the Soviet changed its mind—Rodzianko could go to the Stavka but only if he dictated the method of abdication if Chkheidze went with him. Since, under Rodzianko's plan, power would pass to Michael II, the Soviet leaders refused to be taken in. Furious and disconcerted, Rodzianko protested his powerlessness everywhere. They would have to wait on the evening's meeting of the leaders of the Soviet and the Duma, when they would attempt to conclude an agreement, unless the armies of Ivanov intervened in the meantime.

Far from remaining inactive, the deputies sought to rally the soldiers. They organized spectacular formations and issued a call to order. After some hesitation, they came up with an answer to the question of what to do with the soldiers: "Return to your barracks, so that we'll know where to find you in case of need." At the "Military Committee," the deputies took their cue from the Soviet representatives, who were its founders. "You put us in the soup, now try to obey," said Rodzianko to Sokolov and Mstislavsky. Thus the Duma representative, Colonel Engelhardt, finally became the "boss" of the committee of which he was President. "We belong to an unlucky party," he confided to Claude Anet, the correspondent for the *Petit Parisien*. "We are the *Girondins.* . . . We are trying to make the soldiers obey. How long will that last? It's all right now, but tomorrow? What's to be done?

Engelhardt vacillated, on the one hand announcing that any officers who attempted to recall the soldiers' weapons would be executed, but on the other hand not placing his troops where they would have to face Ivanov's. Instead, he put them at the disposal of Grand Duke Michael and other highly placed notables. Rodzianko betrayed his secret thoughts by asking the soldiers to return their weapons to their officers, who wanted to take advantage of them. Some shots were exchanged. Then a group of soldiers who were far from knowing what was going on arrived at the Tauride Palace to present its grievances and demands. Thus was born the "First Prikaze" (General Order Number One).

GENERAL ORDER NUMBER ONE
Colonel Engelhardt relates:

Some soldiers, apparently delegated by their comrades, asked me to issue an order containing some rather moderate demands,

to be sure, but which included the idea of regimental committees. I went to see Rodzianko and Guchkov and explained that
these soldiers had come to see me as the Duma representative,
and that they hadn't been across the street to the Soviet.
Guchkov and Rodzianko told the soldiers that their demands
were ill-timed. I met one of them who told me in parting:
"Well, all the better. This way we'll write the order ourselves."

That morning the Soviet had taken up the problems of the
army. Regimental delegates were preparing an appeal and an order
intended for the garrison. Sukhanov and Steklov were drafting a
proclamation calling for unity. The soldiers would keep their
weapons and they would be asked to stop lynching their officers.
With these texts put in order, the Soviet had just opened the
debate on the question of power when the delegates who had been
to Engelhardt arrived. Shlyapnikov recognized the Anarchist F.
Linde among them. He saw them surround Sokolov, who was
standing to one side, putting the finishing touches on the text of
the Soviet appeal. At their dictation, Sokolov transcribed their
complaints. Thus was born General Order Number One. In some
ways, it replaced the text prepared by the "Military Committee."

Endowing off-duty soldiers with the civil and political rights of
every citizen, the order annulled everything which was vexatious
in the regulations of the old Russian army. It put the units of the
capital under the political authority of the Soviet and stipulated
that the Duma's decisions were to be considered executive only
when they did not run contrary to those of the Soviet. In answer
to the machinations of the Duma, Article 5 specified: "In no case
should the weapon stocks be turned over to the officers, even if
they should summon them."

Much less stringent than Engelhardt's order, which passed un-
noticed, General Order Number One nevertheless had much greater repercussions. The Soviet Assembly passed it by acclamation,
because it differed little from the work of the Committee. Later it
declared it had had nothing to do with the drafting of this order,
which strictly speaking was true. But, as Zlokazov justly empha-
sizes, General Order Number One nevertheless expressed the will
of the soldiers of the Soviet, even if they were not really its
authors. That evening the text became known to the Duma. "My
blood turned to water when I saw it," wrote Sulgin; "it was the
death of the army." The General Order reduced to naught the
Duma's attempt to take control over the soldiers in the capital.
The Duma Committee found itself alone, far from the Tsar's
armies, faced with the Soviet whose shadow loomed ever larger. If

it didn't want to be obliterated, it would have to agree to negotiate.

AT THE SOVIET:
The Joys and Worries of Victory

Readier by habit to analyze their defeats in endless palavers than to address the crowds like conquering heroes, the Soviet leaders appeared far from triumphant. Perpetual worriers, they wondered what measures they could take to fight the thirteen convoys of troops, which, it was said, were marching on Petrograd. The sudden disappearance of all government resistance looked suspicious. Was it the prelude to terrible repressive measures? Forty years later, Zenzinov still remembered the fear of that night of February 28 to March 1. The Soviet felt quite helpless. Except for the bands which came to offer their lives for the Revolution, the only protection they had was the mob which attended their sessions as if on a holiday. Then everybody went home.

But they had to deliberate, decide, and act.

On the right, Potressov and Zenzinov, in the majority, considered that since this Revolution was "bourgeois," the Duma should take charge of the government; they would be glad to let the Socialists eventually participate. V. Bogdanov argued that this participation should not be delayed; otherwise the cabinet which emerged from the Duma would remain faithful to the Tsar.

The majority disagreed with Bogdanov's view. As long as Russia hadn't the means to achieve a real Socialist revolution, they felt, along with Sukhanov, that the participation of the Socialists in the government could only accentuate the anxiety of the workers, hinder their emancipation, denigrate the Socialist leaders. "There could only be a really Socialist revolution if Russia were backed by a Socialist Europe. In the meantime, it was necessary both that the tax-paying Russians [*classes censitaires*, those who paid their dues in kind—in U.S., sharecroppers] accept power and that the revolutionaries make sure of minimal guarantees so that they could reach the next stage of the revolution." Thus Sukhanov, Grinevich, and Chkheidze wanted to uphold the government as long as it practiced a policy in harmony with the aims of the "democrats." They also wanted to be able to reject "undesirable ministers." In order to remove all doubts about the régime, Sukhanov went as far as to recommend the nomination of Michael as Regent.

Such a position irritated Kerensky extremely, and he condemned those leaders "who declared dogmatically that in keeping

56

with the principles of 'scientific' Socialism, Revolutionary Democracy should not take part in a 'bourgeois' government. He himself was strongly tempted to take part as 'Ambassador of Democracy.' He sensed that the overriding public opinion favored 'a representation of all shades of political opinion at the core of government, with Soviet control, if necessary.' "

At the extreme left, the Anarchists, the Bolsheviks, and the Inter-Borough Liaison Committees, with Unitarian tendencies, felt that these concessions to the bourgeoisie were senseless. The masses had the power; why should they give it up? After March 2nd, the Bolshevik Zaslavsky popularized the slogan "All Power to the Soviets." It was his opinion that "this hope of seeing the bourgeoisie achieve the objectives of the working class and the country was damaging."

"We wanted an intra-Socialist program, a decision about stopping the war," noted a pamphlet circulated at that time. "The Socialists should seize power without installing Socialism immediately," added Shlyapnikov; "that is where we weren't Maximalists." In any case, at the Committee meeting the Bolsheviks never said a word and the other Social-Democrats were astonished. When it came to the vote, they supported nonparticipation with conditional approval. Chkheidze and Sukhanov's viewpoint carried by the vote of thirteen to eight. With this vote, the Soviet once more recognized the legitimacy of the government which the Duma was about to form. It would only support it "insofar as it kept to a program with which the Soviet agreed."

The Committee then enumerated its own proposals. They wanted to keep them modest so as not to frighten the bourgeois ministers. The simplest thing to do was to take up the traditional demands of the liberal parties—amnesty, formation of a Constituent Assembly, etc.—and not say anything about the Socialist goals—the eight-hour day, land reform, peace. Under these conditions, agreement was possible. However, neither the Soviet leaders nor the Duma Committee considered the game won. They decided to confer in the evening on the question of power. But at this time no one was sure of the final victory of the Revolution. The leaders of the Soviet credited the Duma with authority because its members had known how to keep up appearances. Thus the appeals of Rodzianko seemed as powerful as those of Chkheidze. Engelhardt had swept Mstislavsky from the leadership of the Military Committee, and Bublikov had announced the victory of the insurrection of Petrograd in the name of the Duma. Moreover, the members of the Soviet were convinced that only the Duma could communicate with the general staff and prevent any counter-revolutionary attempt. Above all, because the Soviet leaders were experts at criticizing and at ease only as members of the opposition, it didn't enter their minds that the road from Siberian jails to the seat of power was so short. They were already inhibited by the idea that they would be in charge of the government.

On their part, the Duma members attributed radical opinions to the Soviet leaders, crediting them with an authority over the masses they only wished they had, as though the uprisings of February 26th, the Rodzianko incident, and General Order Number One had been their doing. The Soviet leaders were conscious of their own powerlessness, but they would not admit it. The Duma members were in the same position, but they were willing to bluff their way. Thus, in contrast to their rivals, the Duma members were fascinated by power and were willing to go to some lengths to obtain it.

At midnight, the thing which united these two "class enemies" in the same hall was fear—fear of the ever-present crowd, with fingers on triggers and as nervous as they; fear of the repression which they were sure would be pitiless. At that moment the Duma dreamed of governing with the army as its sword and the Soviet as its buckler, while the Soviet dreamed of putting the Duma at the helm with a pistol at its head to make them go where they wanted. But did it know where that was?

THE SOVIET-DUMA MEETING

Sukhanov reported:

There wasn't the same chaos as in our place, but the room nevertheless gave the impression of disorder. It was dirty and smoky, with cigar-butts, bottles, and dirty glasses scattered about. There were also numberless plates, half empty, with all kinds of left-overs. Our eyes glittered with envy and it all made us hungry.

On the left, at the end of the room, Rodzianko was seated, drinking mineral water. Milyukov faced him at a parallel table. He had a pile of papers, notes, and telegrams before him. Farther on, Nekrassov was seated near the entrance. In front of him were four or five unknown people, perhaps spectators. In the middle of the room, between Rodzianko's and Nekrassov's tables, the armchairs and chairs were occupied by the future premier, Prince Lvov, [I. V.] Godnev, Shydlovsky, and another Lvov [V. N. Lvov], the future procurator of the Holy Synod, who was later to be Kornilov's envoy to Kerensky. Behind, standing, pacing, was Sulgin.

During the meeting most of those present were silent. Prince Lvov especially, the "head" of the future government, never said a word during the whole evening. . . . Kerensky, plunged in deep meditation, also took no part in the conversation. . . .

The conversation, naturally, began with the reign of anarchy. One after the other, Rodzianko, Milyukov, and Nekrassov began to describe the horrors they had seen. . . . They told us what we well knew—the assaults on the officers, the pogroms. . . . They were trying to infect us with their feelings in order to get us to participate later in the reestablishment of order.

Quickly they realized they were taking unnecessary trouble. Not only didn't we try to excuse anarchy in any way, but we were in complete agreement with them about the harm it was doing to the Revolution. The Duma leaders then passed on to direct proposals about our contacts, cooperation, support.

Sukhanov then explained that on all these points the Soviet was in agreement. He was even in the process of having an "appeal to the soldiers" printed, although that was not the objective of the meeting, which was, rather, the formation of a government.

Steklov then outlined the demands of the Soviet. Everyone intently listened, except Kerensky, who was "lost in his thoughts and seemed totally indifferent." Sukhanov described the scene:

Steklov tried to show how our demands made sense, demonstrating and proving that they were both rational and acceptable. With historical digressions, giving examples drawn from Western European experience, he insisted especially on the necessity of converting the army to a civil basis. He expected that on this point he would encounter opposition and attempted to show that this demand was perfectly compatible with the need to leave the army its ability to fight. Its power would not be reduced, but on the contrary reinforced. . . .

Worry and wonder began to show on the faces of the audience. But, as well as I can remember, Nekrassov remained completely serene and the face of Milyukov showed signs of a deep satisfaction. . . . He had been expecting that they were going to force a policy of peace on him and he was greatly relieved.

Milyukov answered the Soviet's demands, declaring that they were acceptable. The amnesty was to be taken for granted, as well as the political freedoms. On the third point—the undetermined nature of the future régime—he was unmovable. "I was not surprised that he took up the defense of the Romanovs," commented

Sukhanov, "but I was surprised that he made it the essential point of the negotiations. Now, I see his point of view, and his shrewdness. . . . He understood that only with a Romanov would he win the coming battle; the rest would follow. He was not greatly frightened by the army's liberty, nor by the idea of a Constituent Assembly."

"Those were your demands," Milyukov then said; "now here are ours." Everyone thought that he would call for the "help" of the Soviet against the disorders. . . . But it wasn't even that. . . . Having taken, by a single stroke, his adversaries' measure, he pushed them a little further away from the power which they were letting slip through their hands. It was enough for Milyukov that the government would be able to proclaim "that it was formed in agreement with the Soviet," and that this text would appear alongside a Soviet proclamation, if possible, on the same page of *Izvestya.* Arrangements were quickly made; Milyukov and Sukhanov exchanged texts and disputed only on two points: the soldiers' rights and the schedule of reforms. It was agreed that the soldiers' rights would be in effect only off duty and that the government would not make use of the military situation to postpone the reforms.

They then took up the question of the composition of the government. The suggestion of Prince Lvov as President, Milyukov for Foreign Affairs, Guchkov for War got a mixed reaction; the proposal of the industrialist Tereshchenko for Finance elicited a certain wonder. None of the other names raised any objections; they were the cabinet one would have expected of the "Progressives" if the "Palace conspiracy" had succeeded. In order to give their government a revolutionary touch, the bourgeoisie insisted on adding Chkheidze and Kerensky, the "bucklers." The former refused point blank. While waiting for Kerensky's answer to his nomination as Minister of Justice (he would have taken Maklakov's place), Milyukov presented his government to the public. Here is the scene as reported by *Izvestya:*

"Ladies and Gentlemen," said Milyukov addressing the crowd assembled in the Catherine Room:

> We are living in an important moment, a historic moment. . . . Only three days ago we were only a modest opposition and the Russian government seemed omnipotent. . . . And now it is we and our friends of the left wing who have been borne by the Revolution, by the army, by the Russian people,

to take this honored place as members of the first government to represent the public. *(Prolonged applause.)*

We must preserve our victory.... But how? The answer is clear and simple; we must organize our victory. And to keep it, we must, before everything else, safeguard the unity which has brought us this victory.... Our interior quarrels must now disappear. We must be united.

To be united. And this applies also to you, officers and soldiers of the great Russian army. Remember that the strength of the army lies in its unity. Preserve this ... to show that it will not be easy to overthrow the first government emanating from the will of the people.... *(Long and loud applause.)*

But the ruse soon showed through:

The victorious soldiers know that they can achieve victory and keep it only by keeping their ties with their officers. *(Prolonged applause and yells in the audience.)* They ask me: Who elected you? No one.... Because if we had to wait for an election by the people, by this time we would have been ousted from power. We have been elected by the Revolution. *(Applause, yells: "Who are the ministers?")* I have no secrets from the people.... I am going to tell you the names. At the head of the government we have put someone who is a symbol of Russian society ... *(Yells: "Rich people.")* and who was persecuted by the old régime. Prince Lvov, President of the *zemtsvos.* *(Yells: "Rich people.")* You say *privileged* ... but the nonprivileged are also represented. I have just learned that my comrade A. F. Kerensky has just accepted a post in the first government of the Russian people.... *(Thunder of applause.)* Do you want to hear the other names? *(Yells: "And you?")* My comrades have entrusted me with the Foreign Affairs of Russia. *(Long and tumultuous applause. The orator bows in all directions.)* Now I am going to give you a name which will raise objections. Alexander Guchkov was my political opponent *(Yells: "Friend.")* during the whole duration of the Duma.... But he is a man of action who saved the Russian army, and at the moment I am speaking to you, he is arranging victory in the streets of the capital. *(Applause.)* What would you have said last night, if instead of posting troops at the railway stations where the troops of repression were expected, he had partaken in your discussions? What would have happened to us? *(Yells: "He's right.")* He will be Minister of War.

Milyukov then announced the names Tereshchenko, Finance;

Nekrassov, Transportation; Andrei Shingarev, Agriculture, and so on.

> Good, that's all you want to know.... *(Yells: "And the program?")* Ah, the program. Well, the only document that shows the program is actually in the hands of the Soviet. We have discussed it with them.... But do you want to know a few points? *(Loud noises and yells: "And the dynasty?")* You speak of the dynasty? I know in advance that my answer won't please everyone. But I'll tell you anyway. The old despot who has led Russia to ruin must voluntarily relinquish the throne; otherwise he will be deposed. *(Applause.)* The power will be turned over to the Regent, Grand Duke Michael Alexandrovich.... *(Prolonged yells of indignation burst out. Exclamations: "Long Live the Republic... Down with the Dynasty....")* The heir will be Alexis.... *(Weak applause, drowned again by yells of indignation: "It's the old dynasty.")* Yes, it's the old dynasty, but we cannot always have what we want.... Soon a constituent assembly will be convoked, with universal suffrage, with secret ballots....

The speaker apologized because he could no longer speak. He was exhausted. He was acclaimed and carried from shoulder to shoulder, and thus left the Catherine Room, worn out. At that moment, on the other side of the Tauride Palace, Kerensky decided to accept the post of Minister of Justice offered him by Prince Lvov.

His political ideas were simple and fairly coherent. During March he thought that the government should arrange, before anything else, for the election of a Constituent Assembly. Given the makeup of Russian society, the peasantry and the town proletariat, who were by a large margin in the majority, would delegate to the Constituent a crushing majority of revolutionaries of all shades. Thus the eventual passage to Socialism would be accomplished according to the principles of the middle class— legally and without violence. Thus Russia would set the unique example of a bloodless revolution. But in order to form a democratically elected Constituent it would be necessary for the day's victors to choose the methods of election. Thus the opposition of the Soviet to the Duma seemed to Kerensky to be completely mistaken. With the resumption of normal activities, wouldn't its control come to be recognized as more and more illusory? Wouldn't the Soviet fall apart of itself, the real power passing to the government and the local bodies? The Soviet's attitude seemed to

Kerensky as absurd as it was dangerous. In spite of the fact that he was its vice-president, he did everything possible to suppress it, predicting its imminent fall. He wanted to force its members to join the government and would not quit until he achieved this. He also thought that the government should have immediately proclaimed the Republic, and he criticized the Soviet for not having forced it to do this on the night of the 1st to 2nd.

Still, when he was asked about the régime he had remained silent. At that time he did not want to alienate the members of the Duma who were about to offer him a ministerial post, or the members of the Executive Committee, who would have been hostile to him in view of the fact that Chkheidze had firmly refused the Labor Ministry. As he had anticipated, this silence earned him the Ministry of Justice after Maklakov declined it. Knowing that on this question of his appointment the Soviet leaders would be immovable, Kerensky decided to force their decision by going over their heads and addressing the Assembly directly. The famous scene well illustrates the manner of Alexander Kerensky, a hero right out of the French Revolution. Arriving unexpectedly in the Assembly room, he asked for the floor:

"Comrades, have you confidence in me? *(Yells from the whole room: "Yes, yes, we have confidence.")* I speak from the bottom of my heart. I am ready to die if necessary. . . . *(Everyone was moved. Silence. Then a long ovation saluted Kerensky.)* Comrades, they are forming the new government and I must answer immediately, without awaiting your formal response to the offer I have received, to accept the Ministry of Justice. *(Thunderous applause; general excitement.)* Comrades, the representatives of the Old Régime are in my hands and I couldn't take it upon myself to let them go. *(Thunderous applause, bravos.)* And so I have accepted the offer of the Ministry of Justice. *(Continued applause, bravos.)* My first decree has been to free all political prisoners without exception and to have the Social-Democratic deputies brought here with all honors. . . . *(Thunderous applause, general enthusiasm.)* Since I took this job before receiving your formal authorization, I resign as vice-president of the Soviet, but I am ready to reassume the job if you judge it necessary. *("Yes, yes." Thunderous applause and yells: "Yes. . . .")* Comrades, by entering in this government, I remain what I have always been—a Republican—and I will be the spokesman of democracy."

A thunder of applause stopped Kerensky. Some isolated voices tried to protest against the fact that he had acted against the formal consent of the Soviet. They were drowned by the unanimous cries of the overwhelming majority of those present, who made an ovation such as had not previously been heard in the Tauride Palace. . . .

At the end of this meeting the two delegations were equally satisfied. For the Soviet this conference was a success insofar as the government obtained power, not from the Tsar, as the Duma had hoped, but from the Soviet itself—that is to say, from the Revolution. They were comforted also by the fact that "this sanction would be valid only *so long as* the policy of the government coincided with the objectives of democracy." For the leaders of the Duma, too, it was a good bargain. The nature of the régime would not be set by the Constituent—a fact which would not exclude the possibility of keeping the Romanovs. Above all the Duma committee could congratulate itself on having obtained what it considered most essential—the recognition by the Revolution of the legitimacy of its own power.

During the night, in the midst of these negotiations, Russky had telephoned Rodzianko, who explained to him that the people now demanded the Tsar's abdication. "And what about the proclamation by the Tsar announcing the nomination of a 'Ministry of Confidence'?" asked Russky.

"I don't know what to tell you. Everything depends on events which are moving speedily," answered Rodzianko. Guchkov arrived, upset by the murder of numerous officers in the capital. They must act to obtain the abdication of Nicholas II before "the rabble" made further demands. He would go to the Stavka instead of Chkheidze, who would be useless; Sulgin would accompany him to assure the safeguarding of the interests of the dynasty. Late that night, the city asleep, the two men left in haste. As they were going to demand the Tsar's abdication, there was no need to hide, so they took the train. But as they were also going to Pskov to assure Grand Duke Michael about his succession to the throne, they omitted to tell the Soviet about this object of their voyage.

5. THE ROMANOV'S ABDICATION

Two unknown factors hovered over the destiny of the Russian Revolution, the Tsar's attitude and that of the Stavka. On the evening of the 1st of March, after five days of shooting, while the government created by the Revolution was being formed, there was very little knowledge about these factors to be had in Petrograd. It was known that Nicholas II had remained deaf to Rodzianko's and Michael's appeals, that he had refused to accept Golytsin's resignation, and that he had ordered General Ivanov to reestablish order in the capital. But no more was known of the Tsar's humor than about the High Command's dispositions.

THE TSAR, THE GENERAL STAFF, AND THE EVENTS IN THE CAPITAL

The Stavka knew of the troubles in Petrograd since February 25th. General Khabalov had described the details of the first riots to General Alexeiev, telling him of the death of Commissar Krylov. For his part, Protopopov had telegraphed General Voiekov, the Palace Commandant, to the effect that the insurrection had left everything in a "chaotic state, but brisk measures had been taken to suppress it." The headquarters staff and the Tsar reacted in the same way. Alexeiev informed General Russky, Commander of the Northern Front, "The situation is serious. Everything must be done to speed the arrival of loyal troops. Our future depends on it." Nicholas II blandly telegraphed Khabalov, "I order the stopping as of tomorrow of these unwarranted troubles in time of war against Germany." Khabalov was, to use his own words, struck by this message as if by a sledge hammer blow. "The Emperor seemed worried, but today he seems gay," noted General Lukomsky. In Nicholas's *Journal intime*, dated February 25, there is nothing about these events, nor on the 26th, when he wrote to his wife, "I hope that Khabalov will know how to stop these disorders quickly. Protopopov must give him clear and precise instructions. The important thing is that old Golytsin doesn't lose his head." His children's illnesses worried him much more than the insurrection, and he told Alexandra that he intended to return to Tsarskoe-Selo in two days.

Sunday, in Petrograd, events unfolded unexpectedly. At noon everything was quiet. The Stavka and the Tsar received reassuring reports. But at eleven o'clock the Tsarina told Nicholas of her uneasiness. In the afternoon there was shooting. Rodzianko, panic-stricken, not knowing of the Tsar's orders to Khabalov, sent Nicholas II his first telegram, which the Emperor whimsically did not answer. "It's the big Rodzianko writing me some fool nonsense; I won't even answer him." It was then 9:53 P.M. In fact, at this hour, the ministers meeting at Golytsin's were hopeful. They rejected the "Maklakov Plan" and were as sure of the future as the revolutionaries were dejected. After deliberating, the Council of Ministers decreed the adjournment of the Duma until April and so informed the Tsar by a telegram dispatched at 1:58 A.M. on the morning of the 27th. Everything seemed in order.

On the 27th, one telegram after another arrived, some contradictory. At 11:12 Monday morning the Empress gave the alarm. She had learned of the mutinies and informed her husband that the news was "worse than ever." Again at 1:03 that afternoon, "we'll have to make concessions." Rodzianko had sent another telegram to the Tsar. They must immediately form a responsible ministry—"tomorrow will be too late." According to Cantacuzene-Speransky, this message was not given the Tsar until the next day. This may be true, but certainly he knew of Alexandra's telegrams. In any case, at the same time, he received reassuring news from Belayev and Khabalov, both telling him of the night's mutinies and asking urgently for reinforcements. But the "harsh measures" evoked by the Minister of War were not enough to alarm Nicholas II. Telegram 196, dispatched at 1:15 P.M., even said, "Have confidence in the early reestablishment of order." The Tsar, who in his *Journal* on the 27th, complains of receiving only "fragmentary" news (in fact, they were not so much fragmentary as contradictory), made no attempt to get better information: "I did not stay long with the report, and in the afternoon, took a walk on the Orcha Road." The only remembrance of that afternoon, on which he played dominoes, was that "the sun shone beautifully."

Until that time, neither the high command nor the Emperor's household had been greatly worried about the events in the capital. But suddenly at 7:35 on the evening of the 27th, the Stavka received a message (telegram 197) from Minister of War Belayev:

SITUATION IN PETROGRAD BECOMES EXTREMELY SERIOUS. THE MUTINIES INCREASE. NO MEANS TO COMBAT THEM. ARRIVAL OF LOYAL CONTINGENTS IS ABSOLUTELY NECESSARY AND THESE IN SUFFICIENT NUMBERS TO BE ABLE TO ACT IN ALL PARTS OF THE CITY.

This time the matter was serious, Alexeiev told the Tsar, who remained silent during dinner. Voiekov, who for three days had been busy nailing some shutters in his apartment, suddenly understood the gravity of the situation and took on a woebegone expression. Having read the telegram, the Tsar consulted his advisors. Alexeiev urged him to grant a constitution; Voiekov opposed it. The Tsar ordered Ivanov to reestablish order in the capital, granting him "full powers" and the title of Dictator of the Petrograd region. He entrusted General Alexeiev with the job of supplying the means to fulfill Ivanov's mission.

Between ten and eleven o'clock Alexeiev communicated with different generals about the methods and means of the aid to be given General Ivanov. Only Russky had objections, feeling that "repressive measures could only aggravate the situation." A few hours earlier Evert had said, "He wasn't playing politics, but some steps had to be taken." He urged Alexeiev to give Rodzianko's telegram to the Tsar. Grand Duke Michael urged Alexeiev to nominate a responsible leader to head the government, and Alexeiev forwarded this advice to the Tsar, who answered "that he thanked him for his advice and that measures had been taken." The Tsar still intended to go, as planned, to Tsarskoe-Selo. Decisions would be made en route. Reinforcements would pour into Petrograd continuously, where Ivanov would arrive the next day or the day after. At 11:25 P.M. Golytsin begged the Tsar to put a popular general at the head of the troops who were still loyal. He also recommended the nomination of a Council President who enjoyed general confidence and then offered to resign. The Tsar answered that he was putting "all necessary powers" at Golytsin's disposal; "as for changes in the composition of the ministry, I don't believe they are admissible under the circumstances," he added.

At this hour the entire city was in the hands of the insurgents. The Tsar continually conferred with Ivanov, who explained to him how he had put down a mutiny in Harbin in 1906. Another time at Kronstadt, some sailors were fighting and he had taken two of them by the collar and ordered them to kneel. The sailors obeyed. Thus ended the brawl, to the dumbfounded admiration of all those present. Ivanov expected to enter Petrograd without bloodshed. "Why, certainly," said the Tsar, who went to bed at three o'clock in the morning. All that evening he showed himself "amiable, kind, and quiet."

On the 28th, ignorant of the turn of events, Alexeiev sent Circular 1813 to all army commanders. He outlined the events of February, termed the capital insurgents "mutineers," and reminded everyone of "his duty to his sovereign." At the moment when the Revolution had completely succeeded, the Imperial train rumbled off toward Tsarskoe-Selo. The Tsar and his staff were still in close harmony. Nicholas II was not so lacking in information as his actions make it seem, but he had no idea of bringing a political solution to the uprising; thus only military measures had been taken. The Tsar's carelessness, his quietly stubborn muddleheaded-ness were really responsible for this extraordinary failure of the whole old régime. But he was not solely responsible. The high command and his entourage, sluggish in their all-powerful posi-tion, were also unconcerned. They did nothing to take care of the situation, one and all imagining it could be handled as of yore—by repression.

IVANOV'S RIDE

The "Dictator" left Mogilev on the morning of the 28th. He expected to go by rail to Tsarskoe-Selo with the St. George's Battalion. There he would look over the situation with the Tsarina while waiting for troops which were to arrive via Gatchina from Pskov and Revel. The first incident occurred at Dno. General Ivanov's train met a convoy out of Petrograd in the station. Excitedly, civilians and soldiers told the "Dictator's" troops about the happenings in the capital. In a moment the general's train was emptied while a curious crowd accumulated on the other plat-form. From his car Ivanov could hear the words "equality, liber-ty." Like the French General Soubise, he went to reclaim his soldiers, but they began laughing when they saw him. The "Dicta-tor" pounced on the closest group; "On your knees!" he bellowed, thinking he was still at Kronstadt ten years earlier. "On your knees ... prisoners!" But at the sound of the whistle the train on the other side started, carrying Ivanov's soldiers to freedom.

Other reinforcements were scheduled to arrive soon; neverthe-less, the information which Ivanov had received from Petrograd made him think. The results of his conversation with Khabalov were very disquieting. In brief, it appeared that the capital was in the hands of the insurgents, that except for a few Guard compa-nies or Cossack cavalry troops, all the troops along with the artillery had gone over to the side of the Revolution.

Thus informed, Ivanov went on his way toward Tsarskoe-Selo. At Vyritsa there was more trouble. This time, the rail workers stopped the general's train. "The track is damaged," they said. Ivanov ordered them to repair it. At Tsarskoe-Selo a disappoint-ment awaited him. The St. George's Regiment, reputed to be the most faithful, let him know that in case of conflict with the inhabitants of the city, who had gone over to the Revolution, they would remain "neutral," because their oath only bound them to defend the "person" of the Tsar. The regiment ran up a white flag.

Agreeing with the Tsarina, Ivanov thought it wiser to return to Gatchina. There he would wait for the fresh troops which he needed so much now.

These troops would have to go through Luga during the night. Around two o'clock in the morning, the railworkers learned that 4,000 "Veronitsi" were coming. The Luga "Committee" met and deliberated, an eye-witness relates. They had no directive from Petrograd. On hand they had, at most, 1,500 soldiers. The "Committee" could count on 300 volunteers, 400 perhaps, but, unluckily, all the cannon were under repair. They decided on a trick. Three Revolutionary "officers" went to the station with an escort. When the train arrived, it was sidetracked and the occupants were ordered not to leave—a useless precaution because the "Veronits" were sound asleep. The insurgents entered the car reserved for the officers, woke them up, told them that the city of Luga and its whole garrison—more than 20,000 men—had gone over to the Revolution, and that all resistance was useless. It was thus that the officers were obliged to yield to "force." Their weapons were removed, the cars carrying the artillery were unhooked, and the troops were returned in the direction from which they had come. Standing on the platform behind them, furious, the mystified officers watched this last maneuver. Too late, the train left in the reverse direction, going away from the capital.

In lieu of troops Ivanov received two telegrams, one from Alexeiev in Mogilev, another from Nicholas II in Pskov. Both told him to suspend operations and to await the arrival of the Tsar. He also learned that Guchkov would meet him somewhere on the way. Without troops or instructions the "Dictator" no longer knew what to do. He wanted at least to reach Gatchina. Alexandrovskaya was occupied by revolutionaries. He had to return by Semrino and change trains at Vyritsa. The railworkers were hilarious. From his command post at Petrograd, V. Lomonosov, "General of the Railways," ordered switches and sabotage (see sketch). As the Tsar was going back from Malaya-Vishera toward Bologoye to go toward Dno and Pskov, Lomonosov had Guchkov's train go by Gatchina to join the Tsar at Pskov. He let Ivanov's train go as far as Semrino. Behind him, so that the troop convoys wouldn't be able to follow him, he had the ties pulled out from between the tracks. Meanwhile at Semrino Ivanov was becoming impatient and demanded his locomotive. Does it take this long to fill it with water? Never mind! Since he wanted one right away, the railwork-

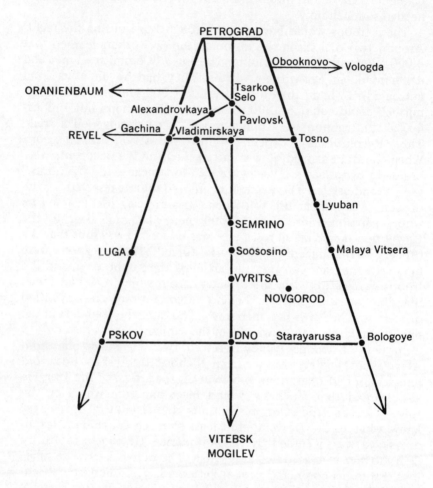

LOMONOSOV'S SKETCH #8

ers gave him one chosen at random. An hour later, between Semrino and Vladimirskaya the "Dictator's" train stopped for lack of water. It never left again. Thus ended Ivanov's expedition.

THE ABDICATION OF NICHOLAS II

During this time the Tsar was rolling toward Tsarskoe-Selo. On the 28th, at around three in the afternoon, he had telegraphed Alexandra, "I hope everything is well. Weather beautiful. Many reinforcements arriving from the front. Love you tenderly. Niki." In the evening, arriving around Bologoye, he learned of the formation of the Rodzianko Cabinet (the Duma Committee), although that did not stop him from confirming to the Tsarina that "will be home tomorrow morning." As the convoy approached Petrograd, rumors were beginning to spread in the train preceding the Emperor's—revolutionaries occupied Lyuban, a bridge in front of Tosno had been blown up, and so on. At Malaya-Vishera the Tsar's suite decided to turn back to Bologoye and go to General Russky's command post of the Northern Front at Pskov. From there it would be easier to lay siege to Petrograd. The Tsar agreed. On the 1st they kept rolling all day, "avoiding the subject of the events." "What a shame," Nicholas II noted blandly. "Impossible to reach Tsarskoe-Selo, but my heart and my thoughts are always there. How painful for my poor Alice to be alone during all these events. . . ."

At that moment, the Empress appealed to Paul, the Tsar's brother and Commander of the Guard. Why didn't he try to bring matters to a head? Instead, Paul had chosen, in agreement with the other Grand Dukes, to draft a manifesto to be submitted to the Tsar. Nicholas II would promise to grant the Russian people a constitutional régime on the signing of a peace treaty with Germany, the Duma would immediately resume its session, and so forth. The Tsarina wrote immediately to Nicholas II not to yield to this pressure. Then she wrote him her last message as Empress— he was never to receive it:

> Everything is against us. Events are occurring with lightning rapidity. It is clear, nevertheless, that they don't want to let you see me so as to make you sign some kind of a paper. And you are alone, without your army, like a mouse caught in a trap. What can you do?

Finally, at eight o'clock in the evening of the 1st of March, the Tsar arrived in Pskov. Russky awaited him impatiently on the station platform. All day Rodzianko's, Alexeiev's, and Ivanov's telegrams had piled up, each one expecting an urgent answer. "Let's dine first," proposed the Tsar.

At Pskov the details of the events in Petrograd were not known, but they were presumed grave. Since the reception of Bublikov's telegram on the 28th they knew that the situation in the capital had taken an irreversible turn. Following Alexeiev's instructions, the high command had dispatched troops toward Petrograd— precisely those that went through Luga the night of the 1st to the 2nd. As at the general headquarters of Mogilev, they thought the future depended on Ivanov's success. The last dispatches from Belayev, although explicit, changed nothing in the conduct of general headquarters or in that of the command post of the North Front at Pskov. Early in the morning of the 1st, Alexeiev received the manifesto from the "Committee for the Reestablishment of Order," which Rodzianko had spent a whole day sending. Alexeiev saw in it a guarantee of "the unshakable character of the monarchic power," and therefore let Ivanov know that his mission would be changed. Feeling reassured as to the nature of the events which had exploded in Petrograd, and anxious only about the effect they would have on the troops in the line, Alexeiev sent a message to the Tsar, asking him to make some concessions and appending to it a proposed manifesto of his own, in which Nicholas II would announce the formation of a "responsible" government under the leadership of Rodzianko. This was at 10:20 on the night of March 1st.

Other similar projects awaited the Tsar at Russky's headquarters. They came from Grand Duke Serge, from Brusilov, from Hanbury-Williams, and from numerous others. As for Russky, he had been much affected by the eruption of Moscow and by Admiral Nepenin's espousal of the Revolution. Convinced that the Tsar had wasted too much time, he became more urgent and Nicholas II gave in after reading Alexeiev's telegram. However, the manifesto failed to mention that the proposed "responsible" government would be responsible to the Duma. Was this a result of Voiekov's influence? Moreover, the Tsar thought that he himself was going to name the Ministers of War, Navy, and Foreign Affairs. Russky had to apply more pressure, and around midnight Nicholas II put himself entirely in his hands. During this time, Russky kept trying to reach Rodzianko by telephone. At 2 o'clock in the morning he was finally able to talk to him. Rodzianko, who was sitting with the Soviet-Duma meeting, explained to Russky that, even if amended, this manifesto would no longer answer to the situation. It was now a question of abdication if they were to save the country from anarchy. Under the circumstances, Russky thought it would be wiser not to issue the manifesto.

Meanwhile Alexeiev learned about what had happened to the Luga battalions. He learned from General Danilov that the Tsar had suspended the order for the march on Petrograd, given two days earlier to General Ivanov (at 5:48 A.M., March 2nd). Knowing exactly the contents of the conversation between Russky and Rodzianko, which had been recorded, Alexeiev, much impressed, intervened to hasten the Tsar's abdication, which he saw as the only way to ensure the continuation of the war and the maintenance of the dynasty. At 10:15 P.M. he made a tour of all the commanders, summarized this conversation for them, and asked them to send telegrams to the Tsar recommending abdication "to save the independence of the country and safeguard the dynasty." Except for Evert, all the generals answered within the hour, "respectfully putting their pistols at their adored monarch's temple." Having read the seven telegrams the Tsar didn't even attempt to resist. He consulted his physician to learn the truth about his son's health and learned that Alexis had little chance of surviving. Then he modified the terms of his abdication and chose his brother Michael as successor. There was a grave question as to whether, legally, the Tsar in abdicating could also give up the crown for his son. Finally, Nicholas II got his way.

Once more, an unexpected event held up the new manifesto. Guchkov and Sulgin, Duma delegates, arrived at Pskov, still hopeful. But they had come in vain. They came in the name of the Duma to force Nicholas II's abdication. Like the military, they thought they must act quickly, "in the interest of the Dynasty." As Sulgin relates:

We bowed, the Emperor saluted and shook our hands. His actions were rather friendly. . . . He sat near a small table placed against a wall covered with green satin. Guchkov sat facing him. I sat at an angle, next to him. Count Frederiks was opposite. Guchkov spoke. He was upset. No doubt he expressed his thoughts clearly, but he had difficulty controlling his emotions and his voice was hollow. The Emperor, facing him, looked straight ahead. His face was calm, expressionless. My eyes never left his face. . . .

Guchkov spoke of what happened at Petrograd. . . . He covered his face with his hands, as if to better concentrate. He did not look at the Emperor and he spoke as though he were talking to himself. It was his conscience which was speaking.

He told the truth. He didn't exaggerate or hold back anything. He told what had been seen at Petrograd. He couldn't say anything else. We didn't know what was going on in the other parts of Russia. *We* have been beaten by Petrograd, not Russia. [Italics added.—M.F.] . . . The Emperor looked straight ahead, inscrutable, calm. The only thing his face seemed to want to say was that these long speeches were useless. Russky came in then. He bowed to the Emperor, without interrupting Guchkov. He sat down between Count Frederiks and me. Guchkov raised his voice. "Perhaps," he suggested, "the answer would be abdication."

Guchkov stopped and the Tsar answered him. After the tremulous speech of Alexandrovich, the Tsar spoke calmly, simply, precisely. . . . He spoke from afar, like a stranger:

"I have decided to abdicate. Until three o'clock yesterday,* I thought first it would be in favor of my son Alexis. But I changed my mind in favor of my brother Michael. I hope that you will understand a father's feelings. . . ."

These last words were spoken very softly. . . . We were absolutely not ready for that. We expected resistance, some outbursts perhaps, not knowing that everything had been decided before our arrival. The Emperor's calm, his apparent indifference, were among the many facts which struck us. . . . He left his Empire like a captain leaving his squadron.

The text of the abdication having been arranged, the Tsar then left for Mogilev. On the station platform the officers held back their tears. Nicholas saluted and with a brisk stride mounted the train. In his notebook he merely noted: "I leave Pskov, my soul oppressed by what has happened. All around me is nothing but treason, cowardice, and deceit!"

MICHAEL ROMANOV'S ABDICATION

During this time Petrograd was seething again. The officers' conduct, Rodzianko's maneuvers, the speeches and the pretences

---

*This word, *yesterday*, gave substance to the eyewitness reports of Francis, Anet, and a few others. At Malaya-Vishera, Voiekov told the Tsar that the Duma was in the hands of bandits and young soldiers and that all they would need would be a few troops to scatter them. Zabel arrived at this time. He showed the Tsar that the situation was much graver than that. Voiekov then proposed opening the lines to let the Germans enter and suppress the Petrograd insurrection. Although drunk, Admiral Nilov became indignant. The Tsar was against this idea, recalling that these were Rasputin's opinions. "Why didn't they tell me," he said angrily. "Why tell me today when everything is lost?" He calmed down and said, "All the better; I'll simply go and live in Livadia."

of Milyukov were now known to all. Once more the irritation was extreme. There was fighting in the streets.

Peshekhonov related:

At my police headquarters you could find locked up on one side Rodzianko's opponents, on the other his adherents. The police were helpless. At one of the meetings the backers of the duma President, more numerous than their opponents, simply had put them under arrest. But on leaving prison, their rivals, now in the majority, arrested the others. . . . But they didn't liberate their own adherents, fearing no doubt that they would be duped.

Disorder was everywhere: "The wheel turns," Count de Chambrun accurately noted, "but here Gracchus Baboeuf appears on the second day. The Russian Revolution is skipping stages."

At the Duma the deputies, now better informed, again felt the current of the civil strife. Rodzianko and Milyukov had tried to deceive the popular movement, but had to back off. The government let it be known that, on the day before, when he spoke of the fate of the dynasty, Milyukov had only been expressing his "personal" views. "Fright was everywhere," relates Lomonosov; "I was in the sanctuary of the Revolution, and instead of heroes, I found only midgets."

In fact, the deputies were aghast at the idea of the population's learning that Michael was going to succeed Nicholas II. Two messengers were sent to the station to intercept Guchkov and Sulgin as soon as they detrained. The deputies were afraid that Guchkov and Sulgin, ignorant of the opinion in the capital, would make public the information they were bringing from Pskov. Rodzianko telephoned immediately to Pskov and Mogilev to stop the dissemination of the act of abdication in favor of Michael, saying it was "a matter of the safety of Russia." Alexeiev and Russky had no inkling of what was going on. "Wasn't it enough that Nicholas had abdicated?" they wondered. "Until the convocation of the Constituent Assembly, it is better to keep still about the Romanovs," explained Rodzianko. "If it were known in the capitol that the Duma and the general staff were agreed about the recognition of Michael II, the results would be disastrous."

Persuaded by this argument, Alexeiev and Russky tried to recall the telegram. Thus Paris and London learned of it, but not Petrograd. As this was occurring, Guchkov and Sulgin arrived at the Petrograd railway station. Thinking that they were conveying good news, they announced that Nicholas II had abdicated and that Michael II was to succeed him. They thought they would be lynched. "Down with the Romanovs. . . . Nicholas . . . Michael . . . It's all the same. . . . White radishes are the same as black. . . . Down with Autocracy." Government agents arrived just in time to rescue them, saving the day by reassuring the public and explaining away the abdication.

During this time, at the Council of Ministers' meeting, Milyukov and Guchkov urged resistance. The government and the Duma had made too many concessions. Petrograd was not all of Russia, and with the help of the army Michael could take over the capital. Shydlovsky assented weakly. Rodzianko, present at the meeting, thought that, on the contrary, the struggle was already lost. It would be better for Michael to abdicate immediately. The government would certainly find the means for a restoration of the monarchy in the following months, and his abdication at least would restore order and give the State back its prerogatives. Nekrassov and Kerensky were against the recognition of Michael II. Guchkov and Milyukov, they thought, were out of touch with reality; they failed to realize that from now on Russia would never accept the Romanovs. They must proclaim the Republic. But Milyukov held fast and even threatened to resign; Guchkov echoed him. As they saw it, the fate of the army as well as the result of the war depended on the nature of the régime. The other ministers did not follow this line of reasoning. They decided to go to Michael to ask him to abdicate; Milyukov managed to persuade them that the minority also should be allowed to express its views to the Grand Duke. And what if he refused to yield to popular pressure? Would the government go so far as to depose him?

Michael was not the stuff that heroes are made of. "Would you guarantee my life in case I took the crown?" he asked Rodzianko immediately. At that moment the issue was decided and Milyukov's entreaties were useless. A jurist, V. Nabokov, so wrote the text of the abdication that the eventual chance of a restoration of the monarchy was left open (another concession to Milyukov and Guchkov). It was decided that both abdications, Michael's and Nicholas's, would be made public simultaneously. Deeply moved, the last Romanov gave his approval, took the pen, and signed unhesitatingly.

Upon hearing this, the city was overjoyed. Again people got together, yelled, and sang. "Now it is finished," said Mstislavsky to a friend, lost in the delirious crowd. He heard a woman's soft voice nearby who told him, "You are wrong, little father. Not enough blood has flowed."

6. THE REVOLUTION IS CONSOLIDATED

Tsarism was brought down and still no one was sure of the fate of the Revolution. The provinces were yet to be heard from, nor the rest of Europe, nor, above all, the High Command. How would it react to the new régime?

THE ATTITUDE OF THE HIGH COMMAND

On the eve of the fall of the Tsar, General Lukomsky thought that in ten days, with 60,000 Guards' bayonets, the capital could be taken over. He did not recommend this action, however, because he thought that first it would be necessary to conclude a separate peace with the Germans, which would discredit the dynasty. Thus it would be better to go along with the Revolution, which would permit the army to go on to victory. Later it would be easier to impose a new régime on the country, a régime which would serve the dynasty's interests. But for these things to come about, several things were necessary. First of all, the officers and men must agree to work together. Neither one nor the other was ready for this, and the high command least of all. Thus, when announcing the formation of a new government, Grand Duke Nicholas withheld from his soldiers the nature of the disturbance and finished his address by having the troops sing "God Protect the Tsar." He also warned, using the formulas which were familiar to him, "That all attempts at disobedience to orders would be dealt with in accordance with the law." The Romanov family was counting on the Grand Duke to take the "whole" matter in hand—a letter from Marie Pavlovna, Nicholas II's aunt, to her son Boris attests to this—and the victors of February would feel the effects of the use that he would make of the Army of the Caucasus. Thus it was only natural that the Soviet and Kerensky got rid of Grand Duke Nicholas, and also of General Evert, who had refused to go along with the new régime.

Suspected by the court of dictatorial aspirations, Alexeiev acted in an equivocal manner on this issue. He announced "that Grand Duke Nicholas had been named Commander-in-Chief by the will of the Tsar and that the new government had been formed as a result of an agreement between the Duma and the Senate," which he knew to be a lie. On March 3rd he issued an "order" against the detachments of revolutionaries in the Northern Army's zone. Having checked with Rodzianko, he specified, "When these so-called delegations appear, we advise against dispersing them, but attempts should be made to capture them and bring them before courts-martial, whose sentences will be executed immediately." A few days later, thinking of the spring offensive, he asked Guchkov to reestablish order in the barracks and the railways, to put new spirit in the fleet, in short to stop the revolutionary action. In spite of the minister's answer that he could only go as far as the Soviet allowed him to, Alexeiev insisted. "In regard to our allies," he said, "it is a question of where you lose the least dignity, by breaking our commitments or withdrawing from them."

Alexeiev passed as one of the more liberal and better informed generals. The Soviet recognized this and didn't dare ask for his dismissal, because the proclamations of the other generals were much more disquieting. For every commander like General Radko-Dmitriev, who played on the revolutionaries' longings for peace in order to threaten them with his thunder, there were ten who hawked the myth of a patriotic revolution whose prime duty was to create the conditions for victory—"the first one being the reestablishment of discipline." Thus General Brusilov, reputed to be a liberal also, said, "These events were the will of God.... Tomorrow, as yesterday, the soldiers must perform their sacred duty toward Him." He concluded, "The Lord will help us save Holy Russia."

The High Command bore itself thus, as if it were merely a matter of a Palace Revolution's having succeeded with a little help from the man in the street. They were irritated by the fact that the disorders continued. Alexeiev didn't want to receive any more "alarmist" messages. In announcing his nomination as Commander of the Petrograd Region, General Kornilov, reputed to be a Republican, had used a formula that was dear to the Duma: "In view of the fact that the old régime had acknowledged itself powerless, a new government has assumed power." Did these officers correctly estimate the meaning of the events in the capital? Certainly not at the beginning; it was just this failure to understand that paralyzed them. Later they wanted to perpetuate their misunderstanding, which was what discredited them in the eyes of the soldiers. The officers suffered most from the anger of the people; for them the night of February 26 lasted more than eight days.

It was in the navy that, relatively speaking, the most horrors were committed. In fact, some mutineers of 1905 were still imprisoned in the fortresses of Revel and Helsingfors, and the hatred of the sailors for the officers of the line surpassed anything found anywhere else. The command remained, more than in the army, faithful to Nicholas II, preferring death to betrayal. There was no communication between the mutineers and the officers. Blood flowed and there were forty victims, among them Admiral Nepenin, although he had been won over to the new régime. Admiral Viren, at Kronstadt, died bravely. "I have lived, serving my Tsar and my country faithfully. I am ready. It's your turn now. Try to give some meaning to your life." He asked to face the firing squad which shot him.

Those who had benefited most from the Tsar's favor were the quickest to espouse the new régime. Grand Duke Cyril set the example, followed by the Cossacks of the Guard, the Palace Police, and His Majesty's Regiment. Those who stayed steadfastly faithful were rare—the Horse Guards of Novgorod; Count Keller; the Beckendorffs; Count Zamoisky, who went on foot to Tsarskoe-Selo to offer his services to the Tsarina; Bunting, Governor of Tver, who committed suicide. Bark, the former Food Minister, had many friends in the new government; they offered him his old portfolio in the new administration, but he refused. "A question of principle," he said.

At the end of a long slumber, Grand Dukes and general officers who owed everything to their Emperor left him without qualms. When they wanted to change back, it was too late.

THE REVOLUTION IN THE PROVINCES

The rallying of the provinces to the side of the Revolution was just as spectacular. "One of the essential facts these days," noted Kerensky, "was the disappearance of all governmental power." In effect, the old power disintegrated all of a piece, leaving not a trace of the vanished régime.

Thanks to Bublikov's telegram, all of Russia learned in a few hours of the fall of the Old Régime. Everywhere, without waiting for directives, the population installed new officials. In the space of a few days there wasn't a town from Minsk to Vladivostok which did not set up its revolutionary administration, Soviet, or Committee of Public Safety. By March 17th, forty-nine cities had organized their soviets. By the 22nd, seventy-seven soviets were in touch with Petrograd, not counting the soldiers' soviets and the factory soviets.

Often events unfolded as at Petrograd, with a rival Soviet forming in opposition to the municipal Duma. This happened at

Zharoslav, Kazan, Nikolaiev, Rostov-on-the-Don, and other cities. In Moscow the balance of forces was the same as in the capital, but there, perhaps acting in a spirit of emulation, the Soviet adopted an extremely radical position. It proclaimed that its role was not only to control the authorities of the city, but also to bring pressure upon them. Most often, the S.R.-Menshevik majority recommended the forming of a local coalition government in which bourgeois, workers, and soldiers would rub elbows. This was the case at Baku, Ivanovo, Nizhniy-Novgorod, Petrozavodsk, Vologda, Astrakhan, Lugansk, etc. The bourgeoisie was hostile to this solution and refused it at Arkhangelsk. An agreement was reached anyway, but not without incident, as at Nizhniy-Novgorod.

Dumaev, one of the working-class leaders of the city, related:

At the beginning, the bourgeoisie got excited. It wanted to organize a *Committee for the Reestablishment of Order* and to put some workers on it who would be acceptable to them. But the workers forced the bourgeoisie to consider the workers not as isolated individuals but as the representatives of an organization. Coming in as delegates of the Soviet to the "Committee," they had to insist that the bourgeoisie take some action against the police. The bourgeoisie whined that it did not want to arrest the governor. It did not want to liberate our comrades either, until it received orders from Rodzianko. A few days later, the Soviet having gone ahead and arrested the governor, the bourgeoisie wanted to replace him with the head of the *zemstvo*. We, the workers, succeeded in requiring that the post not be confided to a single person, but to a board. We finally won and thus a committee was formed with seven members—three bourgeois, three workers, and one soldier.

Whenever a coalition was formed, the representatives of the bourgeoisie were often in the minority, but the balance was often subtly loaded. At Vologda, for instance, the "Governmental Committee" was made up of five representatives of the city, three workers, three peasants, two representatives of the cooperatives, and representatives of the various parties (two S.R., two S.D., two K.D.). At Penza, where the workers were badly organized, the "coalition" was made up by the bourgeois, who were thus able to keep a majority in fact. At Krasnoyarsk, under the leadership of Sverdlov, where the revolutionaries were in force—at least when the militant wing was led by the Bolsheviks—the soviet refused to collaborate with the municipal Duma and immediately went to war against it and the provisional government. At Samara they cut off the telephones of the bourgeois who were former members of the old administration. At Irkustk, once the commander was arrested, the power belonged to the soviet and the bourgeoisie remained completely passive. At Kronstadt it tried to organize a "Provisional Committee," but this "Abortion Committee," as the sailors called it, soon had to leave the field to the most revolutionary elements.

At this time the Kiev case attracted attention. As in many cities, a soviet was formed opposing the municipal Duma. The Menshevik and S.R. majority wanted to show their confidence in the government. The Bolsheviks opposed them and left the meeting, declaring that the soviet was betraying the working class. From then on, they were to pursue different objectives.

The municipal Duma only kept its authority where the workers' presence guaranteed the bourgeoisie the appearance of power. The bourgeoisie overestimated its strength; in the provinces, where it could not lean on general policies, it lost its hold rapidly.

Some of the high functionaries of the Old Régime withdrew, others tried to resist. The mayor of Lugansk complained to Petrograd that a "soviet" wanted to change the make-up of a Municipal Council. The police commissioner of Schlussenburg thought the activities of the committees "comic," and they had all the trouble in the world getting rid of him. There were some arrests, but in general the Revolution was tolerant. In Petrograd Kerensky had personally saved many lives. History will testify to this. In the provinces the new leaders had respect for human life. Thus, at Stavropol the soviet decided that no one could be locked up for more than twenty-four hours without appearing before a court. On the whole, Justice, born in February, committed few excesses. It did not repay the Tsarist repression one one-hundredth of what it had inflicted on the revolutionaries; nevertheless, some of them were shot. Those of Elisavetgrad left testimony:

We, the policemen of Elisavetgrad, salute the soviet and the government and congratulate them on having caused the triumph of liberty, so long in coming. About to die, we prostrate ourselves before the Russian people and beg them to forgive all the evil which we unwittingly committed in the performance of our duties.

We are accused of causing troubles and pogroms. We swear by our wives and our children that this is not true. . . . Truly we rejoice that tomorrow they will have a better life than ours and we cast our curses on the policemen of Petrograd who fired machine guns on the starving people.... It would have been sweet to die from enemy bullets, our souls at peace, our children proud of us.

Everything was done to avoid making a martyr of the Tsar. In March the Emperor and his family were put in protective custody at Tsarskoe-Selo. Then negotiations were undertaken to ensure their exile. There was a question of taking the Imperial family to Great Britain. Later Sir George Buchanan, the British ambassador, claimed that he did not obstruct this project, yet it seems that it was the British government which greeted this proposal unfavorably, fearing it would alienate the new Russia. The presence of Nicholas II thirty kilometers from the capital gave rise to some incidents, so that the government and the Soviet decided to move the Imperial family to Tobolsk. In August the threat of counter-revolution made this move urgent. In the meantime Kerensky had caused a law to be passed abolishing the death penalty in order to spare Nicholas II in case the Revolution decided to try him.

From then on, nothing stood in the way of the complete triumph of the men of February. The only thing which remained was recognition by the foreign powers. The Allied ambassadors thought that the Provisional Government was going to triumph over the Soviet, and, since Milyukov was in favor of a war to the finish, they explained to their leaders that the Allied interest lay in supporting the new régime. The Allied powers redoubled messages of friendship. But they were not unconditional. On March 9th, Alexeiev wrote, "If we don't attack, the Allies will cut off our supplies." Rarely did he show such sagacity. That day, in effect, England stopped its deliveries of artillery matériel to Russia. France did not deliver one single airplane (she had promised three hundred) in March and April 1917. On March 8th, the American ambassador, David R. Francis, who had taken the initiative on recognition, nevertheless telegraphed Secretary of State Robert Lansing: "Agree to no loan to Provisional Government without assurance that it will continue war until victory and no separate peace." This was all the more mystifying since at this time America was not yet at war.

On March 23, 1917, the funeral of the victims of the Revolution took place on the Field of Mars; it was an impressive ceremony celebrating the victory of February.

Marylin Markovitch related:

Suddenly, the distant strains of a band playing a funeral march are heard. Slowly, with measured, deliberate step, the parade approaches. At the head, the militiamen, then the caskets, draped in red on the workers' shoulders. Then, in perfect close formation, the workers' organizations, the men and women students, the crowd of parents, friends, strangers marching in step, in a long, calm file, religious, without priests, the first civil burial in Orthodox Russia.

The revolutionary funeral march gives musical expression to words which, within his own breast, everyone repeats with intense emotion, yet without tears.

> *You have fallen, victims of the final struggle,*
> *For the love of the people.*
> *You have sacrificed all for the people,*
> *For its life, its honor, its liberty.*
> *Farewell, brothers, who have gone*
> *Your honorable and glorious way.*

★

CHAPTER THREE

THE PROJECTS OF THE RULING CLASSES AND THE REVOLUTIONARY ORGANIZATIONS

The success of the Revolution was as unexpected as its outbreak. Rid of Tsarism with one blow, the Russian people exploded with the joy which follows a long wait. After the first few days, a more profound contentment followed the initial elation, as if, reassured, everyone had the feeling that Russia was free, she and her 130 million citizens; as if everyone, by magic, had reached political majority. Suddenly the dream of liberty was turned into the reality of 130 million individual enthusiasts, who became so many specialized reformers, each with his plan for reforming the country. Thousands of telegrams, motions, and letters, addressed to the government, the Duma, the Soviet, and the Nation, expressed this hope.

What aspirations were in these messages, and in what measure did they correspond to the projects of the voting classes, to the programs of the political parties and other organizations, which for more than twenty years pretended to defend the interest of the population? This was an exceptional moment—a few weeks during which neither the parties nor the organizations, which had been disorganized by the Tsarist reaction, was in a position to intercede and take charge of these aspirations. Thus ideas were expressed freely in or out of accord with the projects of the professional revolutionaries. The event is without parallel; in 1789 the wishes of the nation had been expressed within the context of the *Ancien Régime*, before the Revolution could erupt and triumph.

1. THE FEELINGS AND PROJECTS OF THE UPPER MIDDLE CLASS AND THE MIDDLE CLASSES

After February, the *grande bourgeoisie* found itself with mixed emotions. Satisfied to find itself in power, it nevertheless disliked the manner in which it had been brought there. Revolutionary in spite of itself, it instinctively adopted the conservative manner. "We must restore the order destroyed by the incapacity and the criminal inactivity of the deposed order," wrote the *Novoe Vremya* on March 5th. At the same time the bourgeoisie thought it would satisfy its old craving to make of Russia a state modeled on the modern West and completely independent of foreign interference. It figured to reinforce its own power, to base its authority on the country's economy, a condition necessary for this program. First it would be necessary to "pursue the war to its victorious end." Nevertheless, the leaders avoided recalling the objects of the war. They knew how touchy opinion was on this subject and contented themselves with affirming the "necessity" of this victory or recalling "Russia's duty to the Belgians and the Serbs, to the Allies."

Truthfully, the bourgeoisie thought that only the state of war could maintain the structures which had survived the February events. It thought also that the war would tighten the solidarity of the Russian ruling classes with the Western bourgeoisie, on whose help it could rely to restrain the mounting forces of the Revolution. This essential line of reasoning was added to the traditional motives of the "imperialist" bourgeoisie.

Cadets and Octobrists urged the formation of a "single power" to conduct the war. In the *Rech*, as in all their newspapers, they never stopped repeating that the two-power structure was making the government's task impossible. "The soviets and other organizations of the masses should only function as means of expression of the will of the people. In no way must they share power."

The progressive bourgeoisie no longer alluded to what, the day before, was its principal demand—the responsibility of the government to the Assembly. Their very cleverness was a fault, in the opinion of Shydlovsky, because the maintenance of principles would have been a help in the reform of the Duma, which could then have been used as a counterweight to the Soviet. In truth, the new leaders could not agree on a course to follow. As Rodzianko clearly saw, the Cadets "wanted no fetters"; they gave up their principles easily. As for the other bourgeois representatives, they thought it would be better to gain time; persuaded that everything would settle itself and that for the time being it would be better for them to tone down their demands, they felt they could bring up this problem of responsibility later. Thus, when on March 10th the government met the representatives of commerce and industry, there was only the question of victory, of rebuilding the Russian economy, and nothing else. The *Torgovo-Promyshlennaya Gazeta*, an organ of the business world, gave "its complete support" to the government.

By a roundabout path those who rallied to the Revolution also abandoned another point in their program, the formation of a constitutional monarchy. In this, too, the Cadets pioneered the way. On March 6th Milyukov was still endorsing Michael. But his friends condemned his obstinacy, which was embarrassing. At the end of March the Cadet convention, with "unanimous enthusiasm," proclaimed its adherence to the Republic. Kokoshkin was charged with adjusting the party principles to the political exigencies of the moment.

He first explained:

The monarchy was not for us the supreme principle which guided our political program. The monarchist régime was not a principle, but a political expedient. . . . On the question of the political régime, we always distinguish the form of the régime from its contents. And it is the nature of the régime which was essential for us. . . .

Three principles guided us: the principle of the inviolability of civil and political rights, the principle of the sovereignty of the people, and finally the principle of social justice. The application of these principles constituted the foundation of our policies. . . .

Formerly, it seemed impractical to justify a republic. . . . After all, we knew that a constitutional monarchy was nothing more than a compromise between absolutism and popular sovereignty, a compromise which, for the majority, was a necessary stage. . . . We thought, moreover, that in practice constitutional monarchy would reduce the gap between absolutism and the republican form of government to insignificance . . . —that, for example, Great Britain is no less free than France, but more so than some South American republics. . . . Eleven years ago, moreover, the population identified the State with a living symbol. . . . This is no longer the case today.

Then, with the outbreak of war, other things entered the picture. . . . The old formula *For Tsar and Country* no longer meant anything, because it seemed that you could not be for the Tsar and the Country, since the Tsar was against the Country. *(Applause.)* The Nation arose and Tsarism was beaten. It was no longer a question of maintaining the Monarchy, but of restoring it. And to restore it, blood had to be shed, as in the past it would have had to have been shed to form a republic. Because now, the fact is that it is a republic which exists.

After this speech by Kokoshkin, the Convention approved the following resolution in the midst of a storm of applause:

Russia must be a Parliamentary Republican Democracy. The legislative power must belong to the national representatives.

The head of the executive must be a President of the Republic, elected for a period determined by the national representatives and governing with the help of a ministry responsible to the people."

The remainder of the political program remained unchanged. It still favored amnesty and all those reforms which in effect would institute in Russia a political society conforming to the ideals of 1789—equality before the law, political freedom, and so on.

The bourgeois program on the question of the nationalism of minorities had been determined on the eve of the Revolution, by the bourgeoisie's struggle against Tsarism. Thus the Cadets came out against federal decentralization and for the right of cultural self-determination. Preparing to conquer the state from within, they did not intend to reinforce the structure. But they also wanted to give it a certain unity, and proposed a formula of integration which would allow the various nations to choose the form as well as the limits. In this they opposed the policy of the former rightist organizations who called for Russification. With regard to Finland and Poland, the Cadets urged the formation of an internally autonomous régime, granted here, agreed to there, by the legislative authorities of the Grand Duchy. Milyukov, who constantly intervened in favor of the nationalists persecuted by Tsarism, saw himself nicknamed the "fervent defender of Finland." In any case, it could be seen that the attitude of Milyukov and his friends had changed as a result of the war and the temptation which circumstances exerted on certain nationalities. In *Rech*, at the beginning of 1917, Milyukov wrote, "The Cadets will, in the Ukrainian question, show an attitude which will be a function of that of the Ukrainians themselves with respect to the war." In January 1917 the fact that he tried to minimize the importance of the "Wilson note" on the rights of small nations was perhaps an indication that a certain misunderstanding could develop as soon as the bourgeoisie applied its program concerning nationalities.

Like all other revolutionary organizations, the bourgeois political parties tried to resolve the agrarian question to their own advantage—that is, economic advantage, inasmuch as the bourgeoisie over the past ten years had developed its involvement in agriculture; and especially political advantage, inasmuch as it appeared that tomorrow the peasant mass would be the essential factor in an electoral confrontation. But only the Cadets and the Octobrists—who expressed themselves through the medium of the *Union of Landowners*—had a real agrarian program. They too had to adapt it to the circumstances.

In the days of Tsarism, the nationalization of the land constituted the agrarian policy principle of the Cadets. According to them, the land would be given to the peasants. They would pay rent to the state, which would give it to the old landowners, who could thus become rentiers of the State. When the program was worked out in 1906, the Cadets thought that it would go into effect only "when the power had passed entirely into the hands of the people." Meanwhile, they urged the formation of a "National Land Bank" which would be available to those who did not own any land (Paragraph 37). It would be made up of monastic lands, fiefs, etc. But the Cadets would have excluded city-owned lands, lands of the *zemstvos*, and the enclosures. Only the large estates and vast uncultivated areas could be expropriated to make up this land bank. The price would be a function of the rentability. Further, they foresaw the establishment of a "minimum" in land, which would vary according to the region and which, once the needs of everyone had been met, would permit the release of the expropriable land. Thus the bourgeoisie would have been able to buy land cheap. All depended on the manner in which the "agrarian committees" would be formed by the government. This would be decided locally. The other problem was to determine which of the lands would be expropriated and the price at which they would be sold. This had be done quickly, "to prevent the outbreak of trouble in the countryside." But while V. Chechinin, V. Elachich, and some others pointed out the necessity of decreeing the nationalization of the land beforehand, if "they wanted to avoid having the parties of the left exploit the peasants' land hunger" (March 23rd, 1917), the majority, preoccupied with political problems, did not want to rush things. The March convention decided nothing which hadn't been defined previously; the countryside remained quiet, so what was the need of hurrying?

On the other hand, the *Union of Landowners* immediately sensed that private property was in danger. Moribund a few years, the *Union* came to life with the February Revolution. Like many other associations, it was born in 1906, having as its objective the protection of the rights of private property, "the foundation of the State and the guarantee of the public welfare." Under the impulse of Octobrists such as Y. Vulfert and V. N. Lvov, it recalled, in the Spring of 1917, that it would give "all possible aid to the government to resolve the agrarian question." It had to show signs of life, having remained dormant for ten years during the time when the Tsarist government, led by Stolypin, rigidly practiced the policy which it had recommended. Re-emerging at this perilous moment, the *Union* recalled: "that the agrarian question should not be settled from the point of view of the interest of one section of the population or another, but solely from the point of the 'general welfare. . . .' That is to say, in the interest of the nation, everything should be done to improve production. Only private property would be able to do this, because large enterprises made the exploitation of the land easier, whereas parceling led to chaos. It should be avoided at all cost." Coming out against confiscation, the *Union* recommended facilitating the task of the peasants who wanted to acquire land. Rural credit would provide for it. As for the selling price, it would be that of the open market. "The proponents of Socialism want to bring the population back to servitude," explained the *Union*, "to distribute the land in order to take it over again later, as soon as the need is felt. But the peasants would no longer be able to acquire new lands, nor hire new farm hands, nor leave their place, as the merchants, the carpenters, or the masons can." This was a clever argument and less equivocal than that of the Cadets, who, in order to cater to the peasantry, used the Socialist tone, although neither the *Union* nor the Cadets, both of whom were interested in the development of "capitalist" property, could see how to reconcile their aspirations with those of the peasants.

First of all, by attaining power, the bourgeoisie hoped to fulfill its economic objectives. The bourgeois program aimed at "intensifying the development of the country." It was necessary to break the shackles which slowed the expansion and hindered the bourgeoisie's gaining a hold on the economic life. In order to make use of its supremacy the bourgeoisie wanted to free itself of the control of the bureaus so much that its leaders saw the Revolution as a process by which the bourgeoisie would wrest from the State the control which it had over the economy.

Half of the national wealth being in its hands, the bourgeoisie thought that its mission was to take over the administration of the whole. In 1916, Rabushinsky had already worked out a plan to that effect, which would have turned over to the business magnates the management of the economy. As did the Socialists—but with opposite ends in view—the bourgeoisie had sketched a theory of the development of Russia which legalized, from a doctrinal point of view, its ambitions. Evoking the change to Socialism, it insisted on the necessity of going through a capitalist stage and stigmatized as "absurd" all premature change—that is to say, all change "before about a hundred years." The *Journal of the Steel Mill Owners* thought this would be possible only "when Socialism would be feasible in all civilized countries at the same time." Thus in its economic plan the bourgeoisie showed a determination which was exactly opposite to the hopes of the revolutionary movement, since, in contrast to the French bourgeoisie, "which at least had confided the administration of the war economy to Socialist Ministers," it sought, on the contrary, to wrest from the State the rights which it had acquired in the administration of the national economy. Boldly facing those who wanted the State to increase its control over production or prices, the bourgeoisie moved resolutely into the fray.

As for the reaction of the Russian people, the bourgeoisie thought, along with Rabushinsky, that it needed only to wait for it to sow its wild oats, then "everything would be all right and no one would get hurt." No doubt concessions would have to be made to the working class, but in any event there was one thing which would not be granted—the administration of business. As for the rest, the bourgeoisie, ready to work for the establishment of social justice, did not specify just what it meant by social justice. Still, circumstances forced it to react when the working class made its first demands, which had to do with the eight-hour day. On March 14th, the *Moscow Committee for Commerce and Industry* broached the subject. Its conclusions were as follows:

> Before the war, the development of production was insuffi-cient, as is well known. But the war has revealed the true state of things in a startling manner. That is why any measure which would have the effect of diminishing production would be undesirable from the government point of view. At the present time, when it is essential to conduct the war to a victorious end, everything should lead, not to a diminution of work produc-tion, but to an increase. The eight-hour day, then, should not be looked on as a slogan, but from the point of view that it could only cause a diminution of production.
> The norms of production are not related in the same manner to work in Russia and in the West. It is not only because there are fewer work days in Russia than in the West, but for the

same number of hours, the production in Russia is less; to this must be added the fact that even in the West the eight-hour day is the exception. The introduction of the eight-hour day in Russia would only accentuate the gap existing between Russian industry, which would become less and less competitive, and Western industry. Russia would thus be weakened as much today as in the future, as much in wartime as in peacetime. This is what gives this question of the eight-hour day its particular quality. It is not a measure which can be taken up at the local level, or even at the governmental level; it is a problem which can be dealt with only at the international level by a collective decision of all Governments.

After these somewhat discouraging considerations, the Committee added:

The reduction in the number of hours of work, reducing in turn the number of things produced, would end necessarily in an increase in price which would affect everyone, especially the workers, who are consumers of manufactured goods. . . . If they were to introduce, of themselves, the eight-hour day, it would be on them that the responsibility would fall for the measures which the government would have to take and which would not necessarily affect the producers as a class.

When the revolution broke out, the Russian bourgeoisie had felt ill at ease. But it had gotten used to this event, which, in the end, had put it in power. To remain there, it did not hesitate to change its mind and abandon the principles on which, for the last twenty years, it had based its actions.

Installed in the government, it prepared plans for the future, convinced like the working class that it would remain in power for a long time. It acted accordingly, neglecting the aspirations of the workers and all those oppressed, since History had taught them that power remains in the end with the triumphant bourgeoisie.

Whenever they expressed their aspirations, the middle classes adopted a position similar to that of the upper middle class. Thus the pharmacists, on March 5th, decided to "support the government insofar as it applied its program effectively." But they invited all the pharmacists from other areas to join a union. Surveyors and chemists, representatives of Piatigorsk, and civil employees of Murmansk similarly expressed their wishes. They wanted better living conditions, but they saw in the revolution the opportunity to bring Russia out of the "anarchy into which Tsarism had plunged it" and to win the war. One group after another, notably the teachers, thought, along with the upper middle class, that the revolution would help out in the winning of the war. Some added that the war should only be conducted "to a logical end, a peace without annexations or contributions." But on the whole, the professors were more ardently patriotic than the researchers and the scientists. The students were divided. Among the technicians, for example, there was a tendency to give their support to the government, and to the Soviet only "insofar as it would control and guarantee the application of governmental decisions." Others, representing the majority at the Psychoneurotic Institute of Petrograd and at the Dental School of Odessa, reversed the proposition. As an organized body, the students did not represent any real power. It was only in the context of the parties that they played a role, the public seeing them as the descendants of the intelligentsia.

2. ARTISTS AND THE INTELLECTUALS

The artists and the intellectuals, more than the others, had long sung the advent of the Revolution. However, after 1905 they were not as confident or as unanimous. "At times the men of the Renaissance," wrote P. Pascal, "have all had premonitions of disaster, even since before the war." "The period of humanism is ended," wrote Biely; "that of Holy Barbarism is come. History will be skipped over. Culture is an empty head from which everything escapes. . . . Soon will come the explosion. . . . The revolutionary individual moves in a circle. . . . The masses become the tools of the sportsmen of the Revolution."

When the February revolution broke out, thinkers and artists reacted quite differently. Some, like Dmitri Merezhkovsky, Zinaida Hippius, Feodor Chaliapin, Peter Struve, Maxim Gorky, etc., after having saluted "the fall of the Holy Russian Empire," lamented and told themselves, "I believe—I want to believe—that all will be well." Their interpretation of revolutionary events somewhat resembled the point of view of the ruling classes, but their perspective was different. Berdyaev felt, like Milyukov, that "the Revolution was fundamentally patriotic. It had not been born because one class rose against another, the workers throwing themselves against the industrialists or the peasants against the landowners, or even because the class antagonisms had been aggravated. The ancient power had fallen because it had not been able to defend Russia." Did he foresee the storm? Berdyaev urged "the union of all Russians," because the bonds which unite them are those of History, more deep-rooted and stronger than the so-called "class" antagonisms, which are a rather recent notion, born abroad. "At the Constituent Assembly," concluded Berdyaev, in *People and Classes in the Revolution*, "the welfare of the people must come before settling the class question. Besides, History teaches that upheavals always end badly for the mass of the people, whether it be June 1848 or the Paris Commune." Gorky's behavior is equally significant. Sukhanov had all the trouble in the world in bringing him before the Soviet, which was preparing a triumphal reception for him. He had only one concern, the creation of a "Commission for the Safeguarding of Historic Monuments." When he was consulted on the 7th of March to organize the funeral for the victims of the revolution, Gorky went to the Soviet all right, but to say in a sulky tone to the delegates who had greeted him with an ovation, "The time for words is past, now it is time to act."

In contrast to the anxiety of these intellectuals was the enthusiasm of the poets. While Vladimir Korolenko addressed a passionate message to the Soviet, Alexander Blok, Sergei Yesenin, and Vladimir Mayakovsky, who quickly adopted the Bolshevik slogans, proclaimed that "now everything is possible."

Some of the underground leaders went along with the thinkers. Mysterious bearers of the Revolution, they enjoyed, on the eve of the Revolution, an unshared authority. Now the spell was broken. In practice it appeared that the militants were not necessarily the most revolutionary. In the turmoil of the March days, they felt the authority slipping from them and they did not partake in the general rejoicing. Their role ended, many of them took refuge in a new exile, that of actors who had become spectators, the last representatives of a finished world.

But the others who threw themselves into the struggle for power differed on the objectives and the nature of the revolution.

3. PROGRAM OF THE REVOLUTIONARY ORGANIZATIONS

Although surprised by the revolution, the revolutionaries were not short of programs. Each party had its own, worked out for long years, discussed and reconsidered in the light of Stolypin's reaction and the war. In truth, since 1906, the Russian political organizations had become more preoccupied first with their role with respect to power, and then with respect to the war, than with the contents of their programs. The methods of the revolutionary struggle and the choice of tactics held a bigger place in the quarrels between factions than did the differences about objectives. As is often the case in revolutionary action, the militants thought more about ways of bringing down the régime than about what they would do themselves once they came to power. This characteristic difference from the situtation in 1789 makes one think that, in contrast to the Russian nineteenth century, the French eighteenth century had as its objective not to overthrow the government, but only its reform.

Be that as it may, the Russian revolutionary movement had to revise its program because the governments of the Stolypin period, authoritarian in their policies, showed themselves to be reformists with regard to institutions and adequate enough modernists from an economic and social point of view, especially in the countryside. The reforms rallied a part of the bourgeoisie and the peasantry to Tsarism, forcing the parties to readjust their programs. Ultimately, the war with the Central Powers forced them to examine more closely the problem of the border nationalities. Finally, when the February Revolution broke out, the existence of the Soviet forced the parties to reconsider the problem of power.

For ten years, everyone considered revolution unavoidable, but no one foresaw how the régime would end. What is more, the militants made a distinction between their maximum program, whose outline they dreamed about, and the more explicit minimum, which they wanted to impose on the powers that be, little by little. At any rate, it was understood that, once won, the Revolution would proceed by stages. "The contents of a revolution, like the outline of its program, depends on the quality and quantity of the consciousness and the active forces capable of being mobilized," was the opinion of Viktor Chernov and the Populists. The Social-Democrats felt that Russia would have to go through certain phases of development before the Socialist Revolution. The process seemed unavoidable to all of them, even though they varied in their opinion about the nature or the duration of the stages to be passed. A whole polemic on the mode of production in Russia had followed.

Only the Anarchists had a different point of view. To the party thesis of transitory states and intermediate stages they opposed their thesis of immediate change, progressing to the true economic and federated community. "The political parties," they said, "depend on the social structure inherited from centuries of outdated régimes—the Asiatic, the feudal, etc.— . . . to arrive at their principles of action. . . . They make believe that the model (i.e., the West) holds constructive ideas. The Anarchists feel, on the contrary, that a new structure requires new methods from the start, and urge their application."

THE POLITICAL PROGRAM

The "maximum" program of the Social-Democrats remained rather vague as long as the "Social Revolution" had not yet triumphed.

After replacing private property in the means of production and exchange by collective production, and after creating a rational organization for the collective process, in order to ensure the well-being and the complete development of all members of society, the proletarian revolution will abolish class distinction and thus liberate oppressed humanity, for it will thereby end all forms of the exploitation of one section of society by another.

"To accomplish this Revolution, the 'dictatorship of the proletariat' must first be established. This would enact the minimum program of the party." From a political point of view, they aimed at the overthrow of autocracy and its replacement by a democratic republic. The Constitution would insure "sovereignty of the people," universal suffrage, the traditional freedoms, the right to question officials, the election of judges, etc. (See text in Appendix.)

The *Populists* also felt that a provisional political régime could be formed during the transition phase in order to stop counter-revolutionary attempts. Like the Social-Democrats, Chernov pictured the establishment of a "dictatorship of workers." This iron government would provide a foundation for the democratic republic, considered as a stage on the road to Socialism, and not merely as the lesser evil. This was the main difference between the Social-Democrats and the Socialist-Revolutionaries, in theory at least. Fundamentally, the Mensheviks had a certain fondness for a democratic republic, but the Bolsheviks wanted to replace it as soon as possible by "the dictatorship of the proletariat."

The Socialist-Revolutionaries defined the terms of the republic to be formed during the transition period often in identical terms. (See text in Appendix.) Similar in many points, these two programs differed, however, on one essential point—the role and the distribution of power. The Social-Democrats awarded it to a sovereign assembly (Article 1), whereas on this point the Socialist-Revolutionaries remained silent. They had no precise program: "We fear the State like the Devil fears holy water," said an S.R. delegate to the first party convention. Without adopting this Anarchist attitude, Chernov and the Socialist-Revolutionaries were wary of the omnipotence of the State and of Social-Democratic "legalism." In fact, they were more concerned with seeing how they could dismantle the centralized power than with planning on whom to award it. In favor of the autonomy of regions, of the provinces, and even of communes, they were thus really more partial to federalism than the Social-Democrats. More hostile to "centralism" than to the State, they disagreed particularly with the Bolsheviks. They differed also from the Social-Democrats in their suspicions about the representative system. Proponents of direct popular legislation, they denied any group the right to pretend to speak in the name of a class or nation. In this they came close to the Anarchists. In this way, too, they differed from the *Trudoviks* and the Cadets, who favored a unicameral parliament. These were important differences, although less serious than those which had broken out about the role of the soviets or those which bore on the peasantry or the question of national minorities.

THE FUTURE OF THE PEASANTS

The parties had to take changes in rural Russia into account. Stolypin's reforms had created five million new landowners, although this accelerating process was abruptly interrupted by the war. At this time, however, there was a large number of discontented peasants. They were all the more envious and bitter because the phenomenal development of the cooperative movement had helped the new landowners to overcome their initial difficulties. These developments completely upset the schemes of the Socialist theorists. Until 1906, Social-Democrats and Populists agreed that the nationalization or socialization of lands was a step on the road to Socialism, but now millions of *moujiks* had become landowners. Would a nationwide expropriation be necessary? This problem was discussed heatedly from 1906 to 1917. The Socialists, who had been unanimous on these questions until then, divided once more—an unexpected result of Stolypin's reforms.

For the Social-Democrats, the main question consisted of defining the nature of these changes. Lenin thought that a "bourgeois" revolution was going on in the countryside, because "the access to property in the general frame of an economy in the process of capitalist development will end in the destruction of the old order founded on serfdom." The class struggle in the countryside would no longer pit the feudal lords against the peasants, but kulaks against the poorer peasants. This conflict would cause all traces of the feudal economy to disappear. The measures recommended by Lenin aimed more at "animating" the peasant than at satisfying his immediate aspirations. Very explicit when it came to analyzing the role of the peasantry in the Revolution, Lenin remained rather vague when it came to measures which might satisfy them. "It would be unreasonable to tie our hands in anticipation," he wrote in 1905 when he urged the nationalization of the land.

On the other hand, P. Maslov, a well-known Menshevik expert, felt that there had not been a true "revolution" in the countryside because the feudal lords and the bureaucrats kept their hold on the administration of men and affairs. Doubting the ability of the peasants to pioneer their way toward a rural democracy, Maslov counted more on the action of the urban proletariat to trigger a real revolutionary process. The countryside should take a "defensive" attitude and let the cities take the initiative. Like other Socialists, Maslov recommended the formation of "agrarian committees," one for each village, on the day when the Revolution would break out. In contrast to Lenin, he did not foresee the creation of special committees for the poor peasants, feeling that all peasants should remain united. These committees would complete the destruction of the Old Régime. They were to play in the countryside the role of soviets in the cities, ensuring the safeguarding of the bourgeois revolution while preparing for the proletarian revolution of the future. Martynov went even further. He judged that Stolypin's reforms would not even be able to annihilate the old methods of production; thus even the bourgeois revolution remained to be accomplished in the countryside. At the other extreme, N. Rozhkov thought that it was already almost accomplished. The "hooliganism of the countryside was not a precursor of the Revolution, but its sequel." In contrast to the Bolsheviks, he deduced that the democratization of the countryside could be done by peaceful means.

Before and after the February Revolution, several points of the Social-Democratic program were subjects of polemics—the delineation of lands susceptible to confiscation, the mode of acquisition (confiscation, purchase, etc.), their destination, and the manner of development. In this connection, four points should be noted.

I. Lenin was practically the only one to urge the nationalization of *all* the lands, crown-lands, church lands, lands of large landowners, and even the small properties born of the Stolypin reforms. He thought that the system of small cultivation was incapable of liberating effectively the peasantry in a mercantile system. Since changing the "title" of property would change nothing, it was necessary to put the peasantry on guard about this "mirage." Lenin also showed that the extension of the system of small properties would reinforce the capitalist régime and play into the hands of the bourgeoisie. This was an old idea, which he had advanced well before 1906. Plekhanov deduced that Lenin wanted to skip the bourgeois revolution stage. The "old Bolsheviks" only wanted to expropriate the large domains, agreeing in this with P. Maslov who thought that to follow Lenin "would make a second Vendée out of Russia" because all the new small property-owners would rally to the counter-revolution. N. Rozhkov urged the nationalization of all the lands, with a view to redistributing them, in order to rally the peasantry to the Revolution instead of turning them away from it. Both he and Maslov thought that the state lands and the large domains were scarce in the heavily settled areas and that there was very little arable land there. They wanted to limit the expropriations of large landholders to the richer territories.

II. It remained to determine the manner of expropriation of the lands. They had to choose between confiscation and indemnification. Formerly in the majority, the proponents of confiscation became rarer as the number of property-owners increased. Rozhkov and Maslov thought that it would not be feasible to grant the new owners their land gratuitously, while others were still paying the arrears on purchases made under Tsarism. They envisioned putting the money from these sales into a national fund or into regional agrarian committees. Only the Bolsheviks favored a free distribution. On March 14, 1917, Mikhail Kalinin took this position in *Pravda*. No one offered to present the case of the expropriated, at least in public.

III. Who would get the lands which were confiscated? The Mensheviks wanted to distribute them to the poor peasants, who would take full possession. However, they planned to entrust the "agrarian committees" with the job of ensuring the rights of the peasant collectivity who would benefit from a sort of eminent domain. In favor of nationalization and hostile to small property-holders, egalitarian or not, Lenin thought these propositions of Maslov, Rozhkov, and N. Valentinov were wrong. He planned to turn all lands over to the central power once the revolution was accomplished and to proceed then to collectivization.

IV. Thus they could choose the development of the most rentable land—that is to say, large-scale cultivation, which would allow the immediate passage from socialization to collectivization. Y. Larin shared these views, preferring, however, to entrust the job of administering the large domains to the municipalities. But the other Mensheviks thought these concepts utopian. There were as many opinions as there were theorists. However, the thesis of P. Maslov was gaining ground among the Bolsheviks. When he wrote the first manifesto on the agrarian question the day after the February Revolution, Kalinin thought it necessary to enumerate the categories of land which should go to the peasants; thus it was not a question of nationalizing them all.

The Populists put the problem of reform in different terms. According to them, the theory of the class struggle found its principle not in the relations between owners and nonowners, but in the unequal distribution of wealth. Thus egalitarianism was the driving force of social struggles and the principle of the revolutionary program of the Populists. There began the differences. While a majority of the militants felt that land should be the "good" of the people *(dostoianie)*, not its property *(sobstvennost)*, and urged the socialization of the means of production, a small minority (the Social-Populists of Peshekhonov) came out in favor of rural democratic régimes, founded on small property-holders. Some here and there wanted to maintain for a time the family form of cultivation, which they felt was better adapted to the peasants' aspirations than collectivization.

> While the process of transformation goes on in industry from work in common to common control of production, in agriculture it goes from collective administration of the means of production to the organization of labor in common. . . . In agriculture [writes Sisko], first, private property must be abolished to concede to each individual his share before proceeding to inaugurate collective labor.

This "share" the *obshchina* would guarantee everyone, with the

State merely overseeing the redistribution. This project implied a revival of the rural community and the abolition of measures taken against the *mir* by Stolypin's administration.

Like the Social-Democrats, the Socialist-Revolutionaries were divided when it came to the question of defining the method of applying these principles. The less weighty polemics were about the evaluation of the "norm" of agrarian units; it could not be the same from one end of Russia to the other. But how was one to establish an equitable parity? All attempts at an ideal equality were suspect, especially S. Maslov's remarks to the effect that it was wrong to apply this principle indiscriminately, since it would result in dismantling the large estates, the most rentable ones.

Other problems were raised, as they were among the Social-Democrats. There was the indemnification of the dispossessed, to which only the "Maximalists" were opposed, and which the other S.R.s approved, "to avoid violence"; there was also the question of the method of confiscation. According to some, this should be defined by the Constituent Assembly, "which would not be the Duma, from which nothing could be expected"; others thought the "agrarian committees" should be empowered to seize the lands. Once the success of the revolution was established, the Populists would have liked to forbid commercial transactions, to abolish private property, and to define the authority of the "agrarian committees." But the "revolutionary legalism" of the S.R.s prevented action "as long as the Constituent had not made a decision," which annoyed the Maximalists as well as the Socialist-Populists, on this issue in agreement for once.

Thus, although reputed to be authorities on the agrarian question, the Populists were as divided as the Social-Democrats. It was the same way with the economic theorists of the "League for Agrarian Reform," sparked by V. Chazanov, where the "politicians," anxious to have the peasants on their side, struggled with the "economists," who were more concerned with the rational development of production. Briefly, in this field which everyone felt to be of prime importance for the Russia of the future, there was chaos.

THE CONDITION OF THE WORKING CLASS

In a country with a "peasant economy," such as Russia, it was normal that theorists would apply themselves more to seeking methods of agrarian reform than to considering the nationalization or the socialization of industry or commerce. Realizing that agrarian reform was a part of the immediate program of the S.R. while the socialization of industry was to be left until later, the extreme left of Populism abandoned the Socialist-Revolutionary Party and formed the "Maximalist" faction. Among the S.D., the preamble of the program of 1903 evoked the day when "it would be possible to substitute Socialist relationships in production for Capitalist relationships in production," but the minimum program required only "protecting the working class against physical and moral breakdown and developing its potential for the struggle for liberation." It was more detailed on this point than the program of the S.R. and demanded:

1. The eight-hour day for all salaried employees.

2. A weekly rest period of at least forty-two consecutive hours.

3. Absolutely no overtime.

4. No night shift (from nine in the evening to ten A.M.).

5. No child labor involving children of school age (up to sixteen years) and the limitation of adolescents (from sixteen to eighteen years) to six hours of labor a day.

6. Interdiction of female labor in establishments which could cause them harm; paid maternity leave for four weeks prior to and six weeks after confinement.

7. The organization of nurseries for infants and small children, granting nursing mothers a half-hour pause every three hours.

8. State-controlled social insurance for overaged or totally or partially disabled workers from a special fund procured by taxes on capitalists.

9. Interdiction of payment in kind.

10. Interdiction of employers' withholding salaries for any reason whatsoever (fines, malfeasance, etc.).

11. The nomination of factory inspectors; the participation of worker delegates elected by the workers and paid by the state.

12. Inspection by worker delegates of sanitary conditions of buildings furnished by the employers for the lodging of workers, such inspection to extend to matters of interior management and site condition—with a view to protecting the employees against employer intrusion in their lives and activities as private citizens.

101

13. The institution of a medical service in all establishments employing wage workers, with such medical service to be completely independent of the employers' control, free for the workers, and to be charged to the employers; the workers' livelihood is to be maintained during illnesses.

14. The institution of penalties for employers' infractions of labor laws.

15. The formation of labor courts in all sections of the economy, to be made up of equal parts of labor and management delegates.

16. Requirements that local governments set up labor offices.

This part of the program did not give rise to much argument, since the theorists thought that at the stage of economic development in which Russia found itself, it was not going to achieve its "bourgeois" revolution. The transformation of the relations of production in the cities was so distant that the accomplishment of the minimum program appeared merely as a pious wish, almost like the maximum program, which was no longer the case in Germany or Great Britain. The betterment of working conditions was an objective which would develop spontaneously, as would the formation of a Communist society, the ultimate objective. Thus there was a difference between the political program and the agrarian program, where, as a result of the 1905 Revolution, the Tsar had been forced to make some reforms. This had changed the boundaries between the "maximum" and "minimum" programs and had required the reevaluation of the political and agrarian programs of the Socialist parties. An identical revision was required with respect to the question of nationalities.

4. THE QUESTION OF THE NATIONALITIES AND THE REVOLUTIONARY PARTIES

THE PROGRAM OF THE NATIONAL ORGANIZATIONS

The question of the nationalities had been of prime importance for about twenty years. This came as a consequence of the development of capitalism in Russia. The penetration of Russians into the whole empire and their presence as a sort of foreign body from ancient Russia were all the more felt with the development of the minerals of the Ukraine and the construction of the Trans-Siberian Railroad. There were more of them to man the outlying territories, where formerly they had only exerted control. It is significant, for example, that the Burio-Mongol nationalist movement originated after 1891 with the construction of the railroad which deprived the nomads of their migratory grazing grounds. This economic development was accompanied by a cultural development resulting from the increase of cultural exchanges, which opened their small closed world to the outside world. The rise was especially quick in the western provinces, which were open toward Europe, and among the Russian Moslems where newspapers and books in Arabic increased infinitely, further encouraging feelings of nationalism. The nationalities resented, from then on, the policy of Russification as an act of aggression. As a result national movements developed with more vigor. In 1905 they were alone among the revolutionary parties in their fight against autocracy. The 1914 War had opened new horizons for them. What did they really want?

The Poles were the most implacable in demanding their independence. But independence would have meant the unification of the three Polands, and the obstacles to this seemed insurmountable. These objectives were nevertheless pursued by the Polish political organizations, even the Socialists, because they had no confidence in the ability of the Russians to pull off a revolution. However, there were two Social-Democratic organizations who held out, that of Rosa Luxemburg and that of Kulszinsky. According to them, independence was at that time a utopian and illusory desire. Only a revolution in the ranks of the Socialist movement, Russian or international, would be able to solve the Polish question. The struggle for independence would deflect the energy of the working classes and be an obstacle to the fundamental objective of authentic revolutionaries—i.e., the building of a Socialist society. The only difference between these two parties was that the first wanted a united Socialist republic and the second favored a democratic republic of a federal type.

Most of the nationalities urged the formation of a federal republic. They then demanded recognition of the right of self-determination and came out in advance for internal autonomy, with some measure of autonomy in external affairs. It was thus with the Finns, who had always had the benefit of some internal autonomy and who bore ill the restrictive measures of Tsarism since 1899. Only a small group of "separatists"—that is to say, proponents of Swedish union—made up an outside nucleus. But they were unable to endanger the position of the proponents of autonomy who, whether Socialist or not, made up the immense majority in the Seim.

It was an assembly of this type which the Estonians, the Letts, and the Lithuanians also wanted. Among the Letts, however, the current of Luxemburgists among the Socialists was so strong that, as in Finland, ultra-nationalism and extreme rightism were indistinguishable.

It was almost the same thing in the Ukraine. However, at Kiev the nationalists seldom went so far as to express separatist opinions. Moreover, they put forth cultural claims. The autonomy hoped for by cultural circles aimed only at guaranteeing local freedoms or a part in the administration of their own province. By a compensation mechanism, the extreme left was not the only one to struggle against these national aspirations. The Mensheviks were not much in favor of it either.*

The same situation existed in Georgia. The Socialists were only concerned with the revolutionary struggle and were wholly integrated in the struggle of the Russian and international Socialist movements. No doubt, they had a lively national feeling. Georgia was the oldest Western nation of the Empire and only came under the Russian protectorate in 1783. In Tiflis, where the reigning bourgeoisie was of Armenian or Russian origin, the struggle against foreign oppression was confused with the revolutionary struggle. The Social-Democrats were thus in favor of a formula involving extraterritorial autonomy** because the federal solution could lead to independence—with the result that Georgia would fall again under the yoke of its feudal nobility. The Georgian Socialist-Revolutionaries, who had no fear of this peril, urged the federal solution. The right, spurred by the nobility, held out for independence, but it carried little weight.

Armenian separatists were rare because the independence of the country would have been ephemeral in view of the Turkish menace. Further, while aiming at recognition of the "Armenian personality," the national movement sought at the same time to keep from alienating the Russians so that they would work for the return of the provinces conquered by the Sultan. The main Armenian political party, the *Dashnaksutium*, hoped that the Tsar would form a Russian federal republic, of which Transcaucasia

---

*This statement is applicable only to Socialists of Ukrainian or Georgian origin. The behavior of the Russian Socialists with regard to the national movements will be examined further on.

**This formula involved a central legislative organization in Petrograd for all matters pertaining to Georgia. Its representatives would be members of the federal parliament. This method particularly suited those nations which had no territorial basis, for instance, the Jews, or those who, like the Armenians, resided more often outside the country of origin.

would be a member. Divided in turn into provinces, Transcaucasia would apply the rule of extraterritorial cultural autonomy to the people which made it up. Such a formula was justified by the dispersal of Armenians in all of Transcaucasia, notably in Georgia. The *Dashnaksutium* appeared as a revolutionary party, a member of the Second International. It had armed groups, especially active in Turkish Armenia. Its methods were similar to those of the Socialist-Revolutionaries. It went all out for the nationalization of the lands, the eight-hour day, etc. However, its ties with the Armenian church and its nationalism made it suspect in the eyes of the other socialist organizations of the Russian Empire. In Armenia itself an Armenian Social-Democratic party and an Armenian Freedom of the People Party were formed against it. Further, many Armenians adhered to the Russian political parties, especially to the Social-Democrats. The *Dashnaksutium* was nevertheless by far the most representative organization in the Armenian national movement.

Among the other people of the Caucasus, particularism was strong, but the religious leaders, often Moslems, felt it was better to stay on good terms with the occupying forces—that is to say, the Cossacks. There wasn't yet, strictly speaking, any nationalist problem. It was the same along the Volga where the Votyaks, the Germans, the Mordovs, and the Maris had a lively consciousness of their identity, but as yet there was no well organized political movement.

Two other national movements were well developed—that of the Jews and that of the Russian Moslems.

Under Alexander II the Jews' position had improved. The abolition of the "Pale" in 1865 led to an assimilation which might have ended the persecutions and the pogroms. But, as in the case of all the various nationalities, the Jews were the victims of the Tsarist reaction at the end of the nineteenth century. With the rebirth of Anti-Semitism (notably in the Ukraine) the Jews had a feeling of rejection from the Russian nation. They became nationally conscious and fought for recognition of their dignity as individuals and of their collective identity.

The Jews' principal political organization, the *Bund*, had existed since 1897. A Socialist organization, a branch of the Social-Democratic movement in Russia, the *Bund* was against nationalism and felt that the Jews would achieve their ends by means of the revolution. As time passed, however, the *Bund* became more and more Pan-Jewish and less and less internationalist. Can one conclude that its claim to be the sole representative of the Jewish

Social-Democrats in Russia was unfounded? Did the Social-Democrats consider that the Jews were not truly a nation? In 1903, the *Bund* split and left the ranks of the Russian S.D. In 1912 it came back into the party when the Mensheviks put cultural extraterritoriality in their program, a solution which suited the Jews in Russia.

The conduct of the *Bund* was equivocal and arguable as far as the more nationalistic circle of Jews was concerned. They had the feeling that Bundists had only a slight degree of Jewish consciousness, with a desire to become assimilated. Some, more attached to their customs, preferred Populism, which traditionally claimed to be a defender of particularism. The majority rather quickly judged that a necessary condition for Jewish freedom was the settlement of the Jewish people on its own territory. Thus the Socialist-Revolutionary Territorial Party (S.E.R.P.) came into being, claiming a territory for the Russian Jews. Jews in this territory would have the benefit of internal autonomy, while Jews living outside would have a special status.

The least compromising had stuck to the Zionist movement, sparked outside Russia mainly by Jews of Russian origin. The creation of a Jewish home in Palestine was the main objective of the Zionists. Founded in 1897, like the *Bund*, the *Poale-Zion* had many proponents in Russia in spite of the fact that the formation of a Jewish state in Palestine seemed utopian. Some groups splintered off, urging the formation of an independent Jewish state, but not necessarily in Palestine. They spoke of South America and of tropical Africa; those who leaned toward Siberia wooed the S.E.R.P.

The *Bund* was thus between two fires. On the one hand there were those who wanted to be not Jews, but revolutionaries (like Trotsky and Martov), and who fought against nationalism; and on the other hand were the Zionists who thought the patriotism of the Bundists lukewarm and doubted that a Socialist régime could solve the Jewish question.

The Moslem national movement did not have either the same contents or the same objectives from one end of Russia to the other. From a cultural standpoint, the heart of the movement was in the Crimea, where Ismael-Bey-Gasprinky earlier had developed a Moslem renewal program. His movement was all the more successful because the nearness of Constantinople accentuated the reluctance of Moslems to accept the Russification program. Trying to be apolitical, this movement nevertheless was close to the Cadet

Party. It was reproached for being culturally conservative and for its loyalty to the established régimes (in Turkey as well as in Russia). It was rapidly overtaken, even in Crimea, by more revolutionary movements. Even before the 1905 Revolution, the center of the national movement had shifted to Kazan. Because the bourgeoisie which led the *Ittifak* was mainly concerned with commercial activities, Tatar capitalism sought a development in area rather than in depth. It was the same with the national movement. Its area extended to Turkestan, which it controlled in part, politically and economically. This movement tried to be Pan-Russian and, in its political program, claimed an autonomous extra-territorial solution for the Moslems. By its nature and its program the *Ittifak* was close to the Cadet Party. But it was caught in a cross-current of Pan-Turk and Pan-Islam movements on the one hand and a Socialist movement tied to the development of an industrial petite-bourgeoisie on the other.

These movements would have accepted political solutions of a similar nature, in contrast to the two Moslem groups of Bashkir and Azerbaidian. The first hoped to escape the double oppression of Russian feudalism and the Tatar bourgeoisie which had replaced it. They wanted a Russian federal-type solution. The second, centered in Baku, competed with the rival influence of Kazan. As in Azerbaidian, the bourgeoisie had first to struggle against the Armenians who were colonizing the country; because the first step was to control the economic life, the bourgeoisie recommended a political solution which would confer territorial autonomy on Azerbaidian.

This movement was less Pan-Turkish than *Ittifak* and less united. It was not the same with Hummet, a Socialist-inspired movement led by Bolsheviks, of whom there were many in the oil wells of the capital (Baku). Its dissemination and its efficiency were limited, but as a Social-Democratic Moslem movement, it was the only one of its kind.

Turkestan was another center of Moslem nationalism. Three forces divided it. First, there was the local bourgeoisie which had feudal relations with the peasants. It lived off the sale of cotton to Russian industries. Related to the *Ulemas*, it had cultural ambitions and was profoundly conservative. Its interests demanded that Turkestan not be taken out of the Russian State. In contrast, the intelligentsia, in contact with the revolutionary movement of Baku and Kazan, urged the formation of a large revolutionary Pan-Turkish state, taking in the Moslem population of the Russian and

Turkish Empires. These two movements competed for the support of the peasants and nomads who for a long time had been dispossessed by and were in revolt against the Russians. Victims of the suppression of 1916, they constituted the group most liable to resort to extremes.

Thus the Moslem national movement was divided by several cleavages—conservative, reformers, unitarians, and regionalists; Pan-Turkish and Pan-Russian. In 1915 a cartoon in *Mazali*, "The Soldiers of Islam," shows this division. The sellers of nine Moslem papers killed each other to find out who was the common foe. Both the strength and the weakness of this national movement lay in its being so alive and aware, yet divided to the point where it was obliterating itself in its internecine struggle.

THE RUSSIAN PARTIES AND THE NATIONALIST MOVEMENT

How did the Russian parties propose to fulfill these aspirations? On the eve of the war they had to include the national question in their program, recognizing the right of self-determination "for the nationalities *making up the Empire*" (italics added). They thought that these claims would last as long as the Tsarist autocracy lasted. When the people would put an end to it, Russians and non-Russians could build tomorrow's society. No one seriously thought that independence would be claimed by anyone except the Poles or the Finns. Wouldn't even they prefer to remain a part of the new revolutionary country rather than fall under the thumb of their bourgeois or feudal lords? All Russians were convinced that the federalist program of the Socialist-Revolutionaries or the democratic concepts of the Social-Democrats were an answer to the aspirations of the peoples of the Empire. The thesis of Lenin and Stalin caused a scandal: the idea of giving all people the right of self-determination, and with it the right to secede, shocked the revolutionary sense of the old Socialists, even if this dialectic approach would permit the dismemberment of the Russian state to go forward while preventing the seizure of the revolutionary apparatus by a "national" party.

Putting forward this thesis during the war, Lenin argued heatedly with Rosa Luxemburg, Pyatakov, Bukharin, and Radek. They felt that the support given to the national movements would end by reinforcing the bourgeoisie in the countries where it had not yet jelled, which amounted to enlarging and consolidating the capitalist world. As long as imperialism reigned the right of self-determination remained utopian, and after the Revolution it

108

would be useless. Why then dull the revolutionary spirit of the masses? These opponents of Lenin felt that the national struggle was legitimate only in colonial countries where the Socialist idea had not yet taken root. To show this, Bukharin refuted arguments which both Lenin and Plekhanov had used.

> The slogan "right of self-determination" (by the creation of a state or the separation from another state) applies in two concrete cases: (1) that of a territory annexed in the course of an imperialist war; (2) that of a country which has lost its sovereignty. In this last case, it is only a modified version of the slogan "defense of country"; if it does not correspond to defense of national frontiers, it is only a catch-phrase devoid of meaning. In this second case the slogan "right of self-determination" always carries within itself the other slogan, "defense of country," because after having achieved independence—which presupposes the right of self-determination—this sovereignty evidently must be defended. . . . (Otherwise why demand it in time of Imperialism when the threats are constant?)

Relying on letters written by Marx to Engels in 1867, Lenin answered that in a certain context the defense of the right of secession could be progressive even if the claimers were reactionary. For example, the Irish revolt contributed to the weakening of British imperialism. In Russia, where the Socialist ideal had reached even the Moslems, the struggle of the national minorities against Tsarism was even more legitimate and must be supported. Ever since 1914, Lenin had gauged the power of the nationalist sentiment and realized its explosive potential. Until then, the Marxian theorists had set up the dogma that the working class, forerunner of the proletariat, would pioneer the way for the Socialist Revolution. The International's mission was to coordinate or direct its actions. The disagreements had to do with the tactics and the role of the peasants in each country. But was this not underestimating the role of another force—the national minorities—which could be of help in bringing down the State? In the same manner as the proletariat, the nationalities were becoming conscious of the oppression which the State weighed on them, as this oppression grew heavier and heavier with the accumulation of capital and the worldwide character of imperialism. The problems brought out by Karl Kautsky and Rosa Luxemburg required a deeper study of the contradictions of imperialism, since the national question could have revolutionary effects, a thing which had not been foreseen before the outbreak of war. Lenin studied these questions at the beginning of 1917, in *State and Socialism*. Looking at the problem as a whole, he laid the foundations of an argument he was unable to complete, the February Revolution having broken out in the meantime. It is significant that the first chapter aimed to show the difference, on the one hand, between the countries of Western Europe, as well as North America and Japan, where the various minority races are numerically insignificant (Switzerland and Belgium being exceptions), and, on the other, Austro-Hungary, Russia, and Turkey, where the minorities constituted more than fifty percent of the population. Thus, according to Lenin, it was unreasonable to treat the problem of national minorities in East and West in the same fashion. Here was a new argument against the "Westernism" of the Luxemburgers or the legitimacy of the International's claims to arbitrate the purely internal problems of the various states.

In 1917 Lenin was thus the only Bolshevik leader who defended the absolute right of self-determination. But the various races did not know this and the Bolsheviks had always been considered opponents of nationalistic claims, although this was no more true of them than of the Mensheviks or the Socialist-Revolutionaries. The future would reveal that this was a case of misunderstanding, but no one foresaw it on the eve of the February Revolution. Everyone was convinced that with the fall of Tsarism all misunderstandings would be straightened out, all academic quarrels about programs would disappear, as would the rivalries of the peoples of Russiá, which had been inflicted by autocracy on the subject people.

Formerly, quarrels about programs hadn't split the revolutionaries as much as disagreements about tactics or the methods of fighting Tsarism. Would it be the same after the fall? All these programs appeared to be related, even if they differed on some main points. There were various schools of thought. The public would have had difficulty locating in which program these catchwords belonged: land for the peasants, public freedoms, decent wages and working conditions for the working class, the right of nationalities to administer their own affairs, equality of all citizens, separation of Church and State. No doubt, the theorists did not all define these things in the same way. Most of the revolutionaries nevertheless held certain values, and the public had a general idea of their common ideals. In the revolutionary programs could be found the ideals of the Revolutions of 1789 and 1848, the

Commune, of Proudhon and the revolutionary syndicalists, of Marx and Bakunin, all mixed together. What remained and what aspirations were expressed spontaneously, when, left to themselves during the first weeks of the Revolution, neither the parties nor the trade-unions were in agreement or able to take the wishes of the populace into account?

★

CHAPTER FOUR

THE DEMANDS OF THE WORKERS, PEASANTS, AND SOLDIERS IN THE RUSSIAN REVOLUTION

1. THE WORKING CLASS

Late coming to the city, branded by the harshness of the Russian countryside, the working class was prompted by truly revolutionary dedication. Grouped in the working-class quarters where it stayed as if in a foreign land, its existence was punctuated only by demonstrations, strikes, and the long quiet recuperation. For the Russian workman to live meant simply not to die—twelve hours of work a day at the Korsovka station in the far north, eleven-and-a-half for the children of Petrograd, and everywhere a miserable wage.

However, in the last few years, invigorated by the propaganda of the various parties, the workers of Russia lived in the hope of the "final struggle." But the war brutally halted this thrust by introducing an instinctive sentiment among the working class to defend its native land. The workers of Russia then had the distinct feeling that this struggle would cause them to be downtrodden more than ever. From then on, their despair was absolute, as was their solitude, because public opinion saved its sympathy for the lot of the soldiers who shed their blood to save the country. Never had the working class been more certain that it was "the wretched of the earth." Also, more than the other classes, it was astounded, whatever part it played in the Revolution, to find itself liberated in a few days from autocracy, its laws, and the past. With Tsarism fallen, the working class found itself with responsibilities. What was it going to ask of the new régime, and how was it going to act with respect to the new authorities?

"It remains now to create a new life, founded on law and equity," wrote the chief of railway workers of the Niamdom Station on the Arkhangelsk Line to the Soviet of Moscow, giving voice to a faith which, in its simplicity, expressed the hope of a host of workers, worn out by the unhappy past: "Mister Kerensky, we ask you to consider that if we address ourselves to you to tell you of our complaints, it is because we can't stand any more. . . ."

This complaint of the workers of Sysestroi, near Ekaterinburg, speaks for itself:

At the factory there is no medical aid and it's four or five versts to the nearest doctor. . . . No usable washbowls, if there were any, no boiling water or even warm water, the baths broken since 1915. For the holidays, provisions are five versts away and must be carried on foot. The cold is terrible. Fines are showered on the workers without their knowing what they are for. . . .

The women workers of Ekaterinodar add:

We work up to ten-and-a-half hours a day and some of us are paid only 1 ruble 20 kopeks. We are forced to undergo a degrading search. There are no facilities whatever for our meals or for cleaning up."

The demands which they make, such as they are, are those of all of Russia:

The eight-hour day.

Wages by the day, not piecework.

Wages for working women of three rubles a day.

No more searches.

Boiling water for meals.

Installation of canteen and toilet facilities.

Improved ventilation in the factory.

Tools to be furnished by the firm, instead of by workers.

Abolishment of child labor.

Minimum wage of 1 ruble 60 kopeks for simple work.

Management to be polite to workers.

No discharge without the approval of the "factory committee."

Weekly payment of wages.

Two weeks' pay in case of dismissal.

This list, more or less the same, is to be found from one end of Russia to the other, more pitiful in the metal-craft factories, textile mills, tobacco and leather factories than in the mines, where the workers, better organized, had been able to obtain some concessions.

In the first place, these petitions express a unanimous wish, the eight-hour day, the only claim which requires a special law. The weariness of the workers would be enough to make it legitimate. But there were other reasons added by the workers of Moscow: "the eight-hour day is a safeguard against unemployment; also, it is required for true freedom."

Ultimately other claims came forth. Thus they hoped that the prisoners of war would receive pay equal to the Russian workers; otherwise they would involuntarily be strike-breakers. At the end of March the problems relating to the war became especially numerous.

"Eight hours' work, eight hours' sleep, eight hours' free time guarantees the workers' participation in public affairs and the times require their close participation."

Often this claim was accompanied by its corollary "and we don't want any overtime," but if overtime is paid at premium rates and the union agrees, there is no objection to the workers accepting it. During the first weeks of the revolution there were few claims for wage increases, as if, like the French workers of 1848, the Russians wanted to make a present of two weeks' work to the Republic. The workers insisted on a guaranteed wage. They wanted no more piecework, but hourly wages, and they also wanted to be hired for a term of a week or two at the minimum. Obviously they were obsessed by the prospect of discharge. The workers were especially fearful this would happen to them after an accident or illness, because when they returned their place would have been taken and they would be without recourse. They also wanted priority given to the institution of a social security system.

From the end of March on, however, wage increase demands took over and increased more and more. In Moscow, on March 9th, they only asked a 20 percent increase; on the 17th, at Kursk, 50 percent; on the 20th, at Kazan, 100 percent. However, in view of the cost of living, these demands remained modest. Evaluated in rubles, they were accompanied by claims of a nature which shows the degree of distress of the workers—two pounds of black bread and a pound of white bread near Moscow, a pair of shoes every six months and another for the child, in a shoe factory near Kharkov, etc.

The claims about pay reveal that the workers were opposed to the idea of equal pay for all, but at the same time there was a tendency to close the gap. Thus at Petrograd they frequently asked 6 to 8 rubles a day for specialized workers, 2.4 to 4.0 rubles for general workers, 1.6 to 2.0 rubles for children. The principle of

THE ASPIRATIONS OF THE WORKING CLASS
TABLE OF STATISTICS
(BASED ON 100 MOTIONS VOTED IN MARCH 1917)*

General Policy	*In Percent*
A. Measures against the Tsar	2
B. Measures against the Old Administration	3
C. Formation of a Democratic Republic	14
D. Universal Suffrage	5
E. Confidence in Government	3
F. Distrust of Government	11
G. Decentralization	0
H. Hasten meeting of Constituent Assembly	12
I. Free Education	3
J. Graduated Tax	0
K. Defense Proclamations	3
L. In favor of Peace without annexations or Revolutionary contributions	3
M. Elimination of Professional Army	1

Problems Pertaining to the Workers	
N. Eight-hour day	51
O. No Overtime (7 times formally, 7 times with the addition "unless better paid")	14
P. Guaranteed Wages and Social Security	11
Q. Pay Raise	18
R. Hiring Question	7
S. Foremen and Choice of Foremen	2
T. Sanitary Conditions	15
U. Factory Committee Role	12
V. Worker Administration	4
W. International Slogans	7
X. Land for the Peasants	9
Y. To learn to wait for pay-raises and various advantages, to be patient	1

*These first hundred motions are valid for the period of March 3 to March 28. They concern factory workers. This inventory was obtained from the following sources: Izvestya 20 motions; Pravda and Soc. Dem., 20 motions; Archives Documents, 60 motions. The regional breakdown is as follows: Petrograd 40 percent, Moscow 25 percent, other cities 35 percent.

"equal pay for equal work for men and women" was often heard. However, the printers of Kharkov were more conservative, demanding that those who earn 40 rubles a week be raised 10 percent. Those workers who earn 80 to 90 rubles a month, should receive 40 rubles a week; 70 to 90 r. per month to get 35 r. per week; 70 to 80 r. per month—30 r. per week; 60 to 70 r. per month—25 r. per week; 50 to 60 r. per month—20 r. per week; less than 50 r. per month—80 r. per month.

Elsewhere, the workers formulated certain wishes concerning their relations with the companies. First, they wanted to be able to control the hiring and firing—in other words, job security. They also wanted to eliminate black-listing. Naturally it was the factory committee which must negotiate these questions with the administration. Its rights and functions were often carefully specified. Thus, in the cable factories of Petrograd, the Committee must:

Authorize overtime.

Organize the election of grievance committee members.

Watch factory sanitary conditions.

Control hiring and firing of workers.

Establish communication with workers of other factories.

Organize meetings.

Look out for the workers' interests with management.

Settle wage problems with management.

Settle with management on the questions of holidays.

Represent the workers with management in all questions of general interest, so that the workers will not have to address themselves individually to it.

Going further, certain factory committees—e.g., at the Arsenal and Erikson's—undertook the management of their companies. As of March it wasn't a question, however, of proceeding with complete takeover, and the actions of the workers do not suggest that it was. It was circumstances which forced the workers to take over the management of their companies, mostly when the firms showed counter-revolutionary tendencies. At the Iyev and Erikson factories and at the Yorsky firm the workers' committees took over. It obtained the accounting records and introduced most of its workers' demands into the regulations, raising the pay by 150 percent.

However, this intrusion into the administration of the business did not constitute a real takeover of production and did not stem from a revolutionary interpretation of the new function of industry in a new society. The workers kept the factory going, seizing it in order to put pressure on management; there was nothing more at this time from the workers' level. Only the bakers and the typesetters, with their old traditions and unfamiliar with the workings of large industry, took up the problem of management starting March 5th. The typographers wanted to control the orders. The bakers decided that in the future "each worker should find the means of using his potential and receive full compensation for his work."

In these petitions, the political catch-phrases are often to be found side by side with economic or professional claims. Thus the Egorov report, which sums up the wishes of 15,000 miners of the Ural, pretty well expresses the viewpoint of thousands of other workers who were not always able to express their ideas as clearly. Speaking of the situation created by the revolution it says:

> While supporting the Provisional Government, we must realize that it is made up of the bourgeoisie. It will only satisfy the demands of the revolutionary people if pressure is brought to bear, heavily. We must watch out for bourgeois deviations in its policies.

In other firms, the formula of the Soviet of Petrograd was adopted, "to support the government only insofar as its policies correspond to the wishes of the people." The workers sometimes asked that the workers' and soldiers' representatives be allowed to exert control over the government. Some of them say they are ready to fight it if necessary, but these are still rare. The formula "all power to the Soviet" does not appear until just before April, although it was approximated on March 4th when the Union Federation of Petrograd proposed that "only the decisions of the Soviet will be carried out." In contrast, the motions of confidence in the government emanating from factories or unions were few. They were most often subscribed to by employees or artisans, rather than workers, and they expressed confidence in the government "only insofar as it applies its program."

Thus it is clear that the working class granted a rather reluctant support at the government level. Railway workers aside, it did not even bother to address motions or resolutions to it. It was to the

Soviet that they were sent, and to Kerensky also, who was sometimes considered as a hostage of the bourgeoisie, sometimes as an advocate of democracy. This reserve is explained if we recall the political objectives of the working class, perfectly expressed by the miners of the Ural:

> The Russian proletariat, the oppressed and defenseless class, owning no property and dependent in everything on capital, can only better its condition if it wrests from the capitalist class most of its political power, if not all. This would only be possible in the structure of a Democratic Republic, with universal suffrage, secret ballot, and equality for all.

This motion agrees with hundreds of others which recall that it is not sufficient merely to ignore "distinctions of race, nationality, or religion. . . ." Suffrage is not truly universal, the women's petitions add, unless discrimination on account of sex is abolished. They enumerate all the requirements for a valid vote, with the miners of the Ural going as far as to specify that the "Republic is truly democratic only when it assures the people Zemlya i Volya (Land and Liberty)."

For others, few in number, this democratic régime was only the first stage on the road to Socialism. The majority only asked "the immediate meeting of a Constituent Assembly and the formation of a Democratic Republic." This Assembly seemed important to the working class, as the bourgeois press liked to emphasize. According to the workers, the fall of Nicholas II was equivalent to the proclamation of a Republic. The whole nation assumed the responsibility for this change. It was not up to the Constituent to make a pronouncement on that score, since the Republic was already an accomplished fact, for Tsarism fell with Nicholas II. The role of the Constituent Assembly was to legislate the new rules for the functioning of the new régime, to ensure the replacement of one régime by another, and to make the new law official. The workers did not think that they were contradicting themselves in asking at the same time for structural reforms and the convocation of the Constituent, inasmuch as the Revolution had marked the triumph of certain principles which were here to stay—the Constituent's role being merely to ratify the methods in conformity with the wishes of the majority. They considered the reasoning of the moderate parties a sort of provocation, when they pretended that no reforms could be undertaken until the Constituent had made its pronouncements. They guessed that this was some sort of subterfuge which they tried to prevent by demanding the immediate meeting of the Constituent Assembly.

United and determined on these questions, the workers were diffident and divided on the problem of the war. "It has the effect of binding the workers to the ruling class," observed the miners of Kuznetz. But they approached the subject prudently, "because many don't understand the slogan *Down with War*." The cry was let out surreptitiously at the close of meetings. But the workers in the chemical plants of the artillery park clamored "*Vive la Guerre*," like the electrical employees of the plants on the northern front. The army of railway employees especially showed themselves to be, on the whole, very patriotic. The Kuznetz miners, who felt that the imperialist war had a class character, thought it necessary to explain that "the introduction of the eight-hour day would not reduce defense production." It even appears that in March there were meetings against the war in the Gudov plants, the Fabergé plants, and others. Only a small minority shared the Internationalists' opinion on the nature of the war, and an even smaller minority determined on a course of action. These last tried not to trample on the patriotic feelings of the workers, who were more sensitive as they approached the front. Some workers, nevertheless, analyzed the nature of the war in the manner of the Zimmerwaldians. In the minority in March, their numbers increased rapidly thereafter. The Urals led the way, because there the ideological struggle unfolded among workers without the interference of the interpreters of bourgeois thought, as they did in Petrograd and Moscow. These miners declared:

Everything said about the war in the bourgeois press, when they call it a Holy War, a War of Liberation, is nothing but lies. It's a question of covering up for those responsible for the war, and camouflaging its aims. It's a question of stirring up enthusiasm of the people for a meaningless slaughter which is only profitable to the merchants, the bankers, and the industrialists.

France, since its defeat by Germany, dreams only of revenge and of undoing the damage which German industrial power is causing her. There's the real reason for the Franco-Russian alliance. The granting of Constantinople, the Straits, Armenia, Galicia, etc., will furnish the Russian dealers with new markets and new sources of raw materials. . . .

With the overthrow of Tsarism, Russian democracy must immediately take steps to bring the war to a speedy end. The government must say publicly that it is ready to sign a peace

119

without annexations or contributions, founded on the emancipation and liberation of the oppressed people.

The Russian Socialists must take the initiative to bring a World Socialist Convention together which will determine how to end the war in the interest of democracy.

Even among these advocates of a speedy end of the war, there was no question of concluding a separate peace with the Central Powers. Like the workers of the Vindavo Station, they thought that the war could be ended only by the international action of the workers.

There were some direct appeals to Germany. The first was dated March 4th, from the Dynamo plant, but each time these appeals were addressed solely to the proletariat, calling for it to act alone. Often the Russians explained to the German workers that the Russian people were not warring against the German people, but against its government (a manner of presentation which was agreeable to the Russian bourgeoisie). They added that if "the German people are deaf to their appeals, the Russians will defend themselves to the last drop of blood."

In contrast, when the Russian workers addressed their proclamations to their comrades in the Allied countries, they seldom called for the transformation of the international war into a civil war. Most often, they urged them only to bring pressure on their governments to propose reasonable peace conditions, following the example of free Russia. "Some limited peace proposals would be in order," was one resolution. Thus the idea of a peace without annexations or contributions gained ground, but the workers slogans had not yet been put in order. The discussions between the militants of the different revolutionary parties in the midst of the workers' soviets helped to clarify these problems of the war and the Revolution.

All these workers' resolutions, aside from those of the railworkers, have some things in common. This is peculiar to them, because the soldiers' and peasants' petitions don't resemble each other as much. The same principle of classification is to be found in the various announcements of demands which came out one by one in the same order from Murmansk to Ekaterinburg, even though orders could not yet have been passed from one to the other, since neither the political parties nor the unions yet had their meetings and the first issues of *Isvestya* had not yet taken the place of the petitions emanating from the factories. The workers of Russia were not only class-conscious, but they knew the fundamental claims of the working-class movement and its leaders. And if they did not know them, they were sufficiently politically educated to ask the soviet of a neighboring town (a frequent case in out of the way factories) to send them a "militant" to "explain the situation." Thus they avoided acting inadvisedly. Some were not as clear-headed as others, as in the case of the workers of the Petinsky section of Kharkov, who sent "fraternal greetings" to *Pravda*, urging the readers of the Bolshevik daily to "defend the country." These rare inconsistencies, limited to the problems of the War, divided the most inveterate militants and left them undecided. As for the others, the solidarity of the worker class is far from being a myth. They formulated demands which were identical everywhere; the influence of Social-Democratic ideology is evident. However, curiously enough, certain parts of the 1903 program interested no one—universal suffrage, decentralization, the independence of judges, and the problem of taxes are hardly mentioned at all, although they appeared more often in the resolutions of the peasants and soldiers.

It can also be seen that the workers' claims aimed only at bettering working conditions, never at changing them. Here the lag between the parties showed up. In the resolutions coming up from the bottom there was hardly ever a question of Socialism. When the workers seized the account books or took over the administration of a firm, it was in order to have a hostage which would enable them to control and force the management to make concessions. The Socialist or Anarchist ideal of a classless society appeared among their demands only rarely, or as a distant goal. Only the printers clearly presented a more equitable "Workers Republic" instead of the "Democratic Republic" mentioned in all the other resolutions.

There was no trace of "Maximalism" in these resolutions, nor even of revisionism; rather, there were concrete demands, imperative, unanimous, unbiased. They had to be met, completely and without delay.

2. THE PEASANTRY

More than any other country, in Russia the peasant had played the leading role in his country. In the West, at the end of the eighteenth century, serfdom was only a remnant of the past, but not in Russia, where its influence was reinforced. The fear of a peasant revolt, the memory of Pugachev and Stenka Razin kept haunting the masters of Russia. In a sense, the 1861 reforms were an attempt to end the insecurity of the countryside. Badly received by a nobility deprived of its rights, the reforms of Alexan-

121

der II in no way exorcized the danger which threatened Russian society. Liberated in theory, but reduced to living on a diminished income, indebted for life, the peasants remained as insubordinate as ever. There was a difference, though—they found in the old rural community *(mir)* a frame for future action. This was all the more dangerous for the State and for the large landowners *(pome-shchiki)* because from then on the ties of man to man were completely ruptured.

After the 1905 Revolution, the reforms of Stolypin appeased a part of the peasantry by helping them to become landowners. The State thus succeeded in dividing and weakening the peasant class. By bringing the *moujiks* out of the *mir*, they broke up the village solidarity and prevented the threat of new uprisings. In effect, in 1914, there were no common aspirations between the new land-owners from the *mir (Obtrubniks)*, the kulaks and the property-less, and the settlers who went to Siberia or Turkestan. Their demands were all nevertheless urgent:

We demand full sovereignty for the people.

We demand extensive decentralization.

We demand the right for the various nationalities to administer their own affairs.

We demand schools, with teaching in the language of the country.

We demand the full control of the people over the governmental functions. There must be no secrets, neither diplomatic nor of any other kind.

We demand the elimination of the professional army, to be replaced by a militia because three years of war have proven that it is not the professional army which defends the country but its millions of reservists.

We demand that the lands pass into the public domain; they should go to the workers and not belong to private individuals.

We demand that the Provisional Government explain to us immediately why the magnates and other property-owners who have thousands of acres of land could wish not to defend their country, thus escaping military service, while we, who own no land, must defend it with our lives.

We demand the immediate elimination of all taxes, direct or indirect, and their replacement by a single graduated income tax.

We demand fuel immediately, because there isn't much wood here but there are government forests and we should be able to use them.

We, the elected of 31 villages and in the name of about 5,000 people, their representatives:

> Ivan Antonov, Dmitri Andreev,
> Pavel Petrov, Alexei Egorov.

It's a far cry from this letter from the peasants of Pskov to the complaints of the workers in Ekaterinodor. "We demand . . ." sets the tone of these messages which the peasants had drafted by the "intelligentsia" of the neighborhood. The appeals and requests were rare, but the demands were many. At this time, the peasant resolutions expressed claims which were more differentiated than those of the workers. They devoted a more important part of their attention to the future of the country than to the particular interests of the peasants. More often than the workers they expressed a desire to punish the masters of the Old Régime.

Generally, one wish which was expressed more often than the others was for the formation of a democratic republic. For the peasants, this implied decentralization, with more power to the soviets and less to the government. Like the workers and the soldiers, the peasants wanted to hasten the meeting of the Constituent Assembly, although this demand disappeared suddenly after the month of April, as if the peasants no longer counted on anyone else to effect their reforms. Asking fairly often for the education of children (ten times against only three times for the workers, they frequently claimed the right to a "decent" existence. Above all, they quickly expressed their desire for a just peace (twenty-four times, against four petitions of a patriotic nature). Sometimes the words they used are unexpected, sometimes revealing:

> We Russians are not Tatars. They have always invaded Russia with their flocks and their tents. We don't want to go and live in Germany, make slaves of their inhabitants, cut up their cattle or their property. . . . And that for two reasons. 1. It is contrary to the Scriptures. 2. It is a two-edged weapon—each one will win in turn and the only outcome will be slaughter.

Of course, the peasants speak first of all of their impatience to own land: "When we take the land from the Kulaks, it's Anarchy. When they take our sons, it's Patriotism."

A few remarks are necessary:

Of the 51 resolutions which explicitly demanded the confiscation of lands, 31 specified that it was not merely a question of government lands or grazing lands, but also of the large estates. Only fifteen demanded that lands be acquired without compensation. Thus, it was not a question of abolishing private property, but of regulating it. The abolition of private property was demanded only seven times, most often near the large cities, probably under the influence of the urban revolutionary circles.

123

THE ASPIRATIONS OF THE PEASANTRY
TABLE OF STATISTICS*

General Policies	*Percent*
A. Measures against the Tsar	4
B. Measures against Old Administration	16
C. Formation of a Democratic Republic	24
D. Universal Suffrage	9
E. Confidence in Government	10 (7 in March)
F. Distrust of Government	10 (in April)
G. Decentralization	12
H. Hasten Meeting of the Constituent	17
I. Free Public Education	10
J. Graduated Income Tax and no other	6
K. Defender Proclamation	4
L. In Favor of a Quick, Just Peace	23
M. Abolition of Professional Army	3
N. Measures of Safeguards against Large Landowners	11

Agricultural Questions	
O. Lowering of Land Rents	17
P. Forbidding Sale of Land until Constituent	13
Q. No Squatting	4
R. The Constituent Will Settle the Questions of Lands and Agrarian Questions	15
S. Seizure of State Lands, Crown Lands (Fiefs)	20

*This table has been compiled from the first one hundred resolutions found among the three hundred documents assembled by the Soviet historians on the agrarian question for the months of March and April. This sample is as good as any other, since there is a correlation between the selection made here and the breakdown of the agrarian troubles between February and October. It should be noted that in the gathering of documents there is an overrepresentation of the Moscow and Vladimir regions (near Moscow) which is due to the greater development of historical research in the capital. Aside from this distortion, the governments of Tula (9 resolutions), Ryazan (6 resolutions), Kaluga, Pskov, and Smolensk are represented in this table by five or more resolutions. These are the regions where the agrarian troubles were the most numerous. Half of these hundred resolutions bear on the regions which saw the most intense agrarian troubles. The rest bear on the most diversified provinces—thirty-three governments are represented out of about fifty for European Russia. It can be estimated that this sample gives an indication of the aspirations of the Russian peasantry.

T. Seizure of State Lands, Crown Lands, and
     Large Estates   31

U. Seizure of Land without Compensation   15

V. Abolition of Private Property   7

W. Socialization of Land, Nationalization   12

X. Give Land Back to the *Obshchina*   2

Y. The Land to those who work it, in
     accordance with their strength (no pay)   18

Z. Egalitarian Status (norm)   8

AA. Administration and distribution of the
       Lands by the Municipalities, Soviets, etc.   15

There were few statements of principle with regard to the seizure of the land. The peasants said only that "the land must belong to those who work it," often specifying the amount of land to allot to each, "according to their strength." They also condemned the use of paid labor, much as one would judge it inadmissable that lands should lay fallow while some poor wretch does not even own a square foot. Thus if they wanted to limit and regulate property rights, it was only to firm it up and legitimize it.

These statistics show the progress which had been made since 1905, when one hundred percent of the resolutions of the "Peasants' Union" demanded the abolition of private property. The reforms of Stolypin had their effect, giving each peasant a taste of what it was like to be a small property-holder. There is another proof of this change in that only two resolutions asked for the return of the land to the *obshchina*. Yet the fact remains that the Russian peasants were not as individualistic as the peasants of the West; more than fifteen resolutions called for the collective organizations to regulate the expropriation and administration of the lands taken from the government or the *pomeshchiki*. They almost always thought in terms of local organizations; thus only two resolutions proposed the administration of the large estates by the central government, and one of these came from the Bolshevik Mihailov Frunze. About twenty resolutions imply a sort of right of the collectives to watch over the equitable distribution of the land. In these resolutions the ideas of the poor peasants and those of the kulaks differ; nevertheless, certain constants appear:

—Landless peasants did not urge the abolition of private property; they wanted to become owners.

—Those who owned land wanted more.

125

—All showed anger on seeing "reserved" land unused.

—The fact that these fallow lands belonged to nonusers seemed scandalous to them.

These reactions are especially violent in the governments of Vladimir, Kursk, and Orel, where half the land hasn't been seeded beyond two *dessyatines* [approx. 5.4 acres—Trans.]. (See table in Appendix.) Moreover, landless peasants and other unfortunates did not want the *pomeshchiki* to use the presence of prisoners of war or refugees on their lands as a pretext for keeping their domains whole, which otherwise could not be put to use. This anxiety weighed more heavily, it seems, than the discontent arising out of the temporary abuse of the land by the *pomeshchiki*. The ideas of the poor peasants showed up clearly in the decisions made by the Executive Committee of Social Organization of the Uezd Ranenbursky (Riazan Government):

Having examined the allocations of lands on the eve of the Spring sowing, the Committee has decided:

1. All fields must be seeded.

2. The land of the owners is available on the spot.

3. The lease is fixed at ten rubles for each unused *dessyatine*, thirty rubles for each cultivated *dessyatine*; taxes and diverse expenses on the land are to be paid by the owners.

4. Expropriated land is divided into parts allocated by drawing lots among those entitled to it.

5. The large landowners will only retain as much land as they can work themselves, without the help of paid labor or prisoners or war.

6. For each landowner's son who has gone to war, he will be allowed one prisoner of war.

7. No one will prevent the large landowners who must furnish the Army with leguminous vegetables at market prices, by agreement with the Executive Committee, from employing farm workers and prisoners of war as required.

8. Areas of the truck gardens of the large landowners must remain the same as last year.

9. The small landowners whose whole land does not exceed forty-five *dessyatines* can use prisoners of war—only one if they have a drafted son, three prisoners for every two drafted—who will work the land until the peace. The owners will cultivate these lands with their own labor.

10. The *volost* executive committee will see to it that the spring sowing is done regularly at the right time.

11. In case of shortage of hands, the local committees and those of the

volost will call on the neighboring population and the Executive Committee of the Uezd.

12. In case of shortage of draft animals, they will be requisitioned from the large landowners at the average price of the last three years.

13. Draft horses will be requisitioned from the large landowners at the rate of the first requisition of 1914.

14. In case of disagreement with the large landowners, the decision of the Uezd Executive Committee, called in as arbiter, will be final.

15. All agreements will be in writing, signed by both parties.

16. In a case where anyone refuses to sign a decision of the Uezd Provisional Executive Committee, it will become effective by the action of the local committees.

17. The right to occupy the land on the aforementioned basis applies to all citizens.

18. Seed for sowing may be requisitioned from the large landowners.

19. A sufficient amount of labor should be left to care for the cattle and for the upkeep of the estates.

20. The number of workers will be set by the local committee in agreement with the owner.

21. All of the land owned by soldiers should be sowed; the local committee will discuss this question.

22. In order to work the lands registered in this or that *volost*, those who will collaborate with their neighbors and the local committees will thus determine before the start of work the amount of land to be distributed and the number of those wishing to acquire it. The distribution of these lands will then be made to those who are willing to work them. [Then follows the method of grouping for the region.] The Petropavlovsk Monastery lands will be joined to the *volost* Kriushovsky.

23. For the requisition of oats, the regulations will be put into effect through the credit associations.

Further, the Committee decided:

1. To ask the citizens to produce as many vegetables as possible.

2. To forbid the cutting of timber.

3. To stop the buying and selling of lands.

4. To stop the activities of the land commissions.

5. To make provision for the guarding of rivers and forests.

6. To provide for the safekeeping of gardens, orchards, cattle—living or dead.

7. All decrees concerning wages to be modified and in the future the current prices will be set by workers.

In other cases, expropriation will not be limited to lands which belong to the Tsar, the monasteries, or Crown lands (fiefs). It also can take in the part of the large estates which the *pomeshchiki* are not using. If they resist, the committee will go further and make sanctions. As for the bourgeois landowners—that is to say, non-farming owners—their lands will be taken "because they don't need them."

As for the small landowner, the takeover is implicit, since the authority of the committee is legitimate; but this did not mean that the peasantry intended to proceed to a collective administration of the soil, only that it felt that the collectivity had the inherent right to assure the equitable distribution of the lands.

Some resolutions, like those of the "First Farmer Assembly of the Briansk Region," showed the wishes of the kulaks, who often controlled the plenary assemblies. They expected to get their share of the redistribution of the aristocratic and imperial estates. However, knowing the influence of the poor peasants, they were afraid of finding themselves among the group of future expropriates. Further, they refused to admit the competence of the local committees, putting their trust instead in the state or the Constituent Assembly to legislate finally. They thought that this procedure would confirm their acquired rights and that the old system would allow them to have their interests well looked after. While awaiting the convocation of the Constituent they made use of the delay by buying and selling, as conditions warranted.

On the other side, small property-owners and landless farmers did not want to wait for the Constituent's session. They demanded that the agrarian committees proceed with the distribution of land or with a revision of labor contracts. Many of the proletarian farmers thought that the lots which would be granted them—free, it was understood—would not permit them to live as independent farmers, at least in the next few years. Consequently they asked that the rent of the land which they would continue to work be lowered immediately. The petty landowners declared for graduated income tax. Thus the problems caused by the delays were not the same for the poor as for the militants, who pretended to legislate for form's sake. The impatience of the landless was replaced by anxiety, then by distrust when they saw the delay in taking action and in discharging disgraced officials. In Petrograd they were playing the rich man's game. "Here, nothing has changed . . ." remarked a village resolution, near Riazan, less than six weeks after the fall of Nicholas II. In other places the peasants themselves already had taken action.

Looking at the farmers' aspirations and the program of the revolutionary parties, one thing is evident—they rarely speak the same language. This wasn't the case with the working class; there was a precise correspondence between the minimum program of the larger parties and their interpretation of the war or the Revolution on the one hand, and the resolutions of the workers on the other. Nothing like this was the case with the peasantry. Only Peshekohnov's small party expressed the peasants' aspirations with any exactness. But who knew this in the countryside? Thus, there was no particular similarity between the peasants' program and that of the Socialist-Revolutionary Party which pretended to represent it. None of the slogans of the different parties were featured in the documents—neither "equal share," nor "nationalization," nor "socialization," nor "municipalization," nor "return to the *obshchina*," nor "abolition of private property" (the latter phrase appeared only seven times in a hundred motions). The expressions which are found, whether from poor farmers or from farmers' assemblies, where the kulaks, of course, benefitted from a certain influence, are rather:

—confiscation of lands (without specifying who was to get them), sometimes limited to government land, more often extended to the large estates.

—the land to those who work it (which gives an indication of their sentiments).

—lowering the ground rents.

—waiting (or not waiting) for the Constituent, etc.

Collectivization was desired only by an infinitesimal minority. The few resolutions which allude to it did not come from the region where the first agrarian trouble occurred both in 1905 and in 1917, but from the *"shody"* situated near the large industrial cities (Shlusselburg, Ustigor, Moscow, etc.). It appears that if the notion of private property was not held in 1905, this was no longer true in 1917, since, thanks to the Stolypin reforms and the war, the peasants had learned about profits and liked it. It was of this change that the Marxist theorists were aware, and it made them doubt the revolutionary fervor of the countryside. In fact, it exacerbated their impatience. However, their lack of political experience and their divisiveness led them to believe they were powerless. Thus the landless peasants passed the most pitiful resolutions, merely asking for bread, as well as the most fiery, as in the Baltic countries. A large number expected only to profit from the government lands and the land grants. They clashed with the contrary expectations of the petty farmers and kulaks, who also expected to benefit from the windfall. The Social-Democratic theorists wondered which would win out among the peasantry— the divisions born of the Stolypin reforms or the hereditary anger against the ruling classes. They had no idea that these effects could reinforce one another. They underestimated the latent revolutionary force of the peasantry which, without preamble, acted from the first day. It looted the big estates, occupied the vacant lands, and set itself up as lord of the manor, more often and faster than has been said. If we make an inventory of the agrarian disorders, it will be seen that up until April 4th there had been only about fifty instances of agrarian troubles in the countryside, almost all in the same region—in March in the districts of Petrograd, Moscow, Kherson, Riazan, and Penza; at the beginning of April in Penza, Riazan, Nizhni-Novgorod, and Saratov. It was the same in the rural areas near the big cities, in the districts of the middle Volga, and on the seacoast. These outbreaks were slight in comparison with those of a similar period in the early months of the Revolution of 1905, but they were considerable if one notes that they occurred ten years later and only in those regions where the Stolypin reforms had not been put into effect. The people in the best position to know, the overseers of large estates, judged the situation to be worse than in 1905. On March 26th one of them, the manager for the Counts Orlov-Dvidov, wrote to the Undersecretary of State for Internal Affairs to let him know his feelings: without doubt, the troubles were of a magnitude and violence never before equaled; the Government should make no mistake about it.

3. THE SOLDIERS' ASPIRATIONS

Essentially made up of farmers, the Russian armies differed from those of the other belligerents, which were more variegated from a social standpoint. The distance between officers and enlisted men was even greater; furthermore, the officer corps not only was distant from the soldiers, but lived apart from civilian society, shut off from the progressive ideas which were then prevalent. Denikin and Kerensky agreed in deploring the poor mentality of the Russian officers, who were no doubt brave but too scornful toward their men. They had set up disciplinary methods which were similar to those employed in penal institutions. It was worse in the Navy. Moreover, like the Allies, the Russian soldiers fought with fervor against two hereditary enemies—the Turk, or Tatar, and the Germans, heirs of the Poles and Catholics. But unlike the Allies, they never had the feeling that their native soil was in danger. The fighting was always on foreign soil. The hardships of the 1914 campaign, the unparalleled horrors of the retreat of 1915, and the feeling of having been the victims of useless slaughter were some of the reasons for the conduct of the soldiers and their demands during the spring and summer of 1917. From the first day the soldiers, the architects of the Revolution in Petrograd, expressed their will in the famous *Prikaze I* (General Order Number One). This proclamation, in answer to the Duma's maneuverings, went to the heart of the discipline question in the army.

ORDER NUMBER ONE

To the Petrograd Regional Garrison, to all soldiers of the Guard, of the Army, of the Artillery, and of the Fleet—to be enforced immediately and rigorously; and to the workers of Petrograd, for their information.

The Workers' and Soldiers' Soviet has decided:

1. A Committee will be elected in all companies, battalions, regiments, installations, batteries, squadrons, and military units of all kinds, and on board vessels of the Fleet, to represent the enlisted personnel of the units mentioned above.

2. In all those military units which have not yet chosen their delegate to the Workers' Soviet, a representative for each company will be elected. Bearing a written certificate, he will present himself to the State Duma on March 2nd, at ten o'clock in the morning.

3. In all policy actions, the military unit obeys the Workers' and Soldiers' Soviet and its committees.

4. The orders of the Military Commission of the State Duma must only be executed in cases where they are not contrary to the orders and decisions of the Workers' and Soldiers' Soviet.

5. Weapons of all kinds, such as rifles, machine guns, armored cars, etc., must be at the disposal and under the control of the company and battalion committees and will in no case be turned over to the officers, even if they are called for.

6. In ranks, and while on duty, the soldiers must observe strict military discipline, but off duty and outside formations,

in their political, civil, and private lives, the soldiers will enjoy the rights of all citizens and these will not be infringed.

The practice of coming to attention on passing a superior officer and the required salute are abolished, off duty.

7. In the same way the formulas reserved for officers, "Your Excellency," "Your Lordship," etc., are abolished. They will be replaced by "Mister General," "Mister Colonel," etc.

The ill-treatment of soldiers by all ranks is forbidden, as is the use of the familiar form in addressing them. Soldiers are held responsible for reporting any infractions of this order, as well as all misunderstandings between the officers and themselves.

This order is to be read to all companies, battalions, regiments, teams, batteries, and other military and auxiliary units.

The Soviet of Workers' and Soldiers' Deputies of Petrograd.

The contents of this order spread rapidly through Russia, in spite of the efforts of the high command to suppress it. It fit so well with the aspirations of the troops that wherever it was known, it was carried out:

Each time I issued an order, [says General Dragomirov in short], the soldiers would answer: *Now that isn't done any more*. One of them, each time, would refer to some printed matter which he held. *No*, he would say, *that isn't done anymore*. And when I wanted to see this printed matter, he refused to give it to me. [Report to General Russky]

Giving Articles 1 and 2 a rather broad interpretation, the soldiers withheld authority from a certain number of officers. The reason alleged by the soldiers of the 5th Section of the 1st Reserve Regiment showed the grievances of the soldiers against the officers:

Captain Popov:

1. Obscene language.
2. Manner of treating soldiers.
3. Unfairness.
4. Caused sick soldiers to work barefoot.

Ensign Novopavlovsk:

1. Obscene language.
2. Incompetence.

132

3. Abusive language and striking soldiers.
4. Excessive and unjust punishment.

Ensign Bodganov:

1. Manner of treatment of soldiers.
2. Demotions with insufficient cause.
3. Abuse of authority.
4. Antipathy to liberation movement.

These grievances were the causes of the violence used against the officers when the troops saw that they refused to admit that a new order had been born. The "return to discipline" which the officers never stopped extolling "created a yawning chasm between officers and men; no matter how much they explained and explained, they weren't even listened to" (Barancov Report). The soldiers were human beings. They wanted their living conditions improved and they wanted the state to recognize their sacrifice and the sufferings of their families who had no other means of support. The 15th Regiment of Light Infantry listed a whole series of claims wherein are found the common anxieties which beset part of the army and the fleet:

1. Improved pay.
—To demand immediately improved pay, which will show the government's interest in the army, thereby encouraging it and reinforcing the defense of free Russia.

—To increase allotments for soldiers' families and to insure them against the loss of the capacity to work, an absolutely indispensable measure. An army assured of the well being of its dependents can devote itself to the fight against the enemy.

—To give certain guarantees to the soldiers who will have become disabled because of the war.

2. Certain functions should be performed by means of elections.

3. The improvement of the soldier's lot, especially in the matter of sanitation.

4. The abolition of military salute and the practice of coming to attention.

5. The forbidding of discussion of political problems in the army, as proposed by the officers' committee, would be a return to the Old Régime.

In fact, as shown in Point 5, the soldiers wanted to be able to express themselves on the problems of the moment at the front as well as at the rear or among civilians. Since they were also workers and peasants, the political and social aspirations of the soldiers were vague. They expressed themselves less uniformly. The resolutions of the soldiers of the front line (and of the sailors) expressed wishes which show a lack of political experience.

1. A soldiers' organization to fight attempts to restore the Old Régime.

2. The organization of the army in such a way that Socialists will be elected to the Constituent.

3. While maintaining an active defense, we demand that steps be taken for peace negotiations between all belligerents.

4. That soldiers' committees control the operations decided on by the general staff.

5. An immediate meeting of the Constituent Assembly, which, by equal and secret vote, will immediately decide on the form of government. We will give our full support to the formation of a democratic republic.

6. Recognition of the freedom of assembly, press, and speech, of the right to form unions and to strike; the extension of political rights to the armed forces.

7. The end of discrimination on account of religion or nationality.

8. Formation of militia, with elected commanders, for the maintenance of local governments.

9. Election of local authorities.

10. Graduated income tax.

11. Separation of Church and State.

12. Confiscation of lands from owners, the State, the Church, etc.; the land to belong to those who work it.

13. The eight-hour day.

14. Social security for workers, providing for old age, disability, sickness, pregnancy.

15. Pension for disabled war veterans.

16. Compulsory education to sixteen years of age.

17. Formation of a League of Nations for Disarmament.

18. The Petrograd Soviet, Defender of the People, will be defended with all our might.

Compared to those of the workers and the peasants, the soldiers' resolutions have some outstanding characteristics.

—At first they took the military rather than the civilian point of view most often; later this would not be the case.

—They came mostly from the rural elements, but they looked out for the general welfare as well as for that of the peasants.

—Their resolutions resembled the workers' resolutions whenever they were signed by a reserve regiment billeted in a large city. "Here in Dvinsk," noted an observer, "it is the workers, in spite of their small number, who show the way."

—Less stereotyped than the workers' resolutions, the soldiers' resolutions made broader claims than those of the civilians—compulsory education, graduated income tax are frequently mentioned.

—In March, the soldiers' wish for peace, a normal feeling, was less forcibly expressed than the peasants' and workers' pacifism. "On this question, it's the wrong time to come out squarely in favor of it," said the Soviet of Novo-Vichuk.

Numerous militant Bolshevik witnesses attested to the reluctance which they encountered when this subject was broached in the soldiers' meetings. In several resolutions the soldiers asked for the commencement of negotiations for a peace without annexations, but these came more often from troops in the rear than from those at the front. They even went so far as to say "for the soldiers, a change of régime means the end of the war." Often, they said they were exasperated by the phrase "War to Victory," which was repeated so often by the officers. There are also many documents in which the soldiers wish to show themselves as worthy of the "responsibilities which the Revolution has put on their shoulders." It was a question of honor between them and their former officers, and they wanted to take away the monopoly of patriotism which the officers had assumed. An account of the fighting around Stockhod, in the middle of March, by one of the participants, shows the soldiers' feelings:

The masks issued us allowed us to withstand two or three waves of a gas attack. There were thirteen of them and we had to fall back on the other side of the river. Discipline, in spite of what has been said, improved in combat because the soldiers had a sense of responsibility. There wasn't a single slacker in time of stress. Everyone, of course, was hoping for an end to the war, but under honorable conditions for Russia.

135

This was the feeling of the majority. Often the soldiers asked the government to start earnest negotiations, but they left the methods to its discretion. However, the attitude of the officers caused them to revise their opinion and had the opposite effect. The soldiers came to oppose even the principle of continuing the war, defensive or not, because they felt that the officers were hoping to revive the old discipline, while their most fervent wish was its elimination.

★

CHAPTER FIVE

THE HOPES OF THE NATIONALITIES IN THE RUSSIAN REVOLUTION

"The Revolution was barely twenty-four hours old," wrote Sholgin, "when the Ukrainians in the capital were already organizing to present their claims." The Moslems of the Duma formed a "bureau" calling for a Convention on the 1st of May with identical aims. Poles, Letts, Jews, Finns, etc., all joined in showing their enthusiasm for the Revolution.

Russian politicians had made commitments to the various nationalities. They had acknowledged the Poles' and Finns' hopes for autonomy and their right of self-determination (samostoyatelnost). They had always defended the Jews and the oppressed minorities. However, it does not look as though they expected they would one day have to apply to all the nationalities these principles which they had advocated, nor to keep all of their promises at once. Moreover, they believed that the attitude of the various minority groups with respect to the Russian state would change under the euphoria induced by a successful revolution.

1. THE RUSSIAN GOVERNMENT FACES THE CLAIMS OF THE POLES AND FINNS

The new régime was not slow in showing its liberality toward the various national minorities. On March 6th, the Provisional Government published a manifesto reestablishing the "legal order" in Finland—that is to say, the status of 1899—thereby admitting that Finnish autonomy was an accomplished fact. It promised to extend the rights of the Seim and of the Finnish government. The Finns were only half satisfied. They noticed that in unilaterally reestablishing the institutions of the past, the Provisional Government was behaving like the heir of the Tsar-Duke instead of proclaiming the sovereignty of the Finnish people. In the Seim opinion was divided. During the February rush, the Socialist bloc, in the majority, came out solidly for the New Russia; its only regret was that the manifesto wasn't more revolutionary. Some Finnish organizations of Petrograd even declared that they "would recognize the Provisional Government only insofar as it carried out the decisions of the Soviet." In Abo the workers proclaimed their solidarity with "their Russian brothers," and their desire "to keep forever the ties which bound them together." However, the Finnish Socialists decried the government's conservatism. Beginning in March, some even made contact with Bolsheviks such as Giuling, Vill, and Kuusinen, who submitted to them a projected agreement between Finland and Russia. Independent, Finland would be bound to Russia by a permanent union on questions of peace, war, and foreign policy. At the beginning of April the Social-Democrat Tokoi said that "a Russian victory would be bad for Finland." To the consternation of the bourgeoisie, he also said that Finland was destined to be Socialistic. From that time the Socialists never stopped clamoring for independence while the moneyed classes did the opposite: in the minority at the Seim, "they clung to the Russian bourgeoisie for dear life."

The future of Poland seemed rather uncertain. Its independence had been recognized by the Germans and Austrians in November 1916, while they still occupied the country. The Franco-Russian agreement of March 11 left the question of the western frontier to Russia's discretion. Opposed to the separation of Poland, Milyukov nevertheless realized that "the creation of an independent Polish state was the price of a durable peace"—an inconsequential statement inasmuch as only the Constituent Assembly could make such a decision, and in the meanwhile the new régime had no hold on Polish territory. The Poles realized all this. The fall of the Tsar brought into the open all the differences which had always been the weakness of the Polish national movement. In Warsaw the State Council, under the influence of the Central Powers, challenged the Russian Constituent's right to decide on the future of Poland, while the left countered by moving closer to the new régime in Petrograd. Polish soldiers in Russia demanded the formation of a national army separate from the Russian forces, which they saw as the only real guarantee of their ultimate independence. Immediately the Luxemburgist extreme left came out against the formation of a Polish corps, considering it a threat to the Revolution. Hostile to some of the conceptions of independence, some of the Polish workers were already cheering "the international solidarity of the proletariat." In April and May, resolutions hostile to the formation of an autonomous Polish army increased:

> Comrades and soldiers. . . . These Polish Nationalist gentlemen are plotting against the Revolution. They call for the formation of a Polish army as though it were a guarantee of

Polish independence. In fact, they have counter-revolutionary objectives in view. This army will sow discord between Russians and Poles, and in case of need will be used as police against the Revolution. The real war is the Civil War. It is only by means of a European Civil War that the Russian and Polish people will achieve true liberty and true independence. Neither the promises of Wilhelm or Charles, nor the guarantees of the Provisional Government will be able to guarantee Polish Independence; nor will the Polish army, fighting under a Polish flag, which can only reinforce the bonds of slavery, here or in Poland.

Comrades, beware of the trap which the enemies of the workers are setting. Do not become the policemen of the bourgeoisie or traitors to liberty. Remain in the ranks of the Russian Revolutionary army, at the head of the European Revolutionary movement.

Down with this fraud.

Down with militarism.

Long live peace and the brotherhood of the peoples of the world.

According to Felix Dzherzhinsky, the Luxemburgists remained in the minority, though the patriots were not any more united for it, since all the factions excommunicated each other. These quarrels remained meaningless as long as the Polish territory remained in the hands of the Central Powers.

The Provisional Government had not shown that it was ready to recognize Polish and Finnish independence. Only the formation of separate armies would have furnished such evidence. But the new leaders of Russia hoped to cool the ardor of the claims of the various nationalities by showing them that a new era had begun, in which these claims would not be needed. The government issued a declaration on March 19, 1917, in answer to the Petrograd Soviet's plea that "the various minorities be allowed to freely develop their nationalities and their cultures." This highly limited declaration listed the prohibited political and other harassments to which the various national groups were subject, and cancelled them. All Russian citizens were given the right to move their domiciles, the right to own property, to enter all professions, to be contractors, civil servants, and electors, to use their national languages in their schools and contracts, and to establish schools. This declaration freed the various nationalities of the discriminatory practices to which they had been subjected as individuals, although they were not given the collective dignity which they would have acquired if their national identity had been recognized. It is true that in the long run such recognition bore in itself the seed of the disintegration of the Russian Empire, which was something the new leaders were not prepared to face.

Some concessions were made "to those who showed impatience." The Lithuanians were promised autonomy by Prince Lvov, and their representative, Ichas, got a post as Undersecretary of Public Works. The Ukrainians, who had just formed a *Rada*, were told that the claims of their assembly would be submitted to the Constituent, which would decide their future. From then on this answer was given to all the national groups. It became the excuse for all refusals and denials.

2. THE JEWISH "NATION" CRUMBLES

The declaration of March 19, 1917, had been worked out as an answer to Jewish claims, according to Milyukov. This did not mean that it was intended to satisfy their demands or those of other nationalities. According to Kerensky, the declaration aimed mainly at the affirmation of the rights of man and the citizen, to show that these rights would be the law in free Russia. This declaration had no effect whatever on the Jewish minority, who did not consider that it was aimed at them. Their demands addressed to Petrograd remained the same after March 19 as before.

On the other hand, the success of the Revolution seemed to alter the conduct of the Russian Jews and to modify their outlook on the national question. The character of the revolutionary movement and that of the Jewish nationalist movement underwent a change. Besides the professed Jews who considered themselves revolutionaries and nothing else, many Jews thereafter ignored their nationalistic claims and blended into the masses of new Russian citizens. Thus the Jewish workers of Tambov and the Jewish soldiers of the 25th and 39th Corps cheered the Revolution and declared themselves "ready to fight to the end to set up Democracy based on Liberty, Equality, and Fraternity." Others showed their confidence in the new régime and expressed wishes of a cultural nature (Jewish schools, etc.) without further submitting them to their organizations.

The Jewish political parties themselves were taken in by this confident and enthusiastic movement. On March 2nd, the Socialist-Revolutionary Territorial Party (S.E.R.P.) addressed a request to the Provisional Government in which the main claim of the movement—i.e., for territory—had disappeared. As for the *Bund*, it endorsed the Constituent Assembly as the supreme authority, "where the representatives of the Jewish proletariat would work with the whole of the working class." Thus it placed itself under the aegis of the Russian Revolution. The leaders of the *Bund* had too many friends among the men of February to doubt their loyalty; they themselves sat with the Soviet, along with Erlich. The struggle of the *Bund* and that of the revolutionaries joined hands, as had been hoped for years. Placing full confidence in the organizations born of the Revolution, the *Bund* joined in the political struggle of the new régime. The *Bund* doubted that the Jews could any longer make claims of a specific or a cultural nature; yet such claims might still be satisfied since everyone agreed on the foundation in Russia of a truly democratic régime. The belief in the future of the Revolution does not of itself explain the position taken by the leaders of the *Bund*. They saw that with the fall of Tsarism, their membership would melt away, with many Jewish workers considering themselves as plain citizens, active henceforth in purely revolutionary organizations. The center of gravity of the Jewish national movement shifted toward the least compromising members, the Zionists, who became the most active and consistent nationalist group.

Insensitive to the merits of the Revolution, the Zionist groups saw the change of régimes only as a chance to obtain the government's support for a Jewish home in Palestine and as a chance to spread the Zionist cause among the Jews of Russia when the Jewish Nationalist Convention met, before the Constituent election. This was exactly what the *Bund* members feared above all. At the Tenth Party Convention they sent out a desperate appeal to their members dispersed among the different Russian political parties. They needed a majority for Socialism to win out over Zionism:

> The Tenth Convention feels the necessity of saying that it considers the participation of Jewish workers in the National Convention as an opportunity to discuss in concrete terms the question of national-cultural autonomy and that it hopes [*sic*] that the representatives of the *Bund* will resist all attempts to promote any other national policy or anything else.

It added:

> The decisions of the Convention cannot be final [literally—can-

not be obligatory] for the working class. The final decision is up to the National Constituent Assembly.

The *Bund* foresaw that in a Pan-Jewish Convention, the Zionists would form a bloc and would work on the independents, who, because of their presence, would consider themselves Jews above all else. For the *Bund*, the triumph of the Revolution was a swan song.

3. THE BALTIC COUNTRIES AND THE UKRAINE: BETWEEN NATION AND REVOLUTION

On March 4th the Letts in the capital said that they were satisfied with the Soviet resolution on the national question; those in Moscow cheered the Soviet and the army. They decided "to support the government to the extent that it set up a democratic republic, convoked a Pan-Russian Constituent, and guaranteed each national group, including the Letts living in Kurland, Livonia, and the three provinces of Vitebsk, the full right of self-determination on a basis of universal suffrage." Revolutionary hopes and special claims interfered with each other considerably, as in the case of the resolutions of the Baltic and Ukrainian communities living in the large cities of Russia, which were in contact with the political organizations. This situation was even more complicated in the lands of these nationalities.

In Latvia, the Peasant Union mobilized its forces first. Rooted in the soil of the countryside, it represented the most conservative interests, held in check by the "Gray Barons" of the Baltic. It formed a council in which twelve landless peasants were neutralized by twelve landowners, four *pomeshchiki*, eight city dwellers, four representatives of the professions, and eight cooperative representatives. This council made claims of a decidedly autonomous nature, worked out in great detail. It made no mention of reforms in Russia. The drive for independence came out more openly in April, when the Lettish Union, in conjunction with the Peasants' Union, had a meeting at Valk. It demanded the formation of a federal democratic republic—"a union of the peoples and a federation of the governments." Latvia would conduct its foreign affairs through Russia, but would have its own state bank. In Point Two the plan specified that in case of a conflict with Russia the Lettish population would have sovereign decision-making powers.

The Lettish Democratic Party and the National-Democratic Party both endorsed the formation of a democratic republic federated with Russia. They had, however, different ideas on how this was to be accomplished. The former wanted to confide to the Pan-Russian Constituent Assembly the authority to define the state assemblies' limitations, "as in the United States or Switzerland." The latter, more autonomous, wanted to entrust this role to a federal tribunal which would make the final decision in cases of conflict between Latvia and Russia. These two parties had a smaller following than the Peasants' Union and the Social-Democrats, both of which were relatively well organized in the industrial cities of Latvia.

Supported by the landless peasants of Latvia and Wolmar, by the Lettish sharpshooters and by the Egersky Guard Battalion, the Lettish Social-Democratic Party put more emphasis on the revolutionary struggle than on the Lettish struggle. It urged the election of a parliament, but only to act on local affairs. According to Dimanshtein, the slogan "Federation" as used by the Lettish right was opposed by another slogan from the left, "Local Autonomy." At the Fifth Social Democratic Convention in Latvia, which did not meet until July, the themes taken up at the session showed a distinctly Leninist tendency on the subject of the February events. They differed somewhat on the question of the future of Latvia, where the Luxemburgist influence, defended by Stuchka and adapted to the special claims of a large part of the population, prevailed. Thus the resolutions of the Fifth Convention said:

> In the interest of the Lettish proletariat, the Assembly came out for a united and indivisible Latvia (that is to say, uniting Livonia, Kurland, Latgalia) and demanded outright self-government in the political as well as the economic and administrative fields.

The power of the Seim was thus defined:

> It would be supreme in local matters, which would entail administrative and legislative functions. The connection with the central authority of Russia would go through the Seim, which would have a representative from the central parliament, without any authority on legislation.

Finally, taking up the old Bolshevik themes on centralism, the resolution ordered the dispatch of Lettish comrades to the Russian Central Committee "because it was necessary to unite all the international Social-Democratic forces hostile to social chauvinism." In an article in *Zihna*, P. Stuchka explained the thoughts

143

of the Lettish Bolsheviks. On the day when a truly Democratic régime would be set up in Russia, the representation of the special interests of the small nations would be assured in the central Parliament and their wishes would be fulfilled. "Those with the most power have the least power," explained Stuchka. Laws enacted by the central government would not have to be duplicated locally; a conflict between a local Parliament and the central Parliament would no longer make sense, because they couldn't imagine a Lettish Republic bound to a Russian monarchy or the reverse. Thus, the advocates of federation were in reality separatists. The attempt to leave Russia meant they had reactionary ideas in the back of their minds, inasmuch as the Soviet Republic was soon to be proclaimed at Petrograd.

All the elements of the left rallied to this autonomous theme, supported as well by the Land Assembly of Livonia, the Municipal Duma of Riga, etc. Zalit argued for it later in the Moscow Assembly. It was intended to show the willingness of the Letts to remain united with their Russian comrades.

In reality, the anti-Russian feelings of the population, which went back to an old tradition, like the counter-revolutionary and pro-German feelings of the Lettish barons and farmers, were noisily expressed when the Kaiser's troops entered Riga in September 1917. They got a welcome which gave the exact measure of the influence of the Social-Democrats, feeble even in the large cities.

In Estonia, the nearness of Petrograd worked in favor of the Social-Democrats and was an obstacle to the expression of national feeling. Nevertheless, the blue, black, and white flag was hoisted at Dorpat, although the actions in favor or Estonian liberty were timid and slow: the term "local autonomy" did not even appear. In March the Interior Minister promulgated a decree which gave *zemstvo* status to Estonia. In paragraph 12 it was specified that the Russian language had to be used in legislative and administrative functions. The reaction of the Estonians was swift. Prompted by the mayor of Revel, a campaign of petitions followed, endorsed by social organizations ranging from football clubs to chess associations. "There is no sense in fooling around when the Revolution has won," commented *Kiir*, the Social-Democratic daily in the Estonian capital. The Left feared, in effect, that the indirect suffrage used in the *zemstvos* would result in an overrepresentation for the bourgeoisie, who, thanks to this decree of the Provisional Government, would lead the Pan-Estonian Convention convoked by the mayor of Revel in any direction it saw fit. Prompted by the Bolsheviks, the Social-Democrats of Estonia questioned the validity of this "high-handed and undemocratic statute." They were followed by the roadworkers, the tailors, the Estonians of Petrograd, etc. The Soviet appeared as the rival of the upcoming Revel meeting. When the Revel convention met, it looked as though its representativeness was unchallengeable, inasmuch as the Soviet sent some delegates and even the Bolsheviks showed up, in order to demand an accounting of the mandates and to disseminate their agrarian program. The teamwork of the Socialists paid off in that thirty percent of the electorate voted for Russian political parties, which added weight to the Estonian Left. On July 3rd, the Estonian National Assembly summed up its activities: while coming out in favor of a federated republic, it left it up to the Russian Constituent Assembly to implement the project. It asked only that the government recognize the right of self-determination of the peoples of Russia and that the Estonian language be introduced in official communications. These were modest demands; the nationalists were to make much greater ones after October, when the Bolsheviks came to power.

In Lithuania national claims were made much more openly. Since 1915 the country had been largely occupied by German troops. The Occupation Authorities permitted the publication of *Dabertis*, a Lithuanian language daily. They were hoping to form, after the war, an "independent" Grand Duchy of Lithuania, "with the German Emperor as Duke." According to Matthias Erzberger, a German Leftist, the Lithuanian *émigrés* in Switzerland mostly approved of this project, which was disowned by those living in the United States. In Russia, Catholic and Lithuanian Social-Democrats had agreed to form a National Council which on March 13th made its claims known—the formation of "a unified Lithuania, an independent administrative unit." A provisional committee was formed, inviting the various minorities—Jews, Poles, etc.—to send delegates to arrange for a Constituent Assembly empowered to "define the form of the Lithuanian government and its relations with the neighboring nationalities." "This was said discretely, but the project went much further," said Milyukov. In effect, the Lithuanians soon said that "only an international peace congress could decide the future of the country." Those were the views of the Right. At the first meeting of the provisional *Seim* in Petrograd in June, the vote was 140 for the Right and 128 for the Left, who in Lithuanian politics were on a par with the Cadets in

145

wishing for a separation under amiable conditions from the new Russia. The Left then split off, rallying the Unitarians, relatives of the Cadets. For them, national aspirations came before the eventual triumph of revolutionary ideals. It was the same in the Ukraine, but there the presence of a strong urban bourgeoisie caused the Left to modify its stand.

Whereas the Ukrainians were merely a fraction of the Soviet in Petrograd, the nationalist organizations of Kiev formed a Central Ukrainian Council, or *Rada*. At the outset, this *Rada* represented a group of intellectuals unconnected with political parties. Its leaders, for the most part members of the old "Association of Ukrainian Progressives," apparently held secret autonomistic ideas, but until then they had contented themselves with demanding freedom for the Ruthenian Church and the usual legal and cultural claims. The first act of the *Rada* was to greet Prince Lvov and "Dear Comrade Kerensky." The appeal which it sent out later went much further:

> Ukrainians, Citizens, Comrades:
> The happy day is here with the Ukraine, enslaved for centuries, begins a new life. Support the new régime because it is bringing liberty to the Ukraine. Get ready for the National Constituent Assembly where the voice of the great Ukrainian people must resound united to defend the autonomy of our native land and the formation of a federal state.

This proclamation, issued in Shevchenko's language (Ukrainian), had such an effect that all the political organizations of Kiev rallied to it, including the Social-Democrats. The *Rada* invited them to a National Council. It was taking the future of the Ukraine in hand.

In April its President, Mikhail Hrushevsky, formerly so restrained, declared:

> Our claims of a year ago are no longer sufficient for our needs or for the solution of the Ukrainian question. At this hour there is no longer a Ukrainian question. We have a great, free Ukrainian people, which is building its future under different conditions—those of liberty.

Soon thereafter the Progressive Union organized a demonstration demanding that the Provisional Government quickly set up a Constituent Assembly to "confirm Ukrainian autonomy." Again the other organizations had to follow, with the Socialist-Revolutionaries demanding from then on the convocation of a Ukrainian Constituent Assembly and the Social-Democrats merely urging "the preservation of unity with our Russian comrades." The National Conference met at the beginning of April to take up these claims. New voices were heard. Some speakers hoped for the presence of Ukrainians at the peace conference, and opposed the territorial claims of the Poles on the northwest part of the country. This headlong rush seemed hard to stop. The working class, bound to the Social-Democrats, was unable to slow it down, because they had influence only in the east and were concerned only with the class struggle, whereas the heart of the Ukraine lay in Kiev and the countryside. "The peasants represent our strongest support," said V. K. Vinnishenko, one of the leaders of the Ukrainian Social-Democrats, "not the scattered, poor peasants, but the well-to-do, hard-working peasants." The latter wanted above all to take over the large estates owned mostly by nobility of Polish descent. On the Ukrainian S.R.'s proposition, the Kiev Soviet favored the formation of a sort of regional land bank, which would proceed to nationalize the big estates, not to socialize them. Such a project could only emphasize the separatist orientation of the Ukrainian movement, which was little inclined to see Petrograd with sovereign authority over the Ukrainian countryside. "We were Socialist in name only," admitted Vinnishenko, "in reality, we were Democrats, Republicans, not Socialists." In Kiev, the soldiers were in charge; conscious of their cultural differences, they liked to recall the outstanding role of the Volhynie Regiment in the Revolution and demanded the formation of a Ukrainian army "to liberate Bukovina and Galicia." They came out for "War to the Finish." This came as a surprise in Petrograd. In Kiev, the formation of a volunteer regiment, the Bodan Khmelnitsky, seemed like defiance of the Russian majority in the Soviet, who had just come out in favor of "peace without annexations or contributions." Enraged on learning that the Poles had obtained from Guchkov permission to form separate military units, the Ukrainian soldiers made their feelings known at the first meeting of the First Military Convention, "representing the 994,300 Ukrainian soldiers who served in the army." They used the language of the *Rada*—the armed *Rada*.

In Byelorussia the autonomist movement had neither force nor determination. An unrepresentative assembly met at Minsk on March 15, made up of about fifteen people. Other truly Byelorussian organizations could muster only about 29,000 votes, barely more than the Bolsheviks. Starting in April, it looked as though the efforts of the clergy to create a national movement would fail. The people turned to the Russian political parties, especially the Socialist-Revolutionaries, whose agrarian program the Peasants' Assembly adopted in April 1917. At this time neither the Germans of the Volga nor the *Mari* had any distinct national feelings. This was not true of the people of the Caucasus.

4. THE CAUCASUS; THE ORDEAL OF NATIONALIST FEELING BY WAR AND REVOLUTION

The Georgian and Armenian patriots knew perfectly well that in the event of a Russian defeat they would fall under the Turkish yoke, that their country, achieving independence, would live in fear of the Azers, in the majority mainly along the Caspian, or the Ossetian and Dagestanian mountaineers. They were not often separatists. Their attitude toward the February Revolution varied, due to differences between the populations of Georgia and of Armenia.

In Armenia the Revolution changed everything from what it had been on the eve of the Revolution. The *Dashnaksutium* had sent a secret mission to the West during the summer of 1915 to look out for Armenian interests at the peace table. After the fall of Nicholas II, these plans were relegated to second place. The men of February had known how to bring down Tsarism; they would surely know how to resolve the national question in Armenia. The *Dashnaksutium* from then on urged patience, in agreement with the Armenian Committee of Petrograd, which was in favor of an extraterritorial solution. Nothing was settled—perhaps because the more active Armenians, merchants for the most part, were scattered throughout Russia.

The Revolution brought the Georgians closer to the Russian revolutionaries. In Tiflis, at the beginning of March, Grand Duke Nicholas received Noah Zhordania and Isidor Ramishvily, Menshevik leaders of the city Soviet. He congratulated them on "being on the side of order." In effect, the change of régime had been accomplished calmly, as Zhordania had foreseen, since the Revolution had not been a class matter, but one of the entire population. The Social-Democrats knew the role that Chkheidze and Irakly Tseretelli were playing in the capital. Other socialist organizations were also brought into the new administration. Nevertheless, there still was not much unanimity, since all the Georgians did not have the same reasons to rejoice. The faithful, believing that with the ouster of the Russian exarch the Georgian bishops would take their place, were undeceived on this matter by the government commission selected for the Caucasus. There was to be no change in the church until the meeting of the Constituent Assembly. That was enough to awaken the Georgian patriotic sensibilities and to bring grist to the conservatives' mill. The latter, influential in the countryside, recalled in *Sakartvelo*, the organ of the National Democratic Party, that Georgia was entitled to administrative and political self-government. From Switzerland, members of the National Committee wired Petrograd demanding the formation of a Georgian Constituent Assembly. In the garrisons soldiers were demanding separate Georgian units. "That can only lead to reaction," was the opinion of the revolutionary soldiers of Koutais and Tiflis.

Already the cities were opposed to the rural areas, which, dominated by the large landowners, thought that the destiny of Georgia should be decided in Georgia itself. The cities, on the other hand, led by the soldiers and workers, thought that Petrograd would do the job all the better since there were Georgians at the head of the government. In fact, the Socialist position was more precarious than it seemed. In the cities the Socialists would soon become alienated if the petite-bourgeoisie weren't protected from Armenian competition. In the countryside the big landowners explained to the little ones that their lot would improve as soon as the Russian colonists were evicted. Identical reasoning prompted the national minorities of Siberia.

5. THE NATIONAL MINORITIES OF SIBERIA AND THE MOSLEM POPULATION

Thanks to Bublikov's telegram, the farthest reaches of Russia heard about the fall of the Tsar as early as March 4th. Less than forty-eight hours later, in China, a Buriat-Mongol Assembly met, decided to support the Provisional Government, and demanded the formation of a *Seim* with legislative powers and territorial autonomy. The Buriat-Mongols demanded with some heat that they be given back their lands confiscated at the time of the construction of the Trans-Siberian railroad. Rather peculiarly, they wanted the authority of the Seim to be extended to the Tunguses and Kazakhs who spoke Mongolian, if these groups wanted to unite with them.

The Yakuts did not have such a lively sense of national solidarity. They saluted the "Russian Comrades," demanded regular payments, a fairer distribution of tea, and especially that the poor children and orphans be looked after "without distinction as to sex or nationality." In spite of the efforts of Grigory Ordzhonikidze, they claimed nothing more than equality in misery with the Russians and the right to be educated in their own language. These pitifully modest proposals were nothing like the claims of the Moslems, who believed that the dream of Pan-Turanian unity was about to come true.

After the February Revolution, the hopes of the Moslem population came out. Quickly the hot and cold of the Revolution gave rise to more serious schisms than ever before. They lasted until the end of the Civil War.

It was the more moderate people—the Moslem deputies of the Duma—who initiated the idea of a meeting of the "Estates-General" of the Moslem nation of Russia, to be held at Moscow on the 1st of May. Were they trying to sweep the other factions of Moslem opinion into line by getting the jump on them? Whatever it was, their outlook was limited. At the public meeting which they organized at Petrograd on March 7th, they remarked that "the organs of the new régime took no note of freedom of religion in their pronouncements." But the change of opinion was so rapid that the originators of the movement—Maksudov, Calikov, Safarov—were left behind, as were the representatives of *Alash-Orda*, at one with the Cadets. One resolution of the Moslem group of the Duma disavowed Maksudov and stated that "the Moslems of Russia do not go along with 'war to the finish' and the 'conquest of Constantinople and the Straits'—slogans which fail to mention the sacred rights of people or liberty, but which show rather that the Cadet party applies two different sets of rules, one for the people of Europe, the other for the people of Asia—namely, the Turks."

In the whole Empire, everything was gotten ready for the May meeting. In one month about ten preliminary conventions were held. The Convention itself was held from May 1st to the 11th in Moscow. More than nine hundred delegates came, representing all the Moslem populations proportionately, as well as cultural societies, military, professors, etc. The Presidium, twelve in all, of which six were Tatars (three from Kazan-Orenburg and two from Baku), one Bashkir, one Osset, one Crimean Turk, one Sart, and one Kirgkhiz. Selima Jakubova was the first woman to preside over a national convention in contemporary Islamic history.

It was woman's status which caused the first skirmishes between the Progressives and Conservatives. The former won, due to the women delegates whom the clerics had vainly tried to exclude from the meeting hall. The resolution which was adopted embodied all the hopes of women in Islamic Russia—absolute equality between sexes, even in political matters "because thus it is written in Scripture"—ending of sequestration of women—"It isn't found in the Koran"—girls' consent to marriage, end of polygamy, abolition of houses of tolerance, etc. (See text in Appendix.) More than two hundred Mullahs protested noisily in the name of morality against the adoption of such a program. They were beaten. Russia thus found herself, owing to the Moslem minority, the country which took the most daring steps toward the liberation of women.

Other resolutions were adopted to maintain separation of Church and State and instruction in Arabic and Russian. They also adopted a program of social reforms similar to the ones urged by Russian Socialists of all shades.

The main debate bore on the political solution of the national Moslem question. For the first time, the Unitarian groups and the Federalist groups found themselves face to face. The former rallied to this motion of Ahmed Salikov, an Osset Menshevik:

1. The organization of the Russian state on a federal-territorial basis makes the solution of the agrarian question difficult. It can only throttle the foundation of national lands fund to be parcelled out to the Moslem farmers. In the outlying regions, this fund can be used for colonization, but the policy of colonization at the expense of the native population must be ended. The excess land—once the natives have acquired their allotted land—must remain as a reserve fund for the local population, which lives in the vicinity. Such a solution can only be resolved at the state level.

2. In the so-called Moslem states, the workers would not know how to profit from Pan-Russian social legislation, since, by definition, in a system of territorial autonomy, such legislation will vary from state to state. In the Eastern regions the immaturity and the disorganization of the working class will keep them in abominable conditions of exploitation. There will be many struggles before the legislature of the state will decree the eight-hour day, social security, disability and unemployment compensation, and other necessary measures.

3. Territorial federalism will lead to the splitting up of Islam.

Each state naturally will try to enclose itself in its own church, which will throttle the union of the Shiites and Sunnites and will lead to heresies.

4. Territorial federalism will make the emancipation of women difficult in Turkestan and the Caucasus because the legislation will be enacted by men who are accustomed to look on women as slaves.

5. Territorial federalism does not solve the national problem. Instead it will cause a multitude of local problems. By its application the Moslems will lose thousands of citizens because those who are living in Russian states will be Russified.

6. Territorial federalism breaks the political front of the Moslems, who are united from a cultural standpoint. It isolates the different branches of the population. It makes uncertain the accomplishment of the two great tasks of Islam—the rebirth of the great Moslem culture of Asia and the liberation of the Moslem people oppressed by Europeans.

7. Territorial federalism in the Western regions only benefits the ruling classes—*khans, beks baev,* and other representatives of the city bourgeoisie and the reactionary clergy who take advantage of the untutored, ignorant masses whom they use to gain power and to perpetuate, on new bases, the old system of exploitation and subjugation.

This resolution reflected the aspirations of the Tatar bourgeoisie of Kazan, who thought they could take the future of the Moslems in Russia in hand. But against them there were those who did not want to fall under the Tatars (Bashkirs, Uzbeks, etc.), those who thought that autonomy would be a better answer to local problems (Azers), and those who saw a little further and wanted in one way or another to separate from the Russian State. They dreamed of independence, or cherished the Pan-Turkish or Pan-Touranian ideal. Also against this motion were those who thought that it did not go far enough, from a revolutionary point of view. Further, they thought that the adoption of it would strengthen the tendency toward class collaboration. It was defeated by a bizarre coalition which mustered 490 votes against it and 271 in favor. Instead, the Convention adopted (by a vote of 446 to 171) the federalist motion of M. A. Rasul-Zade of Baku:

1. The Pan-Russian Convention of Moslems feels that the solution in the best interests of the Moslem population is a democratic federated republic with a territorial base. Only the national groups without set territories will enjoy national cultural autonomy.

2. To settle the religious and common cultural problems and to coordinate the actions of the Moslem nationalities, a Pan-Moslem body with legislative functions for all Russia will be created.

The implementation of Point Two implied the formation of a provisional central body. By forming it without delay, the Convention showed its desire not to break with the minorities. But the Tatars at that time were few, and with the decisions made in Moscow the Moslem solidarity was broken up. The triumph of particularism meant the end of the Pan-Moslem dream, as conceived by the Tatars. What is more, this struggle in Moscow revealed another line of cleavage which had not existed before 1917—that which pitted the reformist against revolutionary nationalists, who wanted to go further and lay the foundations of "extremist Pan-Islamism." The three main objectives were:

1. The fight against Tatar feudalism and Moslem traditionalism.
2. The national liberation of the Moslems from Russian domination.
3. The extension of Socialism to the whole Islamic world.

Actually, these revolutionary nationalists were not very numerous. Behind Mulla-Nur Vahitov, from Kazan, they willingly worked with the Bolsheviks. Soon they were to aid in the triumph of the October Revolution.

The measures taken by the Provisional Government in the first few days were necessary, but they did not go far enough. The government drew up bills on the future of Finland and Poland, although no one could be sure they would be honored. It made a few promises to the Ukraine and Lithuania, gave *zemstvo* status to Estonia, proclaimed the rights of all individual citizens, and made an appeal for confidence. The Constituent Assembly would do the rest. A certain number of Jews, even *Bundists*, could be satisfied with these measures, as could the Armenians, who shared the ideals of the Men of February, and of course the Georgians, whom circumstances had swept to power. The Tatar bourgeoisie of Kazan, sympathetic at first, was irritated by the Milyukov proposals about the Turks and Constantinople. Several Finnish and Baltic Social-Democrats for similar reasons went the same way. For many of the national minorities, acceptance of the program of the Men of February was as hard as if, Ukrainians apart, they had not taken part in the triumph of the Revolution. Not having themselves won their own liberty, these national groups wanted recognition, which stiffened their stand. Those whom the Revolution frightened became uncompromising nationalists. They refused to grant the Russian Constituent Assembly the authority to legislate for the whole empire, or they thought the Provisional Government was useless. In any case, they all wanted guarantees, mainly the right to form separate military forces. The most militant revolutionaries were hostile to this demand. Everyone would judge the new régime by its attitude on this question which, for the minorities, was the crucial test.

SUMMARY OF PART ONE

The February Revolution differs from the October Revolution in its spontaneity. It was the result of a ferment induced mostly by the propaganda of the political parties. But they did not themselves lead the Revolution, and in that sense Trotsky was right when he said, with Zavadsky, that it was "anonymous."

The first few hours of the Soviet show signs of improvisation. It wasn't made by demonstrators, but by political prisoners just out of jail who were unacquainted with the events which they intended to lead in a definite direction. Those who joined them still wondered, on the eve of the Revolution, about the origin and extent of this movement which was to put them in power. These men played no particular role during the days preceding the formation of the Soviet, for it was only the day before that they had decided to take part in the movement.

To the initial Menshevik-dominated group, as we saw, a few Populists and Socialist-Revolutionaries attached themselves. These men had memories of the First Russian Revolution and wanted to form a Soviet again, as in 1905. In agreement with Chkheidze, Skobelev, and Kerensky, they acted in accordance with a plan which they knew by heart. "We were living as in a dream. . . . And as in all dreams, we acted our parts smoothly and glibly."

The most valid outward sign of the spontaneous action of the masses, the Soviet, would supply the spark to set off the "bourgeois revolution." At the Duma there were three deputies of the extreme Left who figured on pushing the assembly into seizing the reigns of power.

As this bourgeois revolution might strengthen the enemies of Socialism, the Mensheviks proposed to help overthrow Tsarism but, while doing so, to take certain precautions to safeguard the future of the proletarian revolution. They thought it necessary to promulgate a series of irreversible reforms which the Soviet would put into effect. A proletarian bastion in bourgeois country, the Soviet would be the tool of the working class in its struggle against the bourgeois government, in which the Socialists would not take part. At the same time, the Soviet would be the strongest bastion in the bourgeois revolution against any attempt to reinstate Tsarism. The initial period of the Soviet was a page in the political history of Menshevism. No doubt Kerensky was little concerned with the niceties of doctrine, and Trotsky was able to say that he bore himself "like a provincial lawyer pleading a political case." The fact remains that by his actions Kerensky furthered the revolution.

If we take stock of the initial activities of the Soviet, we see, surprisingly, that it made no political decisions, that it never assumed power, and that several times it capitulated to the Duma. Certainly danger threatened, it was believed, so that it was more urgent to organize the defense of the Revolution, to join hands, than to proclaim its objectives and prepare for the next stage. But would it not have been better to assume more power? The members of the Committee chose to remain silent, to let the Constituent set up the new régime, as if the Revolution had never occurred! To explain their attitude, the Defensists used tactical arguments: in order to save the Revolution, first the Germans had to be crushed—that is to say, the war must be continued—then reforms would come. The Internationalists claimed that by making extremist decisions, they would stampede the bourgeoisie into making common cause with the Tsar and would thereby aid in crushing the Revolution. These tactical reasons put them in the same position as the Defensists, whom they had accused the day before of wanting to "castrate" the coming revolution. Another paradox was added by Trotsky's analysis: "The power is in the hands of the Socialists," he wrote, "but their only worry is whether the bourgeoisie, politically isolated, hated by the masses, and hostile to the Revolution, would accept the reins of power. Its assent must be achieved at all cost. It was not the bourgeois who renounced their program, but the Socialists." The description is apt. Trotsky goes further, lumping together different Socialist groups who did not share the same reasons. The fact remains, as we saw, that it was "with relief" that the literary committee learned that the Duma had assumed power. Sukhanov said it and Plekhanov confirmed it. "Steklov clapped his hands," specified

155

Peshekhonov, an observation which showed plainly the hesitancy of the Socialists, giving up all pretence to sovereignty, but congratulating themselves on belonging to the Duma. The second paradox shown by Trotsky was that the Duma would accept power from the Socialists only on condition "that the Monarchy would acquiesce." The insignificance of the Socialists went even further. By not assuming power, the Soviet acted as though it did not consider itself a product of the Revolution. At the most, it was a body in the employ of the bourgeois revolution, and because of this fact it permitted the Duma to head its own committees, recognizing its authority by delegating two of its members, both from its executive committee (Kerensky and Chkheidze).

Traditionally, in the histories of the Russian Revolution, it is usually shown that the two bodies born on February 27, 1917, were matched against each other. Conflicts were certainly not lacking between them. But in order to understand them, it must be recalled that from the first their relations were very complicated. If the Duma's hostility to the Soviet was complete and instantaneous, the opposite is not true. Not only did the soviets work with the Duma, but they admired its dominating position. Moreover, they thought of themselves as a brake to keep the Revolution from becoming the foundation of a bourgeois dictatorship. A few, in the minority, were silent and reserved in view of the state of things.

The Bolshevik plan was to help in the formation of a Provisional Revolutionary Government which would lead the newborn republican régime. Learning of the formation of the Soviet, the Bolsheviks had to modify their tactics, to adapt to the situation. The first dilatory maneuver having failed, they had to collaborate with these Socialist Patriots who were in the midst of this Soviet which was not of their making. However, as Lenin had reiterated since 1905, the Soviet must not be considered, once it came into being, as a rival of the Party, but as a revolutionary link which the Bolsheviks could use to transmit their ideas to the masses. Consequently they must try to get the greatest possible party representation into it. On February 27th, between 6 and 9 o'clock in the evening, Shlyapnikov telephoned everybody in the party—with less success than his rival Defensists, he admits candidly. Circumstances having gone against them, the Bolsheviks immediately urged new elections. In the meantime, they took no part whatever in policy questions, not even working on the committees. However, they introduced the soldiers into the Soviet, because the fate of the soldiers was tied to the Revolution and because the soldiers could help them achieve their policy goal of an immediate peace. They also insisted on the need for neighborhood committees, which they hoped to be able to control. It was in these boroughs that they would create some real soviets—that is to say, soviets in which the Bolsheviks would be in the majority, because they alone urged a truly revolutionary policy.

The sudden collapse of the Tsarist régime was the result of the mass uprisings. Unable to grasp the idea of the power of this movement, Nicholas II and the general staff had decided to try to liquidate it by suppression. But the Ivanov plan misfired and they surrendered unconditionally. Then the General Staff changed its mind; it thought that there had been a Palace Revolution in the streets and it sided with the supposed victors, Michael and the Duma, as if atoning for the disaster of 1905 and 1915. When it saw its mistake and felt the breath of the populace down its neck, the officer corps closed ranks and became the reserve of the counter-revolution. Its success depended upon the continuation of the war, which it owed to the Duma's action.

The Duma had taken full advantage of the Soviet leaders' timidity. It had seized the reins with the intention of holding them and channeling the course of the Revolution to its own ends. But it made the mistake of thinking that the soviets were leading the Revolution and that, once throttled, they would cause no trouble, leaving the Duma as master of the field. It was just the opposite: the Revolution was controlling the soviets and it could take back from the Duma or from the government the power it had entrusted to them. The question remained, would the government and the soviets be able to fulfill the hopes of Russia?

Sorting out the aspirations of the workers, the peasants, the soldiers, the ruling class, and the various nationalities brings out certain facts:

1. On the one hand, there was the determination of the working class to ensure the guarantees which would make for the improvement of its lot in the future, perhaps even going as far as a "proletarian revolution." On the other hand, there was the bourgeoisie's illusion that it had inherited the mantle of power and that it would keep it for several decades. The uncompromising attitude of the property-owners was matched by the vigilance of the workers—a situation which was not conducive to "class collaboration." It was clear that the groups or political parties which were

urging collaboration—and this includes workers as well as members of the propertied classes—were going against the mainstream, against the wishes of the people they were supposed to represent.

2. The peasants were much more radical than the workers, once Tsarism was toppled. Thirty-one of their first one hundred petitions urged the use of violence against their oppressors, former or present, as opposed to only five such petitions from the workers. The countryside also seemed more committed to acting in a revolutionary fashion. Not once in their motions did they suggest that land reform could proceed by stages. Revolution meant suspension of the old laws, drawing up of new ones, and satisfying their land hunger; not waiting, but acting. The main thing was to get some property, to get more if you already have some, and to redistribute the land more equitably. When they proposed confiscation of the large estates, it was to redistribute them. For the peasants there was no clash between private property worked by the family and the collective administration of the land entrusted to a committee elected by the community. For the workers, control of the means of production remained an abstraction. They wanted to control the functions and the administration of the factories in order to secure improvements of their situation, but they were not thinking of changing that situation. One day maybe the State would take over the factories and they would belong to the workers, but they did not see how this was to be accomplished. This was not their motivating force, as the redistribution of large estates was with the peasants. The peasant knew very well how his situation would change when he acquired his land, whereas the worker had no idea of how to act as a captain of industry. It was not easy for him to imagine what to do in a revolutionary situation. His mind was paralyzed, and even if his resentment was as great toward his class enemy as that of the peasant, this would not have mattered because he did not know what to do with it. Later the political parties would teach him and give him the means.

3. The impatience of the national minorities worried the revolutionaries more than it irritated them. The Russian revolutionaries were at this point convinced that they would do such a good job that they had no inkling that there could be a difference between their objectives and those of the nationalists, since, as the heirs of the Revolutions of 1789, 1848, 1871, and 1905, they saw their role in universal terms. This was a sad mistake which became apparent from the first days in Finland, in Poland, and soon

elsewhere. Only some of the Jews, Georgians, and Armenians rallied unconditionally around the new régime.

4. On the national question, at this time, only Lenin had opinions which were similar to those of a large part of the national minorities themselves. On the other hand, like most theorists, he misunderstood the objectives of the peasants completely. This did not matter, inasmuch as the people of the countryside and the various nationalities had very little knowledge of the party programs and the militants had very vague ideas about the real aspirations of the populace. On the other hand, there was a real affinity between the ideas of the working class and those of the Social-Democrats, whose divergent tendencies the workers tried to ignore. At best some were considered more radical, others more moderate.

5. Finally, weary of war, the Russian people were ready nevertheless to bear the vicissitudes of a new campaign if it were clear that the new régime would do everything possible to conclude a just peace. If the enemy refused, he would be fought until he consented. The conduct of the officers and the ruling classes thus figured only indirectly in the "peace at any price" sentiment. They refused to admit that a new relationship had to be established between the troops and their leaders, between property-owners and the disinherited. They became obnoxious with their demands that the war be waged until victory. The workers saw in it a trick to resurrect the past by prolonging the war.

Russia had expressed some hopes, and from here on in it would be hard to ignore them. Every day in every town and village there wasn't a single Russian, man or woman, who didn't shout them in improvised meetings. Briefly, it was a matter of building a new order, without privileges, where equity, competence, and rectitude would rule; an unsullied, kind Republic, with pity for the weak and without rancor for the wicked; a just democracy from which scoundrels would be banished. At the moment, it meant that the Russians wanted to do the impossible: to put an end to the miseries of war, the harshness of everyday life—which was less bearable in Russia than elsewhere—and the old order's social and political inequities. However, they knew that they were not all of the same purpose and that they could not decide their future alone, for they were bound to the rest of the world by the war. On the one side were friends, on the other enemies. The enemies were always the same: Turks and Teutons. They were also associated with other nations by commercial and financial ties, at one with all combatants, as with all those who fought for peace. On their side, circumstances had brought to the government men who were aware of the tragic destiny of their country and were trying to administer it more efficiently than their predecessors. Face to face with them in the Soviet were the experts in the art of criticism, leaders who had shown themselves apt at skirmishing with the forces which had brought the Revolution about. But this did not mean very much since governmental power inhibited them, whereas the Russian in the street considered himself able to run the country—ready to quarrel with the government or the Soviet alike, if they disagreed with him.

Lenin alone, against everyone else, proclaimed himself opposed to the government, against his own party leaders. Instinctively he isolated himself, adopting the only course which brought him into agreement with the masses. To have a command of the situation it was not enough to be able to see clearly. Even the shrewdest had to know what to do! History had willed that it would be precisely the one organized party, the Bolsheviks, which would have a leader with the vision and the ability to modify his earlier ideas completely to fit the circumstances.

PART TWO

★

THE DEFEAT OF
THE FEBRUARY REVOLUTION

CHAPTER SIX

THE START AND THE OPERATION OF THE NEW RÉGIME

"The Revolution is not a four-hand piano recital," wrote I. N. Steinberg. Still, the bourgeoisie and the masses wanted hegemony. The bourgeoisie, the master of the government, groped for the support of the phantom Duma while the people, the master in the country, drew their strength from the soviets.

The Revolution had been made by the people, but, technically, the ruling classes had known how to take the initiative. On February 27th, the formation of the Committee for the Reestablishment of Order had preceded the official formation of the Soviet by a few hours. On the 28th the Committee declared that it had seized the reins of the government. On March 2nd it was into their hands that the Romanovs abdicated. They wanted to keep this advantage and to proceed as though there had been no Revolution. Thus the old laws still would have been in effect and the soviets would have been illegitimate. Nevertheless, they existed and inherited the Duma's authority; they could veto the government's decisions.

The Soviet and the Duma Committee had made an agreement. Would it hold up? Would the contestants be able to respect the rules and overcome the forces on each side which were hostile to all compromise? Not for long—soon they were to set off the crises of April and July, then October, then the Civil War.

1. THE GOVERNMENT BODIES AND THE FUNCTIONING OF THE RÉGIME

THE GOVERNMENT

In the government those who were there knew each other well. They had been in the know on the "palace conspiracy" against Nicholas II. Belonging to the cultured society of St. Petersburg, they were not professional revolutionaries and had already demonstrated their miscellaneous talents—Milyukov as a historian, Kerensky as a political lawyer, Guchkov and Prince Lvov as administrators. Well-bred men, they belonged more to the sensitive world of Chekov than to the dramatic universe of Dostoyevsky. Thrilled by the thought of attaining so much power, they had never sought it—except perhaps for Milyukov and Kerensky. None of them had ever known exile or the hatred of men in the past. By this very fact, they were able neither to feel the humiliation which the people felt nor to express it as strongly as they did. Those who had lived in exile for a long time knew more about it. (Only Kerensky had spent some time in prison.)

They had always wished for the formation of a parliamentary type of government, as in the West. In seizing the reins of power, in March 1917, they did not propose to upset the social and economic order, but to show themselves as orderly men in the context of a regenerated government. They wanted to leave the reforms up to the Constituent Assembly. Their task was to put in order and modernize a country which the neglect of Tsarism had thrown into a woeful state. If they had accomplished this they would have well merited the praise of their country.

Prompted by a concern for the common welfare, they wanted to show the world that change could be accomplished smoothly and peacefully, something which had never been done before. At the council meetings they kept up a polite relationship with each other and shared the same objectives, albeit with different methods of accomplishing them. According to Manuilov, Milyukov, and Guchkov, any concession to "the masses" would lead to ruin. They were the personification of "the resistance," just as their opposite number, the triumvirate of Nekrassov, Tereshchenko, and Kerensky, led "the movement."

The first group expected to put the bourgeois program in effect using Cadet tactics. To overcome the Soviet, they went into battle with determination, overestimating their power, without bothering to resuscitate the Duma. The "resistance" hoped to be able to make use of the revolutionary enthusiasm of the masses while making some small concessions to the Soviet. It wanted to win the war above anything else and to give credit for it to the new régime. In order to do so order must be restored promptly. Guchkov doubted that the prosecution of the war could prevent the collapse of the old social and economical order. At the Ministers' Council when "he spoke softly, his eyes looking off into the distance, evoking the army's fate, you could feel his hopeless despair." He would have preferred to sign a peace in order to be able to institute reforms which would exorcise the specter of violence. His friends thought he was too pessimistic and he never spoke publicly about his feelings. He never became alienated from his colleagues, and he sought, without conviction, to revive the army's sagging morale. Later, when he became convinced that there was nothing more he could do, he resigned.

Milyukov, on the other hand, counted on the war to choke off the Revolution or to legitimize the postponement of reforms until peacetime. The government had had to promise not to use the military situation as an excuse for delaying them. The "resistance," nevertheless, thought it could use the principles of the masses against them by claiming that only a Constituent Assembly had the power to initiate reforms, and the war made it difficult to form one quickly.

The "movement" also wanted to abridge the Soviet's authority. They saw no reason for its existence, now that the Revolution had triumphed. They wanted its leaders to take part in the government, but were turned down. Meanwhile the "movement" men would have liked to make some spectacular reforms and to immediately apply the remedies demanded by the masses. Then the Soviet would no longer be able to play the part of an irresponsible opposition, and would disappear. The "movement" men also thought that increasing reforms was the only way that they could give the country the will to win the war; in this they agreed with the "masses."

United by the membership in the Masons* the triumvirate got along well. Nekrassov tried to win the members of the Cadet Party over to a more open policy than that of Milyukov. Tereshchenko flirted with the conciliators. Kerensky dominated them, thanks to his aptitude for building up a personal relationship with his peers and others. He had a persuasive voice. However, his tantrums became unbearable and people wondered whether he wasn't going too far with his histrionics. He seemed so sincere, so earnest that many forgave him his fits and even his slyness. He was also loved because he symbolized the grandeur of the February days, this man of 1789 who felt, more than the others, the grandeur and the euphoria of the triumphant Revolution. When on March 29, 1917, the "Grandmother of the Revolution," eighty-year-old Catherine Brechko-Breshkovskaya, came back to Petrograd, an immense crowd waited for her. She spoke of the Revolution, of the ideal of liberty. The emotion was intense. She turned to Kerensky, clasped his hand, embraced him, and as though passing the burden on to him, added: "Comrade, yes, we love you and will die with you."

As for the President, Prince Lvov, he was a "just and inoffensive" man. His prestige as former President of the *Zemstves*, gave him, in spite of his feebleness, a certain authority. He was distin-

---

*With Tsarism toppled, Free-Mason solidarity was no longer needed; besides, it could no longer be effective in the maelstrom of the Revolution. (Interview with Kerensky, September 1963.)

guished, devoted to his country, and extremely benevolent. He viewed the emancipation of the Russian people kindly, for he saw in it the confirmation of an old conviction—the Slav's mission to accomplish an authentic humanitarian revolution. In the government he always ruled in favor of the "movement," to the surprise and ire of Milyukov and his friends. Even Kerensky thought he was too conciliatory toward the Soviet.

THE DUMA

Forgetting that a Revolution had broken the bonds which tied the government to the Duma, some ministers tried to revive it and to perpetuate the fiction of the cabinet's responsibility to the Duma. But the majority of the ministers wanted to be answerable to no one. The government assured the survival of the commissions born on the 27th of February and permitted the Duma Committee to create some new ones, like that on relations with cities, or the army commission, whose instigators, Maslennikov, Smiakov, and Zhanuskevitch tried to counteract the soviets' actions. It did nothing more, and in spite of its President, Rodzianko, who was now very popular, it was doomed. Shydlovsky and Prince Mansyrev described the death throes:

At the beginning, bound by its origin, the government asked for and received recognition from the Duma. It made it accept the cabinet changes. Then it only asked for advice about its action. Then it advised it of its demands. After that it wasn't even consulted any more.

Here is the epitaph:

On the first day the revolutionaries occupied only one room of the Taurides Palace, then one or two others. Then they occupied the cafeteria, the post office, the left wing of the building, the chancery, the President's office. Soon there were only the library and the administration office remaining. Farewell, Duma! We have faded away and can never come back.

The most vigorous part had left and the Duma was breathing its last. It was apparent to everyone that it was the Soviet which had become the Parliament of the Revolution.

THE SOVIETS

The Executive Committee* had existed before the Petrograd Soviet, and had been reelected on the evening of the 27th of February. In accordance with decisions made that day, the parties delegated two representatives each to that body, which numbered about forty members from that date on. Among them were nine soldiers, who gradually dropped out. Chkheidze presided there in his undecided way, much as Prince Lvov did in the Council of Ministers. Overwhelmed by his feeling of responsibility, he studiously avoided committing himself when it came to policies. But he became the Committee watchdog once the vote was taken, and he went to great lengths to safeguard the will of the majority. Nikolai Nikolaievich Sukhanov, the most influential theorist on the Committee, steered toward international Menshevism. A friend of Gorky, Martov, and Kerensky, he was the only one to have a coherent picture of the problems of the Russian Revolution. The volumes of *Notes* which he left attest to his lucidity and his sense of history. But he was not a good speaker and because of this had no prestige. The opposite was true of Steklov, who had nothing to say himself but knew how to express the thoughts of others effectively. He was tireless and often led the debate, thus seeming to be the leader of the Committee. During the first few weeks no dominant personality emerged. Kerensky never attended the Committee meetings in spite of the fact he was its Vice President. Shlyapnikov was silent. In mid-March all this changed with the arrival of Tseretelli and A. R. Gotz from Siberia, two respected leaders of the Mensheviks and the Populists.**

*Executive Committee Permanent Members:

Anarchist	Bleishman
Social-Democrats	
Bolsheviks:	Shlyapnikov, Zalutsky
	Stalin (mid-March)
Unitarians:	Zhurenev
Menshevik-Internationalists:	Grinevich, Pankov, Kapelinsky, Sokolovsky
No party:	Sukhanov, Steklov, Sokolov
Menshevik-Defensists:	Chkheidze (President), Skobelev, Gvozdev, Bogdanov, Batursky
Socialist-Revolutionaries	
Internationalist:	Alexandrovich
Defensists:	Zenzinov, Rusanov
Socialist-Populists:	Peshekhonov, Chernolussky
Trudoviks	Kerensky (Vice President), Bramson, Chaikovsky, Stankevich
Cooperative Movement	Grohman, Frankorussky
Bund (Jewish)	Lieber, Erlich
Lettish Social-Democrats	Stuchka, Kozlovsky
(affiliated with Bolsheviks)	
Later put on Committee	Tseretelli, Dan, Woitinsky, Gotz, Charnov

**After March 21, they switched the Committee policy toward the Right; see pp. 190ff.

In the Committee, the Defensists dominated, but the Internationalists were a steady bloc. Their restraint was noted by foreign observers during the demonstrations. The Committee members were hesitant about broaching the subject of the war, which loomed threateningly. There was also a majority, not including Trudoviks and Populists, which defied the government. There were endless problems about the relationship of the Soviet and the cabinet. Kerensky was supposed to take care of this, but he was reluctant to do so. He wanted to take his cue directly from public opinion. From then on, the Soviet refused to back Kerensky's position, since he refused to be their representative—a state of affairs which made for uneasiness. Thus, because of a lack of communications, the cabinet and the Soviet complained of being presented with actions already completed. On March 8th, 1917, the Soviet decided to name a Liaison Committee to the cabinet. Kerensky considered this an insult. Named were Chkheidze, Skobelev, Steklov, Sokolov, and Filippovsky. At the first meeting Sokolov became incensed because he had heard that the cabinet wanted to have the Constituent meet in Moscow in order to remove it from the powerful influence of the capital. He was six months ahead of the times. Then Manuilov exploded: he would never accept any supervision of his administration. The Liaison Committee reproached the cabinet in turn for having nominated Alexeiev without consulting the Soviet. The cabinet's answer was to submit a certain number of decisions to it. The five side-stepped the issues, saying that they had no mandates on these questions. The Soviet discussed the functions and the powers of the "Liaison Commission." In accordance with Steklov's advice, it was decided that they would make written reports on the cabinet's activities; the Soviet would then decide what position to take. These reports were not to be considered as an agreement between the two powers—which is what the cabinet would have liked—but as a sort of petition which the Soviet could ponder. Unable to determine a clear policy, the members contented themselves with the position of an irresponsible opposition. "They'll leave, I tell you, they'll leave," cautioned Kerensky, speaking of the members of the cabinet. In fact, later, they did leave. They were not forced out by the Soviet, but by the masses. Wasn't the Soviet representing them?

"Among the masses the only idea of organization that took root," wrote Peshekhonov, "was that left over from 1905, the formation of soviets." It is a fact that Russia was covered by a network of soviets before a single party had a meeting. The trade unions had never had much stability in Russia. In the middle of March they came out only with a campaign of endorsements. The cooperative movement, "the third form of the workers' movement," was more developed. But like the political parties it delegated two of its leaders, Grohman and Frankorussky, to the Soviet leadership. Could the soviets of Petrograd and the countryside henceforth be considered representative?

Reunited for the first time on the evening of the 27th of February, the Soviet Assembly had been elected by roll call of the original group: One representative for each thousand workers in the large plants, one delegate for each plant of less than a thousand workers. Ultimately, they added one soldier representative for each company. They did not foresee that soon 2,000 soldier-delegates would form a bloc alongside the workers, who only numbered 850. This was a form of voting which the Bolsheviks criticized because, according to them, it discriminated against the large bodies in favor of the smaller ones, in which the Mensheviks ruled. Shlyapnikov asked for a different method of representation, as did the Socialist-Revolutionaries and the Anarchists in Moscow.

At the last count, it came out that the large factories, with 87 percent of the workers of the capital, had 484 delegates to the Soviet, and the others, with 13 percent of the workers, had 422. There certainly was an overrepresentation of the old type of workers, those of small firms. This was no accident because the voting Committee was well informed about the political make up of the Petrograd firms.

The representatives of the large plants were also conciliatory. In the vote on the question of the agreement between the Soviet and the Duma Committee it was 1000 for, with only 15 following the Bolsheviks who wanted to reject the proposal. It was the same on the 5th, when they voted on returning to work. Was the Bolshevik power a myth? Was it the form of representation which was faulty? Did the differentiation between Bolsheviks and Mensheviks hold only for the leaders? It would seem as though the workers elected delegates who went along with the Central Soviet. During these first days the Bolsheviks pulled long faces. "The hostility against us was fairly general," noted Shlyapnikov. The factories were electing delegates who went along with the movement. The militant Bolsheviks were nevertheless few in number. At the meeting of the "Factory Committees" in Moscow, fourteen delegates represented 750 Bolsheviks. There were at this time twenty-four

169

factory committees in the region, with an average of thirty Bolsheviks per factory.

The Committee did not worry very much about these recriminations. They were more worried about the number of soldiers; they didn't know what their political opinions were, but they noticed that often they formed a bloc. Were they going to control the Revolution? On March 4th, there was talk of reorganizing the Soviet, the Mandate Commission being in no position to get rid of the surplus delegates. At the March 18th meeting, Bogdanov was to make a report on this question. Only the workers were invited. The soldiers were to meet the next day, separately, to resolve current problems. Bogdanov proposed a new method of representation—one delegate for each 2,000 citizens (workers and soldiers) and one delegate for each organization or union—which could only mean the workers. Thus the purpose of the reorganization was to diminish the soldiers' representation.

In the provinces too, the soldiers were more or less shunted aside in the running of the Soviet and their representation diminished. Research concerning the cities of Vologda, Nizhni-Novgorod, Grozny, Odessa, Riazan, Yaroslav, and Ekaterinburg shows that the soviets were wholly controlled by the working class or its leaders: 173 soldiers (and 8 officers) had seats out of a total of 1,487 members. Another shows that for 44 soviets in the Moscow region there were 100 soldiers and 34 officers out of 4,743 members. No doubt the military was not proportionately as large in these cities as in Petrograd. The fact remains that, in view of the role which they played in the March days, the soldiers could consider that they were excluded. A large part of the working population itself was not always represented in the Soviet—only half of that of Nizhni-Novgorod, and the national minorities were represented even less, for the soviets were almost exclusively made up of Russians. The bureaus were even less representative; in Petrograd the intellectuals dominated and there were fewer than ten workers out of forty members. Also in the Middle-Volga (Saratov Region), the intellectuals made up more than fifty percent of a convention of workers' soviets of the region.

Still, the representativeness of the Soviet was never challenged, because any segment of the population which thought it was being discriminated against would make up an independent Soviet. It was that way with workers of the Bolshevik strongholds of Vyborg, Narva, Schlusselburg, Kronstadt, and especially the twelve boroughs of the capital, which each made up an autonomous soviet, jealously independent of the Petrograd Soviet, to which they nevertheless sent delegates. In Kiev, the Bolsheviks left the Soviet flamboyantly, seceded, and formed their own organization. In Kronstadt there were several soviets which fought each other mercilessly. Elsewhere, soldiers' soviets were formed wherever and whenever the soldiers thought they were being slighted. There were thus, in the Moscow region, 35 soldiers' soviets alongside 68 workers' and other soviets. In Kursk, they even had an officers' soviet. In the same manner, the various national minorities formed their own soviets—in the Ukraine, Byelorussia, Turkestan, and the Caucasus. Each community, each group, each minority was likely to form itself into an autonomous body and bargain on equal terms with the government and other revolutionary bodies.

In the cities as well as in the countryside, the independent soviets bore the mark of the Russian workers' genius. The method of representation, the constitutional bodies (bureaus, commissions, etc.), the means of action (workers' militia, petitions, etc.) were so many creations which gave the Russian Revolution its style. A new law was born, founded on equity and respect for the individual and his work. Thus the workers substituted their own mores for the teachings handed them by the state, the church, and the intelligentsia. We have seen that this new humanism was not lacking in generosity.

The necessity for federating the soviets became quickly apparent. Those in the provinces saw that they could thereby take part in the carrying out of the decisions made at the summit; the Petrograd Soviet thought it could consolidate its position and lessen the effects of decentralization. Less than a month later, the first Pan-Russian Convention of Soviets was held at Petrograd. Those were the days of adulation for Chkheidze and Kerensky, the successful leaders of February. There was much talk of fraternity, liberty, unity, and sixteen members of the provincial soviets became members of the already overcrowded Committee. Already, the soviets were ceasing to act on their own volition: their members acted on their parties' instructions.

DEMOCRACY AND DUAL POWER

If the Soviet belonged to the revolutionary tradition, "dual power" only had Menshevism in back of it. One whole wing of the democratic camp rejected it. It was the same on the other side; the cabinet, the bourgeoisie, and the general staff wanted a single authority. Opinion was divided between those who, following the

Soviet majority, wanted to apply the new rules to the democratic game, and those who contested it and wanted to change it.

Among those who favored dual power, there were first the Mensheviks, the theorists. According to them, the soviets were to help in the consolidation of democracy; to watch over the cabinet and keep it on the straight and narrow path, away from reaction, the common enemy; to interpret the will of the masses and impose it on the leaders. "Alone," explained *Izvestya*, "the democratic forces are incapable of governing and *reaction* would exploit the smallest error committed by the Soviet." Total isolation would lead to self-destruction. As Tseretelli wrote later, "The cabinet should have complete power, as long as it reinforced the Revolution. If it takes the way of compromises we'll disown it." Two editorials of the *Rabochaya Gazeta*, a Party daily, added:

> This government is provisional; it is to last only until the Constituent. It is Revolutionary, it is a government. It has thus full power over the Army and the Revolutionary People.

Then, addressing the government itself:

> Act, Tear down, Build up.
> Arrest the Imperial Family. Name new officials and replace the old ones who are no longer suitable. Introduce a democratic system in the army. Establish civil equality before law, make all freedoms legal, abolish all discriminations. If the government does its duty, if it begins to act, if it leads the struggle against the old régime to the end, then it will have the confidence of the people.
> Members of the Provisional Government, the proletariat and the army await your orders to consolidate the Revolution and make Russia a democracy.

Immediately after the Revolution, the Mensheviks were divided into several factions. Those who dominated the Soviet Committee were distinctly Zimmerwaldian, in the minority in the Party. The majority changed sides when Tseretelli returned. Those who dominated the party from then on did not want to be confused with the "Social Patriots" of the Yedintsvo group (Plekhanov, Leon Deutsch).

It is hard to appraise the number of Menshevik followers because they called themselves only Social-Democrats, without specifying their leanings. They had distinct organizations in fifteen cities where they were bargaining for unification with the Bolsheviks, but the facts are lacking for defining the Menshevik program in February 1917. Their influence was dwindling in the Caucasus. Elsewhere the traditional image holds true—a feeble network of militants but a large following, since in the soviets on the whole the Mensheviks in league with the S.R.s were in the majority—14 against 3 Bolsheviks in Petrograd, 13 against 3 in Moscow, etc.

The Socialist-Revolutionaries were also elected in large numbers, but in the truly workers' soviets they were less numerous than the Mensheviks. The reverse was true in the soldiers' soviets, and they often had an absolute majority of delegates in the peasants' soviets. However, of the big parties, the Socialist-Revolutionaries were the least organized. To make up a quorum, on March 2 at the Party's Convention, they accepted "anybody." At Tselyabinsk, a city of more than 50,000 inhabitants, there was only one member. Factional quarrels divided them even more than the Social-Democrats. There was nothing in common between Zenzinov, a moderate member of the Bureau, a "Defensist," and a friend of Kerensky, and Alexandrovich, a "Defeatist" and a crony of the Bolsheviks, who was chosen over him at the February 27 elections. At the March 2nd meeting the two clashed violently about the tract against the army officers. The moderates won out and Alexandrovich was roundly abused, but not publicly. From then on Alexandrovich and his friends held themselves aloof. They were impatiently waiting the return of Chernov and Natanson (Bobrov). The majority supported the cabinet "in view of the counter-revolutionary threat," and "as long as it followed the announced program." The motion of the Petrograd group of the S.R. added that it considered the workers' control of the government essential and hailed the appointment to the Ministry of Justice of Kerensky, a defender of the people and of freedom. It added that they must oppose anyone who was against a workers' government. In Moscow the Socialist-Revolutionaries urged the Soviet to put pressure on the government. *Delo Naroda's* first editorial said that it was a serious error to think that the decision to support the government was dictated by purely negative motives, such as the fear of a counter-revolution, inasmuch as the government had promised that it would not use the military situation as an excuse for delaying promised reforms. This nonparticipating conditional support was not accompanied by the usual fraternal salute to Kerensky.

In contrast, the Trudoviks' support was unconditional. In their appeal, they warned against party quarrels and urged solidarity.

Kerensky's party claimed that the government had been formed by the Duma. In this way the Trudoviks opposed the Socialist-Populists, who were delegated to the Soviet in their name and had closer ties to the revolutionary world. The Cooperative Movement was also unanimous in supporting the government. But it soon split. The consumers' cooperatives and the peasants' cooperatives collaborated daily with the authorities; they continued to be a link between the revolutionary masses, the city, and the small village bourgeoisie. The workers' cooperatives, on the contrary, were a branch of the working-class movement. Their leaders accepted class collaboration with bad grace, but they did it for the same reasons as the Mensheviks. However, these workers' cooperatives, the only ones represented at the Soviet, remained neutral in the quarrels between workers' parties, thus incurring the displeasure of the Bolsheviks.

The Trade Unions were weak in Russia and it was through the soviets that the workers' energy was channeled. In a few months, however, a thousand unions were formed. Most of their debates were about whether they were going to act with the parties and which ones—an old story. The railworkers, the spearhead of the movement, moved mostly with the Menshevik Right, the miners and the metalworkers with the Bolsheviks.

Thus, most of the revolutionary organizations leaned toward collaboration with the government, while the workers' opinion was more reserved. There were, however, many militants who had a hostile attitude toward this dual power structure.

The Cadets did not belong in the democratic camp, but nevertheless they took part in its activities. The difference between Cadets, Trudoviks, and Socialist-Populists, who all belonged in the same circles, is sometimes hard to fathom. There was an invisible separation between Trudoviks and Cadets caused by the fact that the Cadets wanted a single power, to be entrusted exclusively to the bourgeoisie. They not only considered the survival of the soviets as a nuisance, but never even admitted that they existed. They did not like the idea of having their leaders as colleagues, as Kerensky said he did. They kept saying that the function of the soviets was to express public opinion, but not to have a share of the power.

The Bolsheviks were of the opposite opinion. Of all the victors, they were the grimmest. This Revolution seemed like everybody's victory, but the workers well knew the deciding role which the soldiers had played. The Bolsheviks had so little influence on the troops that they had the greatest trouble in finding a speaker who could be recognized by them well enough to speak to them. Furthermore, conscious of the weakness of their organization, they tried to strengthen it. It was a task which they found distasteful and dull now that the Tsar had fallen and their rivals and enemies, the Mensheviks, were in control of the Soviet. It was a painful shock to them to find that they were so few. They were even more upset when on the 2nd of March only fifteen delegates voted against the Soviet-Duma agreement. A faction of the Party, prompted by Shutko (from Vyborg), then proposed starting a new uprising of the workers' boroughs, this time against the government; Molotov and Kalinin supported Shutko, as did Shlyapnikov, on condition that it be unarmed. However, on the appointed day, the Bolshevik leader was absent and nothing happened. There was another group who, along with Stuchka, Schmidt, etc., wanted to do it another way. The Bolsheviks passed a resolution showing their distrust of the government, which was "at bottom, counter-revolutionary, and with which no agreement could be reached." The majority succeeded in holding up publication of this motion until March 9th and rejected a bureau motion in favor of a revolutionary government.

All collaboration with the government was out. The Bolshevik Party delegates to the Soviet voted against the formation of a Liaison Commission. The Bolsheviks, mistrusting everyone, could only be brought to cooperate by convincing them that "it was necessary to support the Soviet." Thus in mid-March the Bolsheviks appeared to be ranked against both the government and the Soviet. But inside the party, Shlyapnikov was the mediator between the advocates of violence and the bureau, which was in favor of "Soviet" democratic methods. Viewing the Soviet as the parliament of the working class, this group hoped to gain a majority and then urge "all power to the soviets."

At this time, Kamenev and Stalin arrived in Petrograd. They reinforced the majority and led them somewhat to the right. The party line was publicized, with militants complaining that *Pravda* contained no articles on theory. The majority appeased them by entrusting Kamenev with the job of defining the party line. Neither he nor Stalin needed this in order to pull off a miniature *coup d'état*. On March 14, 1917, in *Pravda*, an editorial by Kamenev outlined in great detail the kind of support which the régime should get. Opposing the Party's Left, he asked, "what purpose would it serve to speed things up, when events were already taking place at such a rapid pace?" According to Kamenev, it was a mistake to act as if the government had to be overthrown because "the important thing was not to seize power, but to know how to keep it." As long as the proletariat was no better organized, such an attitude was wrong.

Stalin saw things in the same way. He showed that "the forces of counter-revolution—not those who aimed for the reestablishment of Tsarism, but those of International Reaction—had not been beaten yet." Systematic opposition was as fruitless as it was inopportune. Kamenev's statements raised a great to-do. Leading the Leftist opposition, Mikhail Olminsky was able to get support from Evgeniya Bosh's report on Lenin's position, as seen through the first *Letter from Afar*. The Petersburg Section even asked for the ouster of Kamenev. But at the Party Conference at the end of March, Stalin's arguments were endorsed. He explained that it was not always a good idea to try to rush things. The Soviet not only controlled the government's actions, it was the prime mover. In any case, the day was coming when dissension would break out between the government and the Soviet. It was necessary to foresee and to prepare for this trial of strength. It would be a blunder to hasten this showdown, because at the moment the government was stronger than it was believed to be. It would be better to give it enough rope to hang itself, which would not take long. Along with B. N. Avilov, who recalled the case of the French proletariat of 1848, who in their impatience resorted to the June insurrection, Stalin and Kamenev thought that premature action would be a serious political error. They prevailed because they kept away from M. K. Muranov, V. D. Bonch-Bruyevich, and Avilov, who came out openly for a war of national defense ("revolutionary defensism"), and also because they had with them those who were anxious about Social-Democratic reunification. At that time the Bolsheviks were somewhat diffident about the question of unity, while the Mensheviks were in favor of it. In fact, there were cities, notably in the Caucasus, where the two factions of Social-Democracy did not even have separate organizations. Many of the militants urged unity of action for all Social-Democrats. There were meetings to this effect in Samara, Novgorod, Smolensk, Kharkov, Tula, Baku, and Tiflis. But in Moscow and Kiev relations quickly became strained, while in Petrograd the idea of a common platform was rejected by the majority of Bolsheviks. They recognized only the "necessity" of reaching an agreement with those Mensheviks who broke with the *Rabochaya Gazeta*, which is surprising since that daily, under the direction of Ermansky, pulled rather to the left on the war question and even went further than Kamenev. Under those circumstances, the negotiations led by Kalinin and Zalevsky led to nothing; they ran aground even before the intervention of Lenin, who was hostile to any unification.

Thus, before Lenin's arrival the party line was lacking in firmness. On one hand, the Kamenev group's success placed the Party far to the right of the center of gravity of the Bolsheviks—even to the right of men such as Sukhanov, Alexandrovich, and Ermansky, who were not Bolsheviks. On the other hand, they would not make an agreement with the Menshevik Internationalists on the pretext that they did not agree about the War—although the Mensheviks had adopted a position neither more nor less "Internationalist" than that of the Bolshevik leadership.

The core felt all the more frustrated since, on its left, the Anarchists could appear as the only unconditional enemies of the régime. The "patriotic" tendencies of Kropotkin's friends only had a small following, most of the militants having approved the Internationalist theses expressed in Petrograd's *Rabocheye Znamenya* and Ukraine's *Nabat*. On March 7th they hailed the Soviet, expressing a wish for representation of their group. They were answered that the question had already been settled in their favor. Sticking with the side of the democratic revolutionaries, they exhorted them to continue the struggle because "to acquire political freedom was one thing, but true freedom was another." "In order to keep from falling under the capitalist yoke, it was essential that the land immediately belong to the peasants and the means of production to the workers." They would thus build a new life, where there would be neither oppressors nor oppressed, neither rich nor poor. To achieve this end, the Anarchists on March 23rd in a pamphlet, from *Rabocheye Znamenya*, demanded the immediate institution of a new form of government and the establishment of communes, as the only way to secure an effective victory over the bourgeoisie. They also demanded that the Revolution decree immediately an end of the war and the destruction of the capitalist order. Only a revolution of this nature would have such a contagiously powerful effect that it could become worldwide. (See text in Appendix.)

At the end of March 1917 only the Anarchists and the Bolshevik minority clearly expressed their position with respect to the government which resulted from the February Revolution. Un-heard in the Soviet, these men had a large following among the masses, and the first actions of the government would cause it to grow even larger.

THE FUNCTIONING OF THE REGIME:
Theory and Fact

The format of the Dual Power was set by the Convention of Soviets at the end of March. Somewhat aggressively, Steklov explained how the régime had been born. Tseretelli made a point: "The Dual Power formula was not fortuitous. The Soviet had chosen to get along with the bourgeoisie. The proletariat had to base its policies on a solid foundation which it would be able to maintain, and not on anything which would be ephemeral. As long as there was a program which united the enormous majority of the working class and the Revolutionary Army, as long as the leaders of the bourgeoisie hadn't deviated from this program, no one was able to say that we were aiming to overthrow the government."

In reality, Tseretelli and most of the Soviet leaders misjudged the mood and the hopes of the warring classes. The Soviet leaders were not yet well enough organized, so that a trial of strength seemed like it would prove fatal in a short time, and on another level than a conflict between forces. In concluding the March 2 agreement, the Soviet and government leaders were only thinking of the contest between them—the Soviet hoping to win out by means of public support, the government by a return to normalcy which would bring back the old habits of obedience to the State and the ruling classes. This was to ignore the phenomenal revolutionary drive which in a few hours had put an end to three centuries of autocracy. Each political party, every political opinion, every ethnic and religious group intended to take over Russia's future and there wasn't a single Russian who didn't have in his pocket a plan ready to reform the country. In these circumstances, the government and the Soviet itself could issue proclamations or pass laws as they wished; they were heeded only insofar as they did not contradict one's own pet project.

Whole parts of the state thus escaped from the authority of the center. In Kiev from the beginning of March, a *Rada* was formed which very soon was acting independently. In turn, several of the various national communities organized themselves and began to pass laws, although they did not necessarily adopt a hostile attitude toward the central power; in the army separate national regiments were formed (Letts, Poles, etc.), even before the question had been considered by the responsible "authorities" (military leaders, government officials, native political figures, etc.). Elsewhere, real autonomous republics were formed, or communes, as at Schlusselburg and Kronstadt, which administered their affairs independently. The *Vossiche Zeitung* counted thirty-six of them which sprang up like mushrooms. But the authority within these new political bodies was splitting up. In Kronstadt there was at first a Movement Committee, and, parallel with it, a Sailors' Committee; then a Workers' Committee was formed for the Port of Kronstadt, then a Soviet of Sailors of the Fortress, and a super-committee which united these last two bodies. Each one acted separately and had substituted itself for the provisional committee which was formed in the first days of the Revolution.

The very foundations of state authority were foundering. This was not a question of anarchy or anarchism, because they derided the state's authority only to place it on fairer foundations or to reinforce it. But at the moment, they judged that it was necessary first to rebel. One day a peasants' assembly decided not to pay the taxes; the next day a factory committee formed a protective militia, or some soldiers refused to take down a barricade as ordered. Peshekhonov, the Soviet commissar in Petersburg, has described how everyone determined to act, decide, and govern on his own—but always in the public interest:

The commissariat, hearing of the existence of a food depot being held by Tsarist authorities, sent two guards. Twenty-four hours later, a big crowd was questioning the sentries. On learning what the matter was, they broke in, looted the depot, loaded the provisions onto trucks they had forcibly requisitioned, and triumphantly brought everything to my commissariat.

2. THE BEGINNINGS OF THE NEW RÉGIME

ITS FIRST ACT

There was a danger that disorders would break out. The Soviet feared this above everything else, but the members of the government were not alarmed, for public opinion would blame the soviets.

In order to set up a true democratic régime, the government appointed special commissions for each project: the organization of the Constituent Assembly, the reform of the administration and the governing institutions, etc. It was turning Russia's future over to Cabinet men, while the future of the Revolution was being decided in the streets. Meanwhile the government issued proclamation after proclamation announcing the abolition of the old political and judicial order. Only Kerensky acted competently. He made a public account of his accomplishments in the Ministry of Justice —the removal of high magistrates, the formation of temporary Courts of Justice, the abolition of the death penalty, etc. But all these measures could only confirm the triumph of the Revolution, and it took Nabokov a long time to work out the amnesty law. Eight days after the fall of the Tsar they were still waiting for it, while everyone wondered why Milyukov had not ordered his lawyers to issue return visas for the *émigrés*.

There were other reasons for grumbling. High officials who had been removed could now be found as "government commissioners." The minister received the representatives of commerce and industry, but the trade unions were not invited. They launched a "Liberty Loan" with great fanfare, but made no social laws, leaving the workers to bargain with management. On the other hand, the government undertook a complete overhaul of its administration, which interested no one. For that, they did not have to wait for the formation of the Constituent, although every time the Soviet proposed a reform, they took refuge in democratic principles, recalling its inabiility to legislate. The national minorities learned this at their expense; and the same was the case with the peasants. They wanted to see the crown lands redistributed. The government had already decided to nationalize them, but it forbade seizure and, after March 9, it took steps to thwart a peasant movement in the Kazan Region. It formed "land committees" whose function it was to carry out the law. But the law was not passed and the government statement indicated that the agrarian question would not be settled soon.

The country had come to a stop for eight days. Already people were queueing up and prices rose again. Price controls set by the Food Commission applied only to bread, meat, milk, and butter. Would it be applied elsewhere than in the capital, if there were shortages? The Government hoped for an end of strikes and the resumption of normal activities, and the majority of the Executive Committee of the Soviet felt the same way. On March 5th Chkheidze made a report along that line, and Pumiansky supported it in the name of the Moscow Soviet. But the workers would not listen; one after the other, the delegates demanded guarantees;

otherwise returning to work amounted to saying that the Revolution was complete, whereas it had hardly begun. The bureau began to feel ill at ease and waver when a soldier expressed his disapproval. The soldiers were in the trenches and the workers should return to work. The military came to support this point of view. The vote, when two fifths of those present were workers, was 1,170 to 30 in favor of returning to work. With this unexpected turn, the bureau had prevailed—thanks to the pressure of the soldiers. Suddenly a specter took shape—was the shadow of the gray coats to rule over the Revolution?

The workers reacted in their own way. In Vyborg, they prepared a demonstration against the Soviet decision. They decided that it was null and void as long as they did not have the eight-hour day, a pay raise, etc. In effect, strikes continued to paralyze about ten firms. On March 8th *Rabochaya Gazeta* launched an appeal to the strikers, claiming that they were discrediting the Soviet by not obeying it. On the 10th the Menshevik newspaper recalled the lessons of 1905: not to rush things, to get well organized before making any demands. On the 14th the Soviet Propaganda Commission launched a new appeal in *Izvestya*, aimed this time at the streetcar workers and transportation workers. But on the 25th the coachmen and truckers still were not working. Before breaking the ice, now fifteen days old, they demanded the nationalization of the transportation industry. "Don't wait till Monday to go back to work," implored the Soviet. It promised to intervene if the heads of firms made no concessions. On the 21st, in the workers' section of the Soviet, Bogdanov noted that the return to work was going badly and that it would probably stay that way if working conditions did not improve. The Soviet then undertook to negotiate with management in the capital. Casting caution to the wind, management accepted the eight-hour day, the formation of factory committees, and grievance committees. Identical agreements were reached at Saratov and in other provincial cities, but for a long time Petrograd was the most progressive. For the Soviet this was an undeniable success. But, in the light of the February events, it looked to the workers like a natural development, certainly not a "victory" inasmuch as this agreement only ratified an accomplished fact. The working classes returned to work only piecemeal, faster in the large factories than in the small ones where the bosses made concessions with ill grace.

The first priority for the new régime was solution of the food problem. According to Shingarev, Minister of Agriculture, there were only two days' food left in reserve in Petrograd and Moscow, which was less than the army had. The price spiral had resumed and Grohman, at the Soviet, was worried about it. According to him, the only way to lower prices was by regulating the economy at the top. The project needed adjustment and, in the meantime, Grohman urged the formation of "state monopolies" in the prime necessities of life. The Soviet endorsed this point of view. Prokopovich, an economist, thought these monopolies desirable, but was of the opinion that only a strong government could swing the deal. But in the government Shingarev opposed the idea. Under pressure from the Soviet, the cooperative movement, the trade unions, etc., a decision was made on this principle affecting wheat. Immediately the banks, who held a large amount of the grain in normal times, became alarmed. On March 19 the first Pan-Russian Convention of Commerce and Industry warned the government that the formation of a wheat monopoly was setting a precedent that would be "the death sentence of the wheat industry." Under pressure of public opinion the government ignored them, but reassured them by affirming that this was only a wartime measure and by raising the price of wheat sixty percent. The law of March 25, 1917, foresaw the creation of local committees at the different levels of government—*uezd, volost,* and municipality. They were given the power to control the distribution of grain and to determine the amounts to be delivered according to the statements of the producers and the needs of the population. The appendix to the law, which set the manner of nomination of the committees, is a fairly good example of the decrees which the Provisional Government used in its anxiety to ensure representation for all Russian social bodies in the democratic bodies born of the Revolution. In this way it could avoid doing business with the Soviet only.

The local food committees will administer food supplies and the organization of agricultural production in accordance with instructions from the Minister of Agriculture, President of the State Food Committee.

Article 2. The local Committees will be made up as follows:

—Three delegates elected from the district *zemstvo* assembly.

—Three delegates elected from the municipal Duma of the district capital.

—One from the local section of the Pan-Russian Union of *Zemstvos.*

—One from the local section of the Pan-Russian Union of Cities.

—One from the local section of the War Industries Committee.

—Five from the local Soviet of Workers or, if there is none, from the hospital or trade union.

—Five from the local peasants' union.

—Six from the local cooperatives (if possible, two from each type of cooperative).

—Two from the local "agricultural association."

—Three from commercial organizations or other bartering organizations.

—One statistical representative from each organization (*zemstvo* and municipality) and one from the agricultural, economic, or public health bodies where these exist.

Articles 3 and 4, which followed, outlined the method of election and the composition of other bodies with more limited powers (*volost* committees, etc.).

Soon after, a law protecting the harvests would guarantee the state against the large landowner's refusing to sow wheat at the prices set by the government. On April 11 the committees were empowered to use the unseeded lands, on condition that they would pay the owners a rent equal to the value of the crop. These measures were accompanied by an appeal from *Izvestya* to the peasants inviting them to produce and work for the good of the Revolution and warning them against the machinations of the *pomeshchiki*. These measures, passed willy-nilly by Shingarev, unquestionably were a success for the new régime and more especially for the Petrograd Soviet. But would they be carried out? At this time they were less concerned about that than the behavior of the soldiers, who were the masters of the situation in the streets.

THE STRUGGLE FOR THE ARMY

In contrast with the *grande bourgeoisie*, the high command had not played the game of rallying to the Revolution. As a result it immediately lost the confidence of the troops and all danger of counter-revolution was apparently averted for the moment. But the government did not know how to rally the soldiers either. It took no spectacular action to reform the army and let it be known that it had no interest in a "revolutionary" army, even if it succeeded in saving the country from invasion. Could it be said that it preferred the return to military tradition over a victory which would put it at the mercy of a reformed army? Or did it believe such a reform impossible in time of war?

The Soviet position was even more precarious. With no hold on the army, it feared that the general staff and the government would take charge. This fear caused it to accede to the troops' demands. But the Committee had so little confidence in the "most counter-revolutionary element of the Revolution" that it looked to the government to keep the army in line. What they dreamed of, really, was that, recovering its cohesion, the army would fight the external enemy, while in the rear the Soviet would take care of the internal enemies and impose its policies on the government.

The "struggle for the army" was a drama in several acts. At the beginning of March, the high command lost the first round. But it retained its functions and was not knocked out. The government and the Soviet fought over its legacy. Who was going to win? On March 1st the Soviet had disclaimed originating General Order Number One. If in the end it assumed the responsibility, it did so reluctantly, not wanting to be blamed for the disorganization of the army by those at the front. Sokolov, presumed author of the General Order, did not brag about it, and Kerensky spoke of "provocation." Shlyapnikov claimed he saw the Anarchist Linde draft the famous text, for which the Bolsheviks never claimed paternity. The next day, Sukhanov wrested from Molotov a package of tracts calling on the soldiers to massacre the officers. Did these libels come from the S.R.-Unitarian Left, or from the Germans in Finland? Whatever it was, the Soviet drafted an appeal to the soldiers for moderation. On the 5th it sent another appeal for cordial relations. In its turn the Moscow Soviet also urged the soldiers not to be too harsh with the officers, even those who had shown hostility toward the people.

As for the government's proclamations, they were countless, but unsuccessful as far as bringing the soldiers in line was concerned. It was then that the officers who had rallied to the Revolution and formed a Union of Republican Officers came to the Soviet with their complaints. The army had become disorganized because the soldiers, misinterpreting General Order Number One, removed some officers and promoted others. Worried about the respectability of the Revolution, the Soviet gave its opinion. It drafted General Order Number Two, which recalled that "the objective of the elections was to designate representatives of the political interests of the army, not the choice of its officers. The delegates' rights were limited to objecting to certain nominations."

This order reaffirmed the other sections of General Order Number One, but it was too late, for the damage had been done. Both Guchkov and the army realized it. The government immediately jumped into the fray. It had tracts published which condemned the authors of General Orders One and Two. "Breaking the oath of allegiance to the Old Régime was unavoidable," they explained to the soldiers, "but the government had been elected by the Duma Committee and then recognized by the Soviet. Therefore they should obey this legally constituted Government." Recognizing the justness of the argument, the Soviet asked Guchkov to endorse the two General Orders. "I'd sooner resign!" replied the minister. He made the point that the drafting of the first General Order had preceded the agreement between the Soviet and the government, and that it was therefore invalid. Not daring to break off relations, the Soviet delegates accepted a compromise: the government and the Soviet would sign a joint appeal which would recognize the validity of General Order Number Two, but only in Petrograd. That was the price asked for its validation. There was no longer any question about General Order Number One. The military section of the Soviet immediately protested against the contents of this "*vozzvanie.*" Sokolov tried to explain that this really was not an amputation but a consolidation, since this "*vozzvanie*" gave legality to the soldiers' decisions. Besides, Guchkov was going to institute other reforms. His embarrassed explanations convinced no one.

As for reforms, Guchkov was able to draw up only Orders 114 and 115 in eight days, while it took him only twenty-four hours to grant special privileges to the Cossacks. Order 114 reminded the officers about the courtesies to be used with the soldiers, nothing more. Order 115 sent the task of working out the details of a reform back to a commission. For the soldiers this was too much. On March 9th the Military Commission of the Soviet caused a Plenary Session of the Assembly to adopt a resolution on the rights of the soldier. It listed his civil and political rights, notably his right of assembly and his right to refuse to partake in religious services. Then the resolution abolished all servile functions which did not serve a useful purpose as far as military efficiency was concerned—i.e., the salute, the use of familiar form of address, the function of orderlies, etc. Relations between soldiers and officers were minutely spelled out. An end was put to corporal punishments, the enumeration of which painted the painful lot of the soldier of the Tsarist army. Loss of rank would be the punishment for those who persisted in the use of corporal punishment. There was nothing revolutionary about this motion, which made no modifications in the structure of the army and said not a word about the nomination of officers. The whole ancient structure remained intact and the only thing which was abolished was the practices which impinged on the dignity of the soldiers.

Guchkov's little action upset the high command, who were thus being dispossessed of their power of lording it over the army.* One can imagine the reactions of the General Staff when it learned of the declarations of the rights of the soldier. It saw red, especially when it learned about the abolition of the military salute. The Ministry of War nevertheless asked Alexeiev to look this regulation over. After all, it had been drafted with the help of a high ranking officer, General Polivanov. Alexeiev refused to have anything to do with it and adjourned the meeting.

The Soviet finally seized this opportunity to regain some of its popularity. In its name *Isvestya* published several articles which were virulently opposed to the Stavka, "the core of the counter-revolution." Then the committee objected to the wording of the new oath which was being required of the military. Was the idea of an oath legitimate? "It was up to the government to make an oath of allegiance to the soldiers," proclaimed a provincial soviet. The Government had to withdraw the oath.

The Soviet and the troops were being drawn closer together, but the ruling classes found a way to draw them apart. A newspaper campaign suddenly announced the imminence of a German offensive. Russia and the Revolution were in danger. The front was demanding reinforcements from Petrograd. "That's not up to me, but to the Soviet," answered Guchkov. This put the Revolution in a delicate position. If the Soviet accepted the stripping of the garrison of the city it ran the risk of turning it over to a "new *Yuan Shih-kai*."** If it refused, the High Command would use it to turn the front-line soldiers, already furious that General Order Number Two was only applicable in Petrograd, against the rear echelon and the civilians. Fearing the worst, the Soviet authorized the High Command to remove some units from the capital, thus losing immediately the little esteem which it had regained. In the

---

*The Navy on the other hand had been democratized by the admirals, who had numerous projects for reorganizing it. Under the aegis of Admiral Koltchak, the Military Committee of Sebastopol drew up a set of laws (regulations) which were published in Isvestya on March 28, 1917.)

**Yuan Shih-kai, Chinese statesman who proclaimed the Republic in China (1913). President of the Republic, he attempted unsuccessfully to have himself proclaimed Emperor.

committee, no one objected, not even the Bolsheviks. They planned the formation of armed groups to take over the defense of the Revolution (the Red Guard) and the departure of the soldiers suited them well enough.

The German attack against Stokhod finally amounted to very little, and the Soviet realized that they had fallen into a trap. Their opponents had been clever enough to congratulate them on the breach of the March 2 agreement, which provided for the maintenance in the capital of the soldiers whose actions had contributed to the fall of Tsarism. In order not to fall into the same trap again, the Soviet decided to establish closer contacts with the front-line soldiers. On March 19th it appointed army commissars, whom it charged with the duty of bringing to the fighting men the greetings of the Revolution.

The counter-revolutionary propaganda was beginning to bear fruit. In the cities, groups of armed soldiers were watching the factories to see that the workers did their job. There were several incidents. This was what the Soviet was afraid of. Were the patriotic appeals going to swing the army into the counter-revolutionary camp? And would the soldiers of the capital think that they would be doing their duty to their country by keeping an eye on the workers?

The Soviet leaders saw the danger. But they did not know what to do as long as the question of the war was not openly brought up. They didn't dare; it was the government which took the initiative.

THE PROBLEM OF THE WAR

Milyukov had not been able to save Tsarism, but at least he wanted to continue the war. He thought that the government would be able to tie the new régime firmly to the Western Democracies and to solidify the social bonds menaced by the February explosion. In pursuing the war to the exhaustion of the enemy—which might also be the exhaustion of the Revolution—he would bring Constantinople as a trophy to the new Russia. In the meantime, by brandishing the danger of Germany, he hoped to divide the victors of February and to incite the army against the workers.

On March 4th Milyukov sent a note to the Russian diplomats abroad, in which the government announced its determination "to strictly observe the international obligations contracted by the Old Régime and its will to fight the war to a victorious end." Reaffirming Russia's ties to its allies, he said he was convinced "that the exaltation which now moved the whole nation would increase its strength and would bring the final triumph of the rejuvenated Russia and its glorious allies that much closer." A circular asked the Russian diplomats to require that the Western chancelleries would state in their answer that they would respect the agreements reached with the former government.

The war aims of Revolutionary Russia thus differed in no way from those of Tsarist Russia, except on one point: Milyukov proposed the creation of an international organization, after the war, which would guarantee peace between all nations—a literary flourish which deceived no one.

Kerensky thought this attitude was dangerous for the government. The Russia of Santa Sophia was dead, and its war aims had died with it. Russia had to be spoken to in a new language. This was not to say that Russia's rights should be ignored in the last; it was just that later, after victory, Russia would be prompted by different feelings. "Meanwhile, say whatever you want, but puff up the soldiers," Guchkov confided to him. Thus Kerensky, in an interview with the *Daily Chronicle*, came out in favor of "internationalizing the Straits." Milyukov protested that Kerensky was only expressing personal views, but the damage was done.

On the democratic side, they well knew that the future of the Revolution depended on the outcome of the war. The fall of Tsarism had changed the nature of the conflict; national defense no longer had the same meaning. Ignoring public opinion, the party leaders tried to avoid this issue. Everyone knew how important it was, but no one dared to take a stand or even to publicize its doubts. Thus at the Menshevik committee meeting on March 6th the Mensheviks took a stand on the war. The *Rabochaya Gazeta* gave this information, but did not say what the position was. On the 8th, it insisted that the cost of war was "unbearable for all the governments concerned, and for poor Russia in particular." The Menshevik Internationalist organ carefully made its feelings known, devoting an editorial each day to one of the various aspects of the conflict. On the 11th, when the bourgeois press announced a coming German attack, the *Rabochaya Gazeta* came out more frankly: "Defend Petrograd, yes; Conquer Tsarigrad [i.e., Constantinople], no." Public opinion would not have accepted a campaign against the war. Thus the Internationalists refused to adopt the Moscow Bolshevik slogan, "In the actual circumstances, the first thing is: Down with the War!" Negotiations toward unity on this question were broken off.

Beside the Bolshevik Left which had decided to make public the struggle against the war, the bureau, more wary, recommended only the transformation of the imperialist war into civil war, asking the proletariat of all countries at war to establish alliances for the immediate cessation of hostilities. But they put this slogan in a little corner of page 3 of *Pravda*. On the 14th, Kamenev took a position opposing that of the Moscow comrades. "Neither disorganization, nor the empty slogan 'Down with War' are worthy passwords," he wrote. On the same day Stalin sent out an appeal for military discipline. The Stockhod alert cast doubt on the peaceful intentions of the German soldiers and the patriotic reawakening which it had elicited showed that the time for defeatist proposals was not yet ripe.

They always came up against the same problems: Had the nature of the war been changed since Tsarism fell? What was the best position for the Revolution—to play it the bourgeois way and fight the war, or to conclude peace, which might bring about a counter-revolution? "We must shout for world peace and not just for peace," urged the Executive Committee of the Moscow Soviet." "War for Freedom" and not "War to Victory" exhorted *Isvestya*. Only rarely did anyone dare to speak of a separate peace, as the Soviet of Ivanovo and a group of soldiers of Kharkov had done; and even here, the former were speaking to the German proletariat and the latter left the responsibility on this matter up to the Constituent.

Uncertainty was widespread, but the Soviet had to take a position now that the government had taken its stand. No one was more aware of these difficulties than Sukhanov. Like Chkheidze, he was haunted by the sight of the troops who daily came to the Soviet, every one of them, with patriotic fervor and in homage to the Revolution, offering him his medals, weeping.

At the very least they would have to draw up a manifesto. Sukhanov called on Gorky, but Gorky, like Romain Rolland, was "too far above the crowd." His text was considered too literary and the Soviet preferred something more political. Without deferring to "democratic tendencies," this appeal declared that "the time has come to make a decisive stand against the acquisitive ambitions of all governments; the time has also come for the people to settle the problem of peace or war." This formula, *Isvestya* reminded its readers, aimed as much at the allies as at the Central Powers. Further, it was a sop to the holders of the "Revolutionary Defensist" position. "We will fight for our liberty," added the manifesto, "against reaction, whether internal or external. The Russian Revolution will not yield to the conquerors' bayonets and will not be defeated by foreign military might." There was a great debate at the Soviet. Steklov made the presentation, which was approved by the Mensheviks Chkheidze and A. T. Chenkely. The Bolshevik delegate Muranov, back from exile, also approved the wording, which met no opposition.

The bourgeoisie retained only the second half of the March 14th appeal, playing upon the commentary Chkheidze made on it the next day. "To you Germans we say: Before speaking of peace, do as we did—overthrow Kaiser Wilhelm." He had improvised this formula in the face of the intervention of the officers and men, who, on the 14th, had thought the appeal would have a bad effect on the morale of the armed forces. The Western press repeated Chkheidze's comment endlessly, which had the effect of dulling the March 14th appeal, as *Isvestya* pointed out on the 18th. *Isvestya* also harped on another point of the Internationalist propaganda—the evils of secret diplomacy. In Russia the March 14th appeal created a stir because of its first half. "It is the Revolution which must be carried to a glorious end," commented the Novo-Nicholayevsk Soviet; the soviets of Nizhni-Novgorod and Riazan called for "the peoples' peace" which would settle things at a "Socialist International Congress." *Isvestya* published an article, "A Second German Swallow." The first had been a "Salute" of the German workers to the February Revolution; the second was the refusal of the Social-Democrats in the Reichstag to vote for the extra appropriation for the war. The democrats, however, still did not have a definite policy; they only knew that they could not go beyond certain limits. When Alexandra Kollontay shouted "Down with the War," she was booed.

Back from Siberia, Irakly Tseretelli, the Menshevik leader, saw immediately that these vacillations were a mortal danger for the Revolution. He had the courage to outline a clear policy which one could either approve or reject:

> The two main questions—that of power and that of the revolution—had already been answered by the Right and the Left. The bourgeoisie said: recognition of our dominance and of our war slogans is problem number one of the Revolution. The Left said: dictatorship of the proletariat and cessation of war for the adoption of revolutionary reforms at home. The first ignored the problems of the Revolution, the second its possibilities. Both led to civil war.

Tseretelli thought, in effect, that the Internationalists were substituting meaningless dogma for the struggle for a program, since they opposed the government without trying to overthrow it, while their catchphrases no more had as their aim fighting the government than opposing it with an alternative policy. His idea was to tie "Revolutionary Defensism" to the struggle for peace. He revealed his position at the March 21 session. The reporter Sukhanov had presented a motion based more on the struggle for peace than on the defense of the Revolution. Tseretelli disagreed. Everything looked as though the Soviet were entrusting the government with the defense of the country, in exchange for which they were forcing it to make peace. According to him, they must at the same time carry on the war, fight for peace, proclaim both sides of this policy, and carry them both out. By urging the Soviet to take immediate action with the government, Tseretelli gave the impression of wanting to have more of a real impact on events than the Internationalists, who were content to merely criticize the leadership or give it advice. He thus outflanked the Internationalist and Bolshevik Left, and won over Lieber and Steklov, who added their voices to those of Chkheidze, Skobelev, etc., and those of the Soviet's Right (Bramson, Tchaikovsky, etc.). Then he convinced his opponents by going a little to the left of the motion adopted that morning. For the Left-Right antagonism, he substituted a dynamic "centrism." On the same day (March 21) the Soviet asked to establish relations with the government.

Milyukov understood the importance of the struggle which was beginning and wanted to consolidate his project before people realized what he was trying to do. Simultaneously in *Rech* and the *New York Times*, he criticized the "peace without annexation or indemnities" formula which some revolutionary organizations were stammering; it was, he said, tied up with German propaganda. "Could the liberation of nationalities of the Turkish or Hapsburg Empires be considered as annexation?" naively asked the Foreign Minister. Without batting an eye, the advocate of the Czechs and Arabs demanded that all the Armenians and Ukrainians be placed under the protection of the Russians, their liberators. As for the acquisition of Constantinople, it could not be considered annexation since it had no bearing on the interests of the Turks, who in spite of five centuries of occupation had never taken roots on the shores of the Bosporus, their presence resting exclusively on the right of conquest, the right of the strongest. The same thing was found in the *New York Times*. However, in the American newspaper, rather than the unification of the Rumanians, Milyukov proposed their "amalgamation in our Ukraine." The democratic press reacted violently.

It was under these conditions that the government received, in the presence of the Duma Committee, the members of the Liaison Commission, who demanded the publication of a note which would define the war aims of the new régime. Milyukov was firmly opposed to this idea, claiming that such a note would be ill-received by the allied governments. But, Skobelev wondered, hadn't Milyukov formerly maintained that it was the territorial demands of Tsarist Russia which had estranged the allies? Guchkov and Shingarev wanted to know if the Soviet would undertake to improve the morale of the soldiers in case the government acquiesced to these demands. "Certainly," the members of the Liaison Commission answered unanimously. Put in the minority, Milyukov had to accede. He held out for making this note in the form of an appeal to the Russian citizenry, which would not imply any demands on the allied governments. With some haggling, the Soviet was able to insert a paragraph which outlined the democrats' program.

> The aim of free Russia is not the domination of other people, or the conquest of their national territories, nor the occupation by force of foreign lands, but the establishment of an enduring peace based on the people's right of self determination. Russia has no desire either to subjugate or to humiliate anyone.

Furthermore, Milyukov twice indicated that Russia "would keep her obligations to her allies" and that "the solution of all problems would be made in conjunction with them"—which considerably changed the meaning of the appeal. As the passage considered essential by the Soviet was surrounded by all sorts of considerations and not at all emphasized in the final draft, the Soviet got the impression that it had been duped. In effect, Milyukov was trying to sneak by. But his hidden thoughts were clear since he immediately sent a secret message to all the Russian ambassadors denying that Russia had renounced her agreements about Constantinople. The bourgeois press played along and claimed to be able to hear the sound of a new Russia in the appeal. The Menshevik and S.R. journals also thought themselves clever in singing about this beautiful success. "A Pyrrhic victory," was the verdict of Sukhanov, who saw all the more clearly and bitterly because his motion had been rejected and he felt a personal resentment.

At the Soviet Congress, the Executive Committee declared the appeal to be a success. The agreement was ratified and Tseretelli's motion won out over that of Kamenev-Kamkov by a vote of 325 to 57 with 20 abstentions. The text reflected the dichotomy to which the majority had subscribed—the struggle for peace and the defense of the Revolution. Insisting on Russia's renunciation of annexations, it called to the people to do as the Soviet had done, to bring pressure on their governments to repudiate all ideas of conquest. If they succeeded peace could not be far away. Meanwhile, respecting the agreement with the government, the Soviet Congress indicated in the motion the necessity "of preserving the combat effectiveness of the army."

PUBLIC OPINION AND THE NEW RÉGIME

At the Soviet Congress seventy-seven votes did not support the bureau's motion. Tseretelli judged that the opposition to the war was due more to weariness than to any internationalist stand. That may have been, but it should be noted that the patriotic demonstrations became rarer and those demanding peace without annexations multiplied. The opposition to war was not as passive as Tseretelli thought, but he was not the only one who misjudged public reaction.

This lag of the militants behind public opinion is found in other areas as well. Already on March 2, the crowd's distrust of the new government was more pronounced than that of the Soviet, where a Right neutralized the already vacillating majority. On March 6th the gap between the policies of the dual power and the ideas of the workers showed up more clearly. In spite of the Soviet's appeals, the workers did not return to work. At the same time a large part of the soldiers of the capital were too busy promulgating the "rights of the soldiers" to worry about the government or the Soviet. In the peace campaign, the initiative did not come from the leading organizations—except for two or three minority notes from the Bolsheviks or Anarchists—but from the workers of the capital and the provinces.

On the question of power the cleavage between the régime and one part of public opinion was becoming complete. "Nothing could be more wrong than to think that in March the two powers were taking opposing stands," wrote Kerensky ten years later. He was right, as was Tseretelli, who thought, at the beginning of

April, that they had never been so close. In truth, a large part of the workers, soldiers, and peasants had already veered away from both the government *and* the Soviet.

What was true in the capital was also true in the countryside. In this respect, the inquiry launched by the "Soviet Regional Bureau" and by the "Provincial Section of the Moscow Soviet" is significant. (See the questionnaire in the Appendix.) The text of the questionnaire shows what interested the Soviet leaders. They wanted to know the representativeness of the locally elected bodies, the relative strength of the different political factions, and the degree of alignment with the policies of the Petrograd Soviet. But there was no question about what interested the workers, or of their demands clamored at all the meetings. Worse still, in asking these soviets to what degree they collaborated with these state bodies, the inquiry seemed to assume class collaboration *a priori*. This was done by most of the Executive Committees, but the motions coming from the "grass-roots" clearly expressed the workers' hostility to such a policy of conciliation. The Soviet leaders had no regard for the will of their constituents; good or bad, their motives were no longer those of the workers. In the structure of the militant republic, the opposition only had fifty-seven votes (and twenty absentions) against a majority of 325. This was not insignificant, for these fifty-seven votes represented more than they seemed to. In periods of crisis it is not necessarily the militants who show themselves to be the most dedicated revolutionaries.

★

CHAPTER SEVEN

THE APRIL CRISIS

1. EUROPE AND THE RUSSIAN REVOLUTION

After the first few days of consternation, Europe wondered about the meaning of the Russian Revolution and the influence it would have on the outcome of the war. No one thought that on the morrow Russia would attempt the first Socialist experiment in history, and that on the day after tomorrow Moscow would become the capital of the Third International.

In Berlin and Vienna there were a few who claimed that the Russian Revolution was a "war-crisis." By taking power, the bourgeoisie was going to lead Russia to "a war to the finish" *(Köln Volkszeitung)*. For those who, the day before, had hoped to conclude peace with Tsarist Russia, the news was bitter. "From here on Russia is a puppet of the British Empire, and February was an English revolution on Russian soil," wrote the *Kölnishche Zeitung*. The *Neues Wiener Journal* and other Viennese dailies took similar positions. The actions of the high command and the government proved that in Berlin and Vienna they were aware of this interpretation of events. The number of German divisions facing the Russians remained the same in April 1917, rose from 72 to 75 in May, and to 78 in June. At this time 48 percent of the Austrian troops and 38 percent of the German troops were marshaled against the Russians.

However, little by little another interpretation came to prevail. Along with the Socialist Left, many believed that "the Russian people, famished and war-weary, were on the point of rising up to demand bread, liberty, and peace, when the Russian liberals in favor of the war rallied to the movement to lead it and exploit it with a view to continuing the war." The Declaration of March 14/27, 1917,* gave weight to this interpretation. In order to exploit the will for peace, the Austro-German general staff refrained from launching a major offensive against Petrograd. It would have catalyzed the patriotic feeling, whereas inactivity would allow disintegration to do its work. Further, the German

---

*Until February 1918 Russia used the Julian calendar, which differed from the calendar in use in Western Europe by thirteen days. Heretofore all dates have been given according to the Julian calendar then in use in Russia. With events involving Western Europeans, however, it has been thought best to use a double notation to avoid any possibility of ambiguity. Thus the notation March 14/27 means March 14 by Russian reckoning and March 27 by the Western European calendar.—Trans.

government aided in every possible way the Russian pacifists who
wanted to return to Russia from Switzerland. Lenin, Martov, and
their Zimmerwaldian friends obtained transit visas in record time—
thirteen days—thanks to the intervention of Bethmann-Hollweg,
the German Prime Minister. At the same time the German Social-
Democrat Scheidenmann and Count Czernin entered publicly in
communication as a result of the March 14 appeal. In April Count
Reventlow hailed the Revolution, and Vienna proposed that the
Provisional Government set up an International Conference on
Peace. But the Russians did not answer these offers any more than
they attached importance to the feelers which the Wilhelmstrasse
sent out to Stockholm and Copenhagen, and to the Bulgarian
address of Maxim Gorky.

Elsewhere, the German government gave *carte blanche* to the
Socialist leaders to talk with the Russian masses. It made use of
the services of "Parvus" (A. L. Helphand), who was formerly
connected with the left wing of the Russian Social-Democrats, but
had now become a Social-Patriot. The German socialists spoke
with the Danish socialist F. Borgberg, who undertook the preliminary steps. Arriving in Petrograd in the middle of April, Borgberg
tried to organize, in the name of the Danish Socialists, an international socialist conference. He gave the Russians the German
Socialists' conditions for peace and explained that the German
general staff remained quiescent on the Russian Front in order to
spare the new régime and to help the pacifist movement. He thus
alienated the "Defensists" as well as the Zimmerwaldians, and
from then on the Soviet showed themselves little disposed to talk
with these groups. Nevertheless, the program of the German socialists was in some respects unacceptable inasmuch as it was concerned only with the "liberation of the Russian part of Poland"
and did not contemplate breaking the *"Burgfriede."* Otherwise,
the Soviet deemed the Danish proposal acceptable. However, they
thought it had a better chance of success if it came from Borgberg.
Thus the Borgberg trip set the stage for the Stockholm Conference.

The negotiations undertaken by the German and Austrian governments were not pressed very far, however, because in the spring
of 1917 the military situation was favorable to the Central Powers.
The Nivelle offensive had been reduced to nothing and the submarine campaign had been a marked success. Further, the failure
of the Sixte-Bourbon negotiations forced Charles I to move cautiously. No doubt, internally, the Revolutionary strikes were at-

tributable to the Russian Revolution, which, Rosa Luxemburg had claimed in March, was "entirely the business of the international proletariat." Would the Revolution sweep all over Europe and hasten the end of the war? At the moment the German high command was not afraid of this. Thus they allowed the Socialists to "play at peace," on the chance that this might help them on the Russian side. These feelers familiarized Russian opinion with the idea of an imminent peace. At least they had the effect of dividing the revolutionists and weakening Russia.

According to the newspapers, the Revolution was acclaimed in Paris, London, and Rome with a burst of enthusiasm. In effect, the Socialists and Liberals were gleeful over the toppling of Tsarism, but conservative opinion was not. It gave credence to a myth that the change of régime had been effected with the consent of Nicholas II and quickly showed its bitterness. The ruling classes declared publicly that the Petrograd Revolution was patriotic in nature. It had been done by the Duma who overthrew the Tsar in order to rid Russia of the German agents who were leading it to ruin. The Tsar was pictured as the innocent victim of the war crisis. Bonar Law, Ribot, and Sonnino spoke of their anguish at seeing him removed from power, and their joy that this Revolution would provide Russia with the means of winning the war. Thus they adopted Milyukov's interpretation of the Revolution. But they didn't believe a word of it. The testimony of Nabokov in London, of Izvolsky in Paris, and of the Japanese ambassadors in the two capitals attests that the governmental circles viewed the Russian Revolution as a catastrophe. This is understandable if the military situation is considered. To be sure, the Battle of Verdun had been won, but at the price of the failure of the Somme Offensive, which they had been counting on to lead to victory. In the East the Germans had celebrated Christmas in Bucharest, and the taking of Bagdad by the English didn't carry the same weight. Elsewhere, the Germans had proclaimed unlimited submarine warfare and the losses which they inflicted on the Allies exceeded all expectations.

Symptomatic of this unease in the West were the increasing Ministerial crises. Asquith was replaced by Lloyd George, Briand by Ribot, while the command of the French armies had passed from Joffre to Nivelle. In Germany, Hindenburg's nomination did not mean the same thing; on the contrary, it meant that the military would have the upper hand in public affairs—another reason for the Allies to be worried. Thus 1917 started inauspiciously; the only hope was America's entry into the war. Meanwhile the fall of Nicholas II was bad news because there hadn't been a more accommodating ally. Moreover, they suspected, from reading the *Times* dispatches, that this Revolution was not entirely a patriotic one. Like Milyukov, they pretended to believe that it was, in order to force the issues and prevent any attempt by the Central Powers to conclude a separate peace with Russia. Hence the immediate recognition of the new government, following the American example. The Allies redoubled their messages of friendship to the Revolution but stopped their deliveries of artillery equipment and pursuit planes.

In Paris and London, the government circles tried to put up a brave front. When they learned that the "maximalists" were pacifists—but not the whole Soviet—they weren't reassured. The press, however, differentiated between Lenin, who was roundly abused, and the Soviet, which was treated kindly. The allied governments hailed the new régime as if nothing at all was the matter. Nivelle sent telegram after telegram to General Alexeiev "demanding" the start of the offensive. This farce couldn't go on. After the Soviet's appeal to the "peoples of the whole world," the governments worried about the turn of events. They thought about opening talks with Prince Lvov:

I telegraphed London and Rome [wrote Ribot] to ask our Allies if they didn't think it would be necessary to ask the Provisional Government to stop their stalling. M. Sonnino was ready to send instructions to this effect, but the Foreign Office thought it would be a better policy not to. In their opinion, the Socialists from France and Great Britain who had gone to Russia should be given time to exert their influence on their political coreligionists.

The idea of utilizing the services of the Socialists came out during the first few days. On March 3rd, in a secret telegram, Buchanan suggested it to the Foreign Office. On the 4th, General Janin, the French military attaché in Petrograd, interceded with Painlevé, and Isvolsky with Milyukov, who spoke about it to Albert Thomas. First the French and English Socialists sent a message to the government, the Duma, and the Soviet to the effect that the French and English ministers and the Labour Party insisted on "victory over the common enemy." (The motion of the French Socialist Party was mum on this point.) Then it was decided to send two delegations to Russia—a special delegation made up of two Socialist ministers, Henderson and Albert Thomas, and another delegation to hail the Revolution in the name of the Western Socialists. In fact, like the preceding one, the Cachin-Moutet-Sanders mission had the objective of charging up the fighting enthusiasm of their Russian ally: "At this time the delegation openly professed its intention to talk sense to the radical Socialists and to counteract Bolshevik propaganda."

In Petrograd, there was no mistaking it. A telegram from the *Independent Labour Party* had preceded the arrival of the "Western Pilgrims." It challenged their representativeness, since the English delegation included no one from the British Socialist Party or the Independent Labour Party. In France, a tract, "Les Bons Apotres" ("The Good Apostles"), from the Zimmerwaldian "Committee for the Resumption of International Relations," added that if Cachin and his friends were thought to have gone to Russia on their own, this was because the Socialist Party hadn't dared to endorse the trip.

After the usual amenities* the allied Socialists immediately sensed the distrust in the air:

> We didn't come to Russia to talk, but to listen [explained Marcel Cachin]. And we object to the allegations of the Swedish press about the aims of our trip. The political principles of the Soviet are those of the Socialist Party. War is being waged against annexations and our party supports the Government only insofar as it carries on a democratic policy.

Marius Moutet hailed "Russian Democracy, which will fight to Victory over Militarism," but Kerensky thought it wise to warn his friends. "I only hope," he declared, speaking of Russian War aims, "that the Allied Socialists will have the same influence on the bourgeois of their countries as do the Russian Socialists."

The next day, at the Soviet, a "Siberian frost" greeted the Allied Socialists. They looked like Shylock's agents, come to get their pound of flesh and blood from the Russian Revolution, Sukhanov commented. They had to justify their representativeness, were informed that the Soviet had wired Paris and London to send Internationalist representatives to Petrograd, and were asked to give assurances about India, Ireland, and Morocco. "But," asked Marius Moutet and Marcel Cachin, worried, "was the release of the colonies to be made a condition for peace?" The Allied Socialists declared that they approved of the Soviet formula, "peace without

*This was the first time that the *Internationale* was sung.

annexations or contributions." In the case of Alsace-Lorraine, there was a misunderstanding; before deciding its fate, according to the Russians, it was necessary to consult the population. The French agreed, but reluctantly. They thought it was up to France, despoiled in 1871, to control the method of the referendum. The Soviet thought, on the contrary, that an international commission should be used, as everywhere else. The Allied Socialists came out against reparations for the victors. However, they thought that war victims should be indemnified by those responsible for the war— i.e., the Germans. According to the Russians, German guilt was clear only in the case of Belgium. War guilt was everyone's, and all the participants should contribute to the reparations. Unanimous in wanting to establish a League of Nations after the war, Russia and her allies could not agree on the method of setting it up. The French delegation thought it would only be possible after the defeat of Germany, while Tseretelli and company thought that an International Socialist Conference could impose peace on all governments. Ultimately they would proceed to set up the League of Nations.

The discussion was renewed upon the arrival of Albert Thomas. The Socialist Minister had begun by declaring in Christiana that "Russian freedom was impossible without military victory." He repeated the same thing to moderate paper *Novo Vremya* on April 11/24, shocking everyone. Constantly flanked by a general and two colonels, the special envoy didn't realize that he owed it to his interpreter, Kerensky, that he was acclaimed with such fervor; when he spoke of "victorious" peace, it became "peace without annexations" in Kerensky's translation. Knowing better, the Russian Socialists reacted otherwise; at the Soviet they took a vote to decide whether or not to receive the French minister.

Thomas had some new things to say. He made it plain that he thought any comparison between the policy of the French Socialists in 1914 and those of the Germans out of place. Neither could they put on the same plane the policies of the "sacred union" in France and the "Burgfriede" in Germany. As far as that went, Thomas added, one could well say that in the Soviet the majority was collaborating with the bourgeois government. Furthermore, the Allied Socialists would permit the German Socialists to attend an international conference only under certain conditions. Above all, Albert Thomas announced that he didn't think such a conference would come to much. If the Russians issued an invitation, the leaders undoubtedly would attend. At best, the German leaders would go to Canossa. What then? These reactions augured poorly for the Tseretelli plan. There was no agreement in sight, either on procedure or on objectives. Even supposing that all the Socialists were to attend a Conference, it was clear that the quarrel between the French and the Germans, for example, was stronger than their quarrel with their own governments. Only the Zimmerwaldian radicals would be able to get along with each other and fight against their respective governments. But precisely these very Allied Socialist missions, just like the Executive Committee, were fighting primarily against "pacifism." On this point they were in complete agreement; from then on, in spite of disagreements, the Allied Socialists received a friendly welcome from the new leadership of the Soviet and from Kerensky. The Russians avoided any idea of a separate peace, and the Allied Socialists quickly forgot the first days' discomfiture and were able to "puff up the soldiers" in a leisurely manner, recalling working class solidarity with the Russian people, etc. Taken up gradually by the unusual spectacle and the exaltation of a successful Revolution, they were converted to the Soviet ideal. Marcel Cachin, especially, more sensitive than the others, felt how weary the Russian soldiers were of the war. He drew his own conclusions, moving closer to the Soviet members. Coming as a shamefaced investigator for his country, he left Russia as an exalted prophet from the homeland of the Revolution.

"I was agreeably surprised," wrote Nekludov, "to see that when they returned from their mission the English and French Socialists seemed to have learned something from the Soviet."

As a minister, Albert Thomas' position was more delicate, but that didn't prevent him from meddling directly in Russian internal matters. But since the direction his action took was in accordance with Soviet polity and was instrumental in Milyukov's ouster, it seemed in the short run as though his mission had helped the *"rapprochement"* of the new régime and the Western democracies. The presence of the Allied missions was a shot in the arm for the Revolutionary Defensists, who found their position strengthened. Nor were the actions of the Central Powers disinterested; indirectly, they worked in the opposite direction. Thus Europe's intervention pulled the Revolution in two opposite directions. By accentuating the radical tendencies, the return of émigré leaders amplified it even further.

2. RETURN OF ÉMIGRÉ LEADERS

April was the time of the return of the famous leaders of the Revolutionary movement, Plekhanov, Kropotkin, Lenin, Chernov. Stars of the second order arrived at the same time, such as the Menshevik Dan and the S.R.s Avxentiev and Natanson. The arrival of the other great Revolutionary leaders occurred at the beginning of May. At the same time, by their writings, Martov, Axelrod, and Trotsky exerted considerable influence beginning in April.

Plekhanov reentered Russia with the Allied Socialist delegation. On March 12/25 he had given *Popolo d'Italia* his interpretation of February events:

> Asiatic Russia is conquered and my country enters triumphantly into the family of the free peoples of Europe. This is so true that the workers have returned to war industries. Thus the War will be fought more vigorously. No doubt the Germans are hoping that the extremists and the moderates will quarrel, thus permitting them to win and restore Tsarism. Opposition to the War is not a Soviet tactic. . . . As for Kerensky, he is a true Socialist.

This defense of Kerensky came as an answer to the attacks of *Avanti*, which was tied in with the Zimmerwaldian Left and which Plekhanov stigmatized in this manner: "They are not Socialists. Their ideology is warmed over, misunderstood Bakunism. It is second-hand Anarchism, second-hand Syndicalism, it is anything you want, but it is not Socialism."

As for their Russian counterparts, "You have no idea what your pacifists are, compared to our Zimmerwaldians," declared Plekhanov to H. M. Hyndman, the British Social Democratic leader. "They are babies compared to us. Our species is frankly and unreservedly pro-German. . . . I'm told that they prefer peace with the restoration of the Romanovs to the continuation of the war. With such people, it will be difficult. Luckily, they are not as influential as they would like to be."

In Petrograd the old leader was triumphantly hailed but was shunted aside from responsible leadership. He was old and sick and the young thought he was in the way. Not having set foot on Russian soil for thirty years, he thought only of defending it, although this was *passé* in the fourth year of War. Tseretelli, Dan, and Chkheidze kept their distance. They didn't want "Social-Chauvinism" to be mistaken for "Revolutionary-Defensism." Left

202

alone with Vera Zasulich, Plekhanov polemicized in *Edinstvo* and, except for a brief moment, played no further role, except as a negative example. If he lived on in the minds of men, it was due mainly to Lenin's attacks. The most moderate factions of the Soviet were thus not helped very much by his return. They got no help from the return of Alexinsky either, for he too was now discredited. Kropotkin's support also had no effect either. The founder of "Scientific Anarchism" was better known in the West than in Russia and his rallying to the patriotic defense in 1917 cost him all his authority in Anarchist circles.

The majority found, in contrast, a resolute ally in Dan, who became inseparable from Tseretelli. The "Left" was expecting much from the return of Martov and Chernov, although they were somewhat apprehensive about it. A letter from Axelrod, an old ally of Martov's, seemed to urge collaboration between the two powers. In March Leonid Martov had defended Chkheidze and Kerensky, who had been attacked in the *Journal du Peuple* by Boris Souvarine. Later, Martov in "A Letter to Citizen Chkheidze" put the Russian Socialists on guard against the coming of the "apostles." Having been burned twice, first by Dan and then by Tseretelli, the Menshevik minority wondered if Martov would go along with them or try to turn them to the Left. The same point could be made about Chernov and Natanson, the two Socialist Revolutionary leaders. Martov at first was reserved; referring to V. Chernov, he had written, "The future belongs to a Workers' Republic. The Russia of the Duma was able to identify itself with it but we don't have to follow them." This observation, written from London, along with Trotsky's proposals in New York and Lenin's in Zurich, were the boldest outside Russia at that time. Chernov thought nevertheless that for the time being the Socialists would benefit by keeping the present régime. He feared a premature convocation of the Constituent; the Socialist parties, disorganized and disunited, especially on the question of the war, would not be able to face the bourgeois parties successfully, even though they more truly represented the wishes of the masses. To delay the date of the elections to the Constituent and try to unite the Socialists, mainly the Populists, was the double aim of Chernov when he arrived in Petrograd. Further, he envisioned making Russia a third power which would impose peace on its Allies as well as its opponents. To arrive at that, it would suffice to make the war seem purposeless by making the Socialists of each country require a program of peace without annexations nor indemnities. Acclaimed by the crowd in the joyful days and greeted by Keren-

sky who had come to see the unrivaled leader of Russian Populism, Victor Chernov quickly became unbearable. Arrogant and
deliberately mysterious, he played the prophet and conspirator,
but no one could see which way he wanted to go. Nevertheless his
authority was such that he was able to exert considerable influence.

Plekhanov arrived in Russia along with the French and English
Socialists; Chernov left England with Avxentiev and Savinkov.
During this time Chicherin did what he could to help Trotsky
return to Russia. He had left New York, but the British authorities
had interned him en route. He had expressed his Zimmerwaldian
intentions in *New Call* well enough so that it was known what he
would do upon his return. The Petrograd Soviet had to intervene
several times with the French and English governments before
they decided to let Trotsky leave, but he wasn't to arrive in
Petrograd until the beginning of May.

During this time, the Russian émigrés in Switzerland were like
caged lions. "What torture it is for us to be chained up like this
during these times," wrote Lenin to Ganetsky. Since they were
sure they would be interned en route, they didn't dare go through
France or Italy. Only Germany remained. Martov suggested this
possibility first, at an émigré meeting where his idea was received
coolly. But Lenin agreed wholeheartedly with him. Natanson endorsed it in the name of the S.R. and Kossovsky for the *Bund*. In
the end, the Internationalists agreed to pass through Germany if
the negotiations were undertaken by the neutrals with the approval of the new Russian régime. In Petrograd, despite the steps taken
by Shlyapnikov and Kollontay, the Soviet did nothing. Finally the
émigrés gave in and decided to let the negotiations with the
German government undertaken by Parvus, then Grimm and Platten, go ahead. In case they succeeded, the allied and neutral
socialists would be asked to furnish bond for their safe passage.
Guilbeaux and some others agreed, but not Romain Rolland.
Allied censorship would not permit publication of either the
reasons or the conditions of the trip through Germany. The
French Foreign Office even tried to get the Swedish government
to arrest the émigrés when they went through Sweden, without
success. On the other hand, the Germans made no objections to
the negotiations and the following agreement was reached:

1. All Russian émigrés could go through Germany, even if
they favored war to the finish.

2. The train transporting them would be considered extra-territorial.

3. The Russians agreed to intercede with their government for the liberation of an equal number of Austro-German prisoners.

These terms were to the advantage of the Central Powers by facilitating the return to Russia of émigrés who for the most part would contribute, they thought, to "the intensification of the demoralization of the army." In effect, most of them had formulated extreme proposals. L. Martov and Axelrod in their "Letter to Comrade Chkheidze," and Lenin in *Avanti* had published, but incompletely, Kollontay's first instructions. Parvus, Grimm, and Platten knew with what determination the Zimmerwaldian "Left" would conduct the struggle for peace, since the first convoy included Lenin, Sokolnikov, and Zinoviev. Parvus sent them a message at Malmo, reminding them of the need for peace talks. He wanted to meet Lenin, but the Bolshevik leader sidestepped him. Already Lenin had made his plans.

"People of our age perhaps will not live to see the final struggle of the coming Revolution," Lenin told the Swiss workers a few weeks before the February explosion. Like everyone else, he was surprised by the announcement of the events in Russia. Krupskaya tells us that he didn't immediately grasp the magnitude of what had happened "because he measured events in terms of his memories of 1905 and said that the task of the moment was to combine the work in the open with underground action." This didn't last. Even before leaving Zurich, he thought that February 27 was the start of the world revolution. On March 3rd he sent Kollontay instructions as specific as they were uncompromising. "Certainly, we will continue to fight 'defensism.' " "We will fight against the Imperialist War of Shingarev, Kerensky, and Company." On the 4th, "No fake alliances with Chkheidze, etc. No agitation *à la Trotsky*." Finally, on the 6th, in the name of the Bolsheviks abroad he sent his first official instructions:

Our tactic—complete distrust, no support for the new government. Kerensky is especially suspect. Our only security is arming the proletariat. Immediate election of the Petrograd Duma. No deals with the other parties. Telegraph this to Petrograd.
Signed: Ulyanov

In his "abridged theses," which were dated the 4th and which would serve as outlines for the *Letters from Afar* and *April Theses*, Lenin indicated again that they shouldn't even think of an agreement with a "Government which would consist only of Kerensky." This uncompromising attitude contrasted so much with that of the Petrograd Bolshevik leaders that only the first of the five *Letters from Afar* was published in *Pravda*, and that only after Lenin's return to Russia. Like the *Letters*, the "Theses" were an analysis of the situation in Russia and the working out of a tactic for going from the first to the second stage of the Revolution.

According to Lenin, three principal political forces had emerged during the February Revolution: (1) the Tsarist Monarchy, with the feudal landowners, the old officials, and the generals; (2) the Russian bourgeoisie of the Octobrists and Cadets, behind which came the petite-bourgeoisie, whose principal representatives were Kerensky and Chkheidze; (3) the Soviet looking for allies among the proletariat and the poor peasantry. With Tsarism toppled, the other two forces were now in an equilibrium represented by the Provisional Government and the Soviet. There was thus a dual power. The proletariat should seek to topple the government, but not right away because this might prove risky. It should be exposed and fought against, as should those who had ceded their power to them—that is to say, the Soviet leaders. Thus Lenin bracketed Kerensky and Chkheidze with the Cadets and the Octobrists. Opposing them he put the Soviet, in spite of the fact that they were its founders.

According to Lenin, the task of the soviets was to lead Russia from the first to the second phase of the Revolution, that of the "revolutionary democratic dictatorship of the workers and peasants." To arrive at that, the soviets should exert their power in the manner of a parallel government and should not be satisfied with just observing the acts of the government. They should have a police force and an administration, for this was the only way to proceed to the effective destruction of the old régime. Lenin thought that the organization of an armed workers' militia was the main task of the soviets. The third *Letter* explained in detail how in Petrograd every citizen should do a day's guard duty every two weeks, with every worker taking a turn. This guard would ensure the political hegemony of the masses. In a conference in Zurich before his departure, Lenin commented on all these themes: the essential task of Social Democracy was to know how to organize the proletariat in a revolutionary manner; by gradually exercising power it would take over from the old régime, of which only the symbol, Tsarism, had been overthrown. The Paris Commune had shown the way, and it should be emulated, but this time all the way. The main problem, peace, was inseparably tied to the problem of power. It was useless to hope that one could force the bourgeoisie to negotiate with the Allies or the Germans. "To ask Guchkov and Milyukov to make peace is to ask a shopkeeper to be honest." To achieve peace, first the working class should seize power with the help of the two forces which had common interests with it—the poor peasantry and the proletariat of the fighting countries. The fifth *Letter*, unfinished, told how this could be brought about; it also showed how the Russian Revolution would lead to the European Revolution.

When he arrived in Petrograd on April 4, 1917, Lenin already had direct knowledge of the situation in Russia. He had read the newspapers of the capital, especially Kamenev's latest editorials in *Pravda*, which he disapproved of violently. For their parts the leaders had an inkling of his position with regard to the war and dual power, but not exactly, because the editors of *Pravda*, worried about the contents of the *Letters from Afar*, hadn't published them. Lenin, they said in sympathetic circles, was not acquainted with the "real" situation in Russia; one would have to wait for his return.

At the Finland Station, Chkheidze had organized a reception in the name of the Soviet. Thanks to Sukhanov, we have a record of this event:

> Advancing with an enormous bouquet in his hands, Lenin literally stumbled against Chkheidze. Chkheidze spoke his welcome speech somberly, maintaining not only the spirit and the letter but also the tone of a lesson in morality:
>
> "Comrade Lenin, in the name of the Petrograd Soviet and the Revolution, we hail your arrival in Russia. But we believe that the main task of Revolutionary Democracy consists now of defending our Revolution against all attempts against it, internal and external. We believe that to accomplish this not disunity but unity is necessary on the part of all Revolutionists. We hope that, in agreement with us, you will pursue these aims."
>
> I was stupified, at a loss. How was one to take this welcome, and this ominous *But?* But Lenin knew how to act. He was there as though nothing that was going on concerned him. He looked in every direction, examining faces, the ceiling. Then turning squarely with his back to the Soviet delegation, he answered:

"Dear Comrades, Soldiers, Sailors, and Workers, I am happy to hail in your persons the victorious Russian Revolution and to salute you as the vanguard of the World Proletarian Army. The predatory imperialist war is the beginning of civil war in all of Europe. It won't be long until Comrade Liebknecht will call for the people to turn the guns against their capitalist exploiters. In Germany everything is in an uproar. Today, or perhaps tomorrow, all of European imperialism may collapse. The Revolution you have made has opened up a new epoch. Long live the World Socialist Revolution!"

That is the scene and speech which marked Lenin's entry into the Revolutionary arena. More than anyone else he resembled at this time the portrait of the ideal Revolutionary, as described by Bakunin and Nechaev:

He has neither personal interests, nor affairs, nor sentiments, nor attachments. His whole being is dedicated to one single end, one idea, one passion—the Revolution. He has freed himself from all ties with the civilized world, renouncing its laws, manners, conventions, and morality. He is their implacable enemy and lives only to destroy them. Anything which contributes to the success of the Revolution is moral, anything which harms it is immoral.

Forty-seven years old, Lenin deserved his nickname, "the Old Man." Thirty years of underground struggle and exile had broken his soul through the trials of waiting and solitude and had stifled the illusions of youth. Lenin had only scorn for the romantic softness of Kerensky, whom he called the "balalaika" of the régime, or for the anxiety of the righteous Tseretelli, "the conscience of the Revolution."

He was accused of Anarchism or of having taken up Trotsky's ideas, but this didn't matter to him. His detractors didn't understand that, for him, an idea was good only when it was effective. The only objective was the seizure of power to accomplish the Socialist Revolution. An action is legitimate only when it puts into practice a theory which has been judged "scientifically correct."

In order to carry out his conceptions of party organization, tactics, and revolutionary objectives, Lenin had broken with Plekhanov, Martov, and Trotsky, one after the other. For a long time he had remained their opponent—not their equal and even less their subordinate, he was rather a seceder. In 1917, the uncontested leader of a diminished but nonetheless hard-core party, he played the game democratically, the only one fighting for the defense of the *April Theses* against all his Bolshevik comrades.

As soon as he arrived in Petrograd, he presented them to his friends. The *April Theses* had the same themes as the *Sketches* and *Letter from Afar*. In them he proclaimed his unconditional hostility to Revolutionary defensism, to the Provisional Government, to the Parliamentary Republic; he urged the seizure of power by the proletariat and the poorer sections of the peasantry, the formation of a Soviet Republic, the substitution of the armed populace for the regular army, fraternization, the nationalization of all lands, the abolition of the police and all officials, and the party's adjustment to its minority situation. Its main task was to explain to the masses "patiently, systematically, and uncompromisingly" the blunders committed by the Soviet majority, and to "unmask the government instead of asking for what amounted to the sowing of illusions." (See complete text in Appendix, Document 27.)

His proposals astonished the political leaders. Milyukov was amused. Reassured, he now thought Lenin need not be feared because his opinions were so extreme. Plekhanov exulted, and for their part Lenin's friends were downcast. "I'm afraid that Ilyich looks as though he's gone crazy," confided Krupskaya to one of her friends. In *Pravda*, Kamenev explained that Lenin had only expressed "personal" opinions, and that the party line was unchanged. In fact, as Shlyapnikov said, Lenin was putting himself "to the left of the Left." He knew it, and said at the Bolshevik Conference that if necessary he would remain in the minority: "One Liebknecht is worth a hundred and ten Defensists like Steklov or Chkheidze." He was immediately attacked in his own party by the "old Bolsheviks," members of the Petrograd Committee, notably Kamenev, Kalinin, and Bagdatev. The latter declared:

Lenin wants nothing less than a European Revolution. He thinks it essential that the Revolution be complete. To apply his minimum program, power must effectively be seized, although not even all the workers are with us. As for giving the people the right of self-determination without first effecting a social revolution, it is foolishness, and this slogan of a general peace concluded between the peoples is absurd. We do not approve of Point Three; on one hand, we would act, but on the other we would denounce the Government—once, twice, and what then? Either we would seize power or the government would fight an all out battle.

209

After saying that he didn't understand why the bourgeoisie couldn't be fought within the confines of the Constituent Assembly, where the workers' and peasants' delegates would be in the majority, Bagdatev concluded that Lenin's theses were at bottom correct, but were not practical and did not constitute an answer to the workers' concrete demands, the eight-hour day and peace.

Thus Lenin first had to take his party in hand. To do this he had a few lieutenants: first there was the "guard," consisting of Zinoviev and Kollontay; then came Shutko, Olminsky, and Molotov, from the capital, along with Shlyapnikov; and finally Stalin, who abandoned the majority to join his leader. In the days that followed it appeared that Lenin's proposals reflected the feelings of a certain number of party organizations in the provinces. In their regional conference, the Bolsheviks of Krasnoyarsk and Samara, behind Valerian Kuibyshev, hewed to the old *Pravda* party line. But those of Moscow, Kharkov, Latvia, and especially the strong Ural federations, prompted by Yakov Sverdlov, adopted resolutions quite similar to the *April Theses*. Lenin's proposals had a tremendous impact because they coincided with the deepest aspirations of one part of the population. The Bolshevik leader had not yet won over his own party, but the country echoed his theses. This was shown when, fifteen days after his arrival, the April Days erupted.

3. THE APRIL DAYS

At the beginning of April, the war question was the main problem. Peasants, workers, and soldiers had been able to satisfy their first aspiration. They had begun to seize the lands and to enforce the eight-hour day, or at least they had broken with the old discipline. But alone they could not resolve the question of the War. Hence they watched the government's every movement. In the cities, especially, there was no motion which didn't bring up the question of the war; political or professional demands became of secondary importance.

An all out fight began between the proponents and opponents of war to the end. The first, few in number, were nevertheless determined. Prompted by such organizations as the *Union of the Army and Fatherland* and the *Union of Soldiers, Students, and Republicans*, they launched a pamphlet war against the worker class beginning in April. Their numbers increased, but not as rapidly as those of their opponents, who were, however, unable to agree on the formulation of a rallying cry.

In the armies the question of discipline and that of the war were inseparable. The Soviet Commissars had won the round and the soldiers obeyed the orders of the officers only when they corresponded to the will of the majority. This was the lesson learned from the "Minsk Congress," the "finale" of the struggle for the political control of the Army. The "anti-congress" inspired by the Moscow government was defeated. It became apparent that the Army would obey only the orders of the Soviet.

Rallied to the idea of a peace without annexations, the soldiers however did not see how to conclude it. This was how the "fraternization" movement came about, "a Revolutionary initiative of the masses" with ill-defined aims. The fraternizations got going in the middle of March and increased until the end of April. Simple but emotional demonstrations occurred where soldiers exchanged biscuits and souvenirs. By scattering them with artillery, the Russian artillery officers earned another reason for the hatred of their soldiers. On April 16th, in *Volna*, the Bolshevik newspaper in Helsingfors, Lenin came out in favor of fraternization "on all fronts." On the 28th, he explained that these fraternizations should be accompanied by a definite political program: "We are not Anarchists and do not think that the war can be ended by simply refusing to fight." The Soviet and *Isvestya* immediately replied by formally condemning fraternization "because it was no longer the Tsar or the landowners that the soldiers were defending, but the Revolution." *Isvestya* added that fraternization was an enemy trap which would be legitimate and would lead to peace only if the Russians were faced with an army which also had accomplished its revolution. Little groups could not attain general peace. The Soviet appeal was heeded. The reports about Frunze's tour attest to this. The Bolshevik leader had left on April 26th to organize the fraternizations. The officers could do nothing about him, but after the Soviet appeal Frunze no longer sought to organize the fraternizations; contenting himself merely with warning the Soviet about the manner in which the command had put an end to them, fundamentally he did not contest the decision. Henceforth incidents of fraternization became rarer. It was no longer with artillery that they were ended, but with rifle fire—proof that the soldiers themselves were hostile to them. At this time the Petrograd Soviet stood as the uncontested leaders. The Bolshevization of the army had not yet begun, inasmuch as fraternizations were ended at the moment when Lenin urged them.

The country's defense was now being undertaken by the democratic movement, and the officers and the command wanted to profit by it. They urged taking the offensive as a way of assuming the ascendancy over the army. "The army seemed ready to take up the struggle," opined a Soviet delegation. Thus the soldiers interrupted Skobelev when he tried to ridicule the officers who had been abused on the 27th of February. It was noted that combatants who expressed themselves in favor of immediate peace were rare. On the other hand, the Duma representatives were unable to pit the front-line soldiers against the workers, as is shown by the greeting extended to Gvozdez. Speaking in the name of the working class, he got more applause than the other speakers. Enthusiastic about the Soviet and becoming politically conscious, the troops nevertheless wondered about the uselessness of the war. Cachin understood this better than the Soviet delegation, who did not see that in asking questions about the best way to conclude peace, the troops were expressing their most heartfelt aspirations, even though afterward they loudly applauded a patriotic speech.

At the front the awareness of the war problem raised special questions—about the duration of hostilities, the choice between offensive or defensive operations, the officers' behavior, the fear that an agrarian reform would proceed during the soldiers' absence. The war aims were less important to them, even though in their thinking they insisted on peace without annexations or contributions, a formula adopted confidently because it came from the Soviet. In the rear, on the contrary, popular opinion was concerned about the war aims. The allied military mission even scoffed about the man in the street mistaking "Anneksia" for the Tsar's daughter and "Kontribucia" for a Black Sea port. They would have been better off if they had concluded that the struggle for peace was quite popular.

The Central Powers' reaction, the Socialist missions to Russia, the return of the émigrés, the tour of the representatives of the Duma and the Soviet were some of the elements which enlivened debate, presented the issues, and opened new horizons.

In the middle of April, two antagonistic demonstrations heightened feelings. First was that of the disabled veterans, who shook their fists at Lenin, whose triumph would have meant that their sacrifice would have been in vain; they demanded war to the end.

Skobelev and Tseretelli were unable to reassure them. Rodzianko earned their cheers. "No," he declared, "we won't try to halt the war now." The next day, April 18th, was May Day by the new calendar. At the call of the Soviet, thousands of banners demanded peace without annexations. Without doubt they had won the battle of the slogans. Would the government act accordingly and put into practice the Declaration of March 27th?

THE MILYUKOV NOTE

Insensitive to the motions of the rabble and its clamorings, Milyukov remained firm in the positions he had taken the first day. He thought them unshakable. In his *Memoirs*, written forty years later, he explains his reasons more clearly than in *History of the Revolution*: a handful of extremists aside, no one dared to demand that Russia withdraw from the war. Since the country remained irrevocably tied to its alliances, to break its past treaties or promises smacked of utopianism, if not of folly: "this was the strength of my position," explains Milyukov. Convinced that the Allied Socialists would never rally to a Zimmerwaldian formula, he thought any modification of foreign policy absurd. To do otherwise would have been to put the war in doubt, and that would have been infamous. In order to go along with public opinion, Milyukov consented to issue the March 27th declaration, but it was intended only for Russian ears. A secret note to the ambassadors specified that the allied agreements remained in force. One sentence of the declaration, by Kokoshkin, specified that "by fully observing the obligations assumed toward its allies, the government would defend the rights of the country"—an obvious allusion to Constantinople. In order to leave no doubts in Paris and London, on April 9th Milyukov sent the *Manchester Guardian* an article explicitly reaffirming the legitimacy of Russia's intentions.

The maneuver backfired. Coming back from England, Chernov assured his friends that in the West no one could see how the March 27th declaration had changed anything about Russia's war aims. He suggested that a note be sent to the Powers. This was how the "Milyukov note" originated.

A Soviet delegation presented itself to the government on April 11th. The ground had been prepared. Naturally, Kerensky was won over, as well as Tereshchenko and Prince Lvov. The most important thing was that Albert Thomas was on the Soviet side. In spite of the advice of Maurice Paléologue, the French ambassador,

Thomas had ranged himself against Milyukov from the start. Buchanan himself was convinced that if they wanted to keep the Revolution on their side they would have to make some concessions, "to heave some ballast," as Marcel Cachin kept saying, "Your Socialists don't make things any easier for me," confided Milyukov to Paléologue. His predictions proved to be somewhat inexact. The very same Socialists could show themselves patriotic in France and Zimmerwaldian in Russia. They had to give in. At the meeting on the 11th, which lasted only a few minutes and was very friendly, the Soviet delegates assured Milyukov that it wasn't a question of loosening ties with the Allies, but of basing them on new principles. At that point the Minister of Foreign Affairs promised to draft a note. In order to force the issue, Kerensky sent out a communiqué announcing its forthcoming publication. At the same time, knowing of the Cadet minister's obstinacy, Chernov started a press campaign against "this Guizot who persists in his dogmatic attitude until History shows him the door." Meanwhile Albert Thomas, wanting to satisfy the Socialists while keeping in touch with the government to which he was an emissary, intervened directly in Russian affairs. He played an important if somewhat ill-defined and equivocal role. "I know the Socialists," he told the allied ambassadors; "they would tear each other to pieces over a formula. You should accept and then modify their interpretation." He told Kerensky that he agreed with him that the allies should change their war aims, but told him to hold off an allied conference to this end because he knew that in France this would be premature. At the same time he led Milyukov to believe that his government's position on this question only needed "clarification." Since Albert Thomas got in touch with him because in the "note" Russia asked for "guarantees and sanctions"—contradictory terms—Milyukov saw in his insistence a confirmation of his own analysis. He didn't understand that he was playing into Albert Thomas' hands. By having kept Kerensky from promoting a revision of allied war aims, Albert Thomas had contributed toward making the Russian Socialists assume a policy of war to the end, but freed of all territorial demands. By helping to regroup the parties opposed to the Cadet minister, he tightened the bonds between Russian Socialism and the Western Democracies.

April 18th, Milyukov sent the Powers the long awaited note. It stressed the impetus which the Revolution would give to the defense of the rights and the principles for which Russia and her

Allies were fighting, and recalled that the government would respect faithfully its obligations assumed toward them. By referring to the March 27 Declaration, Milyukov was able to avoid saying anything about the wishes of the Russian people to avoid annexations. There was not a word about the desire of "democratic Russia" for "peace without annexations or contributions." On the contrary, he spoke of "guarantees and sanctions" which the Allies would set up later to establish a durable peace. (See Appendix, Text 29.)

THE CRISIS ERUPTS

In democratic circles the "Milyukov Note" made them see red. They even thought it was done deliberately in order to provoke a showdown between the Soviet and the military. "It was a slap in the face," repeated Bogdanov. Chkheidze lamented, "Milyukov is the evil genius of the Revolution." On the 19th the alarm was sounded. At the Mikhailovsky Theater, Kerensky spoke of resigning, while in the working circles a campaign of petitions was suddenly started. It swept the whole country. Mostly they asked for the dismissal of Milyukov, while affirming confidence in the Soviet and the need for tightening its control over the government.

Then the *faubourgs* of the capital came to life. F. Linde dragged them along behind the 180th Infantry Regiment. This Anarchist—one of the authors of General Order Number One—was also a Defensist. He feared that the "Note" could lead only to the collapse of the army by stirring up arguments. There was only one way to prevent such a disaster: the Soviet should take over the Foreign Affairs of the Revolution. That was the aim of the demonstration. They shouted: "Down with Milyukov!" "Down with Aggression!" "Down with the Provisional Government!" But on the red banners of the demonstrators, many of whom were Bolsheviks, could be seen, "All Power to the Soviet."

These angry demonstrations broke out in the already charged climate of the Disabled Veterans Day and the May Day celebration. The Right also was mobilized. Would there be an armed conflict? That's what was feared at the Soviet, where they were ignorant of the aims and the nature of the demonstration which was going on. The atmosphere was tense when the debate began. Yurenev and Shlyapnikov proposed sending out an appeal to the masses. Kamenev refused: "He does not want to couple the Bolsheviks to an appeal whose objective would be to force the government to institute a foreign policy which would come not

from the masses, but from the opportunistic Soviet majority." At
the other end, they feared, along with Chernov, that in the event
of an untimely demonstration in the working class districts, some
"obscure forces" would show their strength. They rather approved
the reasoning of Tseretelli, Chkheidze, Dan, and Gotz, who wanted to avoid a civil war at all costs. Unmistakably condemning
Milyukov's note, they demanded a formal disavowal. They declared themselves ready to impose their policy on the government.
Tseretelli showed that the "appeal to the masses is a dangerous
tool," "that the Soviet is strong enough by itself to force the
government to yield." Stankevitch, Kerensky's friend, explained it
from the rostrum:

> What good is it, Comrades, to demonstrate? Against whom are
> you going to use force? Because in the end, you are the force
> and it is the masses which are behind you. Hold on, look!
> [Stankevitch turned around, pointing to the clock, and the
> whole Assembly turned with him.] It is now five minutes to
> seven. Decide that the Government is no longer, that it must
> resign. We will call them on the telephone and in five minutes it
> will have left office. What good is violence, demonstrations, civil
> war?

This speech made a tremendous impression. Won over by it, and
reinforced by Soviet approval, Chkheidze, Skobelev, Woitinsky,
and a few others left to appear before the demonstrators to tell
them how their actions were endangering the Revolution. At the
same time, their friends got busy on the telephones to call the
capital's regiments to dissuade them from participating in the
movement. The Soviet was taking over.

In fact, that very evening its Executive Committee met the
members of the government and the Duma delegates. Alarmed by
the troubles and anxious to reach an agreement with them, the
Soviet delegates didn't want the newspapermen present at the
meeting, nor for *Izvestya* to print the statements of the opposition.

"We realize that the Soviet no longer has confidence in us,"
declared Prince Lvov, "but the Government has done nothing to
earn this mistrust. Since we no longer have your support, we are
ready to leave." A long account of the situation by each of the
ministers followed. "To listen to them," wrote Stalin, "to save the
country, it was only necessary to overcome the soldiers (Guchkov), to overcome the peasants (Shingarev), to overcome the

workers (all ministers). Support us in this difficult task, they said in substance, help us to fight the war (Milyukov), and everything will be well. Otherwise, we're leaving." Though sketchy and distorted, this testimony gives a good idea of the proposals which were made. It doesn't show everyone's anxiety, nor their concern with the gravity of responsibilities which they carried. There was Guchkov, depressed by the disintegration of the army which he was supposed to lead to victory; and Milyukov, convinced that any other "Note" would have shorn Russia of the confidence of her Allies. As for the Soviet delegates, they felt the hot breath of civil war on their necks. They were all worried and, Tseretelli insists, unanimous in wanting to avoid anything which lessened the chance of reaching an agreement. When Kamenev said that calm could be restored only by turning the power over to the workers, some ministers took him at his word. The Bolshevik leader hastily pointed out that he only meant in principle. The Bolshevik faction did not want to overthrow the government just yet. They sought a solution which would satisfy the Soviet without humiliating Milyukov. "Maybe," asked Chernov, grimacing and unctuous, "the Minister of Foreign Affairs might draft another note and then take over as Minister of National Education?" Milyukov refused. Then Tseretelli and Nekrassov drafted it themselves, leaving it to him to make it public.

But on the afternoon of the 21st, ignoring the result of these negotiations and deciding to show their determination, the working districts took to the street at the call of *Pravda* and *Soldatskaya Pravda*. "The time has come to seize power, the first of the preliminaries needed for the conclusion of a democratic peace." Further on, Lenin added: "The government must vacate the premises and yield to the Soviet." Kalinin and Kamenev thought this policy risky. It was, at the least, pulling the demonstration further to the "left" than its participants intended. The banners of the organizations included "Down with the Provisional Government" and "All Power to the Soviets," while most of the motions of the masses only asked for the removal of the "capitalist ministers." Some of the demonstrators were armed, but "mostly for show," as one of them said. The presence of several women bore witness to the fact that no one thought of bloodshed. To make an impression on public opinion, renew the insurrectional tradition, change government policy, sustain the Soviet, and force it to stand up for itself—those were the objectives of the demonstration. Chkheidze learned to his chagrin that it wouldn't do to try to stop the

217

demonstration. He appeared before the demonstrators to give them the good news that an agreement had been reached with the government that morning but had to flee from the scene. The demonstrators went on, having decided to seize the capital for a few hours. Imagine their surprise, when at the corner of Nevsky and Sadovaya, they saw some counter-demonstrators, obviously organized themselves, perched on trucks and quite menacing. In the crowd there were some outcries against Lenin. Quickly, tension gripped the crowd. Knowing that in this neighborhood the bystanders favored them, the counter-demonstrators—students and officers—attacked in small groups, tearing the pennants and flags from the workers. Shots rang out from the buildings. "Help, Comrades, help! To arms!" yelled the groups which had been shot at. The scuffle went on into the night. There were some dead and wounded.

Meanwhile, a few hundred meters away, General Kornilov, the Commandant of the Capital's garrison, had posted himself behind the Marie Palace, ready to intervene, in spite of the fact that the day before he had been formally forbidden to do so. But the soldiers, suspicious, refused to march against the workers. They wanted an order from the Soviet. Warned, the Soviet replied immediately that it was certain they were being deceived. In the future, for better security, they were to obey only orders signed by two members of the Soviet Bureau. The provocation, more or less planned, had failed. Kornilov resigned.

It had been a close call. On the 22nd the Soviet published in *Izvestya* two appeals addressed to the soldiers and the workers. The first were reminded that everything depended on them; the second that an armed demonstration was dangerous. In a few hours the whole city was placarded with appeals from the Soviet. Its authority was strengthened by the event, inasmuch as Petrograd resumed its usual appearance after the 22nd. The Bolsheviks, on the other hand, had overplayed their hand. Lenin recognized it a few days later in "Crisis Lessons"; they had gone "too far to the left." Their stock went down in democratic circles where Kamenev was jeered.

The same day, the *Explanatory Note* drafted by the government and the Soviet appeared. By saying that the *Note* had been adopted unanimously, Milyukov put Kerensky in a difficult position. Further, the government's "rectification" indicated clearly that Russia wanted no territorial annexation; above all, it showed that by "sanctions and guarantees" it meant armament limitations, international tribunals, etc. The Soviet congratulated itself on the results obtained, recalling its determination to force the government to undertake talks with a view to peace founded on the principle of "no annexations or contributions." The Bureau's motion was approved by 2000 votes against 13, which included Alexandra Kollontay and Leonid Kamenev.

It was a narrow victory if one admits, along with Milyukov, that after all "this modest explanation" didn't mean too much in comparison to the power of the movement triggered by the April 18th note. Milyukov didn't even resign, and it is not known if he bothered to send the explanatory *Note* to the foreign powers. "I won a great victory and conceded nothing," Milyukov told the *New York Times*. That's what he thought; "I won too much," he confided a few weeks later to Albert Thomas. Nevertheless, he had made himself undesirable, and it wasn't long before they made him realize it.

4. MILYUKOV'S FALL AND THE FORMATION OF THE COALITION GOVERNMENT
THE PROBLEM OF POWER

Once more, the question of power had reared itself in the "Milyukov Note" affair. The Soviet Executive Committee accused the Liaison Committee of having failed by letting Milyukov send his note abroad. Kerensky was reproached for his negligence. He answered that at least he had avoided the worst by suppressing the sentence in which Milyukov promised not to sign any peace before victory. But he wasn't let off the hook and that didn't improve his relations with the Soviet.

This quarrel cast a doubt on the functioning of the régime. Everyone thought that "things can't go on like this." But what was to be done? The Cadets and the Bolsheviks wanted a drastic solution, but compromise won out in the end. Ten days later the crisis was over, leaving the Right and the Bolsheviks temporarily at loose ends.

Following the April demonstrations, the Cadets took the offensive. In the name of the Government, Kokoshkin was charged by Milyukov with the job of drafting an "Appeal to the Nation." He was to call for calm and throw the responsibility for the troubles on the Soviet. Prince Lvov, more reasonable, struck out that part of it. But Milyukov and Manuilov protested. Consulted about the solution of the power crisis, they presented as an alternative to a coalition government, "which would weaken the government," a policy based on the repudiation of dual power, the sacking of Kerensky, and the struggle against the opposition. The Prince disapproved. To the great dismay of his "resistance" ministers, he wanted to be one of the animators of the "movement." At the memorial meeting for the Four Dumas, he didn't even mention the conflict between the Soviet and the government. In spite of Rodzianko, the Right left no stone unturned because this meeting was to be the signal for the start of the great offensive. Sulgin was aggressive, generating the enthusiasm of these famous men who, for the first time (and the last), heard the great swashbuckler publicly run through the Soviet. Using his own words to declaim Milyukov's speech against Tsarism, Sulgin enumerated the facts which demonstrated the régime's ineptitude, after each one of which he asked: "Was this stupidity or treason?" He concluded, to a burst of applause: "Each one was stupidity; together they spell treason." Tseretelli answered that such talk as Sulgin made would lead to civil war; only an agreement between the Soviet and the government could prevent it. Rudely recalled to reality, the members of the Four Dumas rallied to those whose prescription was wiser. The first great offensive against democracy had failed.

From then on, the ruling classes felt that there could be safety only in the closest collaboration between the Soviet and the government. Prince Lvov, Tereshchenko, and their cohorts could be stopped only if a number of Socialists entered the government. Their idea was to back themselves by the forces of democracy; thus the "revolutionary" bourgeois would no longer bear the responsibilities of power alone. United, moderate Socialists and enlightened bourgeois would resist the combined assaults of the extreme Left, the "resistance," and reaction. Some of the moderates rallied to the mainstream; in *Russkaya Slova*, Evgen Trubetskoy launched a press campaign to that effect.

On the Left, after some maneuvering, a policy of "class collaboration" won out also, but not everyone went along. At the Soviet meeting of the 29th of April, in accordance with the rallying cry of Lenin, Feodotov had tried to persuade the Assembly to assume full power. The delegates' reaction made it plain that this was premature. The majority did not question the principle of dual power; they only wanted to improve the régime's performance. The idea that only a coalition Government would be able to accomplish this was beginning to take root. This wasn't the first day of the Revolution, when the democratic forces were disorganized. The soviets were now able either to collaborate or match strength on equal terms with the agents of the government. Participation in the government would be a step toward a more complete change of régime which the constituent would inaugurate later. The example of Western democracies supported this idea. Wouldn't Revolutionary Russia insure its stability by imitating them?

Once more, it was Kerensky who took the initiative. April 26th, he stated in *Delo Naroda*, the Socialist-Revolutionary daily, "Democracy had become stronger and could no longer be kept out of the government. Its representatives had the right to assume power owing to direct elections by the organizations which they represented." The "advocate of Democracy" calculated the danger of letting himself become isolated, and, ridding himself of the domination of the *trudoviks* and S.R.s, he hoped to tighten the ties between the Socialist and the bourgeois parties. This idea was discussed at the Soviet. Every day the partisans of the coalition increased—among the "working-class rank and file, but not the higher staff" Bogdanov pointed out on the 27th. The small shop-owners and the circles which gravitated around the Soviet also moved in this direction. At the very least, the government had acquired some support. "It comes to the same thing, whether one becomes a part of the government or carries it on one's shoulders," Stalin remarked ironically. The S.R.s thought the same. Prompted by Gotz, they now militated in favor of participation. They thought that with the support of the peasants and soldiers the "party" would be invincible. It wasn't even necessary, as Sukhanov and the Left S.R.s urged, to have the majority of the ministries; for the threat of civil war legitimized the presence of Socialists in the government. Tseretelli was tempted to follow his friend Gotz and rally the Mensheviks. But behind Martov, most of the party leaders remained hostile. Dan even thought it was slanderous to assert that the Mensheviks could soon take part in the government. In reality, some were sorely tempted to accept, but they were afraid of being outflanked by the Bolsheviks. This was a danger of which Gotz and Chernov were unaware at the time, due to the vagaries of the Left Socialist Revolutionaries. The Menshevik leaders gave some reasons. "Our party represents Russia in no way," explained Chkheidze, seconded by Bogdanov; "Russia is a peasant country; to enlarge the seat of power is to include not only the Mensheviks, but the S.R.s and the Populists." He also gave another justification: "In the actual state of political forces, the participation of the Mensheviks in the government would raise vain hopes among the working class." Gotz and Chernov answered that the S.R. would participate in the government only if the Mensheviks were included. Then Tseretelli offered a compromise: the democratic movement could be represented in the government, if not by members of the Soviet, at least by trade unionists and members of the cooperatives. This suggestion was turned down and Tseretelli announced that he was opposed to participation. He found himself in the camp of the Bolsheviks and the Left S.R.s, like Kamkov and Pumpyansky who thought that "making up a coalition ministry would weaken Revolutionary enthusiasm and allow the spirit of the coalition to triumph before the meeting of the Constituent, which should be avoided." After long discussion, participation was rejected by a vote of 24 to 22, with 8 abstentions. Prince Lvov was disappointed. Kerensky was indignant: "Those who were in power had no roots in the nation, and those who represented the will of the people refused to govern."

While this was going on, Guchkov resigned. He had met a Soviet delegation some time earlier and concluded that, between the Soviet and the General Staff, his position was untenable. He thought that the war could not be pursued under these conditions. But he didn't want to break with his friends and had kept silent. The April crisis along with Kornilov's departure convinced him that he no longer had a useful role to play. As a last gesture against the Soviet, he resigned.

It was thought that this was a signal. Some of the ministers spoke of wholesale resignations in the Cabinet. Public opinion buzzed again. Colonel Zhakubovich, representing the Petrograd garrison, approached the Soviet to tell them that there was only one way to prevent a crisis: "the Soviet, who alone had authority in the eyes of the army, must become a part of the government." Had he acted spontaneously? His intervention was accompanied by a series of petitions coming from the garrison, and this was enough to bring back the Mensheviks. "In view of the pressure of the democratic elements and the army," they rallied to the idea of a coalition. "Three days ago," explained Chkheidze, "I said that I could not assume the responsibility of recommending that the Executive Committee send delegates to the Government. Now I have changed my opinion and cannot recommend that it not do so." Tseretelli had given the word on the coalition question; thereafter, none of the reasons given by the Mensheviks on April 28th were considered. It was decided and there was no more debate. Tseretelli spoke of "anarchy and ruin, the machinations of the bourgeois right, the desire of the bourgeois left to collaborate more closely with democratic movement, the necessity of creating at any price a strong coalition government, which would benefit from the support of the masses." The stage was set, commented Sukhanov. Almost alone this time, the Bolsheviks voted "against" with a few Mensheviks and some Leftist S.R.s. Participation won by a vote of 44 to 19.

Even before coming into existence, the coalition rested on a misunderstanding: "The bourgeoisie was relieved to be able to substitute collaboration with the masses for control by the masses." For their part, the masses saw only that, for the first time in Russian history, Socialists were seated on government benches. They also noted that the Soviet had refused power offered them by the workers only to accept it from the soldiers.

THE FORMATION OF THE COALITION GOVERNMENT

In accordance with the usual procedure of a parliamentary-type ministerial crisis, the negotiations for the formation of a coalition government went in two steps—program discussion and bargaining on the formation of a cabinet.

In the name of the Soviet, Dan and Tseretelli drafted the program which they intended to present to the Provisional Government for its approval. Essentially it was twofold: first, the struggle to open negotiations and conclude peace without annexations or contributions, based on the principle of the peoples' right of self-determination; second, strengthening the army by democratization in order to prevent the defeat of Russia and its allies, which could damage the cause of the people and of peace. They didn't even have time to discuss the other points of the project, which bore on the struggle against economic chaos, the defense of workers' rights, and the implementation of agrarian reform. The main thing was the formulation of a foreign policy. Only what concerned the struggle for peace was debated. The Bolsheviks wanted to threaten the allies with a revelation of the secret treaties made with them if they didn't agree to "peace without annexations or contributions." Tseretelli was against this, claiming that it wouldn't be fair since they couldn't divulge the treaties concluded between the Germans and their allies. He prevailed.

Prince Lvov altered the Soviet text; thus the communiqué published after the agreement insisted on the continuity of the government and on the revolutionary quality of the cabinet formed in March. The new government would merely accentuate certain features of the previous government's policies. Tseretelli accepted all these amendments.

The massive participation of Socialists in the government assumed such importance that the moment they thought they had won the essential point—the principle of peace without annexations or contributions—the rest became unimportant. Kamenev himself confidently told Tseretelli: "After all, in the organization of the coalition, of which I don't approve, we couldn't have done any better." At the Soviet, the negotiators were greeted with enthusiasm. Only Zinoviev raised a few objections on behalf of the Bolsheviks, to the effect that there were no provisions in the initial declaration for the immediate initiation of peace negotiations. Woitinsky answered that the Soviet program had found no response among the Allies. Consequently, to start peace negotiations without referring first to Paris, London, or Rome amounted to signing a separate peace. He had touched Bolshevik policy in its most sensitive spot. Zinoviev was booed and the resolution was adopted by more than 2000 votes against about one hundred.

The formation of a government remained to be accomplished. At the Soviet they had already discussed a preliminary problem: should the democratic representatives be in the majority in the coalition government? Sukhanov, Chernov, and a few other Socialist Revolutionaries thought so. The Mensheviks, inhibited by the Bolshevik excommunications, made the point that since the Socialist ministers would be responsible to the Soviet, it mattered little whether or not they were in the majority. They won. The narrative which Stankevich has left of the negotiations which followed recalls in all its details a ministerial crisis in the West:

"Officially, the negotiations took place at Prince Lvov's on Theater Street. But only the definite compromise was agreed on there. Meanwhile the decisions had been made elsewhere. Every phase of the negotiations, every proposal, every amendment called for a pause so that the members of the government and the representatives of the [Soviet] Committee could agree among themselves. Aside from these sessions, there were meetings with the Cadet Party, which was holding its convention then. From the beginning the Cadets made up a series of basic demands: to have as many representatives with the government as the democratic parties, and that the government draft a manifesto condemning Anarchy. But the tone of the note which the K.D.s proposed was evidently unacceptable to the Committee members. The Cadets also wanted the Ministry of Agriculture.

There were contradictory forces at work in the Soviet. The

Committee there was under the influence of Steklov, and his leaders were all in the delegation. He drew up all sorts of conditions and formal demands: in the future all the most important ministries should be in the hands of the "democrats" —i.e., War, Interior, Foreign Affairs, and Agriculture.

In addition to these two main forces there were some secondary ones. In the midst of heated discussion, the representatives of the Peasant Congress came to present their desiderata. The Socialist-Revolutionaries also revealed theirs, in the form of an ultimatum: "Chernov in Agriculture." Then the Populists: "Anybody except Chernov in Agriculture." Chkheidze insisted that Tseretelli remain with the Soviet, where he was indispensable. But the government wanted him in the Cabinet, considering him the only worthwhile democratic representative. The military put up Palchinsky for War. Skobelev wanted the Navy. But the government wanted Kerensky to combine War and Navy. They could find no ministry for Tseretelli and no candidate for Justice. To all this was added the influence from the front. Alexeiev, the commander-in-chief, and the other front-line commanders, Dragomirov, Gurko, and Brusilov, arrived in Petrograd where they made vindictive speeches.

Meeting after meeting was held without results. Every day a Plenary Session of the Soviet met to keep abreast of events, and each day it was duly informed. Finally on the night of May 5th the situation was so confused that all hope of reaching an agreement was abandoned. A Soviet delegation and one from the peasants' committee were meeting at Prince Lvov's. In another room, the government was meeting. Kerensky and Nekrassov ran from one to the other, mediating. But hour by hour the situation became increasingly confused and desperate. They had exhausted every possible solution. Each proposal met with a chain of all sorts of difficulties which were soon to become familiar. The nervous tension became acute, and no one attempted to control either his agitation or his irritation. Problems were no longer even discussed. Everyone spoke, or rather shouted, without rising from his seat. Chernov, disheveled and out of control, was berating little Peshekhonov, whom he had trapped in a corner. Gvozdev had something definite to say: he was indignant about all this noise. Even Tseretelli lost his temper; he was screaming something at Chkheidze, when suddenly Kerensky appeared. "A solution has been found," he announced.

The combination he spoke of was nothing new and there were many flaws in it. But everyone was happy to get out of it. No one objected. The grumblers had to keep quiet. The coalition Government was formed. The Soviet had accepted both continuing the war and assuming power.

Prince Lvov remained as President and also took over Interior; Milyukov was thrown out by his own friends, the Cadets, who nevertheless accepted Nekrassov (Transport), Shingarev (Finance), Manuilov (Education), and Shakovsky (Social Security) in the ministry. There they would fight for their program. Thus, while denying the principle of the Socialist ministers' responsibility to the Soviet, the Cadets thought it perfectly legitimate that their friends should be responsible to their party.

Chernov had refused Foreign Affairs because the tone of the government statement was not sufficiently Zimmerwaldian; he got Agriculture. Skobelev, who dreamed of Navy, got Labor; Peshekhonov, Food; Tseretelli, Post Office. In the final tally, Foreign Affairs fell to the lively Tereshchenko, while Kerensky assumed War and Navy. Thus the Socialists "had desperately fought against control, and they had won." Three men dominated the new cabinet—Tseretelli, Chernov, and Kerensky. Between the first two, who were at ease only among the militants, and the War Minister, who was above the parties and liked to address the public directly, no communication was possible. Each one went his own way. The reign of the coalition would reflect this.

In February, bourgeois political circles and the advance guard of the working class had quickly been won over by the success of the Revolution—the former because they had been unsuccessful in their attempted palace revolution, and the latter because the February events had not been only their doing but had also been the victory of the civilians and soldiers who had realized the proper role of the working class and had accomplished the Revolution.

In April, they all sought what they thought was their rightful place in the political scene—Milyukov by imposing a foreign policy on the country, and the extreme Left by reviving insurrectionary techniques. But the facts reminded everyone that there was a gap between their ideals and reality. Milyukov only seemed to have the power and the masses weren't following their Anarcho-Bolshevik advance guard.

During April many parties also wanted to settle some scores— the resistance bourgeoisie against revolutionary democracy, and the bourgeoisie in the movement; the Revolutionary advance guard against the Soviet leaders. The first quarrel was only a phantom fight, but the other foreshadowed the coming crises.

CHAPTER EIGHT

THE COALITION EXPERIMENT
(MAY–JUNE 1917)

Paradoxically, the soviets and the government were endorsing a policy of "class collaboration" at the very moment when the more advanced elements of the working class and the fighting bourgeoisie came face to face, each rejecting any conciliatory policy. Public opinion nevertheless went along with those who counseled moderation. Russia was chasing the dream of February, a bloodless Revolution. At the end of May, universal suffrage confirmed this verdict and it looked then as though Russia would steer toward a democratic régime in which the soviets would function as a People's Parliament.

The objective of the new government combination was to reinforce the state's authority. But they soon got the feeling that state power had been weakened still further and that the duality of power was reinforced rather than diminished. Only the roles had been changed. It was no longer the Soviet which opposed the coalition. Their place was taken by the officers' associations, the management associations, and, on the other side, the Anarchists and the Bolsheviks. Neither one represented much, but they expressed so forcibly the real aspirations and the anger of the populace, that the "conciliators," powerless to solve the problems of the war or the Revolution, soon drifted aimlessly, taunted by opponents who long before had predicted their failure.

1. THE PARTIES, PUBLIC OPINION, AND THE COALITION

Russian political movements, badgered under Tsarism and astounded by the February Revolution, blossomed forth in the free atmosphere of Spring 1917. The municipal elections, the preparations for the Soviet Congress, and the Constituent Assembly made them define their position with respect to the régime, the war, and the Revolution. Most of the major parties held their meetings during the April days, a few weeks before the municipal elections, which were the first electoral confrontation between the régime and the free population. Russia was serving its apprenticeship in parliamentary democracy.

Cadet Party decisions were the ones most eagerly awaited, since they might have cast a doubt on the future of the coalition, if the majority refused to approve the participation of its members in the second Lvov Cabinet, and if it adopted the systematic opposition urged by Milyukov. Elected President of the Convention, the ex-Minister of Foreign Affairs showed that outside of the counter-revolutionary current, two schools of thought predominated—those who wanted to "preserve and consolidate the gains of the Revolution," and those who wanted "the Revolution to go further." Nekrassov agreed with this estimate, but he asked heatedly "Where is one to draw the line between the former tendency, which Milyukov considered creative, and the latter, which he considered destructive?" There was no doubt in the resigned minister's mind but that the destructive tendency began with the ministers who remained in the government. Nekrassov, on the contrary, thought that the creative tendency included all the members of the new Lvov Cabinet. The Convention agreed, considering that "participation in the government was the surest way to protect the country against counter-revolution," and hoping that "the participation of the groups more on the Left, now responsible for the nation's future, would ensure the government's strength and stability. It would also end the dual power, which had been fatal to the army and the nation." Nekrassov also got the party to promise him unconditional support, because it was precisely that which he recently had chided the Soviet about. From then on, the final motion retained only the points of the government declaration which suited them—i.e., the need for a military offensive, respecting agreements with the Allies, etc. Under these conditions, the Cadet Party endorsement was a mere formality and one had the feeling that it expressed only a forced sympathy toward the government.

On the other hand the adherence of the S.R.s, Mensheviks, Trudoviks, and Social-Populists was unequivocal, although even they were divided. At this time, the opponents of the newly formed government were only a small minority. Among the Social-ist-Revolutionaries, they were to be found on the left. Behind Boris Kamkov, Maria Spiridovana, and M. Natanson, the "Grand-father" of the Russian Revolution, this Populist faction urged a firmer attitude toward the Allies, going so far as to threaten to sign a separate armistice. They also wanted the whole government to be responsible to the Soviet, not just the Socialist ministers. Above all, having kept their taste for clandestine and secret doings, the members of this group couldn't see themselves participating side by side with bourgeois and aristocrats in a government. They sympathized wholeheartedly with the rallying cries of the Bolsheviks. At the other end, another minority, led by Avxentiev, Sorokin, S. Maslov, and C. Brechko-Breshkovskaya, the "Grandmother" of the Revolution, thought that the party should give the government its complete support. She judged Chernov harshly, because in his columns of the *Delo-Naroda* he already had criticized the policies of a government of which they were a part. Closely tied to the *Privyz* group and the cooperative movement, this "Right" published *Volya-Naroda*, to which the Socialist-Populists contributed. In order to carry more weight in the midst of the Populist movement, she hoped to unite with the Socialist-Populists and admit the Trudoviks in a large, moderate party. But they were very much in the minority in comparison with the center, which was itself divided into two factions, one further to the left behind Chernov, the other more moderate, with Kerensky as standard bearer and Zenzinov and Avxentiev as advocates. Thus the party had no unity, being invaded "on the right by the Philistines, on the left by the demagogues," as Chernov put it. People became S.R.s in order to make a career of the Revolution and, according to some, the Socialism of the new S.R.s was somewhat doubtful. Its organization was particularly weak; they claimed a million members, but on the 1st of July they could only count 22,696 militants for 30 percent of the sections, the others existing only on paper. The party program, formulated uncompromisingly, was as vague as it had been in the past.

The Socialist-Populists freely accused the Socialist-Revolutionaries of being a lot of hot air. The party leaders, Peshekhonov and Myakotin, hoped for a more modest but more realizable program. They hoped for an elected government which would put this program in effect before anarchy set in. They wanted to hasten the transformation of the country into a democracy of small property owners, which would have satisfied the rural elements and consolidated the régime. They also wanted the workers to participate in the administration of the firms, for if they were put into positions of responsibility, they could appreciate the problems of the crisis and unemployment. This party had a rather feeble following; they could only muster representatives of 36 organizations, whereas the S.R.s, who claimed 436, could muster 136. Therefore they sought to fuse with other small parties belonging to the Populist tradition. Actually, these militants already had a single organization, the *Edinstvo*, in Saratov, Nizhny-Novgorod, Omsk, etc., but in the center the party thought Plekhanov too chauvinistic and Marxist. The party leaders rather favored Kerensky and the friends of *Volya Naroda*.

Negotiations were undertaken for the organization of a large Populist movement. Chernov was not unfavorable to this idea, but he set too many conditions. For its part, the Right Center of the S.R.s thought the alliance incongruous. Indeed, they were themselves trying to separate from the rest of the S.R.s. In the end only the Social Populists united with the Trudoviks, in spite of the fact that the former thought the latter too close to the Cadets and too attached to the idea of "Russian unity." A bipartisan committee was formed and nominated Tchaikovsky, a Trudovik, to be president of the new group, called "Labor Socialist Populist." The first articles in its organ, *Narodnoe Slovo*, came out strongly against the Bolsheviks. It accused Lenin's party of demagoguery. It criticized the Soviet conduct as well; according to Myakotin, they "should be the representatives of the proletariat and the army, not the whole country.... They sometimes spoke in the name of the proletariat, sometimes in the name of the country. The Soviet didn't have to play the role of a "power" any more, decreeing general orders or discussing the wording of government statements. Now that it had recognized the government program as its own, it should not ignore it or paralyze it, but support it." This criticism fundamentally was the same as what the Right of the S.R. itself said about the Soviet.

At the Menshevik Congress, starting May 9th, 54 organizations were represented—27 under the Menshevik banner, the others as Social Democrats. They debated stormily on the subject of Menshevik participation in the Coalition Government, pointlessly, since they had been presented with an accomplished fact. But when they wanted to go on record, Larine, Martov, and company realized that they were only a small minority, since the triumvirate of Dan, Tseretelli, and Chkheidze was astute enough to entrust the moral support to Gurev, the editor of *Rabochaya Gazeta* who leaned rather to the left. The proponents of coalition won by a vote of 44 to 11, with 13 abstentions. In view of these circumstances Larine wanted to split off, but Leonid Martov dissuaded him. He thought that, thus isolated, the minority would be quickly absorbed by the Bolsheviks. He had his way and remained the respected leader of this small "faction" to which Sukhanov belonged.

The Unitarians of Trotsky and Lunacharsky made exactly the opposite choice; resolutely taking an Internationalist stand and fighting against Revolutionary Defensism, a "Russian variety of Social-Patriotism," they urged breaking off from the Defensists and took with them part of the Polish and Lettish Social Democrats. Their relations with the *Novaya Zhizn* group having foundered on these questions, they had their own journal, *Vpered*, a bi-weekly in which could be found the by-lines of Balabanova, Uritsky, Manuilsky, A. Bogdanov (Malinovsky), and Zhurenev.

When the former leader of the Soviet of 1905 arrived in the capital at the beginning of May, the democrats had just ratified the formation of a coalition government; Trotsky expressed some reservations, but mildly. He wanted more information before taking a fighting stance. In contrast with Lenin, Trotsky had no ready plan for passing to the second stage of the Revolution. The positions which he had taken in the United States and those which he broadcast in his *Peace Program*, published in May 1917, were fairly close to the *April Theses* as far as foreign policy and the attitude to be adopted toward the government were concerned. He had written relatively little on the agrarian question and on matters concerning the problem of the national minorities he put himself definitely in favor of the formation of a United States of Europe.

In Petrograd, Trotsky had only the support of the liaison committee of the working class quarters. His staff seemed more reliable than his troops since the Unitarians could count on only three thousand workers. Thus Trotsky was tempted to collaborate with the Bolsheviks. Lenin sponsored his entry into the organizations tied to the Party. A spark-plug like him was needed and his dynamism would counteract the conciliatory tendencies of the other members of the Central Committee. From June on, Trotsky considered himself a member of the Party, which annoyed the "Old Guard." He said at that time to the English journalist Dosch-Fleurot:

> What is our program if we assume power? We Bolsheviks want an immediate peace. We would prefer not to conclude a separate peace, but the mass of soldiers refuse to spend another winter in the trenches. We propose to seize power and try to bring the Revolution to Germany. If we can't, well then, we'll still have to fight, but the new army will be proletarian. We will begin by giving the people what they fought the Revolution for. We insist on immediate action.

Between those of the left who tolerated the coalition while

condemning it, and those who broke off all relations with its members, the line was imperceptible, as it was between the Martov faction and that of Trotsky, but it was nevertheless impassable.

The Conference held from April 24 to 29, 1917, set the seal on the assumption of Bolshevik Party leadership by Lenin and the adoption of the *April Theses* as the Party platform. Kamenev, Rykov, and Zinoviev vainly tried to soften its interpretation— Kamenev by showing the utopian character of the Leninist scheme, essentially founded on the hypothesis of an European Revolution; Rykov by declaring his reluctance to brand as enemies all the Social-Democrat comrades who didn't accept these ideas; and Zinoviev by trying to convince the audience that it was still possible to believe in a revival of the International. No one listened to them. The April events, the support of Sverdlov as well as of the large provincial federations, the existence of a schismatic tendency among the Mensheviks, the rallying of the Unitarians to ideas similar to those of Lenin, the militants' hostility to the coalition experiment, the frustrated feeling of a large part of the general public—all these things made for the unconditional acceptance of Lenin's *Theses.* At the Seventh Pan-Russian Bolshevik Conference in May, he was defeated only on the question of the break with the Second International, and justly. With its ideological unity affirmed, the Bolshevik Party appeared to be the most homogeneous political organization at the moment. From one end of Russia to the other, twelve big dailies tirelessly took up the rallying cries broadcast by *Pravda, Soldatskaya Pravda,* and *Social-Democrat.* The tracts of May 1st, the Party program, the pamphlets *Soldiers and Workers, Why There Is No Bread, The High Cost of Living,* were spread by thousands of copies in the rear and at the front.* The superiority of a centralized Party was evident since no other organization could spread its slogans with such telling effect. There was hardly any vacillation except on two points: participation in the administration of the municipalities and collaboration with the Mensheviks. Although everyone commented on it, the actual reenforcement of the Bolshevik ranks was rather modest. An inquiry made by the Moscow Regional Bureau of the Party revealed that the number of militants did not exceed 11,000 for the region, less than 3 percent of the workers. It reached 6,000 in the Urals in April and 2,000 in the North Baltic region. However, these numbers grew steadily, while the rival organiza-

---

*Around June 25, *Pravda* claimed that it was printing 90,000 to 95,000 copies (in a justification for obtaining the deferment from the army of its contributors). To that must be added 15,000 copies distributed at the front, and another 63,000 copies of *Soldiers' Pravda* on top of that.

tions had no such growth. Moreover, it was noted that the Bolshevik cells were irreducible; they were swarming and every day new ones were formed, notably in the army and the fleet. In mid-June, at the Pan-Russian Bolshevik Conference of military organizations from the front, led by Krylenko, they counted 26,000 members in about sixty organizations. Still slack, the Bolshevik network was made up of steel strands. For its defense, it had the *Red Guard*, organized at the end of April over the protest of Plekhanov and some Soviet leaders, notably Tseretelli.

With rare exceptions, the Bolsheviki stood alone in the electoral contest. They accepted making common cause only with the Trotsky-Lunacharsky internationalist group. They united with the Anarchists every time they quarreled with the Coalition, but concluded agreements with them only about the administration of local affairs, nothing more.

All political parties were represented in the Soviet, but, while waiting for the elections to the Pan-Russian Congress of Soviets, no one knew exactly what his following among the masses was. In the Petrograd Soviet—now enlarged by the permanent representatives from the provinces—the proponents of the Coalition had won handily and thus attained approval of their policies. It was the same in most of the large soviets in the provinces dominated by the Mensheviks and the S.R.s. On the other hand, the Soviets of Krasnoyarsk and Ivanovo, some others in the Moscow region, and those of the Urals and the Donbas, dominated by Bolsheviks, opposed the Coalition. Some others, without committing themselves, were content to demand "all power to the soviets," "the end of the imperialist war," and "workers' control of production," especially in the Urals.

At the First Congress of Russian Peasants' Soviets, meeting at the beginning of May, the Socialist-Revolutionaries were masters. The entrance of the Socialists into the government was noisily approved. They decided to print several million copies of Bunakov's speech in favor of the war and to launch an appeal against desertion. They thought, along with the editor of *Den*, that the Congress would furnish the "great party" with the organizational staff it needed. The conciliators' theses won with even larger majorities than at the Workers' and Soldiers' Soviets. When the Bolsheviks proposed the publication of the secret treaties, they got only ten votes.

Under these conditions, the governmental coalition went into the municipal elections without too many qualms. Its success was undeniable.

	Voters	Cadets	S.R.-Mensh.	Bolsheviks
PETROGRAD				
May 29–30	790,475	172,215	276,213	159,986
	801 seats	185 seats	299 seats	156 seats

	Voters	Cadets	Populists	S.R.-Mensh.	Bolsheviks
MOSCOW					
June 27	646,568	108,781	11,086	374,885–	75,409
				76,407	
				451,292	

However, at the time, they didn't see that the vote included almost 45 percent abstentions. It was noted, on the other hand, that the coalition supremacy was less marked in the countryside than among the political parties. In Petrograd, the two opposition parties together were as strong as the Coalition. The Cadets were considered as big losers although they got nearly a quarter of the vote in Petrograd. It also appeared that in Russia, the bourgeoisie was not pulling in large segments of the population. The electoral future of the "resistance" was very doubtful. How could they get back the power they had lost? The Bolsheviks were also considered losers. But they had as many votes as the Mensheviks in Moscow, and one fifth of the votes in Petrograd, which was nearly a third of the "democratic" vote. It was not so little.

Aside from the Bolsheviks, the political leaders of February attached no importance to these municipal elections. In their *Memoirs*, written after the event, they never even mention them. They were not enthralled either about the preparations for the election to the Constituent, even though the parties on the "democratic" side were protesting the slowness of the government's action in this area. In effect, with the committee still deliberating, they had to wait until June 2nd to find out what the electoral law was to be (they preferred proportional representation to majority voting), and until June 14th to know the date of the elections, which was set for September 17th.

2. THE COALITION'S FOREIGN POLICY

The government statement of May 3rd marked a decisive change. It was no longer only the Soviet, but also the government which undertook a policy of "peace without annexations or contributions." On the other hand, the democratic leaders aimed to ensure the country's defense and to help in the regeneration of Russia's military might. Never had the objectives of the Soviet and the government been more in accord. In the ministry, the two promoters of the new policy, Tseretelli and Tereshchenko, got along famously, while everyone trusted in the new War Minister, Kerensky, to ensure rebirth in the Revolutionary spirit in the army.

PRINCIPLES AND METHODS

The peace without annexations or contributions formula lent itself to equivocations. Prince Lvov told *Rech* that it was not a question of abandoning the territories which German militarism had occupied, nor of forgetting their obligations to the Belgians, Rumanians, and Serbs, any more than to the French and Belgian people reduced to slavery. However, there was no longer any question of respecting the treaties signed prior to February. Did that mean that by renouncing Constantinople without explicitly saying so, Petrograd intended also to make the Allies renounce their annexation projects? Immediately this raised the question of Alsace-Lorraine. The return of these two provinces to France was not annexation, but "dis-annexation," claimed the bourgeois press. Plekhanov thought the same, recalling that in 1871 Marx and Engels thought the cession of these provinces "null and void." In the Soviet the majority said that the inhabitants would have to be consulted "because in fifty years life had changed radically in Alsace-Lorraine, and with it, the inclinations of the people." This was the very reason the Social-Patriots of France were opposed to any kind of referendum, since immigration and intermarriage had changed the make-up of the population. "It would be neither just nor easy to leave the question up to universal suffrage," claimed *Rech*. But the Left, showing its feelings, would not compromise: "What if the Alsatians-Lorraines, to end the war, preferred to remain German and enjoy a large measure of autonomy?" Wasn't it "the obstinacy of the French bourgeoisie in wanting to take back Alsace-Lorraine which caused the prolongation of the war, threatening all Europe as well as Alsace-Lorraine itself with total ruin?"

This problem was argued for a long time. Since the formula "peace without annexations or contributions" could mean the *status quo ante bellum*, Plekhanov suggested to end it with ". . . founded on the right of self-determination." This time everyone agreed. Only the Bolsheviks wanted to push this principle to its logical extreme. Kamenev wrote: "This does not sanction the right of the Great Powers to acquire colonies. As a preliminary to peace, the troops must be withdrawn from Alsace-Lorraine, Belgium, Poland, Serbia, Macedonia, Salonica, Persia, Ireland, Egypt, and Bosnia, in order to give the oppressed nations complete freedom in the setting of their own boundaries." And as for Russia: "This means the abandonment of Finland, Poland, Turkestan, the Ukraine, etc." And, he concluded: "Such a peace could not be set by capitalist governments, but must be imposed by the proletarian masses on the imperialist bourgeoisie."

The architect and theoretician of Russia's new foreign policy was Tseretelli. The Menshevik leader thought that the Western Powers' appetite would be curbed by the United States' entrance into the war and the February Revolution. Thus Russia's renunciation of her Constantinople claims could serve the cause of Democratic peace. He sincerely believed that a peace could be concluded. In Russia, the Soviet should promote a peace policy to be adopted and followed by the ministers and political parties. The Soviet would encourage the government to intervene with the Allies so that they would proclaim war aims in conformity with the May 3rd statement. In Petrograd the presence of the Zimmerwaldians in the government insured the success of this policy. But since no one could be sure about the Central Powers or the Allies, Russian Democracy should strengthen Socialist action in the belligerent countries and revive the International, in which Tseretelli had "a Messianic faith." A conference of all Socialist parties in Stockholm would initiate a peace program which they would try to impose on their respective countries. In Russia this had already been done; it remained to be done elsewhere. Thus the struggle would be waged on two planes—on the level of relations between governments, and on the level of relations between Socialist parties; furthermore, each party would be charged with taking steps with its government.

Tseretelli and Tereshchenko got along very well. It was decided that the Soviet would help organize a meeting between the various governments, while the government would intercede with the Allies to facilitate a meeting of the Socialists in Stockholm. Tereshchenko went ahead and tried to sound a new note in Russia's foreign relations. His statements went as far as the democrats could expect. In June, after having proposed that the Allies mutually revise their war aims, he stated: "The governments' policies must come closer to conforming with the hopes of Democracy. To that end, Socialist Conferences will lay the foundations on which policy will be established."

But while Tereshchenko was willing to bind the government's policy by the decisions of Russian democracy, he doubted that this would be the case elsewhere. Basically, he hoped to find the means for an acceptable peace, but counted more on the agreements between governments than on the action of the Socialist parties. He saw in the Sixte-Bourbon negotiations a sign of general weariness which could only intensify, and he believed it could be the first step toward a general peace. In the meanwhile he hoped to obtain from the Allies some sign which would lead the Russians to believe that all ideas of annexation had been abandoned, but he doubted their sincerity in this matter.

The Tseretelli-Tereshchenko policy, though supported by a majority of the Soviet, elsewhere met with skepticism and hostility; as *Rech* wrote on May 15: "The Stockholm Socialist meetings should be viewed coolly and calmly. The old International was unable to keep us out of the war. Discredited and crumbling, the International will never be able to undertake the establishment of general peace."

At the other end, the *Edintsvo* group, like the Bolsheviks and the Internationalists, took the coming meeting seriously. "We don't fraternize with the German Socialists, they are excluded," wrote Plekhanov, who like Milyukov and Ribot, saw the Conference as a "trap we must be careful to avoid."

The Bolsheviks took a position which at first glance seemed like Plekhanov's. Lenin, Radek, and Zinoviev thought that the Revolution in Germany was imminent. Hence the Bolsheviks imagined that "the Kaiser's Socialists" were interested in promoting a peace conference which would save Germany from revolution. They concluded that the Stockholm meeting had a counter-revolutionary implication since its success would end in a general peace signed by the governments in office, which would reinforce the capitalist régime instead of toppling it. Karl Radek showed the dialectic nature of the new international relations: German imperialism wanted peace with Russia in order to consolidate the Lvov-Kerensky régime, but if the Russian Revolution wanted to defend itself against German imperialism, it would have to submit to the bourgeoisie, its internal enemy. But the bourgeoisie must be fought, in order to set the example for the German proletariat to fight its own oppressors. "Just as we can't beat our internal foe, Capital, allied to the external foe, World Capitalism and the property-owning classes, so we can't beat the external foe allied to our internal foe." To believe that Stockholm would succeed was a dream anyway, in Bolshevik opinion, because the governments would never agree to a peace without annexations or contributions which the Stockholm Conference could not force them to, all the more, since the Socialist leaders of the European governments were a party to it. The skirmishing which would go on would be nothing but trickery, according to Radovsky: "The Socialist leaders favor the sacred union of classes, a principle wrought by the enemies of the working class who have beguiled the worker aristocracy. He who extends a hand to Henderson and Thomas, extends it at the same time to Lloyd George and Ribot, and to the French and English bankers."

Against Stockholm, the Bolsheviks were equally opposed to a separate peace which would "only benefit the German capitalist bandits" and would ruin the chance of a Revolution in Berlin.

"We must reject . . . separate peace with the German capitalists as well as alliance with the Anglo-French capitalists. Russia's only allies are the oppressed classes of Europe and the enslaved nations of Asia," wrote *Pravda*, and Lenin added: "Let's send our troops East and show that we fight for the liberation of the people of Asia not with words but with deeds."

The representatives of the International faction had ideas fairly close to this and more explicit on the method of attaining their aims: "We must have peace at any cost," said Lunacharsky. "We also must present the Allies an armistice proposal with our peace conditions and we must stop the fighting on all fronts. . . . We will not sign a separate peace, but we will proclaim a cessation of hostilities."

This was a scheme which Lenin and Trotsky would take up six months later. This rejection of a separate peace, like the hope for a European Revolution, was sincere; Tchudnovsky, an Internationalist, even stated in *Vpered*, that it was the government itself which would bear the responsibility for a separate peace. Russia was opposed to the war and events would force her to lay down her arms as soon as a pacifist Government could find the means of achieving a general peace, if not between Governments, then at least between the people.

Leon Trotsky prophesied: "They say that the hope for a European Revolution is utopian. But if it doesn't occur somehow, Russian freedom will be killed by the united forces of our allies and our enemies. He who doesn't believe in the possibility of such a Revolution must expect the collapse of our freedom."

The objective was the formation of a United States of Europe.

238

To attain it, the European War had to be transformed into a European Civil War. Like Lenin, Trotsky thought that the most direct way to accomplish this was to resume the fraternization campaign.

These positions seemed so extreme that some Bolsheviks, like Kamenev, wouldn't go along with them. They thought, as Martov and Chernov did, that they should go to Stockholm even if a Revolution were to break out in Berlin. At least they could revive the International, which, stimulated by the Russian example, would once again find the means for a Socialist Revolution. To arrive at that pass all they needed to do was to make their decisions sufficiently compelling. While waiting for the Socialists to break into all the governments, Russia should not sign a separate peace, but should "wage a separate war," unless, by some miracle, the Allies were to agree to her conception of peace. In favor of Stockholm and opposed to the formation of a Third International, this minority criticized the government's policy of trying to get along with the Allies; in any case, they were sure it wouldn't work.

RELATIONS WITH THE ALLIES

The new foreign policy of the Revolution was founded on several evaluations. It was thought that the Socialist Left would influence the Parliamentary Socialists to steer their governments toward the left. For his part, the Foreign Minister, leaning on Wilson's statements, would urge a revision of war aims. Thus the advocates of imperialistic war, disowned by Washington, Petrograd, and Stockholm, would be forced to yield, and gradually the Allies would fall into line with the Soviet position.

The Western Chancelleries' answer to Tereshchenko's note and the March 27 Declaration disconcerted the Revolutionaries. The Western Powers recognized the justice of the Russian democratic principles and even the advantage of resuming talks on Allied war aims, but these concessions were accompanied by such conditions that the *Rabochaya Gazeta* could say that "the Allies wanted to put old merchandise under new labels." The Menshevik journal added:

"The Chamber," Ribot said, "has rejected the trap of enticing formulas coming not from Petrograd, but from some other sphere, the source of which is all too apparent. . . . What must the Russian Revolution answer to this declaration of war from the French bourgeoisie?"

It was Wilson's answer especially which upset the democratic camp. The American President was distinctly opposed to the Russian ideas, saying publicly "that a peace without victory would strengthen German imperialism, which wants a compromise peace." This time it was the Soviet journal which attacked this "vague and sonorous" note: "It's not the kind of language to use when speaking to Russian democracy," concluded *Izvestya*. "The note was a settling of accounts between Wilson the pacifist by Wilson at war," Chernov remarked ironically.

"The ground was cut from under Tereshchenko's feet," observed Milyukov. He had been right, like Lenin. From then on Russia could declare herself "free of all commitments." Following Bazarov in *Novayza Zhizn*, the Left S.R.s came out in that direction in *Zemlya i Volya*:

"If our way is blocked by bourgeois obstinacy, we will quietly go another way, to the end, knowing our cause is just."

"Separate way," "separate war"—this was the first indication of a split between Petrograd and the West. What provoked it was the casual way the Allies went their own way militarily and diplomatically, ignoring the aspirations of the new Russia. Two years earlier, at the time of the Dardanelles expedition, the Russians already had wondered if the Allies hadn't begun again the operation of the preceding century, occupying Constantinople to keep the Bosporus from them. Then there had been the installation of a Franco-Anglo-Serbian camp in Salonica, forcing the hand of the King of Greece. This violation of neutrality, the military occupation of the country, and the decisions made unilaterally without consulting Russian interests—Tereshchenko protested against such actions, but feebly. For him the main opponent was the "external and internal" enemy. He even justified the "Athens Coup" by "the enormous responsibilities and the great sacrifices made by France in Macedonia." He alibied for the Allies in Albania, where the Italians had just disembarked and where there were reasons to believe they would install themselves as conquerors. The minister assured the Soviet that the future of the country would conform with the principles of the May 6 Declaration, that the occupation was only of a military nature. The opposition wasn't so sure: "The Russian government should dissociate itself definitely from this policy of banditry as practiced by the Allies," said *Vpered* on June 22, 1917. The ire against the bourgeois leaders, accomplices in these matters, mounted.

The government couldn't even argue that the Allies were solicitous inasmuch as economic aid, already reduced by a third at the

time of the Petrograd Conference in January, was further diminished without the Allied mission's intervening in favor of the needs
of the Russians. On the contrary, caught short by the Revolution
and powerless to slow the disintegration of the army in spite of
their efforts, the mission chiefs, Colonel Knox and General Janin,
had a tendency to treat the Russians suspiciously, and took their
offensive as a personal matter. With their ill-concealed irritation at
the turn of events, they contributed to the deterioration of relations between Petrograd and the Western capitals, harassing the
government and the high command and multiplying their pessimistic reports about the future of the alliance. In short, they were
already thinking in terms of intervention, and those Russians who
were faithful to England and France deplored this behavior,
which, in the end, alienated public support instead of increasing it.

Furthermore, Janin asked that "the most glorious" French
regiments send fraternal messages to their Russian brothers in arms
telling of the need to fight to victory. Then he asked that he be
sent the military regulations of the time of the French Revolution
with "the prescription against desertion. I remember that some of
Hoche's were very strict, and Gouvion-St.-Cyr speaks of the harshness of the service in the Rhine-Moselle Army," added Janin, who
wanted to know once more "how many were shot in the French
Army," etc.

Moreover, on the southwest front, the mission supported the
Rumanians against the Russians, under pretext that they were
helping overthrow King Ferdinand. They sent them enormous
quantities of both heavy and tactical matériel, which was sorely
needed by the Russians. This made them indignant, because Ferdinand's conduct had been rather equivocal up to the time of the
success of the Brusilov offensive. The marked sympathy of the
Rumanian officers for the Central Powers was notorious.

Another reason for discord was the Russian wheat deliveries.
The Allied mission saw that the promised amount hadn't been
furnished and they planned, by way of sanction, to hold down
matériel deliveries. The Russian government protested, showing
that the disorganization had been inherited from Tsarism, that it
was the cause of the Revolution, whereas in France everything was
functioning normally. Russia should be helped to remedy the
situation. The Allied mission proved intractable and got the promise that the original quantities would be delivered. Nevertheless, it
. planned to put pressure on the government "in case its ultimate
efforts should prove insufficient"—for example, if they didn't send

the needed locomotives. Albert Thomas tried to put an end to this form of blackmail by sending many telegrams to Paris to the effect that they should help the new régime as much as possible.

To tell the truth, the cooling of relations between Russia and her Allies had preceded the fall of Tsarism. The new régime addressed itself first to Japan and then to the United States when it needed financial support. It put all its hopes in the Root mission, which arrived in Vladivostok in May with the principal aim of reorganizing the transport system. During this time Baxmatev had been sent to Washington to implore American aid and rekindle the good relations between the two democracies. However, American relations with France and England were closer than the Russians had imagined. The Americans had set continued Russian participation in the war as a condition for their entering it themselves. Already disconcerted by Wilson's answer to their "note," the members of the government and of the Soviet understood that American aid would carry the same demands as that of France and England. The Soviet, from then on, put all its hopes in the success of the Stockholm Conference.

STOCKHOLM CONFERENCE PREPARATIONS
Soviet policy rested mainly on the success of the Conference. Ignoring the objections of Plekhanov and Lenin, Tseretelli was the tireless conciliator. He had to fight hostility and skepticism in order for the Conference even to meet; in the government, the vigilant Kerensky kept an eye on him. At the beginning of June Tseretelli almost scored. But if he had succeeded, it then would have been necessary to obtain the capitulation of the governments to the International. But they didn't have to worry about a thing because, after much rigmarole, the Conference wasn't held. This failure had a dramatic influence on the outcome of the Revolution.

The idea of assembling an international conference of Socialists originated with the February Revolution; Axelrod in Switzerland and Lieber in Petrograd seem to have been the first to propose it. Branting, a Swedish Allied sympathizer, came to Russia at the end of March to discuss it. He thought the thing was possible, provided that the initiative came not from the neutral, reputedly Germanophile, Socialists, but from Revolutionary Russia. Otherwise, its failure was preordained, because the allied Socialists would never think of answering an invitation extended by Troelstra, Grimm, or Borgberg.

Yet it was precisely Borgberg who came to Russia bearing proposals. He was acting in the name of the Danish Socialists who, in order to force the hand of the International Socialist Bureau, wanted to hasten the meeting of a conference. The allied Socialists in Russia at the time protested loudly. Therefore, as Branting advised, the Soviet took it upon itself to begin proceedings.

Borgberg proceedings overlapped with those of the Holland Socialist group, who, in league with the Scandinavians, launched on April 9/22 an invitation to a conference set for May 15 under the aegis of the International Socialist Bureau. Camille Huysmans had reluctantly gone along with it, knowing that any premature action would alienate the allied Socialists. Actually, on April 13/26, the Labor Party declined, followed by the French Socialists on April 14/27, and then by the Belgians. The Bolsheviks and the Spartacists objected in turn to this meeting's being held under the auspices of the International Socialist Bureau.

Undaunted, these two groups formed a Holland-Scandinavian Committee with Huysmans as secretary. He reiterated the invitation April 27/May 8 for the May 27th/June 10th. This was coincident with the Russian decision to be in Stockholm as the inviting power.

There was a big debate in the course of which a motion by Dan carried, over the objections of the *Edinstvo* group and of the Russian, Lettish, and Polish Bolsheviks. A call for a Conference was then issued. There were no exclusions. On the contrary, the Soviet "considered it essential that all shades of Socialist opinion without exception should come to the meeting." They cut out from the appeal a part of Point 2, which limited the invitation to Socialist groups which accepted the platform of the March 14/27 appeal.

During this time the Berne Committee had invited the Zimmer-wald Conference participants to meet in order to examine the situation created by the Russian Revolution. Should the decisions made at Kienthal be reconsidered? Should the Left accept participation in an international meeting with the leaders of warring countries? Spartacists and Bolsheviks had already rejected C. Huysmans' first invitation, but the situation had changed since the Holland-Scandinavian Committee's invitation came along with the Soviet invitation. Perhaps the allied Socialists would revise their position.

The first talks with the allied Socialists had taken place before Milyukov's fall. At the time it appeared that they would not accept meeting with the German leaders under any circumstances, at least as long as they didn't repudiate the *Burgfriede*. However, carried along by the exuberance of the Revolution, the French Socialists gradually relaxed their stand: "Listen to their talk. They are completely Russified. . . . It looks as though they understand that the Russian Revolution brings a new life into the world," said *Rabochaya Gazeta*, who had previously never been suspected of being oversympathetic toward Cachin or Moutet. Albert Thomas himself had conceded a great deal to the soviets, including the Alsace-Lorraine question. In the end, would these French Socialists, when they got back to their own country, rally their comrades to the Stockholm idea, which had already been advocated by the "minorities"? Much impressed by the April crisis, Milyukov's fall, and the Soviet victory, they were increasingly won over to the Tseretelli policy. However, they hesitated about going to Stockholm unless they could set the conditions; above all, the English and the Belgians needed convincing.

"The Cadets' program seems very radical to me," Vandervelde confided upon his arrival in Petrograd. Like his friends de Brouckère and de Man, he was too far removed from the Soviet viewpoint to be able to agree with them. Especially on the Stockholm question, the Belgians were intractable. They would never sit at the same table with "the Kaiser's Socialists." Like Plekhanov, they were an advance guard of the "Social Patriots," but when they talked of little Belgium's misfortunes, no one held their uncompromising stand against them.

Henderson had rejoined the Labor Party Delegation around the middle of May. The great powers conferred on him by Lloyd George meant, they thought, that the British government was better disposed toward Russian democracy. The Russians knew that Henderson had suggested that MacDonald accompany him. This gesture was in his favor and the Soviet were even more impressed when he gave Konovalov, the Minister of Industry, a lesson in applied Socialist economics.

Lloyd George and the British government took a more definite position than the French; the submarine war had never been deadlier, and in view of this peril, the British Government could not neglect any opportunities that this Conference might offer them. However, Henderson was even more intractable than Albert Thomas on the method of its convocation. He was willing for the Labor Party to change its decisions opposing the meeting of the International before the end of the war, but he was absolutely opposed to participating in it with German Socialist deputies as long as they would not disavow the *Burgfriede* policy. He thought that no democratic movement could develop in Germany until militarism had been crushed. Thus the decisions made at Stockholm should not be binding on the delegates since they would not be applied in Germany. The Russians hadn't expected such determination. As Tseretelli reported:

> He spoke to me of the resistance which Stockholm would meet among the workers. I was astonished, saying that with Buchanan I didn't get this feeling. "He's not the one who has to meet Scheidenmann, but I am," answered Henderson.

The obstinacy of the allied Socialists irritated the Russian democrats. "You're making things difficult for our propaganda at the front in the face of an offensive," warned Kerensky, with no effect. Tseretelli was desperate. "By refusing to come," he said, almost with tears in his eyes, "you deprive us of the brightest ray of hope we have."

"A chasm separates us from the Allied Socialist deputies," stated *Trud* in Moscow. This was an extreme judgment, but partly true, although the distance from the other Socialist groups was not so great. Thus the peace conditions of the German deputies undoubtedly were contrary to the spirit of March 14/17, but Scheidenmann's party had set no conditions for the Stockholm meeting. He said he was ready to talk and had already made up a delegation. It was the same with V. Adler's Austrian Social-Democrat delegation. On the other hand, the national minorities in the midst of the Austro-Hungarian Social Democrats refused to go to Stockholm, which was a paradox, since the liberation of the Slavic people of Central Europe was one of the permanent war aims of Russia.

In contrast the German and Austro-German minority faction welcomed the Stockholm Conference enthusiastically and had good relations with Martov and Tseretelli. In Russia they enjoyed great prestige, having in their ranks the most famous representatives of international Socialism—Haase, Kautsky, Bernstein, Hilferding, and Adler. The Russians counted on their support because these minority leaders had decided that Socialist participation in the government was "legitimate," as Kautsky explained to the *Birzhevya Vedemosty* correspondent, "even in terms of the resolutions of the Congress of 1900." The agreement with Tseretelli and his associates went even further, since Kautsky, from the perspective of the world revolution, approved of the offensive being readied by the Russian high command. "Inaction on the Russian Front raises the morale of the conquerors. An offensive would make the Socialists' task easier." Haase, but not Lebedour, agreed with Kautsky. According to Lebedour, "this offensive would be the start of Bonapartism in Russia and of chauvinism in Germany." With that, the views of the minority leaders were obviously the same as Tseretelli's followers, notably on the Alsace-Lorraine question. It remained to be seen if the German minority Socialists would agree to sit at the same Conference as the "Kaiser's Socialists," a question unresolved at the beginning of summer.

The support of the French and English minority factions was also obtained. In Paris they had agreed with the German minority on the question of a referendum in Alsace-Lorraine, which was the main thing. As for MacDonald, he had given Vandervelde a letter for the Russian Socialists which very nearly expressed Tseretelli's views on war and peace.

While this was going on, with Cachin's and Moutet's return to Paris, the majority changed sides among the French Socialists, becoming staunch supporters of the Stockholm Conference (May 15/28, 1917). Having achieved this agreement among the neutral Socialists, the Italian party, and the minorities (now majorities) of England, Germany, and France, the Soviet decided to bypass the demands of the allied Socialist delegates. Thinking that it was no longer necessary to underwrite all sorts of conditions, it launched a call to the Socialist organizations and trade unions on May 20/June 2, fixing the Stockholm Conference for June 28. Albert Thomas, de Brouckère, and Henderson protested immediately in a joint letter. This decision had been made before the allied Socialists and the Soviet had found a means of agreement. The allied Socialists pointed out to the Soviet that they didn't see why they should have to break up the "Sacred Union" while the Soviet was continuing with it in its own way. The discussion ended there. Then Henderson forwarded an invitation from the Labor Party to the Soviet for an inter-allied meeting to be held in London in July. There the French, Russians, Belgians, etc. would make preparations for Stockholm. The Soviet Policy Committee pointed out that the Soviet should act autonomously in its capacity as an organizing power and refused the British invitation. At most the Russian Socialists would attend this conference, but not as participants.

"It made the Cadets very happy that this incident had the effect of decidedly chilling the relations between the Socialists and us," noted Tseretelli. Still it was a friendly break. Afterward each made conciliatory gestures. The French stopped demanding the absence of the German Socialists as a condition for the meeting, and the Russian Socialists decided to send mandated delegates to London. Leaving Petrograd at the beginning of June, Albert Thomas told Tseretelli: "We will go to Stockholm, not because we think it possible to talk to the German Socialists, but so that the whole working class world can decide which side is right."

Back in Great Britain, Henderson was even friendlier toward the Soviet. Only the Belgians were intractable.

The participation of the main majority parties thus seemed assured, as well as that of the minority parties. Were they going to see Socialist unity reconstituted at Stockholm? Of course, the Zimmerwaldian Left remained opposed to participation, but after the Soviet vote, wouldn't they also have to reconsider their position? In mid May, Grimm, secretary of the Berne Committee, arrived in Petrograd and a meeting of the Russian Zimmerwaldians was held under his auspices. It was a question of finding out if they would agree to attend a meeting with majority leaders who were connected with capitalist governments. Lenin, Zinoviev, and Trotsky were against it, feeling that any peace concluded before the proletariat seized power would be counter-revolutionary. They were against any collaboration between Socialists and the government and recalled the decisions made at Kienthal in order to get the Berne Committee to oppose the principle of Coalition. Grimm and the leftist internationalists such as Martov, Rakovsky, Kamkov, and some others thought on the contrary that peace had to be concluded to save the Revolution. Only the united action of the Socialists could impose such a peace. The leftists, helped by the momentum of the Revolution, would carry the other Socialists headlong into a truly revolutionary policy. To achieve this end it was necessary that a discussion be undertaken about Socialist responsibilities for the start of the war and that the motions passed at Stockholm be implemented.

Lenin had predicted that the allied Socialists would refuse to come to Stockholm. He had dreams of a revolution in Germany. Since his attitude was based on these two assumptions and since events had proved him wrong so far, it was more and more difficult for him to maintain his hostile attitude toward both the imperialist war and the Stockholm Conference. He pointed out that the decisions of Kienthal forbade the Zimmerwaldians to sit in a meeting with the majority leaders. Grimm's opinion was that the meeting would not be representative enough to make binding decisions. Thus it was decided to hold a Third Zimmerwaldian meeting, prior to the Stockholm meeting, to decide on this matter. Meanwhile, they agreed to send delegates as observers. Lenin preferred to stand alone in his revolutionary extremism rather than to be in the minority and powerless amidst an International Socialist meeting. This uncompromising attitude worried his friends, especially Kamenev. He naively hoped for a success at Stockholm; in this he was much closer to democrats such as Martov and Sukhanov than to Lenin or Trotsky. They mocked the whole affair, proposing that the Bolshevik seats should have signs placed on them saying "Reserved for Bolshevik Delegates whom Lenin Forbade to Attend." These vagaries did not help the Stockholm cause, and the "Grimm Affair" further helped to discredit it.

Grimm, who was secretary of the Berne Commission, wanted to go to Petrograd to see whether or not and in what manner the Zimmerwaldians would take part in the Stockholm Conference. To everyone's astonishment, Milyukov refused him a visa. "I would have agreed even to Borgberg, an avowed Germanophile," Milyukov told Tseretelli, "but with Grimm it's different. In public he pretends to be in favor of a general peace, but I have proof he is a German agent." In fact, this "proof" consisted only of the fact that Grimm had spoken with the German authorities in Switzerland about the return of the Russian émigrés in their country. With Milyukov gone, Tereshchenko was more reasonable; "although Grimm was listed by the Allies as an undesirable," wasn't he an Internationalist of the Left? In reality, Grimm was well known in Socialist circles; Tseretelli and Skovelev could vouch for him. Martov and Axelrod were his personal friends. In Petrograd, he ran into the double opposition of Plekhanov's friends and Lenin's. Wasn't he closely associated with Kautsky, and hadn't he come to work for the success of the Stockholm Conference? they asked.

Suddenly, on June 3rd there was a scandal. Tereschenko let it be known among his colleagues in the government that a telegram had just been intercepted. The sender, Federal Counselor Hoffmann, was sending Grimm Germany's peace proposals for Russia. This was proof that under cover of his Berne Committee functions, Grimm was an agent of the German government. His friends protested. Hoffmann had simply taken advantage of his trustfulness; no doubt he was trying to discredit Grimm by sending him answers to questions which no one had ever asked. Meeting at Tseretelli's, Grimm's friends were surprised to note that he refused to disavow Hoffmann; he only stated that "if the German Government wanted to achieve its imperialist aims in this manner, this was an act of provocation." Grimm's friends, especially Martov, were upset. His past record spoke for him, but why didn't he give the lie to Hoffmann? Tseretelli and Skobelev were not satisfied with his explanation, and Grimm was deported from Russia on May 31/June 13, 1917.

The affair had loud repercussions. The bourgeoisie crowed, for it was now "proven" that the Zimmerwaldians were German agents. The Leninists, who had never approved of the Grimm-Martov line, were also happy. Further, Grimm was a "friend" of the Soviet leaders. "Learn to clean up your own doorstep," Zinoviev told the "Socialist ministers," who were so quick to see Lenin as an agent of the German government. Playing to the gallery, he nevertheless became indignant that a "poor internationalist" comrade was expelled without a hearing. The Mensheviks were all the more embarrassed because they still esteemed Grimm but could not explain his conduct. Until his departure, he had kept absolutely silent, so that none of his friends, either privately or publicly, could take up his defense. The truth came out piecemeal later.

On June 3/16, after arriving in Sweden, Grimm resigned as secretary of the Berne Commission and asked for exoneration. He admitted then that Hoffmann's letter was an answer to a telegram sent him at the end of May. The Commission acquitted Grimm of the main charge against him: he was not a German agent. However, it could be said that he had acted carelessly by not acquainting either Balabanova (his traveling companion for the month) or any other member of the Berne Commission with his doings. On June 30 it was revealed that the letter which Grimm addressed to Hoffmann had asked that he be told of Germany's conditions for peace; Hoffmann in his reply gave Germany's war aims. In the letter he also said that only a German offensive could cause the pending negotiations to miscarry.

Later, abroad, Grimm told the whole truth to his former friend, Leonid Martov. He had given in to his numerous friends in the Socialist world, thinking that he could play a decisive role in promoting peace. If he helped conclude a separate peace between

Germany and Russia, a general peace might follow—a grandiose idea with which Robert Grimm intoxicated himself. Buffeted between the peace of the diplomats and the peace of Stockholm, he let himself be persuaded to play a personal role which was not in keeping with Zimmerwaldian Socialism. In that sense he was disloyal to his comrades. Eventually the German documents revealed that the Wilhelmstrasse let him act because he could have oriented Zimmerwald against the Allies. But they didn't believe that he could succeed.

The Grimm Affair threw a bad light on the Stockholm Conference. It looked as though one of the principal promoters of the Conference had had contacts with the Wilhelmstrasse. The Left and the Right both made the most of the general hostility toward a separate peace. Since Stockholm was something promoted by German-loving Socialists, the peace which would follow would be treasonous—toward the Allies, as some saw it, and toward the Revolution in the eyes of others. It killed the Conference because the three Swedes who took Grimm's place at the Secretariat of the Berne Committee were well to the Left of Grimm and they did nothing toward reaching an agreement between Balbanova, Radek, and the members of the Hollando-Scandinavian committee.

From then on, the hostility of the allied governments toward Stockholm became more pronounced. It was encouraged by moderate Socialists—that is, by Americans such as V. Berger, or Englishmen and Frenchmen like Hyndman, V. Fisher, and A. Varenne. Secretary of State Lansing refused to grant visas to the American delegates to go to Stockholm. Ribot did the same thing at the instigation of the high command, notably Marshall Pétain. In Great Britain, Lloyd George gave the okay, but the Sailors' Union opposed Ramsey MacDonald's departure for Russia. A strike prevented him from leaving, and this incident was widely publicized. In Russia they came to the conclusion that France and England were a thousand miles from the Revolution predicted by the Bolsheviks. Socialist-Revolutionaries and Mensheviks would probably have been more firm toward them, if it hadn't been for the fact that the Bolsheviks were acquiring new vigor in Russia. This was an intolerable situation for the Menshevik leaders to adapt themselves to. Under these conditions everything had to be reconsidered.

At the end of June, a Russian delegation met the Hollando-Scandinavian committee in Stockholm, but they thought it would be better not to get down to business until later. In the meantime, the Russians communicated with the German Socialists. They made a gesture toward the majority party by withdrawing from the plan to examine the question of the Socialists' responsibility for the start of the war, a concession which the moderates considered monstrous. Acting as conciliator, Rusanov got the minority parties (Haase for Germany, F. Adler for Austria) to agree to accept the decisions of the majority. "A hollow victory," thought Branting, since neither the English nor the French—if they came—would subscribe to such a condition. This was not unimportant for the ambassadors of Russian democracy; with their eye on Petrograd, they wanted above all not to make a single move which might give the Bolsheviks a pretext for a rupture.

Prompted by Radek, Balabanova, and Ganetsky, the Zimmerwaldian Left rejected these compromises. They were so convinced that on the morrow Germany, Italy, and Austria would rise up and insure the triumph of the European Revolution that they refused to take part in any negotiations which would involve these "social traitors." When Kamenev, in Petrograd, opined that their rigidness was excessive, not to say clumsy or imprudent, Lenin scolded him severely.

Hollando-Scandinavians and Russians in Stockholm had decided to set their meeting for August 15. Meanwhile new pilgrims, Goldenberg, Rusanov, Erlich, and Smirnov, went west to fan the Stockholm fires. It was flickering in France, where Propaganda Minister Henry Franklin-Bouillon and Premier Georges Clemenceau attacked "the peace Argonauts" vigorously. In Great Britain they had to go back on the agreement with the Center about the question of the Socialists' responsibility for the start of the war. Henderson would not hear of the obligatory nature of the Stockholm decisions. Along with de Broglie and Renaudel it was agreed that the Conference would make recommendations and each party could follow them or not. An agreement was arduously worked out on this basis and they decided to move the Conference from the 15th of August to September 9th. In Italy, the Russians got a warm welcome and the Socialist Party agreed to participate in Stockholm in spite of the connection with the "Berne Commission."

The spell had been broken for a long time and so was the enthusiasm which would have led to the Conference's success. In Russia, in the face of the attacks from the Left and Right, no one was interested anymore. Even before the last blow delivered by the Kerensky government, the Conference was dead in the minds as well as in the hearts—dead even before it was born.

Thus the peace policy of the Russian leaders had failed completely. But there was still the second part of their program to be fulfilled. Would the army be regenerated and instilled with the will to fight the foreign enemy of the Revolution?

3. MINISTER OF WAR KERENSKY'S ACTIONS

Never had an army reached such a stage of disintegration. The deserters weren't even counted any more; in one day in May, a roundup netted 1,300 in Zhitomir, 3,000 at Astrakhan, and several thousand at Ekaterinoslav. In some sectors all discipline had disappeared. More and more, even the principle of the war was argued. Bolshevik propaganda was gaining ground unceasingly. If a change were noted, it was that the troops' adherence was moving continuously in the direction of the ideas of the extreme left. There were more and more purely political motions in favor of "All Power to the Soviet." This was no longer anarchy, but the harbinger of a revolt against all those who wanted war to the finish. In Moscow, *Soldat-Grazhdanin (Citizen Soldier)* echoed the anger of the soldiers presaging new storms:

> "Until the end," croaks the crow, picking the human bones on the battlefield. What does he care about the old mother who awaits the return of her son or the octogenarian who with trembling hand leads the plow?
> "War to the End," cries the student to thousands of people on the public square and assures them that our hardships are due to the Germans. During this time, his father, who has sold oats at sixteen rubles a pud, sits in a noisy cabaret where he maintains the same ideas.
> "To the End" clamor the agents of the allied governments while touring the battlefields strewn with the bodies of the proletarians. Can the soldier in the trenches cry "War to the end"? No. He says something else:
> Until the end of the war, we'll be without food.
> Until the end of the war, Russia won't be free.
> Comrades, let him who cries "War to the End" be sent to the front lines. Then we'll see what he says. . . .

On May 4th, a meeting in Petrograd united the members of the high command and the government which had been formed that very day. Alexander Kerensky, new Minister of War, presided. Alexeiev, Brusilov, Dragomirov, and Gurko summed up the situation. It was, except for Brusilov, a long diatribe against the Revolution. Gurko was the most violent. He and Alexeiev thought that the Soviet were responsible for the disorders. Their slogans had caused the army to disintegrate with all their talk about the "rights of soldiers." As Gurko explained: "Discipline is more important to victory than the knowledge of war aims. During the South African War, the regular army was more stoic than the contingent of volunteers who knew what they were fighting for."

Gurko thought that it was not possible to continue the war under these conditions; it would be better to sign the peace. Alexeiev thought that they could remedy the situation with some drastic measures. They would have to have the courage not to promulgate the famous declaration of the rights of soldiers and even to abolish General Order Number One. Some measures had to be taken in order to isolate the army in the capital. This would enable them to get the soldiers under control. They must understand that the Revolution was over and that the Era of Reconstruction had begun. "A Revolution is not decreed or interrupted by a General Order," explained Skobelev. But they would no more listen to him than to Tseretelli who asked, "Where was the authority of the High Command before the existence of the Soviet—that is to say, during the February events?" Kerensky put an end to the debate. It wasn't a question of "who was responsible for what," but of finding solutions to the questions. He would think about it. At least it looked as though the military was not contesting the authority of the new government and was better disposed toward Kerensky than toward Guchkov.

The new War Minister immediately took some spectacular steps. They were meant to show the troops that he was changing the policies of his predecessor. By forbidding the officers to resign from their positions and promulgating the "Declaration of the Rights of the Soldier" he wanted to show his oneness with the troops and to demonstrate that he didn't care about the objections of the general staff. He followed up in the same spirit by making a series of changes in the general staff. Gurko, Dragomirov, Zhudenich, and some others were relieved of their commands while Alexeiev was replaced by Brusilov at the head of the Army, and Gutor took Brusilov's place at the head of the Armies of the Southwest.

In fact, most of these measures were destined to cause changes because the officers, instead of resigning, now formed associations

253

and prepared for combat. As for the Declaration, Kerensky promulgated it as soon as he was in charge, after first expunging all the articles which would have changed the old army into a revolutionary army. Thus he reinstated Point 14 which authorized the command, during combat, to take all measures, "including the use of armed force against subordinates who disobey orders." In Point 18, the right to nominate and replace leaders was given exclusively to the Command, and the "Committee" no longer had the right to recommend or reject a nomination, as it had in Polivanov's proposal. The extreme left saw the maneuver and Zinoviev denounced this trickery in *Pravda*. But he was unable to judge any better than the members of the government just how far Kerensky veered from the policy of his predecessor—a series of concessions reluctantly and grudgingly granted—in thinking that in order to revive the army, not innovations, but a frankly authoritarian and conservative policy was needed. He saw clearly the problems of the commanders: "To command troops when the means of Command has been lost, to prepare them for action when action to them meant betrayal or counter-revolution, to be forced to tolerate the Bolshevik's poisonous propaganda, to feel the weight of the suspicion of the representatives of Soviet democracy—all this after three years of hard and miserable combat."

To restore the army's fighting ability, Kerensky wanted to present it personally with the Revolution's warmest greetings. He would explain to the soldiers the reason for their sacrifice and if necessary he would counter thousands of arguments with those who opposed him. Under the skeptical and mocking gaze of the officers and Bolshevik soldiers, he went forth into the arena where millions of *"aficionados"* wanted to see him in action. He earned the nickname of "Chief Persuader." The effect was somewhat startling and some of his experiences belong in an anthology. The first happened in the capital, before his departure; to the Congress of Delegates from the Front Kerensky demonstrated his exceptional oratorical gifts:

I didn't come here to salute you. That was done long ago, but to tell you this briefly.

My heart and soul have lost their composure. I am worried and I will tell you frankly why, whatever may be the consequences for me and whatever I may be accused of. The rebirth of the country depends on freedom and on a sense of responsibility. Things cannot go on like this and we cannot save the country this way. I know: most of the fault is with the Old

Régime. Hundreds of years of slavery have not only corrupted the régime, but have also destroyed everyone's sense of responsibility.

Comrades, for ten years you have been suffering in silence. You knew how to fulfill the obligations thrust upon you by a hated régime. You could even shoot the people when the régime ordered it. What has happened now? Can't you suffer any longer? Or has Free Russia become a nation of revolted slaves? *(Loud hubbub in the audience.)*

Yes, Comrades, I don't know—no, I don't know how to lie to people. I don't know how to hide the truth.

Ah! Comrades, it is too bad I didn't die two months ago. . . .

Then I would have died with the sweetest dreams. A new life had begun for my country, forever. There would be no need for whips or sticks in order to make people respect one another.

After having shown the need to fight for peace and defense of country—for in order "to fraternize, they would also have to fraternize on the French front"—Kerensky, speaking over the frantic applause of the audience, concluded:

The country's destiny is in your hands, and the country is in danger. You have tasted the wine of liberty and you have become a bit intoxicated. What we need is sobriety, discipline. You should go down in history so that we could write on your headstones: "They died, but they were never slaves."

The first steps taken, he left immediately for the front and made a grand tour. He wanted to instill the offensive spirit—an impossible task, if ever there was one, but one he wanted to try.

In *The Catastrophe*, he related:

It was in Kamenech-Podolsk. . . . The playground was full of soldier-delegates from the farthest reaches. They were tired, their eyes were feverish, and the tension was extreme. . . . You could see that these people had suffered a severe shock. They couldn't reason normally. They were looking for a new meaning to their lives in the trenches. Listening to the speeches of the delegates, of the soldiers' committees, of Brusilov himself, of the Bolsheviks led by Krylenko, I felt the pulse of the army.

After three years of terrible suffering, millions of soldiers, dead-tired by the hardships of war, suddenly asked themselves these two questions: What are we dying for? Do we have to die?

You can endure anything, as long as you don't think, as long as you don't think of the war aims, or as long as you have the feeling that the sacrifice is unavoidable and necessary, as long as the objective isn't even discussed. . . .

You can't think of war aims under enemy fire. . . . No Army could stand that.

Fundamentally, the persecution of the officers, the mutinies, the Bolshevization of units, the endless meetings—everything that destroyed the army—were merely the expression of its fight for life. The soldier perceived suddenly that there was the justification of his own weakness, his goodwill, his horror of this terrible nightmare. . . . To save the country, the army had to have willingness to die.

A famous incident—that of the little soldier—took place in the front lines of the Army of the Southwest.

General Radko-Dmitriev told me: "There is an agitator in a regiment who can't be contained. He demoralizes the whole regiment with his reasoning about the land. How would you like to meet him?"

The soldiers surrounded us. They were tired, in bad humor. We started to chat. Standing off to the side, the little soldier who had caught the ear of the regiment said nothing. His buddies pushed him: "Go ahead. Tell the Minister all that." He didn't want to talk. Finally he made up his mind. "You said that we must fight so that the peasants can have the land," he said. "But what would I do with this land if I were dead?"

I saw right away that all discussion was useless. I couldn't make myself set up an opposition between private interest and the sacrifice of all. But he must be answered. Faced with such an argument, all reasoning broke down. An emotional shock had to be created instead of trying to convince him.

Quietly I walked toward the little soldier and then, turning toward General Radko-Dmitriev, I said: "General, I order you to release this soldier immediately, so that he can return to his village. So that it will be known that the Russian Revolution has no use for cowards."

The little soldier turned white, said nothing, then fainted. The effect was profound and he asked to remain with his comrades. . . .

Kerensky's presence created a show that no one wanted to miss. Sometimes gay, sometimes sad, always sincere and persuasive, the War Minister had no equal when it came to mesmerizing even the worst disposed audience. When he arrived at Kamenech-Podolsk, Krylenko, an old Bolshevik from way back, had the soldier assembly well under control. Brusilov was worried about it. Wouldn't it be better to cancel this meeting? But when Kerensky spoke, the audience was spellbound. Russia's hardships and the need for devotion were expressed with such eloquence that even Krylenko wept. Kerensky won: "I had come out against the offensive," answered Krylenko, ". . . but if Comrade Kerensky orders it, even if my company won't leave its trench, I'll go and mount the offensive, alone if necessary. . . ."

The results obtained in one month can be judged from the reports of some officers:

WEEK OF MAY 18, BEFORE KERENSKY'S COMING

1. OPERATIONAL ORDERS UNACCOMPLISHED

In spite of the orders of the Commander of the Seventh Siberian Division, the 26th and 27th Siberian Light Infantry Regiments refused to take their position. The Division Commander's exhortations were fruitless.

The 67th Siberian Light Infantry (17th Siberian Division) refused to change position. In the end, the Commander of the 17th got the 66th to agree to move, except for three companies.

Moved during the night of May 20, the companies of the 25th, under threat of the riflemen of the 25th and 26th, came back and were integrated with the men of the 66th. Then, during the night, the Commander of the 7th Division, General Bogdanovich, the 26th Regimental Commander, Colonel Sersnev, and the 3rd Battalion Commander of the 26th Regiment were arrested. They were reprimanded for not being successful in having the movement order annulled. Then they were released. The 26th and 27th are at the breaking point. The steps taken by the Corps and the Military Committee had no effect.

The 707th Infantry refused to carry out the order concerning the 177th Division and to assume its position in spite of the fact that the order had been issued three times. The crowd of soldiers, aided by some officers, proceeded to arrest the 177th Division Commander, General Lyubitsky, who was executed. Reason for refusal: the soldiers do not want to leave a quiet sector for another, unknown and possibly dangerous. The elected "Council" of the 31st Corps decided to arrest the leaders and bring them to court. In case of a fourth refusal of this Order, they would be disbanded and its members proclaimed "enemies of the nation." They would be deprived of all political and property rights. May 23rd, threatened with disbandment, the 707th obeyed.

The same thing happened to the 517th of Batum. On May 24th trouble broke out in some of the Regiments of the 12th and 13th Siberian Light Infantry Divisions. The Regiments refused to move to the operational zone. After the appeals of the 7th Army Commissar, B. Savinkov, on May 25th, all of the 48th Regiment moved in, as did half of the 45th, but the 46th refused. In the 13th Division, the 50th moved in, with a few exceptions. The 51st promised to move on the 26th, the 49th did not advance according to schedule, and the 52nd refused to move and arrested all of its officers.

The Provisional Government has decided to disband the 46th, 47th, 45th, and 52nd Regiments and to bring to trial the soldiers and officers responsible for the disorders.

2. TROUBLES AND ARRESTS OF COMMANDERS

On May 18th, at 8 P.M., a contingent of soldiers of the 1st and 3rd Battalions of the 607th Regiment arrested the Regimental Commander, Colonel Kochkin. Due to the action of General Dubinin, 6th Grenadier Division Commander, Colonel Kochkin was released at 10 P.M., but in order to avoid further trouble, he has been relieved of his command.

3. FRATERNIZATION

On May 8th the enemy tried twice to fraternize with elements of the 9th Siberian Grenadier Regiment, as if they had authority from its Command to start negotiations with the soviets of Petrograd and Kiev. The Austrians yelled from their trenches that they wanted peace with Russia and that if Germany continued to oppose it, they would turn their guns on them. Our men having fired a few rounds, the negotiations came to an end.

4. DESERTION

Left 80.—Returned 3.

SITUATION THREE WEEKS LATER, AFTER KERENSKY'S VISIT

GENERAL SITUATION

According to the latest information, the situation almost everywhere in the 7th Army has improved markedly, although somewhat slower in the 3rd Caucasian Corps.

In the 8th Army, the mood is generally satisfactory. The situation is better and the effect of Bolshevik propaganda has been nullified. Discipline is tighter and fighting spirit is revived. In all the armies the mood shows itself to be more stable, but no one knows how long it will last. The Committees have been requested to take advantage of these circumstances, which may not last, and take up the offensive.

In the 7th Army, the 12th and 13th Siberian Light Infantry Divisions refuse to fight. The operational orders are not carried out. Violations are noted. The men refuse to allow the disbanding of the reserve regiments in the rest areas. No amount of persuasion has succeeded. On agreement between the Commander and the Commissar of the 7th Army, the villages where the infantrymen are located have been occupied by cavalry. Since they refused to give up their weapons and surrender their leaders, some units of the 12th Division occupied the neighboring villages. At 10 P.M. 400 or 500 riflemen laid down their arms.

The incident can be considered closed.

Elsewhere there were no further serious breaches of discipline. In a few companies, some sections balked, but after discussion with Committee members an agreement was reached. In the 5th Don Division, the 29th Cossack Regiment stated that they no longer had confidence in nine of their officers who wanted to lead them into the attack. The Military Delegates came. In the 5th Siberian Corps, a company and a half of the 87th Regiment refused to go into the attack and was disbanded at the same time as the 88th. Elsewhere everything is in order.

At the National Conference of Bolshevik military units, June 16, 1917, Krylenko, back from the Southwest Front, made a report about the morale of these armies which confirmed the commander's diagnosis.

The mass of soldiers is still unorganized although they tend to Bolshevism. Several regiments say they won't go into the attack. Kerensky has a good reputation, even among the Bolsheviks who are struggling against the March SR's. Fraternization has ceased, but fighting has not been resumed. They are thinking seriously about the attack and shock units are being formed. Desertions have stopped, but the soldiers do not come back from leaves. Companies have less than a hundred effectives.

In Cadet Gronsky's opinion "there were even fewer soldiers who want peace now than before the revolution." It is certain, after all, that the motions on the need "not to weaken the army's ability to conduct active operations" did not come only from the officers. However, it appeared that the army's combativeness only showed up where Kerensky had been. Where he had not been—in the 10th Army, for example—the troops were melting away, with a most deleterious effect on morale. They refused to consider an offensive. The morale was even worse in the 5th and 2nd Armies where at any moment mutinies were likely to break out. "The 2nd is worst of all," wrote Denikin to Brusilov; the two of them alone had 140,000 deserters in the last half of May. On the other hand, 109,000 soldiers rejoined their units by the 15th of May, and some of the Minister of War's successes seemed outstanding. Nevertheless, Brusilov asked him on June 11, "If it was worthwhile to prepare to mount an offensive with such morale."

Kerensky had said several times that he had no illusions about the effectiveness of his campaign. Chernov explained that "for an offensive to succeed, it was no good if you had to push the army forward; it should move of itself. In order to obtain this result, one would have to begin by democratizing it." He also repeated that an unsuccessful offensive might start a counter-revolution. Kerensky nevertheless overestimated the powers of his eloquence and "infectious patriotism." It is true that he was under pressure on the right from the officer corps of the Stavka and especially from the Allied Military Mission led by Colonel Knox. Knox badgered him as he had badgered his predecessor, all the while thinking that the Russian Army was dead, "Dead as Queen Anne." A victim of his own delusions, assailed by recriminations, and tempted to emulate Carnot, Kerensky finally ordered an offensive.

The "June 18 Battalions" sallied forth and at first met with success, but it was a flash in the pan. With Galicz fallen, the offensive petered out and stopped. Their honor with the Allies was safe. Russian paid for it with many thousand dead.*

To win it would take a new army. But a professional army would have crushed the Revolution and a mass army would have smothered the new government. Thus Kerensky preferred to maintain the old military system. He hoped to instill new sentiments into the officers and men. He did not proceed with the much awaited democratization, but was satisfied with the replacement of a few officers. In the end his plan went awry. Surprisingly enough, he remained popular. In the eyes of the soldiers he was

*The order for the offensive is dated June 16.

the victorious Revolution, and the fact that he was ordering the generals around made them happy. Perhaps he did not do what they expected of him, but his presence alone reminded them that henceforth they were free men.

With the initial momentum gone, Kerensky's soldiers fell back in disorder. They were no longer the soldiers of '14, naive enough to die "for the Tsar," but the mutineers of '17, determined this time not to die except in a good cause. The Coalition Government had given them neither peace nor land nor brotherhood. Was this failure all the fault of Kaiser Wilhelm? The Bolsheviks said not, that the bourgeois ministers were just as much to blame. Consequently they should be overthrown, like Tsarism. Weren't they the ones who, while doing nothing about peace, were opposed to all reforms and condemned workers and peasants to misery?

★

CHAPTER NINE

THE COALITION EXPERIMENT (CONTINUED)

4. THE CITIES: THE CLASS WAR

MANAGEMENT AND THE WORKERS' DEMANDS

Believing in the coming of a new society, the working class naively expressed its aspirations for a better life. Its demands were very modest—pay above the subsistence level, the forty-hour week, better working conditions in the factories, job security.

The strikes in March had had no specific aims, no specific demands. They were an extension of the spirit of the Revolution and indicated the meaning which the working class understood by the events of February. The management class of the capital understood full well; after March 11th, it had subscribed to an agreement with the Soviet and granted the workers a certain number of concessions. But the wage hikes were not forthcoming and the workers had to submit demands for their pay for the Revolutionary days. The increases were granted, but they were given out parsimoniously and very slowly. In the capital and at Moscow, management was not too slow, but it was different in the provinces, notably in the Vladimir region, the Ukraine, and the Urals. Elsewhere, the small employers beat around the bush and gave little. They would have had to double wages for the workers to recover their purchasing power of the early war years, and to triple them if the Revolution was to achieve a higher standard of living. Only high-level management in the chemical industry was able to make the attempt.

The situation was the same with the other claims of the workers. It wasn't only the eight-hour day which most often had to be fought over. In fact, after waiting vainly for a management answer, the workers themselves initiated the forty-hour week. At the beginning of May this movement spread, but at the Trade Union Conference on June 28 the final motion still asked for a decree making the eight-hour day obligatory. Thus, four months after the Revolution the most popular claim by far still had not been granted. And there was worse: in the Donets, management still used child labor.

Viktor Chernov clearly showed how management fought the factory committees, whose functioning was one of the fundamental demands of the working class:

They acted unscrupulously. The law said that the committees had full power to represent the interest of the workers with management in everything which concerned the relationship between workers and management—pay, working hours, discipline, etc. The employers refused to acknowledge the "etc." Contrary to the meaning evident in the enumeration, they maintained that the questions of hiring and firing were excluded. Whereas the law stated explicitly in paragraph 16 that "*all* disputes concerning relations between employers and workers should be brought before the grievance committees," the employers wanted to exclude the question of hiring. The industrialists of the south even went so far as to claim that industry could not survive unless all freedom was granted to the employers. Those of the Urals stated that no factory administration would acknowledge the mastery of any committee over the factory, nor would they do as the committee wished.

In February the bourgeoisie thought that once the flush of the victory of the Revolution over Tsarism had passed, the Russian people would return to their peaceful ways. It made concessions, accepting a few financial sacrifices. Thus in Petrograd the Industrial and Manufacturing Association estimated that, in comparison to 1916, pay had risen 83 percent in heavy industry, 163 percent in metallurgy, 126 in leather, and 200 in chemicals. But these figures were challenged, and outside the capital they were hardly applicable at all. From the time of the first Provisional Government, management had answered the working-class demands with loud lamentations. They claimed that they could not grant the raises asked for. It was true that for some who were already threatened with insolvency, an effort of this kind, coming at a time when they had enough trouble as it was, would have been too much for them. The peculiar position of Russian industry made it very vulnerable; it had few resources and its financial independence was reduced. Its dependence on foreign capital left it no room for maneuvering. The financial troubles of the time were added to the impossibility of obtaining raw materials. Some factories had had to close down before February for lack of coal and textiles. It got worse in the following months. The industrial machine was turning slower and slower. The demands for pay increases, partially satisfied, acted like a branding iron on the industrialists. But the bourgeoisie was not satisfied to talk about its powerlessness to meet these demands; it challenged their legitimacy. N. N. Kutler, Council President of the Representatives of Industry, stated: "The workers who until this day agreed to work more than forty hours now refuse. It would seem desirable not only to not legalize the eight-hour day, but on the contrary to require that where this demand has already been put into practice it be replaced by a longer work day."

Above all, management refused the guaranteed wage, saying "No work, no pay." This was a serious matter since supply difficulties deprived the factories of their normal supplies of fuel or other essential materials. Would the workers be paid only when the plant was functioning normally? "The Union of Moscow Industrialists" asked the government for some concrete help, but other industries already decided that it was no longer possible to function under these conditions. Some plants closed down.

A series of strikes started up again. The workers had already forgotten the work schedules under the Tsar. The bourgeoisie thought they had too many meetings, parades, and conferences; everything was an excuse for debate. As soon as a question came up concerning the job, work stopped and everyone had his say in these shop meetings. Of course, at quitting time everyone expected to be paid. Lack of concern and disregard for regulations all added to the clashes with the bosses, who had little self-control left. One of them was publicly assaulted. What was the world coming to?

Management asked the Government to put a quick stop to this turbulence; there was no time to lose. The middle-class businessmen had their own economic program which would bear no delays and no setbacks. They wanted to reorganize production and thought that the time for social reform should come later. The behavior of the working class was beginning to get on their nerves; it seemed as though the workers would never be satisfied. What was the government going to do about it?

In agreeing to enter the government, the socialist ministers had a three-point economic and social program: the establishment of an arbitration procedure to settle conflicts between workers and employers; state control of production and distribution; rigid control of war profits, with excess profits to be used to finance the "social" expenses. Evidently this program was copied from the English, for Arthur Henderson had convinced his friends of its efficacy when he was in Russia. Much impressed, Tseretelli, Chernov, and Skobelev had asked Russian management to copy the British example. Nekrassov, Konovalov, and Tereshchenko, the liberal bourgeois representatives in the government, had made no objections, but Shingarev doubted that Russian employers were ready to make the sacrifices it entailed.

After the April events, the government's statement of May 5 expressed the agreement concluded between the old government and the Soviet. The workers were promised some measures to safeguard their employment, but on the other hand the statement condemned "all the anarchistic and violent illegal acts which were disorganizing the country." The foundations of an economic policy were laid: "The Provisional Government will struggle resolutely and firmly against the economic disorganization of the country by systematically setting up governmental control of production, transportation, trade, and the distribution of consumer goods and, in case of need, even industrial organization."

Very discreet on the subject of problems bearing on job security, the government did not go beyond the preceding government, which had done nothing. The principal innovation had been the law of April 23 which set up the "Factory Committees," but this was in reality only the recognition of an accomplished fact. It was always the factory committees or the soviets who negotiated the terms of the agreement between workers and employers. The government had no objection to this procedure, which had been recommended by the Petrograd Soviet. On April 23 the Central Grievance Committee set a minimum wage of five rubles a day for men and four rubles for women, but the government would not guarantee that this agreement would be enforced.

Management interpreted this passiveness correctly and appealed to the State. It asked the government to let it be known that "in the absence of any new laws, the old laws remained in effect." It was significant that in spite of repeated demands from the workers, no eight-hour law was passed.

In favor of the arbitration procedure, Labor Minister Skobelev wrote a law regularizing the use of "grievance committees" in management-worker disputes. He also instituted "Work Committees" made up of equal proportions of workers and managers, which would facilitate agreements between the representatives of management and workers. Auerbach, a member of this commission on the management side, left evidence about the proceedings of these meetings chaired by the minister:

Thanks to their vast erudition, the worker delegates reinforced their arguments with references to laws and customs of all countries, with convention resolutions, etc. The reports which preceded the spelling out of their legal proposals had been carefully prepared. It was evident that everything had been thought of and put in order. Our avowed opponents, the workers' section of the committee, were armed to the teeth. At the first meeting we were deluged with excerpts, examples, formulas, and they did it quite effortlessly. . . . It looked as though we were beaten before the battle began.

Auerbach then reports how management was able to overcome its dismay and to keep ahead of the worker delegates:

All the projects introduced by the delegates entailed considerable expense for the Treasury. The employers started to demonstrate what each improvement won by the Revolution would cost the country. Their calculations panicked their opponents. . . . Even on the questions which were incontestable, such as sickness insurance, old age insurance, we just shrugged our shoulders asking how they could proceed at the national level without upsetting the whole economy.

Thus the employers tried to stall for time, arguing about their financial difficulties and their inability to satisfy the workers' demands. They would only agree to set up some commissions which would study the workers' proposals—"sterile victories" Auerbach noted later. A few months later, the Bolsheviks would find all these projects of social reform all worked out, so that it would seem to observers that the difference between them and the "conciliators" was that they acted speedily. The Socialist ministers deplored this show of bad faith because it played into the hands of the Bolsheviks.

To tell the truth, the Socialist Ministers were counting heavily on State control which would permit them to nationalize production and distribution and to increase the availability of the management class and the country's potential. Since the Socialist Ministers failed to make management listen to reason on the social reform plan, the economic takeover by the State was more urgently needed than ever. The war had shown the economic weaknesses of Russia, and they had to be corrected or everyone would suffer. On May 16 the Soviet reminded the government that they wanted it to take "immediate, complete, and systematic" control of the economy. It urged the setting up of government monopolies on wheat, meat, salt, and leather, and State control of coal mining, oil-drilling, and financial institutions, as well as of metal, sugar, and paper production. It recommended price stabilization. The bourgeoisie thought they were dreaming of Utopia. "Don't expect us to become infected with your democratic mood or that we'll believe in your slogans," stated the South Russian industrialists. Skobelev, the

Socialist Minister of Labor, reassured them immediately: "When we speak of State intervention in the regulation and control of production, we are not thinking of socializing production nor of state socialism, but of the introduction of minimum economic measures required for the country, such as have already been introduced in England."

That was Minister of Industry Konovalov's understanding, when he signed the statement of May 5. In April he had himself mentioned the need for government control. The committees which he envisioned were to help in the coordination of industrial production. These State organizations were to centralize and disseminate orders. Some of the industrial leaders were in favor of such a project because they would favor the industrialists who were on good terms with the ministerial team in power. As a concession to the spirit of the revolution, Konovalov intended that the committees would be open to "everyone," not only to Management and government. He intended also to put a limit on war profits and on wages. He immediately came into conflict with both the extreme left and management. The former thought that he was dreaming; and the latter refused to understand what Stepanov had clearly explained—"that it was in the best interest of free enterprise to have State control," because the State had been under control of the bourgeoisie since February and was trying to resist the assault of those who urged the immediate establishment of Socialism. When he resigned because of his failure, Konovalov blamed "the outrageous demands of the workers" and held them responsible for his departure; because the Socialist circles had not been able to choke off revolutionary activities, he preferred to pass the reins to someone else and leave the way open for a Socialist experiment. At the Soviet, there was consternation. Konovalov did his worst, but nevertheless the Mensheviks and S.R.s put the blame on Lenin as being partly responsible for his departure.

In fact, management thought the hope of an agreement with the Soviet was an illusion. Some thought that a Socialist experiment would produce such chaos that the sooner it was tried the better, but most refused to compromise. With Konovalov gone, the government did not think it wise to publish the report of his successor, V. Stepanov. Konovalov had thought the "state control" which the Soviet wanted to impose on industry impractical, but Stepanov declared on June 8 that "the changeover to Socialism was impossible at the moment." "Still," he added, "the State can create monopolies, if not in industry, at least in commerce."

267

This didn't look anything like what the Socialists meant by state control. Stepanov had borrowed an idea from the industrialist Palchinsky, who had shown the need to create organizations wherein the manufacturers would be represented and whose role would be the rationalization of production. Already, for defense orders, they had to go through the *Prodamet* and *Krovlya* trusts, for railroad material through *Prodvagon*. Stepanov wanted to widen the system and Nekrassov to coordinate the actions of the railroad companies and those of the flour mills, already grouped into a cartel which produced 75 percent of the national output. In brief, as Volobuev remarked, the Provisional Government "legalized these private associations by blanketing them with the State's authority."

Nevertheless, most of the producers were opposed to this project. Since the Socialists in the government were in favor of it, they saw it as a stage toward nationalization. Others were afraid that it would end in a limitation of profits, that the project would change the industrialists into employees, or that the process of centralization would end in socialization. There were some attempts to improve the system in the mills, with no important result. Further, what was done had nothing to do with the sort of control the Soviet had in mind. They were at the stage of declarations of principle and protests. At the Congress of Soviets at the end of June, Grohman insisted that "the industrialists' opposition to government intervention be crushed."

If almost nothing was done in the area of control of production, some steps were taken to improve distribution. True, management would favor this because the rationalization of sales would help in allocation of coal and raw materials; at least this was the case with the manufacturers of machine-tools. The government acted more vigorously in the case of textiles distribution, which were the principal means of exchange in the countryside. If they wanted the peasants to deliver the agricultural products, they had to have cloth. Under the pressure of need and spurred by Food Minister Peshekhonov, the government reorganized the distribution of cotton and wool supplies. Producers and wholesalers were opposed to the project, and the wholesalers finally cornered fifty percent of the market; the rest was sold at a price which was taxed at fifty percent of the price on the open market. The establishment of this state monopoly allowed for rationing, but the moderate press already was speaking of "the murder of the cotton industry and the liquidation of commercial enterprises." In leather also a monopoly of sales was established, in spite of the producers' resistance, but for lack of credits which were not distributed in time, the committee charged with the organization of the monopoly was unable to carry out its task. The monopolies on leather and sugar were established, with the objective of consolidating the wheat monopoly and the policies adopted with regard to the agricultural community.

The Provisional Government had no well established policy about finances. They expected, no doubt, to fight inflation, increase state revenues, and better control the expenditures, but there was no overall plan and as usual it set up a commission to study the methods of fiscal reform. Meanwhile it promised all the creditors of the State, both Russian and foreign, that it would honor its contracts and the commitments of the former régime.

In order to meet the immediate needs of the Treasury, the business circles accepted the principle of· limiting excess profits. S. I. Chetverikov, a Moscow industrialist, was named President of this commission, which included S. N. Tretzhakov, another industrialist. But the project failed. The government expected much from the "Liberty Loans"; the objective of this good-will loan was to resolve the initial difficulties of the new State's treasury, to prove that it was backed by the country's power. Eventually the Allies might lend a financial hand. The Soviet agreed to help with the loan at the end of April, which caused a great deal of controversy. There was talk of a deal, since it occurred at about the time of Milyukov's fall. The results of the Liberty Loan were rather feeble, because a large part of the upper middle class refused to subscribe. "It is a shame," said *Den*, the most moderate of the Socialist journals; "on the minister's first list the upper bourgeoisie is conspicuous by its absence. There are deserters at the Front and there are those at the rear as well." In effect, in Moscow all the textile magnates together had subscribed 43 million rubles, a small sum in view of the 10 million rubles which sugar banker Zharosinsky alone gave. The loan raised only a few hundreds of million rubles, while Tereshchenko hoped to raise three or four billion, and according to Tugan-Baronovsky, about fifteen billion were available.

The bourgeoisie stated that it intended to practice a policy of "equal sacrifice," which meant that it would increase its contribution and accept some financial sacrifices by limitings its profits only if the working class would agree to reduce its demands and quit its campaign for increased wages. The May 5 declaration increased its irritation because it was aimed at the magnates and the war profiteers. (See text 32 in Appendix.)

Tereshchenko's successor in the Finance Ministry, Andrei Shingarev, ran into the "money wall." The subscriptions to the Liberty Loan diminished; the banks were beginning to ruin the country's finances by aiding the flight of capital. The value of the ruble took a nose-dive, which had its effect on potential foreign loans. Paper money circulation was increased in four months from 10 to 13 billion rubles.

The bourgeois ministers were caught between two fires. On one side, their Socialist colleagues and the Soviet urged them to take steps against the shirkers in the rear; on the other, while hoping that their banker friends would help them in their troubles, they knew that "the capitalists would give nothing as long as anarchy reigned." "The small trickle of tax revenues, the failure of the Liberty Loan, the liquidation of property in Russia, and the acquisition of property abroad are the symptoms of the financial panic in Petrograd," the American Consul Winship wrote to his government.

With the hostility and the recalcitrance of the business circles mounting and the pressure from the Soviets increasing, the government decided to take coercive measures against reluctant capitalists. The first solution thought of was a forced loan; apparently first proposed by Peshekhonov, it had several backers in the Soviet. However, Shingarev thought it would be the wrong time to kill the goose which laid the golden eggs. It wasn't rejected but was put off to a later date.

The freezing of funds was the first effective measure taken against the owners. Tax reform was getting nowhere. Everything went along as though the government was expecting the businessmen to rally to its policy of class cooperation—that is, to a régime which was still under their control. But the privileged classes remained deaf to Shingarev's appeals. Skobelev criticized their attitude publicly. The conflict with the government coincided with the increase of the agitation of the factory committees. He declared that the bosses had only one way to remain in charge of their businesses—by giving up their profits to the State. In agreement for once, Plekhanov and Lenin condemned this demagogic statement. But it had its effect. More people knew about the industrialists' war profits and a kind of anger arose against the selfishness of the propertied class. In order to protect them, Shingarev drafted a circular forbidding the control of banking

270

activities for social organization purposes; he did not want commercial secrets revealed. In the civil war atmosphere of June, he understood the need for concessions to public opinion. The law of June 12, 1917, hit the revenues of 1917 pretty hard, while the tax on the war profits of the years 1916-17 reached 90 percent in some cases. This was harsher in appearance than in reality. It affected profits, not capital, and it didn't provide for the creation of a controlling body. Above all, by giving the interested parties a long delay for payment (until April 1, 1918), it allowed them to find means to escape payment through transferral and banking operations. Business circles nevertheless protested violently against the law of June 12. Palchinsky and Bublikov attacked it in the "Special Defense Committee." In order to have it abrogated, they explained that, from a patriotic as well as a practical standpoint, by striking so heavily against the industrialists who furnished the necessary weapons for the country's defense, the government was creating an insurmountable obstacle for the manufacture of necessary material for a successful offensive. General Polivalov supported them in this.

THE BEGINNING OF THE CLASS WAR:
THE FACTORY COMMITTEE MOVEMENT

The Coalition Government had not attained its two objectives, the establishment of state control and the implementation of a democratic financial policy. The Socialist ministers had fought uselessly, but the working classes weren't interested in that; they had never been in favor of state control or a more equitable fiscal policy. On the other hand, the government had taken no legislative steps toward the eight-hour day or toward solving any of the problems of conflict with employees; thus the strikes took on a slight anti-government tinge.

	March	April	May	June
Number of governments in which there were no strikes (out of 75)	16	11	6	1
Number of Strikes (12 to 15 governments, including Moscow, but not Petrograd)	141	231	298	402

The big surge came in May. The working class returned to the tradition of 1905, which had been interrupted by reaction and the war. The February events were not only the work of the working class but concerned the whole of Russia, but now things were different; these strikes belonged to the working class and to it alone. In February the workers had demonstrated to show their discontent about certain things, i.e., poverty, the rise in prices, the harshness of life, the horrors of war. These reasons were still valid, but the strikes now took in much more territory, which was still undefined, but would be revealed gradually.

Management's answer was the lockout. Some businesses slowed down due to the supply problem, which might have justified laying off workers; others closed. It remained to be seen if the shortage of raw materials was an excuse and they were trying to make the workers see the error of their ways. According to the payrolls of 70 factories who laid off workers between April and October, about fifty employers explained this action was due to supply shortages, while about twenty blamed the workers' demands. But according to an investigation made by *Torgovo Promyshlennaya Gazeta* which came out in the spring, at a time when the bourgeoisie had complete faith in its power, the proportions are reversed. It appears that from the end of April, 75 plants already had closed down in Petrograd—54 in order to counter the revolutionary workers' pressure, and 21 due to supply shortages. Regardless, the workers took the lockouts as a declaration of war. For example, in the Urals these lockouts occurred as soon as there was a threat of worker control. A statement from the "Industrialists Committee" focusing their demands on six points, confirms this opinion:

1. The State to have full control, but take no steps which would interfere with the carrying out of the laws.
2. Any attempt, even partial, to put into practice Socialist principles is noxious. The introduction of workers in the management of a company leads to anarchy.
3. Management-worker relations must be regulated by mixed tribunals.
4. No raise in pay.
5. If the government cannot understand this position, lockouts will be necessary, "in spite of the employers' best intentions."
6. Some shutdowns are already unavoidable.

Thus the origin of the lockout was not due to supply shortages. It was not even due to the individual initiative of an employer, as in the spring, but was in answer to a plan worked out during the summer in the Ukraine, in Moscow, and in the Urals by some committees of industrialists. In May and June new plants were closed down every day. *Den* was not taken in. On June 17 it wrote: "If in some cases, the shutdowns are caused by raw material shortages, in many others they are to intimidate the workers and the Provisional Government."

The factories now closed wholesale, according to plan. All legal precautions were taken so that the workers could not claim damages. Because the alleged reasons for this action were blamed on governmental mismanagement—shortage of fuel, etc.—responsibility for the care of the unemployed fell on the shoulders of the State. They were far from job security and the long awaited pay raises.

In *Delo Naroda*, Viktor Chernov condemned this conspiracy which he compared to "bourgeois Bolshevism":

> In this conspiracy against the country, the industrialists are not far behind. . . . Look at this regulation worked out by the *Council of the Industrialists' Association.* Its members are forbidden any innovation in their companies without the consent of the Council. They agree to be bound by it and to deposit twenty-five rubles per employee as a guarantee. This isn't an industrialists association, it's a society of bourgeois Carbonari with an iron discipline. This is an action of the Knight Templars of Industry. It is bourgeois "Bolshevism."

Individually the Socialist ministers condemned the lockouts while calling it bourgeois Bolshevism. Together they did nothing against the offenders. On June 20 the Soviet intervened and set rigid rules for lockouts. It was a defense measure, which did not take into account the mood of the working class, which found in the factory committees an instrument more to its liking in the struggle against management.

THE FACTORY COMMITTEES

One of the main demands of the working class was the recognition and enlargement of the powers of the factory committees. Their function was to defend the workers' rights and to aid in improving their material and psychological position. They were their representatives and they were to meet on equal terms with the employers. At the company level, they would administer their affairs and protect them from the employers, just as at the national level the grievance committees would regulate the conflicts inside each branch of production. The law set the position of

273

the factory committees. It outlined the methods of election and set the limit of their powers. But it avoided the often expressed question of the freedom of the individual worker to refuse the services of the committee if he preferred to defend himself alone against management. Otherwise, the April 23 Law was pretty much what the workers had demanded. It made provisions so that management could not discharge committee members without a previous agreement.

In fact, the workers hadn't waited for the formulation of this law to organize "company committees," as is shown in their documents. From April on, these committees appear frequently. Depending on circumstances, they presented their demands directly to the administration of the plant or asked for the intervention of the local soviet. In any case, it seemed that in each large company the trade union section, the factory soviet, or its delegates from the city soviet, coexisted with the factory committee. The latter was the most energetic and took the place of the soviet, which dealt in high-level policies, or of the trade union, whose members always had to check with the national headquarters before acting. The factory committee directly defended the workers' interests.*

The committees were not much in evidence in March and April because during that period management had reached a number of agreements with the Soviet on the question of returning to work, the eight-hour day, and some pay increases. But starting in April, taking advantage of the conciliatory attitude of the government and the Soviet, management stiffened its attitude. Then the factory committees intervened in a revolutionary manner. In April and May they demanded supervision of the accounts of the companies to check as to whether or not they were in position to grant pay raises for the workers. Thus they learned that a large locomotive firm, whose management claimed that it was unable to grant a pay raise amounting to an annual 36,000 rubles, had earned two and a half million rubles' profit the year before.

Because management was taking steps to bring pressure on the workers and claimed that it could not keep up business as usual, the committees demanded, in their second move, to verify if the factory could no longer function regularly. The committee then set up its control over the administration of the firm. Sometimes, when the employer had already shut down the plant, the commit-

*This was not the case with the railworkers, where the reason for having a national union is self-evident.

tee undertook administering it. Condemning the economic sabotage by management, would the workers take charge of the country's economy?

"Normal economic relations are abolished," remarked *Rech* in mid-May. In effect, the committees were demanding supervision of the administration of the firms in all Russia—their third stage—and in turn, as Management had done before them, they issued "communiqués" which they labeled "in the public interest":

> The workers' and employees' committees of the *Dynamo* factory, noting the total neglect and poor administration of the management of the factory, have noticed the attempts to shut it down and then blame the workers for it. *Considering that the factory shutdown at this moment is a direct blow to national defense* [emphasis added—M.F.] and hastens the economic breakdown, they are uniting all their efforts to prevent a work interruption and improve production. They are reporting these facts to the Instructions Commission. . . . On this basis, workers and employees of the factory think it is essential to institute a greater control on the activities of the factory and on those responsible for its leadership.

The committees were able to take over the administration, as they did in some of the firms in the capital. But they quickly realized that a lone committee was powerless because the ruling class reacted by cancelling orders or the delivery of raw materials. The competence and the authority of the committees grew nevertheless. At this time, when they had as yet acted only in a scattered fashion, they already appeared as the most threatening institution for the capitalist system. At the moment when the employers began to see a safeguard in "state control," the factory committees took a step forward and coordinated their activities at the regional and national levels. Petrograd once more led the way, and starting in May they called a meeting of the factory committees of the capital. More than three hundred thousand workers were represented by 499 delegates mandated by 367 firms—an impressive number, considering that in all there were 670 firms working on defense, with 305,000 workers. Only 131 factories were lacking representatives. The trade unions and social organizations mandated 69 delegates. The delegates from the metallurgical industry represented almost two thirds of the workers present, an absolute majority. For the most part, they now professed Bolshevik opinions.

From the start the Bureau took an anti-employer position. V. M. Levin, an unaffiliated delegate, depicted the situation in the industry thus:

The worker movement in Russia has gone beyond the old limits of workers' actions. It is on a new track. The Factory Committees are *forced*, willy-nilly, to interfere in the economic life of the firms because otherwise the firms would have ceased to function. All industry in Petrograd is suffering from a fuel crisis. But the administration does nothing to remedy the situation. The workers are threatened with starvation due to unemployment. It's up to them to show initiative where the management has failed to do so. And only an organization uniting the factory committees can do this.

Thus was the idea of a new form of "worker control" born. S. M. Schwartz notes justly that this represented no real danger for the employers because they still owned the companies. This control did not change the nature of the productive relationships; it aimed only at ensuring the workers their salaries and decent living conditions. In a way, it tried to ensure the survival of the company, even though it was capitalistic.

The employers' hostility to such a project is understandable, for they saw it as an attack on their monopoly of administration. But the Mensheviks were also opposed to it. Skobelev explained to the Conference members that an administration without governmental control would remain a shadow. He was supported on the left by Avilov, from *Novaya Zhizn*. The truth was that the Mensheviks feared that their "state control" would lose its efficacy if it were counterbalanced by control at the bottom and by a federation of committees all controlled by the Bolsheviks. They were going against the current, and Zinoviev easily won with the Leninist theses on worker control. His motion noted the complete disintegration of the economy and criticized the means adopted by the government for solving the economic crisis:

It is not by bureaucratic means—that is to say, by the creation of organizations dominated by capitalists and officials —nor by retaining the profits of the capitalists, nor by safeguarding their full powers over production or their financial omnipotence that we will find the means to avoid disaster. The salvation of the country demands that we put full trust in the workers, not by words but by actions.
We shouldn't demand or expect revolutionary measure from these organizations. . . .

276

The way to salvation can only be found in the establishment of an effective worker control over production and distribution. In order to do this, it is essential: 1. That the worker organizations (trade unions, soviets, factory committees) should be guaranteed at least two thirds of the votes in the central units; 2. That the factory and plant committees have the right to participate in the control of each company, that they be allowed to examine the accounts and the banking operations.

Acknowledged in some cases, this control must be systematically extended.

This motion also recommended the introduction of the Labor Service and the creation of a workers' militia and ended by declaring that the implementation of all these measures would only be possible when "all power belonged to the soviet." This motion carried by 335 votes against 86 in favor of Cherevanin's motion. The last paragraph was approved by a 190 to 131 vote; a central committee for all the factory committees, with a Bolshevik majority, was then elected.

These decisions moved in the direction of the aspirations of the working class. They brought the Bolsheviks and the workers closer together while alienating them from the Mensheviks and Socialist ministers, who were seen as "proponents of bourgeois interests." The adoption of the Bolshevik resolution weakened the capitalist structure by getting at the base of the relations of production. As a matter of fact, the Bolshevik position was purely tactical. Once in control of the Bureau, they never intervened through the Council in the economic struggle and only used it in the political struggle. From then on, they had control points which allowed them to control the direction of the worker movement. At the Convention of the Factory Committees, they became the apostles of independence of the movement, with the support of Levin, while the Mensheviks defended the trade union prerogatives and were opposed to it. A little later, while in control of the Council, they put the project under wraps. It was mid-June; they had become masters of the trade unions before dominating the Petrograd Soviet itself and the independence of the movement of the Factory Committees no longer interested the Bolsheviks.

The Government and its Menshevik ministers were more energetic in the struggle against worker control than in the struggle with management. Stepanov in the government and Grinevich at the Trade Union Congress both condemned this fact. At the end of June, Skobelev launched a resounding appeal against the factory committees' actions. Its only effect was to destroy whatever

277

confidence the workers had left in the Ministers. Graver decisions had been made before that. At the beginning of May, Acting Minister Savin had suggested closing factories in which workers were trying to exert control. In June, he labeled "undesirable" an agreement reached at the Slyussarenko plants, where two workers were to sit with the directors' council. Savin thought that this would set a precedent. Then Skobelev decided that mixed commissions should not intervene in the administration of companies. At the time of the leather conflict, he came out against the intrusions of factory committees, and when they refused to dissolve, the government stopped the orders for the factories which they controlled and stopped the delivery of raw materials, just as the management had done. In more serious cases the government cut them off, all the while declaring itself opposed to such measures in general. This is what happened to the Brenner factories, as well as the Guzhon works, which management had decided to close down in spite of a decision to the contrary by the arbitration commission. Three months earlier, such a decision would have been hailed as a revolutionary victory against the perpetrators of the lockout. Coming at a time when the factory committees were seizing the companies threatened by management shutdown, the sequestration seemed like a conservative measure which broke the momentum of working-class domination in early June 1917.

5. IN THE COUNTRYSIDE: THE FIRST DISORDERS

In the Capital, the government and public opinion had their eyes on the rise of Bolshevism, the factional strife, the war, and the conflict between workers and employers. They had no inkling of the importance of the slower movement which was starting in the countryside and among the national minorities. In the spring, the peasant movement began, fully aware of its aspirations. The nationalities purused their aims more vigorously, but no one paid any attention. The national question, like the agrarian question, was a source of prime concern to the theorists and tacticians of the Revolution, but these questions seemed too delicate to be resolved just then, and they were left to the Constituent. The revolutionary theoreticians did not take into account either the impatience of the peasants or the demands of the minorities, their attention being focused on other problems. Thus the various circles reacted with irritation to the unexpected and intemperate actions which occurred on all sides. In the long run, this blindness was to lead to the explosion of the Russian State and to the breakdown of its economy. These events, along with the political and moral crisis, would lead between June and November to the sweeping away of the Old Régime, both economically and socially.

THE PEASANTS' ACTIONS

The ideas of the countryside were forcefully expressed at the very beginning of the revolution. (See Chapter IV.) The *mujiks* wanted to become landowners, if they weren't already, to enclose their lots as had already been done by those who were better off, to increase them at the expense of unworked or underdeveloped land. They no longer wanted to work for anyone else and wanted to be their own masters. If they work the farms of landowners, they expected the revolution to lower the land rent and to make a more equitable use of the forests and pastures. They trusted the local Committees to put into effect a redistribution of the wealth which would allow everyone to develop according to his potentialities and would leave the land only to those who worked it.

The peasants' impatience is explained by the long wait and by a whole history of suffering. As the provinces more open to commerce saw a peasant bourgeoisie gradually evolve into more prosperous circumstances, and this development gradually extended to the central provinces, the luck of this minority made the rest of the peasants envious. Stolypin's reforms not only gave birth to a rural bourgeoisie and turned the *mujiks*' hopes toward private ownership, but they also destroyed the old village community, and with it the old family ties. This disintegration had far-reaching effects. Each man, using his freedom as best he knew how, started working for himself. During the first four months of 1917 there were as many isolated acts as collective acts against the old order.

Because it had not received the land by distribution decree, the peasantry started to act in March. Slow to start, it took four months to reach the climax which was so violent as to sweep away the régime born in February.

The *mujiks* started by appropriating the vacant lands and those which were fallow. Further, they seized the cordwood and the haystacks which they themselves had made, judging them fair game. They seized equipment which belonged to the landowners since they were the ones who used it. The count of violations of the established order has been meticulously kept:

	March	April	May	June	Total
Land Seizures	2	51	59	136	248
Trees Felled & Lumber Theft	34	18	19	71	142
Hay Seizures	—	1	11	280	292
Equipment Theft	?	10	7	71	88
Sundry & Total	57	174	236	577	1044

The *mujiks* also proceeded to arrest some people. In the Penza Region, they put an end to the obstreperous actions of a neighborhood *kulak*, among others:

> He held us under the yoke for many years, refusing deliberately to grant us right of way at any price, so that, since we were obliged to pass through his lands, he fined us. . . . He refused to sell us land and then granted them to neighboring *kulaks* rather than us, who asked for them. For many decades we had only the brackish water from his factories to drink. Because of that already in 1905 there were troubles and some of our brethren were condemned to terms in prison. Bakulin, a reactionary monarchist, is a member of the "Union of Russian People"; it would be dangerous to allow him to remain at large.

Along with this, some village committees were organized and prepared to grant the immediate demands of the peasantry, to legalize the first steps taken collectively. The dispositions adopted by the assemblies of peasant-delegates of the Samara and Ryazan Provinces are very interesting from this point of view. It was understood that they were temporary measures and that the determination of the method of possession of the land was to be left to the Constituent Assembly. All land transactions were to be stopped immediately, especially the transfer of communal lands to *otrubniks* (peasants who had left the *mir*). Everything was to be favorable to the seeding of land and to making the best use of the material available. Thus they planned to force the large landowners to seed the maximum amount of land, to put the pastures and the uncultivated land under control of committees or associations, that they would pay a tax equal to that of 1914, plus 75 percent, but not more. To ensure fairness, numerous guarantees were granted to those who had cultivated other people's land for more than ten years. They planned to create at the *volost* level new arbitration tribunals whose decrees would be law until the Constituent Assembly should set up a new agrarian system.

The landowners reacted immediately. Criticising individual actions, they wanted them referred to the traditional channels and called on the Provisional Government to take action against the spread of anarchy in the countryside. Often the large landowners interrupted the sowing, imitating the industrialists who used the lockout. They even resorted to fictitious sales to foreign nationals, which exasperated the peasants. A report of a Vice-President of the Saratov government established the responsibility of each side in the controversy:

> There is neither jacquerie nor murder nor looting of estates, except in a few isolated instances of confiscation of the weapons of former high officials who were dispossessed. Sometimes the overseers have been replaced or arrested and put at the mercy of the *Volost* committee. More often, prisoners of war have been given peasants' holdings. The *Volost* committees have the peasants' confidence. They issue decrees and determine which part of the land the landowners are to seed. They reevaluate the land rents, and the new estimates are given to the owners. The same goes for the equipment and the seed. Here and there, it happens that they use the landowners' horses for the heavy work. . . . Often the conflict is aggravated by the landowners because they refuse to acknowledge the *Volost* committee's legality, confirmed by the Revolution.

The big landowners refused to lower the land rent. The Povarov peasants in the Pereyaslovsky District complained to the Moscow Soviet, "Our proprietor makes us wait hours and hours and then says nothing doing." Elsewhere a forestry director warned the Government Commissar that the peasants were furious that the estate forests had not been distributed, because they learned that elsewhere the distribution of the great estates had been effected.

At the beginning of April, the Tver peasants sent the government a message which showed their bitterness. "The land continues to be governed by the old laws, the estates as well as the crown lands and the monastic lands. The people have lost all faith in the new government."

> We have been told that we have given our most treasured possession, our sons, to save the country. There are as many as six men from one family on active duty. The old government took our horses, our cows; they were slaughtered and the meat rotted and no one gained thereby. Our children must not lay down their arms as long as the land hasn't been given, to the last plot, to the working people, as long as we aren't able to save the

Russian land from famine. Let us cultivate new lands, and in five to ten years the country will become so rich that Russia will be unrecognizable. We have so much wheat that we don't know where to put it since the government forbade us to sell it two years ago. We could feed the whole Tver government and Petrograd also for five months. But no one will buy our grain, so it rots. Send us some buyers and we'll sell it to them with pleasure. We also have plenty of potatoes.

THE NEW RÉGIME'S ANSWER

In its initial reaction, the government had refused to send the troops demanded by the landowners. On April 4 it decided to act, probably because the amount of lands seized had mounted steeply, going from 9 in March to 51 in April. It was feared that the population would proceed to the land distribution before the method of reform could be established by the Constituent Assembly. But it was precisely the reiterated appeals of the government which irritated the peasants. They would have preferred that it legislate without further ado. The government had already decided to nationalize the crown lands and the departmental lands, but immediately specified that they should not be seized as long as the agrarian reform had not been formulated. In April the government planned to take certain steps, satisfactory no doubt, but still conservative. All land transactions were thereupon suspended and Stolypin's reforms were interrupted. Locally the lands came provisionally under the jurisdiction of the "Land Committees," the makeup of which was similar to that of the Committee on the Wheat Monopoly and was open to criticism. What is more, the actions which they might take were in doubt and the *mujiks* wondered if they were aimed at the owners or themselves.

The agrarian question was of such importance that the government would have preferred that the coming reforms not be put in doubt. As usual, a sweeping law first instituted some "land committees" at the local, regional, and national levels. And again, their makeup caused some concern. The worst of it was that the first session would not be held until May 19, and then it was only decided that the task of the national committee would be to gather information, to propose legislation, and to help with provisional arbitration wherever conflicts arose.

By that time, numerous agrarian committees had been set up spontaneously and at various levels. Their composition did not conform to the norms set by the law and it was doubtful that the actions taken at the lower levels would be validated at the next level. To this source of conflict was added the discord between those who wanted to let the local revolutionary organs act and those who urged the coordination of action coming from the Central Committee. Whole collectives, such as that of the Cossacks of the Don, refused to admit the legitimacy of an agrarian reform which concerned them. Several times they recalled that they had acquired their lands by force of arms and there was no question of giving them back. On this question, their motion of June 15, 1917, was explicit. When the Central Land Committee met, the discussions about the agrarian question had been reopened for quite some time. The positions taken by different categories of poor rural peasants, *kulaks*, landowners, and Cossacks were firm. The chances for an agreement were slim, and the chances of applying it even slimmer.

When the political parties met, the extent of the movement in the countryside had been known for some time. While locally the pressure exerted by the small peasants and the landowners moved in opposite directions, in the city the parties started up their old quarrels. However, they no longer opposed each other on the nature of the reforms, but rather on the attitude to be taken about the actions of the peasant movement. Thus the program adopted by the Cadets in May 1917 resembled that of the Socialist-Revolutionaries so much that Prince Trubetskoy and I. Flinkel accused the party leaders of acting with the same demagoguery as their opponents. In effect the Cadets wanted to forbid the reassignment of lands and denounced the suppression of the commons (*obshchina*). They even planned to give the landless peasants the surplus from those landowners whose holdings exceeded the norm, although the actual terms remained to be set. Finally, this proposal of Efimovich was rejected, but there were 33 delegates who approved it against 74 opposed, with about 30 abstentions. Instead of confiscation (with the State indemnifying the expropriated), the party rallied to the idea of forced sales without compensation. The confiscated land would be put into a fund for distribution by the State. They thought they could overcome all obstacles by imposing a progressive land tax. Only a small minority of the Cadets continued to uphold the rights of inequality, and they were no longer listened to. Differing from the S.R.'s program, however, these proposals were only valid in the regions where the minimal norms had not been reached by the local population. Elsewhere, it was possible to own more. Efimovich and Gronsky spoke in favor of forced confiscation of all lands which exceeded the norm but got no response.

The Socialist-Revolutionaries continued to extoll equality. At the Soviet Peasants' Congress where Avxentiev was elected President they urged nationalization without compensation and in accordance with egalitarian principles. Chernov expected to entrust the revived *obshchina* with the administration of the land. To attain perfect equity, he analyzed the principles which should rule in evaluating the norm: it would be necessary to carefully limit the available lands, to classify the terrain, to take an inventory of demands, to supply what was needed, and to figure out the best way to utilize the rest. However, the S.R.s were quite aware of the rights of the communities, especially the Cossacks, who would fiercely defend their privileges. "Only a small minority of the Cossacks understand that when they behave thus, they are alienating themselves from the population," deplored *Delo Naroda*.

While the Mensheviks brought nothing new to the discussion, the Bolsheviks adopted a position opposed to those majority parties. Lenin urged, as before, the seizure of all land without indemnity, always avoiding having to specify how it would be used; above all he urged the peasants to act without delay, asking only that they act through the offices of the local agrarian committees. It can't be said whether this intrusion at the peasants' Congress on May 22 had any effect on the provinces. In Petrograd, they were furious; "If Lenin didn't exist," exclaimed Lieber at the Soviet, "the bourgeoisie would have invented him."

In fact, the Central Agrarian Committee had come out in favor of a Pan-Russian solution to the question. The decisions made locally were only provisional and the local committees would be placed under a central body. Chernov, the Agriculture Minister, thus favored a policy which gave the peasants the impression that their activities were controlled, while the Bolsheviks egged them on to act. The Minister had formally come out "against all seizures and illegal violence." He repeated: "Our slogan is land through the Constituent." He acted in accordance with the Central Land Committee and the Congress of Peasant Soviets, hoping that the land survey would be straightened out quickly and the norms calculated in such a manner that the equity and the productivity would be reconciled. The Provisional Government was nevertheless opposed to any and all measures which Chernov wanted to take to show his solicitude for the peasants. He was thus in the minority when he wanted to forbid land transactions and his colleague in the Ministry of Justice, P. N. Perevertsev, pointedly declared that such transactions were legal. Chernov was also unable to promulgate a law which would permit the villages to use the grazing grounds (meadows). He couldn't even offer the peasants freedom to fish where the rights were reserved for private associations. At the Council, he was in complete disagreement with Peshekhonov, who had diametrically opposed views on the agrarian question, and with his other colleagues, who thought his conduct was demagogic. Thus, two months after assuming office, Chernov had succeeded only in having the reforms of Stolypin abolished. Since there were no indications that anything was going to change, the peasants began to act on their own. In June they seized the hay stocks, and soon this action spilled over from the troubled areas into central Russia.

The other ministers not only had different views from Chernov's, but their functions caused them to see the agrarian question from another angle. They wanted to reestablish the economic cycle. According to Peshekhonov, the unrest in the provinces was due to the fact that they got no compensation for their work. Blocking the flow of transactions would only increase the anxiety of the peasant landholders, thus compounding the evil instead of curing it. Shingarev told the Food Congress on May 21 that it wasn't wheat which was lacking, thus confirming the most widely circulated rumors. "There is grain in all the provinces," he declared. Nevertheless, the wheat was not forthcoming in spite of the establishment of the monopoly. According to Peshekhonov, that was due to the poor distribution of the "Food Committees." Where there were shortages there were committees, but not where there was abundance because there the peasants hadn't felt the need to hoard. The harvests piled up, to their great discontent. If anyone wanted to buy it, there was no guarantee that the peasants would deliver the food because they wanted to be able to acquire products from the city. Since production in the city was diminishing, there was a danger that the countryside would not deliver anything.

The opponents of reform were familiar with these doldrums. For lack of qualified personnel they had to use the good offices of the banks to make the wheat monopoly work. Behind them, merchants and financiers made the law, and they were reluctant to deliver the wheat at a fixed price. The inventory of stocks aroused the suspicions of the landowners who hid their wheat and hoarded it. In July, these inventories had been completed in only a few jurisdictions. According to an investigation of sixteen provinces by the Moscow Soviet, the price set by law was in effect in only two provinces.

The peasants' anger mounted by extending their destruction further. The local Committees were gradually overcome by poor peasants, and more often by soldiers, who gave added force to the peasants' demonstrations. The Russian countryside was overrun by disorders, adding a new threat to the dangers of the war, of the class struggle in the cities, and of the revolt of the national minorities.

The immediate effect was to irritate the population of the large cities which, four months after the fall of the Tsar, were worse fed than in February. Along with this, prices continued to rise in accordance with the laws of the open market. They had risen an average of 112 percent, while wages had only risen 53 percent. In his memorandum of June 8, 1917, V. Stepanov drew a sad picture of the Russian economy. "The desperate situation of transportation, paralyzed by strikes and lockouts in the coal mines, the rise in prices, the exhaustion of raw material stocks, the food shortage, and finally the bitterness of the struggle between capital and labor turn the conflict of interests between groups into economic chaos." In the south of Russia, out of 48 furnaces, only 33 were in use on June 23. The same situation in the Martin furnaces. The number of useable locomotives diminished. There was only ten days' fuel left, and the railroads took coal that was reserved for consumers. It was real chaos and disaster was at hand.

6. THE RUSSIAN REVOLUTION
AND THE NATIONAL MINORITIES

Between February and July, the national movement had spread from one end of Russia to the other. But for a long time, Petrograd heard nothing about it, except for what concerned the Ukraine and Finland. No doubt, the interruption of Maksudov, a Tatar, at the Cadets' Congress at the end of March created a stir (he scored Russian imperialism and its attacks on Turkish Islam), but its importance went unnoted. Nor did anyone note the first Pan-Moslem Congress of Kazan on May 1st, or the events in Latvia. As for the steps taken in Turkestan, they had to do with restoring order in a situation troubled by the mountaineers, and the amnesty offered them looked very much like subjection. No one in authority in Petrograd pictured this colonial question from the viewpoint of the minorities. It was the same way originally with the Ukraine. In Petrograd, says Chernov, no one gave a thought to the *Rada* established on March 2nd; they had eyes only for the Kiev Soviet and its demands for immediate peace. Practically everywhere the soviets, made up almost exclusively of Russians, took up all sorts of problems, but not that of the national minorities. In the Petrograd Soviet it was out of a sense of fairness, by majority vote, that an Armenian delegate was admitted. Elsewhere, there were many representatives of the *Bund*, the Poles, and Latvians, but little importance was attached to the national problems which they might bring up.

The revolutionaries in the capital were misinformed about these matters; to tell the truth, they weren't interested. The federal problem, for them, concerned only the Baltic countries, Georgia, Armenia, and even Finland. In July the Pan-Moslem Congress launched an appeal, noting specifically that "the new Russia paid no more attention than the old to the problems of the Moslems, and that the press—the Conservatives as well as the Liberals and Socialists—was trying to stifle this Second Congress. Only one official pamphlet alluded to it, and that was to say it should be dealt with severely." At the Soviet Congress in June, the Estonians had voiced some complaints of the same kind, which could be found in the Crimea as well.

The Russians in the various countries of the Empire ceaselessly warned of the activities of the nationalists, labeling them as reactionary. The non-Ukrainian groups of Kiev (the soviet, etc.) scored the *Rada*, insisting that it was not representative—an argument also used elsewhere. The Helsingfors Soviet, made up exclusively of Russians—as were most of the soviets, in Kazan, Tiflis, and other cities—supported the Provisional Government unconditionally against Finnish "*provocateurs*" paid by Germany. In Alma-Ata, the Russian Peasant Congress proposed "isolating the natives and strengthening the garrisons in order to overcome national antagonism." As far as the national movement was concerned, the same type of castigation was used from the Zimmerwaldian extreme Left to the reactionary extreme Right: "Chauvinists and petit-bourgeois, nothing else."

The attitude of the Soldiers' Soviet showed what kind of reception the claims of the national minorities would get. We know that they demanded the organization of a national army of separate regiments. After March 20, the Petrograd Soviet rejected this principle, the idea then being the formation of a revolutionary army. In May, "in the midst of the yelling," it rejected the Ukrainians' demand with the cry of "reaction." It was not altogether an alibi because in demanding the organization of autonomous regiments, the nationalists gave the government to understand that they would be devoid of Bolshevik elements. Nevertheless, the soviets of Reval (Estonia) and of Moscow, the Russian garrison of Kiev in particular opposed this demand to which the nationalists attached so much importance for the same reason. The Petrograd Soviet only made an exception in the case of the already existing Lettish regiments. At the end of May they still opposed the formation of a Polish army, which would be "an instrument of the reaction to stifle Polish freedom after the liberation."

The political parties had great difficulty in reconciling their program with their "defensism," all the while taking into account the pressure of the national minorities as well as that of the Great Russians.

The right and K.D.s (Cadets) quickly became alarmed by the weakening of authority at the borders and the aspirations toward federalism. "It is only when the autonomous parties of Russia all have attained the level of Russian civilization that it will be possible to plan for federalism," explained *Birzhevye Vedomosty*, while *Novoe Vremya* worried about the demands of the minority regiments, wondering about the manner of yielding. "After the troops, it will be the foreign policy." In *Russkaya Volya* (Right) as in *Rech* (K.D.), it was shown that the Finns and Ukrainians were playing into the Germans' hands and should be dealt with harshly. In the minds of the K.D.s, the problem of Finnish liberty and that of a German attack were closely linked.

The different meetings of the K.D. party allow us to see how the perspectives of the bourgeoisie were narrowed in proportion as the disagreements between the national minorities and the Russian government multiplied. The K.D.s had always been hostile to federalism, "which weakened the State," showing the nationalities that such a régime would be an illusion in view of the disproportion existing between Great Russian and those that were federated with it. In 1906 they urged extra-territorial cultural autonomy, but allowed that local governmental bodies might have control of the cultural institutions; they also admitted the principle of local laws. Kokoshkin's report of May 13, 1917, does not mention local laws, except in administrative matters. He recommended that Russia not be cut up, but agreed to primary school instruction in the local language. In July the Nolde report excluded all territorial autonomy because it would end in the oppression of the national minorities (Jews, Germans, Russian Ukrainians). The report recommends that the central government be entrusted with giving each nationality its laws and regulations. It proposed the constitution of "National Leagues" with proportional representation guaranteed, which would thus take their part in the legislative work. To what extent the K.D.s were moving against the stream could be judged when, at the end of July, Minister of National Education A. M. Manuilov alluded at length to his recent scholarly work in Ukrainian and proposed his project of spelling reform.

The attitude of the Socialists was more ambiguous. As "Defensists" they could not, like the K.D.s, tolerate the least weakening of the State, especially since they were in charge of it. Henceforth, they saw themselves forced to postpone the application of their principles, casting aside former fellow travelers and now allied with the Monarchist Right! Most of them underestimated the national question to such an extent that in the Petrograd Soviet it didn't even rate a special commission. They asked the national minorities to forget their needs in the name of the "safety of the Revolution," a favorite theme with Kerensky.

The Socialist-Revolutionaries found themselves in a most delicate situation, along with Kerensky and Chernov, now that they were in the government precisely because they had always been ardent defenders of the nationalists, especially the Ukrainians. At first the party tried to finagle. At the April Congress the national question was practically made to vanish. In May the reports of Vishnyak and Chernov were looked forward to, since the moment had come for the S.R.s to set a policy and apply it. Vishnyak came out in favor of a federal constitution of the Swiss type with a collective executive. A *Bundesstaat* and not a *Staatesbund*, explained Radkey. But it would be largely autonomous, since the Ukraine, for example, would have its own regiments, currency, etc. The minorities would be granted personal extra-territorial autonomy. Only Poland would be independent. Three months earlier these proposals would have been accepted enthusiastically. But the straddling of the issues by the S.R.s was revealed suddenly when the question of the representation of the national minorities at the Constituent was brought up. On the 6th, Chernov wrote in *Delo Naroda* that they must not, as in the *Rada* of the Ukraine, settle questions unilaterally. Nevertheless, at the S.R. Congress his motion had precisely this result since it rejected the principle of an autonomous Ukrainian representation—which the Greater Russians would have argued against—in favor of a proportional representation which would have made the Russians "unilaterally" masters of the destinies of the national minorities.

In the *Rabochaya Gazeta* the Mensheviks made a special case for Finland, urging after April a direct agreement between the Seim and the Constituent Assembly. In June they chided the government for its inertia. But in the case of the Ukraine they were intractable, "because this national movement showed nationalist and bourgeois qualities wherein bourgeois and peasants were fighting the Soviets. Further, federalism found allies there among the reactionaries like A. Sholgin." The Armenians and Jews being loyalists, and Menshevism being at home among the Georgians, the Social-Democrat Defensists freely condemned this Ukrainian movement which was completely alien to them.

In June, at the Soviet Congress, the Menshevik point of view was revealed by Lieber and Woitinsky. "At this time," explained Lieber, "there is not so much the need for making an agreement on the rights of people, as for fighting to protect those rights. To speak of self-determination is meaningless as long as no guarantee has been found for harmonious relations between nations." What was meant was that they should fight together to vanquish the Central Powers, who were enemies of freedom of the people. Then, in the structure of a Europe freed from the threat of German imperialism, one could discuss the structure to be founded on the principle of the rights of peoples. In order that the nationalities would not think that these theories were alibis for Greater Russian chauvinism, Woitinsky asked the Congress to adopt "the general principle granting each nation autonomy." But the Mensheviks "opposed any separate attempt to settle the national question, such as would be produced at a Little Russian Congress," because only the Constituent could settle this ticklish question.

On Menshevism's left, men like Martov, Natanson, and the *Novya Zhizn* group spoke more plainly. They thought that the rights of peoples formula was vague and would only serve as justification for annexations. They thought that from the Ukraine to the Caucasus, all talk of popular will was nothing but fraud as long as a truly democratic régime had not been established. In this, they came closer to certain national movements, notably the Moslems, who rejected referendums as well as the democratic or representative method without, however, specifying how autonomy or independence could be achieved. But essentially, they were very close to the Bolsheviks.

Among the Bolsheviks, Lenin's theses ended by being carried at the April Conference. Recognizing the right of secession by the national minorities, the resolution called for a large measure of regional autonomy (without specifying for which "nations"), and categorically rejected the idea of national cultural autonomy. However, this text took into account the point of view of the Luxemburgists who, behind Pyatakov and, to a lesser degree, Stalin, thought that subordinating the Revolution to the problem of the national minority groups was heresy. Kamenev in May, and Alexandra Kollontay, at the Soviet Congress in June, specified which nations the Bolsheviks were thinking of—Finland, Poland, Armenia, the Ukraine, and Turkestan. Strident in their denunciation of the Provisional Government's policy, the Bolsheviks were less precise when it came to tell *how and when* their resolutions were to be turned into actions. For Finland, from March on they recommended an agreement between the representatives of the two countries. The others were left dangling. There were indications that the Bolsheviks rejected the right of secession as part of the peace, but this was never spelled out. Two things were clear:

1. The discrepancy between the ideas which were adopted at the Congress and the attitude of the Bolsheviks who came from the national minorities. The latter often had condemned the reactionary and petit-bourgeois attitude of the nationalist demonstrations in the Ukraine and Kazan, considering them as an obstacle to the progress of the Revolution. They ended up by endorsing Lenin's theses.

2. The astonishment of the other Socialists caused by this turnabout of the Bolsheviks, although it was true that up until the April Congress Lenin was the only one to stand up for the right of secession, which won out.

Viktor Chernov regretted later that the pressure of the national minorities, "which could have been a constructive force, was transformed into a destructive force." Up until the end of June he blamed this on himself and his friends, who had let their opportunity pass. The Bolsheviks, on the contrary, knew how to seize it, and from then on they were able to exploit the national minorities.

All these uncertainties were evident at the Petrograd Soviet. On April 25 they had come out in favor of cultural autonomy for the minorities, which was far less than the national groups wanted. However, at the Soviet Congress in mid-June, circumstances caused a shift to the left. First there was the proclamation of the first *Universal* in Kiev, June 10; reactionary or not, Ukrainian nationalism seemed like a force to be reckoned with. Then there was the stand taken by the Bolsheviks, with its astonishing political realism which put everything in doubt; the parade of affiliated Social-Democratic parties (Lettish, Lithuanian, etc.) which rallied to the Bolshevik position, adding to the Nationalist organizations, considerably modified the relations among the forces at precisely the moment when there was about to be a showdown between the February Régime and all its opponents. At the Congress, the majority of speakers criticized the policies of the Provisional Government for not following the development of the Revolution. The final resolution expressed all the contradictions between the position taken previously and the needs of the political struggle, which required that the national groups not be alienated. Its formulators expressed exactly the Mensheviks' position: the national question should be viewed from a revolutionary standpoint. The foremost consideration was safeguarding the Revolution so that the rights which would be voted by the Constituent could be guaranteed. This was Kerensky's theme. However—and this was the first step to the left—"to strengthen the triumph of the Revolution and democratic cohesion among the national groups," Russia should immediately work toward a decentralized administration and give free rein to democratic impulses coming from the national minorities. Above all—and this was an important innovation—the Socialist organizations unanimously asked the government to recognize all peoples' right of self-determination up to and including secession. The motion also asked the government to take certain minor steps of a cultural nature. In the last point, the resolution unequivocally condemned all unilateral solutions of the national question prior to the Constituent, as well as steps by minorities which could lead to quarrels among them which in the end would weaken the Revolution. This was aimed especially at the Ukrainian Russians. The same evasion was noted in the case of Finland, for it was pointed out that, since no definite ruling would be valid without the approval of the Constituent, any resolution could only be an informal agreement. The sovereignty of the Seim was thus recognized, after a fashion. The motion invited the Finnish democracy to help reinforce the Russian Revolution, which alone could effectively guarantee its liberty. In the Ukraine, the Soviet promised Ukrainian Revolutionary Democracy its full support when the subject was to be debated in the Constituent. It suggested the creation of a representative body for the Ukrainian people and suggested that the Provisional Government get together with the Ukrainians for its formation.

Thus public opinion almost unanimously refused to give unconditional satisfaction to the national groups. Those who were impatient were accused of complicity with the enemy or being
counter-revolutionary. From then on it was no longer necessary to
take into account the pressure which the West could exert on the
government to explain its attitude toward its minority groups, for
this pressure merely added to the pressure emanating from Russian
Democracy itself. The government could not oppose it, especially
when, at the beginning of summer, the revolutionary forces of the
new Russia tried, as a matter of tactics, to conciliate the national
minorities. It is difficult to evaluate this foreign influence, which
was counterbalanced by the Stockholm Conference where the
nationalities were able to make themselves heard in a set-up of
which Russian Democracy could not very well be suspicious.

As at Lausanne a year earlier, the Conference was overrun by the
representatives from the Russian national minorities, especially
Poles, Balts, and Jews. Since it was a Peace Conference, gathered
on the instigation of Socialist organizations, the national groups
tried to bring the debate to their own ground. A questionnaire was
drawn up, to be sent to all the delegations, asking them if there
was any clash between the objectives of the minorities and the
principles of Socialism. Point 6 asked "if the war should continue
until people achieved the right of self-determination." A delegation from Georgia, led by Mikhail Tserethelli and Maxhaveli addressed a memorandum to the Hollando-Scandinavian delegation
in which it opined "that independence would have to be achieved
if one wanted Socialism, because as long as oppression reigned, the
proletariat would always ally itself to the bourgeoisie." But since
most of the oppressed minorities of Austro-Hungary stayed away
from Stockholm, and since everyone was looking for the friendship of the "Russian revolutionaries," the representatives of the
Russian national minorities got scant notice from either the belligerents or the neutrals.

Another thing which made for inertia was the hope in which
they then lived that the peace attempts would prove successful,
either through diplomatic means or through the pressure of the
Socialists on their governments; then all the delicate questions
could be resolved. And there was also the fear that since each
national group had demands to make, all of them would end up
seceding.

If in the cultural sphere the government could grant the national
groups some satisfaction, the needs of war clashed with the demands in the military sphere, which would have hastened the

disintegration of the imperial army if they had been granted. Until the offensive, the bourgeois and Socialist ministers were opposed to these demands. Here Kerensky rejoined the Soviet and the Bolsheviks in their distrust of armies which the Revolution might no longer control. Several times the government forbade meetings of military congresses. It was also opposed to the formation of minority-group military units. Vainly, as has been seen, it permitted the formation of a Ukrainian regiment on May 18. If this concession had been made a few weeks earlier, it would have unleashed chaos, Chernov remarked twenty years later. Coming so much later, it seemed laughable.

There remain only the political demands to be considered. Until July it was in the Ukraine and Finland that they were most violent. Chernov has shown that the Ukrainian national movement was rooted in the soil. No doubt it was led by bourgeois and intellectuals, but they were leading a struggle which coincided with that of all the landholders, large and small, who feared that any land reform would put an end to their privileged position. This is what gave the Ukrainian movement its irresistible force. The Social-Democrats—the urban Russians—could see nothing in this movement. At the Soviet, they fought against it, just like the bourgeois of the capital, whose interest led them toward the industrialization of the region. Only the Social-Revolutionaries (Russian and Ukrainian), who were rather strong locally, wanted to conciliate each faction. They were overcome. In the capital the Ukrainians' projects vanished in the sands of a government controlled by the K.D.s.

In May 1917 a Ukrainian delegation nominated by the *Rada* arrived in Petrograd. Even the Socialist newspapers refused to accept their motions, and after waiting patiently for three days, the Soviet Bureau sent them back. In fact, only the Judicial Commission received them, to the bitter dismay of the delegates. Here point by point is the reception which was granted to the demands of the *Rada*:

> *Question.* Recognition of the principle of self-determination.
> *Answer.* The Provisional Government has not the power. Only the Constituent has this power.
> *Q.* The Ukraine's participation in the Peace Conference.
> *A.* It is illegal, since the Ukraine is not a state.
> *Q.* Nomination of a Ukrainian minister to Petrograd.
> *A.* Impossible since the frontiers of the Ukraine have not yet been set.

Q. Formation of Ukrainian Military Units.

A. Powerlessness. That depends on the War Ministry.

Q. Ukrainianization of official functions and teaching of Ukrainian language.

A. To be studied; but if this is approved, it will have to be financed locally.

Briefly, the government let it be known that it was in favor of national cultural self-determination and that it was willing to recognize the Ukraine's "personality"—and that was all.

Convinced by the K.D., Populist, Socialist, and other leaders that they had nothing to expect from "Russian democracy," the delegates returned to Kiev. Hrushevsky took his cue from these events and had the *Rada* proclaim its first *Universal*—that is, its first sovereign law—on June 10/23, 1917. It resounded like a thunderclap in Petrograd, generating more anger than anything else. At the Soviet, however, with a showdown coming up, they wanted to avoid any mistakes. The government was blamed for letting things come to such a pass. Kerensky wanted to keep in touch with his Ukrainian friends and went to Kiev, where he signed a face-saving agreement with the *Rada*, against the advice of the bourgeois ministers. By this agreement, the Provisional Government recognized the existence of a "General Secretariat" for the Ukraine, whose members would be named by the *Rada* with Petrograd's agreement. The functions of this body would be set immediately and the Constituent would register the agreement. The principle of the referendum in Ukraine was also granted.

The K.D. ministers resigned, furious that a "definitive" agreement had been signed which presented the government with an accomplished fact and set a dangerous precedent.

The relations with Finland were of a different sort. At the Helsingfors Seim the Socialist bloc was in the majority. At the beginning of the Revolution it had sided with the new Russia, Finnish opinion's only regret being that the March Manifesto was not more revolutionary. When it appeared that the February Revolution partly endorsed Tsarist policy, the Finnish Socialists scored its conservatism.

With respect to the Finns, the government went from understanding to reservation. When the Judicial Commission ruled that the legislative acts of Finland, formerly submitted to the Tsar, now came under the jurisdiction of the Provisional Government, even Kerensky did not protest. Still, on May 24 he left to the

295

Constituent the task of deciding about future relations between Finland and Russia—which in this case was a step backward.

Then the government slipped into repressive measures by forbidding certain exports into Finland. No doubt this move was in answer to a Seim decision not to pay any more taxes to a government "which continued the war." The tone was set and the government reacted to Finnish acts more violently than did the soviets, who had sent a delegation to Helsingfors. It came back very much upset by the Finnish demands. Their Diet was arranging a set of laws planned since March on the subject of relations with Russia, but they made no mention of Russian sovereignty or of the role of the governor. To avoid any misunderstanding, Tokoy went over the heads of the government and the Soviet Bureau, directly to Russian people offering the help of the Finnish Socialist, "if the principle of independence was but admitted." The maneuver makes sense if one ties it in with the evolution noted at the Soviet Congress and if one considers it in the context of the preparation for the July events. In fact, on June 30 *Izvestya* published an article favoring the Finns. With the July uprising, the Finnish Social-Democrats in the Seim, seeing that the declaration of sovereignty would not have to be ratified by the Russian government, passed a law proclaiming *de facto* independence. The hatred of Russian was such that they could use it to draw some bourgeois deputies over to their side, thereby giving the revolutionary struggle the national dimension which ensured its success.

Finland wanted to secede because the February Revolution had not been revolutionary enough. The Ukraine, on the other hand, wanted to separate from it because it augured October.

★

CHAPTER TEN

THE REVOLUTION GOES ON

At the opening of the First Soviet Congress in early June, it was already apparent that the Coalition had failed. Only Kerensky gave the impression that he would attain his objective: to reorganize the army and to lead it to the offensive. But in the city as in the country, in Greater Russia as well as among the racial minorities, the policy of conciliation and waiting had failed. The State's authority was crumbling, the economy came to a standstill, people were angry, and the leaders confused.

The specter of civil war haunted the assembly room at the moment when the democracy movement, in full regalia, paraded its electoral victory. Unanimous in combating the schemes of the counter-revolution, it was divided when it learned that behind the threats of Bolsheviks and Anarchists, the masses backed the most radical revolutionaries. Should they be struck down under the pretext that, since the return of Lenin, they had put themselves outside the family of revolutionaries? Or perhaps it was the Republic of Militants who, with the Revolution accomplished, no longer represented the will of the Nation? There was no debate to decide. With the events of June and July, a period of crises began which was to topple the régime.

1. THE DISORDER INCREASES

Everything which represented the State was rejected as a remnant of Tsarism. In the first place, the government was suspect inasmuch as it was an institution; it was contrasted to the Soviet, even though it was the Socialist leaders of the Soviet who were the government's ministers. Furthermore, each city opposed its own soviet to that of the capital. By law, they were all equal, so why couldn't each soviet administer its own affairs? But on their own side each collective pitted the popular "base" against the local soviet. In effect, there were always some militants ready to contest the decisions made the day before. In a way, it was the representative régime which was the cause, for didn't the Revolution mean direct, immediate government? When some debates were held in the Army of the Southwest to decide on a régime for the Russia of the future, the overwhelming majority of soldiers were opposed to

297

the election of a president of the republic. Any delegation of power was denounced, all authority was unbearable. Thus the State's armor was flying to pieces. The populace only obeyed the orders which they agreed with. Certain soviets, the Kiev *Rada*, and the soviets of the state-communes now acted as though they were sovereign, with entire collectives governing themselves as they pleased.

All this was not necessarily against the Provisional Government. On the contrary, "any measure taken by the government against 'anarchy' invariably provoked the distrust from the public although they tolerated the same measures if they were taken by the 'local authorities.' " There was little chance that this action would correspond with the instructions of the government.

The month of June saw an increase in these acts of rebellion. Two cases especially became famous, that of Kronstadt and that of the *Villa Durnovo*, which was the doing of Anarchists. With these two revolts, born in the full fire of the Revolution, it was no longer only the Provisional Government's authority which was baffled, but that of the supreme body of the Revolution, the Congress of Soviets, as well.

At Kronstadt, the various revolutionary bodies which came into being during March had ended by uniting. The Soviet was now dominated by followers of Trotsky, Lunacharsky, S. G. Rozhal, and F. F. Rasknolnikov. They were supported by a consistent majority of 100 Bolsheviks, 68 unaffiliated, mostly internationalists, 91 centrist or leftist S.R.s, along with 5 Mensheviks. No agreement was possible with the government's commissar, Pepelyaev (K.D.), and a conflict of authority then became unavoidable. It quickly turned into a violent quarrel when the question of the fate of the naval officers interned in March came up. Should they be freed before being tried? Regardless of the government's position, the sailors were unyielding. They were holding their former tormentors and pitilessly applied the regulations to them. They wouldn't think of entrusting the job to anyone else; it was a personal matter with them. Pepelyaev ended by resigning in May 1917, for he had been powerless to free the officers.

The Soviet Executive Committee investigated the matter. They proposed to take over the administration of the citadel. Immediately, the Kronstadt Soviet decided by a vote of 210 to 40 that it would "seize power." As long as the Congress of Soviets had not been held, Kronstadt's soviet was by law the equal of Petrograd's. In his report, Anissimov, delegated by Petrograd, called such behavior "regrettable. . . . for the [Kronstadt] certainly demonstrated an unswerving fidelity toward the Revolution, but its energies were on the wrong track." Skobelev and Tseretelli were charged with explaining all this to the Kronstadt Soviet. They were coolly received. They explained that the soviets by themselves did not have the power, and that they had delegated some of their members to the Coalition Government, to which the Kronstadt Soviet, like the others should submit.

"What if we refuse?" asked Rozhal.

"You will be treated like insurgents," answered Tseretelli.

The Kronstadt Soviet Committee acknowledged the justice of this position. But the assembly balked, claiming that its representatives had only expressed their opinions and that no resolution had been passed. Then at the Peasants' Congress, Tseretelli threatened Kronstadt with his thunder. "The Kronstadt proceedings were harming the Revolution. The peasants would refuse to deliver food to the city if the city didn't rally to the side of the people." Yielding to the threat, on May 24 Kronstadt finally voted a resolution recognizing the authority of the Government "until such time as the Soviet would seize power." But the naval officers remained in prison.*

"What many label *Anarchy* is merely the expression of the people's thoughts expressed in a primitive fashion. These events are only inevitable manifestations of the Revolution," Nekrassov concluded. His point of view coincided with that of Kamenev and Lenin. Nekrassov had urged moderation, but his Socialist colleagues, fearing that Kronstadt would set a precedent, acted harshly. Kronstadt did not forgive them.

In Petrograd itself other incidents had occurred which pitted the government against some workmen's organizations, often led by Anarchists. Thus, on June 3, the workers' groups occupied the buildings of *Russkaya Volya*, Protopopov's old daily. In a pamphlet, the Anarchists explained that in a time of Revolution, the survival of *Russkaya Volya* was a constant provocation. Henceforth the daily would belong to the people, no longer to the "henchmen of German and Russian capitalism." Under the influence of Chkheidze, the Congress of Soviets denounced the Anarchists, had some of them arrested, and returned the newspaper's premises to its former owners. In deciding on this action there were only three dissenting votes and eight abstentions.

*On June 13 the Kronstadt Soviet freed Admiral Kossygin and surrendered two high-ranking officers to the Minister of Justice.

The *Villa Durnovo* affair had a greater effect. The Anarchists seized this hotel, which had belonged to a minister of the Tsar. Various rumors were going around about the *Villa Durnovo*; at the very least, it was said, the hotel held weapons readied by the Vyborg inhabitants for an assault on the régime. Perevertsev, the Minister of Justice, issued an expulsion warrant whose only effect was to cause a strike in about thirty factories. But the occupants did not leave the premises and there was no doubt about their intentions. An investigating committee was named and the affair was immediately brought before the Congress of Soviets. It turned out that, far from being an Anarchist lair, the *Villa Durnovo* was only a sort of community house where the residents of Vyborg had installed their trade unions and other organizations; the workers' children were playing in the gardens.

At the Congress of Soviets the reporter Gegechkory, supported by Gotz, nevertheless considered that force should be used only when sanctioned by revolutionary law; otherwise, explained Perevertsev, there would be no government. This time the Bolsheviks and Internationalists rebelled, because, explained Kamenev, "this is not a matter like that of the *Russkaya Volya*, an act committed by an irresponsible group"; it is the whole working population of Vyborg which has taken over the *Villa Durnovo*. This opened a debate on the question of revolutionary legality, which soon merged with the discussion going on at the Soviet Congress about the question of power. Led by Chernov, the majority voted against Kamenev and Lunacharsky, condemning the acts of Vyborg. Here were more enemies which the government would encounter later.

2. COUNTER-REVOLUTION RAISES ITS HEAD

A powerful press campaign during the month of May denounced the anarchy which reigned over the country. In this category they lumped together the banditry in the Kizhinev region, the pogroms which were on the increase, the breaches of discipline in the army and navy, as well as the political conflicts which neutralized governmental authority. The various presses vied with each other in fabricating stories to discredit the Bolsheviks and magnify the anarchy in the country. On May 9, for example, it was announced that the Ienesseisk Soviet had declared a state of siege, that the peasants were seizing the land in Bessarabia, Orel, and Samara. On the 12th the Director of the Kiev militia had launched an appeal to deserters; there were nearly four hundred bandits among them and the soldiers had committed some depredations on the Volga, near Tsarytsin. On the 13th they announced "an order of the day" from the Minister of War against drunkenness and looting and the increasing anarchy in Bessarabia and Riazan, "where the fields had not been sowed." Bandits had been seen on the same day in Kishinev and Narva, while the next day it was announced that alcohol stocks in Astrakhan were destroyed. Then came the sinister announcement of pogroms at Nizhni-Novgorod in Bessarabia, where soldiers allegedly had taken an active part. On the 21st the troubles extended to Orianenbaum, and a state of siege was declared in Tomsk. It was learned also that a certain Corporal Filipov, with deserting soldiers, had founded a "republic" in the Southwest, the Nigulsky Republic. Corporal Shilov in the Caucasus had also founded a "republic." "He administered it in accordance with Bolshevik principles and on several occasions had praised the German soldiers." At Elabuge, Chuhlom, Poshehone, Pereyaslavskaya, etc., other "republics" had thus been created. The reports of these incidents, more often than not, were just alarmist noises that added to the confusion which was already bad enough. B. Bezrabotny, in *Vpered*, named the newspapermen of the PTA Agency as the ones responsible.

This campaign of false information coincided with an anti-Semitic flareup. Beyond the pogroms of Nizhni-Novgorod, Elisavetgrad, Kishnev, and some cities in the Ukraine, the movement gained ground in military circles. In Moscow a regiment refused to have Jewish officers and would not allow speakers sent by the Soviet to address them "because it [the Soviet] was in the hands of the Jews." At Ekaterinodar students formed a "Slav Group" for the purpose of disseminating anti-Semitic propaganda in the countryside. The prosecutor of the Court of Appeals of Petrograd, worried about the mounting anti-Semitism and the increasing number of pogroms, asked the government to enact a special law against incitement to murder and looting. The movement had grown to such proportions in the southwest and the south that the Soviet Central Committee decided at the end of June to send fifteen of its members to the Ukraine, Bessarabia, and Odessa to check it. There was a question of putting the fight against anti-Semitism under Bolshevik auspices. Maxim Gorky, worried, launched several appeals in *Novaya Zhizn:*

There are two Jews behind the Bolshevist-Anarchists, says one.

—More like three.

—Several people say seven and are sure that these seven Simons will upset the Temple inhabited by 170 million Russians.

—But aren't there more Jews among the Mensheviks?

—Nobody wants to acknowledge it—all Jews are Anarchists.

This Rightist campaign sought to discredit the Revolution by exaggerating its excesses and then blaming them all on the Bolsheviks and the Anarchists, "all Jews." Increasingly, it leaned on organized forces such as the Church, the Cossacks, the Stavka Officers' Congress. The right-wing movement had several publications, among which were *Groza*, *Vechernaya Vremya*, and one newspaper with a large circulation, *Malenkaya Gazeta*, which every day branded the soviets as "guilty of having put the proletariat forward as a sort of special nobility, with the rest of the population as outcasts."

The action was still not well defined. In March the Holy Synod had launched an appeal to the believers to support the Provisional Government. N. N. Lvov removed two Archbishops from office, Pitirim and Makari, and the new government prepared a draft of a charter of the rights of the Russian Church. However, as N. N. Lvov showed at the Diocesian Conference of Nizhni-Novgorod, "the Old Régime's administration was not the only enemy of church freedom; the church hierarchy had the same attitude." In effect, when the Pan-Russian Clerical Conference met in June 1917, it appeared that in spite of the nominations, mutations, and promotions effected by the procurator, the large majority of the Congress was opposed to the separation of Church and State and demanded recognition of the "preeminance" of the Orthodox Church, refusing to admit the lay principle. The writer of *Vserossysky Tserkovno-Osshchestvenny* was dismissed for deploring the conservatism of the large majority of the Orthodox clergy. The Pan-Russian meeting of the Orthodox Church was to be held in August. There was no doubt as to the political orientation of its members. They braved the hostility of the population, especially the peasants, "who were ready to forgive the landowners, the officials, the merchants, but not the priests." The clergy tried to revive the peasants' devotion to the Tsar; according to *Volskoe Slovo*, a priest from Buguronslansky had threatened to horsewhip the Cossacks who had overthrown the Tsar. "The time of the

Anti-Christ has come. Do you not see that you should confess and not revolt against God?" Another priest at Simbirsk said that the Revolution was the work of Satan. A third, at Kostroma, announced that "without the Tsar there could be no God, that schools and churches would be closed."

Of course, there were reprisals. Synod printing presses were requisitioned, and on June 14 the Voronezh Soviet had Archbishop Tikhon arrested. He was the fifth in a few weeks, and the government had him released. On June 18 the campaign against the Soviet expanded beyond the provincial level. *Novoe Vremya* published an article by Andrei, Bishop of Ufa, *ci-devant* Prince Ukhomsky, entitled "The Key to Salvation." Uniting right-thinking and earnest men around the Church, the Bishop of Ufa asked the faithful "not to go to the people with speeches in German, like Lenin and Grimm, or speeches in French—this was a defect of the Intelligentsia—but in Russian, the language in which the people had learned to believe in God." The most counter-revolutionary element seems to have been the "old believers," who were openly Monarchist and whom the former President of the "Patriotic League" urged to join the Cadets; the former editor of *Russkaya Znamya*, Zolotnikov, a notorious anti-Semite, asked them to unite with the Cossacks who at this time appeared to be taking the lead of the reaction.

The Cossacks thought that the February victors showed a lack of gratitude toward them and feared the effects of the Revolution: the land would be apportioned and they would be the first to suffer. The resolutions which were passed at the Cossack Congress in mid-June indicated that they would stand for no change in the status of their lands and that they would, if necessary, defend their interests by force of arms. On the war question, they adopted some vigorous motions in favor of the offensive, against fraternization and any separate peace. They also demanded "punishment of the enemy" and, along with Makarenko, who was wildly applauded, they declared that "they would know how to bring certain people in line by means of the lash." These threats were aimed at Lenin and the Bolsheviks and encouraged by some responsible politicians such as Guchkov who, on June 7, told them: "There has been talk of de-Cossacking the Cossacks; it would be better if we were Cossackized. . . ."

The same feelings were to be found among the Officer Corps. The Revolution was in part directed against them, and they wanted to regain their rank, privileges, and grade. They had always lived under the impression that Providence had put Russia's desti-

ny in their hands and that they had failed in February. For them
the Revolution had been a test in which they were constantly
humiliated and many considered themselves debased. The order
entrusted to the military had been destroyed by civilians and
soldiers who no longer accepted their authority. The officers were
ready to go through thick and thin to recover their lost honor and
were moved by such hatred of the régime which was a witness to
their shame that they ended by forgetting their duties as soldiers.

Some of them rallied to the Revolution, but for the most part
these were not the professionals. Others formed "associations"
whose purpose was a return to the old order. The Association of
Officers of the 3rd Siberian stated it quite simply. However,
Tsarism was so discredited that all of them called themselves
Republicans. But what they wanted in reality was the foundation
of an authoritarian régime under the aegis of the army. The
Cossacks and some national minority units were still "loyal," and
others would follow. They counted on Admiral Koltchak and
General Kornilov to win support for the movement; they also
called themselves Republicans. Meanwhile, the Stavka Officers'
Congress passed a resolution embodying their determination to
put a stop to the deterioration of military discipline.

According to them, the causes of the disintegration of the
Army were:

1. The complete disappearance of the martial spirit.

   a. Desire for conclusion of peace, even at the price of sacrificing the
      national interest;
   b. Refusal to undertake even light military operations;
   c. Neglect of duty and indifference on guard duty;
   d. Fraternization even to the point of shooting at those who opposed it.

2. The breakdown of discipline.

   a. Refusal at the front to carry out orders or agreements after negotia-
      tions;
   b. Tendency to replace Commanders by more amenable elected com-
      manders;
   c. Insubordination;
   d. Decisions made collectively.

3. Nullification of Commander's authority.

4. Distrust of officers who didn't approve of "peace at any price."

5. Outbreaks of scurvy and other diseases due to malnutrition.

In their final motion, the Stavka officers stated:

1. The Congress acknowledges that there appears among a large part of the population and in an overwhelming majority of the army a strong feeling in favor of the cessation of hostilities.

It insists on an energetic pursuit of the war in agreement with the Allies.

It favors a peace founded on the rights of the people with guarantees of peace for Russia and evacuation of occupied territories.

2. It rejects the suggestion that Russia not have access to the Mediterranean. The only guaranty of freedom of passage is general disarmament if Russia does not have military control of the Straits.

It is up to the government to establish the conditions for peace.

What is needed is a single, firm government.

3. [Point Three is illegible.]

4. No interference by "military committees," but respect for military channels.

5. The principle of the election of officers is inadmissible.

In June this action of the officers was not yet seditious, but it would become so when the democratic left won out over the "conciliators."

The Right's action had two objectives: an immediate offensive, which it thought would commit Russia to the war and allow the military to regain its authority; and creation of a strong régime which would put an end to anarchy and reestablish a government by men who believed in order.

At the beginning of June the Duma met in closed session. It endorsed this program, putting the accent on an immediate offensive. That was its swan song.

Conscious that the next few days would be decisive for Russia's fate for several decades, the members of the Duma, in Special Session, consider it their duty to warn the public against the conclusion of a separate peace which would be the basest betrayal and would change Russia into a German colony.

They considered also that only an immediate offensive in accord with the Allies is the pledge of a quick end of the war and the strengthening of the liberties won by the people.

It was the new Right Press which launched the campaign "for a strong régime" while avowing themselves "profoundly Republican." "I left the government because it was powerless," sallied

Guchkov a few days after his resignation. That was the start, and from then on the *Malenkaya Gazeta* sounded the alarm, relayed by the *Novoe Vremya*. "Kerensky, Lvov, and Chkheidze would have liked to eestablish order, but one cannot expect the impossible. . . ." The Right "was looking for a Cavaignac."*

> "The dictatorship of the proletariat" in the capital will end by bringing on a protest in the whole country. These shaven Samsons who destroy everything without creating anything will perish themselves in the ruins of the Temple.

Demanding that Price Lvov yield in favor of Admiral Koltchak, the *Malenkaya Gazeta* issued a warning which recalled a famous precedent from the French Revolution: "And if Petrograd will not support it, let the government move to Moscow. Moscow will support it. As for Petrograd, let it perish."

The tone became more strident. Taking up a motion of the *Stavka* Officers' Congress, the *Malenkaya Gazeta* daily demanded the arrest of Lenin: "It is ridiculous for the reader to calmly read in *Pravda* that ten Ministers should be arrested while he trembles when he reads in *Malenkaya Gazeta* that Lenin should be arrested."

The Right called for a demonstration against the government, which was guilty of weakness. In fact, the idea of a counter-revolution had won over quite a section of moderate opinion. Milyukov declared: "At the moment there is no danger of counter-revolution, but there could be if the disloyal Socialists come to power."

Thus, as in 1848, the moderates slipped into reaction while proclaiming themselves Republicans.

3. DEMOCRACY'S BIG SHOW

When the Soviet Congress met on June 3, 1917, the atmosphere was one of exasperation caused by the quarrels of the Grimm Affair, the *Villa Durnovo* incidents, the press campaign against "Anarchy," and the call for a dictator. Moreover, the democratic movement was hopelessly split. On all questions one could find adherents of the Bolsheviks and Internationalists and a few Leftist S.R.s on one side, and on the other the defenders of the Coalition.

The results of the elections in the democratic organizations were impatiently awaited; 20,323,000 people took part in this

*Minister of War Louis Eugène Cavaignac quelled the 1848 Insurrection in Paris.—Trans.

nationwide contest. For 17,500,000 of them the breakdown was as follows:

Workers	5,100,000
Soldiers	8,149,000
Peasants	4,239,000

According to the Mandates' Commission Report, the breakdown of the organizations represented was follows:

Soviets or Organizations grouping Workers, Soldiers, and Peasants	305
Soviets or Workers' and Soldiers' Organizations (including some peasants)	172 (72)
Workers' Soviets	24
Soldiers' Soviets	17

In the election 1090 delegates were elected, of whom 822 were voting and 268 nonvoting delegates representing those organizations or soviets with less than 25,000 members. Their breakdown gives an accurate picture of the range of political opinions among the masses:

Socialist-Revolutionaries	285
Menshevik Social-Democrats	248
Unitarian Social-Democrats	10
Internationalist Social-Democrats	32
Bolsheviks	105
Unaffiliated Socialists	73
Bund	10
Edinstvo Social-Democrats	3
Socialist-Populists	3
Trudoviks	5
United Social-Democrat and Socialist-Revolutionary Platform	2
Anarchists-Communists	1

The Coalition backers thus had a large majority. At the time of voting, the opposition (which started to include the Left S.R.s) never exceeded 160 votes out of 1,090 and 125 out of 777 when the votes were counted; it was therefore insignificant.

Those in the majority nevertheless had the feeling that, in spite of the fact that they controlled the soviets, they had no such control over the public. But they imagined the danger as coming more from the Right rather than from the Left through a misreading of signs which they repeated in April, in June-July, and several other times. Lenin had felt it. "Public opinion is more to the left than our Left," he said. He followed it, egging it on, flanked by Trotsky and others.

When the Congress of Soviets opened, Trotsky, Lenin, and Lunacharsky took the initiative on the question of power. Lunacharsky proposed that the Congress immediately assume the role of a Revolutionary Convention, applying literally the Bolshevik slogan, "All Power to the Soviets." Trotsky, criticizing the government, went on in the same vein. As far as he was concerned, he considered it a sign of progress that the government belonged to "Twelve Peshekhonovs." Finally Lenin, in a famed retort, admonished Tseretelli:

> The Citizen Minister of Post and Telegraph has just said that the situation is so complex that there isn't a political party in Russia which expresses explicitly the wish to take on, alone, all power. To that my answer is: "Such a party exists. No party has the right to refuse the power and our party does not refuse it. It is ready to assume full power at any time."

There was applause, but it was smothered by laughter. Then Lenin went over the party's economic program and proposed to arrest "fifty or a hundred of our richest millionaires." They guffawed over these proposals. Was this Marxism? But seeing things in a clearer light, observers wondered: So, although they were in the minority at the Soviet Congress, the Bolsheviks were willing to assume power, *alone*. . . . Instead of urging the socialization of the means of production, they spoke of "arresting" the capitalist millionaires. . . . They organized their own militia, the *Red Guards*. What relation was there between the party program, its tactics, its revolutionary methods, and the Social-Democratic tradition? They were all the more anxious about this question since the Bolshevik following was increasing.

Kerensky then interrupted and was much applauded:

> You have spoken of 1792 and 1905. . . . How did 1792 end in France? By the fall of the Republic and the rise of a dictator. And 1905? By the triumph of reaction! Now in Russia we are doing again what has been experienced already. We must prevent what happened after 1792 and keep intact the gains of the Revolution so that Comrade Lenin, who was abroad, might still be able to speak and not be forced to flee again to Switzerland. . . .

What does he recommend? Arresting the Russian capitalists? *(Laughter.)* Has Marxism taught such childishness? Any Marxist will tell you that capitalism is international and that the arrest of a few capitalists in a given state will not change the capitalist laws of a bare subsistence level in any given period. You Bolsheviks prescribe childish remedies—*arrest, kill, destroy*. Are you Socialists or policemen of the Old Régime?

Then Chernov and Lieber ranged themselves against the Bolsheviks, while Martov, on the contrary, attacked the Government about its handling of the Greek situation. The vote was a foregone conclusion. The Menshevik-S.R. resolution was carried by a vote of 543 to 126, with 52 abstentions and 65 absentees. The motion declared that putting power in the hands of only the bourgeoisie would be a blow to the Revolution and that the seizure of power by the soviets would be a weakening of it. Thus the Congress expressed its complete confidence in the Coalition Government to obtain a general peace without annexations or indemnities based on the right of self-determination of the people; to continue with the democratization of the army and improve its combat efficiency; to take energetic steps, in agreement with the working masses, to remedy the economic and financial situation and the food shortages; and to fight any revolutionary attempts, regulate the worker and agrarian questions in accord with the masses, and hasten the meeting of the Constituent Assembly.

Birzhevya-Vedemosty judged that the Congress was coming along very nicely. They had yelled "Hurrah for the Army, Hurrah for the Revolution, Hurrah for the International." But they also had yelled, "Hurrah for Russia," and it was the first time that this had come from the mouth of the democrats. The financial journal added: "By moving the democratic movement closer to the government, the Congress has removed the masses from Bolshevism, Zimmerwaldism, and Anarchy."

With these motions passed, the majority left the Congress hall satisfied, and was soon shocked to read in *Pravda* a call for a mass demonstration the very next day. Was the principle of the majority no longer respected by the masses? What game were these Bolsheviks playing by demonstrating against the soviets while demanding that all power be given to them? The majority did not have the time to discuss it. It only realized, a little late, that it controlled the militants but was unable to control the masses.

4. THE JUNE DEMONSTRATIONS

After five weeks in power, the Coalition could claim small success: Economic channels were blocked, there was an open social crisis in the cities and a latent one in the countryside, a disturbing political unease, and the discontent of the national minorities was rumbling threateningly. Only Kerensky seemed to be able to put new life into the army, but it was just this success that gave the Revolution a new start.

Worried because they saw themselves back in the old rut, and disturbed by the calls for resuming active military operations, the soldiers of the capital wanted to prevent a return of the Old Order. The logic of Kerensky's activities would end with their having to relieve their comrades at the front. "Freedom is disappearing," declared the soldiers to the *Social-Demokrat*. Would they unconsciously return to the old discipline?

On May 23 about thirty Bolshevik soldiers met to organize a campaign against Kerensky's policy. B. Nevsky and Nikolai Podvoysky submitted this proposal to the Party Central Committee on June 6, showing that some elements of the 180th Machine-Gun Regiment, the Pavlovsky, and the 6th Engineers, backed by the Kronstadt sailors, were determined to demonstrate. They might as well organize a demonstration under the auspices of the Party. They counted on 40,000 participants. Viktor Nogin and Kamenev thought that this would not be enough and that they could not organize a real demonstration in two days. Impressed by the optimism of Nevsky and Podvoysky, Lenin and Sverdlov came out in favor of the proposal, but on condition that the workers would participate. Zinoviev did not think that they would want to. "These questions do not affect the workers as directly as the soldiers," vouched Stalin; however, he did not think that they should oppose the demonstration. R. A. Abramovich explained why it was hard to evaluate the mood of the masses, although it seemed that for the moment they were calmer; events would have to awaken the working class. The people were saying: "You talk, act like advisors, and fail to act. On April 21st the masses came out into the streets and you called them adventurers. As long as the demonstration takes place under our banners, the results do not matter. At least we will have the soldiers with us, even if the workers will not have anything to do with the demonstration. Otherwise, it is the soldiers who will leave us in the lurch."

With the idea of a demonstration accepted, it remained to

define its objectives. Elena Stassova, Stalin, and Nevsky thought that it should be allowed to proceed no matter what happened. Ivan Smilga suggested the occupation of strategic points such as the railway station. Zinoviev and Kamenev were opposed to any demonstration whatever. Lenin thought that they should let events take their course.

On June 9 the following appeal was sent to *Pravda* to be addressed to the workers and soldiers of Petrograd on June 10:

> Russia is undergoing a time of trials.
>
> The war, which has caused millions of casualties, goes on. It is deliberately being prolonged by these banker millionaires who are enriched by it.
>
> The industrial depression, brought on by the war, leads to the closing of factories and planned unemployment. In order to earn fantastic profits, the capitalists use the lockout.
>
> The bread shortage and other food shortages are getting worse. The spiralling prices are strangling the people and the process goes on in accordance with the whims of the speculators.
>
> The sinister specter of famine is all around.
>
> At the same time, the clouds of counter-revolution are growing larger.
>
> On June 3rd, the Duma, which helped the Tsar to stifle the people, wanted to drown the newly won freedom in a sea of blood.
>
> The Council of State, who furnished the Tsar with murderous ministers, is weaving new machinations in the shadows for the purpose of reducing and paralyzing the people in the name of law.
>
> The Provisional Government, placed between the Tsarist Duma and the Soviet deputies, with ten bourgeois ministers, is under the influence of the landowners and capitalists, from all indications.
>
> Instead of guaranteeing the rights of soldiers, Kerensky's "statement" violates these rights on some very crucial points.
>
> Instead of ratifying the soldiers' freedoms won on the day of the Revolution, new orders threaten them with forced labor.
>
> Instead of consolidating the freedoms won by the citizens, people are locked up without trial, homes are invaded, and new interpretations of Article 129 threaten forced labor.
>
> Instead of fighting counter-revolution, the unleashing of the counter-revolutionaries and their riotings are tolerated.
>
> The breakdown is worsening and nothing is done to prevent it.
>
> The war goes on and nothing is done to stop it.

Famine is threatening more than ever and nothing is done to prevent it.

There is nothing strange about these counter-revolutionaries becoming more and more overbearing, urging the repression of soldiers, sailors, workers, and peasants.

Comrades,

We must not endure this silently. It is criminal not to speak up.

Already the workers are determined to protest.

We are free citizens. We have the right to say what we think and must use this right before it is too late.

We have the right to demonstrate peacefully. Let us then demonstrate peacefully to make our needs and aspirations known.

Let our banners flutter victorious and frighten the enemies of Liberty and Socialism.

Let our call, the call to the Sons of the Revolution, be heard by all inhabitants of Russia, to the joy of the oppressed.

Workers, join the soldiers and support their legitimate demands. Remember, they helped you during the days of the Revolution.

Into the streets, Comrades.

Soldiers, extend a hand to the workers and uphold their just demands. The strength of the Revolution lies in the union of the workers and soldiers. Today, no regiment, no division should stay in barracks.

Into the streets, Comrades.

Line up in an orderly way in the streets of the Capital.

Express your wishes calmly and confidently, as befits the strong.

Down with the Tsarist Duma.

Down with the Council of State.

Down with the ten capitalist ministers.

All power to the All-Russian Soviet of Workers, Soldiers and Peasants.

Re-examine the "orders" against the soldiers and sailors.

Down with industrial anarchy and capitalist lockouts.

Long live control and organization of industry.

The time has come to stop the war. Let the Soviet of Deputies set the conditions for a just peace.

Neither separate peace with Wilhelm, nor secret treaties with English and French capitalists.

Bread, Peace and Liberty.

The RSDRP Central Committee.

The RSDRP Petersburg Committee.

The Military Section of C.C. and C.P. of RSDRP.

The Central Committee of the Factory Committees of Petrograd.

The Executive Committee of the Trade Union Central Bureau.

The Bolshevik Section of the Workers Soviet and of the S.D.
of Petrograd.

The *Pravda* Staff.

The *Soldatskaya Pravda* Staff.

At the Soviet Congress, the discussion was started again on the
question of the war, when Chkheidze, visibly moved, took the
floor. He had just learned that a demonstration was planned for
the next day. The soviets had not been alerted, he said; organized
by the Bolsheviks, it could have no other object than to force the
hand of the supreme body of Democracy. Chkheidze concluded
by asking the Soviet to assume their responsibilities. The Bolsheviks were absent, which confirmed that they were planning something. The Assembly grumbled, roared; it was a question of a real
"betrayal of the Revolution."

Dan took charge, helped by Gotz, Chkheidze, and Tseretelli.
Quickly, the four drafted an appeal to the workers and soldiers to
warn them against Bolshevik provocation. All members of the
Soviet Bureau signed it, except Kamenev and Nogin who were
absent, and Lunacharsky. He was the only one to defend the
Bolsheviks; the Internationalist leader dissuaded the Assembly
from making a decision without being better informed. But
Chkheidze had already sent emissaries to the workers' quarters and
to the suburbs. At one o'clock in the morning the emissaries
returned to tell the thunderstruck Assembly that in the meetings
organized by the Bolsheviks the overthrow of the government was
being openly advocated. It had seemed to them, however, that
there were other meetings being held at the same time which
would have put an end to the Bolsheviks or in any case were
opposed to any demonstration which might be organized under
their auspices. At the Soviet, Leonid Martov put the accent on
another threat: condemning the adventurist attitude of the Bolsheviks, he argued that its effect would be to "incite an unwanted
intervention from the front." Weinstein burst out with: "You
might as well say that a beast is savage because it defends itself
when attacked. . . ." But Martov reaffirmed his condemnation,
claiming that the Bolshevik demonstration was bad because it was
going to cause a reaction.

Was it the unanimity of the Congress, the fear of a

counter-demonstration, or of an intervention by the Front, or did Lenin have a feeling that the masses were still undecided? Whatever the reason, he canceled the demonstration. In *Pravda*, in place of the appeal, there was a blank space. The soldiers and the Red Guard showed their discontent. They declared that they were not obeying the Soviet appeal, but the orders of the Bolshevik Party. If they were asked to go into town the next day, the "Guard" would march in defiance of any orders to the contrary. No matter, it was a victory for the Soviet.

At the Congress Policy Commission, on the 12th, they examined the events of those two days. What steps should be taken to prevent another attempt by the Bolsheviks on the will of the people? Tseretelli surprised his colleagues, who had never seen him so anxious to strike hard and fast. A constant threat to democracy, the "Red Guard" must be dissolved, he contended. He proposed that the Commission give the order to the Military Section to disarm it. Gotz, Lieber, and M. S. Ermolayev supported this demand, but it was disapproved through Dan's intervention. Supported by Hinchuk and Bogdanov, Dan showed that such a measure would exasperate the working-class quarters and drive them toward Bolshevism. Tseretelli then wanted to try to get his proposition approved by the Sections Assembly. This time his own supporters deserted him. He thundered once more against the "Bolshevik conspiracy," a permanent threat to democracy, but this only alienated him from the rest. The time had come for Kamenev to play the part of the outraged victim. "Mr. Minister, if what you have just said is anything other than mere empty talk, have me arrested immediately."

The Bolsheviks raised a din at Kamenev's remark and all got up and left the meeting with a great show. Then Lunacharsky intervened. "The Bolsheviks could not have intended to overthrow democracy," he said, "because they condemn 'Blanquism.'"* Knowing that the delegates did not want to divide the Revolution, he urged clemency, making himself the spokesman of unity. Many moderate Socialists ranged themselves on his side. Shapiro, among them, said that they should not be treated like reactionaries. "They are just overgrown children," added another delegate; "they should be forgiven for letting themselves get carried away." Keren-

*In Marxist theory, Blanquism is the attempt by a Revolutionary minority to seize power by force when conditions for assuming power have not been met. According to Lunacharsky, it would have been Blanquism since the majority of the revolutionaries were opposed to the Soviet's assuming absolute power, let alone the Bolsheviks. He differed with Lenin in that he did not realize the shifting of opinion among the masses and the growing power of the more advanced wing—which was precisely the most important point to Lenin.

sky, Avxentiev, and Znamensky supported Tseretelli. "It was to be an armed demonstration," observed the Minister of War, but he did not recommend any extreme measures. But the tone became more heated with the interjections of Vilenkin and Lieber. Vilenkin, the Fifth Army representative, asked, "Was it all right that, just at the moment when the Front needed weapons, they were found in the hands of those who wanted to end the war, even though the democratic majority thought the war was legitimate?" Lieber took up Tseretelli's proposal again and urged disarming the Bolsheviks. The masses should not be led to believe that democracy meant the reign of machine guns; if it did, all would be lost. "Lackeys," shouted Martov. It was not up to the Socialists to take steps against the workers. Kerensky and Perevertsev agreed; their opposition to the Bolsheviks should not go so far as to divide the revolutionaries. Going back to his position of two days before, Martov remarked that the demonstration was not the doing of the Bolshevik Party, but of one whole segment of the proletarian population. Thus the fault was the government's for having been so slow in accomplishing the expected reforms. Then Lunacharsky said that he no longer considered the June 10th attempt to be in error and Trotsky added that "the party of the proletariat cannot oppose the demands of the proletariat." The demonstration was legitimate, as was the position of the Bolsheviks. Dan sneered: "Is it enough to proclaim louder than the others that one is the 'party of the proletariat' in order to be 'the party of the proletariat'? The great majority of the workers still belong to other parties. . . ."

Things had already been decided. There was a majority hostile to the Bolsheviks, but it refused to use force against them. The Dan-Bogdanov-Hinchuk resolution carried; in the name of Revolutionary Democracy, it condemned the abortive June 10 demonstration: "Because no measures had been taken to prevent an armed demonstration which might have triggered tragic incidents, this could have led to bloodshed."

Further it came out against:

—All calls for demonstrations organized against the will of the Soviet.
—All demonstrations organized by parties without the knowledge of the Soviet.
—All armed demonstrations not under the auspices of the institutions of the people as a whole.

The Bolsheviks protested immediately, claiming that the Soviet was not respecting the rights of minorities. "The majorities change . . .," remarked Bulkin, "one tyranny follows another. . . ."

Aware of these arguments and, according to Tseretelli, "from then on spiritually defeated," Bogdanov and Dan thought that something should be done to counteract this demonstration; accordingly, they considered the idea of organizing another demonstration in the name of the Soviet for the following Sunday. Once more the Bolsheviks walked out of the meeting, and no one knew what they would do on the scheduled day. *Izvestya* indicated the objectives and the spirit of the June 18 demonstration:

1. The aim of the demonstration was to show the unity of revolutionary forces.

2. They must attest to their aspiration for a general peace.

3. The slogan to be: A Democratic Republic through the Constituent Assembly.

4. The demonstration must be peaceful.

5. Consequently it is the citizens' duty to avoid disorder.

6. It is the duty of everybody, without exception, to come to the demonstration unarmed.

What happened on June 18 was in a sense a surprise. The Soviet leaders expected to see before them the usual parade one saw on big popular holidays, a routine demonstration such as had been seen many times during the Revolution. It was a beautiful day, but there were not many demonstrators—in fact, "less demonstrators than placards." When the marchers came by, the leaders were struck by the overwhelming number of Bolshevik slogans: "Down with the six Capitalist Ministers," "All Power to the Soviets," "Reestablish the Declaration of the Rights of the Soldier," "Down with the Offensive," "Down with the Counter-Revolution," "Long Live the People's Peace," "Long Live the Workers' Control of Production," "Down with the Lockout." There were, of course, banners with "Long Live the Socialist Ministers," "Believe in Kerensky," and "Support the Provisional Government," but they were submerged by the others. The progress of Bolshevization was suddenly apparent.

Lenin's party certainly had planned for this June 18 demonstration carefully, delaying by a week the planned demonstration which had been canceled. They had more support than they had had in April from the committees of the working-class quarters, who were well aware of the threat of reaction. The Mensheviks and S.R.s, on the other hand, had not had time to organize marchers as well or to mobilize their people or arm them with slogans. Nevertheless, this explanation, offered by the losers, does not explain the apathy of the public. It was not so much that the public failed to answer the Soviet invitation because it was tired, disillusioned, or indifferent, as it was that the street now belonged to the Bolsheviks, whose organization outclassed that of its rivals. June 18 was a Bolshevik triumph and a disaster for the Mensheviks and S.R.s. A few days before, Lenin told the Petrograd Committee of the Bolshevik Party:

> Today the Revolution has gone into a new phase of its development. At first our peaceful demonstration was forbidden for three days. Now they want to forbid it for the duration of the Congress. They expect us to submit to the decisions of the Congress and they threaten to exclude us. But we prefer arrest to renunciation of the freedom to agitate.
>
> Tseretelli, who has revealed himself as a true counter-revolutionary in his speeches, declared that Bolshevism must be fought not with words, but by depriving them of any and all technical means at their disposal. This is the plan of bourgeois revolutions: first arm the proletariat, then disarm it so that it will go no further. If they had to forbid a peaceful demonstration, it is because the situation is very grave.
>
> Frantic and furious, he has demanded that the Bolshevik Party be banned by Revolutionary Democracy. The workers must tell themselves, calmly, THAT THERE CAN BE NO MORE QUESTION OF A PEACEFUL DEMONSTRATION.
>
> To the attack unleashed against us, the proletariat can answer with utmost calm, prudence, firmness, and organization, WHILE REMEMBERING WELL THAT THE TIME FOR PEACEFUL DEMONSTRATIONS IS PAST.

After June 18 a new era began in the history of the Revolution.

CONCLUSION

At the end of June the Right spoke openly of installing a strong-man in power. Nevertheless, it hesitated to attempt a *Putsch* and thought that it could better achieve its ends by sabotaging the economy, which would have the effect of turning public opinion against the incompetent ministers. At the other end, the Bolsheviks no longer planned to act through the channels of representative democracy, since Lenin had declared that the hour of peaceful demonstration was past.

"History will tell us that after the reign of Nicholas the Bloody came that of Tseretelli the Cruel," shouted Polyansky at the Soviet Congress. History, which searches in vain for traces of this Bolshevik after the purges of the 1920s, certifies in the margin next to this oratorical remark that in fact some Mensheviks and Socialist-Revolutionaries thought of using restraints against their rebelling brothers. Indeed, it had already been done in the countryside. At the end of June the Odessa Soviet confiscated an Anarchist journal. In Rostov, however, the roles were reversed— the Bolsheviks dispersed a democratic demonstration in favor of the Loan. Thus violence had not yet become anybody's monopoly, and it is useless to try to figure out who began it.

Rather, we should wonder about the causes of such a failure. How could a handful of malcontents at the events of March proliferate to the point where they were everywhere in the nation, dividing themselves between the two equally balanced extremes of public opinion, and with such cries of hatred against both the government and the Soviet leaders who had only one idea in mind—to lead the Revolution to an end without bloodshed?

The era of revolutionary enthusiasm certainly was over. Events had not fulfilled the nation's hopes. From the first Trotsky had compared the February events to the Revolution of 1848. In a sense he was right—the long wait, the explosion, the exuberance. Then would come the first disillusions, the first obstacles, the call for arbitration, the intervention of the military. The "June events" took place, but in Russia they lasted from July to September, and instead of December 2 they had October.

Others have compared February 1917 with 1792 and, in retrospect, 1905 with 1789. These comparisons were not merely intellectually stimulating; they also indicated fairly accurately how the observers of that time pictured the future of the Revolution. They saw clearly that the hopes of some were antagonistic to those of others, that they would have international implications, and that their realizations were tied to the fate of the war and the European Revolution. Did they also see the obstacles which Russia's past bequeathed to the Revolution's future?

After February, one could see, on the one hand, the working class's determination to ensure the guarantees which would make it possible to proceed to the proletarian revolution, and on the other, the certainty with which the bourgeoisie considered that it would reign for many decades to come. The property-owners' determination was opposed by the workers' watchfulness, a state of affairs which was hardly conducive to "class collaboration." It is clear that those who urged conciliation, among the bosses as well as among the workers, were going counter to the deeper feelings of the social groups which they pretended to represent.

It was nevertheless the "conciliators" who came to power and kept it. Anxious to safeguard the future of the new régime, the victors of February thought that their unity was essential for the task. But the more the Revolution settled into its pattern, the more the conciliators feared they would be submerged by the advocates of no-compromise. They knew that the *Girondins* were followed by the *Montagnards*,* but what they wanted to avoid at all costs was another Bonaparte. Paralyzed by this threat, they did not dare to act and were able neither to impose social peace in the cities, nor to proceed with agrarian reform, nor to settle the national minorities question, nor above all to resolve the problem of the war. They were afraid that their program would be disapproved, but it was their timidity in carrying it out which was held against them. The fate of the Socialist-Revolutionaries shows this uncertainty; and they went out of style as soon as the terrorist "Grand Old Party" had lost its claws. They had grown on a younger rival, the Bolshevik Party, which henceforth drew the votes. Falling out of favor because of all these failures, the conciliators lost the confidence of the people as quickly as they had won it. During June and July the Menshevik and S.R. leaders were almost lynched by the mob. Their bourgeois colleagues in the government were booed several times by officers' gatherings.

Even if they had succeeded in realizing some of the nation's

*In the French Revolution, the *Girondins* were moderates who dominated the National Assembly until they were ousted and then were executed by the more radical *Montagnards*.—Trans.

hopes, they inevitably would have failed at the next stage. Not only were the aspirations of the various groups at odds, but it was impossible to achieve them at the time.

The bourgeoisie wanted to take charge of the future of the country, but, faced with the demands of the working class, they did not have the means to make the concessions which the most clear-sighted of them deemed essential. In the textile industry it was a question of a social class of long standing, but in other sectors of the economy the upper middle industrial class had not yet had time to accumulate large profits as in Great Britain and France. As a debtor it was so short of resources it controlled only a fraction of the capital which it was using. Working on such a small margin, it did not have the maneuverability to convert its production and it maintained a certain Louis-Phillippe mentality. Impoverished and indebted, this bourgeoisie had to look for a new creditor at the very moment when it had taken charge of the nation's economy. America was willing to help on the condition that it would continue the war, although America itself had not yet entered the war against the Central Powers. This clearly shows Russia's dependence on the West, as well as the solidarity between Washington, London, and Paris. Here was the first stumbling block.

The last to enter the modernization race, the Russian economy had the handicap of being both dependent and frail; furthermore, it had started on a very low level and its economic backwardness was evident in all phases. During the last years of Tsarism it had made spectacular progress, but measuring it in percentages is deceiving. In mechanical industrial matters, for example, it should be noted that at a time when the great powers were exporters, the Russia of Nicholas II furnished only 12 percent of the steam engines it required, which were few. In most indexes of progress—the average rate of increase of agricultural productivity, consumption of raw cotton, per capita cast-iron production, the railway development index, and per capita power consumption—Russia was a long way behind the ten great powers of the period. Not only was she half a century behind France and the United States, but no one saw how she could catch up.

Under these circumstances, the men of February had a difficult time trying to regenerate the Russian economy in the space of a few months. Their powerlessness on the economic level was accompanied by their inability to improve the living conditions of the workers or to come up with new solutions to the social problem.

The workers' aspirations for a more dignified life were also unrealizable. If they even pretended to look interested in the administration of their company, the management took it as an attempt to usurp its most sacred rights; if they succeeded in gaining control, the company would immediately falter, with the connivance of other employers if necessary. In brief, by the end of the spring of 1917 the workers were no longer willing to resign themselves to their fate. The leaders of "their" party assured them that there were solutions to the problems—state control or worker control would end by taming capitalism and setting up Socialism. But the Soviet leaders did not try to impose their views and yielded to the blackmail of those economic experts who predicted that if they interfered, the Russian economy would perish for good. Then the workers turned to the Bolsheviks who, certain that Revolution would break out in Germany on the morrow, were equally convinced that nothing could then stop a successful Socialist experiment in Russia. The Bolsheviks also acquired the support of the noncombatant soldiers by approving of their decision not to return to the front. In addition, they earned the good-will of the countryside by encouraging the peasants to act without waiting for the Constituent, while their Menshevik and Socialist-Revolutionary rivals gave the impression of being opposed to the spontaneity of the Revolution.

The situation was the same way on the political level. The former subjects of the Tsar did not intend to be deprived of their rights as citizens, which they conceived to be quite considerable. Everything which represented the State was abhorred as a survival of the hated past. The government, opposed by the Soviet, was suspect, as were any decisions which one did not participate in making. The smallest provincial Soviet considered itself by right the equal of the large Petrograd Soviet, although for its part the minority did not consider itself bound by the decisions of the majority. It immediately organized into autonomous units and decided, in all sovereignty, the problems which divided the nation. This is what made the representative régime questionable. At the municipal elections in May and June 1917, the first freely held in Russia, there were 40 percent abstentions. For the citizens of the new Russia, the question was not one of being better governed or of choosing another form of being governed, but of being self-governing. Any delegation of power was excoriated, any authority unbearable. The Russians called themselves Social-Democrats or Socialist-Revolutionaries or something else, but in reality their actions were anarchistic, although few of them were conscious of it, since Anarchist propaganda got no response.

Perhaps this is the explanation of the relative failure of the Soviet. Accepted as the agents of the destruction of the Old Order, they were rejected as soon as they came under party control, because, opposed to any form of parliamentarianism, the Russians wanted the power to decide for themselves about their own fate. Indeed, coercing others shocked them almost as much as being coerced; thus, while they approved the Soviet policy, they reproved their leaders who wanted to force Kronstadt to apply it. At this time nothing seemed more odious to them than centralized power. Since the actions of the Soviet Congress were aimed precisely at controlling the revolutionary activities of the country, it is understandable why the slogan "All power to the Soviets" did not receive unanimous acceptance, except in the army, where, more than anywhere else, forms of the past survived. No doubt the soviets were dominated by the "conciliators" for a long time, but even after June, when they were being Bolshevized, the Lenin slogan was not very popular. By that time the factory councils and agrarian committees, in closer touch with the grass roots, were already looming as rivals of the Soviet.*

This posed a paradox. Because they controlled the Soviet, it was the Mensheviks and the Socialist-Revolutionaries who played the role of a centralizing party, as a result of which they rapidly lost popularity. But not the Bolsheviks, whose orientation only the initiated knew, and which at this time, far from being monolithic, was splintered into hostile groups like all the other bodies. The public thought, on the contrary, that their action was always directed toward the disintegration of the Old Order, the governmental power, the authority of the soviets. At the moment, it was in this direction that the forces of the Russian Revolution leaned.

Ten centuries of tyranny had made their momentum irresistable. Under these conditions, how could the team of the men of February channel this torrent? First it was necessary to be united, strong, and wise; but, in contrast to the delegates to the Constituent Assembly in 1789, the new masters of Russia were not the elite of the nation. It was the fall of Tsarism, the circumstances of

*For the same reasons the great slogan of the early days had been forgotten—The meeting of a sovereign Constituent Assembly.

the advent of the new régime which made them famous. Moreover, from the start they were divided, first because the objectives of the tenant farmers (in U.S., sharecroppers) and the masses were irreconcilable, then because unity did not exist on either side. In February 1917 Russia inherited a hundred years of hatred of Tsarism, and it did not take long to see that she also inherited thirty years of party hatreds.

Apparently the victors of February were quarreling about the nature of the Revolution, its tasks, and its objectives; in reality everything boiled down to one thing: what part of the past should be preserved? Milyukov wanted to rejuvenate the State, Kerensky to revive the army, Tereshchenko to reassure the Allies, Shingarev to reestablish finances, Chernov to rebuild the old party, Tseretelli to restore the authority of the Second International, Skobelev to put everybody to work, Gorky to safeguard the historical monuments, and everybody to reestablish relations between governors and governed. Were these men so short-sighted that they could not see that these objectives had no bearing on the aspirations of the people? With eyes fixed on the front lines, observing the increase of Bolshevik influence, doing in their dreams the things which their Western equivalents were doing, they forgot that in Europe the nations had not undergone changes without tremors or violence. They did not see that in any case the European experience was not a suitable model, inasmuch as out of it had come the war, with perhaps more revolutions to come in the future. With the successful Revolution—their Revolution—they thought more of protecting that which they had acquired—the State, the new institutions, their powers—than of leading the way to a radical social change. Overnight, unconsciously, they had assumed the behavior of true conservatives.

At the time, it was the same with the citizens of the new Republic, who were often more energetic than their leaders, more revolutionary, and in any case less willing to compromise and more Bolshevik than the Bolsheviks. They could show themselves very old-fashioned, a tendency they inherited from long oppression. Thus, although they were quick to want liberty for all, they did not realize, Russians that they were, that they were oppressing other peoples; although they were democrats, they deprived entire minorities of their rights. In the Ukraine, the authors of the most heart-rending proclamations about human destiny were the same ones who, the next day, incited pogroms and meted out summary judgments. Through a lack of consistency which is sometimes found in history, others opposed those in power only because they thought they were too feeble, or they demanded at the same time the manpower to work their lands and the elimination of private property. Thus the society was sometimes behind, sometimes ahead of those who would lead it.

Finally, there was this other fact. Up until this time, workers, peasants, and national minorities had been the pawns in the fight against the aristocracy. Suddenly, one and all revealed themselves as citizens fully conscious of their rights. Then a part of the leaders of the revolutionary movement took fright. Foreseeing that they were going to lose their positions when the new society of their dreams would come into being, they clung to their shreds of authority. What anguish gripped the prophets of the Revolution on the day when, Tsarism conquered, all Russia sang its gladness! Caught in the contradictions of the Revolution, the war, and the reaction, unable to overcome them, they believed that their intellectuality and socialist militancy would permit them to say "no" to the hopes of the masses, that Russia would follow them and would unfailingly recognize in them the men of character who should be at the head of the government. It didn't happen that way. After a few more developments—the July events, the Kornilov Affair, the October Insurrection—the Citizens' Republic swept the Militants' Republic aside, putting at their head those who had not opposed the movement.

These Bolsheviks, who were often older and more deeply branded with the imprint of their ancestors than the "conciliators" whom they replaced in popular favor—could they perceive more acutely the anger of the populace, or were they just more willing to play a nihilistic role? Coming out of the darkness of exile or emigration, they knew how to associate with the movement, how to adapt their program to circumstances, and how to act with enough determination and ability to seize the torch of Revolution. They had known how to be patient, to wait for it. They were to hold it for a long time.

DOCUMENTS

1. MARX, ENGELS, AND THE REVOLUTION IN RUSSIA

If Russia tends to become a capitalist nation in the manner of the nations of Western Europe—and during the last few years, she has been to considerable pains in this direction—she will not succeed without first having changed a good part of her peasants into proletarians; and after that, once brought into the bosom of the capitalist system, she will suffer its inexorable laws, like the other vile nations.

Marx, Answers to Mikhailovsky (1877)

The fact that Russia is the last country reached by large capitalist industry, and the fact that she is at the same time the country with the largest peasant population, will make the upheaval caused by this transformation more acute here than elsewhere. The process of replacing some 500,000 *pomeshchiki* (landowners) and some 80 million peasants by a new class of bourgeois landowners could only be effected in the midst of terrible upheavals and suffering. But History is the most terrifying of the gods, who leads her triumphant chariot over the piles of corpses, not only in the wars, but also in the course of an apparently peaceful development. . . .

Engels, Letter to Danielson (1893)

2. BAKUNIN AND "COMMUNISM" (1867)

I detest Communism, because it is the denial of liberty and I cannot conceive of anything human without liberty. I am not a Communist because Communism concentrates and assimilates all the powers of society into the State, because it must end in the concentration of property in the hands of the State, whereas I want to abolish the State, the complete extermination of the principle of authority and the tutelage of the State, which under the pretense of rendering Man more civil and moral, has until now enslaved, oppressed, exploited, and depraved him. I want the organization of society and collectivization or socialization of property from the bottom to the top by means of free association, and not from the top to the bottom by any authoritative means in any form. Wanting the abolition of the State, I want the abolition

325

of hereditary property rights, which is but an institution of the State, an extension of the principle of the State. That is why I am a collectivist and not at all Communist.

3. PROGRAM OF THE SOCIAL-DEMOCRATIC PARTY (1906)

1. Autocracy of the people—that is to say, the concentration of the supreme authority of the State in the hands of a unicameral Legislative Assembly, made up of representatives of the people.

2. Equal and direct universal suffrage for all citizens at least twenty-one years of age, for the election of the Legislative Assembly as well as of all bodies of local administration. The vote by secret ballot; the right of all voters to be elected to all representative bodies; parliaments to be elected every two years. Compensation to the representatives of the people.

3. Broad powers for the local administrations. Regional autonomy for all places which differ in manner of life and in the makeup of their populations.

4. Inviolability of the individual and his residence.

5. Unlimited freedom of conscience, speech, press, assembly, strike, and association.

6. Freedom of movement and choice of profession.

7. Abolition of castes, and absolute equality of all citizens without distinction as to sex, religion, race, or nationality.

8. The right of the population to receive instruction in its mother tongue, in schools to be built at the expense of the State and local bodies. The right of all citizens to speak in their native language at meetings. The introduction of the native language on the same level as the official language in all local bodies, public and governmental.

9. The right of self-determination for all nationalities within the State.

10. The right of every individual to sue officials in a court of law.

11. The election of judges by the people.

12. Replacement of the standing army by the people armed.

13. Separation of Church and State as well as of School and Church.

14. Free and professional instruction, general and compulsory for all children of both sexes to the age of sixteen. The free issue by the State of food, clothing, and school books to needy children.

As an avowed condition for the democratization of our national economy, the Workers' Social-Democratic Party of Russia demands the abolition of all hidden taxes and the establishment of the graduated income and inheritance tax.

4. POLITICAL PROGRAM OF THE SOCIALIST-REVOLUTIONARY PARTY (1906)

—Recognition of the inalienable rights of Man and the Citizen. Full freedom of conscience, speech, press, assembly, and association; freedom to move, to choose an occupation, to strike collectively; inviolability of the individual and the domicile; complete electoral rights of all persons twenty years of age, without distinction as to sex, religion, or nationality, on the basis of direct suffrage, by secret ballot.

—Establishment on these bases of a Democratic Republic with broad self-government of regions and communities in towns as well as in rural areas; with the possibility of a broad application of federal relations between the different nationalities; recognition of their inalienable right of self-determination; proportional representation; direct popular legislation (by referendum as well as parliamentary initiative).

—Eligibility, revocability, and responsibility of all officials, including deputies and judges.

—Free process of law.*

—Instruction to be secular and obligatory for everyone.

—In regions of mixed populations, the right of each nationality to its share of the budget proportional to its population, for cultural ends, and the right of each to administer its share.

—Absolute separation of Church and State, religion being recognized as a private matter.

—Abolition of the standing army and its transformation into a Militia of the People.

5. KARL LIEBNECHT'S REPORT ON THE HORRORS OF RUSSIAN PRISONS

An incomplete statistical report from official sources shows the following: Condemned to death for political "crimes" between 1906 and 1910—3,735 persons, or one sixth of all those tried in public trials; executed—3,741 persons.

*In the fiscal sense.—Trans.

327

The enormity of these figures is evident when you consider that in the period from 1825 to 1905—that is, during the eighty years that preceded the Revolution—only a total of 625 "political" prisoners were condemned to death and only 191 were actually executed.

During the first five years of the constitutional era, the number of death sentences increased 180-fold. During this same time in Germany the number of executions averaged around fifteen a year.

Between 1906 and 1910, trials for political infractions resulted in the condemnation of 37,735 persons, of whom 8,640 were sentenced to hard labor—not counting 5,735 sentenced to death— 4,144 to labor camps, 1,292 to labor battalions, and 1,858 to "compulsory colonization"; each convict was also deprived of all civil rights.

"Compulsory colonization" consists of deporting people, bereft of all help, into barren inhospitable deserts. This method differs little from that used by the Regiment of Young Turks to neutralize the dogs of Old Constantinople. The "colonization" regions are among the least hospitable and the coldest on earth—a cold of minus 30 to 50 degrees Centigrade prevails for several months in many places. It is there that the "colonists," reduced by want to a state of savagery, must try to struggle for their miserable subsistence by the most primitive means and without the aid of a single kopek. There are women and children among them. Frequently this sentence is meted out for the sole crime of belonging to the Social-Democratic Party. Today there are five or six thousand of these exiles!

To the sentences by courts must be added an enormous number of sentences to prison and exile by administrative authorities.

The prisons and houses of detention, of which the most infamous are those of Serentui, Akatui, Tobolsk, Orel, Zharoslav, and Moscow (Butyki Prison), have today, according to official figures, which disregard the minimum requirements for prisoner health, "room" for about 140,000 prisoners. The number is almost fifty percent more than there were three or four years ago. In 1913 there were an average of 220,000 people, sometimes rising to as much as 250,000. Since then the number has risen even higher—in spite of the famous Jubilee amnesty, which benefited common criminals also. Often the prisoners are piled in closer together than cattle in barns, so close together that they have to take turns sleeping. During a large part of their term the hard-labor prisoners at Katorga Prison are chained and often they are even deprived of the leather inserts under the chains so that the irons resting on naked flesh cause abrasions and sores.

For food, the prisoners are allotted ten kopeks per head per day. It goes without saying that this is not enough to feed men, especially those living under interior and exterior conditions as abnormal as those of Russian prisoners. A large part of this trifling sum still remains in the hands of those thieving bandits who make up Russian bureaucracy, while the rest is spent most often on miserable food whose preparation defies description.

Clothed in rags, dirty and insufficient from any standpoint, their most elementary hygienic needs are neglected. It seems unbelievable that humans could live under such abominable and miserable conditions, even for a few weeks. Often it is forbidden to open the drafts to aerate the place. The exercise periods are systematically cut down or eliminated altogether. In most cases the work, without which all deprivation of freedom becomes unbearable, even under favorable conditions, has been eliminated. Only the most obnoxious and unhealthful kinds of work are permitted, such as the carding of wool. Even in cases where political prisoners had the right to perform occupational work of their own, it was forbidden in most cases at Katorga.

In view of all this, the state of health of the prisoners is fearful. Consumption, dysentery, typhus, and scurvy are the great killers. Mortality is excessively high. Consumption accounts for 55 percent of the deaths.

But the barbarity does not stop there. The prisoners are systematically abused, especially the political ones, by putting them in the same cells with the common criminals and turning them over to the tyranny of the most evil among them, who are apparently the favorites of the prison administration. Vile insults and humiliations are their daily lot. They are badly treated from morning till night, from the start of their imprisonment. Over their heads hangs the threat of a barbarous disciplinary system which makes use of the dark cell and beatings, which the Ministry of Justice and the Police have just recently decided are once again essential. These medieval tortures are the order of the day in many Houses of Correction. Thus do they smother what little dignity and self-respect are left to those who have not succumbed to the epidemics and bullets of the guards who, posted before the windows of the cells, are ready to shoot. The only thing left is escape by death for those who want to free themselves of this miserable existence.

Thus there have been veritable epidemics of suicides added to those of sickness.

6. WARTIME: DEFENSE INDUSTRY COMPANIES

TOTAL: 5,200	Employing 1,947,000 workers		On 1/1/1917 Increase of 164,000 (9.2%) over 1915	
Regions	Number of Companies	%	Number of Workers	%
Moscow	1,228	23.3	845,198	43.4
Petrograd	670	12.7	304,134	15.6
Ural	477	9.0	289,650	14.9
Ekaterinoslav	275	5.2	136,718	7.0
Nizhni-Novgorod	305	5.8	85,264	4.3
Odessa	504	9.4	69,857	3.6
Rostov	293	5.5	59,602	3.1
Siberia	933	17.8	42,806	2.2
Karkhov	201	3.8	33,897	1.7
Caucasus	204	3.8	30,638	1.6
Revel	41	0.8	28,277	1.5
Kiev	147	2.8	21,889	1.1

For the Moscow and Petrograd regions, the figures are for only about 90 percent of the companies. They are incomplete for the Ekaterinoslav Region. As can be seen, the first four regions employ about 80 percent of the defense workers. It can also be seen that the Moscow Region has proportionately the largest companies, followed by those of the Urals.* The smallest are in Siberia.

7. RUSSIAN WORKERS AND THE WAR

A LETTER FROM ALEXANDER SHLYAPNIKOV TO PIETER TROELSTRA *
COPENHAGEN, 1914

You have asked me about the opinion of Russian Socialist workers on the subject of the war declared by the Germans on the Tsar of Russia and I hasten to answer right away.

First, dear Comrade, I must tell you that the declaration of war found us in the midst of a revolutionary push. There were some politico-economic strikes in St. Petersburg, Moscow, Riga, Baku,

---

*In Petrograd the Putilov factories increased from 13,510 to 26,564 workers, the Lessner Companies from 1,289 to 7,927, etc.

*We are reproducing here the text of this letter written in French, without changing the spelling. Dots indicate deletions. Troelstra was a Dutch Socialist who belonged to the International Bureau.

and numerous other industrial centers. In St. Petersburg in particular the movement was most violent. Several days before the declaration of war, the worker masses erected barricades for the defense of life and liberty threatened by the brutal police of our country. During the first days of mobilization, demonstrations were held and in numerous places the mobilized were surrounded by demonstrators who, chanting revolutionary songs, accompanied them to their point of departure.

That day we did not believe that war was possible. We knew that on the other side of the border, in a freer country, there were powerful workers' organizations which would try to prevent war, which would not allow themselves to be led to fight others in a horrible slaughter. And our will to resist war was with them. But the news that we got became worse and worse.

We were amazed to see the German Socialist Party, or rather that part of it which was in Parliament, vote the military credits. This betrayal untied the hands of the opportunists in all countries. And here we were witness to the most horrible tragedy imaginable. It was the leaders of the workers' organizations who offered their support, morally and materially, to the Imperialist undertakings of the bourgeoisie. The class struggle no longer exists for those people who now fight not for themselves but always for the freedom of others. . . .

. . .

You have told me that the German Socialists are wondering that we are not glad about the Declaration of War by the German Government against Tsarism. This wonder is only a hypocritical cover up for their own treason. . . .

. . .

You have also asked a question about whether the Russian Socialists have changed since the war with Japan in their attitude towards war and Tsarism. The major part of the workers have remained faithful to the principle of "War against War" but for the moment, in this war, they are alone. . . .

. . .

There is one more contrast [with 1905]. The Manchurian undertaking . . . was only of small interest to the nationalist capitalists. Hence the discontent. It has been looked upon as a dynastic enterprise of the *camarilla*.

Today, these same capitalists and numerous intellectuals of all hues repeat that this war concerns the vital interests of our country. This means that our industry wants more independence,

331

that it wants to get out from under the wing of German Capitalism imposed by the commercial treaty of 1904, to the disadvantage of our national industry. Agriculture wants better outlets, and both want the outlet of the Dardanelle Straits, closed to us by our present Allies?

Alexander Shlyapnikov

8. THE SOCIAL-DEMOCRATIC MINORITY AND THE WAR

THE ZALEZHSKY ORDER OF THE DAY—
Paris, Spring 1915

The war actually is an Imperialist conflict which ends by destroying the productive forces, increases the misery of the working masses, and reinforces political reaction and militarism in all phases of social life. For the world of the proletarian movement, there is only one course to take—the uncompromising struggle against the Imperialist efforts of the bourgeoisie. The international proletariat can only conduct this struggle under the banner of the class struggle. The struggle for the democratization of Russia is one of the most important missions of the proletarian movement.

The war today is developing in the context of the capitalist community, and the proletariat, during the time of the International, unfolded its activities in the context of the nationalist organizations. The party officials of the proletariat deviated from the principle of the class struggle, the idea of international solidarity of the proletariat, and broke up the International. A fatal consequence of this deviation from principles is that the proletarian organizations have submitted more and more to the imperialist policies . . . which leads to the breakup of the class policy of the proletariat.

The elements which united on the basis of the revolutionary action of the proletariat against the War want to reawaken the class consciousness of the workers. Only these elements can oppose the nationalistic appeals. . . .

We reject any attempt to build a bridge between the Internationalists and the Social-Patriots. All Russian revolutionaries of all shades are asked to join the true Internationalists.

THE ZIMMERWALD MANIFESTO (OCTOBER 7, 1915)

PROLETARIANS OF EUROPE!

Here the war has already lasted more than a year! Millions of corpses cover the battlefields. Millions of men will be crippled for the rest of their lives. *Europe has become a gigantic slaughterhouse of men*. The whole civilization created by the work of several generations is doomed to destruction. The most savage barbarism today triumphs over everything which until now was the pride of humanity.

Whatever the immediate cause of the starting of this war, one thing is certain: *the war which has caused all this chaos is the product of Imperialism*. It is the outcome of the will of the Capitalist classes of every nation to live off the exploitation of human toil and the natural wealth of the universe. In such a manner that the economically backward or politically weak nations fall under the yoke of the Great Powers who attempt, in this war, to remake the map of the world by blood and iron, in accordance with their interests.

It is thus that peoples and entire nations such as Belgium, Poland, the Balkan States, and Armenia run the risk of being annexed totally or in part by the simple device of compensations.

The motives of the war appear in all their nakedness as events unfold. Bit by bit the veil falls which has hidden the significance of this universal disaster from the minds of the people.

The capitalists of all countries, who coin from the blood of the people the red money of the profits of war, maintain that the war is in defense of the Fatherland, of Democracy, to liberate oppressed nations. They lie. *The truth is that in fact they bury under the destroyed hearths the freedom of their own people as well as the independence of the other nations*. New chains, new charges—that will be the result of this war, and it is the proletariat of all countries, victor and vanquished, which will bear them.

Improvement in well-being, they said, when the war began.

Misery and privation, unemployment and spiralling costs of living, sickness, epidemics—such are the real results. For decades the cost of the war will absorb the better part of the effort of the people, will compromise the improvement in social conditions, and will impede all progress.

Bankruptcy of civilization, economic depression, political reaction—those are the benefits of this terrible struggle of the people.

Thus the war reveals the true character of modern capitalism, which is incompatible not only with the interests of the working classes and the demands of historical evolution, but also with the most elementary conditions of the human community.

The institutions of the capitalist régime which controlled the fate of the people, the governments—monarchies or republics— secret diplomacy, the powerful management organizations, the bourgeois parties, the capitalist press, the Church—on all these falls the responsibility for this war born of a social order which nurtures them, which they defend, and which serves their interests.

WORKERS!

Yesterday you were exploited, dispossessed, and scorned. But when it came to sending you to slaughter and death you were called brothers, comrades. And now that militarism has mutilated you, torn you apart, humiliated you, crushed you, the ruling classes demand that you give up your rights, your ideals—in a word, to submit to slavery in the social sphere. You are bereft of the opportunity of expressing your opinions, your feelings, your suffering. You are forbidden to formulate your demands and defend them. The press throttled, the freedoms and political rights trodden underfoot: this is the reign of a military dictatorship with an iron fist.

We can no longer, should no longer, remain passive in the face of this situation which threatens the future of Europe and Humanity.

For many years, the Socialist proletariat has led the fight against militarism. With growing apprehension, its representatives concerned themselves about the dangers of imperialistic wars in their national conventions, a danger becoming more threatening every day. In Stuttgart, in Copenhagen, in Basle, the Conventions have outlined the path which the proletariat should follow.

But Socialist parties and workers' organizations in certain countries, while contributing to the formation of these decisions, have ignored, from the beginning of the war, the obligations which were incumbent on them. Their representatives have led the workers to give up the class struggle, the only effective means of proletarian emancipation. They granted the ruling classes the war credits. They put themselves at the disposal of the governments for various duties. They tried, through their press and their representatives, to persuade the neutrals of the worth of the government's policies in their respective countries. They supplied Socialist ministers to the government as hostages for the "Sacred Union." *By this very fact, they have accepted, before the working class, a share of the responsibility for the present and future burdens of this war, its aims and methods.* And inasmuch as each party, separately, failed in its task, the highest representative of the Socialist organizations of all countries, the International, has failed in *its* task.

It is because of these facts that the working class, which had not yielded to the general hysteria, has not yet found in the second year of this slaughter of the people, the means of undertaking simultaneously in all countries an active struggle for peace.

In this intolerable situation, We, Representatives of the Socialist Parties, Trade Unions, or the minorities of these bodies, German, French, Italian, Russian, Polish, Lettish, Rumanian, Bulgarian, Swedish, Norwegian, Dutch and Swiss, We, who do not put ourselves on the level of national solidarity with our exploiters, but who have remained faithful to International solidarity of the proletariat and the class struggle, have gathered together to tie the bonds torn asunder in International relations, to call upon the working class to become aware of itself and to lead it in the fight for Peace.

This fight is the fight for Liberty, for the brotherhood of Man, for Socialism. We must undertake this fight for Peace, for a peace without annexations or war indemnities. But such a peace is only possible if all thoughts of violation of the rights and freedom of the people are condemned. It must not lead to the occupation of entire countries, nor to any partial annexations. No annexations, either avowed or secret, no economic obligations, which because of the loss of autonomy which they entail, are even less tolerable. The people's right of self-determination must be the unshakable foundation of nation-to-nation relations.

PROLETARIANS!

Since the war was unleashed, you have put all your power, your courage, your endurance at the service of the owning classes to kill each other. Today, you must, remaining on the field of the class war, act in your own behalf, for the sacred aim of Socialism, for the emancipation of the oppressed people and the enslaved classes.

It is the duty and the task of the Socialists of the belligerent countries to take up this struggle with all their might. It is the duty and the task of the Socialists of the neutral countries to help their brothers by any and all means in this struggle against blood-thirsty barbarism.

Never in the history of the world has there been a more urgent, noble, higher task. Its accomplishment must be our common aim. No sacrifice is too great, no burden too heavy to attain this end—the reestablishment of Peace among Nations.

Men and women workers, mothers and fathers, widows and

orphans, wounded and crippled, to all of you who suffer from this war and by this war, we say: Over the border, the battlefields, the countryside and the shattered cities—*Proletarians of all countries, unite!*

Zimmerwald (Switzerland) September 1915. In the name of the International Socialist Conference,

For the German Delegation—Georg Ledebour, Adolph Hoffman

For the French Delegation—A. Bourderon, A. Merrheim

For the Italian Delegation—G. E. Modigliani, Constantino Lazzari

For the Russian Delegation—N. Lenin, Paul Axelrod, M. Bobrov

For the Polish Delegation—St. Lapinski, A. Varski, Cz. Ganetsky

For the Balkan Socialist Federation—In the name of the Rumanian Delegation—C. Rakovsky; In the Name of the Bulgarian Delegation—Vassil Kolarov

For the Swedish and Norwegian Delegation—Z. Höglund, Ture Nermad

For the Dutch Delegation—H. Roland Holst

For the Swiss Delegation—Robert Grimm, Charles Naine

10. RESOLUTIONS PASSED AT THE KIENTHAL CONFERENCE (24-30 APRIL 1916)

THE PROLETARIAT AND PEACE

In conclusion, the following Resolution was unanimously adopted.

I.

1. The present war is the result of Imperialist antagonisms resulting from the development of the Capitalist Régime. The Imperialist powers are exploiting, in their own interest, the unsolved Nationalist problems, the dynastic aspirations, and all that survives from the feudal past. The real aim of the war is to cause a new distribution of colonies and to secure the submission of the economically backward nations.

2. The War, unable to eliminate the Capitalist Régime nor its Imperialist inclinations, cannot eliminate the causes of future wars either. It strengthens financial oligarchy. It is unable to solve the old problems of Nationality and to end the struggle for World

Hegemony. On the contrary, it complicates all these problems and creates new antagonisms which emphasize even more the economic and political reaction, sowing the seeds of future wars.

3. This is why, in claiming that the War will end in a lasting peace, the Governments and their bourgeois Social-nationalist agents either do not take into account the necessary conditions for the realization of this end or willfully misrepresent the truth. In a Capitalist Régime, the annexations, the economic and political alliances of the Imperialist states, can no more ensure a lasting peace than can the Courts of Compulsory Arbitration, the limitation of debate, and what is called the Democratization of foreign policy.

4. Forcible annexations cause hatred among people and produce new causes of conflict and collision. Political alliances and coalitions of Imperialist Powers are only the means of prolonging and extending the economic war by causing ever graver world conflagrations.

5. The projects tending to suppress the dangers of war by a general limitation of armaments, by compulsory arbitration, presuppose the existence of a real force capable of balancing the antagonistic interests of the states—and of imposing its authority on them. But such sanctions and such authority do not exist, and the Capitalist development, which aggravates the antagonism between the middle classes of the different countries and their coalitions, gives no hope that we shall see the coming of such a mediating power. True Democratic control of foreign policy presupposes a complete Democratization of the modern State. The proletariat would find there a weapon usable in its struggle against Imperialism, but never a decisive means of changing diplomacy into an instrument for peace.

6. It is for these reasons that the working class must reject the fanciful proposals of the bourgeois pacifists and Socialist-Nationalists who substitute new illusions for old. They lure the masses by turning them away from the Class War and following the "to-the-end" policy.

II

7. If the Capitalist Régime is unable to ensure lasting peace, only Socialism will create the necessary conditions for its realization. In effect, by abolishing private property in the means of production, Socialism simultaneously eliminates the exploitation of the working class by the owner classes, the oppression of the

people, and, by this very fact, the causes of War. That is why the struggle for a lasting peace is, in short, but the struggle for the realization of Socialism.

8. Each time the working class gives up the class war by fraternizing with its exploiters or by subordinating its hopes to those of the Governments and the ruling classes, it steps backward from its goal—the realization of a lasting peace. By acting thus, the working class entrusts the Capitalist classes and the bourgeois Governments with a task which only it can lead to a successful end. Still worse, it donates to the War the slaughter of all that is best, and dooms to destruction the healthiest and most capable elements, which in War as in Peace should be used primarily in the fight for Socialism.

III

9. In accordance with the decisions of the International Congresses of Stuttgart, Copenhagen, and Basle, the proletariat's attitude with respect to the War should not be determined by the military or strategic situation of the belligerent countries. The primary duty of the proletariat is thus to demand, as of now, an immediate Armistice to begin Peace Negotiations.

10. If this appeal find an answer in the ranks of the International proletariat, the working class, by promoting vigorous action whose aim will be the overthrow of Capitalist domination, will succeed in hastening the end of the war and in influencing the conditions for peace. If the working class ignores this appeal, the Peace conditions will be set by the Governments, the diplomats, and the ruling classes without regard for the interest and hopes of the people.

11. In the Revolutionary struggle of the masses for the Socialist aspirations and the liberation of humanity from the plague of military Capitalism, the proletariat must at the same time oppose all hopes of annexations. The proletariat does not consider the political setup before the War to be in the interest of the people, but is opposed to any and all arbitrary resettlements of frontiers, even in cases where, under the pretext of the liberation of people, they should want to establish bogus States with fictional freedom which are in reality under subjection. Socialism itself tends to eliminate all national oppression by the political and economic union of people on a Democratic basis—a union which could not be made under the Capitalistic system. But it is just these annexations, whatever their shape, that make this task difficult, while by

splitting the nations and incorporating them into the great Capitalist powers they make the proletarian struggle more arduous.

12. Until Socialism has brought freedom and equal rights to all people, the constant duty of the proletariat is to fight against all national oppression and all violence against weaker nations, to obtain by the class war their self-determination on a completely Democratic basis as well as the protection of National minorities.

13. The war reparations demanded by the Imperial Powers are irreconcilable with the interests of the proletariat. In the same manner as the ruling classes attempt to put the expenses of war on the shoulders of their working classes, they will try to thrust the weight of the war reparations on the proletariat of the losers. This state of affairs will be as nefarious to the workers of the victorious country, because the worsening of the social and economic burdens of the working class of a given country have inevitable repercussions on the proletariat of other countries and make the International class war that much harder. The action of the proletariat of one nation does not consist of throwing the economic and financial burden of War on the workers of another country, but of setting the burdens on the property-owners of all countries by the abolition of the public debt.

14. The fight against War and Imperialism will intensify as a result of the suffering and ruination caused by the plagues of the Imperialist era. Socialism will develop and direct the movement of the masses against the high cost of living, for the demands of the agricultural workers, against unemployment, new taxes, and political reaction until it ends in the International class struggle and the final triumph of the proletariat.

11. THE MAKLAKOV PARABLE

You are in a car speeding crazily along a narrow crooked road alongside a precipice. . . . Suddenly you realize that the driver cannot drive. Perhaps its because he does not know how to drive under strenuous circumstances, perhaps because he is tired and has lost control of himself—whatever it is, if he stays at the wheel disaster is inevitable. Luckily, there are people in the car who know how to drive. Someone will have to take his place as soon as possible. But it is dangerous when the car is going at such speed. Then, either blindly or because of professional pride, the chauffeur refuses to relinquish the wheel and let anyone else drive. What is to be done? . . . A single move will cause the car to hurtle off into space. You know it and he knows it. He laughs at your anxiety, your powerlessness. "You wouldn't dare!" He is right. You wouldn't.... Better still! Not only will you not bother him, but you will help him with advice. And you would be right. That is what you have to do. But what will you feel when you note that even with your help the chauffeur will not be able to pull through, and if your mother, seeing the danger, should beg for you to do something, and, not understanding your passive attitude, should accuse you of cowardly indifference?

12. THE PROGRAM OF THE "PROGRESSIVIST BLOC"

The undersigned representatives of the Parties and Groups of the Imperial Duma and the Council of State, convinced that only a strong, firm, and active Government can lead Russia to victory and only a Government depending on the confidence of the people can organize an active cooperation with all citizens, have arrived at the conclusion that to accomplish this most essential and important task, the following conditions must be met:

The formation of a United Government, made up of people who have the confidence of the Nation and who are in agreement with the Legislative bodies, in order to put into effect, as soon as possible, a definite program.

A definite change in the methods employed by the government until now, which were founded on a distrust of innovations, especially:

a. A strict adherence to legal principles in administration.

b. An end to dual authority in civil and military matters which are not concerned directly with military operations.

c. An overhaul of local administrative personnel.

d. An intelligent and coherent policy with regard to civil peace and an end to race and class antagonisms.

For the implementation of such a policy, the following measures must be undertaken in the Law and in the Administration:

1. By means of amnesty, our Ruler will put an end to all prosecutions for political or religious reason which are uncomplicated by criminal actions. Remission of punishment and restoration of civil rights must accompany this step, including the right to vote in the Duma *zemstvo*, and municipal council elections . . . excepting traitors and spies.

2. The return of all exiles by administrative order (that is to say, those sentenced without trial for political reasons).

340

3. Absolute cessation of religious persecution in any form whatever, under any pretext, and abrogation of religious persecution circulars, limiting and modifying the meaning of the April 17, 1905 Decree.

4. An act on the Russian-Polish question which would promulgate: the abrogation of the limitation on the rights of Poles in Russian territory; the preparation and immediate introduction of a law concerning Polish autonomy; and the simultaneous revision of legislation concerning property in Poland.

5. The beginning of abolition of measures against Jews—particularly, preparing for the abolition of the "Pale"* and facilitating Jews' access to the schools and universities—and the abrogation of limits on choice of profession, the restoration of the Jewish press.

6. A policy of appeasement in the Finnish question—particularly a change of administrative personnel in the Senate and the end of prosecution of officials.

7. Restoration of the press of Little Russia (Ukrainian), a review of the cases of inhabitants of Galicia arrested or exiled (to Siberia, for example), and the freeing of those arrested without cause.

8. Restoration of the trade union activities and the end of persecution of the Workers' representatives in the Health Insurance Mutuals under pretext that they belong to illegal organizations; the restoration of the workers' press.

9. An agreement by the Government with the legislative organizations for the introduction as soon as possible of the following: *a.* Laws pertaining to national defense, army supply, the care of wounded, refugee aid, and other questions immediately concerning the war; *b.* An immediate legislative program for victory and internal security; equal opportunity for the peasants to attain a rank equal to that of the other classes; the introduction of township *zemstvos*; the Revision of the 1890 *Zemstvos Law* and of the Municipal Law of 1892; the introduction of the *zemstvo* organizations in the outlying provinces, such as Siberia, Archangelsk, the Don Region, the Caucasus, etc.

Laws concerning cooperatives, vacations for employees in private enterprise, the bettering of working conditions for the postal employees, the reinforcement of bans on alcohol; the authorization of conventions of unions of *zemstvos*. The introduction of Justices of the Peace in the provinces where formerly there weren't any because of financial reasons. The putting into effect of the necessary steps to implement the program indicated above. . . .

Summer 1915

13. STRUVE MEMORANDUM ON THE RUSSIAN SITUATION: FEBRUARY 7, 1917**

Two facts stand out in the internal affairs of Russia today:

1. Economic difficulties due to the War;

2. A widening conflict between Crown and People.

*Discriminatory law.

**Extract from Samuel Hoar, *The Fourth Seal* (London 1930), pp. 188-192.

The importance of the first requires no explanation, but it is impossible to separate it from the second factor, the political unrest.

The political unrest has become acute and crystallized. It is evident that in order to conduct the war vigorously to a victorious end, unity must prevail, founded on a compromise between the various interests and their subordination to the national interest. No one doubts that the whole nation has felt the need for this unity and has made this need felt both by itself and through its representatives. But the Crown has not drawn the proper conclusions from this state of affairs, failing to set a policy to meet this situation caused by the war; on the contrary, it defies public opinion, losing precious time for national unity, discouraging true patriots, and building up the hopes of those who dream of a weakened Russia among the Great Powers. It can not be emphasized enough that the reactionary policy of the Crown weakens those very elements which are the most moderate, cutting the ground from under the feet of the most patriotic elements and opening the way for the nihilistic forces.

From this fact comes the feeling, shared by all of Russia and even profoundly affecting the officers' corps, that the conflict between the Crown and the people has done nothing but put Russia in a truly Revolutionary mood. The patriotic elements of society and the Army are quite conscious of the enormous historic responsibility which attaches to an internal conflict in time of war, and it is only for this reason that calm reigns in the nation where every thinking person is continually thinking of and discussing the present situation and the tragic difficulties. The difficulty is all the greater in that the consensus is that highly placed persons in the Crown's entourage are pro-German. This opinion cannot be uprooted by merely making empty phrases. Only a government reorganized in such a way that it would gain the confidence of the population could clear the unhealthy air of suspicion and fear that is actually sapping the nation's strength.

No matter what the disagreement, it should not be brought out before strangers, even Allies. Because we must now maintain solidarity between Allies, the ordinary considerations which are perhaps necessary in time of peace no longer hold and are senseless in the present situation.

All well-intentioned persons in responsible policy-making positions only want the Crown not to commit an irrevocable though baseless act by dissolving the Imperial Duma under the pretext that its term has expired and that a new one must be elected. Such an act would endanger the Crown's future and would weaken the stabilizing elements which have united in order to fight the War to a victorious end. In these events, a fatal role is being played by the present Minister of the Interior, who has lost the good opinion of his colleagues of all shades of opinion and can be considered to be psychologically abnormal.

It should be noted that the old slogan "Down With Bureaucracy" has lost its significance; in the present conflict the best elements of the bureaucracy are on the side of the people.

Such is the actual state of affairs in Russia.

(Report sent to Lord Milner,
at the time of the Petrograd
Conference.)

14. A LETTER FROM ALEXANDRA TO NICHOLAS II

My Darling,

I let you go with my heart torn by anxiety. What a horrible time we are living in. . . . God has burdened you with a terribly heavy cross to bear. I am, I suffer with you. . . . But what can I do? Pray . . . pray and pray again. Our dear friend in the world beyond also prays for you.

The situation seems to improve. Only, darling, be firm. Show some authority, that's what the Russians need. You have been kind. Make them feel your fist now.

I bless you, I embrace you and hold your poor head tightly against my breast. . . . Do you feel my arms about you, my lips tenderly against yours, inseparably?

(Around February 24, 1917)

15. *IZVESTYA'S* APPEAL TO THE POPULATION OF PETROGRAD AND RUSSIA

The Old Order has led the country to ruin and the population to starvation. It was impossible to bear any longer and the inhabitants of Petrograd came out into the streets to show their dissatisfaction. They were received with gunfire. Instead of bread, they got lead; the Tsar's Ministers gave them lead.

But the soldiers did not want to act against the people and they turned against the Government. Together they seized the arsenals, the guns, and some important organs of power.

The fight goes on and must go on to the end. The old forces must be defeated to yield their place to a Government of the People. The salvation of Russia depends on it.

In order to win this fight for Democracy, the people must create its own organs of Government. Yesterday, February 27th, a Soviet of Workers' Deputies was formed, made up of the representatives of the factories, workshops, parties, Democratic and Socialist organizations. The Soviet, ensconced in the Duma, has set as its main task; the organization of the people and the fight for the consolidation of political freedom and Government of the People.

The Soviet has named commissars to establish the authority of the people in the working-class quarters of the Capital. We ask the entire population to rally to the Soviet immediately, to organize local committees in the working-class quarters, and to take over the conduct of local affairs.

All together, with forces united, we will win in order to sweep the old government from office and set up a Constituent Assembly on the basis of equal, secret, and direct universal suffrage.

The Soviet of Workers' Deputies

16. THE BOLSHEVIK MANIFESTO OF FEBRUARY 27, 1917

Citizens! The citadels of Russian Tsarism have fallen. The prosperity of the Tsarist band, built upon the bones of the people, has collapsed. The capital is in the hands of the insurgent people! The Revolutionary troops have come over to the Insurgents. The Revolutionary Army and Proletariat must save the country from defeat and the certain bankruptcy assigned to it by the Tsarist government.

At the cost of enormous efforts, of blood and the life of its sons, the Russian people have shaken off its ancient slavery.

The job of the Working Class and the Revolutionary Army is to create a Provisional Revolutionary Government which will lead the New Regime, the New Republican Regime.

The Provisional Revolutionary Government must establish provisional laws which will safeguard the freedom and rights of the people, confiscate the Monastery Estates and Crown lands and turn them over to the people, institute the eight-hour day, and convoke the Constituent Assembly on the basis of direct, equal, and secret universal suffrage.

The Provisional Revolutionary Government must ensure without delay the provisioning of the people and the army. To that effect, all provisions now stocked by the old Government and municipalities must be confiscated.

The Hydra of reaction might still rear its head. The task of the people and their Revolutionary Government is to repress all counter-Revolutionary attempts against the people.

The immediate urgent task of the Provisional Revolutionary Government is to establish relations with the proletariat of the belligerent countries with a view to the struggle of the proletariat of all countries against their oppressors and their slave masters, against the Governments of Tsarist type and the Capitalist cliques, and with a view to immediate cessation of the bloody slaughter inflicted on the enslaved people.

The workers of the factories and plants as well as the insurgent troops must choose, without delay, their representatives to the Provisional Revolutionary Government which must be established by the Revolutionary Insurgent people and the Army.

Citizens, Soldiers, wives, and mothers! Into the fray! Into the open fight against Tsarist power and its henchmen!

Everywhere in Russia, the Red Flag of Insurrection is raised! Everywhere in Russia, take up the cause of liberty, overthrow the Tsarist flunkies, call the soldiers to the struggle.

Everywhere in Russia, in the cities and the countryside, create the Government of the Revolutionary People.

Citizens! By the unanimous and fraternal efforts of the insurgents we have consolidated the new order born of liberty out of the corpse of autocracy!

Forward! There is no turning back! Fight without mercy!

Follow the Red Flag of the Revolution!

Long live the Democratic Republic!

Long live the Revolutionary working class!

Long live the Revolutionary people and the Insurgent Army!

17. THE ABDICATION OF NICHOLAS II

By the grace of God, we, Nicholas II, Emperor of All Russia, Tsar of Poland, Grand-Duke of Finland, etc., to all our faithful subjects, be it known:

In these days of the great struggle against the foe outside who has for three years tried to subjugate our country, God has seen fit to try Russia with another terrible ordeal. Internal disturbances threaten us with dire consequences on the ultimate end of this stubborn war. The destiny of Russia, the honor of our heroic

Army, the happiness of the people, the whole future of our dear country demand that the War be concluded victoriously at any price.

Our cruel enemy is in the last throes and the moment is near when our valiant army in conjunction with our glorious Allies will defeat it finally.

In these crucial days in the life of Russia, we think we can in all conscience facilitate the union and the organization of all her forces for a quick victory.

That is why, in agreement with the Imperial Duma, we think it best to abdicate the throne and give up Supreme Power.

Not wishing to become separated from our beloved son, we bequeath our heritage to our brother, the Grand Duke Michael Alexandrovitch, with our blessing when he assumes the Throne. We ask him to govern in unison with the representatives of the nation sitting in the legislative organs and to swear an allegiance to them in the name of our beloved country.

We appeal to the loyal sons of Russia, asking them to fulfill their sacred patriotic duty by obeying the Tsar in this painful moment of national trial, and to help him, along with the representatives of the nation, to guide the Russian State on the road to glory and prosperity.

God help Russia!

March 2, 1917

18. THE FIRST STATEMENT OF THE
PROVISIONAL GOVERNMENT

Citizens of the Russian State,

An important event has taken place. By the powerful impulse of the Russian people, the old order has been overthrown. A new free Russia has been born. The overthrow crowns many years of struggle.

By the act of October 17, 1905, under pressure of the uprisen population, Russia saw itself promised Constitutional liberties. These promises were not kept. The Duma—the mouthpiece of the hopes of the populace—was dissolved. The second Duma suffered the same fate. Unable to break the popular will, the Government decided, by the Act of June 3, 1907, to withdraw from the people a part of its rights to participate in legislation, which had previously been granted. In the course of nine long years the people were deprived, one by one, of the rights which it had acquired. Once

346

more the country was plunged into the void of arbitrary absolutism. All attempts to reason with the Government were fruitless and the Great World Conflict into which Mother Russia was dragged by the enemy found her in a state of moral bankruptcy, indifferent to the future, a stranger to her people, and drowned in corruption.

Neither the heroic efforts of the Army, crushed under the weight of the internal chaos, nor the appeals of the representatives of the people, who united in face of the peril which threatened the nation, were able to lead the ex-Emperor or his Government on the way to an agreement with the people. And when Russia, because of the illegal and fatal action of its leaders, found itself faced with the gravest dangers, the nation has been forced to take power into its own hands. In its unanimity, the Revolutionary enthusiasm of the people, fully conscious of the gravity of the moment, and the determination of the Duma together have created the Provisional Government. The Provisional Government holds sacred its duty and responsibility to satisfy the hopes of the population and to lead the country on the bright road to a free and civil Régime.

The Government believes that the spirit of profound patriotism shown during the fight against the Old Order will inspire our valiant soldiers on the battlefield. For its part, it will do all that is possible to furnish the Army with the necessities for victory in war. The Government will consider the ties to its allies sacred and will observe to the letter its agreements with our allies.

While taking all measures for the defense of the country against its external enemy, the Government will consider it its main duty to permit the expression of the will of the people in what concerns the choice of a political regime and will convoke the Constituent Assembly as soon as possible on the basis of universal, direct, equal, and secret suffrage, guaranteeing equal participation in the elections to the valiant defenders of the land of our forefathers who are now shedding their blood on the battlefield. The Constituent Assembly will promulgate the fundamental laws which guarantee the country its inalienable rights to justice, freedom, and equality.

Understanding the gravity of this absence of rights which oppresses the Nation and constitutes an obstacle to the creative drive of the people at a time of national upheaval, the Provisional Government deems it necessary to furnish the country immediately, even before the convocation of the Constituent Assembly, with laws which will ensure civil rights and equality, which will allow all citizens to contribute freely to a creative undertaking for the benefit of all. The Government will also undertake the promulgation of laws which will ensure that everyone will partake equally in the elections of bodies for self-government on the basis of universal suffrage.

In the moment of national liberation, the whole country will recall with gratitude those who, while defending their religious and political convictions, fell victim to the Old Régime. And the Provisional Government considers it a pleasant duty to recall from exile and prison, with all honors, those who suffered for the good of the country.

In fulfilling these tasks, the Provisional Government is actuated by the conviction that it is thus carrying out the will of the people, and that the whole country will support it in its loyal efforts to ensure the well-being of Russia. This conviction gives it courage. The Provisional Government considers that only the warm support of the whole population will guarantee the triumph of the new order.

March 6, 1917

19. AN ANARCHIST TRACT (MARCH 23, 1917)

It is the destructive spirit which is the creative spirit.	The liberation of the workers will be the work of the workers themselves.

THE AIMS AND TASKS OF THE REVOLUTION

The Russian Revolution is going forward rapidly and it can now be said that the Government of Guchkov-Milyukov's days are numbered. The people have risen to decisively announce their will to go to the end, to total victory. They know from experience that a half Revolution will be answered by a reaction, a total reaction.

There are at this time in Petrograd two Governments—the Ministry of Guchkov-Milyukov which hastened to proclaim itself "sovereign," and the Soviet of Workers' and Soldiers' Deputies. The second is holding the bridle of the first. The power in fact is in the hands of the Revolution; Guchkov and Milyukov squirm helplessly in their powerful grasp, recalling with nostalgia the "good old days" of Nicholas the Bloody, and sign with trembling hands the decrees of the Workers' and Soldiers' Deputies Soviet. They play the role of sorry buffoons, which History mockingly has draped with scarlet red robes. These robes do not suit them and they would like to shed them, but cruel History will not allow it and holds them firmly.

It has been two weeks since the Revolution was born, and more than once in this short period the bourgeoisie has tried to deceive and betray it. Having had to chase the Blood-Stained Tsar from the Throne, "worried about the welfare of the people," it wanted to save the tottering Romanov throne and called the Tsar's brother Michael to reign and govern. But the Soviet of Workers' and Soldiers' Deputies was against it. And Michael prudently stepped aside, pretending to submit to the "will of the people." To guarantee the Army's fidelity, those gentlemen, Msrss. Milyukov and Guchkov, contrived to have that proven satrap, Chief of the Black Hundred, Grand Duke Nicholas Nicholaevitch, nominated as Supreme Commander. But the Soviet of Workers' and Soldiers' Deputies again refused. And the Grand Duke, who had his own conception of the will of the people, whom he submitted to the knout and bayonet, this time submitted himself. To bury the Constituent Assembly the Guchkov and Milyukov clique states it will be assembled "after the war." But the Soviet of Workers' and Soldiers' Deputies decided unequivocally that it would be assembled within two months. And this band of professional traitors prudently affixed their signature "within two months." In the Guchkov-Milyukov camp they are beginning to understand not only that they will not be in a position to subjugate distant Constantinople, but also that perhaps they will have to lose territories which they formerly considered inalienable. In the "Noble Allies'" camp a legitimate fear is mounting. They are beginning to repeat to the Milyukovs that a "strong power" is needed. But now the Milyukovs are powerless, without strength. The Revolution has crushed them, bled them. They are preparing to stop it and kill it. They are merely a living corpse in its hands.

But this living corpse can still recuperate if it isn't finished off. The Russian Revolution has innumerable and grandiose possibilities before it, but a great peril threatens it. The greatest peril is standing still, even for a moment. By stopping its motion for a moment, the Revolution will give the reactionary forces the opportunity to organize. And that is what the Revolution must avoid above everything else. Like a storm, it must sweep everything out, reducing those powers of darkness to nothing; otherwise it is they who will destroy it.

The existence side by side of two centralized governments, in spite of the evident predominance of the Revolutionary Government, is wholly abnormal as well as perilous for the Revolution. The immediate problem of the Revolution is to free itself of any and all centralized power, to attain full decentralization with the flag of the Social Revolution as the main unifier.

It must declare itself Maximalist and Social, prepare itself for the Communist revolution, immediately decree the end of the war and end of the capitalist order, and by direct revolutionary action affirm and reinforce its socialist dedication. The moral authority of such a revolution will be tremendous and the whole working class to a man will rise along with it.

It is only a revolution of this kind which can recklessly disregard the peril of a military disintegration. With lightning-like speed it will go to the farthest reaches of the globe and will be greeted everywhere joyfully by the people and will ensure the liberation of enslaved humanity.

The uprisen people is subjected at present to various and sundry pressures. Caught in a dilemma, the bourgeoisie is trying to persuade it of the need for policy reforms and obsequiously suggests that it is up to a Constituent Assembly to determine the new régime, to which it would allegedly submit in the future. It hopes thus to be able to make use of religious and dynastic prejudices to reinforce its own dominance. Further, it nourishes the secret hope of exploiting the patriotic sentiment and the State feeling of the populace to prolong this criminal war.

At the side of the bourgeoisie stands international Social-Democracy. One of its tendencies, called social-patriotism, is on all fours with the bourgeoisie. It is also imperialistic, warlike, and in fact conservative. It calls the workers to massacre each other, a war "to the end," telling them that the hour of revolution is not yet at hand, that "the country must be saved," and it calls on the people to unite under the flag of the Guchkovs and Milyukovs, as formerly they called on them to unite under the banners of Nicholas the Bloody.

Another section of Social-Democracy is divided from the imperialist bourgeoisie on the question of the war. In the domain of foreign policy it puts forward bourgeois pacifist slogans demanding the end of the war and the conclusion of a "peace without annexations." But its program is close to that of the imperialist bourgeoisie. Right now it demands a republic, but it would settle for a constitutional monarchy. Now, with freedom gained, it has even stopped talking of a social revolution and talks only of the need to set up, in the Constituent, the greatest reforms possible. Casting aside the erroneous premise that the revolution is "bourgeois," it uses the tactics of pressure on the bourgeoisie, the tactics of Plekhanov in 1906, to "push the bourgeoisie to the Left."

It is only the most insignificant part of Social-Democracy which remains faithful to Socialism and calls on the people to change the present revolution into a social revolution. But its ideas are not completely thought out, even somewhat equivocal, because in spite of its socialist concepts, it has in reserve the bourgeois alternative. It does not reject the minimum program and in case of the failure of the Social Revolution, it would easily settle for bourgeois democratic reforms which would guarantee it, in the future, the possibility of class collaboration with the bourgeoisie in the context of relatively liberal institutions.

What are our tasks in the present revolution? They stem from our anarchist concepts. We are the eternal and irreconcilable foes of Capital. We believe that there can be no true freedom without the abolition of the Capitalist order and the State. We must make the people understand that the increase in its political rights will not change its subjection in fact. We must show the people the uselessness and the absurdity of the "pushing the bourgeoisie to the Left" tactic. Our historic task is to push the proletariat to the Left so that it will push the bourgeoisie over the cliff.

The byword of "Constituent Assembly," defended by Social-Democracy, is a bourgeois slogan. Its objective is not the elimination of the exploitation of the people by the bourgeoisie, but a compromise with the bourgeoisie which would give this exploitation a new political form. Despite its revolutionary appearance, the Soviet of Workers' and Soldiers' Deputies will not liberate the workers if by its acts it does not put into effect a maximalist, anticapitalist program.

The liberation of the workers can only be accomplished by a social revolution and the realization of this is the most urgent task of the workers of Russia. The Russian Revolution must have a free hand and it must decentralize itself. Its salvation rests solely in the immediate setting up and public announcement of the Communist régime and increased direct action. All of Russia must be made into a network of sovereign revolutionary communes, which by occupying the land and factories will expropriate the bourgeoisie, abolishing private property.

It is only this social revolution which can lead the workers to victory over the bourgeoisie and complete emancipation. A reform of the bourgeois state, even going as far as the extreme limits of democracy will allow, will not free the workers, but will only lead to a new victory of the bourgeoisie over the masses.

Long Live the Social Revolution.
Long Live the Anarchist Communism.

351

20. THE ABOLITION OF DISCRIMINATIONS BASED ON NATIONALITY, RELIGION, AND SOCIAL ORIGIN

With the firm conviction that in a free country all citizens must be equal before the law and that popular conscience cannot tolerate restrictions caused by their faith or origin,
The Provisional Government has decreed:

All discrimination existing because of the present laws concerning the rights of citizens and due to their adherence to a religion or sect or their membership in a national group are abolished.

Consequently

All laws and regulations concerning the whole of Russia or any part of it which were based on religion, sect, or nationality are abolished pertaining to discrimination and intervention, as concerns,

1. Installation, residence, movement;

2. The acquisition of property and other rights concerning the ownership of movable and stationary property as well as the ownership, use, and the administration of these properties and the right to mortgage them;

3. The participation in all crafts, industrial or commercial, including mining, as well as making contracts with the government or public auction;

4. Participation in corporations and other commercial associations, as well as the right to take positions, elected or paid, in these companies or associations;

5. The hiring of servants, employees, foremen, workers, or apprentices;

6. Civil and military service, procedure and conditions for performing this service, participation in elections and municipal self-government and other public organizations; the right to perform all the duties tied to these functions;

7. Admission to all teaching institutions, private, public, and governmental— to complete one's studies, to receive promotions, as well as to teach or educate;

8. The right to perform the duties of tutor, trustee, and juror;

9. The use of languages or dialects other than Russian in business matters, private instruction, and private accounting.

10. The present law is effective on the date of its formulation.

Prince Lvov, Minister President,
March 20, 1917

21. THE SOVIET'S APPEAL TO THE PEOPLES OF THE ENTIRE WORLD

March 14, 1917

Proletarian Comrades, Workers of All Countries!

We, Russian soldiers and workers, united in the Soviet of Workers' and Soldiers' Deputies, send you hearty greetings and inform you of a great event. Russian Democracy has overthrown the Tsar's despotism and entered wholly into the family of nations as an equal member and a powerful force in the struggle for our complete liberation. Our victory is a great victory for Liberty and Democracy. The pillar of reaction in the world, "the policeman of Europe," is no more.

May it be buried forever. Long live Freedom. Long live the solidarity of the International Proletariat and Tong live the fight for final victory.

Our work is not yet done. Some shadows of the Old Régime are still with us and many are the enemies who are gathering their forces to smash the Russian Revolution. Nevertheless, our success is considerable. The people of Russia will express their will in a Constituent Assembly which will soon be convoked on the basis of direct, equal, secret, universal suffrage. It can be predicted with confidence that a democratic republic will be set up in Russia. The Russian people now have complete political liberty. It can affirm its complete power in internal as well as external affairs.

Thus, in appealing to all the people ruined and wrecked by this monstrous war, we say that the hour is at hand for a decisive struggle against the territorial ambitions of the governments of all countries. The time has come for the people to make the decisions about matters concerning questions of war and peace.

Conscious of its revolutionary power, Russian Democracy proclaims its opposition to the conquering policy of the ruling classes by all means and invites the people of Europe to take common decisive action in favor of peace.

We appeal also to the proletarian brothers of the Austro-German coalition and especially to the German proletariat. Since the first days of war, they have assured us that they took up arms in the defense of European civilization threatened by Asiatic despotism. Many of you saw some justification in the support which they gave to the war, but this justification is no longer valid.

Russian democracy cannot be a threat to freedom and civilization.

We will resolutely defend our liberty against all the attempts of reaction, both internal and external. The Russian Revolution will not retreat before the bayonets of the conquerors and will not let itself be crushed by foreign armies.

But we appeal to you. Throw off the yoke of your semi-autocratic government, as the Russian people have swept Tsarist autocracy from office. Refuse to be the tools of conquest and violence in the hands of monarchs, landholders, and bankers. Then uniting our efforts to yours, we will stop the horrible slaughter which is the shame of humanity and has darkened the great hours of the birth of Russian liberty.

Workers of all countries, extending our brotherly hands above the mountains of corpses of our dead, above the rivers of tears and innocently shed blood, above the still smoking ruins of our villages and towns, above the destroyed treasures, we appeal to you to restore international unity. That is the guarantee of our future victories and the complete liberation of humanity.

Proletarians of all countries, unite!

The Soviet of Workers' and Soldiers' Deputies of Petrograd

22. LETTER FROM A GROUP OF SOLDIERS OF THE 202ND MOUNTAIN REGIMENT

In these great days of the glory of Russian democracy, we salute you, revolutionary workers and soldiers, united in this struggle for liberation from Tsarist oppression. We write to you from a distant Front to bring you our thoughts, our aspirations, our interpretation of revolutionary events, and also to get your thoughts on how soldiers should act in these decisive days of the fight with Despotism, and especially what attitude we should take toward this weighty legacy inherited from the Romanovs, the war.

We have not yet been able to organize, and that is why this letter expresses the opinion of only a small group which does its work in the democratic spirit. Because the regiment is in the front line, it is impossible to organize units to represent the soldiers at the present time. As soon as we are relieved we will take the necessary steps to organize some soldiers' committees.

As for the character and the tasks of revolutionaries, we state that the overwhelming majority of the Army, insofar as our group is a miniature of the whole regiment, thinks of the present revolution as democratic, its aim being the emancipation of the people and the formation of a government which would stifle any monarchistic or bourgeois counter-revolutionary attempts. Such a régime could only be a democratic republic. To prevent any bourgeois machination we must organize the Working Class and the Revolutionary Army and demand that the Provisional Government not wait for the Constituent to proclaim a republic.

The work of the dark powers of the counter-revolution has already begun. Later, when we can speak in the name of the Regiment, we will tell you the names of those who are trying to spread trouble in the minds of the soldiers and to foment among them hostility to democracy and the Soviet in particular. In words, they identify themselves with the Provisional Government and send them greetings. It is easier to fight the flunkies of the old régime than these political jesuits who pretend to be the friends of the people.

In the Provisional Government's program there isn't a word about the peasantry. In order to prevent the use of the Army, made up largely of peasants, as a counter-revolutionary force, it is essential that slogans aimed at the peasants be introduced into it, and that the Provisional Government also include the agrarian question in its program.

In matters concerning the conduct of the war, we consider that as long as "dear Cousin" is leading the German nation, all agitation against national defense, at the front as well as the rear, is inopportune. In truth we are weary, the people are in misery, at the end of their rope, and no one doubts that a quick end of the war is essential. But for that, the Soviet and other workers' organizations in authority must take the first steps and establish contact with the workers' parties of the Allied and Enemy powers, to hasten the end of the war and the conclusion of peace.

There, where Sazonov, Bethmann-Hollweg, and Lloyd George have failed, Kerensky, Guesde, and Liebknecht must succeed. But until then the Russian Army must hold off the external foe.

In conclusion, we beg you to establish close ties with us by receiving our delegates and sending us your publications. Once more, we salute you and wish every success for the working class in its heroic fight for liberty.

March 10, 1917

23. A RESOLUTION ON THE AGRARIAN QUESTION

The Assembly of the Voronezh Government, formed by the representatives of the *Volost* Committees, having heard the reports and debates on the agrarian question declares:

1. All land must be transferred to the people;

2. Land property must be abolished;

3. The development of land belongs equally to all those who work it;

4. The land is taken from its owners without compensation;

5. The seizure of land should not be effected before the Constituent Assembly.

The Assembly deems indispensable and urgent the promulgation by the Provisional Government of the following laws:

1. Freeze all land transactions (purchase, sale, mortgage);

2. Give the "land committees" the right to work the lands not in use by the owners;

3. Take steps to furnish the land committees with the necessary agricultural tools to work the land;

4. The land committees must be given the right to regulate farming and the pay of the agricultural workers, to control the working of holdings in order to assure the maximum production of foodstuffs;

5. The Provisional Government must promulgate a law countermanding that on the common grounds, strengthening the farmers' position, and regulating the use of the tools of production;

6. The land committees must ensure the preservation of forests, fishing territories, and other productive lands against pillaging in order to insure their equal use by all people.

Resolution unanimously passed at Voronezh
April 9, 1917
(This resolution was printed and edited by the Voronezh Committee of the Socialist-Revolutionary Party.)

24. WOMEN'S ASPIRATIONS IN RUSSIAN ISLAMIC COUNTRIES

1. According to the Koran, men and women are equal.

2. In the Sacred Texts, women have as much right as men to participate in political or social affairs; their rights are thus in conformity with the Scriptures.

3. In the Koran there is no cloistering of women.

356

4. It being understood that the full flowering of countries is closely tied to equality for all, including women, in the nation ... , the Assembly has decided: Moslem women will have equal political rights with the men. They will benefit from the same electoral rights as the men and will be eligible for the Constituent Assembly.

5. For the women, electoral rights and eligibility are new. Up to now, the Moslems have not taken part in public affairs and that is why it would be impossible to exclude the possibility of reluctance on the part of the women themselves and their husbands, when it comes to implementing this right. In order not to lose the women's vote, which is half of the country's, the Assembly makes the following resolution: "Going to the ballot box is a moral duty for every woman. The votes of the men and the women must be separated and the votes tallied."

6. Given that among Moslems of Russia, the sale of girls and the marriage of sons without the consent of each party leads to marital discord and a painful situation for the children ... , the Assembly decides for the good of future generations: "At the time of marriage ceremonies, the bride and groom must be present."

7. When disagreement arises between man and wife and when the wife wants a divorce, the husband often ... keeps his wife by force. Such a constraint is an indignity and seriously endangers the education of the children. Keeping in mind the rights of women and the spirit of the needs which require the education of the children of future generations, the Assembly decides that "in case of marital discord, the woman's right of divorce must be mentioned in the marriage contract at the time of its formulation."

8. In Turkestan, the Caucasus, and Kazakhstan, girls are married at the age of eleven and twelve. Such early marriages ruin the female body and end in premature deaths of women as well as in the birth of frail children and in the debilitating of the nation. Thus the Assembly has decided that in Russia girls shall not be married before the age of sixteen.

9. It often happens that men, not content with one wife, take another, thinking that it is only a case of changing partners; then they divorce their first wife without reason or cause. Because this is a cause for unhappiness for women, the Assembly has decided—"At the time of the marriage settlement, the man must agree not to marry another woman ... , or to give the first some compensation."

10. ... Recommend that the betrothed undergo a premarital physical examination.

11. In Kazakhstan, the fathers sell their daughters while still young (*kalym*). Later, when she wants a divorce, she must pay back the *kalym*. This *kalym* is completely different from the dowry which is given to the wife, whereas the *kalym* is given to the father. In other words, the *kalym* is a present to the father, as price for his daughter. To guard the rights of the Kirghiz woman ... the Assembly has decided to abolish the *kalym*.

12. Different circumstances cause women to become prostitutes. Later, there are those who try in every way to regain their liberty, but the prostitution regulations are such that they are deprived of respect and their disgrace is public. The Assembly demands then ... the suppression of houses of toleration and those laws concerning prostitution.

357

25. INQUIRY OF THE PROVINCIAL AND REGIONAL SOVIET OF MOSCOW CONCERNING SOVIET ACTIVITY AND ORGANIZATION

	Vologda	Groznyi	Nizhni-Novgorod	Riazan	Odessa	Zharoslav	Ekater-inburg
Number of factories	5			14		135	
Number of Workers	15-18,000	20,000	50,000		90,000	30,000	
Who are electors	Factories	Factories	Var.	All		Workers etc.	
Did Women Vote?	Yes	500	Yes	100	15,000	Yes	
How many Companies represented	5	Those with more than 100 workers		14		70	
How many workers	15-18,000		25,000		90,000	20,000	
Electoral Quotient	1-200	1-100	1 plus 1 each 1000	1 each co.	1-100	1-250 1-500	1-100
Are Employees Rep.?	Yes 25	Yes 12	Yes	4	Yes	2	
Administration	No	No	Yes	2	No	No	
Women on Soviet	3	4	3	3	40	5	
Soldiers	65	80	10	3	Yes	5	
Officers	No	6	1	1			
Number of Members in Soviet	150	170	135	30	900	87	15

	Vologda	Groznyi	Nizhni-Novgorod	Riazan	Odessa	Zharoslav	Ekater-inenburg	
Political Parties Represented								
S.D.	Yes	Only	Yes	Yes	S.D. & Poale	Bolsh Mensh Bund	10	
S.R.	Yes	Yes			Yes	Zion & Uk		5
Others	K.D.		Bund					
Participation in Social Organizations								
Number of members of political committee of city, number of Soviet members	25/8	84/12	135/35	200/25	180/10	103/25		
Food Commission members, Number of Soviet	5/5	6				Varied	9/2	
Militia Commission, number of Soviet members	3/1			All			5/1	
Resolutions passed on the War	Yes	Yes	Yes	Yes	Yes	Banned	Yes	
8 hr day	Yes	Yes	Yes	Yes	Yes	Banned		
On relations with Govt.	Yes	Yes	Yes	Yes	No			
On economic questions	Yes	No			No	Yes		

	Vologda	Groznyi	Nizhni-Novgorod	Riazan	Odessa	Zharoslav	Ekater-inenburg
Other questions							
Improvement since Revolution	8 hr. raise	8 hr. 35 R @ mos.	8 hr. some raise	8 hr.	8 hr. raise	8 hr.	
How many factories have committees	All		All	20	Most of large 25	70	
Trade Unions	7	10	8			2	7
Which Parties are organized	S.D. S.R. K.D.	S.D. S.R. K.D. Dashnak	3 S.D. 2 S.R. Bund	S.R. K.D. Bund	Mensh P.Z.* Bund S.D. Uk.	Bolsh. Bund S.R. Mensh.	S.D. S.R.

*P.Z. = Poale-Zion.

26. FIFTH "LETTER FROM AFAR"*

1. To be able to go in the most judicious manner from the stage following the revolution or to the second revolution, which . . .

2. . . . must transfer the government power from the hands of the government of the property-owners and capitalists (the Guchkovs, Lvovs, Milyukovs, Kerenskys) to the hands of the government of the workers and poor peasants;

3. This latter government must be organized along the lines of the Soviet of Workers' and Peasants' Deputies;

4. It must abolish in all bourgeois states the old machinery of state—army, police, bureaucracy—this being replaced by:

5. An organization not of the mass, but of all the people armed.

*This letter was not published until after Lenin's death.

6. Only such a government—as much by its class content (revolutionary-democratic dictatorship of the proletariat and peasantry) and by its controlling organization (the proletarian militia)—will be in a condition to successfully solve the extraordinarily difficult and unquestionably most urgent tasks: to conclude peace, but not an imperialist peace such as one could make without a proletarian revolution in a whole series of countries;

7. In Russia the victory of the proletariat can only be achieved in the very near future only if, in the first stage, it acquires the support of most of the peasantry in its struggle for the confiscation of all land;

8. In conjunction with the peasant revolution and on the basis of its possibility, it will be necessary, with the support of the poor peasants, to pass to the stage of the control of production and distribution of the principal products, the inauguration of compulsory labor, which will be a stage on the road to Socialism;

9. The question of the inauguration in the countryside of soviets of Workers' Deputies—that is to say, of soviets of agricultural workers, as distinguished from soviets of peasants' deputies—is, under these conditions, of the utmost urgency. . . .

End of March 1917

27. THE APRIL THESES

1. Our attitude about the war—which on the Russian side, under the new government of Lvov and Co., by reason of the capitalist nature of the government, has unquestionably remained a war of imperialistic banditry—permits no concessions, even minimal ones, for "revolutionary defensism."

In a revolutionary war, which would truly justify revolutionary defensism, the conscientious proletariat can only assent on condition: *a.* that power will pass into the hands of proletariat and the poor elements of the peasantry, close to the proletariat; *b.* of the actual renunciation, not merely by word, of all annexations; *c.* of the complete, actual breaking off of connections with capitalist interests.

Given the undeniable good faith of large layers of partisans of revolutionary defensism, who tolerate the war only because of necessity and not for conquests, and given that these masses have been deceived by the bourgeoisie, it is important to explain their error to them with great care, patience, and perseverance, and to explain to them the unbreakable ties between Capital and the imperialist war, to prove to them that without the overthrow of Capital it is impossible to end the war with a truly democratic peace which is not imposed by force.

The organization of the widest possible propaganda of these views in the regular Army.

Fraternization.

2. What is peculiar to Russian activity is the transition from the first stage of the revolution, which has given power to the bourgeoisie by reason of the insufficient realization of the proletariat's organization and consciousness, to the second stage, which must put power into the hands of the proletariat and the poor strata of the peasantry.

This transition is characterized on the one hand by maximum legality (Russia is at this moment the freest belligerent country in the world), and on the other by the absence of violence directed against the masses, and finally by the unthinking confidence of the masses with regard to the government of the capitalists, the worst enemies of peace and socialism.

This peculiar situation demands that we know how to adapt ourselves to the special conditions for the work of the Party among the immense proletarian masses, who are barely politically conscious.

3. No support whatever for the Provisional Government, proof of the lying character of all its promises, especially those concerning renunciation of annexations. To unmask the government instead of "demanding"—which is unthinkable, because it creates illusions—that this government, government of capitalists, cease being imperialistic.

4. To recognize that our party is in the minority, and at this moment a feeble minority, in most of the Soviets of Workers' Deputies, faced by the bloc of all the petit-bourgeois opportunists who are amenable to the influence of the bourgeoisie and who extend this influence over the proletariat, from Socialist Populists, going through the Socialist-Revolutionaries up to the organization commission (Chkheidze, Tseretelli, etc., Steklov, etc.). To explain to the masses that the Soviets of Workers' Deputies are the only possible form of revolutionary government, and that consequently our task, as long as this government remains under the influence of the bourgeoisie, can only be to explain patiently, systematically, doggedly, to the masses the tactical errors of the Soviets, explanations being adapted to their practical needs.

As long as we are in the minority, we do the job of criticizing, of pointing out errors, while postulating at the same time the need for the transfer of power to the Soviets of Workers' Deputies, so that the masses will be emancipated by the experience of their mistakes.

5. We do not need a parliamentary republic—going back to that after the Soviets of Workers' Deputies would be a step backward—but a republic of Soviets of Workers', Farm Laborers', and Peasants' Deputies, for the whole country, from top to bottom.

Abolition of Police, Army, and Civil Service (that is to say, the substitution of the people armed for the Regular Army).

Hiring and dismissal at any time of all Civil Servants; their compensation should not be more than that of the average good workman.

6. In the agrarian program, the center of gravity to be carried over to the Soviets of Agricultural Workers' Deputies.

Confiscation of all property of landed property holders.

Nationalization of all lands in the country. The lands will be put at the disposal of local Soviets of Agricultural Workers' and Peasants' Deputies. Organization of Soviets of Poor Peasants' Deputies. Creation in all large estates (250 to 750 acres, taking into account local and other conditions and the advice of local organizations) of model methods of farming under the control of the Soviets of Farm Workers' Deputies and working for the community.

7. Immediate amalgamation of all of the country's banks into one national bank under the control of the Soviets of Workers' Deputies.

8. Not the setting up of socialism as the immediate task, but simply the immediate transition to control of production and the distribution of products by the Soviets of Workers' Deputies.

9. Party Tasks:

a. Immediate convocation of Party Congress;

b. Modify Party program, mainly:

1. On Imperialism and the Imperialist War;

2. On the attitude toward the State and our demand for a "Commune State" (that is to say, a State of which the Paris Commune was the forerunner);

3. Correction of the old minimum program, which is obsolete.

c. Change the Party name (instead of "Social Democratic," in which the official leaders—"Defensists" and "undecided Kautskists"—have betrayed Socialism the world over and gone over to the bourgeoisie, it should be called the Communist Party.

10. Reactivate the International.

28. FRATERNIZATION: THE FRUNZE TOUR

To General V. I. Gurko:

An agitator from the Petrograd Soviet, Dmitri Petrovich Mihailov, armed with authorization dated April 25, No. 126, has visited our division. Among other things, he urges fraternization with the Germans and only today has organized fraternizations in the 220th Regiment. They have spread to the 218th. The officers' arguments have been unavailing. Does Mihailov really have such authority to act thus? Forwarded to Headquarters.

General Cheglov

In view of the formal disapproval by the Petrograd Soviet of all fraternization at the Front, affirmed by the appeal of April 30, Mihailov must realize that he is contravening said declaration.

... It would be advisable to persuade the "Front Committee" to arrest Mihailov pending clarification by the Soviet.

General Gurko

Following your telegram of May 2. Due to impossibility of acting by force, have been unable to arrest Mihailov. In the 55th Division he is agitating against the officers, wants them replaced by elected officers.

It has already been done in some regiments.

Something must absolutely be done to cause the Petrograd Soviet to recall Mihailov by telegram to end this disintegration which is beginning in this army Corps.

Chief of Staff for Alexeiev

May 1st, German and Russian soldiers mingled in great numbers in the midst of open trenches. At this meeting, the Germans came with their officers and participated immediately in the elaboration of motions on the war and peace and international relations. This meeting made a great impression on everyone. The Russian officers and soldiers almost unanimously acknowledged the usefulness of meetings of this type, but the high command and general staff forbid them, threatening to have the participants shot. The repercussions could be grave, because this sows discord between the officers and men and the spreading of Soviet slogans meets with a stubborn resistance on the part of the High Command.

Mihailov

29. THE MILYUKOV NOTE

On March 27th the Provisional Government published an appeal to the citizens with an exposé of the Free Russian Government's views on the question of the present war. The Minister of Foreign Affairs has asked me to forward this document to you with the following observations:

Our enemies have tried recently to sow discord between ourselves and our Allies by spreading the absurd rumor that Russia was ready to conclude a separate peace with the Central Powers. The text of the accompanying document contradicts better than anything else such a fabrication. You will note that the general considerations expressed by the Provisional Government tally fully with the high ideals proclaimed by the most eminent statesmen of the Allied countries and which are so strikingly expressed by the president of our new ally, the great republic from overseas. The government of the Old Order evidently was not even able to understand and share these views on the nature of this war—a war of liberation—on the setting of enduring bases for peaceful coexistence, on the right of peoples' self-determination, etc. But Free Russia can now speak the same language as the advanced democracies and she hastens to add her voice to those of her Allies. Moved by this new spirit of free democracy, the proposals of the Provisional Government evidently cannot lead anyone to think that the revolution would lead to a weakening of Russia's role in the fight made in common with her Allies.

On the contrary, the hope of the whole population to fight the war to a decisive end has only been reinforced by the awareness of everyone's responsibility. This aspiration has become more effective since it ends in a mission which everyone feels acutely—to rid the mother country of the enemy which has invaded her territories.

It goes without saying, as it is written in the accompanying document, that the Provisional Government, while defending our country's rights, will fully observe the obligations undertaken toward her Allies.

With continued confidence in a victorious end to the war, in full accord with our allies, we are also persuaded that all the questions raised by the war will be resolved by the conclusion of a durable peace and that, moved by such aspirations, the progressive democracies will find the means to obtain these guaranties and sanctions which are essential to the prevention of new blood-spilling conflicts.

30. APPEAL FROM THE EXECUTIVE COMMITTEE OF THE SOVIET OF WORKERS' AND SOLDIERS' DEPUTIES TO ALL CITIZENS

Citizens,

At a time when the fate of the country is being decided, every thoughtless step is dangerous. The demonstrations against the Government's note on foreign policy have led to fights in the streets. People were injured and killed.

In the name of the revolution, to keep it from disorders which threaten it, we appeal to you and ask you sincerely:

Be calm, orderly and disciplined.

The Soviet of Workers' and Soldiers' Deputies is in session. Trust them; they will find the means to satisfy your demands.

But during this time, let no one disturb the peaceful course of Free Russia.

Comrade Soldiers,

Do not go into the streets armed, except at the call of the Russian Committee. Only the Political Committee has the right to decide. Every movement order (except for routine movements) must come from the Political Committee, set with its seal, and countersigned by at least two of the following names: Chkheidze, Skobelev, Binasik, Fillipovsky, Skalov, Goldman, Bogdanov.

Confirm every order by telephoning 104-06.

Comrade Workers and Militiamen,

Your weapons must only be used to defend the revolution. They are not needed in either meetings or demonstrations, in such places they are even dangerous to the cause of liberty. Do not bring your weapons when you go to a meeting or a demonstration.

The Executive Committee calls on all organizations to help it maintain order and calm.

The use of force against citizens in Free Russia is no longer policy. Disorders only benefit the revolution's enemies. Whoever stirs disorder is an enemy of the people.

April 21, 1917
The Executive Committee of the Soviet
of Workers' and Soldiers' Deputies.

31. DECREE OF THE PETROGRAD SOVIET OF WORKERS' AND SOLDIERS' DEPUTIES

On April 21st, at the time of a street demonstration, some instigators fired on unarmed citizens, causing some deaths and injuries.

Given the violent agitation which reigns and is apt to give rise to conflicts between different groups of demonstrators, the Soviet of Workers' and Soldiers' Deputies meeting in General Assembly April 21st, has decided unanimously, in order to prevent troubles which threaten the revolution, that:

1. Meetings and street demonstrations should be forbidden for the next two days.

2. Anyone who calls for a demonstration during those two days, makes use of weapons, even for the firing into the air, shall be considered a criminal and a traitor to the revolution.

3. The facts of the shooting on April 21st shall be submitted to a careful investigation by the Political Committee of the Soviet of Deputies and Soldiers.

The Petrograd Soviet of Workers' and Soldiers' Deputies.
April 22nd, 1917

32. THE GOVERNMENT DECLARATION OF MAY 5TH, 1917

COALITION GOVERNMENT PLATFORM

The Provisional Government, reinforced and reorganized with representatives of revolutionary democracy, declares that it will put all its efforts into translating its ideals of liberty, equality, and fraternity into fact, ideals originating at the birth of the great Russian Revolution.

The Provisional Government is especially unanimous in defending the fundamental lines of its future acts in the following areas:

1. In its foreign policy, the Provisional Government, rejecting, along with the rest of the country, any idea of a separate peace, adopts openly the objective of the reestablishment of general peace, whose objective will not be the domination of other nations, nor the conquest of their territories, but a peace without annexations or indemnities, founded on the right of self-determination. With the firm conviction that the fall of the Tsarist régime and the consolidation of democratic principles in our internal and external policies will create among the democratic allies new aspirations in favor of a stable peace and the brotherhood of nations, the Provisional Government will take the necessary steps to reach an agreement with the allies based on the declaration of March 27th.

2. Convinced that the defeat of Russia and her allies would not only be a calamity for the Russian people but would also have the effect of making world peace founded on the above principles impossible, the Provisional Government firmly believes that the

revolutionary Army will not allow the German troops to defeat our Western Allies and then throw all their might against us. The reinforcement of democratic principles in the Army and the development of its military might, both offensive and defensive, will be the most important task of the Provisional Government.

3. The Provisional Government will resolutely and firmly combat the economic breakdown of the country by the inauguration of a more systematic government control of production, transportation, exchange, distribution of consumer goods, and, in case of need, will resort to the organization of production.

4. Energetic steps for the protection of labor will be taken in every possible way.

5. The question of land transfer to the workers will be left up to the Constituent Assembly and, proceeding to this end, preliminary steps will be taken to assure the greatest possible production of cereals and the maximum development of the land in the national interest and that of the working population.

6. Seeking to inaugurate a series of reforms in the financial system, and to found them on democratic principles, the Provisional Government will pay particular attention to an increase in the direct taxation of the rich (inheritance, excess war profits, property taxes, etc.).

7. Efforts will be made to introduce and develop democratic institutions and self-government as rapidly as possible.

8. The Provisional Government will do everything possible also to ensure as soon as possible the convening of a Constituent Assembly in Petrograd.

Determined to put all its efforts toward the realization of this program, the Provisional Government emphatically declares that a successful job can be done only if it has the full and absolute confidence of the whole revolutionary people and the opportunity to exert the full powers of its office to strengthen the revolution's victory and to ensure its ultimate development.

Addressing a firm and urgent appeal to all citizens for the safekeeping of the undivided power in the hands of the Provisional Government, it declares that it will take firm measures for the country's salvation against any counter-revolutionary attempts, and against illegal, anarchistic or violent acts whose objective is to disorganize the country and prepare the way for a counter-revolution.

The Provisional Government is convinced that in acting thus, it has the firm support of all those who hold Russian freedom dear.

May 5, 1917.
Prince Lvov.

33. PAN-RUSSIAN ASSEMBLY OF PEASANTS' DEPUTIES ON THE AGRARIAN QUESTION

The Pan-Russian Assembly of Peasants' Deputies proclaims to the entire Russian peasantry that henceforth not only the solution of the agrarian question by the Constituent, but also the preparatory work, the work of the local or central land committees, will pass into the hands of the workers themselves. For this reason, the first task—the most important and also that which will entail the most profound effects on the most progressive part of the peasantry—is the organization of elections in the *zemstvos* of villages and districts and the establishment of land committees in relation to these *zemstvos*. The task given to these committees in the preparation for land reform is founded on the following principles: the transfer to the nation for free and equitable use, without compensation, of all lands belonging now to the State, monasteries, churches, and private persons.

Believing firmly in the strength of the peasantry, its sense of organization, and its intelligence, the Pan-Russian Congress of Peasants' Deputies is absolutely convinced that the private ownership of land, with its forests, power, and mineral resources, will be abolished by the National Constituent Assembly which will establish a fundamental law on the land, the conditions for its transfer to the workers, its use and distribution.

The Congress of Pan-Russian Peasants' Deputies is also convinced that in all the land committees, from the villages to the central committee, the workers will be able, thanks to the elective system, to arrange the land reform, oriented toward the emancipation from the liens of private property, without redemption.

The Pan-Russian Congress of Peasants' Deputies deems it necessary for the Provisional Government to make a definite, unequivocal statement which will reassure everyone that on this question it will permit no one to oppose the popular will. The Pan-Russian Congress of Peasants' Deputies expects that the Provisional Government will help, to the limit of its power, the free expression of the working people's opinion on this important question, and that it will stop anyone who places personal interest above national interest from interfering with this debate.

The Pan-Russian Congress of Peasants' Deputies has decided, in the matter of the utilization of lands and their products, that until the Constituent Assembly solves the agrarian question:

1. It is essential to put an end to the food crisis and to struggle against the economic chaos which has swept over the country during these trying and exhausting years of the global conflict.

369

This requires that private enterprise and the vested interests let the general welfare—that of the people as well as that of the State—set the pace.

2. That all lands—and where conditions warrant, the means of irrigation, waters, etc.—come under the direction of the Land Committees who will have the right to issue regulations regarding the cultivation, sowing, harvesting, haymaking, etc.

3. Due to the labor shortage caused by the drafting of a large part of the agricultural force, which is especially critical during the peak periods, the crews of workingmen under contract but available and the prisoners of war must be made available to the land committees and not be restricted to a few landholders, but distributed in the best interests of the working people.

4. In view of the cattle shortage and the wear and tear on agricultural implements, it is essential that energetic steps be taken to requisition and make full use of all the implements which are available in Russia. In the same manner, given the mobilization of a large number of draft horses and the shortage of them—critical in the working of the land—as well as the shortage of draft animals, it is essential that they be fully utilized.

5. The harvest of hay and grain, their conservation, the fishing, woodcutting, lumber operations, and other forest operations must be put under the control of the land committees and other social organizations to keep private interests from stockpiling or hoarding.

6. The establishment of lease, their payment, the setting of agricultural workers' wages, and all these questions are entirely in the hands of the local committees. In litigation cases, the rents accrued, with deductions made for the payment of taxes, must be paid into the local treasury until the meeting of the Constituent.

7. Until the promulgation of nationwide laws, the local committees will be free to initiate steps on the above-mentioned questions, it being understood that any interference from the government or district commissars will be excluded, as belonging to the landed property-holder class.

8. In order to maintain in its entirety the amount of land available for the coming land reform, it is necessary that the land committees exert control to rule out without exception and with the utmost formality any and all sale or purchase of land, mortgage, inheritance until the meeting of the Constituent Assembly.

All transactions concluded after the 1st of March until the promulgation of this embargo will be considered null and void.

The Pan-Russian Congress of Peasants' Deputies deems that only these principles and fundamentals make possible the establishment of a new agrarian order, established by Free Russia, which will unite into a single family, under the aegis of the Workers' Government, without distinction as to nationality, religion, or class, Greater Russians and Ukrainians, peasants and Moslems, peasants and Cossacks, inhabitants of Russia and outsiders, communities and individuals, on whom depend and who will profit from the great reforms.

The Pan-Russian Congress of Peasants' Deputies calls on the peasants and agricultural workers of all Russia to vote in the election of the Constituent Assembly for the candidates who come out in favor of the nationalization of land without compensation and in keeping with the principles of equality.

It asks the whole peasant population to remain calm, but to work steadfastly and with determination for the legal realization of its most cherished wishes, which from the beginning of time has been expressed in the formula, dear to all peasants—Land and Liberty.

34. PRISONERS OF WAR AND REFUGEES EMPLOYED IN PEASANT HOLDINGS

Type of Property	Farm hands	Refugees	PWs	Ratio of PWs & refugees to farm hands
Peasant Holdings	8,221	69	19	1.1%
Large Estates	168	12	22	20.8%
Total	8,389	81	41	1.5%

PERCENTAGE OF SOWN LAND AMONG PEASANT HOLDINGS IN VLADIMIR DISTRICT

Sown Areas	Percent of holdings
Fallow	12.9
2.7 acres or less sown	14.7
from 2.7 to 5.4 acres	22.2
from 5.4 to 10.8 acres	30.3
from 10.8 to 16.2 acres	12.5
from 16.2 to 43.2 and over	7.4
	100%

35. REPRESENTATION BREAKDOWN OF THE DELEGATES
TO THE FIRST CONFERENCE
OF THE PETROGRAD FACTORY COMMITTEES

Industries	Number of Delegates	Number of Factory Committee Representatives	Number of Workers Represented at Conference	Companies Represented	Number of Companies Not Represented
Metallurgical plants	261	172	238,711	134	38
Textile plants	32	26	17,916	15	11
Clothing Manu- facturers	2	2			2
Paper Mills	3	3	988	2	1
Print Shops	32	30	4,981	17	13
Foundries	1	1			1
Shoe Factories	8	7	7,105	6	1
Leather	5	4	2,096	3	1
Railway Materials	8	2	4,532	2	
Electrical Equipment	10	9	4,202	2	7
Streetcar Barns	6	4	5,368	3	1
Sawmills	9	8	1,300	3	5
Carpenter Shops	8	7	1,006	6	1
Tobacco	10	6	2,631	2	4
Tubes and Sockets	3	3	670	2	4
Airplanes	10	8	2,152	4	4
Chemical Industries	4	4	330	2	12
Miscellaneous Small Industries	25	21	20,074	9	2
Ditto	52	41	22,602	20	21
Sheet Metal	4	3	99	1	2
Gas and Petroleum	6	6	654	3	3
TOTAL	499	367	337,467	236	131
Social Organi- zations (10)	18				
Trade Unions (10)	16				
Various Organi- zations (8)	22				
Armed Forces (6)	8				
Press Repre- sentatives	5				
GRAND TOTAL	568	367	337,467	236	131

FIRST OMNIBUS DECLARATION OF THE RADA

Kiev, June, 10, 1917

Ukrainian People, Peasants, Workers, Laborers:

Through your will, we have become the Central Ukrainian Rada, the repository of the rights and liberties of Ukrainia.

Your best sons, elected from the villages, factories, and regiments of all the Ukrainian communities, we have been elected, we, the Central Ukrainian Rada. They have put their trust in us to uphold these rights and these freedoms.

Your elected express their will thus:

The Ukraine to be free, with some attachments to all Russia, without a complete rupture with the Russian State, so that the Ukrainian people will be able to manage their own future in their own territory. A Ukrainian National Assembly to be elected by universal equal, secret, and direct suffrage, and to establish order and install a régime in Ukrainia. Only our Ukrainian Assembly will have the right to issue laws which will be the foundation of this régime.

The laws which will install the régime for the whole Russian State must emanate from a Pan-Russian parliament.

No one knows better than we what our needs be and which laws will suit us best. No one knows better than our peasants how to manage our lands. . . .

Thus spoke those who elected us to represent the whole Ukraine.

Having spoken thus, they elected the Ukrainain Central Rada and told us to lead the people, to guarantee their rights and create a new order in a free and autonomous Ukraine.

We, the Ukrainian Central Rada, fulfilling the wish of our people, take up the heavy burden of constructing a new life and set to work.

We had hoped that the Russian Central Provisional Government would help us, so that together we could organize our country.

But the Russian Provisional Government has rejected all our demands. . . .

We sent our delegates to Petrograd to present our demands to the Russian Provisional Government. The main ones were as follows:

The Russian Provisional Government to declare publicly, by a special act, that it is not opposed to Ukrainian National freedom, to its people's right to autonomy.

The Central Russian Government to have in its cabinet a commissar for Ukrainian Affairs for all questions relative to the Ukraine.

The local authority in the Ukraine to be a representative of the Russian Central Government, the Commissar in the Ukraine to be elected by us.

A part of the money collected by the Treasury in the Ukraine to be returned to the Ukrainians so that they may finance their national and cultural needs.

All of these demands have been rejected by the Central Russian Government. . . .

Now, Ukrainian People, thus we are forced to build our own future. . . .

Henceforth, every village, group of villages, and community which upholds the interest of the Ukrainian People must maintain very close relations with the Central Rada.

Wherever, for any reason, administrative authority remains in the hands of people hostile to Ukrainianization, we prescribe that the Ukrainian citizens should, after informing themselves, elect another administration. Where Ukrainians live side by side with citizens of other nationalities, we propose that the Ukrainians establish relations and conclude agreements with the democratic organizations of those groups which are non-Ukrainian, and that together they set up foundations for a new life. . . .

. . . Later, these laws will be brought before the Pan Russian Assembly for approval.

We need strength in order to be able to act. . . . And for the success of our undertaking, we need, before everything else, money. Until now the Ukrainians offered everything available to the Russian treasury, and the Ukrainian people . . . got nothing in return.

Consequently, the Ukrainian Central Rada orders that all the citizens of the countryside and cities, that all private and public institutions henceforth pay, from the 1st of July, a special tax . . . into the treasury of the Ukrainian Rada.

Ukrainians, your future is in your hands. In this hour of trial, disorder, and dislocation, prove by your unanimity and your national feeling that a nation of wheat producers can proudly and with dignity hold its own with any powerful and organized country.

37. A TRACT FROM THE "PLEKHANOV" GROUP (JUNE 1917)

RUSSIAN WORKERS' SOCIAL-DEMOCRATIC PARTY

Men and Women Workers, Soldiers, Sailors, Citizens, Revolutionaries of Petrograd . . .

The Assembly of the Soviets of Workers' and Soldiers' Deputies calls on you for a demonstration Sunday, June 18th, in honor of those who died fighting for the people's cause.

You will all answer this call. All of you will go into the streets, whatever your opinions, your feelings. The great Revolution has liberated Russia from Tsarism's yoke, which had turned her over to her enemies.

In the place of the old despotic régime, the Revolution has placed a new revolutionary power. It is the unified power of the Provisional Government. It is the power which rests on the democratic organization of Soviet of Workers, Soldiers, and Peasants.

But the success of the Revolution is not yet complete. Internal friction and perils threaten it. These dangers must be overcome. All the friends of liberty must rally round the Provisional Government. Support it. Help it to set up the National Constituent Assembly.

Today, the word for everyone must be:

Long live a stable revolutionary power.

Long live the United Government and the Constituent Assembly.

The gravest peril to the Revolution comes from the external enemy. A victory by the German Army would mean for us the reestablishment of Tsarism, economic enslavement, and social stagnation. The duty of every revolutionary, every citizen, the duty of all workers and soldiers is to do everything possible to prevent the war ending this way. Reaction has betrayed the country and led to negotiations with the enemy for a truce and separate peace.

The Revolution has assumed the unwavering defense of the country. The observance of the obligations to the democracies and the allied workers has been sealed in blood. Democracy cannot renege. It can only fight for a peace which will ruin German Imperialism and strike a mortal blow at the imperialism of all countries. This peace will guarantee the right to self-determination and the free growth of all people.

But there is but one way to arrive at this honorable peace. To the armed force of the oppressor, there is only one answer—force. Only an offensive on all allied fronts will force the Germans to abandon their plans of conquest.

Only this offensive will lead us to a peace which we want soon. Meanwhile, neither peace nor armistice.

Meanwhile, war to the end, in the name of the freedom of all people.

Long live a peace which will ensure a happy ending to this war.

Long live the Union of all revolutionary forces.

Long live World Democracy.

Long live the Russian Workers Social-Democratic Party.

Go, demonstrate June 18th.

The Petrograd Committee of the Pan-Russian
"Edintsvo" Organization.

SOURCES FOR DOCUMENTS
(Numbers in square brackets refer to items in the Bibliography)

MARX, ENGELS, AND THE REVOLUTION IN RUSSIA (p. 325) —texts taken from K. Papaioannou [299] pp. 236 and 237.

BAKUNIN AND "COMMUNISM" (1867) (p. 325)—a text from A. Sergent and C. Harmel, *Histoire de l'anarchie*, (Paris, 1949) p. 364.

PROGRAM OF THE SOCIAL-DEMOCRATIC PARTY (1906) (p. 326)—translation from *Contrat Social*, (1961) pp. 286ff.

POLITICAL PROGRAM OF THE SOCIALIST-REVOLUTION-ARY PARTY (1906) (p. 327)—*Programma Partii Sots-Rev.* (Petrograd, 1917, 13 pp.) pp. 9–10.

KARL LIEBKNECHT'S REPORT ON THE HORRORS OF RUSSIAN PRISONS (p. 327)—taken from G. Haupt, *Le Congrès manqué* (Paris, 1965), pp. 239–49).

WARTIME: DEFENSE INDUSTRY COMPANIES (p. 330)— taken from *Ek. Pol.* [24] II, pp. 17–18. At Petrograd, the Putilov factory went from 13,510 to 26,564 workers, the Lessner enterprise from 1,289 to 7,927 workers (quoted in M. K. Potekhin, in *Istoriya SSSR*, V, (1965) p. 235).

RUSSIAN WORKERS AND THE WAR (p. 330)—Troelstra Archive, Amsterdam [13] (unpublished document).

THE SOCIAL-DEMOCRATIC MINORITY AND THE WAR (p. 332)—*Archives Nationales* [14] F7, 13074 (unpublished document).

THE ZIMMERWALD MANIFESTO (OCTOBER 7, 1915) (p. 332) —taken from Rosmer, *Le Mouvement ouvrier et la guerre*, I, pp. 379–82.

RESOLUTIONS PASSED AT THE KIENTHAL CONFERENCE (24–30 APRIL 1916) (p. 336)—translation following Rosmer, *op. cit.*, II, p. 233.

THE MAKLAKOV PARABLE (p. 339)—*Russkie Vedomosty*, October 1915. Translation F. X. Coquin [278] p. 21.

THE PROGRAM OF THE "PROGRESSIVIST BLOC" (p. 340)— *ARR* [27] XVIII, p. 109f.

STRUVE MEMORANDUM ON THE RUSSIAN SITUATION: FEBRUARY 7, 1917 (p. 341)—taken from Samuel Hoare, *The Fourth Seal* (London, 1930) pp. 188–92.

A LETTER FROM ALEXANDRA TO NICHOLAS II (p. 343)— Alexandra, *Lettres à l'empereur Nicolas II* (Paris, 1924).

IZVESTYA'S APPEAL TO THE POPULATION OF PETRO- GRAD AND RUSSIA (p. 343)—*Izvestya*, 28 February 1917.

THE BOLSHEVIK MANIFESTO OF FEBRUARY 27, 1917 (p. 344)—*HRR* [126] p. 92.

THE ABDICATION OF NICHOLAS II (p. 345)—*Doc. Ker.* [35] p. 104.

THE FIRST STATEMENT OF THE PROVISIONAL GOVERN- MENT (p. 346)—*Izvestya*, 7 March 1917.

AN ANARCHIST TRACT (MARCH 23, 1917) (p. 348)—unpub- lished pamphlet in the Bibliothèque de documentation internationale contemporaine (BDIC).

THE ABOLITION OF DISCRIMINATIONS BASED ON NATION- ALITY, RELIGION, AND SOCIAL ORIGIN (p. 352)—*Doc. Ker* [35] I, p. 211.

THE SOVIET'S APPEAL TO THE PEOPLES OF THE ENTIRE WORLD (p. 353)—*K narodam vsego mira* [136].

LETTER FROM A GROUP OF SOLDIERS OF THE 202nd MOUNTAIN REGIMENT (p. 354) GAORSSLo [12] 7384, 9, 244, 63a and b (unpublished document).

A RESOLUTION ON THE AGRARIAN QUESTION (p. 356)— *ibid.*, 7384, 7, 24, 2–3 (unpublished document).

WOMEN'S ASPIRATIONS IN RUSSIAN ISLAMIC COUNTRIES (p. 356)—Dimanshteyn [364] pp. 296–8.

INQUIRY OF THE PROVINCIAL AND REGIONAL SOVIET OF MOSCOW CONCERNING SOVIET ACTIVITY AND ORGAN- IZATION (p. 358)—this table is based on the enquiry published in *Dok.* [20] pp. 320–33; In their answers, the Soviets sometimes confused the number of delegates with that of the official staff, the number of enterprises with the number of factories.

FIFTH "LETTER FROM AFAR" (p. 360)—Lenin [129] XXIII, 331 (extract).

THE APRIL THESIS (p. 361)—*ibid.*, XXIV, 3.

FRATERNIZATION: THE FRUNZE TOUR (p. 364)—extracts from *Dok. Apr.* [21] pp. 481–565, and from *Dok. Mai.* [22] pp. 329–89.

THE MILYUKOV NOTE (p. 365)—*Dok. Apr.* [21] pp. 725–6.

APPEAL FROM THE EXECUTIVE COMMITTEE OF THE SOVIET OF WORKERS' AND SOLDIERS' DEPUTIES TO ALL CITIZENS (p. 366)—unpublished pamphlet in the BDIC.

DECREE OF THE PETROGRAD SOVIET OF WORKERS' AND SOLDIERS' DEPUTIES (p. 366)—placard from the BDIC.

GOVERNMENT DECLARATION OF MAY 5th, 1917 (p. 367)— *Vestnik vremennogo pravitel'stva*, 6 May 1917.

PAN-RUSSIAN ASSEMBLY OF PEASANTS' DEPUTIES ON THE AGRARIAN QUESTION (p. 369)—*Delo Naroda*, 26 May 1917.

PRISONERS OF WAR AND REFUGEES EMPLOYED IN PEASANT HOLDINGS (p. 371)—taken from *Severnie Zapiski* (1917), no. 1, p. 184 in Trapeznikov [348] p. 294, and Usatova [350] p. 7.

REPRESENTATION BREAKDOWN OF THE DELEGATES TO THE FIRST CONFERENCE OF THE PETROGRAD FAC-TORY COMMITTEES (p. 372)—*Dok. Mai.* [22] p. 293.

FIRST OMNIBUS DECLARATION OF THE RADA (p. 373)— Dimanshteyn [364] p. 161.

A TRACT FROM THE "PLEKHANOV" GROUP (JUNE 1917) (p. 375)—unpublished pamphlet in the BDIC.

NOTES
(Numbers in square brackets refer to items in the Bibliography)

CHAPTER ONE

FROM WAR TO REVOLUTION

Page 5
Russia's revolutionaries—"Theses on the War", of 5 or 6 September 1914, in Gankin & Fisher [37] pp. 140–1; similarly V. I. Lenin, *Socialism and War*.

Nashe Slovo—Archives Nationales [14] Série F.7, *fonds* 13074; cf. A. Rosmer, *Le Mouvement ouvrier pendant la première guerre mondiale* (2 vols., Paris, 1936 and 1959) I, p. 245.

absolutely opposed—Badaev [167].

Only a few factories—Tseretelli [127] p. 10.

Westerners and Slavophiles—this summary of the revolutionary movement up to 1914 is based on works [280–322] of the Bibliography.

Page 9
reform of the country—this is based on observations by Cyril E. Black in [292].

developed public education—education proceeded more democratically than the régime led people to believe; cf. Johnson [360a].

Page 10
able to count them—see Bibliography, particularly works [364ff].

Page 11
his own ideology—there is a good description of exiled Russia in Krupskaya [217] and in Wolfe [282]; see also N. Valentinov, *Mes Rencontres avec Lénine* (French trans., Paris, 1963).

Page 14
small part of the population—Florinsky [289] p. 165; there is a good discussion in Haimson [293].

Page 15
MORE ILLUSIONS—see the general works on economy and society, nos. [286ff].

period of time—A. Gershenkron, "The Rate of Industrial Growth of

Russia since 1885", *Journal of Economic History*, VII, Supplement (1947) pp. 144–74.

American analogues—Florinsky [289].

Page 16

chief economic role—M.-L. Lavigne, "Le Plan de M. Rjabusinskij: un projet de concentration industrielle en 1916", *Cahiers du monde russe et soviétique*, 1964, i, pp. 90–105.

in 1913—*Russian Co-Operator*, May 1917.

a clear advantage—cf. the essay by P. Sorlin, "Lénine et le problème paysan en 1917", *Annales ESC*, 1964, 2, pp. 250–81. [349].

273 per thousand—for consumption, life expectancy etc., see Kerblay [341] p. 329f; also the review *Russia*, no. 6, September 1917, which gives figures for consumption in Russian pounds (*funt*). (1 *funt* = 400 gr.)

other raw materials—Bairoch, "Niveaux de croissance au XIXe siècle", *Annales ESC*, 1965, 6, pp. 1091–118.

Page 17

war with Germany—Volobuev [354].

excellent condition—cf. the works on the Russian Army, and Falkenhayn's memoirs [193a].

The closing of the Dardanelles—cf. Danilov [189] for an account of the campaigns; and Golovine [195] who attempts to explain the problems of the Russian Army.

Page 18

joy and relief—A. I. Denikin, *Ocherki russkoy smuty*, I, ii, p. 29.

events of 1915—cf. Ferro [370].

Page 19

A. V. Krivoshein—in Florinsky [289] pp. 214–15.

that of 1914—Trapeznikov [348] p. 216; *Russia*, no. 6 (September 1917); also Zagorsky, *State Control of Industry in Russia during the War* (Yale U.P., 1927) p. 51f.

made in Russia—on German penetration, see a curious article by Kulisher in *Russko-Angliyski vestnik*, I (January 1917) p. 10.

Page 20

Russian railroads—cf. Yoffe [410].

allies' interests—*ibid*.

[price-table]—*Dok. Apr.* [21] p. 341; and enquiry of 6 April 1917 in GAORSSMo [11b] 683,3,14.

Page 21

typographers—Leiberov and Skaratan [357] pp. 46–58.

[family budget table]—*Sotsial-Demokrat* (Kharkov) 15 April 1917.

Page 22

[wages table]—figures quoted by Florinsky following Strümilin [289] pp. 126, 158–64.

lost no time in filling—on the end of Nicholas II's reign, besides G. Katkov's *Russia 1917. The February Revolution*, Longmans, Londoy 1967, pp. xxviii, 489, the following should be consulted: Florinsky [289]; Charques [290]; Pares [291]; also C. de Grunwald, *Le Règne de Nicolas II* (Paris, 1966).

Page 24

good weather—*ibid;* also Nicholas II [241].

Page 25

"Committee of War Industries"—see Florinsky [289].

France at Verdun—cf. Yoffe [410] pp. 28–32. The allies believed the same, at the Petrograd conference held late in 1916.

ten million members—*Russian Co-Operator*, April and May 1917.

commented Milyukov—see Florinsky [289]; Charques [290]; Pares [291]; de Grunwald, op. cit.

Page 27

make it more liberal—the text of this "parable" is Document 11, p. 339.

a separate peace—Francis [194] p. 62.

"government against the people"—*Doc. Ker.* [35] I, P. 16.

Page 28

chosen sides—in addition Florinsky [289] etc as above, see Alexandre [161] p. 243.

prosecution of the war—Stankevitch [259] pp. 64–5.

"disrupting the movement"—according to Pumiansky: cf. Axelrod Archive [13] August 1916, file 7-28-9.

Page 29

too chauvinistic—*Samozashchita* [58]. Some of the anarchists followed Kropotkin, accepting his views.

Social-Chauvinists—cf. the Zalevski manifesto, Document 8, p. 332. somewhat firmer tone—*Vozrozdhenie* [62] p. 6; Gankin and Fisher [37]; also Grimm Archive [13] file B.125 (message from Avdeev, 26 September 1915).

Page 30

Martov and his friends—see *Zadacha* [63] 21 August–3 September 1917; *Proletariat i Voyna*, November 1915. Similarly, Grimm Archive [13] file B.93 (letter from Lunacharski to Grimm, 13 September 1916) and Axelrod Archive [13] file 7-28-9 (letter from Maisky to Axelrod, 8 September 1916).

revolutionary war—Gankin and Fisher [37] pp. 206–7.
(*Who Needs the War?*)—*ibid.;* Axelrod Archive [13].

Page 31

"class enemy"—Axelrod Archive [13] file 18-8-1 (letter from Axelrod to Larin, 26 April 1915); Kautsky Archive [13] file D.16, 418–422 (letter from Martov to Kautsky, 31 January 1917).

helping war victims—see sources in previous note and the Grimm Archive [13] file G.17; in question are the groups "Samozashchita", "Nash Golos" (Samara), the "Regional Committee of the Caucasus Social Democrats", the Chkheidze faction, the "Organizing Committee", and another group, inadequately described. See also Dvinov [304] pp. 201–5; *Samozashchita* [58].

January 1917—Dvinov [304] pp. 126–217; Axelrod Archive [13] file 12-49-10 (letter from Uritsky to Axelrod, 21 March 1916).

Page 32

lead to revolution—cf. letter from Lenin to Shlyapnikov in Gankin and Fisher [37] p. 252.

savage of hunger riots—*Politicheskoe polozhenie Russii nakanune fevral'skoy revolyutsii v zhandarskom oveshchenii, KA* [26] XXV, p. 14.

Page 33

continuation of the war—*ibid.*

when the war was over—*ibid.*

"patriotic appeals"—Mansyrev [227] *passim.*

CHAPTER TWO
THE FALL OF THE ANCIEN RÉGIME

Page 35

("there isn't any more")—the chief eye-witness accounts and works on the insurrection are to be found in the Bibliography, nos. [160ff]. without aiding them—Blok [169] pp. 78ff.

Kerensky and Shlyapnikov had words—Yurenev [210] 2, pp. 114–43.

Page 36

followed the parade—*Journal de Petrograd*, 5–18 March 1917.
"It looked like a holiday"—Markovitch [228].

reformed on the other side—this is clear from Anet's eye-witness account [165], from Houghtelling [197], and from the contemporary account in the *Journal de Petrograd*.

wondered what it meant—in Kayurov [202].

Page 37

of the day's events—Mansyrev [227] p. 262; Vinogradoff [270] p. 536.
remained unanswered—in de Bienstock, *La Revolution russe* (Paris, 1918).

Page 38

not knowing what to think—there is an excellent analysis of the events of 25 February by I. P. Leiberov in *Octyabr'* [324].

known to be unpopular—E. Semenov, "La Révolution à Petrograd", *Monde slave*, 1917, I.

we had to shoot—*Padenie* [28] p. 220.

Page 39

crushing one another—quoted in *HRR* [126] I, p. 81.

Page 40

popular general like Alexeiev—Mel'gunov [128] p. 150.

no fifth day—Kayurov [202]; Sukhanov [120]; Yurenev [210], *passim*.

gravity of the situation—S. P. Mel'gunov, *Legenda o separatnom mire* (Paris, 1957) shows that some government circles did have the idea of provoking anti-war demonstrations in order to justify, to the Allies, demands for a separate peace; but that these were no more than backstairs gossip, of no practical consequence.

Would this be enough—text in Koutchine, *La Révolution de fevrier en Russie* (Paris, 1937) p. 93.

insurrection . . . could succeed—*HRR* [126] I, p. 81.

taken decisive action—Kayurov [201] p. 105.

make up a government—*Dok.* [20] pp. 5–6.

paralyze Tsarism—Shylapnikov [125] p. 103.

revolution could not succeed—*ibid.*, p. 52. Shlyapnikov certainly foresaw, in February, a "storm", but did not imagine a revolution could succeed.

showed the opposite—*Imperialism, the Highest State of Capitalism* had appeared early in 1917, only in a limited and toned-down edition (cf. Lenin, *Oeuvres choisies* (foreign language edn.) I, ii, p. 615).

Page 41
Skobelev or their friends—cf. Gankin and Fisher [37] p. 252 (letter from Lenin to Shlyapnikov, September–October 1916).

Nikolai Sukhanov—Sukhanov [120] pp. 94–5.

a prepared plan—the historian Burdzhalov [327] pp. 40–2, shows that the pamphlet traditionally dated "26 March"—which is discussed later—should in fact be dated 27 March, i.e. was written after the revolution had succeeded.

Populists to Defeatists—cf. Kerensky [210] p. 20; Zenzinov [274] XXXIV, p. 207.

any joint resolutions—Ermansky, for this day, notes the need "to organize the masses"; cf. Ermansky [193] p. 148.

"take extreme measures"—Vinogradoff [270] p. 557.

under all circumstances—Sukhanov [120] English edn., p. 15.

amounts to nothing—Kerensky [124] pp. 236–7.

propaganda in the factories—Zenzinov [274].

Page 42
nothing had been decided—Yurenev [210] p. 138.

walked on the street—Trotsky [121] I, p. 125.

sign of things to come—Blok [169].

by the entrance—*HRR* [126] I, p. 85.

Page 43
forty thousand rifles—Blok [169].

floating over the palace—de Chambrun [181].

Page 44

on the Monarch—*Doc. Ker.* [35] I, p. 40.

WILL BE TOO LATE—*ibid.*, p. 42.

suggestions to offer—Walter [323]; *Doc. Ker.* [35] I, pp. 45–8.

hold their heads high—E. Semenov, "La Revolution à Petrograd", *Monde slave*, 1917.

Page 45

its dissolution—more precisely, the Tsar suspended the session until May. Just the same, the Duma and the public talked of "dissolution". "the Mob"—Shulgin [256] p. 92.

says Kerensky—Kerensky always claimed the honour of having directed the insurgent regiments towards the Duma—perhaps through Sokolov.

save the situation—Kerensky [210] p. 26.

tell us what to do—Perevalov [246].

Suddenly Kerensky roared—Cherkasky [134].

with a new government—Knox [215] II, p. 557.

"they are finally deciding!"—Cherkasky [134] p. 34.

The Workers' Group—see Chapter 1.

workers and soldiers—Shlyapnikov [125] p. 119.

answer this question—Cherkasky [134].

Page 46

could meet somewhere else—Kerensky [210] p. 27.

proclaim itself the Soviet—Mansyrev [227] p. 268.

What's wanted from me—Shulgin [256] p. 96.

Bordanov, Breido—Mstislavsky [236] p. 22; Dan [187] p. 291.

from the *Bund*—for the *Bund*, see Chapter 1.

Sokolovsky—is this Shatrov or Vladimirov? Outlawed revolutionaries frequently changed their pseudonyms and it is often difficult to identify them.

Pankov—it is difficult to tell whether Alexandrovich was a member of the pre-Soviet at 3 p.m. An attempt has been made to draw up a list of those present in Ferro [330].

nine o'clock that evening—Shlyapnikov [125] p. 117.

Tauride Palace—for the large factories, one delegate per thousand workers, and one delegate per factory for those containing less than a thousand workers.

Newsmen's Committee—Kerensky [210].

Page 47

rebellious soldiers—Zenzinov [274] XXXV, p. 217.

in the preceding days—cf. Anet [165].

available to protect it—see Chapter 3.

first prisoners, well guarded—Mstislavsky [236], from which some good sections have been translated in Walter [314] pp. 157–62.

by Burdzhalov—Burdzhalov [327].

after the army's uprising—according to the text in *HRR* [126] I, p. 92: "The revolutionary troops have gone over to the insurgents." Supplement No. 1—some manifestoes were put up as early as the evening of the 27th; cf. Kayurov [201] p. 167.

formation of a Soviet—Shlyapnikov [125]; Sukhanov [120] English edn., p. 43.

Soviet of 3 P.M.—apparently between noon and 1 p.m.

work out the revolution with them—Trotsky [121] p. 229; *HRR* [126].

Page 48

center of the city—cf. Peshekhonov [248].

the idea of the Soviet—cf. Chermensky [328]. At Vyborg they even went on to elect for a Soviet. The Finland Station was to be the command point for future activity.

but the Soviet as well—see the text of the Bolshevik manifesto, Document 16, p. 344.

Made up of leaders—according to Milyukov, Kerensky adhered to this only with reserve: he thought the committee too attached to juridical fictions; Milyukov [122] ed. Alexiev p. 175.

Page 49

Petrograd the next day—see Blok [169].

2,000 soldiers—*ibid.*, pp. 108–11.

Marie Palace—the seat of government.

Stavka—general headquarters.

mounting the stairs—cf. Ferro [330] p. 369.

Page 50

a voting voice—it included Ehrlikh, Gvozdev and Sokolov.

only provisional—the Menshevik Ermansky says that the delegates had been elected "God knows how". His book was written in 1927—by this time he had become a Bolshevik. On this aspect of the matter, see Chermensky [328].

two hundred and fifty observers—this is discussed in Ferro [330] p. 370.

the democratic camp—Shlyapnikov [125].

The independents thus—see Razgon [333].

Grinevich—Sukhanov [120] I, pp. 120–5; discussion in Ferro [330].

the others came later—the Mensheviks chose Bogdanov and Batursky; the S.-R.s Rusanov and Zenzinov; the Bolsheviks Molotov and Zalutsky.

a Constituent Assembly—apart from the supply committees and the literary and military committees, Peshekhonov [248] speaks of a finance committee. See also Sukhanov [120] English edn., p. 64. The text of this appeal is Document 15, p. 343.

Page 51

insofar as it did not—Rodzianko [253] ed. Alexiev, p. 45.

triumph for the Duma—on all this, Shalyapnikov [125] pp. 122–8.

soldiers in the Soviet—according to Zaslavsky.

majority overruled them—cf. Chermensky [328] p. 11.

THE TWO-POWER STRUCTURE—apart from *KA* [26] XXI, pp. 1–78 and XXII, pp. 1–40, where there are over 300 telegrams and telephone conversations intercepted by the censor, the eye-witness accounts of Boldyrev, Bublikov, Lukomsky, Lomonosov etc., quoted in the Bibliography (nos. [161ff]) are of value. Mel'gunov's work [128] covers this and the succeeding paragraph.

Page 52

AT THE NAVY MINISTRY—Blok [169] p. 125.

most "loyal" troops—*Kut.* [25] p. 14.

machine-gun the crowds—Mel'gunov [128] pp. 163–8 goes deeply into this question and concludes that the whole thing is a legend: there were no machine-guns. But he does not use Lomonosov's account [219]: "In December my cousin Michael told me that they were teaching the police force to use [these weapons]." De Chambrun

[181] who was in the street at the time, writes (p. 58): "At that time—about five p.m. on 28th February—the police began to disappear: they went up on the roofs to their combat posts, for—incredible as it may seem—machine-guns had been set up on top of the houses to clear the street." None the less, no machine-gun was ever discovered.

crossed bayonets—Kerensky [203] and [210].

Page 53

reorganize the government—D. Lloyd George, *War Memoirs* (1936) III, p. 162.

act cautiously—Paléologue [244] p. 113; *Kut.* [25] p. 25; *KA* [26] (1927) p. 111; Houghtelling [197] p. 125.

Duma had assumed power—Bublikov [174] pp. 20–1.

hadn't been a revolution—*ARR* [27] III, p. 252; *KA* [26] XXI, p. 36.

to accompany him—Sukhanov [120] I, p. 112.

Page 54

armies of Ivanov—on this—confused—affair, see especially the accounts by Sukhanov, Milyukov, Shydlovsky cited in the Bibliography and discussed in Mel'gunov [128] pp. 50–61.

he was President—*KA* [26] XLII, p. 62.

Grand Duke Michael—*Izvestya*, 2 March 1917, p. 2, col 1; *KA* [26] XLII, p. 102; *Vozrozdhenie* [62] XXIV (1952) pp. 141–5. Soldiers arrived, to guard Michael (information given by A. S. Mateev, Michael's secretary). Engelhardt's text is in *Doc. Ker.* [35] I, p. 62.

General Order Number One—on this, see the article by G. I. Zlokazov in *Octyabr'* [324], which shows, amongst other things, that the Soviet leaders hardly intervened to make sure their own militia survived; see also V. I. Miller, *Istoriya SSR* (1966) VI, pp. 26–44.

Page 55

write the order ourselves—Knox [215] p. 558.

text of the Soviet appeal—Shlyapnikov [125] I, p. 174.

"Military Committee'—*ibid.*, p. 171.

Engelhardt's order—see p. 54.

Page 56

marching on Petrograd—*Kut.* [25] p. 25.

March 1—Zenzinov [274] p. 219.

Page 57

Chkheidze and Sukhanov's—Sukhanov [120] I, pp. 104–5; Shlyapnikov [125] I, p. 81; Zenzinov [274] p. 266; Zaslavsky, "Pervaya legal'naya K.P.", *Prol. Rev.* (1923) pp. 135–56. See also Mel'gunov [128] p. 23.

Page 58

know where that was?—*ibid.*, and likewise Mstislavsky [236] p. 55f.

Page 60

postpone the reforms—Sukhanov [120].

Page 62

the Catherine Room—*Doc. Ker.* [35] I, pp. 129–32.

Page 63

the Assembly directly—conversation with Kerensky, September 1963.

Page 64

Tauride Palace—*Doc. Ker.* [35] I, pp. 128–9, following *Izvestya*.
interests of the dynasty—*ARR* [27] III, pp. 253–8; Shulgin [256] pp. 238–76.

Page 65

Tsarskoe-Selo—*KA* [26] II, p. 10; *Journal intime de Nicholas II* (Paris, 1934) p. 91f; Nolde [242] p. 127; Mel'gunov [128] p. 141.

Page 66

sun shone beautifully—*ibid.*, similarly Blok [169] p. 100f; *KA* [26] XXI, p. 8; also Cantacuzene-Speransky, *Revolutionary Days* (London, 1920).

Page 68

by repression—*KA* [26] XXI, pp. 1–78 (partularly pp. 8–23) and XXIII, p. 251; also *ARR* [27] II, pp. 18—19. "Officers should reinforce their supervision of the men, should start conversations on patriotic themes" was an order of General Omelyanovich, March 1917, cf. GAORSSLo [12] 7384, 9,244,4.

Ivanov's soldiers to freedom—*ibid.*; Blok [169] p. 132f.

side of the Revolution—*KA* [26] XXI, pp. 20–1; Trotsky [121] pp. 89–90.

Page 69

away from the capital—this is based on Mel'gunov's account [128] pp. 139–90.

Page 71

Ivanov's expedition—the reconstruction of Ivanov's venture is based on Blok [169] p. 125f; Anet [165] I, p. 102; Francis [194] p. 67f; and above all on Lomonosov [219], as well as the sources indicated above.

Page 72

"Let's dine first"—up to the arrival in Pskov, see the same sources particularly *KA* [26] XXI and XXIII; Blok [169] and the *Journal* of Nicholas II.

Page 73

Nicholas II got his way—for events in Pskov, see the same sources, also Denikine [191] p. 191; the memoirs of Grand-Duke Andrey in *KA* [26] XXVI, pp. 185–210; Lukomsky [221]. General Boldyrev's memoirs in *KA* [26] XXIII are particularly valuable. See also Francis [194] pp. 77–9; and Anet [165] I, p. 101.

Page 74

cowardice and deceit!—to the same works should be added Shul'gin [256] pp. 238–76; *ARR* [27] II, p. 26; Rodzianko [253] p. 43; *Journal* of Nicholas II, p. 93.

Page 75

would be duped—Peshekhonov [248] ed. Alexiev, p. 451.

succeed Nicholas II—this was learned in Moscow, where protest telegrams were addressed to the Soviet, GAORSSMo [11b] 66, 3, 914, 1ff.

Page 77

Blood has flowed—to the accounts of Kerensky, Sukhanov, Shul'gin, Milyukov, Rodzianko and Lukomsky cited in the Bibliography, and Guchkov in *Padenie* [28], should be added Lomonosov [219] pp. 66f; and Msitislavsky [236].

high command least of all—see *KA* [26], especially Boldyrev's account; similarly Shlyapnikov [125]; *Doc.Ker.* [35].

General Evert—Shlyapnikov [125] II, pp. 62–4 and 244, 248. In Tiflis, Nicholas succeeded tolerably well as the municipal Duma addressed a message to Rodzianko on 2 March, stating their con-

THE RUSSIAN REVOLUTION OF FEBRUARY 1917

viction that "His Imperial Majesty will give his powerful support in the creation of a new order". TSGIAL [12b] 1278, 5, 1293, 103–7.

Page 78

withdrawing from them—Shlyapnikov [125] II, pp. 83–5 and 236–7; *KA* [26] XXIII, p. 254; *Doc.Ker.* [35] II, p. 850.

Holy Russia—Shlyapnikov [125] II, pp. 244–5.

more than eight days—there were exceptions. Sometimes officers and men fraternized, cf. TSGIAL [12b] 1278, 5, 1284, 98ff.

Page 79

squad which shot him—Naida, *Revolyutsionnoe dvizhenie v tsarkom flote* (Moscow, 1948, 608 pp.)

"A question of principle"—Paléologue [244] III, p. 112; Grand-Duke Cyril, *My Life in Russian Service* (London, 1939, 286 pp.) pp. 209–10; Denikine [191] French edn.; p. 52; Cantacuzene-Speranski, 66. op. cit., p. 124; Korostovets [216] p. 269; GAORSSLo [12] 7384, 9, 142, 12.

factory soviets—*Kut.* [25] p. 219. In April, 83 of them published a newspaper, TSGAORSSSR [11] 6978, I, 362, 20–1.

Page 81

different objectives—*Dok.* [20] p. 308f; also Tseretelli [127] I, pp. 17–25.

Page 82

children proud of us—*Dok.* [20] e.g. pp. 229 and 262; GAORSSLo [12] 7384, 9, 161, 29–30.

to Tobolsk—from April, the Petrograd Soviet received from the provinces motions inviting it to incarcerate the Tsar in a fortress, cf. GAORSSLo [12] 7384, 7, 36, 51.

decided to try him—on this question, see the memoirs of Buchanan and his daughter [175] and [176]; Kerensky [202], [205], [206], [207] should also be consulted. On the Soviet's attitude, see *Dok.* [20] p. 235; also GAORSSLo [12] 7384, 7, 36, 51.

not yet at war—on recognition, see Warth [407]; Yoffe [410]; *Istorichesky Arkhiv* (1955) 3, p. 153; *Kut.* [25] p. 129. At the end of March, in fact, a high official of the Russian embassy in London wrote to Tereshchenko: "A financial appeal to the USA will tie America more firmly to the Allied cause." TSGAORSSSR [11] 3, 1, 326, 37.

Page 83

glorious way—Markovitch [228].

CHAPTER THREE
THE PROJECTS
Page 84
Thousands of telegrams—*Izvestya*, organ of the Soviet, received 14,000 in a fortnight (*Izvestya*, 17 March 1917, p. 7, col. 1). This chapter and the two succeeding chapters are based on extensive reading of the press and archival sources, some unpublished, some published by the USSR. A description of these is to be found in the Bibliography, nos [11]–[13], [20]–[26], [29]–[37] and [46]–[60] incl.

Page 85
its victorious end—motions of the municipal Dumas to this effect are unanimous; cf. the Saratov region, TSGIAL [12b] 1278, 5, 1264; for the Crimea, *ibid.*, 1278, 5, 1293; for the Ekaterinoslav region *ibid.*, 1278, 5, 1267.

to the Allies—*Russkie Vedomosty*, 2 March 1917 (quoted in *Doc. Ker.* [35] I, p. 143); *Dok.* [20] p. 535.

must they share power—on 25 March 1917, at a Cadet meeting: Morokhovets [347] p. 132.

counterweight to the Soviet—Shidlovsky [255] p. 288. For its part, the "Coal Committee" wrote to Konovalov that: "the only way to put an end to anarchy is to rally patriotic feeling round the Duma", TSGAORSSSR [11] 3, 1, 324, 47 and 49.

gave up their principles easily—Rodzianko [253] Alexiev ed. p. 57. "its complete support"—*Torgovo-promyshlennaya Gazeta*, 10 March 1917, in *Dok.* [20] pp. 432–4.

Page 86
still endorsing Michael—*KA* [26] V, p. 114.

Page 87
political freedom and so on—*Rech'*, 27 March 1917; see also Kokoshkin [138b] pp. 4–8 and 21.

question of the nationalism—cf. Ferro [370].

Page 88
agrarian policy principle—cf. Morokhovets [347] pp. 131–53.

rentiers of the State—Maslov [141].

the February Revolution—Morokhovets [347] pp. 153–65.

Page 89

avoided at all cost—*ibid.*

economic objectives—this is based on Volobuev [354].

Page 90

management of the economy—cf. Lavigne, "Le Plan de M. Rjabuš-
insky", op. cit., pp. 90–105.

countries at the same time—Volobuev [354].

to Socialist Ministers—a remark of Volobuev's.

administration of business—cf. letter from an engineer to his
manager, in *Ek. Pol.* [24] I.

Page 91

producers as a class—*Ek. Pol.* [24] I, p. 161; similarly TSGAORSSSR
[11] 3, 1, 292, 20.

to join a union—*Izvestya*, 7 March 1917, p. 5.

Page 92

descendants of the intelligentsia—*ibid.;* also 9 March 1917, p. 4; and
21 March 1917, p. 6. See also TSGIAL [12b] 1278, 5, 1247 (100 items)
and 1278, 5, 1259 (101 items); and TSGAORSSSR [11] 1244,1,15,138.

sportsmen of the Revolution—quoted in P. Pascal "Les Grands
Courants de la pensée russe contemporaine", *Cahiers du monde russe
et soviétique*, 1962, I, p. 59f.

Page 93

now it is time to act—*Izvestya*, 9 March 1917, p. 3.

everything is possible—*ibid.*, 14 March 1917, p. 4; P. Pascal, op. cit.

Stolypin's reaction—there is no overall work on the party pro-
gramme, but Morokhovets' book [347] though supposed to be
restricted to the agrarian question, in fact gives a good overall view.
To this should be added the works on Marxism, Social-Democracy,
Populism and Anarchism indicated in the general section of the
Bibliography.

Page 94

Russia had followed—cf. Morokhovets [347] pp. 74–6. On the point
of means of production and the Marxist scheme of social evolution,
see Wittfogel [302] and the discussion provoked by his work.

Page 95

urge their application—cf. Voline [192] p. 154; Guérin [319].

of society by another—*Contrat Social*, September 1961, V, no. 5, pp. 286–9.

Page 96

distribution of power—cf. *Programma partii sotsialistov-revolyutsionerov* (Petrograd, 1917, 13 pp.) pp. 9 and 10.

first party convention—quoted in Radkey [297] p. 45f.

unicameral parliament—cf. Peshekhonov [147] and [147a]. For the *trudoviki*, see *Byulleten'* [42].

national minorities—for disagreements on the role of the Soviets, see p. 56f.

Stolypin's reforms—to the work of Morokhovets [347] should be added Maslov's pamphlet [141].

Page 99

nationalizing them all—on the Social-Democrats, the following works should be added to those already used: Vasilev [158], Melshcheryakov [142], Trapeznikov [348], Owen [346] pp. 88–132, and Sorlin [349]. On the S.-R.s, besides Morokhovets [347] and Radkey [297], see Chernov [134b] and Peshekhonov [147f]; also Larin, *Voyna i zemel'ny vopros* (Geneva, 1915).

collective labor—Sisko, quoted in Morokhovets [347] p. 79.

Page 100

agreement for once—see in particular the works of Radkey [297], and Peshekhonov [147] and [147b].

development of production—cf. B. Kerblay, "Au Carrefour des théoriciens", V. Chayanov, *Cahiers du monde russe et soviétique*, 1964, 4, pp. 411–61.

of industry or commerce—the phrase "peasant economy" is used in the sense defined by D. Thorner in *Annales ESC*, 1956, 3.

Page 102

labor offices—cf. *Contrat Social*, September 1961, V, no. 5, pp. 286–9.

PROGRAM OF THE NATIONAL ORGANIZATIONS—see the Bibliography, nos. [364ff] to which should be added, for the period before 1914, Seton-Watson [287].

Page 108

internecine struggle—cf. Dimanshteyn [364]; Bennigsen-Quelquejay [401].

fulfill these aspirations—see Chapter 1, p. 9; also Ferro [369].

Page 109

not yet taken root—the principal texts are in Gankin and Fisher [37].

threats are constant—Point 6 of the BUKHARIN MOTION (with Bosh, Pyatakov) drawn up by Bukharin. This text is not in Gankin and Fisher and exists only in the introduction written by Dimanshteyn to his collection of documents [364] pp. xxx and xxxi.

Page 110

of the various states—*Leninsky Sbornik*.

on the subject people—cf. Minor [234].

CHAPTER FOUR

THE DEMANDS

Page 112

the unhappy past—3 March 1917, at the Moscow Soviet (GAORSSMo [11b] 66, 3, 262, 15).

we can't stand any more—19 March 1917, to Kerensky (*Dok.* [20] p. 251).

Page 113

knowing what they are for—7 March 1917, the Gryuntal factories to the Moscow Soviet (*ibid.*, p. 572).

for cleaning up—16 March 1917, at the Petrograd Soviet (*ibid.*, p. 509).

those of all of Russia—women, anticipating equality, made the same claims as the men; cf. the congress of women workers in the Dynamo, Skorokhod factories, etc.; cf. *Pravda*, 9 March 1917.

in case of dismissal—abolition of night shifts was also demanded. On the conditions of work in the Titushin copper factories see *Dok.* [20] p. 534.

obtain some concessions—on tobacco, see the 23-point demands in *Izvestya*, 9 March 1917, p. 6.

Page 114

requires a special law—for instance at Petrograd and Ufa; cf. *Dok.* [20] pp. 387, 466, 514.

for true freedom—15 March 1917, at the Alsvang factories in Moscow (*Sotsial-Demokrat*, 15 March 1917).

their close participation—the precise demands were often "from 8 a.m. to noon, and from 1 p.m. to 5.30 p.m."; sometimes they added "only six hours on Saturdays and holidays". The workers of the Skorokhod in Petrograd expected non-stop work: *Dok.* [20] p. 491.

would be without recourse—there are several examples.

demands remained modest—see the tables in Chapter 1.

shoe factory near Kharkov—at the "Korona" factories in Kharkov and the "Skorokhod" ones in Moscow; cf. *Dok.* [20] p. 529.

Page 116
for men and women—several figures, on the lines of those above, are given by way of example here.

80r. per month—*Sotsial-Demokrat* (Moscow), 24 March 1917.

eliminate black-listing—*Izvestya*, 11 March 1917, p. 6.

cable factories in Petrograd—*Dok.* [20] pp. 483 and 583.

address themselves individually to it—in the Petrograd radio factories, establishment of an assurance scheme was often demanded; cf. *Dok.* [20] p. 493. Often, "friendly funds" were also sought.

Arsenal and Erikson's—for instance, at the first electricity station in Petrograd (*Kut.* [25] I, p. 71).

pay by 150 percent—*Dok.* [20] pp. 473 and 475; for the Sestronets factories, p. 469.

Page 117
compensation for his work—*Izvestya*, 7 March 1917, p. 5, col. 3; 22 March 1917, p. 5.

deviations in its policies—*Dok.* [20] p. 305.

Soviet will be carried out—*ibid.*, p. 460.

or unions were few—printers and workmen from the Rodniky factory.

applies its program—*Izvestya*, 8 March 1917, p. 5; 7 March 1917, p. 5.

Page 118
equality for all—*Dok.* [20] p. 305.

formation of a Democratic Republic—*Izvestya*, 5 March 1917, p. 5.

Page 119
the miners of Kuznetz—*Pravda*, 14 March 1917; *Dok.* [20] p. 500.

Down with War—Sotsial-Demokrat (Moscow), 1 March 1917.

the close of meetings—at the Kramer factories, cf. *Sotsial-Demokrat*, 12 March 1917.

very patriotic—*ibid.;* TSGIAL [12b] 1278, 5, 1251.

Fabergé plants and others—*Izvestya,* 7 March 1917, p. 3.

Page 120

in the interest of democracy—*Dok.* [20] pp. 305–7.

action of the workers—*Dok.* [20] p. 486.

last drop of blood—*Izvestya,* 14 March 1917, p. 7.

example of free Russia—the Zamoskovskirechy meeting is exceptional.

some things in common—usually, it was the railwaymen and artisans who declared their confidence in the provisional government and took the patriotic line, cf. TSGIAL [12b] 1278, 5, 1321.

Page 121

"defend the country"—not published in *Pravda* but in *Dok.* [20] p. 477.

Social-Democratic ideology—instead of enumerating demands, the Alatyr workers merely referred to the minimum demands of the Social-Democratic party, cf. GAORSSMo [11b] 66, 3, 262, 33.

"Workers' Republic"—*Izvestya,* 7 March 1917, p. 5, col. 3.

leading role in his country—cf. N. Vermenitsev, *Krest'yanskoe dvizhenie mezdhu fevral'skoy i oktabyr'skoy revolyutsiy* (Moscow, 1928) p. 178; and Kotel'nikov [31] pp. 362–80.

Page 122

Alexei Egorov—on 9 April 1917: peasants of Vyshgorodechka *volost'* in the Pskov *guberniya* (*Dok. Apr.* [21] pp. 582–80).

Page 123

outcome will be slaughter—peasants of the Semetska *volost'* in Nizhny-Novgorod *guberniya* (*Dok. Apr.* [21] p. 574).

it's Patriotism—letter to *Izvestya* in *Dok. Apr.* [21] p. 659.

Page 125

small property-holder—cf. S. M. Doubrovski, "Le Mouvement paysan en 1905–1907", *La Révolution russe de 1905,* Cahier 5 of *Recherches soviétiques,* ed. P. Angrand (Paris, 1956). See especially p. 100.

Page 126

beyond two *dessyatines*—following the *Atlas: sel'skoe khozyaystvo i kustarnaya promyshlennost'*, quoted and reproduced in Usatova [350] p. 7.

not want the *pomeshchiki*—proportionally, the *pomeshchiki* had at their disposal twenty times as many prisoners-of-war as small cultivators: cf. Trapeznikov [348] p. 294.

Page 127
current prices will be set by workers—*Dok. Apr.* [21] p. 691.

Page 128
they don't need them—26 March 1917, in the village of Dubno, near Petrograd (*Dok. Apr.* [21] p. 693).

equitable distribution of the lands—cf. the resolutions of the Samara region peasant assembly; these arranged soil utilization until new legislation appeared.

Briansk Region—26 and 27 April 1917, *Dok. Apr.* [21] p. 673f.

Constituent's session—the village of Gorka-Vereiska in Moscow *guberniya*, *Dok. Apr.* [21] p. 630.

fall of Nicholas II—10 April 1917, the village of Giblitsa in Ryazan *guberniya*, *Dok. Apr.* [21] p. 589.

Page 130
on the seacoast—cf. TSGAORSSSR [11] 3,1,302.

worse than in 1905—near Samara, and similarly near Archangel'sk, *Dok.* [20] pp. 687–9.

make no mistake about it—*Dok.* [20] p. 692.

Page 132
Deputies of Petrograd—from the translation in *HRR* [126] pp. 97–8.

[Report to General Russky]—5 March 1917, *Dok.* [20] pp. 613–4.

Page 133
antipathy to liberation movement—6 March 1917: officers of the 1st Infantry Regiment (*Dok.* [20] p. 617).

(Barancov Report)—report of General Kaledin, Caucasus Army (*Dok.* [20] p. 639).

no other means of support—see the soldiers' letters, GAORSSLo [12] 7384, 9, files 143, 149, 244, 267, 564.

to the Old Régime—*Dok.* [20] p. 639.

Page 134

with all our might—*Pravda*, 21 March 1917.

Page 135

who show the way—*Dok.* [20] p. 613.

broached in the soldiers' meetings—on 8 March 1918, the soldiers of the 6th Artillery Park asked the Petrograd Soviet if they ought not consider as *agents provocateurs* men who who talked of making peace or who supported the striking workers (GAORSSLo [12] 7384, 9, 244, 33).

peace without annexations—often, sailors expressed themselves more strongly. From 4 March, those of the Helsingfors experimental center "demand that the government should address officially to the German people a Note inviting them to overthrow the Kaiser and begin peace negotiations", TSGIAL [12b] 1278,5,1329,1–4.

means the end of the war—*Dok.* [20] p. 627.

so often by the officers—this was usually so when the motion came from a soviet of both officers and men, for instance in the 5th Infantry Division etc. (TSGAORSSSR [11] 1244,1,15,111).

honorable conditions for Russia—*Dok.* [20] p. 654.

Page 136

start earnest negotiations—see the letter of a group of soldiers in the Caucasus Army, Document 22, p. 354.

its elimination—"The officers have . . . understood in no way what our revolution means", noted the soldiers and NCOs of the Kiev fortress garrison, GAORSSLo [12] 7384, 9, 228, 7.

CHAPTER FIVE
THE HOPES

Page 137

present their claims—Choulgine [392] p. 54.

(*samostoyatelnost*)—*KA* [26] (1927) V, p. 124.

Finnish government—*Kut.* [25] I, p. 72; Dimanshteyn [364] pp. 68–9; Milyukov [132] p. 141.

wasn't more revolutionary—Soderhelm Henning [381] p. 16.

decisions of the Soviet—*Izvestya*, 8 March 1917, p. 8.

Page 138

bound them together—*Golos Pravdy* (Kronstadt), *Dok.* [20] p. 731 (19 March 1917).

for dear life—Dimanshteyn [364] pp. 204–8.

hold on Polish territory—*KA* [26] (1927) V, p. 114; also Filasiewicz [373].

the Polish national movement—none the less, the government received telegrams expressing thanks (see TSGAORSSSR [11] 3, 1, 364, 178ff).

the future of Poland—Filasiewicz [373] pp. xx and 154.

new régime in Petrograd—*Dok. pol.* [371] pp. 36–8.

ultimate independence—*Dok. Apr.* [21] pp. 697ff.

a threat to the Revolution—*Dok. pol.* [371] pp. 39–40. For instance, it refused to participate in the demonstrations arranged by the "national" organizations for 26 March, in Moscow.

solidarity of the proletariat—*Izvestya*, 4 March 1917.

autonomous Polish army increased—*Dok. pol.* [371] pp. 51–2.

Page 139

brotherhood of the peoples of the world—motion of the Polish Social-Democrats in Krasnoyarsk, quoted in *Dok. Apr.* [21] p. 270.

hands of the Central Powers—*Dok. pol.* [371] pp. 53. Milyukov's political calculations regarding Poland have been given more detailed analysis in Ferro [370].

to establish schools—Milyukov [233] p. 62. The text is Document 29, p. 365.

Page 140

who showed impatience—Kerensky's expression.

according to Milyukov—Milyukov [233] p. 62.

law in free Russia—conversation with Kerensky in September 1963. after March 19 as before—the Jews of Moscow were the only exception (TSGAORSSSR [11] 3, 1, 364, 171).

and Fraternity—*Izvestya*, 12 March 1917; GAORSSLo [12] 7384, 9, 143,60. and 7384, 9, 161, 17.

to their organizations—*Izvestya*, 22 March 1917.

Page 141

had disappeared—*Izvestya*, 8 March 1917.

whole of the working class—Dimanshteyn [364] pp. 277–9; *Izvestya*, 9 April 1917.

consistent nationalist group—the telegrams from *Poale-Zion* overwhelm, in numbers, those from the *Bund* (TSGIAL [12b] *fond* 1278; GAORSSLo [12] *fond* 7384).

the Constituent election—Dimanshteyn [364] pp. 379 (in May). In the first weeks of the revolution, some sections of *Poale-Zion* (in Poltava, Gomel', etc.) none the less came round to a "Russian" solution for the Jewish problem (GAORSSMo [11b] 66,3,292,42 and 51 etc).

Page 142

National Constituent Assembly—Dimanshteyn [364] p. 379.

basis of universal suffrage—*Izvestya*, 4 March 1917. The letters of Pskov likewise demanded "liberation" of Courland (TSGAORSSSR [11] 3, 1, 364, 142).

reforms in Russia—*Dok.* [20] p. 716.

decision-making powers—*ibid.*, pp. 716–21; Dimanshteyn [364] p. 230.

Page 143

industrial cities of Latvia—*ibid.*, p. 234.

"Local Autonomy"—*ibid.*, p. 325; *Dok.* [21] pp. 706–10; Dimanshteyn [364] pp. 224–5.

power of the Seim—Dimanshteyn [364] pp. 239ff.

Page 144

with their Russian comrades—*ibid.*, p. 241.

even in the large cities—see the film sequence of the German entry into Riga in *La Grande Guerre* (Pathé, Paris, 1965) and *Trente Ans d'histoire* (Pathé, Paris, 1964).

term "local autonomy"—*Dok.* [20] p. 726.

Page 145

upcoming Revel meeting—Dimanshteyn [364] *passim*.

Bolsheviks came to power—*Rech'*, 14 July 1917.

those living in the United States—*Doc. Ker.* [35] p. 407.

the future of the country—Dimanshteyn [364] pp. 261–3.

Page 146

triumph of revolutionary ideals—*Novaya Zhizn'* reviewed this, published in *Doc. Mai.* [22] p. 463.

legal and cultural claims—the "Union of Progressive Ukrainians" sent a full memorandum to the government in March (TSGAORSSSR [11] 3, 1, 35, 1–4; Choulgine [392] p. 57f.

formation of a federal state—the texts are in Dimanshteyn [364] p. 132.

those of liberty—quoted by Pipes [365] p. 54.

"confirm Ukrainian autonomy"—Dimanshteyn [364] p. 134.

Page 147

with our Russian comrades—*Dok.* [20] p. 730; Dimanshteyn [364] pp. 132–3.

northwest part of the country—*ibid.*, pp. 136–7.

Republicans, not Socialists—*Kut.* [25] p. 192; Dimanshteyn [364] pp. 122–4 and 128; Pipes [365] p. 57.

Bukovina and Galicia—the "progressives" had already formed their attitude towards this: cf. *Dok.* [20] p. 730.

without annexations or contributions—*Izvestya*, 14 March 1917, p. 6. There were also demonstrations for peace on the part of the Social-Democrats; cf. *Izvestya*, 7 March 1917, and Chapter 6.

who served in the army—*Dok. Mai.* [22] p. 445. The Ukrainian pilots took the same line (*Dok.* [20] p. 735).

the armed *Rada*—on the Ukraine, see Pidhainy [388].

about fifteen people—Pipes [365] p. 73.

more than the Bolsheviks—Vakar [393] p. 97.

Page 148

adopted in April 1917—Dimanshteyn [364] pp. 267, 270 etc.

at the peace table—on the Zavrev mission, see Karemzadeh [394].

scattered throughout Russia—Dimanshteyn [364] pp. 401–2; *Dok.* [20] p. 733; wireless dispatch, 18 May 1917, in *Bulletin de presse de Petrograd* [43].

on the side of order—Karemzadeh [394] p. 33.

of the entire population—Zhordania [397] pp. 5–7.

the new administration—*Dok.* [20] p. 757.

Page 149

the conservatives' mill—Karemzadeh [394] p. 35f.

Georgian Constituent Assembly—telegram from Mikhail Tserethelli, in *Annales des Nationalités*, no. 3/1, 1917, p. 83.

Koutais and Tiflis—21 March 1917, *Dok.* [20] p. 732.

minorities of Siberia—Dimashteyn—[364] p. 492.

wanted to unite with them—*ibid.*, pp. 431–2.

Page 150

in their own language—motion of 12 April 1917, in Dimanshteyn [364] p. 437; and *Dok.* [20] p. 303. A "Workmen's Committee" demanded "installation of socialism", GAORSSLo[12]7384, 9, 161, 6.

the 1st of May—Zenkovski [404] p. 140.

no note of freedom of religion—*Izvestya*, 12 March 1917, p. 3.

one with the Cadets—*Kut.* [25] p. 253.

namely, the Turks—*Russkaya Volya*, 28 March 1917; *Golos Dagestana* 30 April 1917, quoted in Dimanshteyn [364] p. 288; and TSGIAL [12b] 1278, 5,1338.

ten preliminary conventions—Van Tatarow, "Der Zusammenschluss der russischen Muhammedaner", *Neue Orient*, June 1917.

professors etc.—Bennigsen, Quelquejay [400] pp. 65–7; Zenkovski [404] pp. 142–58.

Page 151

Islamic history—Van Tatarow, op. cit., p. 268.

liberation of women—Dimanshteyn [364] pp. 296–8.

Socialists of all shades—Bennigsen, Quelquejay [400].

Page 152

exploitation and subjugation—Dimanshteyn [364] pp. 295–6.

Page 153

a Pan-Moslem body—the translation is Quelquejay's; the text is in Dimanshteyn [364] p. 194.

the whole Islamic world—Bennigsen, Quelquejay [400] *passim*.

CHAPTER SIX

THE START AND THE OPERATION OF THE NEW RÉGIME
Page 163

I. N. Steinberg—Steinberg [260].

the Romanovs abdicated—Chernov [179].

made an agreement—Sukhanov [120] I, *passim*.

Page 164

praise of their country—conversation with Kerensky, September 1963.

"the movement"—Nabokov [237] p. 40f.

using Cadet tactics—Bublikov [174] p. 39.

Page 165

will die with you—*Izvestya*, 29 March 1917, p. 3.

Page 166

conciliatory toward the Soviet—Nabokov [237] p. 36.

the cabinet's responsibility—this was Konovalov's case (TSGAORSSSR [11] 3, 1, 324, 37).

consulted any more—Shidlovsky [255].

can never come back—Mansyrev [227].

Page 167

THE SOVIETS—see the work of Anweiler [329].

Page 168

made for uneasiness—Kerensky [204] p. 256.

cautioned Kerensky—Sukhanov [120] II, pp. 209–11 and 323–33.

formation of soviets—Peshekhonov [248] p. 461.

Page 169

Anarchists in Moscow—for the Bolsheviks, see Chapter 2; for the S.-R.s, see *Izvestya*, 4 March 1917, p. 5, col. 3. This passage is missing —the only one—in the *Dokumenty* [34b] p. 414. For the Anarchists, see GAORSSMo [11b] 66, 3, 262, 26.

Petrograd firms—Zlokazov [331] pp. 103ff.

large plants were also conciliatory—Artenev [332] pp. 122–8.

noted Shlyapnikov—Shlyapnikov [125] p. 199.

Page 170

Bolsheviks per factory—*Sotsial-Demokrat*, 18 March 1917.

number of soldiers—Sukhanov [120] II, p. 226.

resolve current problems—*Pravda* and *Izvestya*, 17 March 1917.

1,487 members—the enquiry, town by town, is published in *Dokumenty* [34b] pp. 320–53. See Document 25, pp. 358–60, a summary of the results for seven towns answering the questionnaire; also An-weiler [329].

half of that of Nizhni-Novgorod—*Dokumenty* [34b] pp. 320–53.

workers' soviets of the region—Razgon [333] pp. 83–123.

Page 171

nevertheless sent delegates—on these sectional soviets, which had an important role after July, see no. [334] in the Bibliography.

not lacking in generosity—on the new law, created by workers and peasants, see Chapter 4 and the work of Tokarev [356].

Page 172

error committed by the Soviet—*Izvestya*, 2 March 1917.

make Russia a democracy—*Rabochaya Gazeta*, 7 March 1917, p. 1.

Page 173

13 against 3 in Moscow—Axelrod Archive [13] 1249–X (letter from Uritsky to Axelrod).

were the least organized—Radkey [297] p. 130.

at Tselyabinsk—Sukhanov [120] II, p. 98; TSGAORSSSR [11] 3, 1, 363, 81.

Chernov and Natanson—*ibid.*

was against a workers' government—*Izvestya*, 8 March 1917, p. 6; Sukhanov [120] II, p. 98.

put pressure on the government—quoted in *Kut.* [25] pp. 58–9.

urged solidarity—*Izvestya*, 4 March 1917, p. 5.

Page 174

reasons as the Mensheviks—cf. review of the Cooperative Movement Congress of 30 March 1917 in *Doc. Ker.* [35] III, pp. 1201–2.

displeasure of the Bolsheviks—see Garvi's unpublished MS. in *Doc. Ker.* [35] II, pp. 752–3.

an old story—N. Glebof, *Le Rôle des syndicats ouvriers dans la révolution russe*, publ. les jeunes socialistes romandes, n.d., 16 pp.; *Dok.* [20] pp. 462 and 471.

metalworkers with the Bolsheviks—see the Naglovsky Ms. in *Doc. Ker.* [35] II, pp. 762–4.

not to have a share of the power—25 March 1917, at a meeting of the Cadet party, quoted in Morokhovets [347] p. 132.

The Bolsheviks were of the opposite—see the general works on the history of the Bolshevik Party, notably Schlesinger [305] and Souvarine, *Staline* [281] pp. 142–6.

Page 175
well enough to speak to them—Shlyapnikov [125] p. 165.

the Soviet-Duma agreement—*ibid.*, I, pp. 167 and 185.

condition that it be unarmed—*ibid.*, p. 199.

in favor of a revolutionary government—*ibid.*, p. 209; *Pravda*, 9 March 1917.

formation of a Liaison Commission—Moscow Archives in *Dok.* [20] p. 45.

"all power to the soviets"—*ibid.*, *Dok.* [20] p. 60.

place at such a rapid pace—*Pravda*, 14 March 1917.

Page 176
know how to keep it—*Dok.* [20] p. 86.

Systematic opposition—*Pravda*, 14 March 1917.

ouster of Kamenev—*Dok.* [20] p. 87f; this is a section of Petrograd on the right bank of the Neva.

serious political error—*Dok.* [20] p. 133.

Tula, Baku, and Tiflis—*Kut.* [25] p. 70.

Rabochaya Gazeta—Moscow Archives, *Dok.* [20]; *Rabochaya Gazeta*.

Page 177
Ukraine's *Nabat*—cf. Makhno [229]; Woodcock and Avakumovitch [320] pp. 388ff; Joll [321] p. 174f.

been settled in their favor—*Izvestya*, 9 March 1917, p. 3, col. 2.

neither rich nor poor—text in Shlyapnikov [125] II, Appendix, p. 295.

Page 178
to overthrow the government—*Izvestya*, 8 April 1917, p. 3, col. 4 and p. 4, col. 1.

Page 179
provisional committee—*Izvestya*, and *Rabochaya Gazeta*, 17 March 1917.

to take down a barricade—Knox [215] p. 574.

everything to my commissariat—Peshekhonov [248] pp. 441–4.

Page 180

abolition of the death penalty—*Doc. Ker.* [35] I, pp. 192ff.

return visas for the *émigrés*—he gave, on the contrary, instructions to hold back *émigrés* on the Allies list of "suspects", that is, the Internationalists, "Bulletin d'information, 20 April 1917", *Service des renseignements généraux, Archives de la Guerre* [14].

trade unions were not invited—*Dok.* [20] p. 434.

which interested no one—*Doc. Ker.* [35] I, pp. 243–50.

decided to nationalize them—*ibid.*, II, pp. 523–4.

in the Kazan Region—*ibid.*, p. 585; *Dok.* [20] p. 431.

would not be settled soon—*Doc. Ker.* [35] II, p. 524.

name of the Moscow Soviet—*Rabochaya Gazeta*, 7 March 1917, p. 2; GAORSSLo [12] 1000, 73, 7, 1–6.

Page 181

thanks to the pressure—*Izvestya*, 6 March 1917, p. 3, col. 4 and 9 March 1917, p. 2.

against the Soviet decision—*Kut.* [25] p. 100.

a pay raise, etc—Moscow Archives, *Dok.* [20] pp. 229–31 and 446.

by not obeying it—*Rabochaya Gazeta*, 8 March 1917, p. 2

before making any demands—*ibid.*, 10 March 1917.

transportation workers—*Izvestya*, 14 March 1917, p. 5.

firms made no concessions—*ibid.*, 28 March 1917, p. 3.

conditions did not improve—*Pravda*, 21 March 1917, p. 3.

grievance committees—text in *Izvestya*, 11 Narch 1917.

an accomplished fact—Sukhanov [120] II, p. 275.

concessions with ill grace—Moscow Archives, *Dok.* [20] pp. 360, 364ff.

solution of the food problem—this is based on Volobuev's remarkable exposition [354] pp. 389ff.

Page 182

principle affecting wheat—TSGAORSSSR [11] 3, 1, 314, 20.

death sentence of the wheat industry—Rodzianko wrote to Shingarev to this effect (TSGAORSSSR [11] 3, 1, 286, 20–21).

price of wheat sixty percent—TSGAORSSSR [11] 3, 1, 314, 215–225.

the needs of the population—*Doc. Ker.* [35] II, pp. 618–9.

Page 183

Articles 3 and 4—*ibid.*, pp. 260–1.

On April 11—*ibid.*, pp. 621–2.

machinations of the *pomeshchiki*—*Izvestya*, 23 April 1917.

Page 184

too harsh with the officers—Shlyapnikov [125] I. p. 89.

delegates' rights were limited—*ibid.*, III, pp. 70–2; *Izvestya*, 5 March 1917, col. 1.

Page 185

legally constituted government—see Shlyapnikov [125] II, pp. 282–3.

That was the price asked—*HRR* [126] I, pp. 115–16.

Orders 114 and 115—text in *Doc. Ker.* [35] II, pp. 853–4.

Page 186

dignity of the soldiers—text and discussion in Shlyapnikov [125] II, pp. 99f. and 283.

Alexeiev refused to have—*Doc. Ker.* [35] II, p. 880.

The Government had to withdraw—*Izvestya*, 10 March 1917, and 14 March 1917; Sukhanov [120] II, p. 179.

answered Guchkov—Moscow Archives, *Dok.* [20] p. 429.

Page 187

departure of the soldiers—Shlyapnikov [125] II, p. 136–8. Since the February days there had been a workers' militia, but it had been more or less integrated into the urban militia set up by the government and entrusted with maintaining order in the capital. See Startsev [363] ch. 2.

greetings of the Revolution—*Doc. Ker.* [35] II, p. 866.

groups of armed soldiers—Sukhanov [120] II, p. 307.

There were several incidents—particularly in Moscow; cf. *Dok.* [20] p. 383.

doing their duty to their country—until April, many of the soldiers' letters maintain that, if the workers complain of having to work over 8 hours a day, soldiers have to stay all 24 hours of the day in the cold of the trenches (GAORSSLo [12] 7384, 9, 259, letters 42ff). Sailors maintained the same (TSGAORSSSR [11] 1244, 1, 15, 118—2nd crew of the Baltic fleet). But there were also soldiers who deplored the misunderstandings that set workers and soldiers against each other (GAORSSMo [11b] 3, 262, 60).

Page 188

its glorious allies—text in *Doc. Ker.* [35] II, p. 1042.

the former government—*Dok.* [20] p. 429.

interview with the *Daily Chronicle*—Kerensky [124] p. 130.

the damage was done—*Daily Chronicle*, 23 March 1917.

Rabochaya Gazeta gave this information—*Rabochaya Gazeta*, 7 March 1917, p. 3.

poor Russia in particular—*ibid.*, 8 March 1917, p. 2.

Conquer Tsarigrad—*ibid.*, 9–11 March 1917.

question were broken off—*ibid.*, 8 March 1917, p. 2.

Page 189

page 3 of *Pravda*—*Pravda*, 10 March 1917.

time for defeatist proposals—*ibid.*, 14 March 1917.

Executive Committee of the Moscow Soviet—Moscow Archives, *Dok.* [20] p. 244.

"War to Victory"—*Izvestya*, 17 March 1917.

matter up to the Constituent—GAORSSLo [12] *fond* 6384; similarly, for the sailors, TSGIAL [12b] 1278,5,1329,1–4.

something more political—Sukhanov [120] II, *passim*.

Page 190

foreign military might—text in *Izvestya*, 14 March 1917; complete text Document 21, p. 353.

met no opposition—*K. Narodam vsego mira* (Petrograd, 1917, 15pp) 12–15.

Novo-Nikolayevsk Soviet—*Dok.* [20] p. 29.

"Socialist International Congress"—*ibid.*, p. 300; Ryazan Archives, *ibid.*, p. 302.

extra appropriation—*Izvestya*, 19 March 1917.

she was booed—Tseretelli [127] I, p. 83.

Both led to civil war—*ibid.*

Page 191

establish relations with the government—Sukhanov [120] II, p. 270; Tseretelli [127] I, pp. 45–59.

without annexation or indemnities—for instance the Ufa Soviet, in *Dok.* [20] p. 303.

right of the strongest—printed in *Doc. Ker.* [35] II, p. 1044.

Page 192

amalgamation in our Ukraine—*New York Times*, 8 April 1917 (26 March old style).

firmly opposed to this idea—Milyukov [122] p. 85.

of the Liaison Committee—Tseretelli [127] I, pp. 59–77 and 66.

to humiliate anyone—*Doc. Ker.* [35] II, p. 1045.

was trying to sneak by—Nabokov [237] pp. 59–60.

Russia had renounced her agreements—*Doc. Ker.* [35] II, p. 1058.

this beautiful success—*Novoe Vremya* and *Rech'*, and "bourgeois" papers, and *Delo Naroda*, 28 March 1917, quoted in Radkey [297] p. 156.

Page 193

combat effectiveness of the Army—*Vserossiyskoe* [34a] p. 291.

CHAPTER SEVEN

THE APRIL CRISIS

Page 195

EUROPE AND THE RUSSIAN REVOLUTION—the present writer is preparing a work on this subject. See also the works cited in the Bibliography, nos. [407ff]. On the recognition of the new régime by the Allies, see Chapter 2, p.82.

Köln. Volkszeitung—*Köln. Volkszeitung*, 16 March 1917, quoted in *Daily Mail*, 17 March 1917.

Kölnische Zeitung—*Kölnische Zeitung*, quoted in *Bulletin periodique de la presse allemande*, 23 June 1917, p. 4.

other Viennese dailies—*Neues Wiener Journal*, quoted by *Le Matin*, 19 March 1917.

78 in June—figures reached by General Buat in *Doc. Ker.* [35] II, p. 921.

against the Russians—figures given in Yoffe [410].

view to continuing the war—*Leipzig Volkszeitung*, quoted in *Bulletin . . . allemande*, 26 March 1917, p. 39. *Vorwärts'* judgements vacillated between these two lines.

disintegration to do its work—see the accounts of Ludendorff and Bethmann Hollweg.

Page 196

the German Prime Minister—cf. the work of Zeman [413] and Fischer [417] ch. 13.

sent out to Stockholm—Kolyshko negotiations in *Doc. Ker.* [35] p. 1065.

and Copenhagen—Kleinov-Trotsky conversations in *Doc. Ker.* [35] p. 1065 (not L. Trotsky).

cf. Maxim Gorky—*Doc. Ker.* [35] p. 1073.

become a Social-Patriot—cf. Zeman and Scharlau [414] pp. 206–35.

Zimmerwaldians—Tseretelli [127] I, p. 279f.

Stockholm Conference—Dan's motion, following the Berne committee's invitation in *KA* [26] 1926, p. 70.

Page 197

business of the international proletariat—Rosa Luxemburg, *Spartakus-Briefe* (Berlin, 1920) quoted in K. Mammach, *Die russische Revolution*, p. 13.

Russian Revolution as a catastrophe—this is evident from the instructions given to the censors, which will be shown in a work at present under preparation by the author.

Page 198

pursuit planes—see Yoffe [410]. Colonel Knox was at the bottom of this measure, see Knox [215] I, p. 575.

put up a brave front—*Gazzeta del Popolo*, 5 April 1917; cf. the incidents related in *Giornale d'Italia*, 17 March 1917.

political coreligionists—Ribot, *Correspondance et Journal et correspondances inedites* (1914–1922) (Paris) p. 230.

Albert Thomas—*KA* [26] III, pp. 67–8; Yoffe [410] p. 116.

Page 199

counteract Bolshevik propaganda—Nekludoff [239] p. 304.

Independent Labour Party—see this war of telegrams in *Izvestya*, 24 April 1917.

dared to endorse this trip—Bantke, *Bor'ba za sozdanie kommunisticheskoy partii Frantsii* (Moscow, 1936) p. 135.

explained Marcel Cachin—Shlyapnikov in *KA* [26] (1926) p. 65.

as do the Russian Socialists—*KA* [26] XV, p. 62; *Doc. Ker.* [35] p. 1051.

Sukhanov commented—Sukhanov [120] III, p. 191.

made a condition for peace—the most detailed account is in *KA* [26] and Tseretelli [127]. Apart from the accounts of Paléologue [244], Buchanan [175] etc., there is a useful interview with M. Moutet in R. Kohn, *La Révolution russe* (Paris, 1963) p. 190.

Page 200

League of Nations—see *KA* [26].

Novoe Vremya—Yoffe [410] p. 120.

in Kerensky's translation—de Chambrun [181].

Page 201

What then?—Tseretelli [127] I, p. 185.

exaltation of a successful Revolution—"They find Moutet too muddled", said General Janin.

homeland of the Revolution—Marsel Kashen (Marcel Cachin), "Moi vstrechi s Leninym", *Novaya i Noveyshaya Istoriya*, 1956–9 p. 26.

learned something from the Soviet—Nekludoff [239] p. 304.

Page 202

he is a true Socialist *Popolo d'Italia*, 25 March 1917.

but it is not Socialism—*ibid.*

influential as they would like to be—*Justice*, 12 April 1917.

Page 203

from the return of Alexinsky—Sukhanov [120] III, p. 153.

Anarchist circles—cf. Woodcock and Avakumovitch [320] p. 388f.

collaboration between the two powers—*Rabochaya Gazeta*, 17 March 1917, p. 2.

Boris Souvarine—*Journal du Peuple*, 19 March 1917.

turn them to the Left—*Berner Tagwacht*, 5 April 1917. These fears were not wholly without foundation: in a letter to Kautsky on 28th March (new style), L. Martov "had confidence in the Siberian exiles, Tseretelli, etc., to give direction to the movement" (Kautsky Archive [13] D.XVI, 418–22).

don't have to follow them—*Avanti*, 2 April 1917.

to face the bourgeois parties—Chernov [179] *passim.*

when he arrived in Petrograd—Sukhanov [120] II, p. 152.

without annexations nor indemnities—Radkey [297] p. 156.

Page 204

until the beginning of May—Deutscher [283] p. 211f. On Chicherin, see Nabokov [237], Warth [407] and *The Call.*

to Ganetsky—Krupskaya [217] pp. 264–5.

But Lenin agreed wholeheartedly—*Leninsky Sbornik,* II, p. 385, quoted in *Kut.* [25] p. 114.

for the *Bund*—*Izvestya,* 5 April 1917, p. 2, col. 1.

but not Romain Rolland—H. Guilbeaux, *La Fin des soviets,* p. 30.

Page 205

Austro-German—text in *Doc. Ker.* [35].

demoralization of the army—on these matters, see Rytich, Zeman [413], Fischer [417] etc.

Comrade Chkheidze—H. Guilbeaux, *Du Kremlin au cherche-midi,* p. 92.

Kollontay's first instructions—the paragraphs on arming the proletariat and non-alliance with other parties are missing.

Lenin had made his plans—quoted in Shub [312] p. 72, following a text in Parvus, *Pravda glaza kolet,* which I have been unable to see. Cf. similarly Zeman and Scharlau [414]. On Lenin's activity from April to July 1917, see the works cited in the Bibliography, mainly Shub, Bruhat, Schlesinger, Schapiro.

underground action—see Krupskaya [217] p. 263f.

Kerensky and Company—Lenin [35] p. 238.

à la Trotsky—quoted in *Kut.* [26] p. 70.

Ulyanov—Lenin [23] p. 287.

Page 206

only of Kerensky—*ibid.,* p. 285.

Page 207

The Paris Commune—*ibid.,* pp. 285–324.

a shopkeeper to be honest—*ibid.,* p. 331f.

have to wait for his return—*Dok. Apr.* [21] *passim.*

Page 208

World Socialist Revolution—Sukhanov [120] pp. 269ff.

Page 209

as though he's gone crazy—quoted by Abramovitch [160] p. 30.

Steklov or Chkheidze—*Dok. Apr.* [21] p. 30f.

fight an all out battle—*ibid.*, pp. 57–9.

Page 210

April Theses—Petrogradskaya obshchegorodskaya vserossiyskaya konferentsia RSDRP (Bol'shevikov) v aprele 1917g (Moscow, 1925) p. 10f.

was the main problem—see Chapter 6; TSGAORSSSR [11] *fondy* 3 and 1235.

Page 211

of a rallying cry—*ibid.; Izvestya*, 11 April 1917, p. 8 and the following days.

the orders of the Soviet—Sukhanov [120] III, p. 81.

attain general peace—*Izvestya*, 30 April 1917.

Page 212

a patriotic speech—Tseretelli [127] English edn., p. 97 and n. 33.

peace was quite popular—cf. Pares [245] p. 427; Knox [215] etc.

Page 213

to halt the war now—Sukhanov [120] III, p. 112.

battle of the slogans—*ibid.* Just the same, he received messages in favour of "war to the bitter end", cf. GAORSSLo [12] 7384, 9, 158.

explains Milyukov—Milyukov [233] pp. 339–40.

the rights of the country—*ibid.*, p. 341.

Russia's war aims—see Chapter 6.

"Milyukov note"—see Chernov [123] and Tseretelli [127] I.

Page 214

Milyukov to Paléologue—Milyukov [233] pp. 354–8.

draft a note—Sukhanov [120] III, p. 270; Tseretelli [127] I, pp. 80–5.

this Guizot—quoted, particularly, in Radkey [297] p. 159.

modify their interpretation—Warth [407] p. 156; Bruce-Lockhart [173] p. 82.

this would be premature—in Yoffe [410] p. 76.

confirmation of his own analysis—Milyukov [233] II, p. 360 and [122] p. 93.

Page 215

a durable peace—*Dok. Apr.* [21] p. 725.

Milyukov is the evil genius—Tseretelli [127] I, p. 87.

Kerensky spoke of resigning—Milyukov [233] p. 362.

control over the government—*Dok. Apr.* [21] pp. 777–830. The messages came from Yaroslav, Smolensk, Tver, Rybinsk, Podol'sk, Tula etc. cf. GAORSSLo [12] 7384, 7, 36, items 29, 33, 37, 40, 63; and *ibid.*, 7384, 9, 564, items 1–13.

aim of the demonstration—Woitinsky [273] pp. 270–1.

"All Power to the Soviet"—*Dok. Apr.* (21) *passim.*

Page 216

the government to yield—Tseretelli [127] I, pp. 77–107.

civil war—quoted in Trotsky [121].

The Soviet was taking over—*Dok. Apr.* [21] p. 730; Woitinsky [273] pp. 271ff.

statements of the opposition—Sukhanov [120] II, p. 280.

ready to leave—Tseretelli [127] I, pp. 194ff.

Page 217

Otherwise, we're leaving—Stalin [257] III, pp. 43–7; *Dok. Apr.* [21] p. 737.

Tseretelli and Nekrassov—Tseretelli [127] I, pp. 77–107.

yield to the Soviet—Lenin in [24] p. 184.

"capitalist ministers"—enquiry (opinion) following *Dok. Apr.* [21] and four daily newspapers in the capital.

as one of them said—Tsernik's account in *Dok. Apr.* [21] p. 742.

Page 218

decided to seize the capital—*ibid.;* Sereda's report in *Dok. Apr.* [21] p. 743; *Izvestya*, 23 April 1917; see also *Delo Naroda*, 25 April 1917.

counter-demonstrators—*Dok. Apr.* [21] pp. 742–7.

dead and wounded—*Delo Naroda*, 25 April 1917. The fight began with the crowd, not the counter-demonstrators.

Kornilov resigned—*Dok. Apr.* [21] *passim.*

Petrograd resumed its—the Soviet received numerous messages of solidarity (GAORSSLo [12] 7384, 7, 36, items 52ff). Most of them accused Milyukov, but some explicitly condemned Leninist propaganda.

Kamenev was jeered—*Pravda* published the more moderate appeals only on 29 April 1917, at a date when Lenin had seen his mistake (cf. Lenin [24] p. 212) cf. also the petition of 7,000 army electricians and Lenin [24] p. 211.

Page 219

international tribunals—text in *Doc. Ker.* [35] II, p. 1100.

"no annexations or contributions"—*ibid.*, pp. 1100–1.

the April 18th note—Milyukov [122] *passim*.

they made him realize it—*ibid.*, [233] *passim*.

his relations with the Soviet—*Protokoly soveta* in [29] pp. 216–18.

Page 220

animators of the "movement"—Tseretelli [127] I, pp. 107–38.

the great offensive—the main speeches are in *Doc. Ker* [35] III, p. 1258f; commentaries in Tseretelli [127] I, pp. 319ff.

together they spell treason—*ibid.*

against democracy had failed—*ibid.* Up to this time, "democracy" had tolerated the survival of the Duma. But from now on, there are increasingly numerous messages demanding its dissolution—thus the officials of the Kiev railway management as early as 27 April 1917 (TSGIAL [12b] 1278, 5, 1231, 198ff).

"resistance" and reaction—Prince Lvov wrote to Chkheidze to support this step (TSGAORSSSR [11] 3, 1, 286, 39).

this was premature—Sukhanov [120] III, p. 389; Tseretelli [127] *passim; Doc. Ker.* [35] pp. 1252ff.

Page 221

gravitated around the Soviet—Tseretelli [127] pp. 107–38.

Stalin remarked ironically—*ibid.*

Mensheviks could soon take part—Milyukov [122] p. 101. He did of course say this on 1 April.

Left Socialist Revolutionaries—a remark of Radkey's.

hopes among the working class—Abramovitch [160] p. 39.

Page 222

which should be avoided—Radkey [297] p. 144.

represented the will of the people—Kerensky [203] p. 269.

As a last gesture—Woitinsky [263] p. 276; *Archives de la Guerre* [16] Na.6, telegram 699.

there was no more debate—Sukhanov [120] III, *passim*.

Page 223
vote of 44 to 19—*ibid*.

collaboration with the masses—Steinberg [260] p. 22.

He prevailed—Tseretelli [127] I, p. 142.

Page 224
accepted all these amendments—Stankevich [259] p. 128.

we couldn't have done any better—Tseretelli [127] I, p. 144.

more than 2000 votes—*ibid*.

They won—see Radkey [297], the best account of the S.-R.s.

Page 225
continuing the war and assuming power—Stankevich [259] pp. 130–2.

Page 226
and they had won—Sukhanov [120] III, p. 410f.

CHAPTER EIGHT

THE COALITION EXPERIMENT

Page 227
a People's Parliament—in May, as in April, the Soviet received numerous motions to this effect, cf. GAORSSLo [12] 7384, 9, files 154, 159, 161.

Page 228
only a forced sympathy—*Rech'* and *Izvestya*, 10 and 11 May 1917.

Page 229
vague as it had been in the past—this is based on Radkey [297] pp. 88 and 232; and *Rezolyutsii* [153]. Kerensky, member of the Trudovik group, maintained his links with the right wing of his old party. Without telling him, his former leaders even wanted him elected to the Presidium. The War Minister was in Moscow when he learnt from the newspapers that he had been both nominated and beaten, when a Left S.-R. accused him of having reintroduced the

death penalty at the front. Chernov, though present at the debate, had not publicly intervened to deny this (conversation with Kerensky, September 1966).

Page 230

Narodnoe Slovo—Protokoly [152].

Right of the S.-R.—Myakotin [146] pp. 7–9; telegram D, June 1917, in *BPP* [43].

Page 231

United States of Europe—Trotsky [155]; *BPP* [43], in the week 9–16 May 1917; Sukhanov [120] IV.

insist on immediate action—Dosch-Fleurot, *Through War and Revolution* (London, 1920, 242pp.) p. 178.

Page 232

No one listened—*Dok. Apr.* [21] pp. 128ff.

with the Second International—Schapiro [306] p. 165.

North Baltic region—*Dok. Apr.* [21] pp. 856 and 885.

Page 233

about sixty organizations—*Dok. Mai.* [22] *passim.*

notably Tseretelli—the existence of a "workers' militia" (see Chapter 6) and the fear that the military would react mistrustfully, meant that formation of Red Guards was delayed—though these had been desired since March and recommended by Lenin in his third "Letter from afar". The April incidents showed how vulnerable workmen were when they organised a pacific demonstration; from then on, no delay was permitted in formation of a Red Guard. On this, see Startsev [363].

organizational staff it needed—BV despatch, 19 May 1917.

Page 234

set for September 17th—neither the Menshevik-S.-R. "majority" not the members of the government were in a hurry to submit themselves to the verdict of universal suffrage. Chernov's motives have been explained (p. 203); despite the promises made on 2 March, Guchkov hoped to put off the elections "until peace", *Bulletin des renseignements généraux, Archives de la guerre* [16] 16 April 1917.

Page 235
Revolutionary spirit in the army—see the Bibliography, nos. [390ff.]
Claimed *Rech—Rech'*, 16 June 1917.
with total ruin—*Rabochaya Gazeta*, 26 May 1917.
right of self-determination—*Edinstvo*, 22 May 1917, in *BPP* [43], 22 May–4 June.

Page 236
setting of their own boundaries—*Pravda*, quoted in *BPP* [43], 14–27 May 1917.

peace that could be concluded—Tseretelli [127] I, p. 256. His friend Abramovitch was not, it seems, as optimistic.

steps with its government—*ibid.*, pp. 169–392; Abramovitch [160] pp. 45ff.

Russia's foreign relations—for instance, with Japan, cf. his conversations with Ushida (in the text, Utsida) in *KA* [26] XXV, p. 149.

policy will be established—Tseretelli [127] I, p. 370; *Doc. Ker.* [35] II, p. 1121.

Page 237
sincerity in this matter—Tseretelli [127] I, p. 343.

skepticism and hostility—cf. the letter from Axelrod printed in *Rabochaya Gazeta*, 27 March 1917, p. 2.

establishment of general peace—*Rech'*, 17–30 May 1917.
be careful to avoid—quoted by Tseretelli [127] I, p. 281.
instead of toppling it—see *Pravda*, 16 June 1917, and a letter, signed "K. R." in *Pravda*, noting the insurrectional movements in Germany (1 July 1917). Chernov also believed this (Tseretelli [127] I, p. 361).

Page 238
our internal foe—Radek, "Die russische Revolution und der Friede", *Zimmerwald* [39], pp. 1864–5, 3 May 1917.

French and English bankers—cf. an article signed "G.R." in *Pravda*, quoted in *BPP* [43] 8–21 June 1917; *Rabochaya Gazeta*, 17 May 1917.

enslaved nations of Asia—BP despatch, 14–27 June 1917; *BPP* [43] 10–23 June 1917.

cessation of hostilities—this theme is taken up several times in *Vperyod*.

between the people—*Vperyod*, 7 June 1917, p. 5.

collapse of our freedom—at the Soviet Congress.

Page 239

fraternization campaign—Trotsky [155].

for a Socialist Revolution—Chernov [123] p. 290.

the Soviet position—Vasyukov [408] has shown how the Provisional Government, though disappointed with Wilson's attitude, none the less came closer to the U.S.A.

March 27 Declaration—the texts are in *Doc. Ker.* [35] II, pp. 1106–10.

The French bourgeoisie—*Rabochaya Gazeta*, 27 May 1917.

Page 240

a compromise peace—Chernov [123] p. 290.

concluded *Izvestya*—*Izvestya*, 21 May 1917.

knowing our cause is just—*Novaya Zhizn'*, 6 June 1917; *Zemlya i Volya*, 30 May 1917.

Page 241

Allied mission's intervening—cf. p. 25.

how many were shot—*Archives de la guerre* [16] Na.6, Carton 4 (coded telegrams).

The marked sympathy—*ibid.*, Cartons 4–9. The question of Russian divisions in France only latterly took on a political aspect.

Page 242

help the new régime—Yoffe [410]; and Janin's telegram of 9 April 1917 (see for instance, *Archives de la guerre* [16] telegram of Thomas, no. 91, Na.6, Carton 4).

American aid would carry—*Kut.* [25] p. 129; *Ek. Pol.* [24] pp. 536ff.

outcome of the Revolution—the most complete account—from the Russian point of view—is in Tseretelli [127] I, pp. 169–341.

Axelrod in Switzerland—*Rabochaya Gazeta*, 27 March 1917, p. 2.

Borgberg—Tseretelli [127] I, p. 272.

Page 243

meeting of a conference—cf. Meynell [419].

International Socialist Bureau—Tseretelli [127] and Meynell [419].

March 14/27 appeal—texts in *Doc. Ker.* [35] II, pp. 1169–72.

Page 244

toward Cachin or Moutet—4 May 1917, in *BPP* [43] 4–17 May 1917.

removed from the Soviet viewpoint—quoted in Warth [407] p. 69.

little Belgium's misfortunes—quoted in Tseretelli [127].

applied Socialist economics—*ibid.*, I, pp. 199ff.

Page 245

answered Henderson—*ibid.*, I, p. 202.

brightest ray of hope—Vandervelde [269] French edn., pp. 237–8.

representatives of international Socialism—hence the petition campaign in favour of Friedrich Adler, condemned to death after assassinating Count Stürgkh, cf. GAORSSLo [12] 7384, 9, file 172.

Congress of 1900—Tseretelli [127] *passim*.

Page 246

"Kaiser's Socialists"—*ibid.*, I, pp. 309ff.

views on war and peace—text in Tseretelli [127] I, pp. 224 (mid-April).

a means of agreement—text in *Doc. Ker.* [35] II, p. 1172.

Page 247

which side is right—Tseretelli [127] I, p. 213.

motions passed at Stockholm—the principal texts will be found in Gankin and Fisher [37] and Tseretelli [127] I, p. 307f.

Page 248

Reserved for Bolshevik Delegates—on this, see Gankin and Fisher [37] and Tseretelli [127] I, pp. 390ff.

"Grimm Affair"—on the Grimm Affair, to the works cited should be added *Doc. Ker.* [35] II, p. 1178, which gives seven documents.

Page 249

Grimm was deported—Tseretelli gives the most complete account [127] pp. 243–56; see also Gankin and Fisher [37] pp. 621ff.

"poor internationalist"—Gankin and Fisher [37] p. 623.

Page 250

disloyal to his comrades—based on Tseretelli's account.

that he could succeed—Zeman [413] pp. 46ff.

Page 251

moderates considered monstrous—Tseretelli [127] pp. 312ff.

Lenin scolded him—*ibid.*

Page 252

thousands at Ekaterinoslav—PTA despatches. On the Army, see nos. [22], [32], [35], [124] in the Bibliography.

Then we'll see what he says—in *Soldat Grazhdanin,* quoted in *BPP* [43], 25 May 1917. This was on old idea that had turned up as early as March, cf. TSGIAL [12b] 1278, 5, 1251, 48.

Page 253

contingent of volunteers—Tseretelli [127] I, p. 406.

toward Guchkov—*ibid.,* p. 412.

Page 254

Polivanov's proposal—Kerensky [124] pp. 183ff.

this trickery in *Pravda*—*Pravda,* 15 May 1917.

and miserable combat—Kerensky [124] p. 195.

Page 255

but they were never slaves—*Doc. Ker.* [35] II, pp. 913–14.

Page 256

willingness to die—Kerensky [124] p. 195.

remain with his comrades—*ibid.,* p. 203.

Page 258

SITUATION THREE WEEKS LATER—*Dok. Mai.* [22] pp. 348–51.

Page 259

Elsewhere everything is in order—*ibid.,* pp. 372–3.

than a hundred effectives—NJ despatch, *BPP* [43].

Page 260

only from the officers—see Tseretelli [127] II, pp. 17ff.

effect on morale—*BPP* [43] 13–26 May 1917.

is worst of all—*Razlozhenie Armii* [32] p. 91.

140,000 deserters—in Yoffe [410] p. 179.

mount an offensive—*ibid.*

"infectious patriotism"—Chernov [123] p. 382.

Kerensky finally ordered—on officer pressure, cf. GAORSSLo [12] 7384, 9, file 228. According to the War Minister, the Allied mission's intervention had little effect (conversation with Kerensky, September 1966).

CHAPTER NINE

THE COALITION EXPERIMENT (CONTINUED)

Page 262

different in the provinces—*Dok. Mai.* [22] pp. 270ff.

high-level management—*Utro-Rossii*, 22 June 1917, in *BPP* [43].

most popular claim by far—BV despatch, 28 June 1917, in *BPP*.

Page 263

as the committee wished—Chernov [123] p. 217.

200 in chemicals—TSGAORSSSR [11] 3, 1, 324, 144.

Page 264

longer work day—*Doc. Ker.* [35] II, p. 717.

"No work, no pay"—*Ek. Pol.* [24] I, pp. 404–5.

was the world coming to—Tseretelli [127] p. 433; *BPP* [43] 23 June 1917.

What was the government—BV despatch, 10 May 1917, in *BPP*.

"social" expenses—Volobuev [354] pp. 19–87.

Page 265

industrial organization—text in *Doc. Ker.* [35] III, p. 1276.

agreement would be enforced—*BPP* [43] 23 April 1917.

eight-hour law was passed—following the factories, the provincial Soviets, in turn, made this demand (TSGAORSSSR [11] 3,1, file 324).

Page 266

upsetting the whole economy—V. A. Auerbakh, 'Revolyutsionnoe obshcestvo po lishnym vospominaniyam", *ARR* [27] XIV, pp. 13–14.

Page 267

introduced in England—quoted in Volobuev [354] p. 65.

Management and government—Sack [254] p. 261.

Page 268

State's authority—*Ek. Pol.* [24] I, p. 167; Volobuev [354] *passim.*

no important result—at the end of April the third extra-ordinary assembly of representatives of the Exchanges of Commerce and Agriculture adopted a project for concentration and co-ordination of the exploitation of solid fuel (TSGAORSSSR [11] 3, 1, 314, 215–25).

manufacturers of machine-tools—on 19 April 1917 Konovalov had written to Prince Lvov that he hoped a monopoly of *sales* of coal would free exchange (TSGAORSSSR [11] 3, 1, 324, 109).

wool supplies—*Doc. Ker.* [35] II, p. 699.

Page 269

committee charged with the—Volobuev [354] pp. 169–299.

agricultural community—see Chapter 6.

policy about finances—Volobuev [354] pp. 300–82.

those at the rear as well—*Den'*, 10 May 1917.

Tugan-Baranovsky—Volobuev [354] p. 318.

Page 270

10 to 13 billion rubles—*Doc. Ker.* [35] II, p. 509.

American Consul Winship—*ibid.*, p. 510.

backers in the Soviet—*Edinstvo*, 24 May 1917; *Pravda*, 16 May 1917.

to a later date—*Doc. Ker.* [35] II, p. 495.

Shingarev's appeals—BV despatch, 3 June 1917, in *BPP* [43].

this demagogic statement—*Edinstvo*, 24 May 1917; *Pravda*, 16 May 1917.

selfishness of the propertied class—*Pravda*, 30 April and 8 June 1917.

Page 271

commercial secrets—*Ek. Pol.* [24] I, p. 219.

banking operations—Volobuev [354] p. 320.

General Polivanov—*Ek. Pol.* [24] p. 1229; *Doc. Ker.* [35] II, p. 500.

conflict with employees—as Minister for Transport, Nekrassov did try to bring the railwaymen into management; he was called "the Bolshevik Minister" and the suggestion failed. Skobelev recognized the right to strike, but this became public only on 28 June—*Birzhevie Vedomosty*, 3 June 1917.

Number of Strikes—*Dok.* [20] pp. 592–600; *Dok. Apr.* [21] pp. 476–80; *Dok. Mai.* [22] pp. 292–300 and 324–7.

Page 272

supply shortages—quoted in *BPP* [43].

declaration of war—TSGAORSSSR [11] 1235, 53, 10, 83–4.

threat of worker control—Volobuev, in *Voprosy istorii* (1962) 6.

Some shutdowns—BV despatch, 2 June 1917, in *BPP*.

Page 273

bourgeois "Bolshevism"—*Delo Naroda*, 23 June 1917.

Page 275

responsible for its leadership—*Dok. Mai.* [22] p. 293.

professed Bolshevik opinions—see Document 35, p. 372.

Page 276

uniting the factory committees—*Vperyod*, no. 2, p. 7; *Doc. Ker.* [35] II, p. 724.

it was capitalistic—*Doc. Ker.* [35] II, pp. 724–6.

Page 277

was then elected—*ibid.; Dok. Mai.* [22] pp. 290–1.

dominating the Petrograd Soviet—*Doc. Ker.* [35] II, pp. 747f. and 762f.

Stepanov in the government—BV despatch, 21 June 1917, in *BPP*.

Page 278

had left in the Ministers—*Doc. Ker.* [35] II, p. 713.

working-class domination—Volobuev [354] *passim*.

Page 279

the Old Régime—Kotel'nikov [31], to which should be added the material of nos. [20–2] in the Bibliography.

started to act in March—since 6 March in the Kazan district, and since 15 March in the Ryazan district, etc (GAORSSLo [12] 7384, 9, 147, 6f).

Page 280

TABLE—figures arrived at following Kotel'nikov [31] p. 363f.

to remain at large—*Dok.* [20] p. 674.

new agrarian system—*ibid.*, pp. 693–7; *Dok. Apr.* [21] p. 588.

Page 281

fictitious sales—for instance, in the Kazan region (TSGAORSSSR [11] 3, 1, 314, 127.

confirmed by the Revolution—*Dok.* [20].

nothing doing—*Dok. Apr.* [21] p. 587.

the great estates—*ibid.*, p. 578.

Page 282

plenty of potatoes—*ibid.*, p. 581.

makeup caused some concern—*Doc. Ker.* [35] II, pp. 528–32.

Page 283

motion of June 15—*BPP* [43] 15 June 1917; *Doc. Ker.* [35] II, p. 597.

actions of the peasant movement—Morokhovets [347] pp. 142ff.

suppression of the commons—BV despatch, 12 May 1917, in *BPP* [43].

uphold the rights of inequality—Morokhovets [347] p. 145f; *Doc. Ker.* [35] II, p. 605.

got no response—Morokhovets [347] pp. 150–64.

Page 284

with egalitarian principles—*Doc. Ker.* [35] II, p. 597.

utilize the rest—Chernov [134b] p. 21.

defend their privileges—the tone of their recriminations differs from that of the prayers addressed by the proprietors affected by land-grabbing (TSGAORSSSR [11] 3, 1, 302, 135f).

Delo Naroda—Delo Naroda, 16 June 1917.

local agrarian committees—Lenin [129] XXIV pp. 501–21.

bourgeoisie would have invented him—BV despatch, 19 April 1917, in *BPP*.

under a central body—*Doc. Ker.* [35] II, p. 544.

land under the Constituent—Chernov [134b] p. 14f.

Page 285

into central Russia—Chernov [123] pp. 233–54.

not deliver anything—*Izvestya*, 7 June 1917.

Page 286

only two provinces—cf. Volobuev [354] *passim;* similarly an enquiry concerning the *gubernii* of Kazan, Simbirsk, Samara, Ufa which confirms Volobuev's analyses (TSGAORSSSR [11] 3, 1, 361. 62–4).

only risen 53 percent—Volobuev [354] pp. 404–44.

into economic chaos—*Ek. Pol.* [24] I, 16; *Doc. Ker.* [35] II, p. 671.

disaster was at hand—*Novaya Zhizn'*, 23 June 1917. The condition of the Russian economy in 1917 will be discussed in a later volume.

AND THE NATIONAL MINORITIES—see the general Bibliography on the nationalities, nos. [364ff.].

importance went unnoted—von Hedenstom, *Geschichte Russlands 1878–1918* (Berlin, 1922) p. 320.

Page 287

the Kiev Soviet—*Kut.* [25] p. 243; Chernov [123] pp. 264–89.

Armenian delegate—*Petrogradsky* [29] p. 224.
which they might bring up—*Kut.* [25] p. 205.
and even Finland—many of the works on federalism published in 1917 take only the case of these countries: cf. A. F. Salikovsky, *Chtoe takoe avtonomiya i federatsia*, and the works of Dolgorukov, Minor [234] etc.

should be dealt with severely—*Neue Orient*, 25 August 1917, p. 455.

in the Crimea—Dimanshteyn [364] p. 100.

argument also used elsewhere—Vakar [393] pp. 97ff.

paid by Germany—Milyukov [122] p. 142; PTA despatch, 23 May 1917, in *BPP*.

strengthening the garrisons—Park [405] according to Belotsky.

Chauvinists and—Pilenko in *Vechernee Vremya*, 16 June 1917 (a rightwing daily).

Petrograd Soviet rejected this—*Kut.* [25] p. 115.

Page 288

devoid of Bolshevik elements—Choulgine [392] pp. 114–15.

Reval (Estonia)—PTA despatch, 22 May 1917, in *BPP* [43].

to which the nationalists attached—BV despatch, 19 April 1917: the Moscow Soviet opposed the formation of Jewish regiments.

existing Lettish elements—BV despatch, 23 April 1917; on 9 May the "military section" reaffirmed its position.

after the liberation—Filasiewicz [373] p. 193.

aspirations towards federalism—*Vechernee Vremya*, 13 June 1917.

plan for federalism—*Birzhevie Vedomosty*, 15 May 1917.

it will be the foreign policy—*Novoe Vremya*, 14 June 1917.

of a German attack—*Russkaya Volya*, 30 June 1917.

Page 289

the legislative work—see the press of 24 July and the following days; Anon. [143] p. 143.

Vishnyak and Chernov—Dimanshteyn [364] p. 67; for the S.-R.s, see Radkey [297] and Minor [234].

Rada of the Ukraine—Dimanshteyn [364] p. 47.

Page 290

destinies of the national minorities—*Delo Naroda*, 16 May 1917.

for its inertia—Dimanshteyn [364] pp. 48,94 etc; *Den'*, 8 May 1917; *Rabochaya Gazeta*, 23 June 1917.

like A. Sholgin—*Rabochaya Gazeta*, 3 and 15 June 1917.

Lieber and Woitinsky—Dimanshteyn [364] pp. 98–116 gives the main documents.

independence could be achieved—interview by foreign journalists, 7 May 1917. The first number of *Novaya Zhizn'* (17 April 1917) anticipated a referendum in the contested areas—in the overall context of a peace-treaty.

Page 291

Lenin's theses—Lenin [129] XXIV, pp. 305–6. See above, pp. 13 and 108.

national cultural autonomy—on the Bolsheviks' position, see Carr [276], Pipes [365] and Boersner [366].

Provisional Government's policy—"Nothing is more insolent than the Government's uncompromising policy towards the Ukraine", said *Pravda*.

representatives of the two countries—cf. Shlyapnikov [125] III, pp. 355–9.

was never spelled out—"Every people must decide for itself with whom it shall go, once the troops have retired", said Lenin to the Soviet on 16 April (*BPP* despatch [43]; the text is not in the *Complete Works*). Kamenev on 13 May, inviting Russia to leave Finland, Poland, Turkestan, etc., added: "All the armies must leave the contested territories" (in *Pravda*).

Ukraine and Kazan—cf. Murkhayamov, *Oktyabr' : national'ny vopros v Tatarii* (1917–18); Kazan, *Tatknigoizdat* (1958); Bennigsen and Quelquejay [400].

secession, which won out—on 22 May 1917, still, while talking in the Soviet of Lunacharsky and Kamenev, Kerensky said "The Bolsheviks, consciously or unconsciously, don't understand the Finns in their notion of separatism". Probably he was badly informed—certainly he despised the Congress—but the judgment was nevertheless significant.

cultural autonomy for the minorities—*Petrogradsky* [29] I, pp. 122–6.

Universal in Kiev—see Document 36, p. 373.

Page 292
national groups not be alienated—text in Dimanshteyn [364] pp. 114 and 599.

Page 293
Russian Democracy itself—cf. Sakya Muni, *Annales des Nationalités*, 6/7 (1917) pp. 145ff.

could not very well be suspicious—see pp. 242 ff. In fact the Americans were putting pressure on the Finns. Clearly the Allies had no interest in letting the Russian Empire disintegrate; they had too many interests in the Ukraine, etc.

if the war should continue—Troelstra Archive [13] file 580.

ally itself to the bourgeoisie—Adler Archive [13] file 421. This is of course not I. Tseretelli.

minorities of Austro-Hungary—see Chapter 8.

delicate questions could be resolved—after the Sixtus negotiations came those of Armand-Reverts, the German proposals to Russia, and the Papal peace offer. On these questions, see Renouvin [418] pp. 475ff.

end up seceding—Socialist thinkers had made little effort, hitherto, to analyse the character of each nationality movement, the nature or the limits of their aspirations.

Page 294
military congresses—28 May and 6 June 1917 to the Ukrainians, and 4 June to the Estonians.

Chernov remarked—Chernov [123] p. 27.

was rooted in the soil—*ibid.*, pp. 268ff.

demands of the *Rada*—Reshetar [387] *passim.*

Page 295

delegates returned to Kiev—A. Shulgin gives an account of the "mission" he carried out with Stebnisky and others, in *L'Ukraine contre Moscou* [392], pp. 114ff.

Ukraine was also granted—cf. Dimanshteyn [364] pp. 62–3; BV despatch, 30 June and 1 July 1917, in *BPP*.

dangerous precedent—it is not within the scope of this book to deal with the problem of whether the Ukrainian question was merely a pretext for the resignation of Cadet ministers.

March Manifesto—Soderhelm-Henning [381] p. 16.

the Provisional Government—PTA despatch, 14 May 1917.

Page 296

future relations between—a few days earlier he had said "Our generosity must not be understood as weakness and only by the Germans."

certain exports into Finland—cf. *Vechernee Vremya*, 23 June 1917; "These measures will perhaps make the Finns more sensible, whether or not they displease the Germans and the defeatists."

reacted to Finnish acts—the government limited itself to ceding the Finnish Senate some of the Tsar's powers.

role of the governor—"The Finns do not appreciate that immediate separation would expose Russia to an attack by German imperialism" wrote *Rabochaya Gazeta*.

for the July events—cf. the declarations of Urjo Sirola and Karl Wiik at Stockholm; Svenska Telegrambyran despatch, in Adler Archive [13] 27 May 1917.

CHAPTER TEN

THE REVOLUTION GOES ON

Page 298

instructions of the government—on 29 May 1917 the post office workers of Nizhny Novgorod refused to send on to Prince Lvov a telegram from the town's industrialists which demanded that the government put an end to anarchy (TSGAORSSSR [11] 3, 1, 304, 204–5).

along with 5 Mensheviks—BV despatch, 20 May 1917, in *BPP* [43].

equal of Petrograd's—BV despatches, 17 and 29 May 1917, in *BPP*. Fort Ino disapproved unanimously of the decision (GAORSSLo [12] 7384, 9, 170, 121).

Page 299

unswerving fidelity—BV despatch, 21 May 1917, in *BPP*.

answered Tseretelli—Tseretelli [127] p. 427f.

the side of the people—BV despatch, 29 May 1918, in *BPP*.

Kronstadt did not forgive them—cf. Raskolnikov [249] *passim*.

often led by Anarchists—Sukhanov [120] IV, p. 285f.

eight abstentions—*Pervy* [30] p. 120.

Page 300

acts of Vyborg—*ibid*.

magnify the anarchy—*Vperyod*, no. 2, p. 6, 7 June 1917.

Orel, and Samara—BV despatches, 9 May 1917; PTA despatch, 12 May 1917, in *BPP* [43].

Page 301

near Tsarytsin—BV despatch, 8 June 1917, in *ibid*.

declared in Tomsk—RV and DV despatches, 17 and 3 June 1917, in *ibid*.

the PTA Agency—*Vperyod*, 7 June 1917.

in the hands of the Jews—*Izvestya* (Moscow) 27 June 1917; RV despatch, 30 June 1917, in *BPP*.

anti-Semitic propagands—RV despatch, 28 June 1917, in *BPP*.

murder and looting—NJ despatch, 2 July 1917, in *BPP*.

under Bolshevik auspices—NJ despatch, 30 June 1917, in *BPP*.

Page 302

all Jews are Anarchists—in the army, an anti-Semitic campaign was under way from the very first days of the Revolution. On 28 February, Lt. Col. Pisarev gave an order to draw up a list of all Jewish NCOs serving in the rear (order 803, in GAORSSLo [12] 7384, 9, 244, 4 reverse side). See also on development of pogroms, GAORSSLo [12] 7384, 7, 36, items 37ff. We are told that, on the eve of the Revolution, the army restrained the populace from pogroms. It wanted them, no doubt, for itself.

The action was still not—Curtiss [360]; *Doc. Ker.* [35] II, pp. 803ff. To these should be added E. S. Osipov, "The Church and the Provisional Government", *Voprosy istorii*, 1964, 6, pp. 65–76.

majority of the Orthodox clergy—*Doc. Ker.* [35] II, pp. 808ff.

Page 303

churches would be closed—BV despatches, 22 May and 20 June 1917, in *BPP*.

lead of the reaction—cf. *Novaya Zhizn'*, 16 June 1917.

we were Cossackized—BV despatch, 14 June 1917, in *BPP*.

Page 304

Officers of the 3rd Siberian—Tseretelli [127] II, p. 27.

Page 305

of officers is inadmissible—Kerensky [124] *passim*.

Page 306

proclaiming themselves Republicans—Milyukov in the Duma. The same point is made by the creation of a "Republican Centre" in June 1917—its motto being "Order, Discipline, Victory". cf. GAORSSLo [12] 3, 1, 292, 314.

Page 307

than 25,000 members—*Arkhiv Okt. Rev.* [30] I, XXVII.

therefore insignificant—*ibid.*, I.

Page 308

"All Power to the Soviets"—*ibid.*, I, pp. 83ff.

smothered by laughter—*ibid.*, I, pp. 67ff.

Page 309

policemen of the Old Régime—*ibid.*, I, pp. 77ff.

65 absentees—*ibid.*, I, pp. 459–60.

Zimmerwaldism and Anarchy—BV despatch, 25 June 1917, in *BPP*.

Page 310

to the old discipline—there were greatly increasing numbers of motions by front line troops against deserters and rear-troops during June (TSGAORSSSR [11] 1244,1, file 15).

who will leave us in the lurch—*Dok. Mai.* [22] pp. 483ff.

Page 311

Lenin thought—*ibid.*, p. 494.

Page 313

Soldatskaya Pravda Staff—*ibid.*, pp. 494–5.

organized under their auspices—cf. TSGAORSSSR [11] 1294,1,15, 211.

to cause a reaction—Tseretelli [127] II, pp. 203–26; Sukhanov [120] *passim.*

Page 315

still belong to other parties—Tseretelli [127] pp. 226–59; and the fundamental accounts of Sukhanov [120] and Chernov [123].

All calls for demonstrations—text in Tseretelli [127] II, p. 224; *Izvestya*, 13 June 1917.

Page 316

"Support the Provisional Government"—*Izvestya*, 20 June 1917.

the threat of reaction—cf. GAORSSLo [12] 47, 1, 3, 36ff.

Page 317

PEACEFUL DEMONSTRATIONS IS PAST—Lenin [129] XXV, p. 79.

SELECT BIBLIOGRAPHY*

I General

II Archival, documentary, newspaper and other primary sources

III Contemporary accounts

IV General works

V Works on particular aspects of the Revolution

(Numbers in square brackets refer to items in this Bibliography)

I. GENERAL

1 *Guide to Russian Reference Books* by Karol Maichel, ed. J. S. G. Simmons, vol. II, Hoover Institution's Bibliographical Series XVIII, (Stanford University Press, California, 1964) 294pp. This is a basic work, referring to all archival guides and bibliographies in Russian and other languages. For the period of the Revolution, pp. 61–78 should be consulted.

2 *Gosudarstvennie arkhivy soyuza SSR. Kratky spravochnik* (*Archives of State, USSR. Short Guide*), Moscow, 1956, 508pp.

3 *Tsentral'nie gosudarstvennie arkhivy oktyabr'skoy revolyutsii i sotsialisticheskogo stroitel'stva: putevoditel'* (*Central Archives of State of the October Revolution and the Construction of Socialism: a Guide*), Moscow, 1946, 347pp.

4 (and 5, the best known guides) Dobranitsky, M: *Sistematichesky ukazatel' literatury po istorii russkoy revolyutsii* (*Systematic Guide ot the Literature of the Russian Revolution*), Moscow, 1926, 182pp. Valuable for little pamphlets published during the Revolution.

5 *Bibliothèque et Musée de la Guerre. Catalogue périodique du fonds russe de la bibliothèque*, ed Alexandra Dumesnil (Paris, 1932) 739pp. The most useful catalogue for study of the war and the Revolution.

6 Postnikov, S. P., *Bibliografia russkoy revolyutsii i grazhdanskoy voyni* (*Bibliography of the Russian Revolution and the Civil War*), Prague, 1938, 445pp. Usefully complements the above for *émigré* literature.

7 Zaleski, E., *Mouvements socialistes et ouvriers. Chronologie et bibliographie. La Russie*, vol. II, Paris, Editions Ouvrières, 1956, 490pp. This is a convenient aid to research, with works classed by date of publication and catalogue-numbers of the larger libraries. It is particularly useful for writers of Russian

---

* Some works published in 1966 appeared after the present volume had gone to press.

origin. For newspapers, it must be used together with the collective library catalogue.

8 Haupt, G., "Ouvrages bibliographiques concernant l'histoire de l'URSS", *Cahiers du monde russe et soviétique*, 1960, pp. 502–13. A useful summary.

9 Shapiro, D. A., *Select Bibliography of Works in English on Russian History 1801–1917*. Oxford, 1962, 106pp. A very well-made selection of the principal English-language works with references to reviews made of them.

10 Horecky, P. L., *Russia and the Soviet Union, a Bibliographical guide to Western-language Publications*, Chicago, 1965, 470pp. A selection of 1960 works with brief critical evaluations of each. The bibliographies of the following works, mentioned below, are particularly valuable: Bezemer [406]; Browder and Kerensky [35]; Gankin and Fisher [37]; Mel'gunov [128]; Pipes [365]; Schapiro [284]; Seton-Watson [287]; Souvarine [281]; Walter [323].

II. ARCHIVAL, DOCUMENTAL, NEWSPAPER AND OTHER PRIMARY SOURCES

11 TsGAORSSSR (Central Archives of the October Revolution) *fondy* 3, 66, 398, 393, 1235, 1244, 1978

11b GAORSSMo. (Moscow regional archives) *fond* 66.

12 GAORSSLo. (Leningrad regional archives) *fondy* 47, 54, 55, 101, 151, 4592, 4601, 4602, 1000, 4600, 4605, 7384, 7389, 8878.

12b TsGIAL (Leningrad historical archives) *fondy* 23, 1405, 1276, 1278. References to the Soviet archives give in succession the place, the *fond* number, the section, the file and the item.

13 Internationaal Instituut voor Geschiedenis Sociale, Amsterdam. Particularly the archives of F. Adler, Axelrod, Grimm, Kautsky, Savinkov and Troelstra.

14 Archives Nationales (Paris): série F.7, *fonds* 13074, 13069, 13349, 13372, 13374, 13089.

15 Archives de la Censure (Paris): Registers kept at the Bibliothèque de documentation internationale contemporaine, Paris.

16 Archives du ministère de la Guerre, Vincennes: Missions militaires en Russie; Missions militaires en Roumanie.

17 Archives de l'Institut d'histoire sociale, Paris.

18 Public Cinema Archives in Ivry, Koblenz and London.

19 Private Cinema Archives of Pathé and Gaumont.

20 *Revolyutsionnoye dvizhenie v Rossii posle sverzheniya samoder-*

zhaviya (*The Revolutionary Movement in Russia after the Fall of the Autocracy*), *Dok.* Moscow, 1957, XXIX, 858pp.

21 *Revolyutsionnoye dvizhenie v aprele* (*The Revolutionary Movement in April*), *Dok. Apr.* Moscow, 1958, XX, 934pp.

22 *Revolyusionnoye dvizhenie v Rossii v mae i iyune 1917g.* (*The Revolutionary Movement in Russia in May and June 1917*), *Dok. Mai.* Moscow, XX, 663pp.

23 *Revolyutsionnoye dvizhenie Rossii v iyule i iyul'sky krizis* (*The Revolutionary Movement in Russia in July and the July Crisis*), *Dok. Jul.* Moscow, 1959, XX, 627pp.
A source of exceptional value, particularly for economic and social history. These four collections should not, however, be used without precaution. See Ferro in *Annales ESC.* 1965, 3 pp. 597–8.

24 *Ekonomicheskoe Polozhenie Rossii nakanune velikoy oktyabr'skoy sotsialisticheskoy revolyutsii* (*The Economic Situation of Russia on the eve of the great Socialist Revolution of October 1917*) *Ek.Pol.* Moscow, 1957, 2 vols. 692 and 654pp.

25 *Velikaya oktyabr'skaya sotsialisticheskaya revolyutsiya: khronika sobitiy* (*The Great Socialist Revolution of October: Chronology of Events*), *Kut.* Moscow, 1957 and 1959, 700 and 663pp. A detailed chronology, with references to document and archives; useful for the development of the revolution in the provinces.

26 *Krasny Arkhiv* (*KA*) Moscow, 1922 41, 106 vols. The "Red archives" constitute the fundamental source for the political history of the revolution

27 *Arkhiv russkoy revolyutsii* (*Archives of the Russian Revolution*) (*ARR*), Berlin, 1921–37, 22 vols. The chief archival collection put together by *émigrés.*

28 *Padenie tsarskogo rezhima: stenografi cheskie otchety* (*The Fall of the Tsarist Régime: stenographic record*) Leningrad, 1924–7, 7 vols. Records of the trial set up by the Provisional Government on the Ministers of the old régime.

29 Pokrovski, M. N. and Yaroklev, Y. A. *Arkhiv oktyabr'skoy revolyutsii 1917g.* (*Archives of the October Revolution, 1917*), Moscow, 1925–39, especially the following volumes:
I. *Petrogradsky sovet rabochikh i soldatskikh deputatov* (*The Petrograd Soviet of Workers' and Soldiers' Deputies*) 1925, 374pp.

30 Ibid. II. *Pervy vserossiysky s'ezd sovetov rabochikh i soldatskikh deputatov* (*First Pan-Russian Assembly of Soviets of Workers' and Soldiers' Deputies*) 2 vols., 1927, 490 and 480pp.

31 Ibid. V. *Krest'yanskoe dvizhenie v 1917g.* (*The Peasant Movement in 1917*) 1927, 440pp.

32 Ibid. VI. *Razlozhenie armii v 1917g.* (*The Dissolution of the Army in 1917*) 1927, 330pp.

33 Ibid. VII. *Rabochee dvizhenie v 1917g.* (*The Workers' Movement in 1917*), 1926, 377 pp.

34 Ibid. VIII. *Burzhuaziya nakanune fevral'skoy revolyutsii* (*The Bourgeoisie on the eve of the February Revolution*) Moscow, 1927, 330 pp.

34a *Vserossiyskoe soveshchanie sovetov* (*Pan-Russian Assembly of Soviets*), Moscow, 1927, 355 pp. These volumes were carefully prepared. Volume II [30] gives a complete record of the first Pan-Russian Congress of Soviets.

34b *Dokumenty velikoy okt. revolyutsii* (*Documents of the great October Revolution*), Moscow, 1927.

35 Browder, R. P. and Kerensky, A. F., *The Provisional Government, 1917* (*Doc. Ker.*) 3 vols., Stanford, 1961, 1875pp. A very useful collection. It reflects the Kerensky interpretation of the Revolution.

36 Golder, F. A., *Documents of Russian History* (London, 1927) 663pp. This first great collection of documents in a western language remains, still, most valuable.

37 Gankin, O. H. and Fisher, H. H., *The Bolsheviks and the World War*, Stanford, 1914, 856pp; reprinted 1960. Fundamental for the history of international pacifism.

38 *Comité organisateur de la conférence socialiste internationale de Stockholm*, preface by C. Huysmans, Stockholm, 1918, 542pp.

39 *Zimmerwald:* a collection of documents prepared by the Amsterdam Institute of Social History, which will shortly be published. (The proofs were kindly given to the present writer by the Secretary of the Institute. The wording of the title had not yet been agreed.) These are two essential collections on the history of the Zimmerwald, Kienthal and Stockholm conferences. See numbers [326, 362, 364].

Newspapers, etc.

40 Zaleski (see [7]) gives a list of newspapers and reviews in Russian dealing with the history of the Revolution (pp. 125–39)

(a) appearing in Russia, or clandestine publication:

41 *Byulleten' izdavaemy ob'edinyonnymi gruppami partii S-Rev.* (*Bulletin published by the united S.-R. groups*).

42 *Byull. moskovskogo komiteta narodno-sotsialisticheskoy* (*trudovoy*) *partii* (*Bulletin of the Moscow Committee of the Populist-Socialist Workers*).

43 *Bulletin de presse de Petrograd* (*BPP*): from 14 April (old style). A work extremely rich in unpublished information. There is now a microfilm edition, with index, by S.I.M., Paris.

44 *Bulletin de presse de Moscou* (from 1 June 1917)

45 *Byloe* (*The Past*), which dates from the 1920s.

46 *Delo Naroda*, the S.-R. daily newspaper.

47 *Edinstvo*, Plekhanov's Social-Democrat daily.

48 *Nachalo*, weekly of the *Edinstvo* group in Omsk.

49 *Izvestya petrogradskogo rabochikh deputatov* (*News of the Soviet of Workers' Deputies in Petrograd*), semi-official Soviet newspaper.

50 *Journal de Petrograd*, an abridged version of the *Bulletin* [43].

51 *Vestnik vrem. Pravitel'stva* (*Provisional Government Newssheet*), semi-official government newspaper.

52 *Novaya Zhizn'*, the newspaper of Gorky and Sukhanov.

53 *Narodnoe slovo*, the Socialist-Populist newspaper.

54 *Pravda*, Bolshevik daily.

55 *Rabochaya Gazeta*, Menshevik daily.

56 *Rech'*, Cadet daily.

57 *Novoe Vremya*, evening newspaper, moderate.

58 *Samozaschchita*, "defensist" publication during the War

59 *Sotsial-Demokrat*, the Bolshevik daily in Moscow.

60 *Volya Naroda*, right S.-R. newspaper.

61 *Vperyod*, bi-weekly of Lunacharsky and Trotsky after 2 June 1917.

62 *Vozrozhdenie Internatsionala i bor'ba za mir* (*Re-birth of the International and Struggle for Peace*), Menshevik.

63 *Zadacha rossiyskogo proletariata* (*The Task of the Russian Proletariat*), Menshevik.

(b) Newspapers appearing outside Russia:

64 *L'Action Française*

65 *L'Homme enchaîné*

66 *Le Populaire du Centre*

67 *Le Journal du Peuple*

68 *Le Temps*

69 *La Victoire*

70 *L'Echo de Paris*

71 *Le Petit Parisien*

72 *Le Bonnet Rouge*

73 *La Croix*

74 *Daily Mail*

75 *Manchester Guardian*

76 *The Times*

77 *Morning Post*
78 *British Citizen and Empire Worker*
79 *Russian Co-Operator*
80 *Clarion*
81 *Labour Leader*
82 *Nation*
83 *New Statesman*
84 *Justice*
85 *Vanguard*
86 *The Call*
87 *Avanti!*
88 *Corriere della Sera*
89 *Idea Nazionale*
90 *Osservatore Romano*
91 *Il Resto di Carlino*
92 *La Stampa*
93 *Critica Sociale*
94 *Journal de Genève*
95 *Demain*
96 *New York Times*
97 *Vorwärts*
98 *Bulletin périodique de la presse allemande*
99 *Bulletin périodique de la presse autrichienne*

(c) Specialist reviews:

100 *Golos minuvshchego* (Populist tendency); after 1922 *Na chuzhoy storone.*
101 *Istoricheskie zapiski* (Moscow)
102 *Proletarskaya revolyutsiya* (1922 et seq.—the first review devoted to the history of the Revolution)
103 *Voprosy Istorii* (Moscow)
104 *Istoriya SSSR* (Moscow)
105 *Novaya i noveyshaya istoriya* (Moscow)
106 *Vozrozhdenie*, Paris
107 *Novy Zhurnal* New York
108 *Slavic Review*, New York
109 *Russian Review*, New York
110 *Cahiers du monde russe et soviétique*, Paris (*CMRS*)
111 *Le Contrat social*, Paris
112 *Le mouvement social*, Paris
113 *Rivista storica del socialismo*, Turin
114 *International Review of Social History*, Amsterdam
115 *Slavonic and East European Review*, London

116 *Survey*, London
117 *La Revue Historique*, Paris
118 *Annales ESC*, Paris
119 *Les Temps Modernes*, Paris

III. CONTEMPORARY ACCOUNTS

1. Basic accounts

These are presented either as "memoirs" or as history. Numbers 120–9 are all essential. The authors involved wrote, for the most part, other works, indicated below with the sign *.

120 Sukhanov, N. *Zapiski o revolyutsii* (*Notes on the Revolution*), 7 vols., Berlin, 1920. Carmichael has translated the chief parts in an excellent English edition, 1 vol., Oxford, 1954, 691pp. There is a French version published in 1966. This is the most penetrating and most complete eye-witness account of the 1917 revolution. The author, among the founders of the Petrograd Soviet, was a Social-Democrat on Martovian lines.

121 Trotsky, L. *Histoire de la Révolution russe*, 2 vols., Paris, 1931, 440pp. and 635pp. The outstanding history of the 1917 revolution. Trotsky concealed his differences with Lenin.

122 Milyukov, D. N. *Istoriya vtoroy revolyutsii* (*History of the Second Revolution*) 3 vols., Sofia, 1921. Milyukov, former foreign minister of the Provisional Government, here writes as a professional historian, but in fact gives a highly contestable version of the February revolution.

123 Chernov, V. *The Great Russian Revolution*, New Haven, 1936, 360pp. A somewhat hasty account by the S.-R. leader.

124 Kerensky, A. F. *The Catastrophe*, New York, 1927, XI, 377pp. The most penetrating and lively of Kerensky's writings.

125 Shlyapnikov, A. *Semnadtsaty god* (*1917*), 3 vols., Moscow, 1923–7. These memoirs of 1917 are in fact interrupted once Lenin arrives. Shylapnikov was a chief Bolshevik in Petrograd.

126 Stalin, Voroshilov, Gorky, Kirov, Zhdanov, Molotov: *Histoire de la Révolution russe*, Moscow, 1936 (French edition in 3 vols.). The Russian version is illustrated, and entitled *Istoriya grazhdanskoy voyni v SSSR*. (*History of the Civil War in the USSR*), 1 vol., Moscow, 1936, 307pp. This is the "official" history, dating from the Stalinist period.

127 Tseretelli, I. *Vospominaniya o russkoy revolyutsii* (*Memories of the Russian Revolution*), 2 vols., Paris, 1963–4, 492 and 426pp. A member of the Menshevik "majority", opposed to Martov's line.

128 Mel'gunov, S. P. *Martovskie Dni* (*The March Days*), Paris, 1961, 449pp. This historian was, in 1917, one of the leaders of the Socialist-Populists.

129 Lenin, V. I. *Sochineniya* (*Works*), 35 vols., Moscow, 4th edition. Unless indicated otherwise, references in the text are to the French edition being published (Lénine, *Oeuvres complètes*, Paris and Moscow, 20 vols. already published).
Sadoul and Serge refer essentially to the period after October: Sadoul, J. *Notes sur la révolution bolchévique* (*oct. 1917–janvier 1919*), Paris, 1919.
Serge, V. *L'An I de la révolution russe*, Paris, 1930.

2. Contemporary accounts

130 A. K. *Komu nuzhna voyna?* (*Who needs the War?*) Helsingfors, 1917, 20pp. A pamphlet written in 1915 or 1916 by Alexandra Kollontai. It supports Lenin's theses.

131 Alexinsky, G. *Voyna i revolyutsiya* (*The War and the Revolution*), Petrograd, 1917, 46pp. Supports Plekhanov's theses.

132 Berdyaev, N. A. *Vozmozhna li sotsial'naya revolyutsiya?* (*Is Social Revolution possible?*), Moscow, 1917, 24pp. Analyses the nature and possibilities of the Revolution.

133 Bogdanov, A.—Malinovsky—*Zadachi rabochikh v revolyutsii* (*The Workers' Tasks in the Revolution*), Moscow, 1917, 36pp. Member of the Bolshevik Party, and also agent of the Tsarist police, Bogdanov should not be confused with his namesake (V. Bogdanov) who was among the founders of the Petrograd Soviet.

133b Bobrovnikov, N. *Chto proizoshlo v Rossii* (*What happened in Russia*), Petrograd, 1917, 36pp.

134 Cherkasky, A. *Pervie dni revolyutsii* (*The First Days of the Revolution*), Petrograd, 1917, 28pp.

134b Chernov, V. *Agrarny vopros i sovremenny moment* (*The Agrarian Question and the Present Situation*), Petrograd, 1917, 77pp. A public lecture presented by the S.-R. leader on his arrival in Petrograd.

135 Gorky, M. *Ein Jahr russische Revolution*, Leipzig, 1918, 78pp. Selection of articles from *Novaya Zhizn'*, in translation.

136 *K Narodam vsego mira* (*To the Peoples of the World*), Petrograd, 1917, 15pp. The Soviet's appeal, 14 March 1917.

137 Ky, *Zadachi professional'nikh soyuzov* (*Tasks of the Unions*), Petrograd, 1917, 18pp.

138 Kizevetter, A. *Prostie rechi o svobode* (*Simple Speeches on Liberty*), Petrograd, 1917, by a Cadet leader.

138b Kokoshkin, F. *Respublika* (*The Republic*). A Cadet leader, rallying to the Republic.

139 Kropotkin, P. *Pis'ma o tekushchikh sobitiyakh* (*Letters on Current Events*), Moscow, 1917, 127pp. Written in England from 1914 to his return to Russia.

140 Larin, Yu. *Voyna i zemel'naya programma* (*The War and the Agrarian Programme*), Moscow, 1917. This reproduces a small work by the same Menshevik theorist, published in Geneva, 1915.

141 Maslov, P. *Politicheskie partii i zemel'ny vopros* (*The Political Parties and the Agrarian Question*), Moscow, 1917, 31pp. The most respected Social-Democrat theorist on land questions.

142 Meshcheryakov, V. *Agrarnaya programma russkikh sotsial-demokratov* (*The Agrarian Programme of the Russian Social-Democrats*), Moscow, 1918, 58pp. A straightforward account.

143 (Milevski), *Les Dangers mortels de la révolution russe*, Paris, 1917, 251pp. Sets out the chief problems of Russian politics.

144 Milyukov, P. and Struve, P. etc. *Russian Realities and Problems*, Cambridge, 1917, 208pp. A collection of articles.

145 Myakotin, V. *Revolyutsiya i ee blizhaishie zadachi* (*The Revolution and its Immediate Tasks*), Moscow, 1917, 16pp.

146 Myakotin, V. *Veliky perevorot i zadachi momenta* (*The Great Overthrow and the Tasks of the Moment*), The Socialist-Populist Programme of Action, by one of their leaders, a historian.

147 Peshekhonov, A. *Pochemy my togda ushli* (*Why we Left*), A further edition of a 1906 pamphlet explaining why the Socialist-Populists formed a party independent of the S.-R.s.

147b Peshekhonov, A. *Pravo na zemlyu* (*The Right to Land*), Petrograd, 1917. The Socialist-Populist agrarian programme.

148 Prizhelaev, Yu. *Zadachi rabochikh v kontrole i organizatsii proizvodstva* (*The Tasks of the Workers in Supervision and Organization of Production*), Petrograd, 1917, 62pp. An S.-R. pamphlet.

148b Petrovich, N. *Chto nuzhno znat' krest'yanstvu* (*What the peasants must know*), Kiev, 1917, 16pp. A Ukrainian S.-R.

150 (*sic:* 149 missing). Plekhanov G. *God na rodine* (*A Year out of Exile*), 2 vols. Paris, 1921, 247 and 270pp. Writings and speeches of 1917–18.

151 *Protokoly zasedaniy s'ezda deputatov Baltiyskogo morya* (*Record of Proceedings of the meetings of the Baltic-Fleet Deputies*), Petrograd, 1917, 17pp.

152 *Protokoly 1-go. vseross. s'ezda narod. sots. partii, VI-go vseross. s'ezda trud. gruppy, 1-go. s'ezda trud.-nar.-sots. partii* 17–23 June,

443

Petrograd, 1917, 208pp. Proceedings of the Trudovik-Populist Congress of Unification.

152b Protopopov, A. *Vospominaniya* (*Memoirs*), *KA*, 1925, X. Written in prison.

153 *Rezolyutsii prinyatie na 3.-m. s'ezde S.-R. v Moskve* (*Resolutions adopted at the 3rd S.-R. Congress in Moscow*), Petrograd, 1917, 16pp.

154 Sorokin, P. *Problema sotsial'nogo ravenstva* (*The Problem of Social Equality*), Petrograd, 1917, 64pp. A right S.-R.

155 Trotsky, L. *Programma mira. K Stokol'mskoy konferentsii* (*A Peace-Programme: the Stockholm Conference*), Petrograd, 1917, 30pp. The first pamphlet published by Trotsky after his return from the USA.

156 *Trudovaya narodno-sotsialisticheskaya partiya., programma* (*Programme of the Socialist-Populist Workers' Party*), Petrograd, 1917, 16pp.

157 Tugan-Baranovsky, M. *Zemel'ny vopros na zapade i v Rossii* (*The Agrarian Question in the West and in Russia*), Petrograd, 1917, 87pp.

158 Vasil'ev, P. *Sotsial-Demokrati i zemel'ny vopros* (*The Social-Democrats and the Agrarian Question*), Odessa, 1917, 16pp.

159 Zinov'ev, G. *Chego khochet sots. dem. Bol'shevik? V voprosakh i otvetakh* (*What does a Bolshevik Social Democrat want? Questions and Answers*), Petrograd, 1917, 16pp. The first Bolshevik catechism? It was written in the summer of 1917.

3. Personal accounts written after 1917

160 Abramovitch, R. *The Soviet Revolution 1917–1939*, London, 1963, 473pp. An account useful for the years after the October Revolution.

161 Grand-Duke Alexandre, *Quand j'étais Grand-duc*, Paris, 1934, 304pp. Demonstrates that he invited the Tsar to carry out reforms.

162 Alexinsky, G. *Du Tsarisme au communisme*, Paris, 1925, 296pp.

163 Alexinsky, G. *La Russie révolutionnaire*, Paris, 1930, A Bolshevik who, in 1914, went "Social-Patriot".

164 Alexinsky, G. *La Vie amère de Maxim Gorky*, Paris, 1950, 285pp.

164b Andrey, Grand Duke: Extracts from his "Diary" in *KA*, 1928, XXVI, pp. 185–210. Important for the abdication.

165 Anet, C. *La Révolution russe*, 4 vols., Paris, 1919. The *Petit*

Parisen correspondent here gives a complete version of his reflections.

166 Axelrod, P. *Die russ. Revolution und die soz. Internationale*, Jena, 1932, 250pp. A collection of articles.

167 Badaev, A. *Les Bolcheviks à la douma*, Paris, 1932, 250pp. By one of the Bolsheviks deported in 1914.

168 Balabanova, A. *My Life as a Rebel*, London, 1938, 324pp. The writer played an important rôle in the Zimmerwald movement, but her memoirs contain little of serious importance.

169 Blok, A. *Les Derniers Jours de l'Ancien Régime*, Paris, 1931. Blok put together a reconstruction of the last days of the Imperial régime, hour by hour. The result is clear, precise, and without commentary.

170 Boldyrev, V. "Diary" in *KA*, XXVII, pp. 250–73. A good analysis of the Staff's reactions during the February Days.

171 Bonch-Bruevich, V. *Na boevykh postakh fev. i okt. revolyutsiy* (*At Combat Post in the February and October Revolutions*), Moscow, 1930, 412pp. Useful for October.

172 Breshkovskaya, K. *Hidden Springs of the Russian Revolution*, Stanford, 1931. By the "grandmother of the revolution".

173 Bruce-Lockhart, R. H. *Memoir of a Secret Agent*, London, 1932. Useful for Allied reactions, especially after July.

174 Bublikov, A. *Russkaya Revolyutsiya* (*The Russian Revolution*), New York, 1918, 100pp. Important work: Bublikov was a member of the Duma.

175 Buchanan, G. *My mission to Russia and other Diplomatic Reminiscences*, 2 vols., London, 1923, 253 and 280pp. The most important of foreign eye-witness accounts of the Revolution.

176 Buchanan, M. "The Foulest Crime in History" in *Saturday Review*, May, 1935. The Ambassador's daughter here recounts what her father could not reveal.

177 Bukharin, N. *Vom Sturtze des Tsarismus bis zum Sturtze der Bourgeoisie*, Zürich, 1918, 20pp. Analyses the meaning of the Revolution.

178 Bukharin, N. and Zinov'ev, G. *Iyul'skie dni* (*The July Days*), Petrograd, 1918, 15pp.

*179 Chernov, V. *Sovety v nashey revolyutsii* (*The Soviets in our Revolution*), Moscow, 1918.

*180 Chernov, V. *Pered burey* (*Before the Storm*), New York, 1953. The analysis of the Soviets' role is useful; the memoirs hasty— [123] being superior.

181 de Chambrun, *Lettres à Marie*, Paris, 1941, 241pp. A lucid and sensitive account by this former attaché of the French Mission.

182 Czernin, O. *In the World War*, London, 1920. Former Austro-Hungarian foreign minister.

183 Chidlovksi, see Shidlovsky [255].

184 Chliapnikov, see Shlyapnikov [126].

185 Choulgine, see Shulgin [256].

186 Dan, F. *K Istorii poslednykh dney vremennogo pravitel'stva (The Last Days of the Provisional Government)* in *Letopis' revolyutsii*, 1923, pp. 161–73.

187 Dan, F. *Proizkhozhdenie Bol'shevizma (The Origins of Bolshevism shevism)*, New York, 1946, 494pp. Important for the period 1905–17.

188 Dan, F., and Martov, L. *Die Geschichte der russischen Sozial-Demokratie*, Berlin, 1926. A fundamental work—the Menshevik interpretation of the history of Russian Social-Democracy.

189 Danilov, Gen. *La Russie pendant la guerre mondiale*, Paris, 1927, 553pp. History of the military operations.

190 Dem'yanov, A. *Moya sluzhba pri vrem. prav. (My Service under the Provisional Government)*, *Arkhiv Russkoy Revolyutsii*, IV, 1922, pp. 55–129.

191 Denikine, Gen. *La Décomposition de l'armée et du pouvoir*, Paris, 1921, 342pp. The first volume—the only one to be translated into French—of this White General's memoirs.

192 Eichenbaum ("Voline"), *La Révolution inconnue*, Paris, 1947, 690pp. Anarchist interpretation of the Revolution.

193 Ermansky, O. *Iz perezhitogo (From the Past)*, Moscow, 1927, 250pp. The author was a Menshevik during the Revolution, Bolshevik when he wrote his memoirs.

193a Falkenhayn, E. von. *Die oberste Heeresleitung 1914–16 in ihren wichtigsten Entschliessungen*, Berlin, 1929. An excellent account of the performance of the Russian Army.

194 Francis, D. R. *Russia from the American Embassy*, New York, 1922. He had no understanding of the revolutionary movement.

195 Golovine, Gen. *The Russian Army in the World War*, New Haven, 1931. The best account of the nature of the army.

196 Gurko, Gen. *Memories and Impressions of War and Revolution*, London, 1918, 347pp. An excellent eye-witness account.

197 Houghtelling, J. *A Diary of the Russian Revolution*, New York, 1918, 195pp. The notes of this American journalist are often unexpected and sometimes useful.

198 Hoare, S. *The Fourth Seal*, London, 1930, 377pp. A member of the Allied Mission to Petrograd in January 1917.

199 Ivanov-Razumnik, *God Revolyutsii (The Revolutionary Year)*, Petrograd, 1918, 204pp. A collection of articles.

200 Janin, Gen. "Au G.Q.G. russe", *Monde slave*, May 1927. Former chief of the French Military Mission in Russia.

201 Yurenev, Y. "Mezhrayonka", *Proletarskaya Revolyutsiya*, 1924, 1, 2, 6. A good account of the activity of this group before Trotsky arrived.

202 Kayurov, V. "Shest' dney revolyutsii" (Six Days of Revolution"), *Prol. Rev.*, 1923, I, pp. 157–70. Classic account of the February days, by a Bolshevik worker.

203 Kerensky, A. F. *The Prelude to Bolshevism*, New York, 1919.

204 Kerensky, A. F. *The Crucifixion of Liberty*, New York, 1934.

205 Kerensky, A. F. *The Road to Tragedy*, London, 1935.

206 *The Kerensky Memoirs. Russian and History's Turning-point*, London, 1966, 550pp.

207 Kerensky, A. F. *Iz daleka (From Afar)*, Paris, 1922.

208 Kerensky, A. F. *Delo Kornilova (The Kornilov Affair)*, Moscow, 1918, 192pp.

209 Kerensky, A. F. *Izbrannie rechi (Selected Speeches)*, Petrograd, 1918.

210 Kerensky, A. F. *La Révolution russe de 1917*, Paris, 1928, 250pp.

211 Kerensky, A. F. *L'Expérience Kerenski*, Paris, 1936, 182pp.

212 Kerensky, A. F. "Quarante Ans après", *Est et Ouest*, 1957, pp. 1–7.
The best Kerensky account is [124]. [204] gives a good overall view, while [207] and [208] are useful. [206] is interesting for the period before 1917 and the months following the October Revolution

213 Kamkov, B. *Chto takie levie S-Ry? (What are the Left S.-R.s?)*, Moscow, 1918, 15pp.

214 Kleinmichel (Countess). *Souvenirs d'un monde englouti*, Paris, 1927. Memoirs of the Imperial Court.

215 Knox, Col. *With the Russian Army*, 2 vols., London 1921, 760pp. The chief of the British Military Mission in Russia.

216 Korostovets, V. *Seed and Harvest*, London, 1931. By an observer close to Cadet circles.

217 Krupskaya, N. *Ma Vie avec Lénine*, Paris, 1933. By Lenin's companion.

218 Krylenko, N. "Fevral'skaya revolyutsiya i staraya armiya", *Prol. Rev.*, 1923, nos. 2 and 3. On agitation in the army.

219 Lomonosov, V. *Memoirs of the Russian Revolution*, New York, 1919, 97pp. The railway engineer who contributed to the failure of Ivanov's mission.

220 Litvinov, M. *The Russian Bolshevik Revolution, its Rise and Meaning*, London, 1919, 54pp.

221 Lukomsky, A. *Memoirs of the Russian Revolution*, 2 vols.,

London, 1922, 301 and 333pp. A good account of the abdication.

222 Lunacharsky, A. "Ideologiya nakanune oktyabrya" ("Ideology on the eve of October"), extract from *Za pyat' let*, Moscow, 1922. A good summary.

223 Luxembourg, R. *La Révolution russe*, 1920, reprinted Paris, 1946. A classic.

224 Maklakov, V. "Fevral'skaya revolyutsiya 1917g." ("The February Revolution of 1917"), *Sovrem. Zapiski*, 1939, pp. 238–56.

225 Maklakov, V. "The Council of Ministers, 24th Feb. 1917", *Novy Zhurnal*, 1946.

226 Maklakov, V. "The Agrarian Question in Russia", *The Russian Review*, 1950. This Cadet lawyer had an active rôle in the abdication of Nicholas and Michael.

227 Mansyrev, Prince. *Moi vospominaniya (Memories)* in *Fevral. Rev.* Alexiev edn., Moscow, 1925, 509pp. One of the best accounts of what happened on 27 February.

228 Markovitch, M. *La Révolution russe par une française*, Paris, 1918. A woman of society: not well informed, but sensitive and perspicacious.

229 Makhno, N. *Russkaya revolyutsiya na Ukraine (The Russian Revolution in the Ukraine)*, Paris, 1920, 1 vol. appeared in French translation, 360pp. Anarchist viewpoint.

230 Matveev, A. "Vospominaniya", *Vozrozhdenie*, 1952. Memoirs of an aide-de-camp of Grand Duke Michael.

231 Mel'gunov, S. P. *Kak bol'sheviki zakhvatili vlast' (How the Bolsheviks took over power)*, Paris, 1953, 391pp. A useful reconstruction.

232 Merejkowski, C. *Vom Krieg zur Revolution*, Munich, 1918, 176pp. A collection of political and literary articles.

233 Milyukov, P. N. *Vospominaniya*, 2 vols., New York, 1955. See especially for the period before 1917; see also [122].

234 Minor, O. S. "Nasional'ny vopros v 1917–18" ("The Nationality Question 1917–18"), *God russkoy revolyutsii*, Moscow, 1918. The S.-R. point of view of the national question.

235 Mordvinov, A. "Otryvky iz vospominaniy" ("Extracts from memoirs"), *Russkaya Letopis'*, V, pp. 65–177. The abdication, by an aide de camp of the Tsar.

236 Mstislavsky, S. *Pyat' dney (Five Days)*, Berlin, 1923, 163pp. An account of five decisive days of the February and October Revolutions by an officer, of S.-R. sympathies, who witnessed and took part in the events of February.

237 Nabokov, V. "Vremennoe Pravitel'stvo" ("The Provisional

Government"), *A.R.R.*, I, 1921, pp. 9–96. He was present at its first meetings.

238 Nabokov, V. *The Ordeal of a Diplomat*, London, 1921. A good piece of observation, by this attaché at the Stockholm embassy.

239 Nekludoff, A. *Diplomatic Reminiscences*, New York, 1920, 350pp. A witness to English reactions to the revolution.

240 Nicholas II, *Letters of the Tsar to the Tsaritsa*, New York, 1929. An English version of the "Lettres" published in *KA*, XX and XII.

241 Nicholas II, *Journal intime*, Paris, 1925, 303pp.

242 Nolde, B. *L'Ancien Régime et la révolution*, Paris, 1928, 220pp. Cadet in sympathy.

243 Noullens, J. *Mon Ambassade en Russie soviétique*, 2 vols., Paris, 1933. Essential for the period after September 1917.

244 Paléologue, M. *La Russie des Tsars pendant la Grande Guerre*, vol. 3, Paris, 1921. Better versed in Court circles than in Opposition ones.

245 Pares, B. *My Russian Memoirs*, London, 1921, 623pp. Knew the Liberals of Petrograd outstandingly well.

246 Perevalov, P. *Narod i armiya v bor'be za svobodu* (*People and Army in the Struggle for Liberty*), Petrograd, 1917, 60pp.

247 Poincaré, R. *Au Service de la France*, 10 vols., Paris, 1926–33.

248 Peshekhonov, A. "Pervie nedeli" ("The First Weeks"), *Na chuzhoy storone*, I, pp. 253–319. A good account of the first days of the Revolution by the Populist leader.

249 Raskol'nikov, *Kronshtadt i Piter* (*Kronstadt and Petersburg*), Moscow, 1925. 280pp. The role of Kronstadt in the Revolution.

250 Reed, J. *Ten Days that Shook the World*, New York, 1922; The "classic" on October.

251 Rhys-Williams, A. *Through the Russian Revolution*, London, 1923. By the historian of the Peace of Brest-Litovsk.

252 Ribot, A. *Journal*, Paris, 1936. French premier during the February Revolution.

253 Rodzyanko, M. "Gosudarstvennaya duma i fevral'skaya 1917g revolyutsiya" (The Duma and the February Revolution"), *ARR*, 1922–6, pp. 5–80. Essential.

254 Sack, A. *The Birth of the Russian Revolution*, New York, 1918. Contains some interesting documents.

255 Shidlovsky, *Vospominaniya*, Berlin, 1932. The author was Vice-President of the Duma in 1917.

255b Shlyapnikov—see [125].

256 Shulnin, A. *Dni* (*Days*), Leningrad, 1925, 228pp. Essential.

257 Stalin, J. *Sochineniya* (*Works*), Vol. 3, Moscow, 1938.

258 Stalin, J. *Na putyakh oktyabrya* (*On the Road to October*), Moscow, 1925, 280pp. Claims that he always agreed with Lenin.

259 Stankevich, V. *Vospominaniya* (*Memoirs*), Berlin, 1921, 353pp. Important—by the trudovik leader, a friend of Kerensky's.

260 Steinberg, I. *Ot fevralya do oktyabrya 1917g.* (*From February to October*), Berlin, 1918, 231pp. A good analysis by a Left S.-R.

261 Tarassov-Rodionov, *La Révolution de février 1917*, Paris, 1930, 338pp. Superficial.

*262 Trotsky, L. *Sochineniya* (*Works*), Vol. 3, part I: 1917, Moscow, 1925, 466pp.

263 Trotsky, L. *Oktyabrskaya revolyutsiya* (*The October Revolution*), Moscow, 1918.

264 Trotsky, L. *Our Revolution*, New York, 1918, 220pp.

265 Trotsky, L. *L'Avènement du bolchévisme*, Paris, 1920.

266 Trotsky, L. *Staline*, Paris, 1948, 620pp. (In an appendix, there is a list of Trotsky's works that have received French translation.)

267 Trotsky, L. *La Révolution défigurée*, 1927, 217pp., reprinted in Trotsky, L. *De la Révolution*, Paris, 1963, preface by P. Broué, pp. 103–47. Apart from [121] already indicated, [262] is important. For a criticism of Trotsky's historical work, see A. Stawar, *Libres Essais marxistes*, Paris, 1963, 279pp., pp. 114–67; and Y. Bourdet, *Communisme et marxisme*, Paris, 1963, 154pp., pp. 13–39.

267b Ceretelli, see Tseretelli [127].

268 Vishyak, M. "Fev. Rev.", *Sovrem. Zapiski*, 1927, XXXI. Populist in sympathy.

269 Vandervelde, E. *Three Aspects of the Russian Revolution*, London, 1918, 220pp. Summarizes a mission to Russia, and author's impressions.

270 Vinogradoff, P. "Some impressions of the Russian Revolution", *Contemporary Review*, May 1917. Impressions of a Russian diplomat in London.

270b Voline, see Eichenbam [192].

271 Witte-Narishkind, V. *A Petrograd pendant la révolution*, Paris, 1925, 219pp. Superficial.

272 Wassiliev, V. "Mes souvenirs", *Monde slave*, 1927. Former chief of the Petrograd police.

273 Woitinsky, W. S. *Stormy Passage*, New York, 1961, 550pp. Interesting on the April crisis and the events thereafter.

273b Jurenev, see Yurenev [201].

274 Zenzinov, V. "Fev. Dni" (The February Days), *Novy Zhurnal*, 1953, and XXXV. Important.

IV. GENERAL WORKS

1. *History of the Revolution*

To the basic contemporary accounts, [120–130], the following should be added:

275 Chamberlin, W. H. *The Russian Revolution*, 2 vols., New York, 1935. The most complete account of the Revolution and the Civil War.

276 Carr, E. H. *The Bolshevik Revolution*, 3 vols., London, 1950–3. Fundamental for the period October 1917–1923.

277 Grenard, F. *La Révolution russe*, Paris, 1931, 386pp. A penetrating analysis of the 1905 and 1917 revolutions.

278 Coquin, F. X. *La Révolution russe*, Paris, 1962 (collection *Que Sais-Je?*). A well-constructed and useful introduction.

279 Carmichael, J. *The Russian Revolution*, London, 1966. A good account of the Revolution.

The publication of a new three-volume work, in Russian, by Mints, has been announced (since published) *Istoriya Velikogo Oktyabrya*.)

2. *Large-scale works, histories of the Bolshevik Party and the Revolutionary Movement, Introductions to the study of the USSR.*

280 Rosenberg, A. *Histoire du bolchevisme*, Paris, 1932, 250pp. A very penetrating study of the subject, from Marx to the Five-Year Plans, by a Communist who left the movement in 1927.

281 Souvarine, B. *Staline*, 1st edn. Paris, 1935. A pioneering work, altogether remarkable, but a one-sided criticism of Lenin's successor.

282 Wolfe, B. D. *Three who made a Revolution*, New York, 1960. The best account of the three Bolshevik leaders before 1917.

283 Deutscher, I. *Trotsky: the Prophet Armed*, Oxford, 1953; first volume of a monumental triology.

284 Schapiro, L. *The Origin of the Communist Autocracy*, London 1955. Essential for the period after October.

285 Friedmann, G. *De la Sainte Russie à l'URSS*, Paris, 1938, 287pp. First sociological comparison of Russia and the USSR.

On Russia before the Revolution:

286 Kovalevski, M. *La Russie sociale*, Paris, 1914, 180pp. A classic.

287 Seton-Watson, H. *The Decline of Imperial Russia*, London, 1952, 406pp. A model analysis.

288 Portal, R. *La Russie de 1894 à 1914*, CDU, Paris, 113pp. An

excellent introduction—originally an advanced lecture-course. I have not been able to use the work of G. Katkov, *February 1917*, London, 1967, 488pp., which examines the circumstances preceding the fall of Nicholas II.

289 Florinsky, M. T. *The End of the Russian Empire*, Yale U.P., 1931, 272pp.

290 Charques, R. *The Twilight of Imperial Russia*, Oxford, 1958, 256pp.

291 Pares, B. *The Fall of the Russian Monarchy*, London, 1939, 510pp. Charques covers the reign of Nicholas II in a lively style. Pares is the most thorough on court intrigues. Florinsky deals only with the years 1914–17—there is a great deal to this work, which can be regarded as complementing Seton-Watson. There have been two debates in the *Slavic Review* on the nature of Russian society in 1913, and the question of social stability. The first of these debates was revived in:

292 Treadgold, D. W. *The Development of the USSR*, Seattle, 1964, 399pp. The other has been taken up in:

293 Haimson, L. The Problem of Social Stability in Urban Russia'', *Slavic Review*, Dec. 1964, pp. 619–53.

On the workers' movement, political parties, ideology:

294 Martov, L., Maslov, P., and Potressov, A. *Obshchestvennoe dvizhenie v Rossii v nachale XX veka* (*The Social Movement in Russia at the Beginning of the 20th Century*), 4 vols., St. Petersburg, 1909–14.

295 Venturi, F. *Il populismo russo*, 2 vols., Turin, 1952. Fundamental studies.

296 Spiridonovitch, A. *Histoire du terrorisme russe*, Paris, 1936, 250pp. By a former chief of police.

297 Radkey, O. *The Agrarian Foes of Bolshevism*, New York, 1958. Extremely valuable: the only history of the S.-R. party.

298 Lichtheim, G. *Marxism. An historical and critical study*. New York, 1961, 412pp. The best synthesis on Marx and Marxism after Marx.

299 Papaioannou, K. *Les marxistes*, Paris, 1965. Selected writings, judiciously chosen with a very valuable commentary.

300 Keep, J. H. L. *The Rise of Social-Democracy in Russia*, Oxford, 1963, 334pp. The most thorough and detailed account of the period before 1905.

301 Haimson, L. *The Russian Marxists and the Origin of Bolshevism*, Cambridge, 1955, 246pp. A good introduction to the political thought of Plekhanov, Axelrod, Lenin, etc.

302 Wittfogel, K. *Oriental Despotism*, Yale U.P., 1963, preface by

P. Vidal-Naquet. Discusses the theories of Lenin and Plekhanov on the future of Russia.

303 Ulam, A. *The Unfinished Revolution: an essay on the source of influence of Marxism and Communism*, New York, 1960, 317pp. On the relationship of Marxism to social evolution.

304 Dvinov, B. *Pervaya mirovaya voyna i rossiyskaya sots. demokratiya (The First World War and Russian Social-Democracy)*, New York, 1962, 239pp. Useful, Menshevik in sympathy.

305 Schlesinger, R. *Il Partito comunista nell' U.R.S.S.* Milan, 1962, 462pp.

306 Schapiro, L. *The Communist Party of the Soviet Union*, London, 1960, 631pp.

307 Broué, P. *Le Parti bolchevik*, Paris, 1964, 619pp. Schlesinger's book is the most thorough on the history of the Revolution, Schapiro on the period before it, Broué on the Stalin era—all three are highly useful, the first two are also reference-works.

308 *Histoire du parti communiste (bolchevik) de l'URSS*, Paris, 1946, 310pp. The Stalinist interpretation of party history.

309 Daniels, R. V. *The Conscience of the Revolution*, Cambridge, 1960, 526pp. A study of opposition to the party leadership, 1903-28.

310 Avrich, P. H. "The History of the Party and Soviet historiography", *Political Science Quarterly*, Dec., 1960.

311 Dewhurst, M. "L'Historiographie soviétique récente et l'histoire de la révolution", *Cahiers du monde russe et soviétique*, 1964, 4, pp. 559–67.

312 Shub, D. *Lenin*, London, 1955.

313 Bruhat, J. *Lénine*, 1952, 381pp.

314 Walter, G. *Lénine*, Paris, 1950.

315 Fisher, L. *Lenin*, New York, 1966.

316 Possony, S. T. *Lenin, the Compulsive Revolutionary*, London, 1966, 480pp. Fisher is most complete, but not very useful on the Revolution, by contrast with Shub, lively, well-informed and not sparing his hero, and Bruhat, faithful to the Leninist tradition.

317 Schwarz, S. *Lénine et le mouvement syndical*, Paris, 1935.

318 Hammond, D. T. *Lenin on Trade Unions and Revolution*, New York, 1957, 153pp.

On anarchism other than Vline and Makhno, already quoted, see

319 Guérin, D. *Les Anarchistes*, Paris, 1966, 230pp.

320 Woodcock, G., and Avakumovitch, I. *The Anarchist Prince*, London, 1950, 463pp.

321 Joll, J. *The Anarchists*, London, 1964, 304pp.

322 *Ni Dieu ni maître, histoire et anthologie de l'anarchie*, Paris, 1966, édition de Delphes.

V. WORKS ON PARTICULAR ASPECTS OF THE REVOLUTION

1. The Fall of Tsarism, and the Formation of Soviets

On the February Days, other than the accounts indicated above, particularly Sukhanov [120], Trotsky [121], Shlyapnikov [125], Mel'gunov [128], Blok [169], Shulgin [256] and the extracts collected in Browder-Kerensky [35] there is an overall study:

323 Walter, G. *Histoire de la révolution russe*, Paris, 1958, 380pp. A very lively account, with numerous documents translated from the Russian and otherwise difficult to acquire. There is a large bibliography.

324 *Oktyabr' i grazhdanskaya voyna v SSSR (October and the Russian Civil War)*, Moscow, 1966, 522pp. A collection of articles. On Soviets, the following should be added:

325 Gorin, P. *Organizatsiya i stroitel'stvo sovetov v 1917g. (The Organization and Construction of Soviets in 1917)*, Moscow, 1928, 476pp. A collection of documents, with a substantial introduction.

326 *Documenty velikoy proletarskoy revolyutsii (Documents of the great Proletarian Revolution)* ed. Gorodetsky, E. N., Razgon, I. M., and Mints, I. I., Moscow, 1938, 378pp. Minutes of the correspondence of the Soviet's Military Committee.

327 Burdzhalov, E. N. "Taktika bol'shevikov v burzhuazno-demokraticheskoy revolyutsii" ("The Bolsheviks' Tactics in the Bourgeois-Democratic Revolution"), *Voprosy istorii*, 1954–6 and 1956–8. Shows the gap between the position of Lenin and that of Stalin before April 1917.

328 Chermensky, E. D. "Fev. burzh-dem. revolyutsiya" ("The Bourgeois-Democratic Revolution"), *Voprosy istorii*, 1950–2. Discusses Burdzhalov's ideas.

329 Anweiler, O. *Die Rätebewegung in Russland 1905–21*, Leyden, 1958, 344pp. A basic work for the study of Soviets, especially from the institutional point of view.

330 Ferro, M. "Les débuts du soviet de Petrograd", *Revue historique*, April–June, 1960, pp. 353–80. Analyses the divergences between revolutionary militants when the Soviet was formed.

331 Zlokazov, G. I. "Sozdanie petrogradskogo soveta" ("The Creation of the Petrograd Soviet"), *Istoriya SSSR*, 1964–5, pp. 103 ff.

332 Artenev, S. A. "Sostav petrog. Soveta" ("Composition of the Petrograd Soviet"), *Istoriya SSSR*, 1964–5, pp. 112 ff.

333 Razgon, A. I. "O sostave sovetov nizhnego povolzh'ya v

marte-apr. 1917g" ("Formation of Soviets in the lower Volga region, March–April 1917"), *Sovety i soyuz rabochego klassa i krest'yanstva v oktyabr'skoy revolyutsii* (*The Soviets and the Unions of Workers and Peasants in the October Revolution*), Moscow, 1964, 226pp. A good provincial monograph.

334 *Rayonnie sovety Petrograda v 1917g* (*The Sectional Soviets of Petrograd in 1917*), 3 vols., Leningrad, 1966. An excellent collection of documents.

2. Economic and social affairs

General works on economy and society

335 Lyashchenko, P. I. *Istoriya narodnogo khozyaistva SSSR* (*History of the Economy of the USSR*), Vol. 2, Moscow, 1948.

336 Baykov, A. *The Development of the Soviet Economic System*, Cambridge, 1947, 514pp.

337 Portal, R. *Les Slaves*, Paris, 1965, 520pp. (mainly pp. 251–325).

338 Gille, B. *Histoire éc. et soc. de la Russie*, Paris, 1949.

339 Sorlin, P. *La Société soviétique*, Paris, 1964, 270pp.

To these overall works, not dealing precisely with the Revolution, should be added the following remarkable articles on two aspects of economic and social affairs:

340 Gershenkron, A. "The Rate of Industrial Growth in Russia since 1885", *Journal of Economic History*, Supp. 7, 1947.

341 Kerblay, B. "L'Evolution de l'alimentation rurale en Russie" (1860–1960), *Annales* ESC, 5, 1962, pp. 885–913.

The peasantry and the agrarian question: two fundamental studies of the agrarian question as a whole:

342 Robinson, G. T. *Rural Russia under the Old Régime*, New York, 1932, 342pp.

343 Florinsky, G. *Agricultural Russia on the eve of the Revolution*, London, 1930, 340pp.

To which should be added the classic article:

344 Pascal, P. "Le Paysan russe", *Revue historique*, 1934, pp. 32–70. In the revolutionary period:

The principal documents may be found in Kotel'nikov [31] and the collections, [20–23] and [35]; to which should be added:

345 Milyutin, M. *Agrarnaya revolyutsiya*, Vol. 2, Moscow, 1927, 231pp. To the overall studies of the peasantry, indicated above, should be added:

346 Owen, L. *The Russian Peasant Movement 1906–1917*, London, 1937, 267pp. There is a relatively large number of works dealing with the agrarian policies of the various parties during the

Revolution; other than the writings on 1917 that cover the agrarian question, particularly Chernov, Larin, Maslov, Peshek-honov, etc., shown above, the following can be used:

347 Morokhovets, A. E. *Agrarnie programmy rossiyskikh partiy v 1917g* (*The Agrarian Programmes of the Russian Parties in 1917*), Leningrad, 1929. Essential.

348 Trapeznikov, S. P. *Agrarny vopros i leniskie agrarnie problemy v trekh revolyutskyakh* (*The Agrarian Question and the Leninist Interpretation of the problems during the three Revolutions*). Overall study.

349 Sorlin, P. "Lénine et le problème paysan en 1917", *Annales ESC*, 1964, 2, pp. 250–81. Shows how Lenin's ideas were adopted to circumstances between February and October 1917.

On life in the countryside during the Revolution, other than works indicated above—mainly [20–22], there is a good regional monograph which, in the absence of an overall survey, must be used:

350 Usatova, A. N. *Agrarnie preobrazovaniya i pervie kommuny vo vladimirskoy gubernii* ("The Agrarian Transformation and the First Communes in Vladimir province"), Vladimir, 1961, 97pp.

On the working class and industry: to the general works on economic affairs shown above, the following should be added:

351 Rashin, A. G. *Formirovanie rabochego klassa Rossii* (*The Formation of the Working Class in Russia*), Moscow 1958. This should be used together with:

352 Fleer, M. *Rabochee dvizhenie v gody voyni* (*The Working-Class Movement during the war-years*), Moscow, 1926, 357pp. Many documents.

353 Grave, G. B. *Burzhuaziya nakanune fev. revolyutsii* (*The Bourgeoisie on the even of the February Revolution*), Moscow, 1927, 303pp. On the composition and activity of the Russian working class on the eve of the Revolution, and throughout 1917, other than the above works, mainly [11–34], see also:

354 Volobuev, P. V. *Ekonomicheskaya politika vrem. pravitel'stva* (*The Economic Policy of the Provisional Government*), Moscow 1962, 483pp. The contents of this excellent work go beyond the title.

355 Volobuev, P. V. *Proletariat i burzhuaziya Rossii v 1917g* (*The Russian Proletariat and Bourgeoisie, 1917*), Moscow, 1964, 352pp. This completes the above, and widens its perspective. These are two essential works; the following, provocative, work ought also to be consulted:

356 Tokarev, Yu. S. *Narodnoe pravotvorchestvo nakanune velik. okt. sots. Rev.* (*The Creation of a Popular Right on the eve of the October Revolution*), Leningrad, 1966, 185pp.
Two articles with useful insight:

357 Leiberov and Shkaratan: "K voprosu o sostave petrogradskikh promyshlennikh rabochika" ("The Composition of the Petrograd Working-Class"), *Voprosy istorii*, 1961–1.

358 Gaponenko. "Rabochy klass nakanune Okt" ("The Working Class on the eve of October"), *Istoricheskie zapiski*, 1963.
See also:

359 Volin, S. *Deyatel'nost' menshevikov v profsoyuzakh pri sov. vlasty* (*The Mensheviks in the Trade Unions under Soviet Power*), New York, 1962, 122pp;
and on the Church and education:

360 Curtiss, J. S. *The Russian Church and the Soviet State*, Boston, 1953.

360a Johnson, W. *Russia's Democratic Heritage*, 1950, 350pp.

The Army, the Navy and the Red Guard: on the history of the Army on the eve of the Revolution, the best work is:

360b Golovine, N. N. *The Russian Army and the War*, Yale U.P., 1931, 287pp.
There are a great many "memoirs", for instance Denikin, Danilov, etc., shown among the eye-witness accounts [160 ff.]; see also the documents on the revolutionary period, notably [32] and the collections already quoted. For the first years of the war, the accounts by German and Austrian generals—particularly Falkenhayn—may be read with profit. There is no overall work on the Army during the revolution. But on the Navy there is:

361 Naida, S. *Revolyutsionnoe dvizhenie v tsarskom flote* (*The Revolutionary Movement in the Tsarist fleet*), Moscow, 1948, 608pp. A good piece on the history of the Revolution in the navy.

362 *Baltiyskie moryaki v podgotovke i provedenii vel. okt. sots. Rev.* (*The Baltic Sailors in the Preparation and Conduct of the Oct. Rev.*), Moscow, 1957, 435pp. A collection of documents.

363 Startsev, V. I. *Ocherki po istorii petrogradskoy Krasnoy gvardii i rabochey militsii* (*Essay on the History of the Petrograd Red Guard and the Workers' Militia*), Leningrad, 1966, 309pp. A model study.

3. Nationality problems

The essential sources will be found in:

364 Dimanshteyn, S. M. *Revolyutsiya i natsional'ny vopros* (*The*

Revolution and the Nationality Question), Vol. 3, Moscow, 1927, 467pp. This should be completed through the documents published in *Dok.* [20–3] and in *Doc. Ker.* [35].

The essential work is:

365 Pipes, R. *The Formation of the Soviet Union*, Harvard U.P., 1954, 355pp.

For the period before 1917, Seton-Watson [307] is an important complement. On the place taken by the nationality question in Party policies, other than Carr [281] see

366 Boersmer, D. *The Bolsheviks and the National and Colonial Question*, Geveva, 1957.

367 Burmistrova, T. Yu. *The Leninist Policy of Proletarian Internationalism during the period of the foundation of the S.D. Party*, Leningrad, 1963 (in Russian).

368 Carrère d'Encausse, H., and Schram, S. *Le Marxisme et l'Asie*, Paris, 1965, 493pp.

369 Ferro, M. "Les soc-rév. et le problème des nationalités", *Le Mouvement social*, No. 45, Oct. 1963, pp. 93–100.

On the nationality question during the war and the nationality-policy of the Provisional Government:

370 Ferro, M. "La Politique des nationalités du gouvernement provisoire", *Cahiers du Monde russe et soviétique*, 1961–2, pp. 131–66.

Poland: The principal documents may be found in Dimanshteyn [364] and *Dok.* [20–23], to be completed with:

371 *Dokumenty i materialy po istorii sov-pol'skikh otnosheniy (Documents and material on the history of Soviet-Polish relations)*, Vol. I, Moscow, 1963, 546pp.

Other than the general works quoted above, see

372 *The Cambridge History of Poland*, 2 vols., London, 1941.

373 Filasiewicz, S. *La Question polonaise pendant la guerre mondiale*, Paris.

374 Blociszewski, J. *La Restauration de la Pologne et la diplomatie européenne, 1914–23*, Paris, 1927.

375 Dmowski, R., in *Russian Realities and Problems* [144].

376 Tserethelli, M. V. *Die Befreiung Polens und das Nationalitätenprinzip bei den Zentralmächten und bei der Entente*, Berne, 1917, 65pp.

377 Pidhainy, O. S. *The Ukrainian-Polish Problem in the Dussikution of the Russian Empire*, Toronto, 1962, 119pp.

Finland: works in Finnish are not accessible to the present writer. Other than works and documents quoted above, the following have been of use:

378 Schybergson. *Politische Geschichte Finnlands,* Gotha, 1925.

379 Wetterhoff, F. *Finnland im Lichte des Weltkriegs,* Berlin, 1916.

380 Delavoix, R. *Essai historique sur la séparation de la Finlande et de la Russie,* Paris, 1932. Mainly legalistic.

381 Soderhelm-Henning. *The Red Insurrection in Finland,* London n.d.

382 Goltz, V. D. *Meine Sendug in Finnland und im Baltikum,* Leipzig, 1920.

Baltic peoples: to the above sources should be added:

383 Page, S. *The Formation of the Baltic States,* Harvard U.P., 1959.

384 Dauge, A. *Latytsi,* Moscow, 1917.

385 Bilmanis, A. A. *A History of Latvia,* Princeton, 1951. Documents.

386 Bossin, A. *La Lithuanie,* Paris, 1933.

Ukraine: to the above sources should be added two important works:

387 Reshetar, J. R. *The Ukrainian Revolution,* Princeton, 1952. Essential, with a large bibliographical appendix.

388 Pidhainy, O. S. *The Formation of the Ukrainian Republic,* Toronto, 1966, 685pp.

Some of the contemporary accounts have use:

389 Doroshenko (publ.). *Velikaya istoriya Ukrainy (The Great History of the Ukraine),* Winnipeg, 1948.

390 Hrushevski, P. *La Lutte sociale et politique en Ukraine,* Paris, 1920.

391 Stebnitski, B. *L'Ukraine et les Ukrainiens,* Berne, 1918.

392 Choulgine, A. *L'Ukraine contre Moscou,* Paris, 1920.

Byelorussia:

393 Vakar, N. P. *Belorussia,* Harvard, 1958.

Armenia, Georgia, Caucasus: to the sources indicated—particularly Dimanshteyn, Pipes and Seton-Watson—should be added:

394 Karemzadeh, F. *The Struggle for Transcaucasia 1917-1919,* New York, 1952, 356pp.

395 Pasdermadjian, *Histoire de l'Arménie,* Paris, 1949 ("Que Sais-Je?" ed.).

396 Garibdganian, "Bolshevik organizations in Armenia, March–October 1917" (in Russian), *Voprosy istorii.* Especially for the period after July.

Georgia: the essential work is:

397 Zhordaniya, N. *Za dva goda* (*Two Years*), Tiflis, 1919. Most of the other works bear on the period October 1917–1920. There is a selection of them in Pipes [365].

Jews: to the sources and books mentioned above should be added the histories of the Social-Democrats and the Bolsheviks. There are two important works:

398 Greenberg, *The Jews in Russia*, 2 vols., New Haven, 1944.
399 Schwarz, S. M. *The Jews in the Soviet Union*, Syracuse, 1951.

Moslems: to the above-mentioned sources should be added:

400 Bennigsen and Quelquejay, *Les Mouvements nationaux chez les musulmans de Russie. Le Sultangaliévisme au Tatarstan*, Paris, 1960, 285pp.
401 Bennigsen and Quelquejay, *La Presse et le mouvement national chez les Musulmans de Russie avant 1920*. Paris, 1964, 386pp.
402 Carrère d'Encausse, H. *Le Mouvement réformiste chez les musulmans: le Turkestan*, Paris, 1966.

Three older works should be mentioned:

403 Mende, G. v. *Der nationale Kampf der Russlandtürken*, Berlin, 1936.
404 Zenkovski, S. A. *Pan-Turkism and Islam in Russia 1905–1920*, Harvard U.P., 1960.
405 Park, A. G. *Bolshevism in Turkestan*, Columbia, 1957.

4. International Relations

On relations between states: the principal documents are in *KA* and the *Documents of Kerensky* (*Doc. Ker.*) already quoted. The "memoirs", mainly of Tseretelli, Milyukov, etc., of the ambassadors and other foreign observers, are also important.

There is a list of them in:

406 Bezemer, J. W. *De Russische Revolutie in westerse Ogen*, Amsterdam, 334pp., in Dutch.

There is a useful summary in:

407 Warth, R. D. *The Allies and the Russian Revolution*, Durham, 1954, with a good bibliography. The work should be compared with:

408 Vasyukov, V. S. *Vneshnyaya politika Vrem. Pravitel'stva* (*The Foreign Policy of the Provisional Government*), Moscow, 1966, 495pp.

409 Adamov, *Konstantinopol' i prolovy* (*Constantinople and the Straits*), 2 vols., Moscow, 1925.

410 Yoffe, A. E. *Russko-frantsuzskie otnosheniya v 1917g.* (*Russian-French Relations in 1917*), Moscow, 1958, 354pp.

411 Ignat'ev, A. V. *Russko-angliyskie otnosheniya nakanune okt. rev.* (*Russo-English Relations on the eve of the Oct. Rev.*), Moscow, 1966, 400pp.

On relations with Germany:

412 Katkov, G. "German Foreign Office Documents in Financial Support to the Bolsheviks in 1917", *International Affairs*, April, 1956.

413 Zeman, Z. A. B. *Germany and the Revolution in Russia*, London, 1958, 157pp.

414 Zeman and Scharlau, *The Merchant of Revolution* (*Parvus-Helphand*), London, 1965, 306pp.

415 Bonnin, G. "Les Bolcheviks et l'argent allemand pendant la première guerre mondiale", *Revue historique*, 1965, pp. 101–27.

For an overall view of the problem of a separate peace during the period of the Provisional Government, from the German viewpoint, see.

416 *L'Allemagne et les problèmes de la paix pendant la première guerre mondiale*, edited with notes by A. Schérer and J. Grunewald; preface by M. Baumont and Pierre Renouvin, 2 vols., 1962 and 1966.

Collections of documents:

417 Fischer, F. *Griff nach der Weltmacht*, Düsseldorf, 1961, 896pp.

As a reference-work:

418 Renouvin, P. *La Crise européenne et la grande guerre*, 4th edn., Paris, 1962, 799pp.

International History of Socialism: the chief documents are in *KA* and particularly Gankin and Fisher [37], and likewise [39]. Among the memoirs, the most complete on these questions is certainly Tseretelli [127]; but there is also much use in Lenin, Trotsky (especially [121]) as they bear on Stockholm. On Stockholm, a good introduction is an article:

419 Meynell, "The Conference of Stockholm", *International Review of Social History*, 1960, 1 and 2.

See also, on the origins of the III Internationale, and the links between the Russian Revolution and the labour movement:

420 Sworakowski, W. S. *The Communist International and its front*

organizations, Stanford, 1965, 496pp., which mentions 2,282 works.

For the period before October:

421 Lazitch, B. *Lénine et la III Internationale*, Geneva, 1951.
422 Fainsod, M. *International Socialism and the World War*, 1935, 238pp.
423 Karliner, M. M. *Rabochee dvizhenie v Anglii v gody pervoy mirvoy voyni* (*The Labour Movement in England during 1914–18*), Moscow, 1961, 480pp., with a bibliography for Great Britain.
424 Kirova, Z. *Rabochee dvizhenie v Italii do 1917g* (*The Labour Movement in Italy to 1917*), Moscow, 1962.
425 Lasch, C. *The American Liberals and the Russian Revolution*, New York, 1962, 284pp.
426 Kriegel, A. *Aux Origines du communisme francais 1914–1920*, Paris, 1964, 2 vols., with an excellent bibliography.
The present writer is himself preparing a work on the European reaction to the Russian Revolution.

INDEX

★

477